Personality

Personality

Seymour Feshbach
Bernard Weiner
University of California, Los Angeles

D. C. Heath and Company · *Lexington, Massachusetts   Toronto*

Consulting Editor: Paul H. Mussen
University of California, Berkeley

Cover photograph: "Masks" © Marie Cosindas, 1966

Published simultaneously in Canada.

Printed in the United States of America.

International Standard Book Number: 0-669-89383-8

Library of Congress Catalog Card Number: 81-81504

To our parents,
Joseph and Fannie Feshbach
and
Julius and Bessie Weiner

1,2 ,3, 6, 8 , 9, 10, 11

Preface

In a sense we are all personality psychologists. We are making an inference about the genetics of personality when we say, "She has her father's personality." We are judging child-rearing practices when we note, "They're good parents." We are noticing the stability of personality characteristics when we complain, "He's always been stubborn!" We also hold our own "theories" of personality with "laws" like "Thin people are introverted" and "Red hair indicates an impulsive personality." Thus, the study of personality is part of our everyday lives, and good students of the subject are better able to adapt to the demands of living in a complex society. As a result, the study of personality is extremely popular at colleges and universities.

Personality is intended for an undergraduate audience at two- and four-year colleges and universities. Because we have avoided unnecessary jargon, an extensive background in psychology is not a prerequisite for the use of this book. We have tried to produce a readable text that is easily understood at the college level. However, respecting most students' intelligence and ability, we have not written "down" to them.

Most textbooks in the field of personality fall into one of two categories. The majority of the texts present in detail many of the theories that have been devised to account for human personality. These texts discuss between ten and twenty-five theories, introducing the readers to all of the concepts and ideas of each theorist in turn. In contrast, the second type of text is narrowly focused, advocating a particular point of view and fitting the many phenomena of personality into a specific perspective. These textbooks are often written by proponents of learning theory approaches, with their special allegiance to behavior modification or social learning, or by humanists, with their great concern for the self and subjective experience. In our opinion, both approaches are unsatisfactory, because they neglect many facets of the field of personality. The study of personality includes many subtopics, as well as theories, and no single theoretical approach can adequately account for the vast array of observations in the field.

In contrast to these two types of approaches, *Personality* takes up many of these subtopics and discusses the views of the major theorists concerning them. This approach allows us to compare various viewpoints on different facets of the field of personality while avoiding advocating any particular theory as "correct" or aligning ourselves with any particular school of thought. This type of text organization also encourages students to think critically and to contrast each theorist's views with those of the others, thus deepening students' understanding and setting the stage for class discussions or papers on the various issues.

Personality has been guided by certain assumptions, as well as by judgments about what a personality textbook should include. Our approach begins with the assumption that there are various interrelated subparts of the field of personality, including theories of personality (Part II), personality development (Part III), personality assessment (Part IV), and personality dynamics (Part V). In addition, the person is a product of both genetic dispositions and the physical and social environment (Part I). Second, we feel that it is necessary to be eclectic rather than to advocate a particular point of view. However, we do accept the idea that there are enduring personality dispositions, or traits, and we contend that the person and the environment are always interacting and contributing to behavior. Third, we feel it essential to present a text based on the experimental findings—that is, a text guided by scientific method and grounded on empirical evidence. Finally, given the myriad of topics available for discussion, we have chosen those that are both central to the field and intrinsically interesting to students. Thus, we have devoted special attention to such areas as self-concept, dreams, hypnosis, aggression, achievement strivings, and personal responsibility. In *Personality,* by means of a thorough analysis of these and other topics, we hope to add to the reader's knowledge by conveying current facts and theories, as well as by dispelling some of the false beliefs held by untrained people. We believe that we have achieved our goals—that *Personality* is inclusive, eclectic, empirical, and challenging—and that at times we have provided a new perspective on the various subtopics of the field of personality.

To aid in the learning process, we have included a number of teaching aids in the text itself. Boxed material highlights interesting anecdotes and examines more specialized topics in detail. Each chapter is followed by both a general and a point-by-point summary that provide a ready overview of the material in that chapter. Thought Questions relate the material in the chapter to the student's everyday experiences. In addition to these in-text aids, the book is accompanied by an *Instructor's Guide,* which contains over 750 multiple-choice and essay-type test items.

We want to thank Kathy Graves and Natalia Hamlyn for their help with the many different tasks involved in completing the manuscript. Robert Kaplan aided with the preparation of the chapters on measurement, and Norma Feshbach provided helpful advice for the developmental section.

S. F.
B. W.

Contents

Personality

Introduction to the Study
of Personality

1

Who am I? What am I really like? How can I get to know what you are really like? How did we become the way we are? Can we ever change? These fundamental questions concerning the nature of personality have always occupied a central place in human thought.

Beliefs and assumptions regarding human behavior and "answers" to the questions above have varied over the years. Some writers have stressed human beings' continuity with the rest of the animal kingdom and their similarity to the higher mammals. This is, of course, the position embodied in Charles Darwin's theory of evolution. Darwin pointed out the similarities in human and infrahuman emotions, including rage, excitement, and contentment. Similarly, other writers have maintained that the actions of both humans and infrahumans are guided primarily by instinct. Conversely, we could stress the more *qualitative differences* between humans and infrahumans, such as the distinctly human capacity for language and thought, the uniqueness of human cultural achievement, and the evidence of self-awareness and personal growth among humans. Furthermore, humankind progresses, transmitting culture and technology through the ages so that the human condition is continually being improved. This sort of growth does not characterize infrahuman species.

However, faith in the progress of humankind's *social* development, as contrasted with sheer *technological* development, has been rudely shaken by atrocities and wars in this century. Perhaps paradoxically, the constant threat of thermonuclear war has further intensified curiosity and concern about what is basic to human personality and what can be changed. Do violent "animal" impulses lurk beneath culture's civilized veneer, impatiently awaiting an opportunity for overt expression? Will self-centered needs override all other values under conditions of economic and social stress?

Psychology cannot yet provide the answers to many of the difficult questions regarding personality. The relatively objective and systematic study of personality is still in its infancy, less than six decades old. Our scientific tools are still quite limited. We have no magical procedures that will reveal the inner depths of our minds. For ethical reasons, we cannot and should not freely experiment with infants, raising them under carefully controlled, laboratory conditions. We do not have the power to alter culture, socioeconomic structures, and other significant features of the human environment that play an important role in personality. Nor do we have the power to alter the human body. For these reasons, we cannot reach the precision of measurement and experimental control in the study of human behavior that characterizes research in physics and chemistry.

Nevertheless, much can be learned by examining personality from an empirical, scientific perspective. At the very least, adoption of a scientific approach enables one to think about personality issues in a more analytic, discriminating manner. There are a great many, often conflicting, current assertions regarding personality. For example, "One's basic personality is formed in the first two years of life" versus "We are constantly changing and growing"; "Personality changes as the situation changes" versus "We are who we are, regardless of context"; "Sex and aggression are the basic human drives" versus "The basic human goal is self-actualization." Research provides us with the data to discriminate between valid and unfounded assertions, between assertions that have yet to be tested and those that are probably not testable.

In this text we will apply a scientific approach to the major theories of personality. We are sympathetic to all of these theoretical positions because of the enormous complexity of the problems with which they attempt to deal. Because theories of personality typically attempt to explain different aspects of human behavior, it is often difficult to call one "better" than another. But one must also be critical when evaluating the relevant evidence and the logic of each theory. We are able to use common scientific criteria to evaluate and compare theories. These criteria include the breadth and comprehensiveness of the theory (how much of the data on personality is explained); the testability of the theory; its degree of empirical support; and its heuristic or generative value. The meaning and applicability of these criteria will become more evident when we discuss different personality theories in Part II.

Our discussion of personality research and theories will be from the perspective of psychologists who are not limited to one particular theory but draw upon a number of them. In our framework, the individual both acts and reacts, has unique aspirations and fantasies, and is conscious of the future as well as the past and the present. We will consider personal behavior within a broad social-cultural context, for one must be sensitive to the powerful effects that the values of the culture, the family, and the larger society exert on behavior. Individuals are social beings, functioning in particular cultural settings. At the same time, one must have some appreciation of the role of genetics and evolution in human behavior. We are also biological creatures shaped by evolution.

A Case History

To illustrate in concrete terms the issues and problems to which the study of personality addresses itself, it is useful to examine individual behaviors over time. For this purpose, we will review the case of a young married couple, Robert and Elaine Cooper, who sought therapy for personal and marital problems. The Coopers' real names and other possible sources of identification have been disguised, but the pertinent features of their lives remain the same.

The Coopers had been married for two years when they first saw a psychologist. Robert was twenty-four, one year older than Elaine. They had met in high school, began living together in their junior year at college, and decided to marry when Robert was admitted to a graduate school of management located in another part of the country. Their immediate reason for seeking help was bickering and quarreling. Elaine expressed concern about Robert's emotional state, describing him as tense and irritable for the previous few months. Robert, on the other hand, complained about Elaine's lack of understanding and flirting with other men, particularly at parties with fellow employees of the public relations firm where she worked.

Robert and Elaine agreed that their relationship had begun to suffer after their graduation from college and their subsequent move. Both had been raised in the community where they attended college and, while they had looked forward to the move, they also had felt some ambivalence about it. According to Elaine, Robert had changed radically after this shift in school and community. Whereas Robert had previously been a relaxed, outgoing, and confident individual, he was now jealous, short-tempered, and moody. He continued to work very hard at his studies, but occasional heavy drinking, which appeared to be on the increase, interfered with his work. Robert acknowledged these changes in himself but attributed them to Elaine's interest in other men.

Robert's early life had been fairly uneventful, with the important exception of his father's death when Robert was six years old. But his mother was a strong, stable woman. With her support, Robert had overcome his grief and found male models in uncles and friends of the family. He was an only child and, although he sometimes missed having siblings, he had a number of close friends throughout his childhood. He did very well in school, was a fair athlete, and had been popular in high school.

Elaine was a middle child, with a brother three years older and a sister two years younger. Her memories of her childhood were filled with constant arguing between her parents, who finally had divorced shortly after Elaine's ninth birthday. As a child, Elaine had always been somewhat shy, a tendency that had become exaggerated after her father left home. While her brother had been very angry and her sister quite sad over their father's leaving, Elaine had manifested little feeling. Partly because of her shyness, she had few childhood friends. She never felt comfortable with her younger sister but was quite attached to her older brother. Her mother and teachers viewed her as a "good" child, compliant and conscientious, rarely troublesome or negative. During her elementary school years, she had been tall and ungainly but had undergone a striking physical transformation in adolescence and had been considered one of the most attractive girls in her high school. Robert was her first boyfriend and her marriage to him fulfilled a lifelong fantasy. She had developed no other relationships with men, although she was quite flattered by the interest men in her office took in her. She could not understand Robert's resentful attitude toward her social interactions at the office, particularly since friends saw her as emerging from her shell. She was very eager to obtain psychological help, in part because of her marital problems and in part because of nightmares she had been experiencing for several months. After eight months of marital and individual therapy, Elaine's nightmares disappeared and both she and Robert felt that their relationship had sufficiently improved to warrant discontinuation of therapy.

We will use the case history of Elaine and Robert Cooper to illuminate the major issues and problems in the field of personality. In turn, articulation of these issues and problems enables us to describe and understand the Coopers' behaviors from a scientific perspective.

Antecedents of Personality

Cultural context.   Robert and Elaine Cooper are products of their own time and culture. Their values and attitudes differ in many ways from those held by their parents and in other cultures. Expectations, norms, values, and prescribed modes of behavior vary both between cultures and within a particular culture. As a result, nationality and socioeconomic status have powerful effects on behavior. Every society is structured by its own pattern of social positions and corresponding social roles. Which position you occupy and which role you are playing at any given time in part determines your behavior. For example, a mature man is not supposed to behave like a child; the behavioral demands on a politician are not the same as those on the average individual; and in most societies the expectancies for women are different from those of men. Social roles also shape behavior in the sense that people usually conform to role expectations. The business executive generally wears a suit to work; the schoolteacher follows appropriate rules in not socializing unduly with students. Social roles not only affect behavior but also influence the way in which people perceive events. A general has a very different perception of war than a private. And we all occupy a number of social positions and roles simultaneously.

The differences in assertiveness between Robert and Elaine must be understood partly in the light of differences in sex roles: the difference in the social behaviors expected of males and females in this society. Until very recently, females were supposed to at least appear to be compliant if they were to be considered feminine; assertiveness was considered a masculine trait. Even with the rise in consciousness of sex stereotypes, the sex typing of behavior still remains. For example, in one study, females and males were depicted displaying the same moderately assertive behavior. Nevertheless, observers saw the females as significantly more aggressive than the males (Freundl, 1977).

Socialization and development.   For a society to function with some degree of harmony, there must be a reasonable fit between the resources, norms, and role prescriptions of the culture and the attitudes, desires, and expectations of the individuals in that culture. One major mechanism by which this fit is accomplished is the process of *socialization.*

From infancy, children are trained to develop the motivations and behaviors that will permit them to adapt effectively to their culture and social group. But within a particular culture's child-rearing structure, there is tremendous room for variation. Parents differ in style and attitude. Some are punitive, while others are permissive. Some are loving, while others are cold. For some, the child is eagerly desired; for others, the child is unwanted. Some parents are capable; others are incompetent. And there are important experiences in childhood beyond the specific behaviors of the parents. Size of family, the child's position in the family, family dislocation, illness, and divorce are all factors that enter into personality development. Beyond the immediate family, there is the availability or absence of accepting relatives and friends, rejecting or accepting peers, and school successes or failures. The influence of many of these factors can be seen in the development of Elaine's and Robert's personalities. Robert had a close relationship with a strong, loving mother, along with the early loss of a father. Elaine was hemmed in by siblings, had parents who could not communicate with her or each other, and felt her father had deserted her.

Children do not automatically develop adult personalities simply by growing older. The socialization process and the manner in which socialization interacts with other childhood experiences and with the individual's biology are central theoretical and empirical issues in the study of personality.

Biological variables.   The impact of culture and the family on the development of human behavior is so powerful that one can too easily overlook the significant role of biology. Humans are biological as well as social creatures. They share some of the characteristics of other mammals although, as humans, they have capacities and attributes that clearly distinguish them from other animals. One important question is the degree to which social behaviors and motivations that are more or less common among human beings are biologically based. Is human violence a function of a "killer instinct" (Ardrey, 1967)? Do humans, like other species that move in packs and herds, have an *instinctive* preference for social groups? Do altruism and cooperation spring from the same sources as in honeybee and ant societies?

In addition to exploring the biological basis for species-wide attributes, there is the equally important issue of the role of biological variables in the development of individual differences in personality. To what extent are particular individuals *born* aggressive, timid, moody, or psychologically vulnerable? There are certainly striking differences in the activity level, irritability, and alertness of infants at birth and there is evidence that these early temperamental differences are linked to later personality differences (Thomas and Chess, 1976). It is thus of interest that Robert was reported to have been a very "easy" and happy infant who slept much of the time, while Elaine cried a great deal as an infant and was not easily pacified.

Animal studies have shown not only that differences in physical characteristics are inherited but also that behavioral differences can be genetically transmitted. At the human level, most psychologists feel there are significant genetic factors involved in differences in intelligence, musical ability, and other capacities or talents. Although there is also good evidence that tendencies to certain forms of mental illness may be inherited, there is considerable debate regarding the importance of genetics (as compared with other factors) in the predisposition to mental illness and in the determination of normal personality differences.

Traits

While the study of personality is concerned with universal human tendencies, the description and analysis of individual differences are also of central interest. Elaine's and Robert's styles of social interaction differed strikingly in their elementary and high school years. Elaine had been shy and somewhat withdrawn, while Robert had been outgoing and comfortable in social situations. Elaine tended to display little emotion compared with her siblings (as in her response to her father's leaving home) and compared with Robert. Still another noteworthy difference between Elaine and Robert was in their reactions to the move. While both eagerly looked forward to the opportunity to

Introversion-extraversion is a central personality trait. Like the people shown here, Elaine's and Robert's characteristic behavior patterns—such as whether they preferred to be alone or to engage in idle conversations with others, for example—differed significantly. (left—Donald Dietz/Stock, Boston; right—James R. Holland/Stock, Boston)

establish their independence and expand their experiences and friendships, Robert became clearly upset and moody following the move, while Elaine became apparently more confident and assertive.

There are, of course, many other points of difference and similarity in Elaine and Robert, but one of the principal objectives of the study of personality is to *select* out of individuals' myriad behaviors those actions that reflect significant personality dimensions. These relatively stable personal characteristics are typically referred to as *traits*. For instance, the tendency to be attentive and interested in one's own thoughts and feelings (*introversion*) versus the tendency to be strongly oriented to other people and social situations (*extraversion*) is one trait on which Elaine and Robert differ. The study of introversion-extraversion and other traits provides a basis for comparison between individuals and, as we will later document, helps account for the uniqueness of each individual. Although personality theorists differ sharply in the value they place on the idea of traits, the search for the key characteristics, or traits, of the person is a significant part of the history of personality.

Behavioral consistency.   One of the striking aspects of the Coopers' life patterns is the apparent inconsistency in their behaviors. Was Elaine shy or was she outgoing? Was she insecure or was she self-confident? Was Robert easygoing or was he depressive and moody? Was he friendly or was he hostile?

Elaine had had great difficulty in expressing her feelings but seemed to be changing; Robert apparently was moving in the opposite direction. One might well wonder what Elaine's and Robert's "real" personalities were. Does their history demonstrate that there is no consistency in behavior, that there are no relatively enduring aspects of personality?

A closer scrutiny of their life histories suggests greater consistency in behavior than is at first apparent. Robert was at ease, open, and friendly in familiar settings, especially childhood home surroundings. But he became very distressed and threatened in new situations that were devoid of those earlier attachments. Robert's behavior therefore was consistent *within specific situations,* as was Elaine's. Furthermore, Robert's ambition remained the same despite situational changes, as demonstrated by his work output in high school, college, and graduate school.

The issue of behavioral consistency, i.e., whether behavior is general over different situations or varies as the situation changes, is a major and controversial question in the study of personality. A number of psychologists maintain that personality traits are highly situation-specific and that it is fruitless to seek broad, general behavior patterns that are descriptive of individuals (see Krasner and Ullman, 1973, p. 489; Mischel, 1968). Still others argue that people are not chameleons, matching their behavior to each particular circumstance. Rather, underlying individual consistencies can be discerned if we analyze the interaction of situations and behavior appropriately (Allport, 1961; Bem and Allen, 1974; Cattell, 1965; Epstein, 1979; Feshbach, 1978). Our own view is that behaviors vary in their degree of generality-specificity, as demonstrated by the generality of Robert's achievement strivings but the relative specificity of his stress reactions. The individual, the trait, and the situation must all be considered when examining the generality or specificity of behavior.

Overall organization of traits.   We have described Elaine's and Robert's personalities as if each consisted of a number of behavior patterns that existed in isolation from the other. In delineating individual differences, one almost inevitably adopts a kind of cataloging approach, enumerating a series of distinct behaviors. Thus, Elaine is described as emotionally unexpressive, introverted, and usually shy, conforming, and somewhat insecure. However, the listing of these traits, while often useful, does an injustice to the unity and overall organization of personality. Elaine's conformity was related to her difficulty in expressing her feelings, which in turn was related to her shyness and insecurity. While, for many people, introversion is not associated with social skills and may merely reflect a strong interest in their own thoughts, feelings, and privacy, this was not the case for Elaine. Her introverted tendencies were in large part a result of her anxiety and insecurity in social situations. Her fear of social rejection made it difficult for her to express feelings, particularly negative ones; this increased her distance and alienation from others.

One can see evidence of the overall organization of various personality traits in Elaine's personality. A similar analysis can be made for Robert. The implications of any particular personality trait depend to a considerable degree on this overall organization.

Personality Measurement

One of the hallmarks of science is measurement. Psychologists, no less than physicists, chemists, and biologists, need to quantify the variables they wish to investigate. That quantification can consist of crude statements of mere "presence" or "absence" or quite precise terms such as "twice as much." When one deals with traits such as Robert's dependency and Elaine's suppressed emotions, the task of measurement becomes especially difficult and challenging. Indeed, some would argue that the task is impossible. According to one eminent scholar (Barzun, 1954, p. 143), "the love of a parent for a child, or any other kind of attachment, repulsion, fear, joy, faith . . . these are realities that are visible, non-material and non-measurable." Yet these are precisely the "realities" that are at the very heart of the study of personality.

Psychologists recognize that personality measures cannot do full justice to the richness and individuality of human beings. The quality and degree of Robert's attachment to his mother and to familiar objects are not readily accessible to observation or adequately expressed in a test score. However, relatively meaningful measurements of the strength of these bonds can be made. Furthermore, one can assess personality dimensions such as desire for achievement, latent hostility, conformity tendencies, and the like. Quantification is essential because it both permits comparison between people on given dimensions and also allows one to determine which factors are associated with these personality dimensions and how strong the associations are.

The measurement of personality traits is a major scientific challenge. There are no X rays available that will penetrate our psyche and reveal our innermost hopes, secrets, and passions. Useful measures have been developed for some facets of personality but not for others. No measure of personality is perfect; psychologists are engaged in an ongoing effort to improve and refine their measuring procedures and tests.

Personality Change

We have briefly discussed a number of factors that influence the development of personality and its measurement. But what about personality *change*? Can we also identify factors that are responsible for change? Just how different can a person become?

It has been said that "the child is father to the man"; that is, early socialization and biological differences determine adult personalities. Many personality theorists support such a position, although others would give equal weight to experiences that occur in grade school, adolescence, and later in life. However, even if one assumes that personality is formed in childhood, it does not necessarily follow that personality cannot change. Psychoanalytic theory, for example, which assigns great importance to the role of early experience in the formation of personality, includes a therapeutic method (psychotherapy) for bringing about some degree of personality change.

Personality traits are, by definition, relatively enduring and stable. The question is how fixed they are. Some behavioral tendencies may take a great deal of time and effort to change, if they can be changed at all, while others may be much more readily modifiable. Through therapy, for example, Elaine showed a significant change in her style of expressing and communicating feelings. In contrast, Robert's strong early dependency and attachments remained largely unchanged, although he did develop insight into this aspect of his personality.

In a sense, most people are constantly engaged in the process of personality change, seeking greater mastery of themselves, opportunities to develop untapped interests and talents, and greater understanding of their social and physical world. This search for identity is not merely an effort to determine what our personality is; it is a process by which we continually develop and change the personality we seek.

Personality Dynamics

There is an intimate relationship between the structure and the dynamics of personality, although the terms refer to different aspects of the study of personality. The *structure* or "anatomy" of personality concerns basic dispositions and interrelationships of the different elements of personality. Personality *dynamics*, on the other hand, is concerned with the meaning and function of behavior. In considering personality dynamics, one looks for the purpose or the objective of an act—*why* the individual behaves the way he or she does. Questions of dynamics are also typically addressed to the immediate situation in which action is taking place, whereas questions concerning the structure of personality generally deal with relatively enduring and stable aspects of behavior.

Robert Cooper's response to the move from his home community to graduate school is an excellent example of personality dynamics. Acknowledgment of dependency was inconsistent with his self-image and thus anxiety provoking for Robert. He was completely unaware of his degree of dependence on his mother and on the "security blanket" of familiar objects and people. He reacted to the separation with extreme distress, which he attributed to his wife's supposed flirtations. Note the dynamic elements in the situation: a change in stimulus situation (his moving), a strong motivation (attachment, dependence), anxiety blocking his recognition of true motives, disruption and distress, and attribution of responsibility for negative feelings to some agent other than the self. We will encounter all of these elements again when we consider in greater detail experimental efforts to clarify dynamic processes.

Elaine's nightmares provide another example of a response to the dynamic interaction between a particular set of personality dispositions and a particular stimulus situation. Elaine began to resent Robert's irritability and jealousy, behaviors that were quite uncharacteristic of him. However, she could barely acknowledge these angry feelings to herself, much less to Robert. To complicate matters, she found herself in a situation in which she was the object of flattery and admiration. While she did not actually seek the attention of other men, she secretly enjoyed this new experience and felt guilty because there was an element of truth in Robert's accusation. Robert's difficult behavior only made these other experiences more pleasant and rewarding, serving to further intensify her guilt. These conflicts emerged during sleep when her guard against sexual feelings toward other men was partially relaxed. The nightmares were the expression of these severe conflicts, anxiety, and guilt. It is evident from these examples that personality dynamics are inextricably connected with personality structure and organization.

A Definition of Personality

We have discussed a number of questions and factors in the study of personality, but we have not yet offered a definition of the term *personality*, except by implication. Personality is not a precise concept, and psychologists are not in complete agreement about all of its connotations. We can, however, propose a definition of personality that you may find helpful. Personality refers to (1) relatively enduring behavior patterns and traits that distinguish people, groups, and cultures; (2) the overall organization and structure of these enduring behavior patterns and traits; and (3) the interactions among these patterns as well as the interactions with the fluctuations in an individual's internal state and the changing external stimulus situation.

Thus, some of the central issues in the field of personality concern the particular traits individuals have; their consistency; the overall organization of these behavior patterns and traits; their measurement; their development; possibilities for change; and, finally, how these stable characteristics of the organism interact with particular situations and with temporary variations in feelings, desires, and other internal states. These are the issues for psychologists in the fields of personality development, assessment, change or therapy, and dynamics.

The History of Personality Study

Many different personality theories have been formulated to deal with the issues raised in the Coopers' case history. These theories did not emerge suddenly from the minds of particular theorists; they have a history and in some instances can be traced directly to positions formulated in earlier centuries. Similarly, modern personality research has a historical context. Many of the issues addressed by contemporary research have been considered in earlier periods, hampered, of course, by the use of more primitive methods and less insight than we have now. To better understand contemporary theoretical and research issues and to appreciate the changes in the way we think about and investigate personality issues, it is helpful to consider their historical background. We can divide the history of personality into roughly three periods:

1. The prescientific era (the Greeks and phrenology).
2. The clinical era (the French influence and psychoanalysis).
3. Modern scientific psychology (the origins of psychological testing, behaviorism, and psychodynamics).

The Prescientific Era

The prescientific era of personality study, which extended until the middle of the nineteenth century, produced a number of interesting ideas, some of which are reflected in contemporary theories. However, until the development of systematic, objective methods of observation and measurement, there was no way to determine the validity of a particular theory, to decide among competing theories, or to compel greater precision in the formulation of propositions and generalizations.

The Greeks.   Consider, for example, the interesting and creative conception of Theophrastus (372–287 B.C.), Aristotle's successor as head of the Lyceum in Athens, who is best known for his collection of personality sketches called "characters." Theophrastus was struck by the observation that, while all of Greece had the same climate and Greeks had the same general upbringing, they did not all have the same personality. He proposed a set of thirty personality types, each one presented in the form of a character vignette with one outstanding personality trait. Each such character sketch opened with a brief definition of the dominant trait and continued with examples of this trait in action (see Box 1.1). Among the characters sketched were the Liar, the Surly Man, the Tasteless Man, and the Flatterer. These exaggerated, unidimensional depictions of character also became common literary devices, as in the romantic heroism of Cervantes's Don Quixote and the blind loyalty of his vassal, Sancho Panza.

Despite our sense that we know people who fit some of these character types, there are many difficulties with Theophrastus' approach. Some of these same difficulties apply to modern character typology. One obvious problem with these unidimensional sketches is that they are caricatures, appropriate perhaps for dramatic purposes but grossly inadequate for objective scientific description. The concept of type has an either-or quality; one is or is not a particular personality type. In contrast, the concept of trait implies a continuum of the quality in question, with some people displaying very little of the trait, others more, and so on. Individuals are more appropriately and accurately described by their position on a continuum of trait dimensions rather than as belonging to one particular type. For example, it is more useful to describe Elaine Cooper in terms of many traits of varying magnitude—

Box 1.1   THE PENURIOUS MAN
                                    Theophrastus

Penuriousness is economy carried beyond all measure. A Penurious Man is one who goes to a debtor to ask for his half-obol interest before the end of the month. At a dinner where expenses are shared, he counts the number of cups each person drinks, and he makes a smaller libation to Artemis than anyone. If someone has made a good bargain on his account and presents him with the bill he says it is too much.

When his servant breaks a pot or a plate, he deducts the value from his food. If his wife drops a copper, he moves furniture, beds, chests and hunts in the curtains. If he has something to sell he puts such a price on it that the buyer has no profit. He forbids anyone to pick a fig in his garden, to walk on his land, to pick up an olive or a date. Every day he goes to see that the boundary marks of his property have not been moved. He will destrain on a debtor and exact compound interest. When he entertains the members of his deme, he is careful to serve very small pieces of meat to them. If he goes marketing, he returns without having bought anything. He forbids his wife to lend anything—neither salt nor lamp-wick nor cinnamon nor marjoram nor meal nor garlands nor cakes for sacrifices. "All these trifles," he says, "mount up in a year." To sum up, the coffers of the penurious men are moldy and the keys rust; they wear cloaks which hardly reach the thigh; a very little oil-bottle supplies them for anointing; they have hair cut short and do not put on their shoes until midday; and when they take their cloak to the fuller they urge him to use plenty of earth so that it will not be spotted so soon.

From *Personality: A Psychological Interpretation* by Gordon W. Allport. Copyright 1937 by Henry Holt & Co., Inc. Renewal © 1965 by Gordon W. Allport. Reprinted by permission of Holt, Rinehart and Winston.

relatively high in introversion, moderately insecure, and so on—than to describe her as a pure introvert.

Aside from the unidimensionality of Theophrastus' character types, one has no way of knowing whether the number of types should be ten or one hundred or one thousand. Five centuries later, in fact, the physician Galen (A.D. 130–200) proposed only a fourfold classificatory system based on Hippocrates' doctrine of the four basic "humors" of the body: black bile, an imaginary fluid; yellow bile, a fluid secreted by the liver; phlegm, secreted by mucous membranes; and blood. Galen's theory of *temperament* asserted that an excess of black bile makes a person melancholic; an excess of yellow bile produces a choleric temperament, quick to anger and action; the predominance of phlegm results in a phlegmatic (calm and stolid) individual; and the predominance of the fourth humor, blood, makes one sanguine (warmhearted and confident). Galen's effort to relate biological characteristics to personality traits anticipates modern theories of the relationship between physique and temperament. But Galen, like Theophrastus, failed to provide any evidence in support of his particular physical and psychological typology. There was no way to determine or measure the dominant humor or temperament, much less demonstrate that particular humors were associated with particular temperaments.

Unfortunately, measurement in itself does not guarantee a scientific basis for a theory; that basis depends on how the measurements are obtained and the ability of other investigators to produce the same findings. When the measurement of personality is based on the judgments of a human observer, then the measurements are subject to serious distortion by possible observer bias. An observer, when viewing an event or another person, does so selectively, attending to some stimuli in the situation and not to others. There is always a danger that the observer may attend primarily to those events and stimuli that support any hypotheses or biases that may be brought to the situation. So, for example, when Robert Cooper described Elaine as flirtatious, his judgment or observation was being biased by his own insecurity.

Phrenology. There are several episodes in the history of psychology that exemplify the fallibility of measurements obtained without controlling for observer bias and other sources of error. None is more telling than the pseudoscientific movement of *phrenology* that achieved wide acceptance during the first half of the nineteenth century. Phrenologists drew conclusions about an individual's personality from minor bumps in the shape of the head. They assumed that the mind could be broken down into twenty-seven essential elements, or faculties, of human nature (Franz Joseph Gall, 1758–1828). Each of these faculties corresponded to enlargements of particular areas on the surface of the brain and skull (see Fig. 1.1, page 16). While some phrenologists were charlatans, many were genuinely convinced that their discipline was a science that employed the same methods as any other natural science. The following excerpt from O. L. Fowler's "Practical Phrenology" is illustrative:

Like all other exact sciences, large portions of it was discovered and brought to its present state of perfection, entirely by induction . . . by an observation and a classification of facts . . . the following is the method adopted by Dr. Gall in the discovering of competitiveness . . . after collecting a promiscuous company of ordinary persons from the streets, he assertained from them which were cowardly and which courageous. He then placed the former by themselves, and proceeded to examine and compare the respective developments of the different portions of their heads, until he assertained that not withstanding the great diversity of shape in other parts, yet the heads of the courageous ones all displayed a fullness and thickness just behind the top of the ear, and that the heads of the cowardly were all thin and depressed in that particular region. This discovery . . . was then applied to innumerable other subjects, until its correctness was fully established.

The errors that led Gall to these completely fallacious conclusions are numerous. He used a questionable self-report procedure to determine who was cowardly and who was courageous and neither recorded his measurements nor determined the variability in his groups. Fowler also cites a number of case histories that are testimonials to the remarkable "success" of the phrenologists' approach. We know, of course, that there are great dangers in

Figure 1.1   A typical phrenological chart, showing the correspondence between parts of the skull and personality and behavioral characteristics. (Courtesy, The Francis A. Countway Library of Medicine, Harvard University)

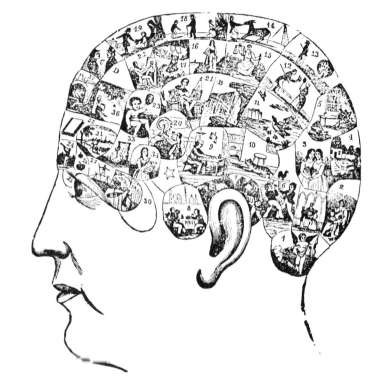

NUMBERING AND DEFINITION
OF THE ORGANS.

1. AMATIVENESS, Sexual and connubial love.
2. PHILOPROGENITIVENESS, Parental love.
3. ADHESIVENESS, Friendship—sociability.
4. UNION FOR LIFE, Love of one only.
5. INHABITIVENESS, Love of home.
6. CONTINUITY, One thing at a time.
6. COMBATIVENESS, Resistance—defence.
7. DESTRUCTIVENESS, Executiveness-force.
8. ALIMENTIVENESS, Appetite, hunger.
9. ACQUISITIVENESS, Accumulation.
10. SECRETIVENESS, Policy—management.
11. CAUTIOUSNESS, Prudence, provision.
12. APPROBATIVENESS, Ambition—display.
13. SELF-ESTEEM, Self-respect—dignity.
13. FIRMNESS, Decision—perseverance.
15. CONSCIENTIOUSNESS, Justice—equity.
16. HOPE, Expectation—enterprise.
17. SPIRITUALITY, Intuition-spiritual revery.
18. VENERATION, Devotion—respect.
19. BENEVOLENCE, Kindness—goodness.
10. CONSTRUCTIVENESS, Mechanical ingenuity
21. IDEALITY, Refinement—taste—purity.
B. SUBLIMITY, Love of grandeur.
22. IMITATION, Copying—patterning.
23. MIRTHFULNESS, Jocoseness—wit—fun.
24. INDIVIDUALITY, Observation.
25. FORM, Recollection of shape.
26. SIZE, Measuring by the eye.
27. WEIGHT, Balancing—climbing.
28. COLOR, Judgment of colors.
29. ORDER, Method—system—arrangement
30. CALCULATION, Mental arithmetic.
31. LOCALITY, Recollection of places.
32. EVENTUALITY, Memory of facts.
33. TIME, Cognizance of duration.
34. TUNE, Music—melody by ear.
35. LANGUAGE, Expression of ideas.
36. CAUSALITY, Applying causes to effects
37. COMPARISON, inductive reasoning.
C. HUMAN NATURE, perception of motives.
D. AGREEABLENESS, Pleasantness—suavity

using anecdotal individual case material as a principal source of evidence. Judging from the popularity of such modern pseudo-sciences as scientology and astrology, the lesson to be learned from phrenology is a difficult one.

The Clinical Era

The French influence.   The clinical analysis of the study of personality had its initial impetus in France. From the beginning of the nineteenth century, psychology in France centered on psychopathology. Inspired by the ideology of the French Revolution, Phillipe Pinel (1745–1826) removed the chains in which mental patients had been kept. His successors introduced other humane practices in the care of the mentally ill. More systematic observations of mental patients were made, resulting in a description of mental disorders. The feeble-minded were seen as a separate group and around the mid-nineteenth century a training school for the feeble-minded was established.

The work of the French with the mentally retarded led in 1905 to Alfred Binet's (1857–1911) development of a test of intelligence to establish a more accurate diagnosis of this disorder. Intelligence testing had a profound effect on the field of personality in that it highlighted the possibility and importance of assessing individual differences.

While one offshoot of French interest in psychopathology was the intelligence test, another was the study and use of hypnosis in the treatment of mental disorders. The distinguished neurologist Jean-Martin Charcot (1825–1893) made hypnosis a respectable, although mysterious, medical treatment for mental disorders. He applied hypnosis to such hysterical behaviors as the loss of bodily function (paralysis of the arm, numbness of the hand, deafness) without apparent organic cause. Charcot also believed that both hypnosis and hysteria were pathological states. A rival French group took the now more commonly accepted view that the phenomena associated with hypnosis were the result of specific suggestions rather than the manifestations of an abnormal psychological state.

French interest in hypnosis and hysteria continued with more detailed studies of *dissociation*, or the split between behavior and awareness that occurs under these conditions. American interest in dissociation was spurred by Morton Prince, who reported a number of intriguing cases of multiple or split personalities. Patients exhibiting amnesias, automatic writing, sleepwalking, and related dissociation symptoms were also studied by Prince. Particularly significant for the emerging field of personality was Prince's founding of the Harvard Psychological Clinic in 1927. Here Henry Murray, Prince's successor, demonstrated how the ideas and observations of Charcot, Prince, and, most importantly, Sigmund Freud could be studied experimentally.

Psychoanalysis.   When Sigmund Freud, the originator of psychoanalysis, completed medical school in 1881, the science of psychology was not yet a decade old. Moreover, the problems with which the infant science was concerned at that time were far removed from the issues central to the study of personality. From the Leipzig laboratory founded by Wilhelm Wundt in 1875 emerged a series of studies in sensation, perception, reaction, attention, and association. These experiments had little to say about human motives, passions, or traits (although at a later point Freud was able to make use of the process of association in a unique and productive way). After a period of involvement in basic research in physiology and neuroanatomy, Freud opened a medical practice in neurology. It soon became evident to him that he could find no organic, neurological cause for the symptoms most of his patients brought to him for treatment.

In collaboration with an older and successful Viennese practitioner, Joseph Breuer, Freud began to make use of such psychological procedures as hypnosis and "talking out one's feelings." In particular, the case of Fraulein Anna O. made a deep impression on him. This twenty-one-year-old woman was a classic case of hysteria. Her limbs were paralyzed, she could not experience feeling or pain in parts of her body, she suffered problems in sight and speech, and she experienced nausea and confusion. Breuer found that these symptoms were relieved when Anna was placed under hypnosis and was encouraged to express her feelings. But he decided to terminate the case when he found that he could not cope with either the strong feelings that Anna began to show toward him or the symptoms she developed when he tried to sever the relationship.

Freud was intrigued with the striking symptom changes Anna displayed. He left Vienna for a period of study with Charcot in Paris and, while working there, observed cases of male hysteria. This contradicted the then-prevailing view that hysteria was a female disorder (the terms *hysteria* and *hysterectomy* both stem from the Greek word for "womb"). When Freud lectured on this topic upon his return to Vienna, he found the medical groups there resistant to his ideas, in part because of the general antagonism between the French and Austrian schools of thought. This early conflict between Freud and organized medicine over clearly observable symptoms helped prepare him for the greater hostility he was to encounter when he proposed even more radical theories about mental illness and normal personality.

In a later chapter, we will consider Freud's ideas in detail. At this point, we only briefly highlight those aspects of Freud's theory that were major innovations in the study of personality.

1. Behavior, according to Freud, is *determined*, arising from natural causes. The principle of *determinism* had been an article of faith for the physical sciences. Its application to biological phenomena was spurred by the work of Charles Darwin, who showed that biological structures that were thought to be accidental or due to divine intervention could be explained by the natural selection of similarities that favored survival. It became meaningful, then, to look for the function or the adaptive value of an organ or a physiological process. Freud extended this principle to psychological phenomena, asking of any behavior or thought: What is its function? What is the cause? Considering Elaine and Robert Cooper, we thus seek the basis for Elaine's nightmares and the reasons for Robert's anxieties after moving to a new community, rather than merely viewing these events as random occurrences without purpose or meaning.

2. Human behavior is governed largely by unconscious processes; that is, significant choices and actions are influenced by feelings and motives of which the individual is unaware. This belief was also reflected in Freud's method of treatment, which encouraged patients to give free associations, to say whatever came into their minds. The belief in the unconscious also gave rise to projective testing methods, in which meaning given to ambiguous stimuli (such as inkblots) is thought to reflect the unconscious needs, wishes, and conflicts of the test taker.

3. Human personality and character are basically determined in the first five years of life. Freud assumed that sexual energies are present at birth and are transformed during the course of development. The assumption of the pri-

macy of the sex drive and the attribution of this motivation to the young child elicited much controversy and many negative reactions.

The ideas proposed by Freud paved the way for the ever-growing field of clinical psychology. In spite of major modification of Freud's ideas, concepts such as determinism, the unconscious, and psychosexual development remain at the core of contemporary psychoanalytic theory.

Modern Scientific Psychology

Origins, of psychological testing.   We have already suggested that Charles Darwin's theory of evolution influenced the emerging field of psychology with its assumption of scientific determinism and its focus on the function or adaptive value of biological structures and processes. Still another implication of the Darwinian model for the study of human personality was the importance of species differences and of individual differences within species. These variations were important in two ways. First, they were transmitted from generation to generation, thus providing a clue to the role of heredity. Second, the variations might have implications for an individual's role in society; that is, some might be "born" to be leaders and others, to be followers.

Sir Francis Galton (1822–1911), a cousin of Charles Darwin, published the first edition of *Hereditary Genius* in 1869, in which he marshaled evidence that eminence ran in families. He then assumed that this familial pattern was due to the inheritance of ability. Galton investigated many aspects of individual differences, such as the richness and range of verbal associations, and developed mental tests to measure these differences. He also proposed the use of physiological measures of blood pressure and heart rate to assess individual differences in emotionality and temperament. In Galton's work we see the beginnings of a movement toward the development of adequate testing procedures.

World War I served as an impetus to the development of personality tests. To screen and classify soldiers, army psychologists constructed the first group-administered intelligence test: the Army Alpha. And since it was not feasible for each recruit to receive an individual psychiatric interview to screen mental disorders, a test including more than one hundred items was developed based on questions that would have been asked in such an interview. This first personality questionnaire was the Woodworth Personal Data Sheet. The test included the following items (Hollingworth, 1920):

- Do you usually feel well and strong?
- Do you ever walk in your sleep?
- Do you have nightmares?

A "no" answer to the first item and a "yes" answer to the second and third items were believed to be indications of psychopathology. If there were many responses in this direction, the soldier was seen by a psychiatrist.

The 1920s and 1930s saw the development of a number of personality tests, some designed to assess psychological disturbances and others to measure individual differences in personal values and personality traits. Testing is now one of the major subdivisions within the field of personality. Before their psychotherapy, the Coopers could have been administered a number of such tests to provide the therapist with information regarding their personality traits and conflicts that might not have become immediately evident in the therapeutic situation.

Behaviorism.   The fields of clinical psychology and personality assessment were born in Europe, particularly France, Austria, and England. But in the early 1900s America began to develop its own special brand of psychology, known as *behaviorism.* Whereas psychoanalysis envisioned the mind as filled with unconscious fantasies and early childhood residues, the behaviorists emptied the mind of its contents, even rejecting the very concept of mind. (It is sometimes said that psychology first lost its soul and then its mind!) In a famous article that appeared in 1913, John B. Watson criticized prevailing psychology as subjective and unreliable; he argued for a *science* of psychology based on objective measures of observable behaviors and of the external, stimulus situation. The task of psychology, he contended, was to (1) predict the response, given the stimulus; (2) identify the stimulus, given the response; and (3) predict the change in the response, given a change in the stimulus. Watson's views on psychoanalysis were especially severe. He predicted that "twenty years from now an analyst using Freudian concepts and Freudian terminology will be placed upon the same plane as a phrenologist" (1930, p. 27). Watson, like Freud, was willing to pursue the implications of his theory and observations wherever they might lead. And, also like Freud, he had a profound influence on the psychology of personality.

The behaviorist school gave rise to several related but competing theories. Further efforts to translate psychoanalytic concepts into a form that could be empirically tested were undertaken by a group of Yale University psychologists influenced by Watson but advocating a more elaborate theoretical perspective. In contrast to Freud, this group stressed the importance of a laboratory-based learning theory. *Learning theory* places great emphasis on the significance of situational factors, postulates few mental processes, and attempts to deal with personality processes within a rigorous and objective experimental framework. The Yale psychologists conducted a number of experiments linking aggression to the occurrence of frustration. The hypothesis of a relation between frustration and aggression was a significant advance over the Freudian position, which postulated an instinctive aggressive drive.

To illuminate the problems faced by the Coopers, these psychologists would attempt to determine the situational conditions, particularly the external rewards, that led to Robert's acquisition of strong dependency behaviors, as well as the punishments that caused conflict over his dependency. They also would explore the rewards and punishments in the current life situation that were maintaining these behavioral patterns. In addition, they might search for the frustrations in Robert's life that were the basis for his jealousy and irritability. These concerns have their roots in the experimental tradition.

Psychodynamics.   Behaviorism and learning theory provided scientific avenues for testing some of Freud's ideas, in the process contributing to the advancement of psychology as a respectable science. But they were not the only ways. Other investigators, such as Henry Murray and Kurt Lewin, adopted the experimental method without accepting many of the restrictions advocated by the behaviorists and learning theorists.

Henry Murray developed a theory of personality that emphasized the full range of human motivations. He also pioneered in the measurement of human motivation and stimulated the experimental analysis of personality dynamics. Murray's well-known measure of motivation, the Thematic Apperception Test (TAT), would be a logical choice to administer to the Coopers because it is particularly effective in uncovering conflicts like the dependency conflict so important in Robert's life.

Kurt Lewin's theory of personality emerged from his background in Gestalt psychology. A basic tenet of the Gestalt school is that the whole, or context, determines the significance of any component of human experience and behavior. Meaning depends further upon how an event is perceived. This is a core belief among *phenomenologists,* who deal with how the person *subjectively* experiences the world. These principles are incorporated into contemporary humanistic psychology, as well as into a large body of research on the dynamics of human motivation.

In sum, the issues and problems of today have clear historical roots in psychology's short, but rich, history. The traditions we have discussed in the preceding pages form the heart of psychology and will be repeatedly examined in the following chapters. These traditions provided the basis for the methods used in dealing with and understanding the Coopers, and they are the essential avenues used to explore the many facets of personality.

An Overview of this Text

In the ensuing chapters we will examine contemporary theoretical and empirical efforts to answer some of the questions raised in the first half of this chapter: questions regarding individual traits; their measurement, development, and change; and the manner in which these traits influence an individual's actions in particular environments. The answers to these questions are guided by the historical concepts and theories discussed in the second half of this chapter: the early search for traits, individual differences, and the uniqueness of each person; concepts from clinical psychology concerning the unconscious; the influence of measurement; the experimental analysis of observable behaviors, learning, and motivational processes; and, finally, the influence of Gestalt psychology on the study of the whole person.

In Part I of the text we examine the role of genetic and social-cultural factors in personality. We then turn from these biological and environmental influences to consider contemporary theories of personality in Part II. In Part III, we look at personality from a developmental perspective, examining how personality develops and changes over the life span. The outcome of this development is considered in Part IV, in which we examine the structure of personality and the tests and procedures used to assess it. Part V is concerned with issues of personality dynamics: motives, conflicts, emotions, and consciousness. Part VI is a series of chapters devoted to more complex personality processes and behaviors, which are examined from the perspective of the earlier chapters; that is, in terms of biological variables, social-cultural factors, theoretical approaches, development and change, structure, measurement, and dynamics.

These areas of study are approached from a particular point of view. We will always try to separate what is known, or the *facts* of personality, from mere speculations or untested ideas. We will try to present the significant developments in the field, examining problems in historical perspective and showing the theoretical significance of various issues. Our approach is generally eclectic, since different theoretical positions seem best suited for different problems. But we do assume that there are enduring personality dispositions. Behavior is complex, and one must often search for underlying dynamics as well as examine thoughts, both conscious and unconscious, and their influence on actions. Because of this complexity, no single concept is sufficient in and of itself to explain the difficult issues in the field of personality.

Summary   This chapter has presented a case history of a young married couple to illustrate some of the areas and issues in the study of personality. The major issues include the identification of key personality traits, their consistency, overall organization, and measurement. Personality psychologists examine how these dispositions are formed by cultural, social, and biological antecedents and how they can be changed. Another key area of investigation for personality psychologists is the dynamics of behavior, or the function of traits manifested in a particular situation for optimum personal adaptation.

Three different traditions in psychology—the assessment of individual differences, clinical psychology, and scientific or experimental psychology—have evolved to address personality issues.

PART I

The Innate and Environmental Determinants of Personality

In Part I we present the context for the emergence of personality. A key question in this area is, "Are we what we are because of nature or because of nurture?" When the question is phrased in this manner, neither answer can be correct, for the choices are not mutually exclusive. There clearly are both inborn and social-cultural influences on the individual. Genetics and environment—nature *and* nurture—regulate and guide each person.

In Chapter 2 we examine some of the innate determinants of personality and behavior. We observe that, as products of a long evolutionary history, human beings are predisposed to certain patterns of behavior. In addition, specific genetic blueprints provide the foundation for personality and behavior.

But it is evident that social learning experiences also have great impact. Individuals brought up in different cultures or social classes behave differently. If one wants to predict what an individual is doing or thinking at a given time, some of the best predictors are the point in history when the individual was born and where he or she is living. In Chapter 3 we examine some of these social and cultural influences, as well as characteristics of the physical environment that have behavioral consequences.

Chapters 2 and 3 do not attempt to give complete accounts of the genetics of personality or the social determinants of action; full courses are devoted to these topics. Rather, we introduce the context of the person: an individual with unique predispositions who is nevertheless modifiable and shaped by surroundings.

Genetic Determinants
of Personality

2

Charles Darwin's controversial conclusion that the human species is the product of a long period of evolution was set forth in *The Origin of Species* and *The Descent of Man*. Darwin proposed a simple, yet powerful, theory to explain the process of evolution: "survival of the fittest." He stated: "Any variation, however slight and from whatever cause proceeding, if it be in any degree of profitability to an individual . . . will tend to the preservation of that individual, and will generally be inherited by its offspring. The offspring, also, will thus have a better chance of surviving" (1869, p. 61). Thus, the theory of evolution is intimately linked with the concept of inheritance—the transmission of characteristics from one generation to another.

In this chapter we examine some of the genetic determinants of personality structure and behavior. Although biochemicals and hormones, brain mechanisms, and other biological factors influence personality, we focus here on the topic of genetics because of the vast research in this area and because it well illustrates the role of biological givens in behavior.

It is helpful to frame a genetic approach to personality within the context of evolutionary theory. Among the questions discussed are: What limitations do inherited characteristics place on learning? Do humans have instincts, or innate urges and unlearned patterns of behavior? What are the tenets of the emerging field of sociobiology? Are there universal facial expressions or behaviors that are exhibited across cultures? And can it be demonstrated scientifically that personality characteristics and behavioral problems are in part genetically influenced? We will present evidence that the answer is yes and that a complete theory of personality must consider innate factors.

The Nature/Nurture Controversy

Limitations on Learning

The notion that personality structure and human behavior might be partially determined by genetically rooted factors has met with some opposition (see

McClearn, 1962). First, many psychologists believe that the possible influence of inborn characteristics or propensities is overcome by humans' vast learning capacities and social experiences. This viewpoint was carried to its extreme by John B. Watson, founder of the behaviorist movement in the United States. Watson argued that a human being is a "blank slate" (*tabula rasa*) at birth.

Give me a dozen healthy infants, well-formed, and my own specified world to bring them up in and I'll guarantee to take any one at random and to train him to become any type of specialist I might select—doctor, lawyer, artist, merchant-chief and, yes, even beggar-man and thief, regardless of his talents, penchants, tendencies, abilities, vocations, and race of his ancestors. (1930, p. 104)

However, a great deal of research evidence casts doubt on Watson's conception. Primarily because of ethical constraints, this research has been conducted with infrahumans rather than with human subjects. Although one must be cautious in extrapolating or generalizing the findings to humans, the human-infrahuman continuity and the fact that humans are also biological creatures with an evolutionary history suggest that the findings do tell us something about human personality and behavior.

Teaching infrahumans tricks. B. F. Skinner and his followers have demonstrated that behavior can be modified through the use of reward; that is, prior responses can be increased in strength through reinforcement. It is possible to train organisms like rats and pigeons to engage in such apparently bizarre behaviors as playing ping-pong by rewarding responses that approximate the behavior that one wishes to produce, until finally the experimenter-designated "correct" response is emitted. This procedure is called *shaping*.

Encouraged by these demonstrations, Breland and Breland (1961) tried to teach behavioral "tricks" to infrahumans for commercial appearances at circuses and on television. However, many of their attempts failed. For example, the Brelands tried to teach pigs to deposit wooden coins in a piggy bank. Once the pigs associated the coins with their food reward, however, it became increasingly difficult to make them deposit the coins. Instead, they would drop and root with their new-found "money."

The Brelands suggested that the learned response (deposit) conflicted with an instinctive tendency. They labeled this process *instinctive drift.* Thus, for example, the rooting response, which the pig instinctively employs in the process of obtaining food, interfered with the banking behavior because the coins became associated with food reward. Similarly, the Brelands found it impossible to teach chicks to play baseball; the chicks chased the ball instead of performing the "correct," learned response of circling the bases. Such a search-and-follow tactic is how chicks typically find food, is instrumental in their survival, and thus conflicts with antagonistic performances. On the basis of these observations, the Brelands wrote a book amusingly entitled *The Misbehavior of Organisms,* to contrast their findings with those reported in Skinner's *The Behavior of Organisms.* The Brelands' experiences clearly demonstrate that innate factors set limits on what behaviors can be learned and performed.

Taste aversions.   Research has also shown that not all stimuli are capable of serving as cues for organisms to engage in certain responses. For example, if a rat is given saccharin-flavored water prior to a shock, that taste will not serve as a signal that shock is forthcoming. However, the saccharin can be an effective signal to learn an induced food poisoning. That is, rats will learn to avoid the saccharin water if drinking is followed by illness, but not if it is followed by shock. On the other hand, lights and sounds are cues that *can* be learned to signal food-related shock; rats will avoid or escape from situations in which such cues are followed by shock (Garcia and Koelling, 1966). These relationships are consistent with evolutionary demands. There is a natural connection between eating and nausea, but not between visual cues and food-related distress.

In sum, it is evident that biological factors play important roles in determining what can and cannot be learned. The simple belief that virtually any response can be learned, as espoused by Watson and perhaps Skinner, clearly is not correct. Although this research has used infrahuman subjects, the postulation of a psychological continuity between humans and infrahumans suggests that this principle also applies in the case of human behavior.

The Role of Genetics

In contrast with those who focus on learning as the primary component in behavior are those who assert that humans follow some preestablished blueprint enacted at the moment of conception. Clearly, if personality and behavior are shaped by learning and experience, then humans are subject to change, for new habits, attitudes, and modes of action can be taught. But if the cause of action is perceived as a fixed and immutable inborn characteristic, it is easy to reach the pessimistic conclusion that change cannot be accomplished.

Still another factor that has discouraged the acceptance of heredity as an influence on personality is the American credo that "all people are created equal." Acceptance of genetic postulates carries the danger of an elitist position asserting that people are created unequal and therefore deserve to remain unequal. Elitists might contend, for example, that because males are *born* more independent and competitive, they should serve in important occupational roles, while women, because they are *born* more dependent and cooperative, should remain in the home, caring for the family. This conviction, even if the genetic assumption were true, ignores the importance of learning and socialization, so highly stressed by Watson and others, and overlooks the great biological variation that is exhibited within such groups as males and females. (Of course, in this instance there is no evidence supporting presumed male-female genetic differences.)

A further corruption of the genetic position has been exhibited by extremists advocating eugenics, or the improvement of the human race by the application of the laws of heredity. In Nazi Germany, for example, eugenicists argued for the extinction of certain individuals and groups in order to produce a more perfect species.

But in spite of learning theorists' arguments and the dangers inherent in applying the principles of heredity, there are some inborn, inherited determinants of personality and behavior. Our commonsense observations that "like begets like" and the vague notion that behavior is due to "human nature" do contain some degree of truth. Behavior is a product of both nature and nurture, i.e., what one brings into the world and how this is influenced by experience. Learning and experience are central explanations of human action, but genetic roots cannot be disregarded.

The passion and political overtones surrounding the nature/nurture controversy make it especially important to think clearly about these issues. In assessing the implications of the studies presented in this chapter, a distinction must be made between scientific and social significance. It is of scientific importance to demonstrate the presence or absence of genetic determinants of such behaviors as dominance, sociability, alcoholism, criminality, and mental disorders. However, it may be that environmental factors are far more important. Moreover, behaviors that have strong genetic determinants still can be modified through learning and experience. For example, phenylketonuria (PKU), a genetic mental deficiency, can be prevented by an environmental factor (early dietary manipulation). This deficiency also is interesting from a genetic viewpoint in that it is virtually unknown among Jews. (On the other hand, Tay-Sachs disease, a lethal central nervous system disorder, is especially prevalent in the Jewish population.)

At the same time, the fact that personality or behavior can be modified through learning does not negate the significance of genetic or biological variables. Watson may have been able to train a child with a genetic tendency toward introversion to become an outgoing, successful salesperson. However, the training may have been more difficult and extensive than it would have been with a child disposed toward extraversion. One would also want to know whether there were any negative side effects of training, whether the individual enjoyed being a salesperson, and so on.

In sum, the relation between genetics and personality is complex, and as students, scientists, and citizens, we need to think sensibly about it. We want to be able to analyze the meaning of such statements as "Mothers have innate mothering instincts" and "Humans have an innate aggressive drive" and to recognize that assertions like "War is due to the human instinct for aggression" are nonsense.

All Humans Are Alike

The Question of Instincts

Instincts are often regarded as genetic givens. An *instinct* or, more appropriately, instinctive behavior can refer to either (1) an unlearned, fixed pattern of activity, such as nest building in birds and web spinning by spiders; or (2) a specific motivational tendency that is inferred from overt behavior. An instinct in this second sense is a potential toward action and is considered an unlearned "want" or "urge" built into the structure of the organism. It is an imperative that "must" find expression, although it does not have to be recognized by the organism. Although the ends, or goals, of instincts (urges) are presumed to be fixed, the means of expression can be quite diverse. For example, Freud suggested that aggressive instincts can be satisfied through war, antisocial behavior, or self-destructive acts.

Genotype versus phenotype.   The notion that an aggressive urge can be satisfied by a variety of behaviors calls attention to an important distinction that is evident throughout this chapter: that of genotype and phenotype. *Phenotype* refers to the observed behavior; *genotype,* to the underlying cause. It is evident that similar phenotypes may reflect quite different genotypes. For example, while two children may both be hitting their father, one may be expressing hatred and the other, playfulness. Or in one case there may be intense anger inhibited by great fear, while in the other there is only mild anger inhibited by mild fear. Conversely, different phenotypes may have similar causes, or genotypes, as when an aggressive urge is expressed in a cruel joke or a self-destructive act. In this chapter genotype refers to the underlying genetic makeup of the individual, while phenotype is an observed behavior or characteristic.

History of the instinct concept.   The notion that human beings are guided by "inner urges" and that such a genotype leads to a variety of phenotypic behaviors was very prevalent in the early part of this century. Psychologists at that time often employed the concept of instinct to account for a broad array of human and infrahuman behavior. Holt (1931, p. 428) satirized the overuse of the word *instinct:* "If he goes with his fellows, it is the 'herd instinct' which activates him; if he walks alone, it is the 'anti-social instinct'; . . . if he twiddles his thumbs, it is the 'thumb-twiddling instinct.' Thus, everything is explained with the facility of magic—word magic." Some even contended that there must be an instinct to believe in instincts!

In the face of such criticisms, the use of instinct as an explanatory construct began to wane (see Beach, 1955). However, in more recent years ethologists, who study animal behavior in natural settings, have presented evidence supporting the notion of internal urges. This concept is perhaps most dramatically illustrated in what has been labeled *vacuum behavior,* or behavior patterns that appear when an appropriate stimulus is *not* present. For example, a starling raised in captivity will sometimes engage in complex sequences of hunting, killing, and even eating prey, even though there is no prey in the cage. The bird thus seems to be acting on an instinctive urge. In a similar manner, caged female birds sometimes take hold of their own feathers and go through the motions of building a nest with them.

Ethologists such as Lorenz (1950) and Tinbergen (1951) account for vacuum behavior by suggesting that such actions have their own energy source. If the action does not occur, the energy accumulates; expressing the action discharges the energy. When energy accumulates, the response is likely to be expressed in inappropriate settings. Hence vacuum behaviors are considered to be goaded by internal agitations or pressures that persist over time.

One might think that the behavior of a captive starling has little to do with complex human actions. Yet Freud contended that humans have an aggressive instinct that increases over time if it is not expressed in action. Indeed, many individuals advocate the creation of socially acceptable channels in which to drain our aggressive energy, such as competition on the football field. This view is examined in detail in subsequent chapters; here we will merely note that the energy models suggested by Lorenz and Tinbergen are not widely accepted (see Hinde, 1960; Lehrman, 1953). Critics argue that the so-called accumulated energy is nowhere to be found. Ethologists, too, have recognized the shortcomings of this mechanical approach, and today few adhere to such energy models.

Instinctive Patterns of Behavior

Recall that instinct, in addition to meaning a genotypic urge, also refers to an unlearned pattern of behavior that is characteristic of all members of a species of the same sex at the same level of development. Birds' responses to mating calls and squirrels' hoarding of food are examples of such unlearned patterns of responses. These behaviors are caused primarily by genetically transmitted physiological states and functions; they are akin to the built-in behaviors exhibited by plants, such as movement toward light. These instinctive behaviors frequently are not single responses, but are action sequences that follow a predetermined, predictable course. Furthermore, the observed behaviors often are crucial for survival and therefore are interpreted in an evolutionary sense. For example, it is known that the stickleback fish will attack any other fish of its color and often any object of this particular color. This behavior results in *species-spacing,* or spreading species members apart so that there is sufficient food available for survival. Distinctive birdsong often also has a species-spacing function.

The *isolation paradigm* is the experimental procedure most often used to demonstrate that behavior is innate. In such studies, infrahuman newborns or infants are reared in isolation so that they cannot observe others or "practice" particular responses. Then they are given the opportunity to engage in a particular behavior. For example, a bird is isolated from other birds of its species, so that it never hears a mating call. Then it is taken from isolation and placed in a situation in which a mating call would be appropriate for other, normally reared birds. If the bird responds, it is exhibiting *innate behavior.* Typically, a response is believed to be innate if it is constant across all

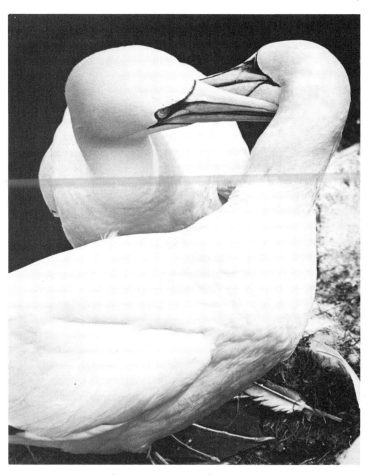

Gannets engaging in a courtship preening ritual, a complex and instinctive pattern of behavior. (© David Urry and Katie Urry/Ardea London)

members of a species, if it appears even when the animal has been raised in isolation, and if it is elicited the first time that the animal is placed in the appropriate environment. Research has demonstrated many such responses, such as birdsong and nest building, and it has been concluded that these responses have strong genetic determinants.

It often is difficult to prove with certainty that a response is innate or unlearned rather than learned and experience-based (see Lehrman, 1970). In addition, the higher the organism is in the infrahuman-human scale, the more likely that the behavior is influenced by learning. Among human beings one might expect to find few unlearned patterns of behavior, other than reflexive responses such as the eyeblink or knee jerk. Although one cannot use the isolation paradigm to identify innate human behaviors, it is quite possible that there are innate reactions—fears, aversions, preferences for particular stimulus situations—that have significance for human personality. Fear of the grotesque or a child's responsiveness to the mother's breast and the warmth of her body are possible examples of such reaction tendencies. Whether behaviors such as maternal care among humans have genetic determinants cannot be demonstrated with certainty, although it is reasonable to suppose that they do. Such an inborn tendency would have great survival value for the species, in that the young would be protected from danger and starvation. It is also important to note that humans might be goaded into such built-in instinctive actions by emotional states, so that one feels "anxiety" for the young or "guilty" about incestuous behavior. These emotions then confer a positive value on actions that are relevant for survival (see Breger, 1974). Even more complex examples of instinctive behavior have been postulated by the sociobiologists

Sociobiology

In recent years a new scientific discipline, *sociobiology,* has sought to establish that even such social behaviors as conformity, altruism, and cheating have a biological or genetic basis (Wilson, 1975, 1977).

Sociobiologists have been guided by the ideas of Darwin. They accept that survival-promoting behavior is passed on from one generation to another. But they contend that perpetuation of the genes, rather than of the individual organism, is the prime evolutionary tendency. For example, a bird may risk its own life to warn the rest of the flock of impending danger. In this manner the individual bird might not survive, but the survival of the others with like genes is aided. Sociobiologists contend that evolution produces organisms that follow this logic and "calculate" genetic gains and losses. One interesting extension of these ideas is that human altruism is expected to decline. Increasing mobility and the breakdown of families have weakened ties with the immediate kin who most share our genetic makeup; thus, we are less likely to sacrifice our own needs to aid others.

These ideas have been invoked to explain some puzzling facts. For example, why should female ants devote their lives to helping the queen to breed, instead of breeding themselves? Sociobiologists have pointed out that female ants actually share more genes in common with their sisters than they would with their own offspring. Thus, in order to perpetuate genes identical to their own, it is in their self-interest to assist the queen in producing more daughters.

Sociobiological concepts have also led to a reinterpretation of various facets of human sexual behavior. The male, sociobiologists argue, has one prime goal: to transmit as many of his own genes as possible to the next generation. On the other hand, the female must invest a great deal of time in each birth and can have only a very limited number of offspring. Thus, males are in general more promiscuous than females because only male promiscuity has much payoff. Furthermore, because females must invest more of themselves in each pregnancy, they are important resources that males must "purchase." As a result, in most cultures older males (who have more necessary resources) marry younger women (who have many years of childbearing left). Sociobiologists point out that males have only one great disadvantage in breeding: they cannot be certain that the offspring is their own. Thus, sexual jealousy is aroused and courtship rituals have emerged to monopolize the female's time. During this extended courtship the male also can determine if the female is already pregnant.

Needless to say, these controversial ideas have angered many individuals and groups. The controversy involves primarily the extension of sociobiological principles to complex human social behaviors. First, the hypotheses regarding humans are supported by relatively little data. In addition, it is obvious that cultural factors greatly influence human actions (see Washburn, 1978). For example, how can sociobiologists account for the fact that today many males undergo voluntary sterilization and the birthrate in many countries is falling so rapidly that there is zero population growth? Why do people perform altruistic acts for individuals unrelated to them (even though it is known that all humans share many genes)? In spite of difficulties in explaining such facts, advocating this extreme biological view, which is also present in part in Freudian psychology, has proved exceedingly provocative and has spurred the interpretation and reinterpretation of a variety of phenomena.

Facial Expressions and Emotions

Darwin argued that human facial expressions are inherited and are modified very little by cultural experience. For example, he pointed out that the baring of teeth by humans in situations of anger and contempt is similar to the display of teeth among carnivores prior to a hostile attack or during an aggressive defense.

A number of studies have attempted to verify Darwin's insight. These studies bear on the biological basis of emotional experience as well as on the universality of emotional displays. Two basic paradigms have been followed in this research area: (1) examining the facial expressions of children born deaf and blind; and (2) analyzing the agreement concerning identification of emotions in different cultures.

A baboon in full threat gesture, with teeth bared. Darwin pointed out that a human snarl has a similar facial pattern and suggested that emotional displays are genetically programed. (Irven Devore/Anthro-Photo)

Investigations reveal that blind and deaf children do display quite normal facial expressions (Eibl-Eibesfeldt, 1970; Freedman, 1964). Hence, these observations tend to support the universalistic, Darwinian explanation of facial expression. Of course, culture plays some role in the control of facial expression and in determining which situations are appropriate for eliciting and displaying particular emotions and facial expressions.

The cross-cultural research has been guided by identification of the so-called basic human emotions. Ekman and Friesen (1975) isolated six primary emotions—fear, surprise, disgust, anger, happiness, and sadness—and also identified the facial muscles associated with these affective (emotional) states. Photographs showing the facial expressions associated with these emotions (Fig. 2.1 shows these for anger and happiness) were then shown to people in five different countries—the United States, Brazil, Chile, Argentina, and Japan—and the subjects were asked to identify the emotion portrayed. Table 2.1 shows the percentage of agreement with the labels supplied by Ekman and Friesen. As Table 2.1 indicates, there is quite high agreement among the five nations. In addition, natives of New Guinea, who did not have reading skills and were not subject to the possible confounding of media exposure, responded similarly to individuals in the other five countries. In sum, it appears that facial expressions of some emotions are to a large extent a genetically based characteristic of the species.

Figure 2.1   Examples of the photographs used to portray the six primary emotions. These faces express anger (left) and happiness (right). (Ekman and Friesen, *Unmasking the Face*, 1975, p. 25. Used by permission. Photographs by Ed Gallob.)

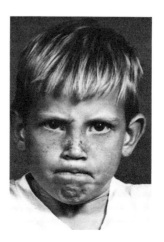

Table 2.1   Percentage agreement in how photograph was judged across cultures

Emotion	United States (n = 99)	Brazil (n = 40)	Chile (n = 119)	Argentina (n = 168)	Japan (n = 29)
Fear	85	67	68	54	66
Disgust	92	97	92	92	90
Happiness	97	95	95	98	100
Anger	67	90	94	90	90

Source: From the book, *Unmasking the Face* by Paul Ekman and Wallace V. Friesen. © 1975 by Prentice-Hall, Inc. Published by Prentice-Hall, Inc., Englewood Cliffs, N.J.

The Incest Taboo

The *incest taboo* is basically a restriction in sexual choice. In Western culture this behavior includes primarily parents and siblings, but also extends to close cousins. Sexual restriction is, of course, not confined to Western cultures; the types of limitations may, however, differ between cultures. As Laing (1965) has pointed out: "A good deal of effort in all societies is given to deciding which bodies may be joined on which occasion and at what age. Persons in all cultures are governed in their actions by an intricate web of injunctions about whose bodies of what sex their own bodies should come into contact with." The generality of the incest taboo, first pointed out by Freud, is considered one of the major observations in the social sciences. Why and how might such a moral rule have arisen? Why do most individuals feel such contempt or disgust when reading of an incestuous relationship?

One function of the incest taboo is to forestall intrafamily rivalry, which could cause jealousy within and disruption of the family. In addition, marriage outside the family often strengthens the involved parties. The alliance of two countries, for example, frequently has been secured by marriage between members of the ruling families. In earlier cultures, intergroup marriage frequently was forced. Service (1966, p. 36) states:

There is but one means of keeping up permanent alliance, and that means is intermarriage. . . . Again and again in the world's history, savage tribes must have had plainly before their minds the simple practical alternative between marrying-out and being killed-out. Even far on in culture, the political value of intermarriage remains. . . . "Then we will give our daughters unto you, and we will take your daughters to us, and we will dwell with you and we will become one people," is a well-known passage of Israelite history.

Finally, and perhaps of greatest importance, genetic research has revealed that inbreeding leads to the expression of genes that reduce fitness, as displayed in mental deficiency or physical abnormality. Outbreeding, on the other hand, counteracts deficiencies and tends to produce "hybrid vigor" (Lindzey, 1967a).

For these many reasons, it has been suggested that inhibitions were erected not only against particular sexual acts, but even against the arousal of certain desires. That is, anticipatory controls over sexual wishes were developed. Over many years these sexual barriers became internalized rules and customs, passed on from generation to generation. Here again we see the possible importance of genetics in influencing complex human behavior.

All Humans Are Unique

Despite cross-cultural similarities and the universality of some behaviors, it can equally well be said that each human is genetically unique. Given the billions of possible inherited gene patterns, each individual is provided with fairly idiosyncratic genetic configurations. The resulting variability in genetic structure is manifested in individual differences in characteristics and behavior. Two basic procedures have been followed in studying the genetic determinants of individual differences. One method is experimental, involving the selective breeding of infrahumans. The other is nonexperimental in the sense that there is no intervention in the lives of its human subjects.

The Experimental Study of Heritability

For many years *selective breeding* has been unsystematically performed on domestic animals to enhance certain temperamental or behavioral characteristics, such as ferocity, docility, hunting ability, and so on. In more systematic laboratory settings, animals exhibiting a high or low degree of a certain behavior, such as emotionality, are selectively bred for generations and the emotionality of subsequent generations is then compared. The experimenter thus performs on a compressed time scale what natural selection is presumed to do during the course of evolution. In natural selection, high or low extremes of a characteristic, or *directional selection,* may be favored. For example, natural selection in oppossums evidently favored inertness in the face of danger; visual aggressive displays or strength and speed are favored in other species. In nature, as in the laboratory, there may also be *balancing selection,* which favors intermediate values of the characteristic in question.

The logic of breeding experiments is straightforward and nicely illustrates what is meant by the concept of heritability. Assume, for example, that we observe a group of animals learning a maze and that they attain scores of 1–10, based on the number of trials before success. That is, one animal learns the maze in a single trial, another takes two trials, a third requires three trials, and so on. Now, for example, we take the "brightest" animals, which require only one trial to learn, and we inbreed them. Of their offspring, we again inbreed the fastest learners. Assume that this procedure is continued for thirty generations. Now, if the thirtieth generation of animals still gives us scores of 1–10 in maze learning, we know that the ability to learn this maze has no heritability. Rather, the differences among the animals are due entirely to environmental factors. Conversely, assume that for this thirtieth generation all the animals learn the maze in one trial. In that case, we would assume that maze learning was due entirely to genetic factors; heritability is the determining factor. In actuality in this situation, the variability among the animals, i.e., their differences in trials to learn, will most likely decrease over generations, but will not disappear entirely. Thus, there will be both genetic and environmental determinants of learning, with the decrease in variability indicating the degree to which this behavior is influenced by genetic factors.

A representative study of selective breeding for a particular ability is illustrated in an investigation by Thompson (1954). Thompson measured the speed with which rats learned a maze for a food reward. Then he bred the low-error (maze-bright) rats with other maze-bright rats, and the high-error (maze-dull) rats with other maze-dull rats. The offspring of these matings were then tested on the maze. This procedure continued for six generations; by the sixth generation, the error scores of the two breeding populations were dramatically different (see Fig. 2.2). It is interesting to note that rats superior in maze learning do not necessarily master other problems as rapidly. Maze learning appears to be a specific ability.

The data in Fig. 2.2 indicate that maze learning is influenced by heredity. But this should not be taken to mean that environmental factors have little or no effect on such learning. Cooper and Zubek (1958) took the strains of rats bred by Thompson and reared them in either enriched or impoverished conditions. The enriched environment contained ramps, tunnels, and many movable objects, whereas the restricted environment included only a food box and a water tin. When the maze learning of the rats was assessed (see Table 2.2), the experimenters found that when the groups were reared in either extreme environment, their performance did not differ greatly. The enriched environment primarily raised the performance of the dull rats, while the restricted environment chiefly lowered the performance of the bright rats. Only

Figure 2.2   The results of selective breeding for maze learning. (Thompson, 1954, p. 217. Used by permission of the Association for Research in Nervous and Mental Disease, Inc., and the author.)

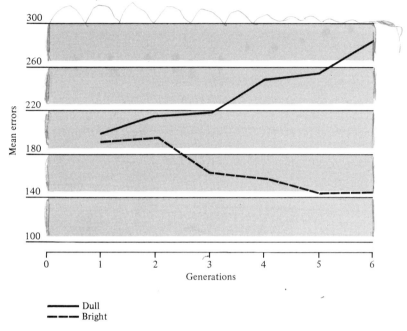

in the normal environment were there differences due to an innate ability factor. Hence, there is nothing absolute about heritability; an organism's individual sensitivity to disparate environmental conditions may either mask or exacerbate inborn tendencies. What is inherited, then, is the way in which the organism responds to the environment, and heritability is in turn a function of the environment in which the behavior is studied.

Table 2.2   Mean error scores for maze-bright and maze-dull rats raised in different environments

Rats	Enriched environment	Normal environment	Restricted environment
Bright	111	117	170
Dull	120	164	170

Source: Adapted from Cooper and Zubek, 1958, pp. 160, 161. Used by permission.

Very similar conclusions regarding heritability have been reached in the study of emotionality. Broadhurst (1961) inbred high- and low-emotionality rats, selected on the basis of their defecation in an open field test. In this procedure, rats are placed in an unfamiliar environment, and emotional responses are inferred from the well-documented fact that fear causes defecation and urination. After six generations of inbreeding, there were dramatic differences between the populations, with the data resembling those reported by Thompson (1954) in terms of the magnitude of group differences and the increasing inequality in emotionality over the generations.

While it seems reasonable that learning ability and even emotionality may have a genetic basis, it is perhaps less sensible to believe that preferences or incentive values have a genetic component, as opposed to being entirely learned. However, breeding experiments have demonstrated that alcohol preference also may be inherited. It has been documented that particular strains of mice choose an alcohol solution over a water solution (Rodgers, 1966), while other strains avoid alcohol and prefer water. Furthermore, when strains with high and low alcohol preference are interbred, the offspring display an intermediate desire for alcohol as opposed to water (Rodgers and McClearn, 1962). Later in this chapter we will suggest that alcoholism among humans might also be determined in part by inborn tendencies.

The Study of Heritability Through Human Research

In contrast to studies of infrahumans, research using human populations is nonexperimental in the sense that there is no intervention or manipulation of variables, because of obvious ethical constraints. Rather, individuals who vary in their degree of genetic relationship, such as foster parents and their children, natural parents and their children, siblings, fraternal twins, and identical twins, are compared and contrasted. Genetic similarity is a function of degree of kinship, so for genetically influenced characteristics, similarity in behavior and character should increase with biological relatedness.

The basic shortcoming of human genetic research is that the environments are not controlled. As a result, it is often impossible to infer with certainty that observed behavioral similarity is a function of biological relatedness and is due to inborn characteristics. In infrahuman research using inbreeding techniques, the environments are controlled and identical for each group.

Consider, for example, a hypothetical research study demonstrating that emotional mothers have highly emotional children, whereas nonemotional mothers have children with low emotionality. These data might be interpreted as demonstrating that emotionality is heritable. However, it is quite possible that these children had different home environments; perhaps highly emotional mothers create unstable environments which produce highly emotional children, while nonemotional mothers establish stable environments which give rise to children low in emotionality. In this investigation, the learning and the genetic contributions to emotionality cannot be separated.

To help interpret the ambiguous results of such family studies, twin and adoption studies are often employed to disentangle genetic and environmental contributions.

The central research separating genetic from environmental contributions to human behavior involves a comparison between twins from different eggs (fraternal, or dizygotic twins) with those from the same egg (identical, or monozygotic twins). The latter type share completely identical gene pools; dizygotic twins, on the average, share only about 50 percent of their genes. Hence, monozygotic (MZ) twins should be more alike in behavior than dizygotic (DZ) twins, if the behavior under study has a genetic component. This hypothesis assumes that the environments of DZ twins are as identical as the environments of MZ twins. However, such an assumption, although reasonable, is not always warranted. Identical twins may have more similar social learning histories; it has been found that they are more likely to dress alike, have common friends, and spend more time together than fraternal twins (Smith, 1965). Thus, even twin studies need to be scrutinized carefully before making inferences about genetic influences on behavior.

In principle, it is possible to study the effects of shared genes by comparing identical twins reared in similar versus different environments. Although such a sample is seldom available, some investigations have examined the similarities of siblings adopted in infancy and reared in foster homes, compared with unrelated individuals reared in these same homes. Any differences in the similarities within these two groups, given that all else is equal, are logically attributable to the genetic similarity of the sibs. Conversely, any differences in the behavior of identical twins show environmental and experiential influences on behavior.

Identical (monozygotic) twins. Evidence indicates that many aspects of their temperament and behavior also will be similar. (Copyright © Harvey Stein, 1978)

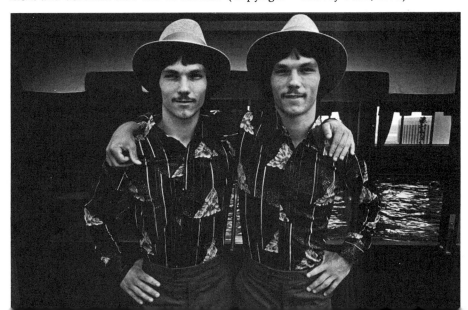

We now turn to some investigations that have compared identical with fraternal twins. First, some personality characteristics of these groups are examined, and then various psychological problems, such as schizophrenia and alcoholism, are analyzed for genetic determination.

Temperament.   *Temperament* may be defined as the "characteristic phenomena of an individual's nature, including his susceptibility to emotional stimulation, his customary strength and speed of response, the quality of his prevailing mood, and all the peculiarities of fluctuation and intensity of mood" (Allport, 1961, p. 34). Buss, Plomin, and Willerman (1973) selected four temperaments to study for heritability: emotionality, activity, sociability, and impulsivity. Twenty-item questionnaires were constructed, with five items for each temperament. These questionnaires were given to mothers of fraternal (DZ) or identical (MZ) twins. The mothers rated items such as "Child cries easily" on a scale of 1 (a little) to 5 (a lot). The items, their corresponding temperaments, and the correlations for the two sets of twins, separated according to sex, are shown in Table 2.3. Table 2.3 reveals that, on virtually all the items, the correlations were higher for the MZ than for the DZ twins of both sexes. However, it must also be mentioned that because the questionnaire used in this investigation had not been previously demonstrated as valid, one must be cautious about full acceptance of the data. For example, the mothers' responses may have been influenced by their own preconceptions of twin behavior, rather than by the twins' actual behavior. The findings do support the hypothesis that these temperaments have a genetic component, but closer examination of the results also demonstrated the effects of the environment on temperament. For example, although not shown in Table 2.3, the correlations for all but the emotionality items decreased sharply from early to late childhood, as revealed when the correlations were examined separately for twins above and below the age of 4½. (Not all researchers, however, have found this decrease in correlation over time.) Furthermore, at times the differences in the correlations between the identical and the fraternal twins are so great (e.g., the correlations for the item "Child tends to be impulsive" are $r = .81$ for the male MZ twins, but $r = 0$ for the male DZ pairs) that environmental influences must have acted to make the fraternal twins less alike.

Introversion-extraversion.   It has been suggested that introversion-extraversion may be the most genetically influenced of the personality traits. Introverts are defined as quiet, retiring, introspective, and not very socially active. Extraverts, on the other hand, are characterized as being outgoing, impulsive, and uninhibited, having many social contacts, and frequently taking part in group activities (Eysenck and Eysenck, 1964).

The best-known theory of introversion-extraversion relates this personality dimension to inherited differences in the functioning of the reticular activating system (RAS). This neurological activating system is located in various areas of the cortex and is responsible for an organism's level of arousal or degree of internal stimulation. Eysenck (1967) has suggested that under nor-

Table 2.3　　Items and correlations on the temperament scales

	Correlations			
	Males		Females	
A priori scale assignment	MZ*	DZ*	MZ*	DZ*
Emotionality				
Child cries easily.	.56	.10	.47	.23
Child has a quick temper.	.34	.10	.40	.70
Child gets upset quickly.	.64	.10	.66	.00
Child is easily frightened.	.58	.11	.70	.00
Child is easygoing or happy-go-lucky.	.46	.00	.38	.00
Activity				
Child is off and running as soon as he wakes up in the morning.	.88	.41	.86	.00
Child is always on the go.	.48	.02	.72	.01
Child cannot sit still long.	.76	.25	.65	.27
Child prefers quiet games such as coloring or block play to more active games.	.77	.00	.21	.03
Child fidgets at meals and similar occasions.	.67	.38	.68	.31
Sociability				
Child makes friends easily.	.74	.26	.47	.00
Child likes to be with others.	.61	.27	.29	.05
Child tends to be shy.	.57	.10	.51	.00
Child is independent.	.58	.25	.44	.24
Child prefers to play by himself rather than with others.	.55	.10	.73	.46
Impulsivity				
Learning self-control is difficult for the child.	.75	.55	.83	.69
Child tends to be impulsive.	.81	.00	.68	.39
Child gets bored easily.	.83	.13	.49	.59
Child learns to resist temptation easily.	.72	.35	.70	.52
Child goes from toy to toy quickly.	.82	.44	.83	.62

Source: A.H. Buss, R. Plomin, and L. Willerman, "The Inheritance of Temperaments," *Journal of Personality, 41,* 1973, p. 517. Copyright 1973, Duke University Press (Durham, NC).

* MZ = monozygotic
　DZ = dizygotic

mal conditions introverts are more highly aroused than extraverts. Somewhat paradoxically, high arousal results in restraints or inhibited behavior because the cortex is exercising control over the more primitive brain centers (see Wilson, 1978). Extraverts, on the other hand, being less normally aroused, are also subject to less cortical control.

Given this physiological conception, one might anticipate a high degree of heritability in this personality dimension; the twin studies support this belief. Several investigations have compared the similarity of MZ and DZ twins on self-report measures of extraversion (see Shields, 1976). These measures contain such items as:

- Do you often long for excitement?
- Are you mostly quiet when you are with people?
- Generally, do you prefer reading to meeting people?

The typical correlations between the test scores of the MZ twins approximate $r = .50$; the usual correlation for the DZ twins is about $r = .20$. The correlation between normal sibs and child-parent pairs is also around $r = .20$. In one study, Shields (1976) found that identical twins separated from each other actually had slightly more similar scores on the extraversion scale than identical twins reared together, as if parents reacted to the twins or they reacted to each other in a manner that would enhance their differences.

Loehlin and Nichols (1976), making use of personality inventory responses, reported data that support the above conclusion. The subjects, twins who had taken the National Merit Scholarship Qualifying Test, were administered a variety of measures, including the California Psychological Inventory (CPI), which consists of eighteen different scales, some of which relate to the introversion-extraversion dimension. On virtually all of these scales the correlations of the scores for the MZ twins approximated $r = .50$; those for the DZ pairs were $r = .20-.30$.

Carey, Goldsmith, Tellegen, and Gottesman (1978) examined a number of twin studies that used the CPI scales and computed the mean correlations for all the investigations (see Table 2.4). It is evident from Table 2.4 that the correlations are much higher for the identical than for the fraternal twins, with the typical difference about $r = .20$. Furthermore, the highest MZ versus DZ heritabilities are for dominance, sociability, social presence, and self-acceptance, which are subscales of extraversion. In sum, it appears that many personality traits may have a genetic component and that the tendency toward introversion or extraversion has the greatest heritability.

Mental illness and social problems.   The twin studies of heritability of personality required the assignment of quantitative degrees of the trait under investigation to the individuals being compared. This number was derived from reports of others, self-reports, or actual observations of behavior. Examination of the genetic determination of mental illness and social problems, on the other hand, involves the assignment of individuals to a category, such as schizophrenic, alcoholic, criminal, and so on. Then the rates of *concordance* (both twins classified in the same category) and *discordance* (twins in different categories) are examined. The genetic hypothesis concerning social problems

Table 2.4   Mean MZ and mean DZ correlations for the eighteen CPI scales

CPI scale	MZ	DZ
Dominance	.59	.31
Capacity for status	.61	.46
Sociability	.54	.21
Social presence	.54	.28
Self-acceptance	.51	.23
Well-being	.46	.31
Responsibility	.49	.33
Socialization	.47	.25
Self-control	.52	.30
Tolerance	.52	.32
Good impression	.48	.23
Communality	.30	.12
Achievement (conformance)	.40	.25
Achievement (independence)	.53	.37
Intellectual efficiency	.54	.38
Psychological mindedness	.43	.21
Flexibility	.50	.30
Femininity	.42	.25

From Carey et al., 1978, p. 307. Reprinted by permission.

is corroborated when higher concordance rates are displayed as a function of biological relatedness.

The mental illness that has been most extensively investigated from a genetic perspective is schizophrenia. Gottesman and Shields (1972) collected data from all the pertinent studies that had been conducted and compared the concordance rates of schizophrenia for fraternal and identical twins. In such studies one starts with a hospitalized schizophrenic, finds out if he or she has a twin, and determines whether or not the twin has ever been or is now hospitalized with the same diagnosis. The name of the investigator, the size of the sample, and the rates of concordance in the studies compiled by Gottesman and Shields are shown in Table 2.5, page 44. The data clearly suggest that schizophrenia has a genetic component.

Table 2.5   Concordance rates in twin studies

Investigator	Date	MZ pairs			DZ pairs		
		n^a	c^a	%	n^a	c^a	%
Luxenburger	1928	19	11	58	13	0	0
Rosanoff et al.	1934	41	25	61	53	7	13
Essen-Möller	1941	11	7	64	27	4	15
Kallmann	1946	174	120	69	296	34	11
Slater	1953	37	24	65	58	8	14
Inouye	1961	55	33	60	11	2	18
Tienari	1963	16		6–36[b]	20		5–14
Kringlen	1967	55		25–38	90		4–10
Fischer et al.	1969	21		24–48	41		10–19
Pollin et al.	1969	80		14–35	146		4–10

Source: I.I. Gottesman and J. Shields, *Schizophrenia and Genetics: A Twin Study Vantage Point* (New York: Academic Press, 1972), pp. 30–31. Reprinted by permission.

[a]n represents the total numbers of pairs; c represents concordant pairs, i.e., those pairs in which both members were schizophrenic.
[b]Range of concordance rates reported by investigators.

In a discussion of the inborn determinants of schizophrenia, a well-known psychologist (Meehl, 1962, p. 827) wrote:

Let me begin by putting a question which I find is almost never answered correctly by our clinical students on PhD orals, and the answer to which they seem to dislike when it is offered. Suppose that you were required to write down a procedure for selecting an individual from the population who would be diagnosed as schizophrenic by a psychiatric staff; you have to wager $1,000 on being right; you may not include in your selection procedure any behavioral fact, such as a symptom or trait, manifested by the individual. What would you write down? So far as I have been able to ascertain, there is only one thing you could write down that would give you a better than even chance of winning such a bet—namely, "Find an individual X who has a schizophrenic identical twin." Admittedly, there are many other facts which would raise your odds somewhat above the low base rate of schizophrenia. You might, for example, identify X by first finding mothers who have certain unhealthy child-rearing attitudes; you might enter a subpopulation defined jointly by such demographic variables as age, size of community, religion, ethnic background, or social class. But these would leave you with a pretty unfair wager, as would the rule, "Find an X who has a fraternal twin, of the same sex, diagnosed as schizophrenic."

Even when sibs and twins are reared apart, there are high concordance rates of schizophrenia (see Rosenthal, 1970). Similarly, manic-depressive psychoses clearly appear to be influenced by inborn characteristics (see Bertelsen, Harvald, and Hauge, 1977; Kallmann, 1958).

Finally, recall that the preference for alcohol differed greatly among strains of mice. Humans also apparently have inborn preferences or susceptibility to alcoholism, for investigations reveal a marked heritability of this problem. (Of course, preference for alcohol among rats and alcoholism among humans should not be considered identical phenomena.) It has long been recognized that alcoholism is a familial disorder in that rates of alcoholism are far higher among relatives of alcoholics than among the general population. Goodwin et al. (1973) even found that where children have been separated from their biological parents at birth or shortly thereafter, the presence of alcoholism in the biological parents is of far greater predictive significance for the development of this disorder in the children than is the presence of alcoholism among the adoptive parents. An offspring of an alcoholic parent is more likely to become an alcoholic even when raised by nonalcoholic foster parents than is an offspring of nonalcoholic parents when raised by alcoholic foster parents. But, even this evidence is not definitive for the genetic determination of drinking; it could be, for instance, that offspring of alcoholics are placed in less desirable homes. The data, however, are highly suggestive of built-in determination of the development of a drinking disorder.

It is not known how this predisposition might be transmitted and to what degree heritability accounts for the transmission of this illness. Furthermore, it is likely that what is inherited is only a breeding ground where social-cultural factors play a role in the manifestation of alcoholism. Indeed, the different rates of alcoholism between males and females and between various ethnic groups point to the crucial role of social-cultural factors in determining who actually becomes an alcoholic. Even in this regard, though, the relative roles of genetics and culture are exceedingly complex. For example, it has been suggested that the Chinese drink little because of a genetic propensity to become ill with alcohol intake. Clearly, then, the disentanglement of genetic from cultural factors cannot be readily resolved, and simple instances of a genetic or a cultural influence, on closer inspection, reveal contributions from the other source.

Classification by Type

Biological givens are often relied on to classify individuals. Later in this text one such classification—gender—is examined in detail. Another biological classification scheme is based on body build. Kretschmer (1925) identified four basic constitutional types: pyknic (short and stocky), athletic (strong and well proportioned), leptosomic (tall and slender), and dysplastic (a mixture of the other three). Kretschmer, who believed that body build is related to mental disorders, reported that schizophrenics are often leptosomic and that manic-depressives are typically pyknic.

Guided by Kretschmer, Sheldon and his colleagues (Sheldon and Stevens, 1942; Sheldon, Stevens, and Tucker, 1940) suggested that there are three fundamental physiques and that each physique is associated with a particular temperament.

Physique	*Temperament*

1. Endomorphy (soft and round; digestive viscera overdeveloped)
2. Mesomorphy (muscular, rectangular, strong)
3. Ectomorphy (long and fragile; large brain and sensitive nervous system)

1. Viscerotonic (relaxed, loves to eat, sociable)
2. Somatotonic (energetic, assertive, courageous)
3. Cerebrotonic (restrained, fearful, introverted, artistic)

Relatively sophisticated rating scales have been developed to assess each of these body types.

The idea that physical type influences personality has received relatively little attention from psychologists. This stems in part from the charlatan image created by palmists and phrenologists (see Chapter 1), as well as from a general reluctance to accept genetic determinism. Nonetheless, there are a number of reasons why body type might influence behavior (see Lindzey, 1967*b*). Some of these reasons implicate social or experiential variables, but others relate directly to genetics.

1. The same experience might influence both physiology and behavior (e.g., maternal overprotection might result in both obesity and overdependence).
2. Factors such as height and weight set limits on behavior as well as influence what behaviors will be rewarded. For example, individuals of a certain biological makeup will be more likely to engage and succeed in sports, which could in turn affect their behavior and self-concept.
3. Society holds certain expectations about the relationship of body characteristics and behavior (e.g., "Fat people are jolly"; "Redheads have hot tempers") that could foster certain biology-behavior linkages.
4. Genetics might influence both physique and behavior. For example, it has been demonstrated that albino mice are especially poor at escape learning (Winston and Lindzey, 1964). In a similar manner, it has been clearly documented that, among humans, mesomorphs are overrepresented among delinquents (see Lindzey, 1967*b*). Furthermore, studies indicating that criminal behavior has higher concordance among identical than among fraternal twins suggest that a common genotype may be influencing this form of socially deviant behavior.

Summary Human beings are the product of a long evolutionary history that predisposes them to behave in certain ways. In addition, genetic makeup is evident in the uniqueness of each person and in the similarity of individuals to other persons of like genetic heritage. These propositions have been subject to a good deal of vigorous experimental research, ranging from selective breeding to human twin studies of schizophrenia. The research has conclusively demonstrated the far-reaching influence of genetics on personality and behavior.

*Specific
Points*

1. A characteristic or a predisposition can be both inherited and modified by environmental factors and experience. For example, early diet manipulation may prevent a genetic mental deficiency known as PKU.
2. *Instinct* has two meanings: (a) an unlearned, fixed pattern of activity such as nest building in birds, and (b) an inner "want" or "urge."
3. The concept of instinct as an inner urge is exemplified by *vacuum behavior*, a behavior pattern undertaken in the absence of the appropriate stimulus. Ethologists have explained these behaviors with the suggestion that energy may accumulate within an organism if a behavior is not expressed.
4. To study whether or not a behavior is innate, the *isolation paradigm* is used. The organism is reared alone and then given the opportunity to engage in the behavior under study.
5. *Sociobiology* seeks to establish that complex social behavior has a biological or genetic basis. The generalization of these conclusions to humans is under question.
6. Some facial expressions appear to be universal. This observation supports the Darwinian belief that expressions are inherited behaviors.
7. The *incest taboo* may have an inherited component, since its function is to strengthen families through forced outbreeding, which lessens the likelihood of certain genetic disorders that increase with inbreeding.
8. *Selective breeding* experiments have demonstrated that specific abilities such as maze learning and traits such as emotionality have genetic components. The offspring in such studies tend to behave similarly to their parents
9. Twin studies comparing identical and fraternal twins have demonstrated that temperament and personality traits like introversion-extraversion have genetic components.
10. Studies of social problems using *concordance* and *discordance* rates have demonstrated a genetic basis for mental illnesses like schizophrenia and for social problems like alcoholism.
11. There is evidence that body type is related to behavior, although it is uncertain whether such a linkage is inherited or is a product of social experience.

*Thought
Questions*

1. What are some of the arguments, pro and con, that might be advanced concerning eugenics and the genetic regulation of marriages?
2. Can you think of any apparently instinctive patterns of behavior in pets you have observed?
3. What might a sociobiologist say about falling in love?
4. What evolutionary changes in human personality do you predict will take place in the future?

Physical, Social, and Cultural Determinants of Personality and Behavior

3

In Chapter 2 we contended that personality structure and behavior are determined in part by a long evolutionary history that predisposes individuals to act in certain ways. People come into the world with genetic givens that influence who and what they are and what they become.

In this chapter we examine the same questions from a totally different perspective: how aspects of the environment into which we are born influence us. These determinants of behavior, which are not genetically transmitted, are part of the impinging physical, social, and cultural milieu. Human beings are versatile in their patterns of adaptation to a variety of physical and social conditions—they dwell in hot or cold climates; they have contrasting social roles; they are brought up in cultures with widely disparate customs and mores. All of these factors produce different modes of behavior. Indeed, it has been said that humans have no nature, only history.

In this chapter we examine two types of influence on personality and behavior: the physical world, such as the climate or architecture; and the social world, such as one's class and one's culture, including the rules and mores of the larger society.

The Physical World

It is convenient to distinguish between two aspects of the physical world: (1) the natural environment, including the climate, availability of resources, existence of nearby bodies of water, and similar factors; and (2) constructed environments such as offices, homes, and hospitals (Altman, 1976).

The Natural Environment

The natural environment makes demands, sets constraints, and provides resources. In short, it has a great deal to do with how we live our lives and thus tends to affect personality greatly. For example, families in extremely cold climates are more likely to sleep in one bed. This sleeping pattern could influence the closeness of the family, sexual attitudes, and related aspects of personality development. Individuals typically are not consciously aware of the importance of physical factors as determinants of personality. Thus, both the natural environment and the biological givens discussed in Chapter 2 exert their effect without the immediate knowledge of those affected.

Climate, subsistence, and settlement patterns. Cross-cultural investigations of the influence of climate on personality nicely illustrate the interlocking of the physical and social worlds. You should be aware that climate is just one example among many (e.g., physical resources, topography, amount of daylight, ionization of the atmosphere) we could have selected to demonstrate personality's broad environmental context. Climate is particularly appropriate for discussion because its effects on personality and behavior have been clearly documented.

Berry (1976) has shown that one manner in which climate affects personality is through the causal chain of climate → settlement pattern → individuals' personalities. Anthropologists have identified four settlement patterns of societies: fully nomadic (move continuously); seminomadic (move regularly but occupy a fixed settlement for a season); semisedentary (move regularly but less often); and fully sedentary (occupy one settlement for a long period of time). These patterns of adaptation are directly related to the manner in which the society subsists. Societies that live by hunting and gathering are semi- or fully nomadic, whereas agricultural societies are semi- or fully sedentary.

Two climatic variables influence both the means of subsistence and the settlement pattern within a society: the average temperature and the amount of rainfall. The temperature level and amount of rain permit organisms to satisfy their subsistence and shelter needs in diverse ways. In the case of both low rainfall and low temperature, as in polar regions, agriculture is impossible. Hence, the means of satisfying basic nutritional needs are hunting and/or fishing, activities that typically require a nomadic existence. Given low rainfall but high temperature, as in desert regions, neither agriculture nor fishing is possible, but hunger can be satisfied by hunting and gathering; this, too, requires mobility. Given high rainfall, however, agricultural activities are possible for the satisfaction of basic needs.

In sum, the natural environmental factors of temperature and rainfall influence the manner in which food needs are met and, in turn, influence patterns of settlement. Furthermore, these disparate methods of need satisfaction require different personality types in order for the society to survive. In agricultural societies, according to Barry, Child, and Bacon (1959, p. 52):

Carelessness in performance of routine duties leads to a threat of hunger, not for the day of carelessness itself but for many months to come. Individual initiative attempts to improve techniques may be feared because no one can tell immediately whether the changes will lead to a greater harvest or to a disastrous failure. Under those conditions, there might well be a premium on obedience to the older and wiser, and on responsibility in faithful performance to the routine laid down by custom for one's economic role.

Furthermore, "growing and harvesting crops on a large scale requires teamwork, and rigid organization may be needed to mobilize and direct the people's efforts toward the common goal of an abundant harvest" (Pelto, 1968, p. 40). On the other hand (Barry, Child, and Bacon, 1959, p. 52):

At an opposite extreme is subsistence through hunting or fishing with no means for extended storing of catch. Here individual initiative and development of high skill seem to be at a premium. Where each day's food comes from that day's catch, variations in the energy and skill exerted in food-getting lead to immediate reward or punishment.

To summarize, societies must cope with disparate environmental demands and may require disparate personality types in order to be successful. Agricultural societies need to bring up children to be reliable and obedient, whereas hunting societies require that their members be self-reliant and autonomous. The research indicates that societies do indeed tend to beget appropriate personalities.

Table 3.1 shows the relationship between degree of food accumulation, which is high in agricultural societies and low in hunting societies, and child-rearing practices that promote responsibility, obedience, and achievement. Table 3.1 clearly reveals that high food-accumulation societies stress compliance (there is a high positive correlation between amount of food accumulation and responsibility and obedience), whereas low food-accumulation societies emphasize assertion and autonomy (there is a high negative correlation between amount of food accumulation and achievement, self-reliance, and autonomy, meaning that the higher the food accumulation, the lower these other variables).

The research therefore suggests dramatic relationships among the natural environment, means of need satisfaction, food accumulation, settlement pattern, and socialization practices (see Table 3.2). Although it seems farfetched and requires an understanding of many mediating variables, it is not entirely incorrect to say that personality is determined by the amount of rainfall!

Table 3.1	Relationship between six child-training practices and degree of food accumulation	

Child-training variables	Boys	Girls
Responsibility	+.74	+.62
Obedience	+.50	+.59
Nurturance	−.01	+.10
Achievement	−.60	−.62
Self-reliance	−.21	−.46
Independence	−.41	−.11

Source: H. Barry, I. Child, and M. Bacon, "Relation of Child Training to Subsistence Economy," *American Anthropologist,* *61,* 1959, p. 57. Reproduced by permission of the American Anthropological Association from the *American Anthropologist* 61 (1):57, 1959.

There have also been laboratory attempts to substantiate the linkages shown in Table 3.2. In one investigation (Berry, 1967), individuals from high and low food-accumulating cultures (respectively, the Temne and Eskimo peoples) were tested for conformity in a controlled laboratory setting. The participants were asked to match the length of various lines and in one condition were given false information about others' responses. It was demonstrated that the Temne (high food accumulators) tended to agree with the alleged responses of others, regardless of the information's correctness. Of course, there may be many interpretations of the observed differences in conformity. However, the findings are in accordance with the hypotheses suggested in Table 3.2, thus contributing to a consistent network of theory, support from field observations, and laboratory findings.

Table 3.2	General overview of relation between ecology and socialization practices	

Rainfall:	Low	High
Subsistence:	Hunting and gathering	Agriculture
Food accumulation:	Low	High
Settlement pattern:	Nomadic	Sedentary
Socialization emphasis:	Assertion	Compliance

Source: Table adapted from "Human Ecology and Cognitive Style," John W. Berry, p. 60, © 1976, Sage Publications, Beverly Hills, with permission of the publisher.

Climate and aggression. We are all familiar with the stereotype that individuals living in a warm climate are much more impulsive and tempestuous than individuals living in a cold climate. The phrase *hot tempered* illustrates this common association between heat and anger. One possible way of obtaining evidence relevant to this belief is to compare the predominant personality types found in such areas as Sweden, Norway, and Siberia with the personality types found in more southern climates, as in Italy, Argentina, and Indonesia. However, there are so many other differences between these populations, including religion, economic well-being, and social history, that one could not reasonably attribute any observed differences in aggression to disparities in climate.

Another approach to this question is to examine the relation *within* a culture between temperature and aggressive behavior. It can be assumed that

Figure 3.1 Frequency of collective violence (riots) as a function of ambient temperature. (Baron and Ransberger, 1978, p. 354. Copyright 1978 by the American Psychological Association. Reprinted by permission.)

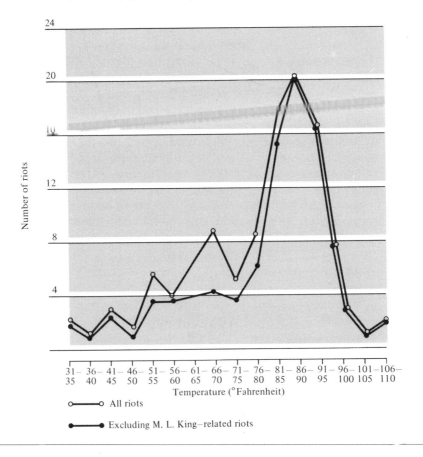

any aggressive display in part reflects a temporary state in the individual, a transient disposition to react with hostility. And it does, in fact, appear that people become more irritable on very hot days. Several investigators have gone beyond this rather unsystematic observation to scientifically examine the effects of temperature on expressed aggression, both in the laboratory and during real-life events (see Baron and Bell, 1975, 1976; Baron and Ransberger, 1978; Griffitt, 1970). There is some evidence substantiating the "long, hot summer" hypothesis, which states that high temperature stimulates violence. In support of this position, it has been shown that more riots occur during the summer than during other seasons. However, there also may be an optimal level of temperature that promotes aggression, with temperature levels above or below this point less likely to instigate aggressive behavior.

To test these ideas, Baron and Ransberger (1978) identified occurrences of collective violence between 1967 and 1971 in which there were (1) arson, looting, or rock throwing; (2) persistence of events for at least one day; (3) participation by sizable crowds; and (4) intervention by law enforcement agencies. They then related the number of such riots to the temperature at the time of the riot. Figure 3.1 reveals that most riots indeed take place when the temperature ranges between seventy-six and ninety degrees Fahrenheit. Temperatures above and below that point are less frequently associated with large-scale violence. The drop in aggression given extremely high temperatures may be due to the fact that there are far fewer days with such extreme heat. On the other hand, it is possible that certain responses incompatible with violence are elicited during excessive heat. Escape from subjective discomfort and sheer exhaustion certainly interfere with hostile activities.

Of course, the underlying cause of riots is not entirely the temperature level. And it could be that warm nights merely facilitate the gathering of the crowds that are necessary for large-scale antisocial actions. But there is no question that heat is one of a number of conditions that promote aggressive expression.

Constructed Environments

The nature of a physical setting promotes a multitude of human actions and feelings. Consider the consequences of working in a windowless office; being confined to a small, dark room; or staying in a cold, impersonal hospital. There are many more research studies about the psychological effects of such constructed physical surroundings than about the natural environment, perhaps because social engineers can change offices and classrooms more readily than the climate or the availability of resources. Again, because of space limitations, we have selected just two examples that illustrate the relationships between behavior and a person's physical context.

Psychiatric wards. What is perhaps most noticeable in a psychiatric ward is the lack of interaction between the patients. They sit alone, wander about by themselves, and remain generally removed from others. Observers attribute

Table 3.3   Total number of verbal interactions during thirty-three five-minute observation periods

	Brief interactions	*Sustained interactions*
Old arrangement	47	36
New arrangement	73	61

Source: Sommer and Ross, 1958, p. 132. Reprinted by permission.

this behavior to the patients' states of mind, describing them as "withdrawn," "out of touch," and "incapable of human interaction."

Sommer and Ross (1958) noticed that even in so-called modern wards, with television sets and good lighting, the furniture tended to be arranged with shoulder-to-shoulder seating along the walls of the room or with chairs placed in back-to-back rows, not unlike seating arrangements in public transportation waiting rooms. Given this placement of furniture, interaction is difficult; the geography of the ward promotes psychological withdrawal. Of course, such furniture arrangements might facilitate cleaning and the movement of food carts, but these positive consequences are far removed from the goals of a mental hospital.

To demonstrate the effects of seating arrangements on interpersonal communication, Sommer and Ross changed the position of the furniture in a psychiatric ward. They had the chairs moved from the walls and placed around tables, so that the seated patients would be facing one another. The attractiveness of the tables was also enhanced with flowers and magazines so that the patients would use them as a focal point. Before these changes and two weeks after the alterations were introduced, Sommer and Ross time-sampled verbal communications on the ward. Table 3.3 indicates that the number of both brief and sustained interactions almost doubled given the new physical context. It is thus evident that one's behavior is determined by the immediate geography and that conclusions about a person cannot be divorced from the physical environment. What was thought to be a manifestation of a basic personality pattern (namely, social withdrawal) was found to be significantly influenced by the organization of the physical surroundings. One wonders what the long-term effects on personality might be if one were raised in a home with furniture arranged as in a typical psychiatric ward!

Office space.   Of course, the physical environment influences communication in normal settings as much as on a psychiatric ward. Wells (1972) demonstrated that working in a large, open office as opposed to a smaller, enclosed space has different consequences for social interaction and friendship patterns.

Wells asked approximately three hundred workers on one floor of a large office building, "With whom would you prefer to work?" Of the respondents, most worked in a large, open area on the floor, but about 33 percent were located in separated and enclosed spaces. Wells reported that:

1. Friendship choices were directly related to the present physical distance, or proximity, between employees.
2. Workers in the smaller areas especially preferred workmates from their own sections, and these choices were reciprocated. Hence, working in smaller areas led to closer-knit groups.
3. The percentages of individuals not chosen by anyone (the social isolates) were higher in smaller work spaces.

In sum, social cohesion is greater in smaller work areas, but such arrangements also foster the development of a subset of lonely individuals who are excluded from the in-group. There is a good deal of evidence, particularly in studies of children, that social exclusion and isolation are related to emotional problems and negative feelings about oneself. Thus, psychological well-being and interpersonal contact can be determined in part by geographical factors that affect social interaction.

Behavior Settings

Roger Barker (1960, 1965, 1968) has said that the best way to predict human behavior is to know where a person is. In a post office, a person behaves "post office–like"; in church, one's behavior is "churchy"; and in classrooms, one acts like a student (or a teacher). Post offices, churches, and schools are all *behavior settings*. A behavior setting has spatial properties and a geographical location, but it also has social properties, such that the setting exists only when people are gathered there to perform certain activities. Hence, a shutdown post office is no longer a behavior setting, even though its physical properties might remain unchanged. Behavior settings vary greatly, from bridge clubs and restaurants to baseball fields and offices. They can be part of the natural environment, such as parks and lakes, or constructed environments, such as schools and offices.

Wicker and Kirmeyer (1977) have described a behavior setting as a place where:

1. One of a number of regularly occurring human activities take place, such as playing bridge at a bridge club or praying in a church.
2. A behavior is coordinated with inanimate objects within the setting, such as card tables at a bridge club or pews in a church.
3. People inhabiting the setting are interchangeable and replaceable. Anyone arriving at a bridge club can enter a game, and Sunday services continue as congregations change. Hence, the behavior exhibited is independent of the particular people within the setting.

Within these settings a variety of personal motivations are satisfied. The motivations of bridge players can vary from aggression and affiliation to achievement and power; the unity of the setting is not derived from the unity of the participants' motivations. But, in spite of motivational differences, the individuals in the setting engage in the same general pattern of behavior.

Overmanning and undermanning.   The relation between the number of people in a setting and the psychological consequences of being part of that setting has been thoroughly investigated. Settings can be *undermanned*, *overmanned*, or have an optimal number of members, each determined by the number of people available to perform a setting's essential functions. A bridge club with three members is undermanned, while a baseball team with one hundred members is overmanned.

Consider, for example, some consequences of participating in a baseball game when your team has only four members instead of the usual nine. As a result of this undermanning, each team member's average value is greater and each person has more obligations. For example, the second baseman must also play first base. There is therefore greater variability and more effort required per player than in an optimally manned setting. Because of these demands, more tension is aroused, more responsibility is assumed, and greater insecurities are manifested. And there are more incidents of personal success and failure.

In general, setting size is correlated with degree of manning. Small towns and small schools, for example, tend to be undermanned, whereas urban areas and large schools are overmanned. As Fig. 3.2 demonstrates, there are relatively more people performing in responsible positions in small than in large environmental contexts.

Overmanning and undermanning generate forces to bring about an optimal level of manning. For example, if a setting is undermanned, there are pressures to remain in and recruit others to the group. On the other hand, if a setting is overmanned, recruiting tends to be reduced, and eligibility standards may be raised. For example, the drama coach may have to plead with

Figure 3.2   Subjective feelings in large and small schools: Relation of degree of undermanning and experiences in behavior settings. (Wicker and Kirmeyer, 1968, p. 259. Used by permission.)

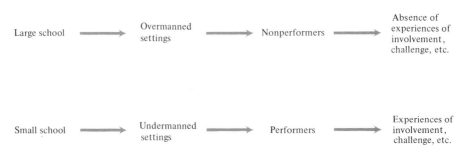

students to participate in a play at a small high school, while at a large school there are tryouts where only the best performers are accepted (see Wicker and Kirmeyer, 1977). These influences on personality and behavior are not consciously perceived by the person rejected from, say, the football team. He is less likely to blame the size of the community than to blame himself and to suffer the psychological consequences of this belief.

Total institutions.   A *total institution* is also a behavior setting, but it has certain unique characteristics not found in the types of settings investigated by Barker. A total institution completely encompasses the individual, forming a barrier to the types of social intercourse that occur outside such a setting. Monasteries, jails, homes for the aged, boarding schools, and military academies are a few examples of total institutions.

Total institutions have certain common characteristics (see Goffman, 1961). First, the individuals in such environments must sleep, play, and work within the same setting. These are generally segmented spheres of activity in the lives of most individuals, but within a total institution one sphere of activity overlaps with others. Second, each phase of life takes place in the company of a large group of others. Frequently sleeping is done in a barracks, food is served in a cafeteria, and so on. In such activities everyone is treated alike and must perform certain essential tasks. Third, activities in an institution are tightly scheduled according to a master plan, with set times to rise, to eat, to exercise, and to sleep. These institutional characteristics result in a bureaucratic society, which requires the hiring of other people for surveillance. What often results is a dichotomous split in the groups within an institution into a large, managed group (*inmates*) and a small supervisory staff. There tends to be great social distance between the groups, who perceive each other according to stereotypes and have severely restricted communications.

The world of the inmate differs greatly from the outside world. When one enters a total institution, all previous roles, such as father or husband, are disrupted. The individual is further depersonalized by the issuance of a uniform, confiscation of belongings, and gathering of personal information, as well as by more subtle touches like doorless toilets, record keeping, and bedchecks. The effects of an institutional setting are so all-encompassing that one can meaningfully speak of an "institutional personality": a persistent manner of behaving compliantly and without emotional involvement.

Of course, there are individual differences in adaptation to the situation. They can be as extreme as psychosis, childlike regression, and depression or as mild as resigned compliance. Most individuals do adjust and build up a system of satisfactions, such as close friendships and cliques. But because of these bonds and the fact that the habits needed to function in the outside world have been lost, inmates face great problems upon leaving an institution. A shift from the top of a small society to the bottom of a larger one may be further demoralizing.

Goffman provides many other fascinating insights into total institutions, but the general message of his work is that, to understand behavior, the environment in which it occurs must be taken into consideration.

Both prisons and military bases can be total institutions, in which members wear the same clothes and perform identical activities. The institutional world also is divided between those in charge and the "inmates." (above—Danny Lyon/Magnum Photos, Inc.; below—Mary Ellen Mark/Archive Pictures, Inc.)

Privacy, Territoriality, and Density

A number of other key concepts have been identified in the study of the relation between the physical world and behavior; among them are privacy, territoriality, and density (Altman, 1975).

Privacy refers to an individual's freedom to choose what is communicated about the self, to control when this communication will take place, and to limit incoming stimulation. It is evident that when large families live in one or two rooms, or even when houses in good neighborhoods are placed too close to one another, feelings of privacy are sacrificed. In such situations one gives up control over unwanted intrusion (see Ittelson, Proshansky, Rivlin, and Winkel, 1974).

Privacy has a number of functions, including the opportunity for self-evaluation, reflection, and planning. Hence, the absence of sufficient privacy can have serious psychological consequences. It comes as no surprise, then, that cultures provide mechanisms for ensuring privacy, such as locks on doors, curtains, and Do Not Disturb signs. Even primitive cultures have privacy mechanisms, including huts that only one sex or one person is allowed to inhabit. At the same time, given some opportunity for privacy, cultures differ markedly in their physical arrangements affecting privacy. Societies that require economic cooperation and shared decision making tend to have physical arrangements that reduce privacy. The Israeli kibbutz is a modern example of such an arrangement where privacy is hard to come by. Societies that emphasize economic competition and individualism, on the other hand, are more likely to have tall fences to separate different families.

The term *territoriality* is derived from the study of infrahumans (see Chapter 2) and assumes that organisms lay claim to a particular territory which they defend from intruders and determine who may or may not enter. A number of infrahuman species, including birds, dogs, and fish, lay claim to territories. Humans also appear to be territorial, although such behavior need not be instinctive. However, common to both humans and infrahumans is the idea that territories encompass a given geographical area, that there is clear ownership of the place, and that the physical location is personalized or marked.

One interesting aspect of territoriality is the reactive behaviors toward intruders or invaders of a territory. Among infrahumans, the defender of a territory is typically the winner of a fight, regardless of the relative physical attributes of the combatants. Among humans, it has been suggested that when in one's own territory one is more dominant, controlling, and powerful.

Edney (1975) experimentally examined whether humans display special behaviors when in a home territory. The study was conducted in college dormitory rooms, where one person was the resident and the other a visitor. Participants who were the residents of a room responded differently to the experimental task than did the visitors, expressing greater feelings of control. In a similar study, Martindale (1971) found that dormitory residents were more successful at a negotiation task when in their own territory. There is

Hong Kong is characterized by high "inside" and "outside" density, which has many consequences for personality and behavior. (Hiroji Kubota/Magnum Photos, Inc.)

thus come truth to the belief that "people's homes are their castles"; behaviors in a home setting do differ from actions in other physical locations, with individuals more likely to behave like "kings" in terms of increased dominance, power, and hostility.

Density refers to the number of people per unit of space and should be distinguished from crowding, which is an experiential reaction or feeling (Stokols, 1972). One can be in a high-density area, such as a stadium during a sporting event, yet not feel crowded. On the other hand, at times "three is a crowd."

Among the numerous distinctions related to density are "inside" density and "outside" density in housing (Zlutnick and Altman, 1972). As shown in Fig. 3.3 an urban dwelling has high outside density, but can have either high or low inside density. It has also proved useful to distinguish social density from spatial density. Social density involves a constant space for a differing number of individuals (e.g., twenty versus one hundred viewers at a movie theater), while spatial density places the same number in differing spaces (e.g., twenty children in a small versus a large room).

Density also has a number of psychological effects, including withdrawal, aggression, and fatigue. Because of these negative consequences, people invoke mechanisms to cope with density. For example, Valins and Baum (1973) report that residents of high-density dormitories avoid others, sit farther away

Figure 3.3   "Inside" and "outside" density. (Zlutnick and Altman, 1972, p. 51.)

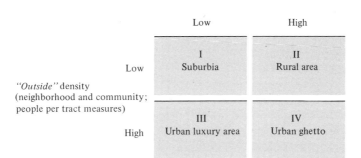

"Inside" density (within residential units; people per room measures)

	Low	High
Low	I Suburbia	II Rural area
High	III Urban luxury area	IV Urban ghetto

"Outside" density (neighborhood and community; people per tract measures)

from strangers in a laboratory setting, and are less comfortable among strangers. They appear to view others negatively, one of the social costs of their high-density living conditions. In a similar manner, Rohe and Patterson (1974) found that as spatial density increased in a daycare center, incidents of expressed hostility also increased.

Effects of the Physical World

Our initial discussion has examined the relationship between the physical or geographical environment and personality. Natural factors such as average temperature and rainfall influence personality by limiting the available means of subsistence and, in turn, determining what personality types are best suited to survive within these environmental constraints. Constructed environments also influence behavior directly. For example, the placement of furniture or the size of a working area can affect interpersonal communication and friendship patterns.

Another aspect of the environment that shapes behavior is the *behavior setting*. Behavior settings can be characterized by the number of people available to perform important functions. If a setting is undermanned, for instance, more tension and uncertainty are aroused, but there is also a greater sense of responsibility and personal acceptance. A total institution is a particular type of behavior setting where communications with the external world are severely restricted.

Finally, the concepts of privacy, or the freedom to choose and control one's communications; territoriality, or claim to a particular geographical space; and density, or the number of people per unit of space, are aspects of the physical environment that have far-reaching psychological consequences on both immediate behavior and long-term adjustment patterns.

The Social World

The physical world of climate, terrain, material structures, and space provides the background for diverse cultures, customs, social structures, and roles. We will treat the social world as if it were independent of the physical world, but in fact the two are as intimately connected as nature and nurture. The structure of a society and its cultural traditions exert powerful influences on the personalities of individuals born into it. Social groups and cultures may live in similar physical settings but display quite different behaviors.

The influence of the social world is especially impressive when one considers that the members of quite different social groups can still be quite similar biologically. The infant born into a preliterate New Guinea tribe and the infant born to a sophisticated Parisian family are genetically more alike than different. Indeed, it has been estimated that human races are fifty times more similar than are human and chimpanzee and that even so-called unrelated individuals share more than 99 percent of their genes (Washburn, 1978). (Of course, these similarities do not deny the possibility of biological differences between cultural groups. Selective mating, which restricts one's choice of partner to one's own social group, can maintain and accentuate any already existing genetic differences between groups.) However, it remains clear that genetic differences between groups are minor compared with the wide range of behaviors exhibited between social classes and cultures. It is primarily social, not biological, factors that cause members of a social group to behave uniquely.

Because of our flexibility, because humans are adjustable and changeable, the disparate norms and values of a society can be transmitted to and accepted by succeeding generations, ensuring the survival of the culture. Each generation must learn to function within the confines and according to the rules of a given society and social group. Our families, peers, schools, churches, and mass media are among the social agents and institutions that determine who and what we are, or our *socialization*. Some of these influences will be examined in later sections of the text where we analyze personality development and specific behavioral patterns. For the present, we again choose an illustrative topic, social class, and consider the relation between this key social variable and personality to demonstrate the binding of the individual and the social world.

Social Class

All societies are to some extent stratified. *Social stratification* is a relatively stable, hierarchical arrangement of groups of individuals, with the "higher" classes within this hierarchy receiving more social and material rewards than the "lower" classes. Individuals within a class typically perform similar occupations and face the same life conditions and problems. As a result, individuals can be assigned to a social class by using indexes such as education, occupation, income, and prestige. All of these class indicators are intertwined, for education provides access to job opportunities, while jobs, in turn, bring increased income, prestige, and power.

The concepts of social class and social status are so complex that some scholars even differentiate between the two, contending that class has implications for one's *chances* in life, while status has implications for one's *style* of life. Here we will not differentiate between the terms, but assume that assignment to a particular class may reveal place of residence, type of job, level of property ownership, amount of education, friends' social status, and related attributes. Class is also associated with such personal characteristics as values, mode of dress, and even style of speech. Because of the pervasive influence of class membership, knowledge of just this variable can reveal much about an individual's personality. Disparate social classes also expose children to different methods of child rearing which influence a variety of personality traits.

Middle versus working class.   There are many contrasts between and implications of middle- and working-class membership in the United States. The middle class often earns income sufficient to permit savings and has both advanced education and marketable skills. Its members have what is called a *conceptual* orientation (Miller and Swanson, 1960), using their mental capacities to solve problems, with their jobs often involving the manipulation of symbols rather than objects. Their life focus is on occupational advancement and competent performance, and their jobs are often quite specialized and responsible.

Members of the working class, on the other hand, typically have more serious financial concerns and not enough salary to permit savings. They are more likely to have on-the-job training than a formal education. Their orientation toward life is considered to be *motoric,* in that they manipulate objects rather than symbols; combat is more likely to take place on a football field than in a debate.

The varied, subtle effects of social class can be seen in the way in which family members communicate with one another, in the precision and richness of their language and thought. Studies carried out in the United States and England (Bernstein, 1962a, 1962b; Hess and Shipman, 1965; Olim, Hess, and Shipman, 1967) have shown that middle-class adults and adolescents use more complex and less stereotyped language in their verbal communications than do lower-class groups, even when intelligence test scores are similar. Evidence that these verbal differences have adaptive consequences is provided in a study in which families from the United States, Puerto Rico, and India were given a problem to solve (Straus, 1968). The problem was to determine the rules of an unfamiliar ballgame played on a small court. In all three national samples, the middle-class families were more successful at the task, displaying greater and more elaborate verbal communications with one another than did the lower-class families.

Given these very broad generalizations (which might, of course, be incorrect for any given individual), what implications are there for the structure of personality and what child-rearing practices might foster personality differences between the classes?

Self-esteem.   First, social class differences are highly associated with inequalities in self-esteem. Occupations such as garbage collector or street sweeper have low standing in our society, even among the incumbents of those occupations (Inkeles and Rossi, 1966). Individuals performing these occupations are aware of how others perceive their work. Indeed, on virtually any measure of self-esteem, differences emerge when individuals are grouped according to social class (see Inkeles, 1968).

These disparities are evident among youths as well as adults. In a study of a large sample of high school juniors and seniors, Rosenberg (1965) found that adolescents from upper social classes have higher self-esteem on the average than do adolescents from lower social classes. Self-esteem, moreover, was positively related to school achievement, occupational expectations, and reported social relationships with peers. Given the critical importance of self-concept and self-esteem for other aspects of personality (see Chapter 10), the fact that social class membership has an impact on self-image is a significant finding.

Discipline patterns.   As might be expected, the social classes differ in their child-rearing practices. Middle-class parents tend to use psychological discipline (withholding of love), while parents of lower-class children are more likely to employ physical punishment (Miller and Swanson, 1960). In addition to using more physical coercion, lower-class mothers impose more restrictions on their children (Waters and Crandall, 1964) and use more negative statements in teaching them (Feshbach, 1973). Psychological discipline in the middle class is often guilt-inducing and leads to both high standards and self-control, whereas the physical discipline of the lower class is in itself a stimulus to later aggression. Furthermore, such behavior provides a model for subsequent aggression and a low degree of self-control.

It may be, of course, that lower-class parents are more punitive and restrictive because their life circumstances make it difficult for them to behave otherwise. The predicament of the lower-class parent is graphically described by Newson and Newson (1976, p. 338):

The mother's ability to be "relaxed" over toilet training, for instance, may be more dependent than she likes to think upon an efficient hot water supply, automatic washing machine and plastic pants, or upon disposable napkins or a good nappy service—or, alternatively, upon a warm sun and a culture pattern that allows children to run naked! It is not so easy to remain calm and accepting as the toddler wets nappy after nappy, if washing them involves boiling up water in a kettle and scrubbing away by hand; nor, indeed, can a mother be quite so "friendly and easy-going about the bathroom" (Spock) if the bathroom doesn't exist and the lavatory is the other side of the back yard or down a flight of tenement stairs and shared with three or four other families of careless habits. Again, whether the pre-school child is expected to stand up for himself and hit back when he is among his peers, or whether he is withdrawn from such conflict by his mother, can be seen as partly, though not entirely, a function of the type of housing occupied by the family, according to whether the child can be withdrawn into his own yard or garden and whether neighbouring entrances are separated by fence or hedge.

Psychopathology.   Severe psychopathology is also distributed unevenly across social classes. There is a general tendency for less-privileged groups to exhibit more mental illness. For example, hospitalization rates for schizophrenia are highest in central city areas of lowest socioeconomic status and the rates diminish as one moves toward the peripheral areas of the city. The class-schizophrenia relationship has been confirmed again and again in major cities all over the world, including, for example, New York, London, Taiwan, and Helsinki (see review in Kohn, 1968), with the relationship strongest in the largest cities. In cities of less than approximately 100,000 people, the relationship disappears.

Why should urban populations manifest such a marked discrepancy in pathology between the social classes? Perhaps the most prevalent explanation—the *stress hypothesis*—is that conditions in lower-class life foster greater stress which, in turn, promotes psychopathology. On the other hand, according to an explanation called the *drift hypothesis,* people who become schizophrenic tend to suffer a decline in status and move to the inner city *after* appearance of the pathology. Thus, schizophrenia may *cause* one to fall into the lower class, rather than the reverse. The weight of the evidence does not support this position, however. Instead of starting with a high-status job and declining, schizophrenics often never seem to have an adequate position.

Although the stress hypothesis is more plausible, it is also subject to a number of problems. In studies in which stress has been equated between classes (a complex and perhaps questionable process in itself), there remain differential incidents of psychosis between the classes. Thus, it appears that the lower classes are less able to cope with stress in general. Kohn (1968, p. 171) asks:

What is there about the conditions of life of the lowest social strata that might make it more difficult for their members to cope with stress? One can think of intriguing possibilities. Their occupational conditions and their limited education gear their thinking processes to the concrete and the habitual; their inexperience in dealing with the abstract may ill-equip them to cope with ambiguity, uncertainty, and unpredictability; their mental processes are apt to be too gross and rigid when flexibility and subtlety are most required. Or, a related hypothesis, the lower- and working-class valuation of conformity to external authority, and devaluation of self-direction, might cripple a man faced with the necessity of suddenly having to rely on himself in an uncertain situation where others cannot be relied on for guidance.

In comparison to schizophrenia, a relatively frequent middle-class pathology is *depression,* which might be considered a form of self-destructiveness. Some suggest that the incidence of depression is relatively high because middle-class Americans blame their failures on themselves, for they have been given plenty of opportunities to succeed. On the other hand, a member of the lower class is more likely to place the blame on social barriers and to experience a different psychological reaction, such as anger or even paranoia (see

Keller and Zavalloni, 1964). However, the even greater prevalence of depression in the lower than in the middle class makes this explanation questionable.

In sum, it is evident that social class affects many aspects of one's personality, including self-esteem, expressive style, and pathology. Individuals with identical genetic patterns will nevertheless differ widely as a result of being raised in different class environments.

Culture

Personality differences between nations and ethnic groups are popularly recognized; there are stereotypes that all the people within a particular group or nation are believed to follow. These differences are ascribed to disparities in *culture,* the modes of acting and feeling, or the set of norms and ideals, that are customary for an entire group. Culture therefore involves consistency in the actions of a larger number of people than does social class.

Not all customs that distinguish one culture from another are equally relevant to personality. The fact that it is taboo in some cultures to eat pork while in other cultures it is taboo to eat beef is probably not germane to personality. It is also important to recognize that there is much more variability in personality than in social customs in any society. Consequently, one finds that only *on the average* are people in one culture more aggressive, ambitious, courageous, or conforming than people in another culture. Although phrases like "the fiery Latin American temperament" or "the inscrutable Oriental mind" have varying degrees of correctness when applied to any particular individual, it is still valid to try to determine whether there are sets of personality attributes that most members of a culture have in common. When such common attributes are found, one can speak of a "national character type," recognizing that there are many individuals within that culture who may not conform to that type.

In certain instances the description of the resources or practices of a culture virtually ensures that there will be personality and behavioral differences between cultural groups. For example (Child, 1968, p. 95):

Suppose we read that a particular society has a very stable economy, with ample food for a longer period always on hand, and efficient and equitable techniques for distributing it. We are strongly tempted to believe that the typical member of that society has little if any anxiety about getting enough to eat. If we read that young children in another society see little of adult men, we will easily believe that some aura of early-instilled femininity will cling to the typical male child as he grows up.

Indeed, our own observations and experiences suggest that people in different cultures appear to be dissimilar in certain essential ways. Crossing borders in Europe, one is met with marked and often alarming differences in people. Clearly, an individual's character is determined by time and place of appearance in history. Let us now briefly consider some examples of cultural differences pertinent to personality which have been convincingly documented from comparative child-rearing and psychopathology studies.

Child rearing.   Cultures, like social classes, differ in the rearing of children: the amount and type of discipline, the presence or absence of one or both parents, the presence or absence of extended families in the household, the time to wean, the type and severity of toilet training, and so on. At times these differences are not striking, inasmuch as parents everywhere are confronted with similar problems in raising their children: "In all societies the helpless infant, getting his food by nursing at his mother's breast . . . , freely evacuating the waste products, exploring his genitals, biting and sucking at will, must be changed into a responsible adult, keeping the rules of his society" (Whiting and Child, 1953, pp. 63–64). Nevertheless, differences do arise in the process by which the human infant is socialized into a particular society; these differences have clear implications for the formation of the personality of the person it will become.

In a pioneering and already classic study, Whiting and Child (1953) used available ethnographic materials to examine the methods of weaning, toilet training, independence training, and regulation of aggression and sexual expression in seventy-five preliterate societies. They found significant and systematic relationships between variations in these child-rearing practices and, for example, beliefs about illness. Societies that severely punished children for aggression tended to believe that illness was caused by such hostile agents as sorcerers, while severity of weaning was associated with the belief that illness was caused by eating or drinking bad food or poison. Furthermore, the practice of isolating or removing ill patients from their homes was more prevalent in societies that punished the child's early expressions of dependency on others.

The child-rearing practices of a culture are inevitably linked to other features of a culture that have psychological significance. In the beginning of this chapter we presented evidence regarding the psychological importance of such features of the physical environment as density and privacy. The circumstances under which children are raised vary quite markedly with respect to those dimensions. In a study of six cultures, Whiting (1966) found that the average number of individuals in a house or courtyard ranged from 7.9 children and 7.5 adults for the Tarong society of the Philippines to 2.8 children and 2.3 adults for a New England community. One can reasonably expect greater autonomy or self-orientation in the New England child and greater social orientation and dependency in the Tarong child. Cultural differences in social independence are also related to sleeping arrangements. Until about the age of fifteen, about half of Japanese children sleep with one or both parents, while a large percentage sleep with one or more siblings (Caudill and Plath, 1966). Sleeping arrangements in Japan foster more familial cohesion and social interdependence than is the case in the United States.

Because cultures are so complex, one cannot readily establish from these correlations precisely which features of a culture cause which behaviors. In addition, the effects of a particular cultural feature depend on many other facets of the culture. Consider, for example, the relationship between father absence and the development of concerns about achievement and accomplishments. Bradburn (1963) examined the relationship between achievement drives among three groups of Turkish males who differed in the age at which they were no longer living with their fathers. Bradburn reported that the sons separated from their fathers at an early age had higher achievement drives. Thus, for example, orphans, who are generally deficient in a number of psychological respects, scored higher than nonorphaned children on an index of achievement concerns. Bradburn pointed out that in Turkish culture, where the father dominates the son, father absence facilitates independence and striving for competence. In America, on the other hand, early father absence tends to decrease measured achievement striving (Veroff, Atkinson, Feld, and Gurin, 1960). In American culture, fathers may be more encouraging than dominating, setting high success standards. Thus, their absence deprives children of a role model and causes lowered achievement concerns. In sum, the absence of the father has quite different consequences on achievement as a function of the role of the father within that culture.

Psychopathology.   Symptoms of mental disorder vary greatly, depending on the cultural context of the disturbed individual. For example, the hysterical symptoms that were so frequent in Vienna at the time of Freud, and so central in the development of Freudian theory, are now rarely in evidence. Similarly, the incidence of manic-depressive psychoses has greatly decreased in America, but not in England. Although care must be taken in all such comparisons because diagnoses are also subject to change, it is quite clear that there are different rates of mental illness between cultures over time.

Mental disorders may vary between cultures because different cultures give rise to different types of conflict and stress or because the mode of expression for disturbance varies as a function of cultural setting. For example, the aged in Ghana have secure positions within the family and are not relegated to a lower status as they grow old. This is not the case in our culture. Thus, in Ghana the tendency toward mental illness is not made worse by aging, while in our culture the aged exhibit a variety of specifically age-related disturbances such as depression.

Pathology takes forms other than mental illness, and again there are marked disparities between cultures. For example, in the Philippines the homicide rate exceeds that in the United States by a factor of six and is forty times that in England (see Chapter 18). It has been suggested that Filipinos tend to place blame on others and to have low impulse control. In accordance with this suggestion, incidences of depression and guilt are particularly low in that culture. As has been suggested in Chapter 2, there are wide disparities in rates of alcoholism between cultural groups. For example, it is well documented that Jews and Chinese have very low rates of drinking problems, while the incidence of alcoholism among the Irish is very high (see Opler, 1959).

In sum, cultural differences in child-rearing and socialization practices abound and may well be responsible for observed cultural differences in personality and pathology.

Summary   In this chapter we have examined some personality determinants that are not genetically transmitted, but rather are products of the world into which an individual is born. These external influences reside in both the physical and the social worlds. The number and variety of these influences are infinite; we have selected just a few examples for illustrative purposes. Among the factors in the physical world that affect behavior, some are found naturally in the environment, such as climate or amount of rainfall, while others are constructed, such as wards, offices, institutions, and other behavior settings. Within the social world, social class and culture are the two overriding determinants of personality structure and behavior, influencing values, child-rearing practices, and mental illness.

Specific Points

1. Climatic conditions of rainfall and temperature in part determine a society's means of subsistence, which in turn affects settlement patterns and the characteristics of individuals needed for the society to survive. Agricultural societies need obedient and responsible members, whereas hunting societies require self-reliant and autonomous members.

2. Climate also affects behaviors, such as aggression.

3. Communication in such constructed environments as psychiatric wards is facilitated by appropriate seating arrangements.

4. Small office spaces tend to both promote social cohesion and foster the development of a subset of isolated individuals who are excluded from the in-group.

5. *Behavior settings* have spatial properties and a geographical location and exist independent of the specific individuals within the setting. The *overmanning* of behavior settings typical of large towns and large schools leads to exclusion, whereas *undermanning* results in increased participation and responsibility.

6. A *total institution* is a behavior setting, such as a prison or monastery, that completely dominates the individual. Living in a total institution has far-reaching psychological consequences.

7. Privacy, the freedom to choose and control incoming communications; territoriality, the claim to a particular space; and density, the number of people per unit of space, are aspects of the physical environment that also have profound psychological effects.

8. *Social stratification* into classes influences self-esteem (lower classes tend to have lower self-esteem) as well as discipline patterns (lower classes are more punitive).

9. Schizophrenia is overrepresented among lower socioeconomic groups. The *drift hypothesis* states that schizophrenia may cause one to fall into the lower class; the *stress hypothesis* implies that lower-class membership increases the likelihood of becoming schizophrenic.

10. Cultures differ in their child-rearing practices, living arrangements, and other factors that result in disparate national or ethnic character types.

Thought Questions

1. If you could arrange the rooms and spatial features of a house in any way you wished, what would be the best arrangement for fostering close, cordial relationships between family members?
2. List some of the behavior settings in which you act. Are they over-manned, undermanned, or optimally manned? Has this influenced your behavior in the settings?
3. How and when have your reactions been affected by being inside or outside your own territory?
4. Based on your own observations, are people in different cultures really "different"?

PART II
Theories of Personality

Part II presents some of the best-known and most influential theories of personality. Among them are Freudian psychoanalytic theory (Chapter 4); descendants of and dissidents from the psychoanalytic conception, including Jung, Adler, Horney, Sullivan, Fromm, and Erikson (Chapter 5); social learning theory (Chapter 6); and cognitive approaches to personality as in the work of Carl Rogers, Abraham Maslow, George Kelly, and other phenomenological theorists (Chapter 7).

These theories differ in many respects, but at the heart of the differences are contrasting basic assumptions about human nature or the essence of human beings. Psychoanalytic theorists such as Freud and his followers believed that individuals strive to reduce inner tension, keeping internal agitation to a minimum at all costs. Humans are, in their view, irrational and instinctive biological beings. Considering the basic subdivisions of personality identified in Chapter 1 (personality assessment, development, change, and dynamics):

1. Inasmuch as individuals are unaware of their need states, personality assessment is conducted by means of indirect or projective techniques.
2. Biological and historical factors are believed to play an essential role in behavior, and individuals progress through a fixed sequence of developmental stages.
3. Personality change must deal with the unconscious and the irrational desires of individuals.
4. Conflicts concerning sexual and aggressive instincts and social inhibitions form the heart of the psychoanalytic study of behavioral dynamics. In addition, the frustration experienced because of unsatisfied desires is directly linked with psychopathology.

In its most extreme form, social learning theory asserts that individuals are mere machines and that the study of personality is part of the more general examination of input-output associations or stimulus-response bonds. Given this basic view of humans, personality assessment, development, change, and dynamics all focus on specific associations:

1. Personality assessment involves the direct recording of behaviors in specific situations.
2. Personality development is based on the formation and strengthening of habits or stimulus-response bonds.

3. Personality change is accomplished by altering stimulus-response connections through the use of rewards to foster acquisition of more functional responses and punishments to extinguish maladaptive responses.
4. Behavioral dynamics involves conflicts between competing habits or response tendencies. Different and incompatible responses may be called forth by the same situation.

In its less extreme form, which we primarily examine in this book, social learning theorists accept the fact that humans are not robots, but thinking organisms whose thoughts influence their actions. However, only a few of the higher mental processes are actually incorporated into their theories. The more moderate social learning theorists also believe that, although reward and punishment do influence performance, learning can take place through mere observation of others, without the direct influence of reward and punishment. Nevertheless, even these less extreme positions reflect a more mechanistic orientation than in the psychoanalytic and cognitive approaches.

Gestalt, phenomenological, and other cognitive approaches to personality often start with the assumption that individuals are scientists seeking to understand their world and to fulfill their innate potentials. Thus:

1. Personality assessment is concerned with understanding how individuals view the world or ascertaining individuals' subjective experiences.
2. Personality development is synonymous with cognitive growth, accompanied by a movement in the direction of higher goals.
3. Personality change involves altering one's view of the world and oneself. A variety of techniques, from group therapy and role playing to more radical forms of sensitivity training that supposedly enhance self awareness, can be employed.
4. Personality dynamics considers the influence beliefs have on actions, focusing on the functional significance of cognitions and subjective meanings.

The theories presented here differ in a number of other respects. Primary among these differences are the phenomena on which they focus and the research methods they have used. Freudian theory led to an examination of defense mechanisms, free associations, dreams, and sexual behavior; social learning theory has examined the effects of different rewards, punishments, and role models on social behaviors; and Gestalt, phenomenological, and other cognitive approaches have been especially concerned with self-concept, self-esteem, self-actualization, and overall human potential. The theories stand side by side, each with unique abilities for accounting for certain observations. As a result, there is not a clear hierarchical ordering of theories, with one "better" in every respect than the others.

Table II.1 summarizes some points of comparison in the theories examined in the next four chapters. It will help you to return to this table as you progress through the chapters and the remainder of the text. Some of the terms in the table may be unfamiliar to you now, but they will be introduced and discussed in subsequent chapters.

Table II.1   Comparison of the major theories of personality

Theory	Chapter	Some major contributors	Focus	Main concepts*	Assessment goal	Assessment instruments	Goals for change
Psycho-analytic	4	Freud	Sexual motivation	Energy, instinct, libido, cathexis, id, ego, superego	Reveal basic unconscious desires	Projective techniques	Insight into desires; new coping techniques
Psycho-analytic Descendants	5	Jung, Adler, Horney, Sullivan, Fromm, Erikson	Personal growth; social motivations	Compensation, archetype, inferiority, neurotic trend, attachments, authoritarianism	Reveal basic unconscious desires	Projective techniques	Insight into desires; new coping techniques
Social Learning	6	Miller, Skinner, Bandura, Mischel, Rotter	Learning and the stimulus situation	Reinforcement, expectancy, value, model	Reveal typical ways of responding and their eliciting stimuli	Behavioral observation and objective instruments	Change habits; develop new responses
Cognitive-Phenomenological	7	Rogers, Maslow, Kelly	Humans as scientists; subjective experience	Unconditional regard, positive self-regard, personal constructs	Reveal perceptions of the world	Objective instruments, open-ended questionnaires	Alter cognitions or views of the world

* Not descriptive of all theorists within a category.

Freud's Psychoanalytic Theory of Personality

4

The greatest figure among personality theorists is Sigmund Freud, the creator of psychoanalysis. Freud's psychoanalytic theory is the most general and best-known conception of personality. His contributions range far beyond psychology; one cannot understand twentieth-century intellectual thought without some knowledge of psychoanalytic theory. Certainly Freud plays a less central role in psychological thinking today than twenty or thirty years ago, but he is by no means relegated to history. Many of his ideas have been absorbed by other personality theorists and incorporated within their theoretical frameworks.

Freud's conception is so vast that it is meaningless to ask whether it is "correct" or "incorrect." Some aspects of the theory have been shown to have reasonable validity, others have no empirical support at all, and still others are beyond empirical test. In this chapter we present an overview of many of Freud's theoretical concepts and examine in detail the area of defense mechanisms in order to illustrate the experimental testing of some of Freud's ideas.

Biography

Sigmund Freud (Fig. 4.1) was born in Freiburg, Moravia (now Austria), on May 6, 1856, and died in London on September 23, 1939. Most of his life was spent in Vienna, which he left only when the Nazis invaded in 1938.

Freud began his scientific career as a neurologist and quickly established a reputation in neurological research and medical investigations. In his medical practice he treated patients with various "nervous" disorders, using conventional medical and physical procedures. Since these treatments often failed, he traveled to Paris in 1885 to study the alleviation of hysterical symptoms through hypnosis (see Chapter 1). But he soon became disenchanted with hypnosis as well; many patients were not susceptible to hypnosis, and the effects of treatment frequently did not carry over to the waking state.

Figure 4.1   Sigmund Freud (1856–1939) with his daughter Anna in 1928. (Mary Evans/Sigmund Freud Copyrights)

Nevertheless, this period was extremely important in Freud's development. First, it was an experimental demonstration during a hypnotic session that provided Freud with key insights into the dynamics of personality. During an experiment conducted by Hippolyte Bernheim, a French physician, a woman was given the posthypnotic suggestion that, after waking, she should walk to the corner of the room and open an umbrella. Upon awakening, and after the designated time had elapsed, she did exactly that. When questioned about the reason for her behavior, she said that she wanted to see if the umbrella was hers. On the basis of this demonstration, Freud realized that conscious reports do not always indicate the real motivation for an act; that is, an action can be determined by forces that are *unconscious*. A second consequence of Freud's introduction to hypnosis was that he began to use a treatment technique, developed by Joseph Breuer, in which hypnotized patients talked about their symptoms. In the process, patients often recovered disturbing memories that seemed to be the unconscious causes of their illnesses.

From this beginning, Freud gradually came on the method of *free association*, during which patients are asked, under normal waking conditions, to tell the analyst everything that comes to mind, regardless of how trivial or embarrassing it may seem. Freud found that these free associations could be systematically related to patients' underlying conflicts and overt symptoms. By listening carefully to verbal associations, he was able to detect consistent themes that were manifestations of unconscious wishes and fears. These themes often involved sexual conflicts. The discovery that much of individual behavior is a compromise between wishes and anticipated fears is another of Freud's central contributions.

Freud and Breuer soon reached a parting of the ways because of Freud's beliefs about the importance of sexual desires in the development of mental illness. Thereafter, Freud primarily worked alone to formulate startling and original ideas about child development, the incest taboo, the interpretation of dreams, the unconscious, and a wealth of other psychological processes and phenomena. Freud initially surrounded himself with disciples, including Carl Jung from Switzerland and Alfred Adler from Austria (see Chapter 5). But

Freud (left, front row) with G. Stanley Hall (middle, front row) at Clark University in 1909. At the right in the first row is Carl Gustav Jung. (Mary Evans/Sigmund Freud Copyrights)

often his interpersonal relationships were stormy and friendships were aborted. His fascinating life history includes his self-analysis, the controversies surrounding his ideas, the founding of the International Psychoanalytic Association, and an invitation to Clark University in Massachusetts (1909) that paved the way for his acceptance after a long period of scientific ostracism. There were a number of reasons why Freud was not initially accepted by the scientific community (see Shakow and Rapaport, 1964). He did not communicate openly with other scientists, having virtually no academic correspondence, and alienated others because of his strong opinions. Furthermore, he did not present carefully accumulated evidence in support of his ideas, even gathering his data in a mysterious and secretive atmosphere closed to all but his patients. Finally, he came from an unknown Jewish family at a time of religious discrimination that prevented him from receiving a university position.

It is of interest to note that Freud was part of a continuing trend toward relegating humans to lower and lower status levels. First, Copernicus took Earth and its inhabitants from the center of the universe; then Darwin established that humans are not unique; finally, Freud contended that individuals are irrational and unaware of their own motivations. Perhaps the next step, currently in progress, will be to make inanimate objects more intelligent than their makers!

Basic Theoretical Concepts

Homeostasis and Hedonism

It is useful to consider Freud's theories within the context of a biological survival model. Given this viewpoint, which borrows much from Darwin, individuals are viewed as striving to satisfy personal needs within a world of limited resources. To satisfy these needs, behaviors must be undertaken that lead to the desired goals, virtually all of which are located in the external world. Thus, individuals must adapt to and function within the world around them.

More specifically, consider a psychological analysis of how behavior is governed by the need for food (although Freud was concerned more with sex and aggression than with tissue deficits). All organisms have a biological need to ingest food, a need made known to the organism because its presence causes discomfort. There is a limited supply of food in the external world, and organisms must compete for these resources. After the organism has engaged in appropriate activities and has eaten, the internal stimulation and pain (e.g., hunger pangs) that accompany food deprivation cease. The organism then feels satisfied and remains in an unmotivated state (at rest) until the next onset of hunger pangs, which follow a cyclical pattern, again generate food-seeking behavior. Freud conceived a similar cyclical model of sexual and aggressive desires and satisfactions.

Two central concepts guided his analysis: homeostasis and hedonism. *Homeostasis* is the tendency toward the maintenance of a relatively stable internal environment. That is, there is a propensity for an organism to remain in a state of equilibrium. If, for example, there is a condition of deprivation because food is absent, then a state of disequilibrium exists, and food-related actions are initiated to return the organism to balance, or equilibrium. *Hedonism*, a doctrine associated with the philosopher Jeremy Bentham (1779), asserts that pleasure and happiness are the chief goals in life. If homeostasis is the governing principle of behavior, then pleasure is the by-product of being in a state of equilibrium, where all one's needs are satisfied.

Freud accepted the doctrine of hedonism and the principle of homeostasis. For Freud, the satisfied individual typically does not pursue any stimulation, since activity indicates some type of dissatisfaction. On the contrary, the presumed ultimate goal of human striving is the absence of tension or need, which is accompanied by quiescence. One logical extension of this position was Freud's postulating a death instinct or *death wish*, for in death there are no unsatisfied desires. This is similar to the alleged desire to "return to the womb," where all needs are fulfilled.

Psychological Energy

Freud was greatly influenced by Hermann von Helmholtz, the German physicist who argued that physiological events could be explained with the mechanical principles of physics and chemistry. Freud contended that all psychological work, whether attaining a goal or just thinking about it, requires the use of energy. Three energy-related concepts are useful in understanding his explanation of human behavior: conservation of energy, entropy, and a distinction between bound (kinetic) and free (potential) energy.

Freud conceived of humans as closed energy systems. That is, there is a constant amount of energy (*libido*) for any given individual. This idea was derived from the principle of the conservation of energy, which states that energy is neither created nor destroyed. One corollary of this law is that if energy is spent performing one function, then it is unavailable for other functions. It will be seen that this corollary plays an important role in Freud's theory.

Entropy refers to the amount of energy that is not available for doing work. According to Freud, some energy is *bound*, kinetic, or "cathected." A *cathexis* (from the Greek *kathexo*, meaning "to occupy") involves an attachment to some desired but unattained object. The attachment or cathexis does not mean that energy literally leaves the person. Rather, there is a feeling of "longing" for the object, and there are repeated thoughts, images, and fantasies about him or her or some substitute object. A cathexis might be only temporary, for if the desired goal is attained, then there is a freeing of energy. As a result of goal attainment, bound energy is transformed into *free* (potential) *energy* that is then available for use in other functions. If all one's desires are fulfilled, then all energy is free. Thus, energy distribution is related to subjective satisfaction or happiness.

Consider, more specifically, how Freud might analyze the situation in which a loved one must go away for a period of time. Because that person is no longer available as a need satisfier, he or she becomes an object of cathexis. Energy is now bound, and the unsatisfied individual might fantasize about being with the loved one, daydream of their reunion, and so on. The binding of energy is unpleasant, reflecting the fact that needs have not been fulfilled. In addition, the bound energy is not available for other activities. The individual might therefore experience a lack of interest in other friends and hobbies. When the longed-for person returns, then needs are again satisfied, the cathected energy is freed to do other work, and there is a state of subjective pleasure. Note, then, how closely the concepts of homeostasis, hedonism, and the various forms of energy are linked in Freud's theory. If an organism is in equilibrium (homeostasis), then all energy is free, and the maximum pleasure is being experienced (hedonism).

It is useful to pause for a moment and ask if it is reasonable to apply these assumptions about energy and energy distribution, borrowed from classic mechanical theories, to human behavior. First, it should be noted that Freud was not unique in considering the role of energy distribution and the accumulation of energy on behavior. As indicated in Chapter 2's discussion of instincts, some ethologists have also assumed that energy may accumulate and that the likelihood of an instinctive response increases if a particular behavior has not been expressed. Freud is unique, however, in conceiving of individuals as closed energy systems, with the amount of energy fixed and presumably inborn.

Freud's statements about energy must be considered basic postulates in his conception; they are not amenable to proof or disproof. In other words, it is not possible to test the notion that there is libidinal energy, or that happiness is associated with free energy, or that we are closed energy systems. But do these postulates or assumptions lead to particular insights and testable hypotheses regarding human behavior? Are these postulates useful in building a theory of human behavior that is both theoretically parsimonious and empirically sound? As will be documented later in this chapter, the answer to these questions depends on what particular aspect of the theory is under consideration.

The Instincts

The hedonistic goals that individuals wish to reach are instinctive, in the sense that instincts are considered internal urges. Freud contended that instincts drive the organism toward action and are represented in the mind as wishes or desires. The *source* of the instincts is bodily metabolism; their *aim* is immediate discharge; and their *objects* typically are external satisfiers.

Freud vacillated in his ideas about instincts, at times postulating one, and at other times two, basic instincts. Initially, he suggested that there are two classes of instincts: those meant to preserve life (hunger) and those directed toward the attainment of pleasure (sex). The sexual instincts also were related to the preservation of the species. In his final analysis he reaffirmed that there are indeed two instincts, but that they are somewhat different from the two he at first postulated. He contended that one instinct represented a life force (*Eros,* or love), while the second represented a death force (*Thanatos,* or death). Freud contended that aggressiveness is one manifestation of the death instinct turned outward. However, the notion of a death instinct, as contrasted with an aggressive instinct, has been accepted by few psychoanalysts. The life instinct, or sexual motivation, was incorporated within Freud's drive-discharge view of behavior. Sexual drives were conceived as biologically rooted, persistent internal stimuli that demand satisfaction. Gratification of sexual desires leads to a state of quiescence, while lack of satisfaction, usually because of an opposing force, could result in maladaptive behaviors and neurotic symptoms.

It is often contended that Freud's concentration on sexual motivation was a result of his living circumstances: repressive Vienna of the late 1800s. But, as indicated in Chapter 2 in connection with the incest taboo, the importance of sexual dilemmas and conflicts appears to be universal, which suggests that powerful drives for sexual expression must be operative in the face of social inhibitions. In addition, Freud pointed to certain clinical findings to defend his concentration on sexual motivation, including his beliefs that neurotic symptoms could be traced to unfulfilled sexual urges and that infants and children also exhibit great interest in sexual matters (Klein, 1969).

Psychological Determinism

Psychological determinism refers to the axiom that thoughts and actions have causes (see also Chapter 1). Freud carried this principle to its extreme, stating not only that *all* psychological events are caused, but also that most of them are caused by unsatisfied desires or drives. Freud maintained that, in order to understand any behavior—be it a neurotic symptom, a free association, or a social act—one must attempt to analyze the motivational function of the behavior.

In one of his earliest publications, Freud singled out three apparently different aspects of normal human behavior—humor, slips of the tongue, and dreams—for special attention. According to Freud, all three behaviors serve the same function: vicarious gratification of a forbidden impulse or an unfulfilled wish. They are hidden means of tension reduction. Consider, for example, the following joke: Standing on a green, one golfer is vigorously choking another to death. A third party arrives on the scene and says casually to the aggressor, "Excuse me, but your grip's all wrong." Freud believed that such a joke evokes laughter because unconscious aggressive urges that are usually prevented from expression are being satisfied through the socially acceptable outlet of a joke. In addition (Volosinov, 1976, pp. 58–59), "a good joke needs a listener; its aim is not only to bypass a prohibition, but also to implicate the listener via laughter, to make the laughing listener an accomplice and, as it were, *socialize* the transgression."

Similarly, such mental lapses as slips of the tongue and forgetting also have psychological determinants.

An error of this sort is said once to have crept into a Social-Democratic newspaper, where, in the account of a festivity, the following words were printed: "Amongst those present was His Highness, the Clown Prince." The next day a correction was attempted. The paper apologized and said: "The sentence should of course have read, the Crow Prince." Again, in a war-correspondent's account of meeting a famous general whose infirmities were pretty well-known, a reference to the general was printed as "this battle-scared veteran." Next day an apology appeared which read "the words of course should have been, the bottle-scarred veteran"! (Freud, 1915, p. 35)

In Freudian theory, dreams are also wish fulfillments, or at least attempts at wish fulfillment, having their origin in sexual and aggressive impulses. Freud argued that the true meaning of a dream, or its *latent* content, is often masked. The *manifest* content of the dream, or what the dreamer reports, is typically a distortion of the "real" dream contents. However, with proper analysis Freud believed that the latent meaning of a dream could be uncovered. He therefore thought that dreams provided the "royal road to the unconscious." Freud also stated that the vicarious satisfaction provided by dreams has the function of preserving sleep. He thought that, in the absence of dreams, unpleasant impulses would disturb and awaken the sleeper (see Chapter 15 for further discussion of the dream state).

Here again one can raise such empirical questions as: Must a "good" joke tap unconscious aggressions and sexual wishes? Are all "Freudian slips" related to unconscious wishes? If I miss an appointment with my girlfriend or with a professor, does it necessarily mean that I did not want to meet with them? Must dreams always fulfill wishes? The answer to these questions appears to be an unqualified "no," but *some* jokes, *some* slips, and *some* dreams do have a motivational basis that are amenable to a Freudian interpretation. Furthermore, Freud's creation of a theory that could interrelate and offer common explanations for such diverse behaviors as jokes, slips of the tongue, and dreams (to which might be added neurotic symptoms, religion, family rivalry, and other behaviors) was a remarkable achievement.

Libido and Developmental Stages

Freud used the term *libido* (Latin for "lust") to stand for the pleasure-seeking instinctive energy that drives human behavior. Freud proposed that sexual impulses undergo four developmental stages: oral, anal, phallic, and genital. During the first year of life, the infant is in the *oral stage,* with libidinal impulses being gratified through the mucous membranes of the mouth (note, then, that Freud might be seen as concerned with sensual pleasure in the broader sense, rather than in the more narrow sexual sense). During the child's second and third years, the *anal-stage* pleasures stemming from the excretion and retention of feces dominate the child's erotic life. Sometime toward the end of the third year and the beginning of the fourth year, the *phallic stage* of development takes place, in which excitation and stimulation of the genital area provides the primary source of erotic pleasure (see also Chapters 8 and 9). This stage ends with the resolution of the so-called Oedipal conflict and is followed by a *latency period* during which children appear relatively unconcerned with sexual matters. Finally, after around the age of twelve, the child enters the *genital stage,* which corresponds to adult sexual concerns and pleasures.

The Oedipal conflict. The psychoanalytic theory about the development of the Oedipal situation is clearest in the case of the male. Around the age of five or six, a boy's sexual impulses are directed toward his mother, and he resents his father, who is perceived as a rival for the mother's affections. Freud labeled this classic rivalry the *Oedipal conflict,* after Sophocles' play in which Oedipus Rex unwittingly kills his father and marries his mother. According to Freud, the boy also fears that his father will retaliate against these sexual impulses by castrating him. Freud considered this fear, labeled *castration anxiety,* to be the prototype of all subsequent anxieties, in which one is flooded with internal stimulation. To reduce castration anxiety and at the same time gratify his feelings toward his mother, the boy identifies with his father, thereby internalizing his idealized perception of his father's attitudes and values. Clearly, the incest taboo is associated with the resolution of the Oedipal situation. In Chapter 2 we outlined a number of survival advantages resulting from this taboo, including outbreeding, which strengthens the group and produces hybrid vigor within the family.

The same process in a girl—the *Electra complex*—takes an analogous, but more complicated form, with the girl jealous of her mother's relationship with her father and ultimately identifying with her mother. This identification is not as complete as the boy's identification with his father, in part because of an already absent penis; consequently, it is presumed in orthodox psychoanalytic theory that women do not develop as strong a moral sense as men do. Freud also asserted that, because of their lack of a penis, women envy men. Indeed, women emerge as the inferior sex in Freud's theorizing, a facet of the theory that is more a figment of male chauvinism than a result of scientific inquiry and certainly not supported by any empirical evidence. (In Freud's defense, however, it must be recalled that at his particular point in history there was great sexual inequality. In addition, Freud clearly was ahead of his time in recognizing and accepting female sexuality at all.)

Freud's reconstruction of the Oedipal situation from the free associations of his adult clients has provided profound theoretical and clinical insights into the nature of family dynamics (see Chapters 8 and 9 for further discussion). Freud may have been incorrect in assuming that the Oedipal conflict is universal and that sexual jealousy is the primary basis for the child's feelings of rivalry. He certainly failed to take into account the effect of such factors as variations in family structure and the death or absence of a parent on the Oedipal situation. However, there is little doubt that even in the most loving of households there are rivalrous elements in the family triangle. How the young son resolves the conflict between his envy and fear of his powerful father and his attachment to his mother, and how the young daughter integrates her envy of a mother to whom she is strongly attached with her desire to be the center of her father's attention, play a central role in subsequent personality development.

Fixation.   Many adult emotional problems were traced by Freud to specific disturbances during the oral, anal, and phallic stages. As a result of these disturbances, libidinal energies become tied up, or *fixated*, at a particular stage of development. It is assumed that the greater the fixation at a given psychosexual stage, the less energy the person has available for mature relationships. Freud used the analogy of an advancing army, with the more troops stationed in the rear guard, the fewer troops available to meet new dangers. When defeated, the more likely the army is to retreat to where it has the greatest number of rear-guard troops (i.e., fixated energy). For example, a child with a strong oral fixation who encounters a major source of frustration during the phallic stage—say, the birth of a sibling—may revert to such oral behaviors as thumb sucking, exaggerated dependency, and, in some cases, nursing.

You might well ask, "Do children really have to pass through such a developmental sequence? Is the retention of feces really the primary source of sensual or libidinal satisfaction for two-year-old children?" Such questions related to developmental stages and sequences will be examined in more detail in Chapters 8 and 9, which focus on the growth of personality. However, at this point it can be said that the experiences of feeding, toilet training, and genital exploration are of major significance for the child's development. What is debatable, however, is Freud's hypothesis that these three areas of bodily activity reflect a common sexual motivation. It is also questionable that oral, anal, and phallic transitions are more central to the child's development than are experiences in other areas, such as attachment and independence training.

Personality Structures

According to Freud, human personality has three components: the id, the ego, and the superego. These structures have specific unique functions as well as distinct operating processes. The id, ego, and superego are not to be found in a specific location in the brain or in the body. Rather, they represent interacting, hypothetical structures, proposed by Freud to explain his observation that behaviors result from compromises between libidinal needs and desires, the restrictions of the environment, and the conscience, or internalized moral values.

The id.   Freud conceived of the *id* as the first system to develop within the person. It is most closely related to the biological realm of sexual and aggressive drives. Since the individual is unaware of these inborn drives, the contents of the id are primarily unconscious (see Fig. 4.2).

The id is the reservoir of all psychological energy, or libido. The availability of this energy allows the id to be directly responsive to bodily needs. Internal bodily tension cannot be tolerated by the id, which functions to discharge any internal tension immediately. Thus, the id operates according to the pleasure principle, or the doctrine of hedonism, seeking immediate pleasure through homeostatic processes and tension reduction. For example,

Figure 4.2   The relationship of the personality structures to the levels of awareness. (Lickhart and Spiegle, 1974, p. 67.)

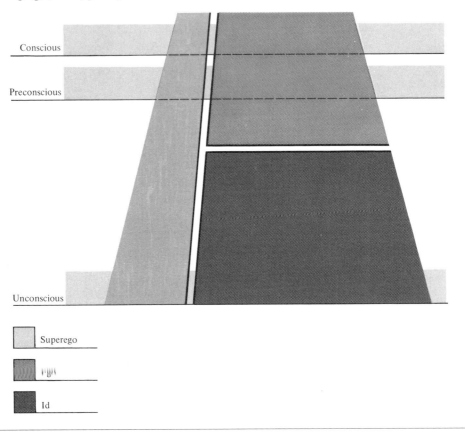

a hungry infant will reflexively suck at a bottle or breast, thus reducing its hunger. Although it must be remembered that Freud was concerned primarily with sexual and aggressive instincts, this automatic action, designed to return the organism to equilibrium, beautifully captures Freud's idea of an id-instigated action.

Id functioning is also characterized by *primary process thought,* a mode of thinking perhaps best known to us through our dream experiences. Primary process thought is illogical and timeless, with reality not distinguished from irreality and hallucinations, for example, not distinguished from actual occurrences. Thus, in the absence of external goal gratification, internal mental acts can be called on to fulfill wishes. The infant, according to Freud, can imagine that it is ingesting milk to reduce tension (see Chapters 14 and 15 for a discussion of imagery). Extensions of this idea suggest that we might dream about great accomplishments in order to satisfy some of our achievement desires, or daydream of attacking someone in order to gratify aggressive needs.

The ego.   It is evident that organisms must learn to differentiate between milk and the idea or the image of milk if they are to survive. Fantasy must be distinguished from reality. In addition, immediate goal gratification sometimes leads to more pain than pleasure, as when sexual or aggressive actions are later punished by society. To handle the problems of discrimination and the necessity of delay, the id develops a new structure that can come to terms with the objective world. Freud labeled this structure the *ego*.

The ego is governed by the reality principle rather than the pleasure principle. This does not mean that hedonism is given up. The ego serves the id in its pursuit of pleasure and tension reduction, but also takes the demands of reality into account. The ego follows the rules of *secondary process thought:* adult thinking that is characterized by logic, time orientation, and a distinction between reality and irreality. The ego also has access to the tools of memory, attention, and the control of motor activity. Thus, its existence provides a means for delaying gratification and planning long-term goals.

The contents of the ego are partially conscious (see Fig. 4.2), but the individual is still not aware of all aspects of ego functioning. Most experience is preconscious (not in consciousness), but nevertheless available from memory storage (see Fig. 4.2). The ego also includes the defense mechanisms, such as repression, that protect one from psychic pain. These defenses, which are generally not part of the conscious experience, will be examined more fully later in this chapter.

The superego.   According to Freud, the *superego* is the last of the three personality structures to develop. The superego has two main functions, both based on built-in reinforcement processes: (1) to reward individuals for acceptable moral behavior and (2) to punish actions that are not socially sanctioned, by creating guilt. The superego thus represents internalized moral codes, often called the conscience. The superego opposes the expression of unacceptable impulses, rather than merely postponing them, as does the ego.

Freud contended that the development of the superego occurs when the child identifies with the same-sex parent. In doing so, the child internalizes moral ideals, takes on appropriate sex-role behaviors, and resolves the Oedipal conflict with the same-sex parent for the affection of the opposite-sex parent (see also Chapter 9).

Integration of the structures.   Freud was greatly influenced by his training in neurology, where he observed a hierarchical ordering of neural structures. For example, just as the onset of some neural firings can inhibit other neural firings, so can the ego inhibit the strivings of the id. Freud conceived of the ego as the executive agency or "highest" structure in a person, which is responsible for final behavioral decisions. In this capacity it must act as a mediator to satisfy the constant demands of the id, be bound by the con-

Figure 4.3   The ego as the mediator of behavior. (Lickhart and Spiegle, 1974, p. 72.)

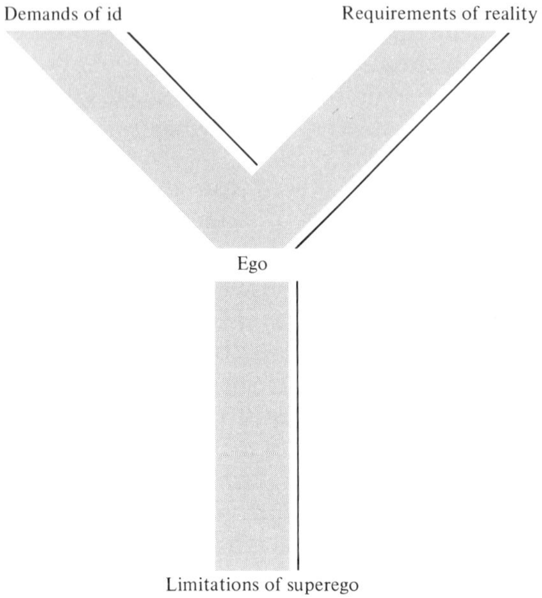

Demands of id   Requirements of reality

Ego

Limitations of superego

straints of reality, and pacify the ideals of the superego (see Fig. 4.3). As Freud (1933, p. 78) noted, "The ego, driven by the id, confined by the super-ego, repulsed by reality, struggles to master its economic task of bringing about harmony among the forces and influences working in and upon it; we can understand how it is that often we cannot suppress a cry: 'Life is not easy.' "[1]

Anxiety

The concept of *anxiety* is of central importance in psychoanalytic theory, inasmuch as the dynamics of behavior revolve around the notion of a conflict between expression and inhibition. Inhibition is an ego function that is intimately associated with the experience of anxiety and, in turn, the defense mechanisms.

---

[1] From *New Introductory Lectures in Psychoanalysis* by Sigmund Freud, Translated by James Strachey. Used with the permission of W. W. Norton & Company, Inc. Copyright © 1965, 1964 by James Strachey; Sigmund Freud Copyrights Ltd., The Institute of Psycho-Analysis, and The Hogarth Press, Ltd., from Volume 22 of *The Complete Psychological Works of Sigmund Freud*, edited and translated by James Strachey.

To understand the relationships among inhibition, anxiety, and the defense mechanisms, it is useful to trace Freud's changing analysis of these concepts. Freud's earliest theorizing argued that anxiety is the result of undischarged libidinal energy. That lack of sexual gratification, which could arise from any number of sources—the absence of wished-for objects, poor relations with others, or, most importantly, inhibitions and repressions—was believed to result in an accumulation of drive energy. The unexpressed libido was then "explosively released in a transformed state, the state of anxiety" (Monte, 1977, p. 120). Anxiety therefore was considered a product of the id, automatically arising from unfulfilled sexual urges.

As Freud gave the ego greater importance in his theory, he reversed this sequence of "repression produces anxiety" to "anxiety produces repression" (Freud, 1926). In a later period in his thinking, Freud contended that when drive expression will lead to more pain than pleasure, the ego "inoculates" itself with anxiety. This anxiety serves as a warning that, if the individual engages in the forbidden activity, then the ego will experience a much greater amount of anxiety than it just felt in very modulated form. The anxiety that will be experienced will be similar to that of an earlier danger situation: the "birth trauma," or the overwhelming helplessness that is first experienced when one leaves the protection of the womb. In order to avoid this state, the ego initiates action, activating defense mechanisms that interfere with and delay drive expression. Freud thus made anxiety an ego signal rather than an id discharge.

Stated somewhat differently, whenever an instinct pushes for expression that might lead to significant punishment or pain, the organism reacts with alarm in the form of anxiety. A defense will then arise, both to prevent immediate goal gratification and to help resolve the conflict by permitting the urge to be expressed in a socially acceptable form. Thus, anxiety can be directly linked to inhibition and psychological defenses.

Defense Mechanisms

It has just been suggested that the ego protects the individual from pain that might be experienced as a consequence of direct sexual or aggressive expression. Because the mechanisms used by the ego have a protective function, some of them are called *defense mechanisms,* or simply *psychological defenses.* Psychological understanding of these defenses was one of Freud's major insights and also one of the important contributions of his daughter, Anna Freud.

The psychological defenses that protect an individual from overwhelming anxiety, punishment, and other unpleasant experiences are sometimes quite obvious. For example, fainting is one mechanism that prevents continued exposure to such aversive sensations as the sight of blood or the feelings that accompany the death of a significant other. Any observer can recognize a faint, and the fainter can later readily comprehend what happened, if not the underlying reason for the loss of consciousness. Thus, Freud would not have considered fainting to be a typical psychological defense. Although it is now accepted that not all defenses must be unconscious, Freud contended that defense mechanisms operate on an unconscious level (see Fig. 4.2), with individuals not consciously aware of the defenses or their functional significance.

Repression and the Unconscious

One of the more provocative, better-known aspects of psychoanalytic theory is the assertion that a significant part of our behavior is governed by forces of which we have no awareness. Our choice of marriage partner, vocation, and even hobbies may reflect the influence of impulses and fears that remain unconscious, or at least inaccessible to consciousness. Memories associated with unacceptable feelings may also be excluded from awareness. When Freud encouraged his patients to recall painful memories and to confront unacceptable feelings, they appeared to resist his efforts. Freud hypothesized that this resistance was a function of an active force that he called *repression,* which acted to keep thoughts unconscious. The unconscious, of course, is not a place or object situated deep in the recesses of the brain; it is, rather, a property of thought and behavior. People are conscious of some of their thoughts and actions and their underlying reasons, while they may be completely unaware of other thoughts, feelings, attitudes, and actions. (See also Chapter 15.)

Freud believed that repression is the most significant defense mechanism, upon which all the other defenses are based. As he rather poetically described it (1933, pp. 305–306):

every mental process . . . first exists in an unconscious state or phase, and only develops out of this into a conscious phase, much as a photograph is first a negative and then becomes a picture through the printing of the positive. But not every negative is made into a positive, and it is just as little necessary that every unconscious mental process should convert itself into a conscious one. It may be best expressed as follows: Each single process belongs in the first place to the unconscious psychical system; from this system it can under certain conditions proceed further into the conscious system.

The crudest conception of these systems is the one we shall find most convenient, a spatial one. The unconscious system may therefore be compared to a large ante-room, in which the various mental excitations are crowding upon one another, like individual beings. Adjoining this is a second, smaller apartment, a sort of reception-room, in which consciousness resides. But on the threshold between the two there stands a personage with the office of door-keeper, who examines the various mental excitations, censors them, and denies them admittance to the reception-room when he disapproves of them. You will see at once that it does not make much difference whether the door-keeper turns any one impulse back at the threshold, or drives it out again once it has entered the reception-room; that is merely a matter of the degree of his vigilance and promptness in recognition. Now this metaphor may be employed to widen our terminology. The excitations in the unconscious, in the ante-chamber, are not visible to consciousness, which is of course in the other room, so to begin with they remain unconscious. When they have pressed forward to the threshold and been turned back by the door-keeper, they are "incapable of becoming conscious"; we call them repressed.[2]

Several different kinds of clinical and experimental observations support the belief that unconscious forces may exert significant influences on human behavior. Freud's analyses of his patients' symptoms, dreams, and associations convinced him that they were usually not conscious of the underlying reasons for their actions. They would repeat the same disastrous relationships, the same failures, the same self-destructive life patterns (e.g., alcoholism and drug addiction) without any awareness of the motivational bases for their behavior. Freud further observed that some people were unconsciously attracted to activities or ideas to which they consciously objected. It has been suggested, for example, that those who lead crusades against pornography and spend a good deal of time reading and viewing pornographic material are often unconsciously drawn to such literature. Hypnosis provides still further clinical data suggesting that behavior can be influenced by unconscious motives (see Chapter 15).

There are numerous clinical reports of instances of repression. One dramatic autobiographical example has been provided by the distinguished psychologist Elsa Frenkl-Brunswick. In one session of her psychoanalysis, undertaken in her early twenties, the analyst commented that her conflict and anxiety reflected a kind of "Cordelia" complex, referring to King Lear's youngest daughter. (Shakespeare's King Lear did not appreciate Cordelia's love for him until late in life.) Frenkl-Brunswick, puzzled by the reference to Cordelia, said that she was unfamiliar with the play, and the analyst had to summarize its highlights. Several years later, when sorting through her personal belongings, she came across some old high school notes on *King Lear*. She had not only studied the play, but also copied down the part of Cordelia, word for word!

The experimental study of repression. In addition to clinical sources of data bearing on unconscious phenomena, there has been a very active study of repression in experimental settings (see Rapaport, 1942; Weiner, 1966). Freud was not very encouraging toward such laboratory investigations, for he felt that his clinical observations provided sufficient evidence and that tests of his ideas could be conducted adequately only during therapeutic sessions. However, others more fully recognized the limitations of drawing inferences where relevant variables are not controlled and where there is opportunity for observer bias.

---

[2] From *New Introductory Lectures in Psychoanalysis* by Sigmund Freud, Translated by James Strachey. Used with the permission of W. W. Norton & Company, Inc. Copyright © 1965, 1964 by James Strachey; Sigmund Freud Copyrights Ltd., The Institute of Psycho-Analysis, and The Hogarth Press, Ltd., from Volume 22 of *The Complete Psychological Works of Sigmund Freud,* edited and translated by James Strachey.

One early technique employed to demonstrate repression was merely asking subjects to recall past events. If they remembered more pleasant than unpleasant experiences, then experimenters inferred that repression was operating to interfere with the memory of unpleasant occurrences. This approach was weak, however, because some of us may indeed have more pleasant than unpleasant experiences. In other words, a subject's recall may be accurate and does not necessarily demonstrate repression.

A second, frequently used procedure in the study of repression is pairing distinctive stimuli, such as digits or words, with pleasant and unpleasant sensations, such as good or bad smells or receiving either money or shock. When subjects are later asked to recall the stimuli, and the stimuli paired with aversive consequences are recalled less often than the stimuli paired with positive consequences, then repression is assumed to have taken place. Note that this procedure is better than merely asking subjects to recall life events, because the positive and negative experiences are controlled and equalized. But, these studies are also deficient on several counts. First, consistent data are not reported. At times there is greater recall of stimuli associated with pleasant experiences; at times the reverse is true. In addition, whenever "repression" is demonstrated, it is difficult to argue that the retrieval of the "forgotten" stimuli is opposed by an active restraining force. The experimental stimuli are far removed from the dangerous sexual and aggressive urges discussed by Freud.

A third research procedure for studying repression examines the recall of successful and failed achievement activities. Since it can be reasoned that it is ego-protective to forget failures, repressive forces should impede the retention of poor performances. Subjects in these experiments are given a number of tasks to solve, half of them too long to solve in the allotted time and half more easily solved. Thus, subjects tend to experience success on half the tasks and failure on the other half. Then they are asked to name the tasks on which they worked. Again, however, the findings are inconsistent: at times recall of the uncompleted tasks is greater, and at times better recall of the completed tasks is reported.

A fourth experimental procedure involves the recall of "complex-related" words. The notion of a complex-related word was first advanced by Carl Jung (see Chapter 5). Jung read subjects lists of words and asked them to respond with the first associations that came to mind for each word (the *word association* technique). Jung noted that some responses were preceded by unusually long pauses and inferred that, in those instances, the stimulus words were related to a particular personality complex, or area of emotional disturbance and personal difficulty. He believed that the stimulus words were therefore associated with repressed and conflictual material. Because of this association, immediate responses were likely to be censored, resulting in a longer latency period before the appearance of the verbalized response.

Some repression studies examine the recall or retention of complex-related words and their associations, compared with words that are unrelated to particular complexes or conflicts. In one investigation (Clemes, 1964), hypnotized subjects first learned a list of complex- and noncomplex-related words and then were given a posthypnotic suggestion that they would forget about half the words. Subsequent testing in a normal waking state revealed that the subjects were indeed able to recall only about half the words and, of crucial importance, the forgotten words were those specified as complex-related. When the hypnotic suggestion was subsequently lifted, the subjects were able to recall almost all the words. This is a reasonable demonstration of Freud's concept of repression and the unconscious because:

1. The material under study was relevant to each subject's area of emotional disturbance, unlike investigations using smells or shocks.
2. An active inhibiting force was introduced, in this case by means of an experimental instruction during hypnosis. This force interfered with the emergence of threatening thoughts into consciousness.
3. The emotionally related words were retrieved into consciousness when the active inhibiting force subsided, in this case because of the removal of the posthypnotic suggestion.

In sum, although there is a great deal of clinical and anecdotal evidence about the notion of repression, many laboratory studies have failed to support it, except in a few well-designed experimental investigations conducted under controlled conditions.

Perceptual Defense

Perceptual defense also refers to a resistance against threatening material. While perceptual defense is not among the ego-protective processes that are usually enumerated when defense mechanisms are presented, it is closely related to denial, which is briefly discussed later in this chapter. Perceptual defense is also similar to repression in that, while repression prevents selected *memories* from becoming conscious, perceptual defense keeps selected *perceptions* from the individual's awareness. This concept has received a vast amount of attention from personality psychologists. Its appeal is due in part to the relationship between perceptual defense and subliminal perception (see also Chapter 15). At one time claims were made that behavior could be controlled by television and movie advertisements processed without the knowledge of the viewer; these ads were flashed quickly across the screen and perceived at a subliminal level, below conscious awareness. These claims, fortunately, are exaggerated.

Nevertheless, there is a great deal of anecdotal and clinical evidence to support the notion of perceptual defense. As is true of repression and many other defense mechanisms, the experimental evidence is not always conclusive but, at the same time, there have been some experimental demonstrations that appear convincing, and new ways of thinking about perceptual defense are adding to its validity.

A controversial experiment.   An investigation conducted by McGinnies (1949) first aroused interest in the experimental study of perceptual defense and best illustrates the goals of research in this area. Subjects were shown words on a tachistoscope, an instrument that allows the exposure of material for durations as short as 0.001 second, so short that the stimuli cannot be identified. Some of the flashed words were neutral, or nonaffective, such as *house* and *flower*, while others were "taboo," such as *whore* and *bitch*. The subjects' task was to identify the words, while the speed of exposure was gradually decreased until the word shown was correctly identified. In addition to word recognition, galvanic skin response (GSR) to the words was recorded. The GSR is a measure of electrical conductance, generally measured from the palm, and is accepted as an index of emotionality. It is one measure taken during a lie detector test, for instance.

Two interesting findings were reported. First, taboo words were recognized later than neutral words. That is, the duration of the flash needed for the perceiver to be able to identify taboo words was greater than that required for neutral words. A second provocative finding was that heightened GSRs were exhibited on trials in which the subjects did not correctly report the flashed taboo word. In other words, emotion was exhibited without conscious word recognition. These findings posed somewhat of a paradox, for how can a perceiver defend against a stimulus unless that stimulus is first perceived? That is, the material must be sufficiently processed to realize that it produces anxiety, but blocked so that the perceiver is not made anxious!

In part because of this apparent logical inconsistency, investigators attempted to discredit the findings of McGinnies and other reports of perceptual defense. Many opponents argued that perceptual defense is nothing more than a response bias. For example, subjects could have been reluctant to *say* the taboo words, particularly if they were somewhat unsure of the correctness of their guess; that is, the results could have been due merely to response suppression. There is also evidence that the frequency of prior exposure to words influences both recognition and what the subject is likely to guess (Howes and Solomon, 1951). Some experimenters argued that the neutral words were much more likely to have been heard or read by the subjects than the taboo words (recall that the experiment took place in the late 1940s). Thus, although the neutral words were more quickly recognized, the results could be due to different exposure frequencies. And finally, it was pointed out that the verbal response was dichotomous; that is, it was scored as either correct or incorrect. On the other hand, the GSR was a continuous measure that allowed for a full range of responses. Thus, for example, an individual could be unsure of whether the exposed word was *bitch* or *bite*. If the subject decided on *bite* while the word was really *bitch*, the answer was scored as incorrect, even though there was likely to be some GSR deflection. It would not be reasonable to label the discrepancy between the incorrect score and the GSR deflection as perceptual defense (see Eriksen, 1958, 1960).

The idea that there are different response systems (e.g., verbal and physiological) has enabled writers like Bandura (1971) to reinterpret apparently unconscious phenomena. Bandura suggested that merely thinking taboo words is not punished, but overtly repeating such words is. Thus, the phenomenon of perceptual defense indicates only that there are differential reinforcement contingencies in the world and that reinforcement controls behavior. One can respond at one level (internally) but not at another level (verbally). The observation of a phenomenon labeled "perceptual defense," Bandura argued, is not proof that unconscious perceptions exist.

Other investigators have come to the defense of perceptual defense, and it appears that none of the counterarguments attempting to do away with the defense concept has been completely adequate (see Dixon, 1971; Erdelyi, 1974). For example, experimenters controlling for frequency of word exposure also report perceptual defense (Dulany, 1957), and perceptual defense is exhibited when methods are used to eliminate a response suppression explanation (e.g., subjects are required to respond with a taboo word to indicate the perception of a neutral word, and vice versa; see Zigler and Yospe, 1960).

Information processing and perceptual defense.   Perceptual defense becomes logically more acceptable when considered within the framework of more contemporary conceptions of *information processing.* It is now evident that many processes are involved between the perception of a stimulus and a final response, or conscious awareness. These processes include stimulus reception, analysis, and transfer into short-term, then long-term, memory storage.

A process akin to perceptual defense can occur at any stage of this multiprocess system. For example, common observation shows that people frequently avoid traumatic input (as during a horror movie) by fixating away from the stimulus, or closing their eyes. In this instance, control over stimulus input is voluntary and conscious, but in other circumstances the avoidance may be neither voluntary nor conscious. For example, it has been documented that pupils expand and contract in different situations as a function of the person's needs and desires (see Hess, 1965), an alteration that influences the perceiver's sensitivity.

In addition, one can scan incoming information and, on the basis of partial analysis, decide whether to encode or to reject the material for additional processing. For example, at a party one might receive different messages in each ear. The contents of one channel can then be rejected, even though this rejected information has been "heard." The message content is thus not transferred into memory. In other words, we can perceive without remembering; many more stimuli are apprehended than are put into memory storage (see Chapter 15). This sort of selectivity analysis can readily account for the more esoteric notion of perceptual defense (see Erdelyi, 1974).

Other Defenses

There are many other defenses against painful, anxiety-producing thoughts and feelings in addition to repression and perceptual defense, such as *rationalization, intellectualization* of impulses to strip them of their emotionality, and *isolation* of ideas to separate them from unacceptable related thoughts and attitudes. College students, because of their generally high verbal abilities, are frequently given to intellectualization: discussing threatening topics such as atomic warfare, future careers, and sexual inadequacy in an overly elaborate, rational manner which spares them the anxiety associated with these topics.

Defenses do not have precisely the same meaning or function for each individual. They differ in their consequences, generality, centrality to an individual's personality organization, degree of usage, and many other key dimensions. Suffice it to say that the manner in which one copes with unacceptable impulses is a key area of concern in the fields of personality and abnormal psychology. A few of the more familiar defense mechanisms are discussed in the following paragraphs.

Denial.   In *denial,* impulses and associated ideas reach awareness, but their implications are rejected or denied. For example, an unwillingness to check on medical symptoms could indicate the presence of denial, as is "gallows humor," the tendency of soldiers to engage in banter and jest as they near an engagement with the enemy. While denial may be functional for soldiers marching off to combat, it can be damaging for the individual. To deny the possible diagnostic implications of a persistent swelling that may be symptomatic of cancer is to risk the possible consequences of failing to take advantage of early treatment. Denial can also result in profound psychological consequences as, for example, when one refuses to acknowledge negative traits in a potential spouse.

Reaction formation.   *Reaction formation* is the manifestation of behavior that is directly opposite to unconscious feelings and attitudes. A parent who defends against unconscious feelings of resentment toward an unwanted child by reacting with overwhelming affection is exhibiting a reaction formation. Since it is nearly the opposite of genuine expression of feeling, reaction formation is often exaggerated, inflexible, and inappropriate.

Projection.   Projection consists of attributing one's own unacceptable, repressed feelings and ideas to others. Experimental studies have shown that perception of others' motives and feelings can be greatly influenced by the perceiver's own feelings and attitudes (Tagiuri, 1969). For example, frightened children are more likely to see other children as frightened (Feshbach and Feshbach 1963; Murray, 1933). In the strictest definition of projection, the individual is completely unconscious of the impulse that is projected. However, although lack of awareness may facilitate projection, it is not a necessary condition for the attribution of one's own feelings and desires to others.

Displacement.   The defense of *displacement* refers to repressed or blocked feelings and actions that are expressed toward an innocent target. In one well-known early study concerned with frustration effects, it was found that children at camp, who were prevented by the camp directors from engaging in a pleasurable activity, attributed fewer favorable traits to minority-group members when judging their characters (Miller and Bugelski, 1948). This defense will be examined in more detail in Chapter 14.

Sublimation.   *Sublimation* is a form of displacement in which an unacceptable, unsatisfied impulse is expressed in a socially acceptable form. Freud suggested, for instance, that unsatisfied sexual impulses could be expressed in highly approved artistic ways.

Individual Differences in Defensive Preferences

As might be anticipated, individuals differ in their defensive reactions to threatening stimuli. Defensive preferences can be distinguished in many ways, according to their complexity, generality, effectiveness, and degree of reality distortion. One individual difference that has received much attention from psychologists is *repression-sensitization* (see Byrne, 1961). It is reasoned that some individuals respond to particular kinds of threats with repression and perceptual defense. In so doing, they avoid anxiety-laden information. Hysterical reactions, including symptoms such as blindness and limb paralysis, are generally associated with the use of repressive defenses. Conversely, it appears that one may cope with a particular threat by using sensitizing defenses. The person then becomes more vigilant to threat and remains in close contact with the stressful material. He or she may then be better able to monitor and control the threat. The constant worrier and the obsessive-compulsive neurotic are examples of the use of sensitizing defensive orientations.

Individual differences in repression-sensitization are generally assessed by means of a true/false, self-report inventory called the R-S scale (Byrne, 1961). Some typical items on the scale, with "True" answers indicating repression, are:

- I don't seem to care what happens to me.
- Often I feel as if there were a tight band about my head.

The items on this measure were taken from the Minnesota Multiphasic Personality Inventory (MMPI, see Chapter 12), and many of the items are also included in popular measures of general anxiety, such as the Manifest Anxiety Scale (MAS). Many investigations have examined the behavioral correlates of different responses to the scale items. It has been found, for example, that repressors, as opposed to people labeled as sensitizors, require longer tachistoscopic exposure before recognizing threatening words, remember more successful tasks than failed tasks, and are slower at learning a list of affective arousing words. Thus, the scale has some empirical validity (see Byrne, 1961).

Although we really know very little about why or how individuals use

Figure 4.4   Effects of defense and vigilance training on perceptual recognition. (Adapted from Dulany, 1957, p. 336. From *Introduction to Personality* by Walter Mischel. Copyright © 1971 by Holt, Rinehart and Winston, Inc. Reprinted by permission of Holt, Rinehart and Winston.)

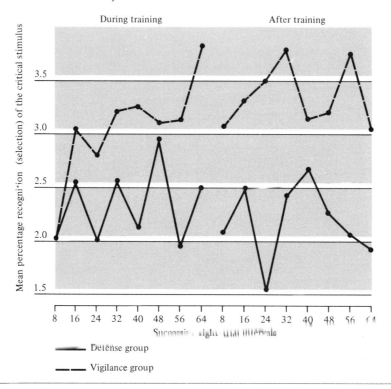

one particular defense rather than another, a research investigation by Dulany (1957) has nicely demonstrated the influence of prior learning on defensive preferences. Dulany simultaneously presented four geometric figures on a tachistoscope below the level of recognition, or below what is termed the *threshold level.* The subjects responded by indicating which figure stood out the most. Half the subjects were given an electric shock whenever they designated one particular, "critical," figure as most visible. The other half were shocked when they did *not* select this critical figure. Thus, the subjects in both groups received experiences designed to promote avoidance (repression) or approach (sensitization) behavior. After the training period, the shock apparatus was disconnected; the subjects were quite aware that the shock was no longer contingent on their response. Then the four figures were again presented for recognition. Dulany found that stated recognition of the critical figure was far greater under the sensitization condition than under the repression condition both during and after training (see Fig. 4.4). In sum, it appears that a prior learning experience that has instrumental or functional significance is one antecedent that may produce different defensive preferences and contrasting coping strategies.

General Evaluation

What, then, can we conclude about Freud's theory of personality? As was stated at the beginning of the chapter, it is useless to ask whether the theory is "correct" or "incorrect." Some of its concepts, such as that of defense mechanisms, have led to a great deal of research and have gained general acceptance. Other concepts, such as the death wish or the postulation of a closed energy system, have generated no research and have few adherents. In general, the theory's most significant contribution is that it provides a language with which to examine human action. It is therefore a most important step toward the development of a theory of personality, a step that builds a foundation for further work. But it is also just a first step and one with many shortcomings. The theory is often vague and without empirical support, concentrating excessively on particular facets of behavior and neglecting other aspects. As a result, it often leads to false interpretations and overgeneralizations.

There is a tendency to ask too much of this theory. People use it to try to explain why we engage in sports, why we are doing poorly in our interpersonal relationships, and why wars take place. At present, it is impossible for any single theory to account for such diverse phenomena with any degree of accuracy. Thus, rather than criticizing and rejecting Freud's theory out of hand, we should accept it for what it is and was: a monumental attempt to account for a great variety of human behavior by means of a few basic concepts and ideas. It has provided abundant insights and will influence psychology and social thought for many years to come.

Summary This chapter has presented some of the basic concepts of Fruedian psychoanalytic theory as well as research bearing on the theory. The concepts examined pertain to the underlying principles of behavior (homeostasis, hedonism, and psychological determinism); energy dynamics (conservation of energy, bound energy, free energy, libido); the structures of personality (id, ego, superego); and the inhibition of action (defense mechanisms). Freudian theory conceives of individuals as caught in a never-ending conflict between instinctive sexual and aggressive drives and the restraints demanded by the social world and internalized ideals. The dynamics of personality emerge from an analysis of this dilemma between expression and inhibition. The theoretical network proposed by Freud has led to major new insights about personality and has generated much new knowledge. This generative aspect of psychoanalytic theory is perhaps its most important contribution.

Specific Points

1. Freud's ideas were spurred by a hypnotic demonstration that motivations are not always conscious and by the use of *free association*, a method initially derived from having hypnotized subjects talk about their symptoms.

2. *Homeostasis* refers to organisms' tendency to maintain a relatively stable internal environment; the doctrine of *hedonism* asserts that pleasure is the chief goal in life. Freud included both homeostasis and hedonism as basic principles in his conception of human behavior.

3. In Freud's system, if all psychological energy is *free*, then all wishes have been attained and there is a subjective state of pleasure.

4. Instincts are primarily sexual internal urges that strive for expression. They have a source (bodily metabolism), an aim (immediate discharge), and objects (satisfiers residing in the external world).

5. According to Freud, all behavior is determined, including jokes, slips of the tongue, and dreams. This is known as the principle of *psychological determinism*.

6. Humans progress through a fixed developmental sequence of *oral, anal, phallic,* and *genital stages.* The *Oedipal conflict*, which concerns the rivalry between a child and the same-sex parent, is resolved during the phallic stage. *Fixation* can result from specific disturbances during any one of the stages.

7. Freud conceived of personality as composed of three structures: *id, ego,* and *superego.* These structures represent the idea that behavior is in part determined by personal (biological) needs, social reality, and internalized ideals. The ego is the "executive" of these structures, responsible for the individual's overall adaptation.

8. *Repression* is the most important of the psychological defenses. Freud represented repression as a force active in keeping thoughts from consciousness. Many experimental investigations have tested this concept, but only a very few well-conceived studies have provided confirming evidence.

9. *Perceptual defense*, which keeps selective threatening perceptions from conscious awareness, has had a lively experimental history. Contemporary approaches such as *information processing* make this concept less mysterious.

10. There are many *defense mechanisms*, including *denial, reaction formation, projection, displacement,* and *sublimation.*

11. Individual differences on the *repression-sensitization* continuum have been identified by means of personality questionnaires.

Thought Questions

1. Has psychoanalytic theory helped you to understand yourself? In what way?
2. Is repression necessarily "bad" for mental health? When, if at all, can repression facilitate psychological adaptation?
3. Freud maintained that hedonism is the chief goal in life. Can you think of times when you acted in a way that did not maximize pleasure? Could Freud have accounted for your behavior?
4. We have all had the experience of closing our eyes to avoid looking at something terrible or frightening. Can you think of any other methods you have used to avoid anxiety and stress?

Psychoanalytic Dissidents
and Descendants

 Although psychoanalysis began with Freud, it certainly did not end there. Psychoanalytic theory has undergone significant change since Freud's death, and Freud himself introduced major theoretical revisions during the course of his lifetime. Thus, any response to the question, "What is psychoanalytic theory?" depends on whether one refers to the early writings of Freud, the later writings of Freud, or more contemporary psychoanalytic theory. To complicate matters further, not only has Freud's theory of psychoanalysis undergone substantial revision, but also several similar, but significantly different, rival theories have emerged. Many contemporary modifications of psychoanalytic theory have come in response to criticisms from these rival theories.

Rivals to Freud

Several of Freud's first rivals were his associates and disciples, including Carl Jung and Alfred Adler. Because of their dissent on basic issues, they separated (or were asked to separate) from Freud with the request that they not call their theories "psychoanalytic." It is not always clear why some of Freud's adherents who proposed theoretical changes were able to retain their identification with classic psychoanalysis, while others decided to separate or were excluded from the psychoanalytic movement. In some instances, both personality and theoretical conflicts appear to have been involved. However, one common element in all the dissident movements is the rejection of libido or sexual motivation as the primary source of human conflict, anxiety, and neurosis. The alternatives to libido theory proposed by Jung (1916) and Adler (1927), as well as by such later dissidents as Horney (1937), Sullivan (1953) and Fromm (1941), are diverse. (Box 5.1 provides a brief statement of some of these alternative motivations.) In response to their proposals, Freud would not deny that people are motivated by inferiority feelings (Adler) or by a need for relatedness to others (Fromm). But for Freud sexual motivation was primary. The possibility that human beings might have different central motives—with libidinal striving primary for some but ambition, pride, or need for affection dominant for others—was an unacceptable solution for Freud

There are several possible reasons Freud held so tenaciously to libido

---

Box 5.1 BASIC HUMAN MOTIVATIONS AS PERCEIVED BY PSYCHOANALYTICALLY ORIENTED THEORISTS

Carl Jung

Striving for self-actualization, as reflected in integrating the "wisdom" of the personal and collective unconscious with the products of conscious experience.

Alfred Adler

Will to power, feelings of inferiority, and striving toward superiority or perfection.

Karen Horney

Basic anxiety, as reflected in exaggerated needs for love (moving toward people), independence (moving away from people), and destruction (moving against people).

Harry Stack Sullivan

The need for security in conjunction with the need for biological satisfactions; postulation of self-dynamism as a major motivational outgrowth of the need for security.

Erich Fromm

The expression of one's human, as contrasted to animal, nature; identity and a stable frame of reference for perceiving and comprehending the world, as reflected in the needs for relatedness to and transcendence of other people and physical nature.

theory. First, there is a certain theoretical simplicity and elegance in proposing one basic motive governing all human behavior, from which all desires and goals emerge. Second, transformations in libidinal or sexual impulses and the management and distribution of that energy, as discussed in Chapter 4, were basic premises in Freud's theory; lessening the importance of these impulses would have required substantial modification of the theory. Third, and here we are speculating about Freud's own psychodynamics, Freud had undergone enormous personal sacrifice in bringing the sexual basis of neurotic symptoms to the attention of medical colleagues and in suggesting the radical notion that young children may have sexual fantasies about their parents. Having sacrificed so much for libidinal theory, he must have been strongly motivated to defend that theory in the face of subsequent criticism.

In this chapter we will review some of the major psychoanalytically based alternative theories as well as some of the developments that have taken place in psychoanalytic theory itself subsequent to Freud. A word of precaution, though, before we review these alternatives: they did not arise from systematic empirical research. They reflect mainly insights, speculations, and assumptions based on each theoretician's own clinical and life experiences. In addition, these theories do not lend themselves to critical empirical comparison, in large part because each stresses a different motivation. Thus, the theories are, in many respects, not *commensurate,* i.e., able to be compared with one another so that one theory may be judged as "best." Rather, each is able to explain some aspects of human behavior better than the others.

The Analytic Psychology of Carl Jung

It would be wrong to presume that the only difference between Freud and his dissenters lay in the motivation believed to be central to human striving. Other revisions, innovations, and concepts were introduced by each theorist. The most comprehensive and formal alternative to Freudian theory is that proposed by Carl Gustav Jung (1875–1961). Jung, like Freud, has had a significant impact on modern thought and was a prolific writer and erudite scholar. Before he pursued a medical and then a psychiatric career, Jung's education and interests lay primarily in humanistic theology, philosophy, anthropology, and archaeology. This orientation became increasingly evident as Jung developed and expounded his own conception of human nature and the limits as well as the possibilities of human potential.

Jung had already begun a promising career as a leading young psychiatrist in Zurich, Switzerland, when he first became attracted to Freud's writings. After a lengthy correspondence with Freud, Jung came to visit him in Vienna in 1906. Freud recognized Jung's brilliance and soon decided that Jung was to be his "crown prince," his successor as head of the psychoanalytic movement. When the International Psychoanalytic Association was founded in 1910, Jung became its first president at Freud's request. But growing theoretical differences began to affect their professional and personal relationship, and Jung withdrew as a member of the association only four years later.

Carl Gustav Jung in his study in 1949. (C. G. Jung, *Word and Image,* ed. Aniela Jaffe, Bollingen Series XCVII, Vol. 2. Copyright © 1979 by Princeton University Press, plate 95, p. 114.)

Jung saw human beings as guided as much by aims and aspirations as by sexual urges. Jung's formulation of a basic human striving for growth and self-actualization was probably the major factor in his rift with Freud. When Freud asked Jung to become the permanent president of the International Psychoanalytic Association, he also asked for a commitment to the overriding importance of the libido, requesting, "Promise me never to abandon the sexual theory. This is the most essential thing of all. You see, we must make a dogma of it, an unshakable bulwark" (Campbell, 1971, p. xviii). But Jung believed that the unconscious instinctual life embraces more than simply sex and aggression; it includes other urges such as the need to create and to self-actualize. These ideas were subsequently incorporated by humanistic psychologists in America, to the extent that Gordon Allport, one of the original leaders of this movement, spent a year under Jung's tutelage.

To distinguish his approach from classic psychoanalysis, Jung called his theory of personality *analytic psychology.* A basic assumption of this theory is that the personality consists of competing forces and structures that must be balanced. For example, each of us, according to Jung, has both masculine and feminine tendencies; however, an integrated personality balances its more masculine aggressiveness with a more feminine sensitivity. In a similar manner, there must be balance between our conscious and our unconscious. Jung thus emphasized conflicts between opposing forces *within* the individual, rather than between the individual and the demands of society or between the individual and reality. For Jung, a self-actualized individual emerges out of the struggle to balance and integrate the various opposing forces that make up the personality.

The collective unconscious.   Jung's interest in archaeology and in ancient cultures and mythology led him to take a much more positive view than Freud of the function of symbols, dreams, and related unconscious processes. One of the most original and controversial concepts in Jung's theory is that of the collective unconscious, which, according to Jung, is the source of much of our vitality, creativity, and neurosis. Jung differentiated the *ego,* or the conscious mind; the *personal unconscious,* which contains repressed memories and desires; and the *collective unconscious,* which includes the psychological residue of the human species' ancestral past. The collective unconscious consists of universal tendencies to respond selectively to particular situations and figures with particular kinds of feelings. Jung contended that "the collective unconscious contains the whole spiritual heritage of mankind's evolution, born anew in the brain structure of each individual" (Campbell, 1971, p. 45).

The collective unconscious is made up of powerful, primordial elements called *archetypes.* Among the many archetypes postulated by Jung are the hero, the wise man, the sun god, the demon, and even each key member of the family. Each archetype is associated with an instinctive tendency to have a particular kind of feeling or thought toward a corresponding object or experience. For example, an infant's image of its mother will consist of aspects of the actual mother infused with the preformed conception of the mother archetype.

Two especially significant archetypes are the animus and anima. The *animus* is the male archetype that is experienced by a woman, while the *anima* is the female archetype experienced by a man. These archetypes imply that, to some extent, women have innate ideas and attitudes about men and that men have innate ideas about women. Thus, for example, a woman's response to a man is, according to Jung, a function of her animus archetype as well as a function of the actual man. The same holds true of a male's perceptions of and reactions to a female.

Two additional archetypes that warrant special mention are the shadow and the persona. The *shadow* is the lower, animal side of human nature, or our darker instincts. The passions and the impulses associated with the shadow, not unlike those of Freud's id, give rise to socially unacceptable thoughts and behaviors. The *persona,* in contrast, is the socially acceptable mask that each person wears in public. The persona archetype, in conjunction with social conventions, makes individuals tend to adopt masks and conceal their real nature. If this archetype is too powerful, then the individual becomes shallow, playing a role and detached from genuine emotional experience. There must be a balance among the persona, the shadow, and the other archetypes. The archetype of the *self* signifies the innate tendency to balance and integrate the diverse components of the person. The primary symbolic representation of the self archetype, according to Jung, is the magic circle, or *mandala.* This symmetrical circle symbolizes human striving for unity and wholeness.

It is interesting to consider the specific examples that Jung invoked as evidence for the archetypes. For example, Freud interpreted a da Vinci paint-

"The Castle" mandala by C. G. Jung, which represents the self-archetype and symbolizes human striving for unity. (C. G. Jung, *Word and Image*, ed. Aniela Jaffe, Bollingen Series XCVII, Vol. 2. Copyright © 1979 by Princeton University Press, plate 78, p. 93.)

ing of Saint Anne with the Virgin Mary and the Christ Child as meaning that Leonardo himself had two role mothers. Jung, on the other hand, contended that it was a manifestation of the collectively shared and inherited archetype of the dual mother, or rebirth. There are many myths about dual descent from both human and divine parents. Heracles, according to Greek legend, was born of mortal parents, but unwillingly adopted by the goddess Hera; the walls of the birth chamber in ancient Egyptian temples depict the second, divine conception of the Pharaoh; and Christ, through his baptism in the Jordan, was reborn (Jung, 1936). Furthermore, in the beginnings of medicine, rites of rebirth were used as a magical means of healing. Jung further notes that a key idea in medieval (and contemporary) occult philosophy is the common infantile fantasy that one's parents are not one's own "real" parents, but merely foster parents. According to Jung, the practice of giving children godfathers and godmothers is another example of the dual-birth motif. He would no doubt cite the phenomenon of the born-again Christian as still further evidence of the power of the dual-mother, or rebirth, archetype.

Archetypes are reflected in the universal symbols, images, themes, myths, and art of Eastern and Western cultures, as well as in dreams and even in the visions and symptoms of psychotics. Archetypes "create myths, religions, and philosophies that characterize and influence whole nations" (Jung, 1936, p. 68), as well as influence individual behaviors. These vast sources provided Jung with the needed "proof" for the existence of archetypes. Note again how Jung's training in archaeology and philosophy influenced his ideas, in contrast with the natural sciences that formed Freud's background.

Leonardo da Vinci's painting "Madonna and St. Anne," which Jung interpreted as illustrating the dual-mother archetype. (Musée Louvre, Cliché des Musées Nationaux, Paris)

It is obvious, however, that the "evidence" on archetype transmission, while interesting, is far from conclusive. The assumption of innate predispositions to react with specific emotions to a limited set of stimuli such as fear of the dark, fear of strangers, and attachment to warm objects is not incompatible with biological theory. However, the notion of a racial inheritance of an extraordinary set of visual, emotional, and behavioral tendencies, based on the acquired experiences of the species, is not acceptable.

Complexes. Another of Jung's important, but less controversial, contributions is the concept of the complex. Our common reference today to a "mother complex" or a "guilt complex" are some examples of how Jung has influenced our everyday vocabulary. A *complex* consists of a set of feelings, ideas, memories, and behaviors organized around a common nuclear element that provides the binding power and "pull" of the complex. For example, an adolescent girl seen in a local clinic was unusually attracted to older men. At the same time, she experienced a great deal of conflict and guilt over these relationships. When directly questioned about her late father, she could relate very few memories of him. And when given a word association test, in which she was to respond with the first association that came into her mind, in response to her father's name she blushed and finally uttered a barely audible sound. This cluster of behaviors is a manifestation of what would be called a father complex.

Jung (1904) discovered evidence of these complexes through a clever adaptation of the word association procedure first devised by Galton. Jung presented lists of words to his patients and determined which words produced irregularity in breathing and changes in skin resistance. From an analysis of the content of these words, he was able to infer the existence of specific complexes. There are now a variety of modern word association procedures based on Jung's method. Typically, subjects are asked to give a verbal response to each stimulus in a list of words. Delays in response time and unusual associations are taken to indicate that the stimulus has special meaning for the subject.

Experimenters have found it possible to induce behaviors similar to complexes through hypnotic techniques, thus lending validation to Jung's idea. For example, Reyker and his associates (Reyker, 1967; Sommershield and Reyker, 1973) induced a sexual complex in hypnotized subjects by administering the posthypnotic suggestion: "After you are awakened, you will not be able to remember anything about the session. However, sexual feelings will well up inside of you whenever words associated with money or metal are mentioned." When subjects were awakened and subsequently presented with words such as *penny, dime,* and *lead,* they manifested a variety of symptoms, including headaches, sweating, guilt, and confusion.

Personality types.   One of Jung's best-known contributions is his personality typology of two basic attitudes, or orientations, toward life: *extraversion* and *introversion.* Both orientations are viewed as existing simultaneously in each person, with one usually dominant. The extravert's energy is directed toward external objects and events, while the introvert is more concerned with inner experiences. The extravert is outgoing and makes friends easily; the introvert frequently prefers solitude and cultivates few relationships. There is a substantial amount of empirical evidence indicating that extraversion-introversion is indeed a significant personality dimension (e.g., Dicks-Mireaux, 1964; Eysenck, 1947; Wilson, 1978). For example, in anxiety-provoking situations, there is evidence that extraverts are much more likely to choose to be with other people than to be alone (Shapiro and Alexander, 1969).

Although Jung's distinction between extraversion and introversion has been confirmed, most investigators now view extraversion-introversion as a single personality dimension along which people vary, in contrast to Jung's conception of a pair of opposing attitudes. For Jung, these attitudes exist simultaneously and in opposition, even though one may dominate the other. When there is exaggerated activity in the service of one attitude (say, when an extravert has spent several days and evenings in social activity), then, Jung believed, psychological activities will occur that are directed toward achieving balance (e.g., the extravert's dreams will have introversion themes). This fundamental psychic mechanism in Jung's theory is referred to as *compensation.* In one interesting experimental test of Jung's conception, some subjects participated in a number of social activities, while others spent the same time in isolation (Dallett, 1973). Subsequent dreams were then analyzed to determine if compensation had occurred. The findings, unfortunately, were not clear. Nevertheless, the investigation points out how one might go about experimentally testing Jung's notion of compensation.

Jung extended his typology to include two other pairs of opposing tendencies: *thinking* versus *feeling* and *sensing* versus *intuiting*. These were considered to be psychological functions describing different ways in which extraverts and introverts deal with and perceive their experiences. *Thinking* is intellectual, leading one to ask how things work. Its opposite function, *feeling*, leads one to ask whether an experience feels good or bad (also see Chapter 15 on left-hemisphere versus right-hemisphere functioning). When the feeling function is dominant, one is oriented toward such emotional responses as love, anger, and pleasure. *Sensing* is a reality function; when it is dominant, one deals with the external world in terms of appearance, as if one were a photographer. On the other hand, when the *intuitive* function is prominent, one is responsive to unconscious images, symbols, and the mysteries of experience. Two personality measures, the Gray-Wheelwright (1964) questionnaire and the Myers-Briggs Type Indicator (Myers, 1962), have been constructed to assess these basic functions and have been considered by some to have utility (Maduro and Wheelwright, 1977). However, as is generally the case in Jungian theory, much more research is needed to establish the validity of this categorization of people according to basic functions.

An overview of Jung's theory.   In sum, it is evident that most of Jung's theory remains at the level of conjecture. In contrast to Freudian theory, which stimulated an enormous and varied body of research, Jung's work (with the exception of introversion-extraversion) has given rise to little systematic research. In addition, his concepts of the collective unconscious and archetypes, besides being in apparent contradiction to biological theory and data, are difficult, if not impossible, to test empirically. Nevertheless, Jung has deepened and expanded our conception of cross-cultural themes, human experience, and human potential. He recognized the positive implications of religious, spiritual, and even mystical experiences for personality growth and can truly be said to be the forerunner of the humanistic movement in psychology (see Chapter 7).

In deviating from Freud's theory, Jung looked further inward, amplifying and reconceptualizing the contents and structure of the psyche. On the other hand, other analysts trained in the psychoanalytic tradition looked outward, maintaining that social motivations, such as the desire for status, approval, and power, can supercede biological urges. Included in this group are such figures as Alfred Adler, Karen Horney, Harry Stack Sullivan, and Erich Fromm. These analysts differ in the particular motivations they believe to be central in human behavior and in how much attention they give to social influence as a determinant of personality. However, these "social theorists" are all sensitive to the role of society in influencing personality and provide valuable, creative insights into personality structure and dynamics.

Alfred Adler's Individual Psychology

Alfred Adler (1870–1937) was a Viennese physician who became associated with Freud shortly after the turn of the century. However, he never fully accepted psychoanalytic theory, and Freud found Adler's criticism difficult to tolerate. Although Adler served as president of the Vienna Psychoanalytic Association in 1910, he severed all relations with psychoanalysis just one year later (Ansbacher and Ansbacher, 1956, 1964). He frequently visited the United States, finally settling in New York in 1933.

A basic tenet of Adler's *individual psychology* is that human beings have an innate social interest (Adler, 1927): it is in the nature of humans to be cooperative and interested in the welfare of other people. This positive, socially oriented image of human nature is in sharp contrast to Freud's depiction of the individual as driven by biological urges that are inevitably in conflict with the requirements of social living. According to Adler, people develop problems because of mistaken goals and patterns of living that block the expression and realization of their social interest—a far cry from Freud's ideas about repression of libidinal impulses.

Striving for superiority.   Closely related to the idea of innate positive social motivation is Adler's assumption of a basic human tendency to strive for superiority. Superiority, for Adler, does not necessarily entail power over others or competitive success, but refers to a more general goal of perfection and self-realization. The human being, in his view, constantly strives to move upward. There is a close similarity between this characterization of human motivation and Jung's postulation of a creative energy force motivating the organism toward wholeness and integration. In the neurotic or emotionally disturbed individual, this positive force is misdirected, manifesting itself in the pursuit of power, prestige, and other selfish goals.

Adler's conception of a force moving individuals in the direction of higher goals was the outcome of his own gradual evolution in thinking. Shortly after his association with psychoanalysis, Adler concluded that aggression was a more significant drive than sexuality. However, whereas aggression alone assumed greater importance in Freudian thought, Adler eventually came to view other motivations as more profound and ultimate. Adler replaced aggression with the striving for power, and both power and aggression were subsequently seen as distortions of a more basic urge for superiority or perfection. It was Adler who coined the term *masculine protest* to describe exaggerated, power-oriented behaviors by men or women in response to feelings of inadequacy and inferiority.

Inferiority.   The concept of inferiority appeared quite early in Adler's writings. Adler noted that many individuals seem to engage in constant efforts to overcome feelings of inferiority. Initially, he interpreted these as reactions to organ inferiority. As a practicing physician he encountered people who attempted to overcome a physical deficit by intensive exercise of the affected organ or by development of a compensatory skill; e.g., the development of acute hearing as a compensation for poor vision. A famous historical example of compensation for organ inferiority is Demosthenes, who stuttered as a child and is said to have practiced speaking with pebbles in his mouth to overcome his handicap. Thus, in spite, or perhaps because of his handicap, Demosthenes became an outstanding Greek orator.

Adler extended the concept of inferiority to its modern usage, which refers to feelings of psychological and social, as well as physical, inadequacy. Feelings of psychological or social inferiority, like those of physical inferiority, might also have positive consequences, as when a young child's feelings of inadequacy compared with an older sib might lead him or her to learn new skills.

Style of life.   The individual's efforts to compensate for real or imagined inferiorities may affect a specific behavior, as in the case of Demosthenes, or the entire organization of personality. Adler referred to the distinctive personality that each of us develops in response to our inferiorities as our *style of life*. Each person is said to have a unique style of life, formed by the age of five, that characterizes the person throughout life and becomes the distinguishing feature of the personality. A related concept is that of the *creative self*, the facet of the individual that provides direction for life by organizing, transforming, and integrating one's experiences. This concept, like some of Jung's notions, is more an affirmation of the human spirit than an explanation of behavior.

An overview of Adler's theory.   In sum, Adler presents a positive image of human nature and its potential. People are motivated by social interest and by creative efforts to attain perfection and overcome inferiority. These positive urges can turn destructive or neurotic because of deficient child-rearing

---

Box 5.2   BIRTH ORDER AND PERSONALITY DEVELOPMENT

One of Adler's most acute clinical observations was of the importance of birth order in determining personality development. The oldest child, having received the parents' individual attention, has the problem of coping with the birth of the second child. Because one common reaction is concern with maintaining power and the status quo, oldest children are likely to be more conservative, responsible, and socially oriented. The second child, competing to be "number one," is likely to be ambitious; the youngest child is often the family "pet," overindulged and spoiled. Although earlier research failed to provide support for these hypotheses, a classic study by Schachter (1959) reawakened interest in this Adlerian hypothesis and stimulated a large body of research indicating that birth order, in conjunction with such variables as family size and sex, does affect personality. Schachter conducted a number of experimental studies on the effect of anxiety on the need to affiliate with others. Subjects who were led to believe that they would be shocked in a coming experimental session chose to wait for the session with people in a similar situation more often than they chose to wait alone. Of special relevance for Adler's views concerning birth order was the finding that, of first-born subjects, 80 percent chose to wait with others while only 31 percent of later-borns chose to do so. This was believed to demonstrate the more social orientation of the first-borns.

practices, like rejection or overindulgence, or because of deficiencies in the larger society. Freud, in comparison, presented a more pessimistic, tragic view of development and considered Adler's psychology shallow and superficial. Although Freud recognized social and familial influences, he believed that people are destined to experience conflict between biological urges and the requirements of a civilized society regardless of the mode of child rearing or the organization of society.

Freud's and Adler's contrasting assumptions about human nature do not lend themselves to empirical examination. Which image one considers more valid depends on one's personal experience and worldview rather than on scientific findings. On the other hand, some of Adler's more limited and clinically based observations have been subject to empirical test and may represent his most enduring contributions to psychology (see Box 5.2).

Karen Horney

Karen Horney (1885–1952) was a European-trained physician and psychoanalyst who had been psychoanalyzed by a disciple of Freud and emigrated to the United States from Berlin in 1932. Horney's first book, *Neurotic Personality of our Times,* was published in 1937 and provoked enormous controversy among psychoanalysts. Her departures from Freudian theory were no less striking than Adler's, and it was evident, from the perspective of Freud's adherents, that she had left the fold to join the ranks of the heretics.

Horney's and Adler's ideas were fundamentally very similar. Horney was optimistic about the possibilities for human growth, satisfaction, and self-realization. She placed greater emphasis on the role of self-enhancement, personal security, and interpersonal (social) motives than on sexual and biological urges as the principal determinants of adjustment and neurosis. However, the specific interpersonal motives and mechanisms that Horney suggested as central to personality differ from those stressed by Adler. For Horney, *neurosis* was best understood as a pattern of response to basic anxiety. Horney described basic anxiety as "the feeling a child has of being isolated and helpless in a potentially hostile world" (Horney, 1945, p. 41). The infant's feeling of helplessness is not inevitable but is dependent on the extent of parental warmth, affection, consistency, and other behaviors that contribute to a child's feeling of security.

Just as she felt that basic anxiety is not inescapable, Horney also took exception to the Freudian notion that penis envy in women is preordained by their biological nature. In general, she disagreed with Freud's psychology of women, contending that he failed to appreciate how the socialization of women fosters problems in self-confidence and leads to an exaggerated dependence on the love relationship.

Horney was sensitive to the various neurotic patterns that frequently exist in adult relationships, which she perceived as strategies that the child develops to reduce the distress of feelings of insecurity and helplessness (that is, of basic anxiety). Finding security in trying to please others, manipulating and exploiting others, and even devaluing oneself are examples of such neurotic patterns. What makes these patterns of behavior neurotic or maladaptive is that they are exaggerated and cannot produce satisfaction. In addition, although one of these modes of behavior might be dominant, they tend to conflict with one another, causing additional tension and distress.

Horney categorized neurotic patterns according to three fundamental types:

1. *Moving toward people*—a neurotic need for approval and affection from others; a need to please and defer to others.
2. *Moving against people*—a neurotic need for power; a need to exploit others and constantly feel superior.
3. *Moving away from people*—a neurotic need to be aloof, detached, uninvolved, completely self-sufficient, and independent of others.

All three neurotic patterns result in self-images that are impossible to live up to and trap both the person and those with whom he or she is involved. These patterns may maintain security, but they also serve as ways of expressing the unconscious hostility and rage to which feelings of helplessness give rise. Horney contended that there is a thin line between acting aloof in a social relationship and rejecting someone. Furthermore, one can control and even injure or psychologically destroy another person by excessive demands for affection, help, and support.

Horney neither formulated a comprehensive theory of personality nor attracted a large group of disciples to promote her ideas. However, her descriptions of neurotic patterns and their underlying mechanisms have been incorporated into many contemporary personality theories that address the problems of neurosis and psychopathology. Her views on the importance of the child's early experience of affection and security are reflected in a wealth of research (Bowlby, 1969; Harlow, 1971; Spitz, 1945; see Chapter 8). At the same time, there remains some question of whether Horney's views of personality are superficial and overoptimistic. It is certainly questionable whether *any* child can escape the rivalries within the family triangle of parents and child or avoid conflicts between self-assertion and pleasing others.

Harry Stack Sullivan

Of all the theorists discussed in this chapter, Harry Stack Sullivan (1892–1949) is the least well known outside the specialized circle of psychiatry and psychology. There are several reasons for his relative obscurity. First, he published only one book describing his theory (although his students and disciples subsequently edited several books based on his lectures and on detailed notebooks that Sullivan had kept). Second, he is difficult to understand in that his writing style is technical, and his ideas are highly compressed, rather unsystematic, and loosely integrated. And, perhaps the most important reason of all, he set himself the extraordinarily difficult task of constructing a theory of personality based on interpersonal relations. Although others, like Horney, also emphasized social relationships, Sullivan was much more radical and thoroughgoing in his social psychological assumptions concerning human nature and its development.

For Sullivan, a person simply did not exist independent of his or her interpersonal relationships. He did not conceptualize the person as having attachments to, desires for, or hostilities toward others. According to Sullivan, we *are* these attachments, these love relationships, and these hostile interactions; the unit of study is the interpersonal situation, not the individual. He believed that individuals develop characteristic interaction patterns in specific situations with real or perceived figures, and that personality is the total of these relatively enduring, recurrent interaction patterns.

According to Sullivan, individuals pursue two basic goals: *satisfaction*, which refers primarily to biological goals; and *security*, which refers to more social needs. When either of these goals is frustrated, the individual experiences tension and anxiety. This can occur as early as the first few weeks of life, in the course of the infant's interaction with the mother. Furthermore, direct frustration is not necessary for the infant to feel threats to its security. Expressions of disapproval by the mother are sufficient, for the infant is said to experience this disapproval through a process of empathy, which, according to Sullivan, is a form of emotional communication between the infant and its significant caretaker. To reduce the anxiety stemming from frustration and parental disapproval, the child develops a set of protective ideas about the self, referring to the self as the "good me" and the "bad me." The greater the threat and anxiety that the individual experiences in the course of development, the greater the discrepancy between these ideas about the self and the individual's true feelings and experiences. We will see that this notion has also been adopted by some of the leading humanistic theorists (see Chapter 7).

On the basis of these early experiences, one develops images not only of oneself but also of significant others. Sullivan used the term *personification* to describe the combination of feelings and perceptions that make up these images. Personifications may persist and influence later behavior. For example, negative experiences with a rejecting father may result in a personification of him as cruel and uncaring; this same personification may then be projected onto other authority figures, distorting their actual behavior and character. Personifications thus provide a link between early and later experiences and account for continuity in interpersonal problems.

Sullivan's propositions regarding the developmental consequences of early ideas about the self and others have a contemporary ring. For example, Sullivan advocated the idea that personality can change throughout life; that middle childhood and adolescence are important developmental periods; that social institutions profoundly influence behavior; and that the child's style of thinking or mode of experiencing the environment undergoes significant developmental changes.

Erich Fromm

The last of the social psychological theorists we will consider in this chapter is Erich Fromm (1900–1980). Fromm, like Adler, Horney, and Sullivan, had psychoanalytic training but, unlike the others, came to psychoanalysis with advanced training in sociology rather than with a medical degree. His background in sociology and the related disciplines of philosophy and political science is reflected in his contribution to the understanding of human personality. Fromm's views present an unusual combination of tough-minded Marxian analysis of the impact of economic institutions on personality structure, with warm, almost romantic humanism. While Freud saw social institutions as a mirror or consequence of basic psychological needs, Fromm perceived the individual as essentially victimized by a harmful society. Fromm, a refugee of Nazi Germany, believed that the attraction of so many Germans to extreme political forms was a consequence of the structure of German society, rather than a reflection of uninhibited biological urges.

Personality and society. Fromm's first book, *Escape from Freedom* (1941), linked changes in basic personality to change in Western society. Fromm suggested that human beings strive for freedom and autonomy but that this very struggle may result in feelings of alienation from nature and society. People need to be free and autonomous, but they also need to feel connected and related to others. The intensity of this conflict and the different ways in

Erich Fromm (1900–1980) at home in Luzern, Switzerland in 1968. (Bill Ray/*Life* Magazine © Time Inc.)

which it is resolved, according to Fromm, are dependent on the economic organization of the society.

In preliterate cultures and feudal societies, the individual had few choices. Behavior and opportunity were fully prescribed by one's tribe or one's social and economic position in society. There was little freedom, but also little alienation. With the Renaissance, however, an individual striving for freedom and independence came to the fore. The Protestant Reformation and the rise of capitalism enhanced and emphasized individual opportunity, freedom of choice, and personal responsibility, but the price for this, Fromm argued, was intense feelings of isolation and loneliness.

How do individuals cope with alienation? One way is to surrender individuality and choice. Fromm described a number of personality mechanisms that are unconsciously adopted to "escape freedom." The first of these, *authoritarianism,* is manifested in either masochistic or sadistic tendencies, terms that do not have sexual connotations, as Freud used them, but refer to ways of relating to authority. The masochist behaves in an excessively helpless, submissive, and dependent manner, whereas the sadist strives to control, dominate, and exploit others. Both strivings are typically found in the same person. A highly authoritarian military structure may foster both traits, with the same individual behaving sadistically toward soldiers of lower rank and masochistically in relation to superior officers. Another escape mechanism that Fromm described is *destructiveness,* in which case a person no longer attempts to relate and reduces feelings of powerlessness and alienation by seeking to weaken others. Finally, one can escape through excessive *conformity* to social rules; by being completely conventional and exactly like others, one can reduce feelings of separateness.

The basic needs.   As Fromm (1955, 1964) developed and elaborated on these ideas in his later work, his humanistic orientation became more evident. The conflict between striving for freedom and striving for security centered on five basic human needs:

1. *A need for relatedness*—to have, care for, share with, and be responsible for others.
2. *A need for transcendence*—to become more creative and rise above one's more animal nature.
3. *A need for rootedness*—to replace our separation from nature with feelings of kinship with others.
4. *A need for identity*—to achieve distinctiveness through one's own efforts or through identification with another person or group.
5. *A need for a frame of reference*—to have a stable structure or framework that will aid in organizing and understanding one's experiences.

Each of these needs can be satisfied in neurotic ways or in a personally and socially productive manner. Again, the social and economic structure of the surrounding society is critical.

Fromm describes five social character types or orientations in modern capitalistic societies which are related to the basic needs: *receptive, exploitative, hoarding, marketing,* and *productive.* The receptive individual achieves security by being taken care of; the exploitative person achieves security by taking what others have; the hoarding orientation is expressed in an attachment to things, or even to thoughts, that can be accumulated; the marketing orientation leads one to find some identity and relatedness through "selling" oneself; and the productive orientation, which is the only truly healthy one, is characterized by the realization of one's potential and maximum development of one's capacities. These orientations presumably are represented in varying degrees in each individual, although one or two of them may dominate. But the ideal—the productive orientation—cannot be fully achieved in contemporary society. One can only hope for some combination of a productive with a nonproductive orientation; for example, through hoarding one can achieve capital that may be used for positive personal and social goals.

We have already seen, in Chapter 3, that social differences can influence personality. However, there is little evidence indicating that Fromm's character structures are linked with particular social structures. Nevertheless, Fromm's theoretical views are stimulating and appealing. In the tradition of social reformers, he argued that through radical change in the social structure one can create a society in which both the individual's and the society's needs can be met. Particularly in his later writings, Fromm proposed that humans are essentially good but become corrupted by civilization, a theme reminiscent of Rousseau's "noble savage." For Fromm, true self-love and the love of others are sides of the same coin. In deriving a humanistic code of ethics, Fromm put the matter most succinctly: "Evil constitutes the crippling of man's powers; vice is irresponsibility toward himself" (Fromm, 1947, p. 20). A judgment on whether this positive and optimistic view of human nature is more "correct" than Freud's pessimistic view will have to await the verdict of posterity.

Psychoanalysis Since Freud

Classic psychoanalysis has never been a static theory. It underwent regular and major changes during the course of Freud's lifetime. For example, the concepts of id, ego, and superego were not introduced until the 1920s, well after Freud had laid the major foundations of his theory. Since Freud's death, psychoanalytic theory has continued to evolve, with new concepts introduced, old ones revised, and new directions taken.

These more recent changes have come from a number of sources. First, psychoanalysis has not been immune to the contributions and criticisms of its dissidents, and efforts have been made to accommodate some of these critiques without altering the basic structure of the theory (Erikson, 1950; Anna Freud, 1946; Kardiner, 1945). Second, psychoanalysis was recognized even by Freud as incomplete. Because it still has areas of inconsistency and ambiguity, a good deal of recent work has been directed toward making the theory more logical and coherent (Hartmann, 1964; Rapaport, 1959; Schafer, 1976). Third, as psychoanalysts experimented with therapeutic techniques and expanded their range of patients, new ideas were introduced to account for their observations (Erikson, 1950; Anna Freud, 1946; Fairbairn, 1952; M. Klein, 1937; Kohut, 1971). Perhaps surprisingly, experimental research has played a very minor role in these changes, even though an enormous number of studies have been directed to the investigation of psychoanalytic propositions (Kline, 1972).

We cannot hope in a few pages or even a few chapters to do justice to the development of psychoanalytic theory during the years since Freud's death. Many of these changes are either technical or involve esoteric controversies of concern only to psychoanalysts. However, there are several directions being taken in contemporary psychoanalytic theory that are of particular interest to students of personality.

1. *The growth of psychoanalytic ego psychology.* Increasing attention is being paid to defense mechanisms; to ego functions such as thinking, perception, and mastery; and to the development of the self and related ego structures. For example, analysts have become as much concerned with coping strategies and modes of adaptation as with basic id-instigated drives. A particularly significant component of this new direction has been objects relations theory, which deals with the child's attachment to and thoughts about people, the effect of these attachments and thoughts on the child's individuality and feelings about the self, and how these factors change during the course of development. For example, a question of interest to objects relations theorists would be the developmental effects of a disturbed relationship with the mother when an infant is six months old versus the same disturbed relationship when the infant is eighteen months old. Note that the focus here is on relationships, not solely on impulse frustration or gratification.

2. *Disenchantment with psychic energy and drive theory.* Modern psychoanalysts do not reject the importance of libidinal impulses and the psychosexual development of the child. However, there has been dissatisfaction with Freud's theory of libidinal energy and its supposed distribution and expenditure. These concepts are far removed from experiences that individuals report and from their perceived sources of conflict. Thus, there have been efforts to bring the theory closer to the perceived world of the patient in therapy.

3. *Greater recognition of the influence of culture and the family.* Although modern psychoanalytic thinking does not attribute the same importance to social variables as do such dissidents as Fromm, Horney, and Sullivan, there is increased acknowledgment of the influence of social institutions on personality. There has been particular interest in the effects of cultural variables on the development of ego functions and self-processes, as evidenced in the writings of Erik Erikson and other psychoanalysts.

The writings of contemporary psychoanalytic theorists reflect these three trends in varying degrees. There is considerable ferment and debate among psychoanalysts over the significance of these theoretical developments. It will become clear in the following pages that contemporary psychoanalysis does not speak with the same unified voice as when Freud was alive and functioning as its principal arbitrator and innovator.

Erik Erikson

Of all the psychoanalytic writers to modify and expand psychoanalytic theory, the best known is Erik H. Erikson (b. 1902). There is some question about whether he should be included among psychoanalytic descendants or psychoanalytic dissidents, with the choice depending on whether one emphasizes the similarities or the differences between his views and those prevailing among post-Freudian analysts. Since Erikson perceived his own views as expanding rather than radically altering Freudian theory, he has been included in this section of the chapter, rather than in the earlier section on alternatives to psychoanalysis.

Before being trained in psychoanalysis by Anna Freud, Erikson was an art teacher in a progressive private school and a graduate of a training program for teachers in the Montessori method. Erikson's educational background, his direct teaching experiences with children, and the Montessori emphasis on the child's development of initiative through play and work are evident in his later theoretical writings. Following the completion of his psychoanalytic training in 1933, Erikson emigrated to the United States. At various times he held positions at Yale, at the University of California in Berkeley, at the Austin Riggs Center (a leading psychoanalytically oriented institute), and at Harvard University. His first book, *Childhood and Society* (1950), was a landmark volume, an impressively creative extension of psychoanalytic theory. It contains the essential ideas that provided the framework for his subsequent theoretical writings (1964, 1968, 1976) and his biographies of Luther (1958) and Gandhi (1969). We see in Erikson's writings an emphasis on ego processes and cultural influences, although the significance of libidinal development and biological factors is not denied.

The stages of development.   The notion of developmental stages was central to Erikson's thought. He viewed the early stages of development in terms similar to Freud's, but he examined these stages from the perspective of the particular kinds of ego processes involved, rather than in terms of biologically determined libidinal tensions. An emphasis on ego processes leads naturally to consideration of social and cultural forces, for the ego is the mediator between personal needs and the demands of social reality. In addition, Erikson did not view the pattern of personality as essentially completed and unchangeable by the time the child enters school. His analysis of development embraced the full life span, from infancy to maturity.

Erikson proposed eight *psychosocial stages* in personality formation, each stage critical for developing certain fundamental personality characteristics

Table 5.1   Erikson's eight stages and their implications for personality structure

Psychosocial stages	*Personality dimensions*
1. Oral-sensory (first year)	Basic trust versus mistrust
2. Muscular-anal (ages 2–3)	Autonomy versus shame and doubt
3. Locomotor-genital (ages 3–5)	Initiative versus guilt
4. Latency (ages 5–12)	Industry versus inferiority
5. Puberty and adolescence	Identity versus role confusion
6. Young adulthood	Intimacy versus isolation
7. Adulthood	Generativity versus stagnation
8. Maturity	Ego integrity versus despair

and preparing the child for later ones. Table 5.1 shows how basic personality dimensions are related to the psychosocial stages. Each stage involves a crisis or developmental problem; if the crisis is adequately resolved, then the individual acquires a healthy component of personality (e.g., trust or personal initiative); if the crisis is not adequately reconciled, then a negative quality (e.g., mistrust or guilt) is acquired. For example, in the earliest, oral-sensory stage the infant interacts mainly with its mother, and the goal of the interaction is primarily the supplying of food. It is the infant's first interaction with the social world, in which it finds out either that basic needs are fulfilled generously and with affection, or that the world is harsh and unpredictable, giving supplies grudgingly and without love. According to Erikson, the infant develops a sense of trust or mistrust toward the world during this period. That is, the infant is becoming a trusting or a mistrustful person. Although later events can alter the basic disposition that has been established, the first experience of fulfilled or unfulfilled expectations is nevertheless of critical importance.

In later work, Erikson (1976) introduced the concept of *ritualization* to describe a culturally patterned activity or social ritual which each stage fosters. In the oral-sensory stage, the mother recognizes the child through personal but culturally ritualized touching, feeling, and other interactions. This constitutes a significant affirmation of the child and of the mutuality between mother and child. This relationship is believed to form the foundation for subsequent adult ritualizations, such as certain religious ceremonies.

An overview of Erikson's work.   Erikson's theoretical formulations are especially appealing to contemporary readers because of his emphasis on factors that underscore a sense of identity and relationships with others. If sexual problems can be said to have been the predominant "hangup" in the Victorian era, then problems of confusion over self-identity can be said to be the predominant concern in modern, technologically advanced Western societies.

Erikson, like Freud, thought that conflict was inevitable in the human struggle, but he had a less tragic and pessimistic conception of the outcome of conflict resolution. Self-insight and control, he felt, are important in coping with the dilemmas of living. In addition, the ability to resolve conflict is substantially augmented by the attributes acquired during development, given a positive resolution of each developmental stage. The mature person evolves the attributes, or "virtues," that help him or her to cope with problems: hope, will, purpose, and competence (the rudiments of virtue developed in the four childhood stages); fidelity (the adolescent virtue); and love, care, and wisdom (the central virtues of adulthood) (see Erikson, 1964). These virtues are reminiscent of Old and New Testament preaching, and it is probably not accidental that Erikson's ideal model of the person has counterparts in Western religious thought.

Erikson's work contains a sensitivity to the problems encountered in the course of development that lends credence to his views. However, his theory has stimulated surprisingly little research. There is no acceptable evidence supporting Erikson's hypotheses regarding stage–personality linkages. Also, Erikson has been criticized for emphasizing ego attributes and conscious impulses while neglecting sexual and aggressive motivations and unconscious forces. But, in spite of these empirical and theoretical criticisms, Erikson's rich, compassionate, and well-articulated views have had wide-ranging influence, far beyond the sphere of psychoanalysis. In addition, he has compelled psychoanalysts to pay greater attention to cultural factors influencing personality, as well as to the developmental problems that individuals must master at every age in the life span.

Psychoanalytic Ego Psychology

In its early formulation, psychoanalytic theory was addressed primarily to issues of libidinal dynamics, psychosexual development, and the expression of unconscious desires in dreams, neurotic symptoms, slips of the tongue, and a variety of other behavioral phenomena. Following World War I, Freud turned his attention to other dimensions of personality and introduced the psychological structures of the id, ego, and superego. The ego, by instigating danger signals, became critical in his concept of defense. Anna Freud then developed and elaborated on the notion of ego defense against threat and considered in detail a variety of mechanisms that children and adults use to reduce threat.

These changes made the ego more central to psychoanalytic theory, but its theoretical status remained unsatisfactory. In classic psychoanalytic theory, all thoughts and actions were derived initially from id desires. Such functions as thinking, perceiving, and mastery, which Freud assigned to the ego system, were secondary processes that arose because of a conflict between reality and the immediate gratification of id impulses. Tying ego functions to the id created theoretical complexities for psychoanalysis, whereas other theories were able to deal with ego functions in a much more straightforward manner. Also, viewing the ego functions as a consequence of conflict and defense tended to make one look at those functions in terms of degree of impairment, rather than as positive, healthy mechanisms for coping with and mastering the environment.

Heinz Hartmann (1958) recognized that for psychoanalysis to become a general psychology, it was necessary to conceive of ego functions as independent of the id-reality conflict. He proposed that ego functions are conflict-free and should be viewed as biological processes that enable human beings to master the various developmental tasks of walking, thinking, concept formation, and motor coordination that are required for effective growth and adaptation. He suggested that ego processes, rather than being derivatives of the id, emerge independent of the id. Because these ego processes were then no longer dependent on drives or conflicts, Hartmann said they had *primary autonomy.* Individuals were believed to derive satisfaction from the pure exercise of their limbs and from acts of perceiving and attending that were analogous to, but independent of, the libidinal pleasure derived from erogenous zones. These ideas provided the theoretical framework for what is currently referred to as *psychoanalytic ego psychology.*

Ego processes become organized into systems or structures that can serve a defensive function, satisfy libidinal impulses, or become instrumental in the satisfaction of other goals. For example, talking can serve a defensive function by obscuring one's true feelings and blocking direct action; satisfy libidinal or oral-sadistic functions, as in the case of sarcasm; and satisfy other goals by serving as an instrument to fame and success, as in the case of a national newscaster. When used instrumentally, these functions are said to acquire *secondary autonomy.* They can become free of the situations and drives that gave rise to them and become significant behaviors in their own right.

Hartmann's work on ego processes and related ideas offered by other psychoanalytic writers (e.g., Rapaport, 1960) contributed significant revisions to psychoanalytic theory. They helped resolve inconsistencies in the theory and provided a more integrated and logical account of normal psychological development. For example, one inconsistency in the earlier theory revolved around the development of the ego. It was said that the id created the ego in order to further its aims of impulse gratification (see Chapter 4). Yet the id, which operates according to primary process thinking, does not differentiate reality from irreality and can hallucinate goal gratification. Thus, why should it create an ego? That is, there is a logical inconsistency between the stated characteristics of id functioning and the need for creation of the ego. By giving the ego its own source of energy and by developing it independently of the id, the psychoanalytic ego psychologists resolved this paradox.

In general, psychoanalytic ego psychology has not offered an empirically tested set of hypotheses and predictions. Rather, its theoretical structure permits the study of curiosity, mastery, and perceptual and cognitive processes without relating these activities to id desires. Thus, researchers with a psychoanalytic ego psychology orientation have turned their attention to the ways in which individuals cope with internal feelings and the external world in nondefensive, as well as in threatening, contexts.

As an example of this type of research, George Klein and his associates (see Gardner et al., 1959) contended that there are systematic individual differences, or *cognitive styles,* in the ways stimuli are perceived. For example, a distinction can be made between *levelers,* who are believed to gloss over perceptual differences, and *sharpeners,* who accentuate these differences. This contrast in cognitive styles is assessed by using a simple perceptual task; levelers, for example, take longer than sharpeners to notice changes introduced by experimenters in the size of simple geometric shapes. There is some debate concerning the generality of this style and its importance for the study of personality; ego psychologists feel that repression is aided by a cognitive style of leveling, although the empirical evidence supporting this belief is weak. Nevertheless, the point to be made is that these studies can stand without reference to classic psychoanalysis.

Another research area explored by psychoanalytic ego psychologists is subliminal perception. Such investigations look at the effects of stimuli presented at levels below the individual's awareness on perceptions, thoughts, and feelings (Luborsky, 1967; Shevrin, 1974; Silverman, 1976; see also Chapter 15).

Psychoanalytic ego psychology, as contrasted with traditional psychoanalytic theory, has also led to interesting and productive research in ego processes in infants and very young children. It has helped psychoanalysts go beyond oral, anal, and genital issues and look at the influence of the type of mothering, the infant's attachment to the mother, and the environment in which the infant is raised on the infant's cognitive and social development. Although the research is not uniquely psychoanalytic in method and implications, the pioneering work in this area has been conducted by psychoanalysts (Escalona, 1968; Mahler, 1958; Ribble, 1943; Spitz, 1945). For example, René Spitz (1945), an early psychoanalytic ego psychologist, drew the attention of psychologists, social workers, and the larger society to the potentially deleterious effects of early institutionalization on the cognitive and emotional development of children. In a classic study, Spitz followed two groups of infants: one raised in an institution where unmarried mothers or adequate substitutes cared for the babies, the other raised in a foundling home with a limited nursing staff (each nurse cared for about ten infants). The foundling home had good hygienic facilities and the infants were not mistreated. Nevertheless, Spitz found dramatic psychological and physical disturbances in this group of children. Thirty-four of the ninety-one babies in the foundling home died within a five-year period, while others displayed various deficits in speech, motor coordination, and other ego functions. While there is some question about the comparability of the babies in the two groups, subsequent work with both humans and infrahumans (Bowlby, 1969; Harlow, 1971) has strongly supported the finding that early attachment plays a critical role in subsequent development.

Objects Relations Theory

It is undoubtedly already evident that the writings of the psychoanalytic ego psychologists are frequently abstract and removed from empirical or clinical observation. The content of *objects relations theory* is even more abstract and remote. Although the ideas put forth by objects relations theorists are often difficult, speculative, and esoteric, they are introduced briefly here because they convey the current views of an influential group of psychoanalysts working in the Freudian tradition.

The essence of objects relations theory is a focus on the infant's attachment to the mother and other figures. These early attachments provide the basis for the infant's ego development from intense attachment to the mother to a distinct, autonomous self. The characteristics of these attachments are believed to provide the basis for the child's subsequent interpersonal relationships.

Melanie Klein.   The potential importance of the infant's early attachments was noted by a number of Freudian analysts who worked with young children. The first systematic theoretical propositions on the role of the infant's social attachments in the development of personality were presented by Melanie Klein (1937). Klein emphasized pre-Oedipal interpersonal experiences, especially mother-child attachment. According to Klein, the infant must pass through two stages of attachment and objects relations during approximately the first year of life. In the first phase, the infant is believed to develop attachments to part objects, such as the mother's breast, and to relate to these objects in terms of gratifications, frustrations, and fears.

Klein agreed with Freud's view on the role of libidinal impulses, but placed even more emphasis than Freud on the importance of aggressive impulses during this period. According to Klein, the child both wishes for the maternal object and is hostile and fearful toward it. The child resolves this conflict by categorizing the world into good and bad objects. This categorization is postulated as a necessary step in the child's ego development. During the next phase, the child begins to integrate objects, no longer splitting them into good and bad components. For instance, the infant now recognizes the mother and relates to the maternal object as a whole rather than as part objects. When the child comes to the realization that good and bad experiences stem from the same object, it must then struggle with feelings of ambivalence. Recognition of the mother as a whole object implies both awareness that she is a separate figure, upon whom one is dependent, as well as awareness of one's separateness. The developmental progress of the infant through these early phases can go awry and become disrupted by hostility and envy if the infant is unloved or if its needs are not gratified.

There is, of course, much more to the theoretical views of Klein and her adherents than this brief description of early objects relations and ego development. Other aspects of Kleinian theory—the importance of dyadic (mother-child) relationships rather than the triangular (mother-father-child) relationships stressed by Freud, the assumption of pre-Oedipal envy of the parent, the projection of unacceptable impulses onto an object, and subsequent identification with that object—extend beyond the scope of this introduction to object relations theory.

While Melanie Klein is a significant figure among psychoanalysts, she has had very little impact on the mainstream of developmental psychology because her views on the infant's emotional life are so extreme. She conceived of "an infant from six to twelve months trying to destroy its mother by every method at the disposal of its sadistic endeavor—with its teeth, nails, and excreta and with the whole of its body, transformed by imagination into all kinds of dangerous weapons" (1937, p. 187). This image rightly elicits skepticism and, like many other psychoanalytic conjectures, is not accompanied by empirical support.

Object representation.   The child not only has feelings toward or libidinal investment in significant objects such as bottle, breast, mother, and father, but also has cognitive images or representations of these objects. These representations may be viewed as the *internalization* of object relations. Feelings and attitudes toward the object become elicited by a representation of the object. However, in the earliest phase, the infant is believed to be unable to differentiate itself from the object (Rapaport, 1950). Mahler (1968) views this primitive level as a period of *symbiosis* in which the infant is attached to and dependent on the mother and cannot differentiate between mother and self. Elements of symbiosis can sometimes be observed in adult relationships; for example, in some marital relationships the partners can no longer determine which feelings and values are their own and which are their spouses'.

Object representations are believed to provide the necessary basis for separation between self and other. They permit the child to tolerate the absence of the mother and of immediate gratification and are the foundation for the development of thinking and symbolic activity. One important element in the process is the development of object constancy. *Perceptual constancy* refers to the recognition and maintenance of a constant representation of a stimulus, even though it is presented at different angles and distances and in varying environments. From a psychoanalytic standpoint, *object constancy* refers to the capacity to evoke a constant representation of an object in its absence, regardless of variations in need for and feelings toward the object. Imagine the child's world if the mother who feeds the child appears different from the mother who disciplines the child, or if each time the mother wears a new dress, she becomes a different person. For psychoanalytic ego psychology, disturbances in object relations are an important antecedent of subsequent neurosis and psychosis.

Psychoanalysis in Flux

The one statement about contemporary psychoanalytic theory that can be made with confidence is that it is in the process of change. New directions in many aspects of the theory are being pursued (Klein, 1967; Kohut, 1971).

One of the most radical departures from traditional psychoanalytic theory has been proposed by Roy Schafer (1976). Schafer stresses the distinction between Freud's clinical insights and his theory (see Klein, 1967). He accepts Freud's theory of infantile sexuality, the importance of the Oedipal situation, the use of defense mechanisms, and similar propositions that are closely related to the reports of people in therapy. However, he rejects Freud's use of psychic energy constructs, of drive, and of terms that imply separate places or entities in the mind. He proposes that "we should not use phrases such as 'a strong ego,' 'the dynamic unconscious,' 'the inner world,' 'libidinal energy,' 'rigid defense,' 'an intense emotion,' 'autonomous ego function,' and 'instinctual drive' " (1976, p. 9). Such phrases make the error of *reification,* that is, making *things* out of or giving life to psychological processes, experiences, and behaviors that are essentially *actions.* We should use verbs and adverbs, he contends, to designate these as processes. For example, instead of saying, "He cannot control his sex drive," we should say, "He readily engaged in sexual actions even when he knew it would be wise not to do so" (1976, p. 28). Phrases such as "internalize an object" and "deeply repressed" attribute to the mind spatial qualities that are properties of physical objects, and such common expressions as "conflict between id and ego" also require translation into action terms.

These changes in the language would alter the entire theoretical framework of psychoanalysis. They eliminate a whole array of theoretical structures and mechanisms, many of which are either controversial or simply vague and ill defined. Needless to say, many of the changes proposed by Schafer have not been acceptable to the main body of psychoanalysts. One problem is that Schafer, in his effort to discard surplus theoretical baggage, seems also to have discarded structural concepts such as ego or self that are needed in order to account for the organization and consistency of behavior. Furthermore, by adhering so closely to an action language, one tends to turn a theory into a collection of descriptive statements rather than an organized set of propositions that lead to specific deductions, predictions, and analytic interpretations.

Although psychoanalysis has profoundly deepened our insight into human experience and behavior, much of the theory is loosely stated and needs to be rooted in clear operations or behavior. In addition, much of the theory has been unresponsive to research. Psychoanalysts do refer to scientific findings, and some are engaged in research inquiries, but psychoanalysts typically do not drop or significantly change a theoretical conjecture simply because of lack of empirical support. They have generally not attempted to separate those aspects of the theory for which there is sound scientific evidence from those portions that remain largely speculative.

Summary   While sexual and aggressive motivations formed the heart of psychoanalytic theory for Sigmund Freud, several of his associates and disciples maintained that other human motivations are central to personality. As a result, they left the psychoanalytic movement and developed rival theories. Jung, the most prominent of these dissidents, formulated an elaborate theory stressing human striving for self-actualization and the balance and integration of competing conscious and unconscious tendencies, including instinctive ideas and feelings inherited from the ancestral past. Adler, Horney, Sullivan, and Fromm constitute a group of dissidents who emphasized the importance of interpersonal relations, social motivation, and the influence of society on personality development.

Significant modifications of classic psychoanalytic theory have also occurred. These changes are characterized by greater attention to positive ego processes of coping and mastery, increased interest in the child's attachment to others, and greater recognition of the influence of the family and culture on personality. Of particular importance are Erikson's concept of psychosocial stages of development; Hartmann's proposal of ego processes emerging independently of the id; and Klein's analysis of object relations and the child's ego development. While it is difficult to predict the outcome of the ferment, it is clear that substantial changes are being made in psychoanalytic theory.

Specific Points

1. According to Jung's *analytic psychology*, each individual has opposing personality tendencies, such as masculine-feminine and introversion-extraversion. The self-actualized individual emerges out of the balance and integration of these opposing forces.
2. The *archetypes* that make up the *collective unconscious* are inherited by all human beings. They are reflected in universal symbols, images, myths, and dreams.
3. Jung conceived of a *complex* as a set of feelings and behaviors organized around a strong, common nuclear element.
4. According to Adler, people are basically motivated by positive social interest and efforts to overcome inferiority. Distortions of positive urges can take place through exaggerated compensation for feelings of inferiority.
5. Horney described three fundamental patterns of response to basic anxiety: moving toward people (exaggerated need for approval); moving against people (hostility, dominance); and moving away from people (aloofness, lack of involvement).
6. According to Sullivan, personality is the total of one's patterns of interpersonal relations. Early ideas about the self and *personification* of others are important mediators of interaction patterns.
7. In Fromm's view, human beings are basically positive, loving creatures whose positive impulses can be warped by society, particularly by an alienating economic system.

8. Erikson described eight *psychosocial stages* from birth to maturity, each of which poses a particular developmental task. The manner in which developmental problems are resolved provides the basis for specific personality characteristics such as basic trust versus mistrust, initiative versus guilt, and identity versus role confusion.

9. One of the consequences of *psychoanalytic ego psychology* has been an increased emphasis on the infant's early attachment to the mother. This attachment and other *object relations* provide the basis for the child's ego development and subsequent interpersonal relationships.

Thought Questions

1. Do you socially present the "real" you and, if not, how do you think your real self differs from your persona?
2. Do you support the Freudian position that society inhibits desires and that people are basically antisocial, or the Adlerian position that society can facilitate personal development and that individuals have social concerns? Why?
3. Assuming that family rivalry is quite common, what other interpretations can you offer of the Oedipal and Electra conflicts besides Freud's hypothesized sexual envy?
4. Do you feel that American society promotes alienation? How might this be changed?

Learning Theory Approaches to Personality

6

Learning theories of personality have their origins in the laboratory, unlike psychoanalytic theories, which are rooted in the clinical interactions between therapists and patients. However, as we will see, the applicability of these learning theories to personality and clinical problems has become the primary source of their vigor and popularity.

Learning theorists have undertaken the ambitious task of not only accounting for personality development on the basis of principles established in the laboratory, but also applying these principles to changing emotionally disturbed, maladaptive behavior patterns. As we will see, therapeutic procedures based on learning theories have indeed been implemented successfully in clinical situations. In fact, one of the most significant developments in the field of clinical psychology has been the vigorous growth of therapies based on learning principles.

In previous chapters, we have seen how a group of psychodynamic, clinically based theories explained personality development and functioning using complex concepts that were difficult to define and evaluate. In the next chapter, we will cover more cognitive theories that are also clinically based and frequently employ complex terminology that is not easily translated into concrete concepts. The concepts used by the learning theorists, however, are simpler and more readily tied to observables. Thus, the learning theorists have in a real sense undertaken the difficult challenge: explaining the phenomena of human personality with a restricted, empirically based vocabulary and a set of well-defined principles. How they have approached this task, the ways in which vocabulary and principles have had to be expanded, and the adequacy of their theoretical accounts of personality are some of the questions to be considered in this chapter.

The learning theories reviewed in this chapter share a number of characteristics, several of them noted earlier (see Chapter 1 and the introduction to Part II):

1. The use of concepts and methods that are closely linked to the laboratory, particularly to the experimental analysis of learning.

2. The assumption that the principal behaviors constituting personality are acquired, or learned, during the course of development. More specifically, an individual's behaviors in a given situation are believed to have been acquired through a history of being rewarded or punished in the same or similar situations. For example, the difference in timidity and aggressiveness between two boys, Robert and John, may be accounted for by differences in their learning histories. Robert may be inhibited and timid because his retreats from threatening social encounters have been rewarded by adults, and his abortive attempts at self-defense have met with punishment from peers. However, John may be a bully at school because his aggressive behavior has been reinforced by his resultant control of others, by his gaining possessions, and by the attention he receives for it. Learning theorists acknowledge that genetic and biological factors may influence individual differences but believe that these are secondary to learning experiences.

3. A theoretical emphasis on observable stimuli and responses. All but the learning theories of personality locate the basic processes of personality inside the individual. Learning theories, however, differ on this point. Some, like Skinner's (1953) operant reinforcement theory, are concerned solely with observables and make no inferences about the mind or what might be occurring inside the organism. Others, like the learning theories of Miller and Dollard (1941) and Bandura (1977), do propose a variety of internal processes that intervene between the onset of the stimulus and the subsequent overt behavior. Nevertheless, even these theories prefer to focus on stimuli and behaviors that are observable to the scientist. They make as few assumptions as possible about mediating elements such as thoughts, feelings, and desires.

4. An emphasis on the importance of the situation as a determinant of action. One of the great controversies in personality research has centered on the role of the situation as a determinant of behavior. How important is the situation compared with the characteristics that an individual brings into it? Whereas personality theorists have by and large paid attention almost exclusively to the attributes of the person, learning theorists have helped to balance

this often one-sided emphasis by demonstrating the influence of situational or environmental factors on behavior. Some learning theorists may have pushed this balance between the situation and the person too far to the other extreme by minimizing the role of dispositional (person) variables. The person-situation controversy is a major issue in the study of personality and will be examined at various points in this text (see especially Chapter 13).

Although there are many similarities among learning theories, there are also major differences among them. These differences, which are in some instances as great as those among the various psychoanalytic and psychodynamic theories, will be considered in detail as we review the major learning theory approaches to personality.

Associationist (Stimulus-Response) Learning Theory

The period from the 1930s through the 1960s was one of ferment and controversy surrounding a few major psychological theories, each one offering hope of explaining much of psychology. One of the most influential of these theories was proposed by Clark Hull (1943, 1951, 1952). Hull and other theorists of this period aimed to formulate a theory of behavior that would adequately encompass most species, from the laboratory rat to the human. Indeed, much of the research support for these theories came from studies of the laboratory rat. Hull was not oblivious to the differences between rat and human, but he believed that there are common requirements imposed on every living organism to satisfy biological needs and to adapt to the environment. Clearly, Darwin was an important influence on Hull, who further assumed that for mammals—whether rats or human beings—the mechanisms governing learning are basically identical. Humans as well as lower animals, according to Hull, are creatures of habit.

Habits and Drives

Habits are stable stimulus-response connections. A dog attacking an intruder on sight, a dolphin soaring above the water in response to a verbal command, and a preschooler regularly crying at the sight of another child with a toy he or she wants are all exhibiting habits. Hull proposed that habits are acquired and strengthened whenever a response that occurs together with a stimulus is accompanied or shortly followed by drive reduction. Drive reduction is thus required for a response to be reinforced. *Drive reduction* refers to a decrease in the intensity of a motivation or drive, as when hunger, thirst, or sex is partially or fully satisfied, or when fear is reduced after a threat is overcome. In addition, the effects of drive reduction supposedly work automatically, so that the lowering of drive strengthens any response that happens to be occurring in that particular stimulus situation.

Hull's own research examined the effects of the reduction of such *primary drives* as thirst and hunger. Since drive reduction in these instances meant that the organism had obtained water when thirsty or food when hungry, the reinforced response was biologically adaptive, aiding the organism in its struggle for survival. But the reinforced response does not have to be instrumental to the attainment of a reward, according to the theory. Irrelevant responses occurring in conjunction with relevant behavior are also expected to be reinforced. For example, a hungry rat that scratches its snout while pressing a bar that releases a food pellet will be more likely to scratch its snout the next time it is hungry and is placed in the same apparatus. B. F. Skinner has suggested that the same mechanism responsible for a hungry rat's pawing at its snout for food, when that response has nothing to do with obtaining a reward, is the basis for superstitious behavior in humans.

The situation is more complex for humans because, in addition to such primary drives as hunger and thirst, there are many *acquired,* or *secondary, drives* such as our desires for love, power, achievement, and money. In addition, people have many learned fears. These secondary drives might even conflict with one another or with primary drives, so that the drive reduction of one motivation may lead to the reinforcement of a behavior that thwarts the satisfaction of other motivations. For example, the response of drinking alcohol may be reinforced by the reduction of painful fears and anxieties. However, habitual drinking may also result in economic loss, family disruptions, and social disgrace; thus, the overall effect of a drinking habit is maladaptive.

Personality Development

Hull provided the basis for a formal theory of learning that could be used to account for both maladaptive and adaptive behavior in humans and infrahumans. Thus, his theory was attractive to psychologists and other behavioral scientists with interests in animal behavior, human personality, and social interaction. For example, sociologists and anthropologists used Hullian principles to analyze how society transmits and maintains particular customs.

Among Hull's associates and students at Yale were John Dollard, a sociologist with an extensive background in cultural anthropology and psychology, and Neal Miller, an experimental psychologist then known for his studies of drive acquisition and reinforcement. These two pioneered in systematically extending and elaborating on Hull's principles to account for personality development, social behavior, and psychopathology (Dollard et al., 1939; Dollard and Miller, 1950; Miller and Dollard, 1941). In recent years the personality theory formulated by Dollard and Miller has declined in popularity, paralleling the decline of Hullian theory from the central position it once occupied in psychology. However, the Dollard-Miller analysis is still useful and has substantially influenced other learning approaches to personality.

It is helpful to consider how the critical concepts in the Dollard-Miller analysis—cue (stimulus), drive, response, and reinforcement—apply to a concrete situation. Assume that a professor typically responds with sarcasm whenever a student answers a question incorrectly. Even after receiving unfavorable feedback and complaints about his behavior, the professor finds it difficult to change. According to the concepts of Dollard and Miller, the *cue* in this situation is an incorrect answer; the *response*, sarcasm. While the cue and the response are obvious, the operative *drive* in this situation and the *reinforcement* are less apparent. The drive could be a need to impress the class and the reinforcement, class laughter; or the drive could be a need for power and the reinforcement, student fear and docility; or the drive might be aggression and the reinforcement, the expression of pain on the face of the unfortunate student. In examining behavior from the perspective of Dollard and Miller, one seeks to establish the cue that is eliciting a response, the drive that has been gratified in the situation, and the reinforcement that reduces the drive.

Cues.   Although the cue that elicited the professor's sarcasm is evident, cues are often so subtle and disguised that neither the respondent nor an outside observer can pinpoint the stimulus that is actually eliciting the behavior. Most of us have experienced feelings of anger or anxiety and have engaged in a compulsive eating binge without being able to identify the stimuli that elicited, or caused, these behaviors. An important task for the clinician dealing with symptoms such as fear, uncontrollable thoughts, and compulsive rituals is to determine the cues that evoke these symptoms. Cues exert a powerful effect on a person's behavior; they "can determine when one will respond and which response one will make" (Dollard and Miller, 1950, p. 32).

Cues can also elicit *mediating responses:* internal, nonobservable responses that are believed to intervene (mediate) between observable stimuli and overt responses. Thoughts, feelings, and the anticipation of events are potential mediating responses which can then serve as cues, eliciting other mediating or overt responses.

Mediating responses can have drive as well as cue functions. For example, for a child who once had been frightened in a dark room by an intruder, any dark area came to elicit the mediating response of fear, through a process of conditioning. Because fear is aversive, the child was driven to reduce the fear, in this case by lighting the room. Thus, the child insisted on sleeping in a well-lit room, never entered a dark area, looked for a flashlight before opening a large closet, and was reluctant to leave the house at night. This process is shown in Fig. 6.1.

Acquired drives.   Fear, as a learned response, is one example of a secondary, or acquired, drive. *Acquired drives* are similar to such primary drives as hunger and thirst in that the organism will strive to reduce them. A response that

Figure 6.1   A mediating response with cue functions.

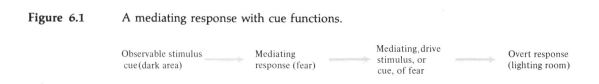

| Observable stimulus cue (dark area) | Mediating response (fear) | Mediating, drive stimulus, or cue, of fear | Overt response (lighting room) |

results in drive reduction will then be reinforced; that is, the probability of that response occurring again in the same situation is increased. This holds true whatever the acquired drive—fear, say, or a need for fame or affiliation.

The cue, or stimulus, value of the fear drive is illustrated by the habits that the darkness-fearing child subsequently developed. He asked his mother to bring along a flashlight whenever he was taken to the dentist, and the dentist found that permitting him to shine a flashlight or placing a bright lamp near the drill helped relax the child. The mediating response of fear was therefore common to both the dental situation and the dark room, and the response of illuminating the area became attached to both the internal cue of fear and the external cue of darkness. That is, when the internal cue (fear) occurred in a context (the dentist's office) other than that in which it was first learned (the dark), the previously learned fear-reducing response (bright light) became generalized to the new context. This process is referred to as *mediated generalization.* Through mediated generalization, very different stimuli—for example, a dark room or a dentist's chair—may come to elicit the same response: use of a flashlight.

Comparison with psychoanalytic theory.   The examples above illustrating the concepts of cue, drive, response, and reinforcement suggest the applicability of Hull's and Dollard and Miller's learning theory to various aspects of psychoanalytic theory. Although stimulus-response learning theory and psychoanalytic theory come from far different traditions, employ different concepts, and differ sharply in methodology and rigor, they share several assumptions about human nature. Psychoanalytic propositions can therefore be translated into the language and structure of learning theory.

Dollard and Miller's learning theory, like psychoanalytic theory, allows for unconscious determinants of behavior; that is, motivations of which the individual is unaware that affect thought and action. In addition, both learning theory and psychoanalytic theory assert that the ability to label these motivations, or the achievement of insight, will produce more adaptive behavior. Both theories also emphasize the role of drives in governing behavior and the significance of motivational conflict as a cause of psychopathology. Still another point of consistency between the two theoretical approaches is their common assumption of the necessity of drive reduction for reinforcement. Both Hull and psychoanalytic theorists see the organism as striving to reduce tension and as acquiring and maintaining tension-reducing behaviors. Finally, both camps believe that behavior follows laws and is determined, thus providing the basis for scientific analysis and prediction of behavior.

Language and repression.   It is illuminating to examine the Dollard-Miller analysis of repression, because it introduces us to the role of language in their theory and, more generally, to the strategies and concepts that experimentally based learning theories use to explore complex psychoanalytic propositions and observations.

Figure 6.2 depicts a number of possible responses that a male with strong sexual conflicts might make when confronted with a sexually attractive female. Between the observable cue of an attractive female stimulus and the observable response, different chains of mediating responses might take place. The overt goal response at the end of the chain reduces the experienced anxiety and is therefore reinforced by anxiety reduction. The figure shows that different overt responses are often mediated by disparate covert cognitive statements. For example, a response of indifference might be preceded by the covert statement of "She bores me"; an aggressive remark might be mediated by the covert appraisal, "I don't like her"; and so on.

These different anxiety responses can affect behavior at different points in the motivational sequence. Thus, the indifference response might move up in the chain and interfere with the sexual response so that sexual arousal does not even occur. This process might be so automatic that the individual is unaware that he is repressing his sexual feelings. Repression also can take place through the individual's mislabeling his sexual response—for example, attributing tension to a forthcoming exam rather than to sexual arousal. The most extreme form of repressive response results in complete avoidance of stimuli that elicit sexual feelings, namely, avoidance of women. Alternatively, one might establish a nonintimate, friendly relationship, a compromise response that permits partial gratification of sexual feelings and reduction of sexual anxiety. But this is still a form of repression in that the individual remains unaware of his sexual feelings. Removal of such repression entails a reduction of anxiety, the experience of sexual feelings, and accurate labeling of those feelings.

Dollard and Miller's incorporation of covert verbal responses in their theoretical analysis anticipated current interest in cognitive behavioral modification, an approach considered later in this chapter. In general, the relative flexibility of their interpretations of Hullian theory has permitted investigators and theorists operating within this framework to address many of the major issues in the study of personality, including frustration, aggression, and conflict (see Chapter 14). The same flexibility, however, made the Dollard and Miller theory vulnerable to criticisms similar to those leveled against psychoanalytic theory, especially since there are too many unobservable concepts that can be made to fit any behavioral outcome. There was also consid-

Figure 6.2   Alternative stimulus-response mediating response chains leading to repression.

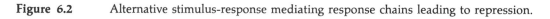
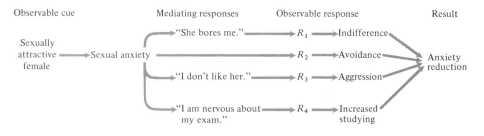

This is one type of activity *not* explained by the concept of drive reduction. (Robert Eckert/EKM-Nepenthe)

erable objection to the principle of drive reduction as a prerequisite for learning. A number of apparent exceptions were noted in which people appeared to seek an increase in drive, such as excitement and activity, with these experiences themselves being reinforcing. In addition, it proved difficult to demonstrate empirically the acquisition of drives other than fear. In general, there was so much dissatisfaction with the drive concept that attention shifted to the analysis of reinforcement. Nevertheless, although the popularity of the Dollard-Miller theory as a whole has waned, many of its concepts have been incorporated into other learning approaches to personality.

Reinforcement Theory

The learning theory of B. F. Skinner dispenses with the mediating, unobservable processes that Hull, Miller, and Dollard posited as occurring inside the organism. The task of psychology, according to Skinner, is to establish lawful relationships between behavior and events in the objective world. Skinner was very precise about what he meant by "lawful" and "objective." Concepts such as tension, feeling, desire, drive, attitude, and intention do not refer to objective, physical events that can be directly observed; they are attributes of a vague entity called the "mind." For Skinner, it was scientifically inappropriate to use nonobjective events as explanations of behavior.

Radical Behaviorism

The *radical behaviorist* position advocated by Skinner had two fundamental components. One asserted that scientific explanation should depend on as few assumptions as possible. Consequently, before assuming the existence of hidden psychological processes, one should first explore the explanatory power of a system based on observables, one that requires no additional assumptions. Skinner noted that when we attribute the "cause" of a behavior to an internal event or tendency, we are doing little more than restating the behavior, instead of explaining it. For example, to say that a child assaults his peers because he is aggressive does not add to our understanding of the assaultive behavior. This statement merely labels or categorizes the behavior.

The second aspect of the radical behaviorist position was more profound in its implications. Skinner's position was that what we commonly refer to as "mind" is either fictional or irrelevant as an explanation of behavior. Skinner contended that human behavior is subject to the same laws as the movement of physical objects and that a sophisticated science, whether of physics or of psychology, should not appeal to mysterious, hidden, inner forces. Skinner (1971, p. 7) wrote:

Although physics soon stopped personifying things in this way, it continued for a long time to speak as if they had wills, impulses, feelings, purposes, and other fragmentary attributes of an indwelling agent. . . . Aristotle argued that a falling body accelerated because it grew more jubilant as it found itself nearer home, and later authorities supposed that a projectile was carried forward by an impetus, sometimes called an "impetuosity." All this was eventually abandoned, and to good effect, but the behavioral sciences still appeal to comparable internal states.

Skinner's response to the question "What is man?" is clear. Humans, for Skinner, are machines. While it is difficult and upsetting for humans to think of themselves as machines, Skinner maintained that such a conception was necessary for both scientific and social progress. Machines do not have feelings and intentions. They have inputs and outputs or, from a psychological perspective, there are environmental events and resulting behaviors. Through a functional analysis of the relationship between specific environmental events and specific reactions, one can explain behavior without referring to mechanisms operating within the organism. Hence, if we observe someone eating, instead of asserting that the person is eating because of hunger, we should link the eating to an antecedent environmental event such as time of food deprivation, the lunch bell's ringing, or the appearance of appetizing food. The objective of functional analysis is to determine which features of the environment are regularly linked to particular behaviors.

Lawfulness and Control

Regularity, the hallmark of a lawful relationship, is the basis for asserting that a particular event is the cause of a particular behavior. Human behavior may often appear chaotic, spontaneous, or free, but according to Skinner, that appearance is only because we have not discovered the events that control the behavior. Skinner deliberately used the word *control* to convey that human behavior is completely determined and predictable, given a knowledge of the stimulus events that are lawfully related to the behavior. A simple example of predictability and control concerns a four-year-old boy who was referred to a clinic because of frequent tantrums. When the child's parents were interviewed, it immediately became evident that the boy threw a tantrum whenever he was frustrated, and that his desperate parents ultimately acceded to his demands, permitting him, for example, to stay up late and watch television. The behavior (tantrum) was reinforced (under the control of) his parents' acquiescence. In a similar manner, the parents' acquiescent behavior was reinforced by the child's stopping the tantrum. When the parents learned to ignore the tantrums, they very rapidly disappeared, or *extinguished*.

Operant Reinforcement

Through the manipulation of reinforcement contingencies—that is, reward, nonreward, or punishment following a response—dramatic changes in behavior may be brought about. Removing reinforcements from previously reinforced responses leads to extinction, while the reinforcement of a response will increase the future likelihood of that response. Responses that operate on the environment so as to change it, while being controlled by these consequences, are called *operants*.

Skinner's principal interest has been in the variables governing operant behavior. The primary factor that he has investigated is scheduling of, or the frequency and patterning of, reinforcement. A reinforcement can be administered after every response, after a specific or variable number of responses, or after a specific or variable time interval. In his first, ground-breaking book, *The Behavior of Organisms,* Skinner (1938) demonstrated lawful, predictable, and quantifiable relationships between different reinforcement schedules and the response rates of the organisms being reinforced. For example, organisms reinforced following every relevant response responded more frequently per unit of time than did organisms given a reward after specified time intervals.

What has all this to do with personality? Skinner and his students have attempted to demonstrate that through appropriate manipulation of reinforcement one can control which responses a human will make and how frequently and vigorously these responses will be made. Personality, then, is viewed simply as the collection of these reinforced operant responses. For Skinner, individual differences in personality are primarily a function of the differences in behaviors that have been reinforced and in the reinforcement schedules governing the emission of those behaviors.

Partial reinforcement.   Although it is frequently argued that the principles of operant reinforcement are less valid because they were derived from studies of rats and pigeons, there is both informal and experimental evidence that humans also respond differentially to different schedules of reinforcement.

The effects of *partial reinforcement* (reward schedules in which the relevant response is reinforced less than 100 percent of the time) certainly apply to humans as well as to infrahumans. Extensive research literature indicates that many partially reinforced responses are even more difficult to extinguish than responses that have had a history of constant reinforcement. Hence, parents who finally decide to ignore, rather than pick up, a child who cries after being put to bed will find that crying will persist much longer if the child was not picked up every time it cried previously. This consequence of partial reinforcement can also account for the seemingly paradoxical behavior of gamblers who keep betting despite heavy losses; they, too, are intermittently reinforced for their behavior.

Partial reinforcement increases the persistence of positive behaviors as well as such problems as crying and gambling. Given certain tasks, a history of successes interspersed with failures leads to greater persistence in the face of subsequent failures than does a history of 100 percent success. This phenomenon has been observed in the laboratory (Nation, Cooney, and Gartrell, 1979), as well as in everyday life. Compare two politicians, for example: one who has met with both success and defeat in running for political office and one who has always been successful. Suppose that they are both then repeatedly defeated at the polls. According to the partial or intermittent reinforcement effect, the politician with a history of unmixed success will probably give up political life sooner than the politician who experienced failure as well as success. In other words, the "trait" of persistence can be developed by providing the learner with tasks that are neither too easy nor too difficult. Intermediate-level tasks allow learners to experience the pain and challenge of frustration, as well as the pleasure and satisfaction of success.

The fact that some partial reinforcement effects generalize to very dissimilar tasks suggests that there are cognitive factors mediating the effects. For example, the subject may be learning an expectancy or a rule, such as, "If I wait long enough, I will eventually succeed." But from a Skinnerian standpoint, the important question is *whether* particular reinforcement schedules lead to predictable effects, not *how* they produce their effects. This is particularly true if the "how" requires reference to private events.

Shaping.   There are many instances in which a desired behavior is never manifested and therefore is not subject to immediate manipulation through reinforcement. For example, pigeons do not automatically peck at disks, just as rats do not walk into a cage and immediately begin pressing levers. Similarly, a timid person may not make the assertive responses that one wishes to encourage, and a child who fears the water is not even going to try engaging in swimming behaviors that can be conveniently reinforced. To facilitate the emission of these responses, the behavior of an organism can be gradually *shaped* through a process of *successive approximations.* For example, a pigeon might be presented food only when it is near a disk. After that behavior is learned, it may receive food only when near the disk with its head raised; later, only when near the disk with its head raised and its beak pointing to the disk. Such successive approximations will continue until, finally, the bird pecks at the disk, at which time a reinforcement is delivered immediately.

Analogous shaping procedures have been applied to human behaviors. In a study designed to increase interpersonal behaviors in severely withdrawn schizophrenics (King, Armitage, and Tilton, 1960), patients were first reinforced with social and material rewards for performing a simple motor response. Subsequently, the task was made more complex, and any verbal response, whether directed toward another person or not, was rewarded. The patients' behavior gradually shifted in the direction of more verbal and social responses. Finally, investigators were able to reinforce the patients when they communicated verbally with other patients. This reinforcement technique proved to be more effective than more traditional therapeutic approaches in fostering social behavior in these patients.

Applications of Reinforcement Theory

Skinnerian psychology is functional and pragmatic. In an important sense, it is less a theory of personality than a system for behavior change and social engineering. It proposes a set of procedures for controlling and shaping behavior and has had a profound impact on a variety of areas, including education, clinical psychology, animal training, and psychopharmacology. Examples of the application of Skinnerian principles to clinical problems have already been cited. Skinnerian methods, sometimes referred to as *behavior modification,* have been used for many different types of behavior difficulties.

Autism. One often finds Skinnerian principles applied to difficult cases that have been unresponsive to other forms of therapy. Work with autistic children, who suffer serious impairment in language and social attachment, is illustrative. Especially distressing to parents is the child's apparent unresponsiveness to and failure to display affection. Other symptoms of autism include stereotyped, ritualized gestures and behaviors (whirling around) and extreme attachment to certain objects. The initial task of determining the environmental stimuli and reinforcements that "control" such behavior has proven very difficult in these cases. A great deal of effort is spent simply determining what is reinforcing for the child, say, a favorite food. After experimenters discover a primary reinforcer, a secondary reinforcer is determined. For example, an experimenter's "yes" or smile might be paired with food so that the experimenter's response can also be used as a reinforcer. Through the use of such techniques, detailed shaping procedures, and many learning trials, it has become possible to train autistic children to acquire some speech and some social skills (Lovaas, 1968). The children are not cured in the sense that they become normal youngsters; however, they do become more manageable and better able to communicate.

Token economies. Procedures based on Skinnerian principles have also been applied in such social settings and organizations as schools, prisons, and hospitals to foster desired behaviors. The *token economy* is one such innovation in organizational rules and procedures, where tokens are used as interim reinforcers that can eventually be exchanged for a preferred reinforcer. The great advantage of tokens is that they allow for great flexibility in reinforcers—from privileges to material objects—thereby permitting individualization of the reinforcement. The first implementation of a token economy, by Ayllon and Azrin (1965), has become a prototype for numerous programs. Schizophrenic patients in a psychiatric ward were reinforced for a designated set of behaviors including grooming themselves, serving meals, and washing dishes. The tokens the patients received when performing the desired responses could be exchanged for such rewards as passes, television privileges, selection of roommates, candy, and cigarettes. As is characteristic of Skinnerian studies, the responses and reinforcers were carefully specified and objectively recorded and quantified through systematic observation procedures. The results demonstrated substantial improvement in patient behavior with the implementation of a token economy. As soon as the reinforcement procedure was discontinued, however, the patients' behaviors deteriorated, returning almost to their initial levels.

The dependence of new behaviors on the maintenance of reinforcement also illustrates one of the limitations of token economies and other behavior modification techniques. The behavior is frequently dependent on being in the same stimulus situation; that is, positive changes do not generalize to new situations (e.g., the home) where the stimulus conditions are different. For these reasons, a group of investigators working with highly aggressive youngsters implemented a behavioral change program directly in the home, the setting in which the most difficulty occurred for these children (Patterson, Cobb, and Ray, 1973). The experimenters attempted to modify the family systems of interaction, altering the patterns of provoking stimuli and the ineffective reinforcements employed by both children and parents.

Programed instruction.   The applicability of Skinnerian principles is by no means restricted to disturbed individuals. In fact, Skinner has described an ideal society based on his principles in which conflicts and discontent would be minimal and individuals would thrive (Skinner, 1948). A less ambitious but still highly important application of Skinnerian principles to normal populations has taken place in educational contexts. The contributions have been of two kinds: (1) the implementation of more effective methods of classroom management, and (2) the development of programed instructional methods. Essentially, *programed instruction* consists of initially presenting material at the individual's level of competence and ensuring that a correct response is given before proceeding to more difficult material. When an error is made, the program guides the person to the appropriate earlier lesson that provided the basis for arriving at a correct response. A major feature of programed instruction is that it can be packaged in texts and booklets to facilitate self-instruction. While there is some debate over the relative effectiveness of programed instruction and how it works, it is a useful addition to available educational methods.

A programed instruction learning device, one of the outgrowths of Skinnerian psychology. (Jean-Claude Lejeune/Stock, Boston)

Limitations of Reinforcement Theory

It is evident that many clinical psychologists find Skinnerian techniques to be useful; research using operant theory and methodology is both vigorous and salient. At the same time, however, there are serious limitations in the Skinnerian model as a comprehensive theory of personality and behavior. One fundamental difficulty is the arbitrary relationship it establishes between the particular response to be reinforced and the particular reward used as a reinforcement. Given a particular reinforcer, such as food, the Skinnerian assumption is that this reinforcer will work equally well or poorly for any individual organism, regardless of the response to be learned. However, as was discussed in Chapter 2, this is not the case. Food is an excellent reinforcer to condition the pecking of a pigeon, but a poor reinforcer when one wants to condition wing movements. Organisms are biologically organized so that there are natural reinforcing consequences for particular behaviors (Breland and Breland, 1961). In a similar manner and more germane to present concerns, reinforcing a child for excellent performance with such external rewards as money or candy may not increase subsequent achievement strivings if his or her goals were intrinsic mastery of the task or a desire for parental affection.

A related theoretical difficulty is the failure to consider factors other than external reinforcers that maintain a preferred response. It may be possible, given patience and a sufficient number of reinforcements, to train a child who is temperamentally introverted to be socially outgoing and extraverted (see also Chapter 2). This child might be superficially indistinguishable from a child who responds quickly to reinforcements for extraverted responses. However, there may be costs to the introverted child that would remain hidden unless explicitly assessed. A child whose behavior was difficult to shift might be less happy and spontaneous and have a lower threshold for frustration as an extravert. Similarly, studies of sex differences (Maccoby and Jacklin, 1974) indicate that boys tend to be more physically aggressive than girls. While one can train girls to be as physically aggressive as boys, such training may have consequences for the girls' personality that extend far beyond the learning of aggressive responses. Because Skinnerians have ignored the structural or organizational aspects of personality, they have given too little attention to the consequences of behavior modification for aspects of personality other than the specific behaviors that are undergoing modification.

In addition, Skinnerians have failed to ask what some psychologists consider to be a central question in personality, namely: Why are particular events or experiences reinforcing? For example, why is one individual attracted to particular kinds of males, why is peer approval a powerful reward for child A but not for child B, and so on?

Nevertheless, whatever one's position on the merits of Skinner's ideas as a theory of personality and human behavior, there is no doubt that Skinner's operant reinforcement theory has made important contributions to psychology. In the area of methodology, it has fostered painstaking observations of situations and behaviors so that one can determine and quantify the precise stimulus events that are linked to specific behaviors. It has also encouraged and provided the methods for systematic evaluation of therapeutic and educational programs, just one small aspect of its many applications. In addition, Skinnerian psychology has had the surprising effect of focusing attention on the detailed study of an individual, rather than on the statistical average of a number of individuals. Skinnerian methods enable one to establish precise relationships over time between changes in individual behavior and changes in reinforcement contingencies and other stimulus events. In the traditional controversy between the clinical and scientific approaches, the clinician has typically emphasized individually based case histories, or what is called *idiographic data.* On the other hand, the scientist has emphasized experimental findings that are normative for an entire population, so-called *nomothetic data.* Skinner has combined aspects of both approaches, studying a single individual with scientific procedures. He has therefore helped to make the systematic study of the individual scientifically respectable.

Social Learning Theory

Although Skinnerians, along with Dollard and Miller, have applied learning principles to complex social behavior, they have been criticized by those learning theorists who are concerned primarily with social behavior. This criticism is based in part on the fact that their analyses are derived from the study of infrahumans. In addition, these critics find fault with Dollard and Miller's emphasis on drives and drive reduction and are especially unsympathetic toward Skinner because of his neglect of cognitive factors in regulating behavior. These shortcomings have been addressed by several related personality approaches which are collectively referred to as *social learning theory.*

Expectancy-Value Theory

The theory proposed by Julian Rotter (1954, 1972) emphasizes the construct of *expectancy*, or an individual's belief in the probability that a specific behavior will lead to satisfactions or valued goals. For example, on the basis of prior experience, a student may have the simultaneous expectancies that diligent study will bring the approval and affection of her parents and the disapproval of her fiancé, who wants to spend more time with her. To predict how hard she will study, one has to know the *reinforcement values* of the goals represented by parental approval and avoidance of her fiancé's disapproval. Each of us has our own hierarchy of values for such common human goals as money, affection, status, entertainment, sex, and power.

The likelihood that a particular behavior will occur, according to Rotter, is a joint function of the person's expectancy that the behavior will lead to one's goals and the values attached to those goals. In other words, people will generally choose actions that, on the basis of previous experience, they expect will lead to valued goals. Hence, children are likely to say "please" in requesting something if previous experience has shown that there is a high probability (expectancy) of getting what they want (highly valued goals) when they do so. Behaviors with low expectancies of satisfaction are not likely to be engaged in unless, under some circumstances, they are associated with high reward. For example, twelve-year-olds are not likely to cry when trying to convince their parents to do something; at this age, they have found that such behavior has low expectancy of bringing satisfaction. But they might cry if crying could result in obtaining some very great satisfaction, such as permission to stay overnight at a friend's house. Characteristics of the specific situation also play a central role in Rotter's theory, inasmuch as expectancy and reinforcement vary according to one's specific environment.

Reinforcement value and expectancy are terms that Rotter uses to refer to specific goals and behaviors. These specific goals commonly cluster into broader categories that are conceptualized as *needs*, such as the needs for recognition and status, dominance, independence, love and affection, physical comfort, and protection-dependency. For any individual these needs will vary in their *need value*, or the value of their satisfaction for that individual. The likelihood, or expectancy, of the behavior one has learned to rely upon to achieve satisfaction of a need is referred to as *freedom of movement*. Low freedom of movement coupled with high need value results in a very frustrated individual who feels ineffective in satisfying an important goal. This particular constellation of factors could result in maladaptive and neurotic behavior, such as engaging in excessive amounts of nonproductive fantasy.

The concepts of need and need value link Rotter's model to psychoanalytic theories, while the expectancy concept provides links with more cognitive motivational theories. Rotter has been critical of psychoanalytic theorists for not recognizing the role of expectancy as a determinant of behavior. No matter how intense a specific desire or instinct postulated by psychoanalysts might be, if an action has zero subjective likelihood of leading to one's goals, then that action will not be undertaken.

Rotter's formulation of the concept of freedom of movement was associated with the development of a scale for measuring generalized expectancy concerning the efficacy of one's efforts. This scale has been intensively used to study the properties of a personality dimension labeled internal versus external control of reinforcement. *Internal control* refers to the individual's belief (expectancy) that he or she can significantly determine whether or not a goal will be reached, while *external control* refers to the belief that fate, or external agents, rather than personal factors, are the most important determinants of goal attainment. The research and applications stimulated by the concept of *locus of control* will be examined in more detail in Chapter 17.

Bandura's Social Learning Theory

Another prominent social learning theory was first proposed by Bandura and Walters (1963) and subsequently developed by Bandura and his students, as well as a number of others (e.g., Mischel, 1968; Wolpe, 1958). It now vies with Skinner's operant reinforcement theory as the principal representative of learning theory approaches to personality. Bandura and Walters placed great emphasis on the consequences of a response—that is, the feedback provided by reward or punishment of a behavior. The Bandura-Walters model also incorporates a number of internal mediating processes, such as attention, covert rehearsal of instructions, self-criticism, and self-reinforcement. A number of different learning mechanisms, especially observational learning, are used to account for the social development of the child. *Observational learning* refers to the acquisition of new behaviors through observation of another person performing them.

Many social responses and personality characteristics are acquired simply by imitating or copying the behavior of the models one observes. The mechanism of imitation as a significant social learning process was discussed by Miller and Dollard in an early book entitled *Social Learning and Imitation* (1941). However, whereas Miller and Dollard gave only secondary attention to observational learning, Bandura and his students have carried out a systematic series of studies investigating the process of imitation or *modeling;* they assigned this process a central role in social learning theory.

Modeling.   When we see a three-year-old boy carrying a briefcase, putting it down, and saying to his mother, "It's been a hard day at the office," we know that the child was not directly taught those behaviors. Rather, he acquired them through observation of his father's behavior, through modeling.

The mechanism of modeling has three properties that give it special significance for the understanding of personality development:

1. Modeling typically involves a social situation (the model and the imitator) and a social relationship. The model can be an actual person or a film or cartoon representation.
2. Modeling is a means by which complex behaviors can be readily acquired. The reinforcement methods proposed by Skinner require careful, time-consuming efforts to shape a complex social behavior. In contrast, imitation can produce very rapid acquisition of social behaviors.
3. Direct reinforcement of imitated behavior is not required for learning to take place.

These properties of modeling have significant consequences for our understanding of behavior change and the process by which children are socialized. According to Bandura (1969, p. 118), "virtually all learning phenomena resulting from direct experiences can occur on a vicarious basis through observation of other persons' behaviors and its consequences to them." Thus, while Skinner would look for reinforcement contingencies in the environment to explain a child's aggressive behavior, Bandura would examine important figures in the child's environment, such as parents, peers, or television heroes, who may serve as aggressive models. In what has become a classic study (Bandura, Ross, and Ross, 1961), nursery school children individually observed an adult engaging in aggressive behavior toward a Bobo doll (a large, inflated plastic clown that uprights itself when knocked down). The adult struck the doll with a mallet and made a number of predetermined aggressive statements such as, "POW! Kick him, sock him down, sock him in the nose!" The child was then mildly frustrated and given an opportunity to play with the Bobo doll while the adults left the room. The degree of modeling displayed by the children was striking, with the children often hitting the doll with exactly the same motions as the model, using precisely the same verbal comments. A comparison of their responses with those of a control group of preschoolers who had merely observed the adult playing with a construction toy revealed much more aggressive behavior in the children who had observed the aggressive model.

A wide variety of behaviors, from self-control and altruistic responses to aggression, can be acquired through modeling. For example, the influence of a model on aiding a "lady in distress" was examined by stationing a woman next to a car with a flat tire. Approximately one-quarter mile closer on the same road, experimenters placed another car with a flat, but this time a young man was helping the female to fix it. The young man thus served as a model. Compared to a control condition without a model, a significantly greater number of drivers stopped to offer assistance to the second woman (Bryan and Test, 1967).

Response acquisition and performance.   Children do not automatically or consistently imitate. Modeling, like other learning processes, is affected by a number of factors. Among the variables that facilitate modeling are similarity in sex between model and observer (Bandura, Ross, and Ross, 1961); the power of the model (Bandura, Ross, and Ross, 1963); and observation of reinforcement of the model's response (Bandura, 1965; Parke and Walters, 1967). In evaluating the effects of these variables, it is essential to distinguish between *acquisition* and *performance* of the response. Different factors determine whether the response is acquired and, if it is acquired, whether it is performed. Learning, or response acquisition, is influenced by attention to the model and by how well one interprets and rehearses the model's behavior (Bandura and Jeffrey, 1973). Performance, however, depends much more on the nature of the reinforcing consequences to the model and the observer.

In a study bearing directly on this acquisition-performance distinction, preschool children observed a filmed model exhibiting aggressive responses. Under one condition, the model was praised and rewarded with treats, while in a second condition the model was severely punished for the aggressive display. A control condition was included in which there were no response consequences to the model. A test of the degree of imitation following the different modeling conditions revealed significantly less modeling by children in the punished-model condition, compared with children observing the model when reward or nothing followed the behavior. To demonstrate that this effect was not due to differences in learning of the response, the children in all three groups were offered highly attractive incentives to reproduce the responses of the model. When positive incentives were introduced, children in all groups performed the response they had observed. Thus, all three groups learned the model's responses equally, but their performance of the response was dependent on the anticipated consequences of that behavior.

Verbalization and rules.   In contrast to Skinner, social learning theorists emphasize the importance of verbalization, rules, and related symbolic processes that are believed to mediate behavior. Rewards and punishments for behaviors are more effective when they are accompanied by explicitly verbalized rules (Liebert and Allen, 1967; Parke, 1970). Research indicates that the acquisition of an operant can be greatly facilitated by informing a subject exactly what kinds of responses are to be positively reinforced (Spielberger and DeNike, 1966). The more we are able to verbalize the stimuli and reinforcing contingencies in our environment, the better we are able to understand and adapt to the environment.

To demonstrate the role of verbalization in observational learning, children witnessed a model engaging in a complex sequence of behaviors. They were asked to verbalize the model's novel responses, watch attentively, or count rapidly. The last condition was included to prevent implicit verbal coding of the model's actions (Bandura, Grusec, and Menlove, 1966). Modeling was highest in the verbalization group, next highest in the attentiveness group, and lowest in the rapid-count condition. Verbal statements that are silently rehearsed also have a significant effect on behavior.

The situation and discriminative cues.   One of the major tenets of social learning theory is that behavior is a function of the situation in which it takes place. Walter Mischel (1968, 1973) has argued cogently and vigorously that the consistency in behavior implied by such concepts as traits or motives is largely illusory. He stated (1968, p. 177) that "response patterns even in highly similar situations often fail to be strongly related. Individuals show far less cross-situational consistency in their behavior than has been assumed." Both Mischel and Bandura reject the "layer" image of personality, the notion that there are basic personality traits underlying the variations observed in overt behavior. If a man is highly aggressive with his peers but docile with his father and other authority figures, social learning theorists would contend that he should not be considered a fundamentally aggressive individual who masks his aggression when dealing with individuals in positions of authority. Rather, they argue, he is more appropriately described as someone who displays different response patterns in different situations. From a social learning standpoint, the similarity of responses in different situations is dependent on similar response consequences, rather than on a generalized drive or trait.

Self-efficacy.   Another point of departure of social learning theory from Skinner's operant theory concerns external versus internal sources of reinforcement. Social learning theorists do not limit reinforcements to external rewards or punishments, but also include self-imposed reinforcing consequences (Bandura, 1977a; Kanfer and Marston, 1963). Human beings have internalized standards of performance which they utilize to evaluate their actions. The self-evaluative statement, "I did well," following a particular test performance is a reinforcement for that performance. One student might make such an evaluation only for a grade of A; another might feel such evaluation was accurate if the grade was C. Conversely, some individuals may be very self-critical, administering self-punishment even though performance might appear excellent to an observer. Depressed adults, for example, tend to evaluate their performances as poorer than the nondepressed do, even for identical accomplishments (Loeb, Beck, Diggory, and Tuthill, 1967).

Feedback from internal and external reinforcements affects one's sense of *self-efficacy*, a concept that has gradually assumed a central role in Bandura's (1977a) thought. Self-efficacy refers to the expectation that one can effectively cope with and master situations, that one can bring about desired outcomes through one's own personal efforts. This clearly relates to Rotter's concept of locus of control, briefly introduced in the previous section. Bandura maintained that the effects of conditioning and modeling therapies are mediated by the change that occurs in one's sense of self-efficacy, or the belief that "I can." In an experiment demonstrating this process, investigators examined the effects of a participant modeling procedure on adults with a severe fear or phobia of snakes. Individuals in the modeling-plus-participation (imitation and snake-handling) condition expressed stronger self-efficacy expectations and subsequently reflected greater mastery over the situation than those in only a modeling group, who had not actively handled a snake. In addition, regardless of experimental condition, the subjects' efficacy expectations were highly correlated with the extent to which they approached the snakes (Bandura, Adams, and Beyer, 1977).

Limitations of Social Learning Theory

Social learning theory, like operant theory, lacks concepts that deal with the organization and structure of personality, concepts that help predict the pattern of interrelationships among the significant components of personality. In general, social learning theory is concerned with the conditions influencing the acquisition and performance of specific responses, rather than with the factors that determine which behaviors or reinforcers are central to the organism. Such questions as the psychological significance of affection, sexuality, the family triangle formed by parents and child, and the developmental shifts in human striving, remain far outside the scope of social learning theories.

Cognitive Behavior Modification

The approaches that have been grouped together under the label of *cognitive behavior modification* stress the role of cognitive factors in mediating behavior and attempt to bring about change through alteration of these cognitions (Mahoney, 1974). There is clearly substantial overlap between cognitive behavior modification and social learning theory, and the two approaches are quite compatible. Their difference lies in emphasis and historical background. Cognitive behavior modification was guided by, yet significantly deviates from, Skinner's operant theory. Although Skinner's radical behavioral position either excludes or minimizes the relevance of internal events, the cognitively oriented behaviorists maintained that one can adhere to the objective spirit of Skinner's approach while investigating the role of such internal processes as images, self-monitoring responses, and perceived responsibility. The processing, storage, and recall of information also enter into the cognitive behavior modification model.

An especially important impetus to this approach has been the development of therapies that clinically modify deviant behaviors by altering the cognitions that mediate these behaviors (Kanfer, 1971; Meichenbaum, 1973; Rimm, 1973). For example, in one therapeutic program, schizophrenics were trained in self-instructional statements that stressed concentration and attention (Meichenbaum and Cameron, 1973). The investigators demonstrated significant improvements in the patients' performance of perceptual and concept tasks, as well as "sick talk" following the training program.

Imagery

During the past decade there has been an upsurge of interest in the role of imagery in both experimental (Paivio, 1971) and clinical (Lazarus, 1971; Wolpe, 1969) psychology. *Imagery*—the pictures that one visualizes—can be used to facilitate memory and to alter feelings and behavior. Wolpe (1958), in his pursuit of behavioral alternatives to psychoanalytic treatment, pioneered in the utilization of imagery for the *systematic desensitization* of anxiety. Wolpe's objective was to train anxious patients to relax while in the presence of anxiety-provoking stimuli. He theorized that the relaxation response inhibits anxiety and therefore will weaken the bond between the anxiety response and threatening stimuli: a process considered to be an example of the more general principle labeled *reciprocal inhibition.*

Wolpe's treatment requires initial training of the client in deep-muscle relaxation and the construction of an *anxiety hierarchy,* consisting of a series of related situations that are graduated according to the degree of evoked anxiety. The patient first imagines the least anxiety-provoking situation in the hierarchy while maintaining a relaxation response, with the procedure then followed successively for each item in the hierarchy until the patient can relax fully while visualizing the situation that had evoked the most anxiety. Wolpe reported substantial clinical success with this treatment and, in the process, stimulated an extensive clinical and experimental literature applying this technique to a variety of problems. While systematic desensitization is much more complex in terms of both effects and mediating processes than merely reciprocal inhibition, the study and use of imagery remains a significant component of the cognitive behavior modification approach.

Other Cognitive Changes

The enormously complex world of images, anticipations, self-perceptions, beliefs, and information offers rich opportunities for changing behavior. We have previously referred to the technique of *self-instruction.* For example, reminding oneself to count to ten before responding in anger is one way in which self-instruction is used to control behavior. Imagery, another cognitive process just discussed in the context of desensitization, can also be used to condition fears and avoidance. For example, one treatment program for obesity required that obese clients visualize appetizing food coupled with a disgust-producing image, a procedure referred to as *aversive imagery* (Cautela, 1977). Aversive imagery has also been used in the treatment of alcoholism (Miller, 1959), smoking (Tongas, 1979), and sexual deviation (Davison, 1968).

The *attribution,* or causal explanation, that individuals make for their success and failure provides another promising area for cognitive intervention. The tendency to attribute failure to one's incompetence, rather than to lack of effort, task difficulty, or luck, is linked to a variety of maladaptive behaviors, ranging from depression (Abramson, Seligman, and Teasdale, 1978; Beck, 1967) to poor school achievement (Dweck, 1975). For example, in one study children with poor frustration tolerance having difficulties in school were trained to ascribe their failures to a lack of effort. Effort, as opposed to ability, is under volitional control and can thus be modified and increased. This perception resulted in a substantial improvement in persistence and performance in the face of failure, compared with children not receiving the attributional retraining (Dweck, 1975; see also Chapter 16).

Still another type of cognitive mediator is the logic and strategy used in problem solving. Cognitive strategies are related not only to intellectual performance, but also to the ability to solve social problems (Shure and Spivack, 1972; Spivack and Levine, 1963). Spivack and Shure (1974) developed a program that trained children to think in terms of means-ends relations, that is, in terms of the probable consequences of various behavioral options. They demonstrated a significant improvement in the behavior of disruptive pre-schoolers who participated in their program.

Although there have been encouraging findings from some cognitive behavior modification programs, others have not been as successful. Saying the right word to oneself does not always produce the desired change; some beliefs are strongly ingrained and resistant to change. Behaviors such as smoking may be so habitual that even changes in beliefs and the recognition that the behavior is harmful may not produce a behavioral change. Much more theory and research are required to determine the conditions under which various cognitive behavior modification procedures will be effective. There is no doubt that there are significant links among cognitions, desires, feelings, and behavior. But the direction of these links—which elements are causes and which are effects—is a difficult issue. Finally, cognitive behavior modification runs the risk of introducing thoughts and responses that are as difficult to define and measure as some of the psychoanalytic concepts that the behavior theorists have so roundly criticized.

Summary

Learning theories of personality are rooted in the experimental laboratory. The objective of these approaches is to apply established principles and concepts of learning and performance to understanding and changing complex human behavior. The learning approaches are committed to the use of rigorous quantitative methods; they tend to be mechanistic in their conception of human behavior; and the learning theorists attribute major importance to the role of reinforcement and observable environmental antecedents of behavior. Although learning theorists in general prefer to discuss observables, the different theories vary markedly in the extent to which they make use of such unobservable constructs as drives, mediating responses, expectancy, and imagery. In recent years, learning theories have tended to expand their use of internal mechanisms, particularly cognitive processes. As the learning theories become more cognitive and incorporate more unobservable constructs, there is some question of whether they will be appreciably different in rigor from more clinical and phenomenological theories.

*Specific
Points*

1. Hullian theory asserted that *habits* are acquired when a stimulus-response pairing is followed by *drive reduction,* for both *primary* and *secondary,* or *acquired, drives.*
2. *Drive, cue* (stimulus), *response,* and *reinforcement* are the key concepts in Dollard and Miller's theory.
3. Through a process of *mediated generalization,* dissimilar situations can come to have an equivalent effect because they elicit common *mediating responses.*
4. According to the Dollard-Miller model, the psychoanalytic mechanism of repression can be explained in terms of such overt responses as mislabel-

ing and avoidance, which are elicited by anxiety-evoking stimuli because they reduce the mediating response of anxiety.

5. For Skinner, the concept of "mind" is illusory. Behavior, according to the radical behaviorist position, is a function of reinforcement. Reinforcement of selected responses determines the kinds of behavior elicited in response to a stimulus, and the schedule of reinforcement determines the rate and persistence of responding.

6. Behaviors that cannot be reinforced because they are rarely manifested can be trained through a gradual process called *shaping,* in which *successive approximations* to the behavior are reinforced until the desired response is made.

7. *Behavior modification* procedures based on Skinnerian principles have been applied in cases of severely disturbed children and adults. Autistic children have been taught to respond to social reinforcers, while schizophrenic patients have shown significant improvement in social behaviors through the application of these principles.

8. One limitation of Skinnerian theory is the assumption that any reinforcer should augment any response. In fact, organisms are biologically and developmentally organized so that certain reinforcers are more appropriate for particular behaviors.

9. Among Rotter's significant contributions are the analyses of the constructs of *expectancy, reinforcement value,* and the *internal* versus *external control* of reinforcement.

10. An important property of *observational learning (modeling)* is that it makes possible the very rapid acquisition of complex social behaviors.

11. A distinction must be made between learning and performance. A child may not display a response that has been acquired through modeling if the model was punished for that behavior, but may display that response given situations in which the fear of punishment is reduced.

12. From a *social learning* standpoint, the similarity of responses in different situations is dependent on similar response consequences, rather than on a generalized drive or trait.

13. The recent development of *cognitive behavior modification* procedures offers a less radical Skinnerian approach to behavioral problems. Cognitive processes such as *imagery, self-instruction,* and *attribution* are utilized in clinical procedures applying Skinnerian and related methods.

Thought Questions

1. A student who received a poor grade on an exam began to avoid studying. Analyze this situation using the key concepts of Dollard and Miller.
2. Would you want to live in a society based on Skinner's principles? What might it be like?
3. Can you think of ways in which you control your own behavior through covert self-instructions?
4. What types of behavioral problems seem most amenable to learning theory treatments? Which ones might be better treated with a psychoanalytic approach?

Phenomenological Theories

7

Many types of personality theories fall within the category of *phenomenology*—the study of subjective experience, or the "meaning" that one gives to events. What these theories have in common is a primary concern with the cognitive, or mental, aspects of behavior and experience. Although most social learning theories have incorporated cognitive variables in their theoretical models, reinforcement mechanisms that influence observable actions remain central to these theories. This is not the case for the phenomenologists. Phenomenological theories are concerned with the "now" of experience, addressing the present situation and its meanings rather than the past and how things came to be the way they are (a central quest for both psychoanalytic and learning theories). Humanistic psychology, one of the more vigorous and influential of the phenomenological approaches, sees the constraints and fears that block full awareness of the "now" of one's experiences as major contributors to neurotic behavior. An important goal of humanistic theories is thus expansion of the individual's consciousness of the present environment and subjective experience.

Theories based on how individuals make sense of the world and themselves are also embraced by phenomenology. The best-known of these theories was formulated by George Kelly, who assumed that individuals go about their everyday activities like scientists, formulating hypotheses about their environments and themselves, gathering information to test these hypotheses, and drawing inferences from the obtained information. Kelly's theory is subsumed within a literature known as *implicit psychology*, which deals with the perceived laws of behavior held by naive observers, or the personality theories of individuals who are untrained psychologists. Other phenomenological approaches to personality, such as Eastern religious philosophies, are not presented here, primarily because they have not yet made sufficient systematic contributions to our understanding of personality and have not generated supporting research evidence.

Humanistic Theory

Prior to the 1960s there were two dominant movements in psychology: psychoanalytic and behaviorist. Sociologists of science suggest that the development of both theoretical perspectives was greatly influenced by cultural factors. Psychoanalytic theory originated in the supposedly repressive society of Vienna around the beginning of the twentieth century, a social milieu that may have accounted in part for the psychoanalytic emphasis on repression, conflict, and neurosis. On the other hand, behaviorism was spawned in turn-of-the-century America. It embraced Darwin's concern with adaptation and function, as well as the belief that behavior is completely modifiable, an assumption consistent with the optimistic psychological climate in America at that time.

Around 1960, a so-called third force in psychology came into existence. This third force, *humanistic psychology*, focused not only on what a person is, but also on what a person has the potential to become. Humanism emerged at a time when people were experiencing alienation and dissatisfaction despite (or perhaps because of) economic and technological success. Many individuals began questioning traditional values, including striving for success and achievement. This emphasis on existential problems naturally gave rise to a more humanistic psychology. Thus, three major theoretical positions in psychology, each having the status of a movement, appear to have arisen directly from the social and cultural themes of their times.

The social precursors to humanistic psychology were in evidence when the Association of Humanistic Psychology was founded in 1962. Four interrelated principles were adopted by the humanists to guide their pursuits:

1. *The experiencing person is of primary interest.* Humanistic psychology begins with the study of individuals in real-life circumstances. Humans are

subjects, rather than mere objects, of study. Psychological research, the humanists contend, cannot be modeled after early physics, in which the objects of study were "out there." The person must be examined and described in terms of personal consciousness, which includes subjective experience and how the individual perceives and values himself or herself. The basic question with which each individual must grapple is "Who am I?" Individuals, as travelers in life, must determine where they are and where they wish to go. As a result, the humanists follow a *holistic* approach, in which experiences are not broken down into component parts like single frames within a film, but the entirety of life is considered.

2. *Human choice, creativity, and self-actualization are the preferred topics of investigation.* Humanists argue that the study of psychologically crippled people has led to a crippled psychology, while the study of lower organisms has yielded an incomplete psychology, devoid of consciousness. The humanists believe that psychologists should study wholesome and healthy individuals, people who are creative and fully functioning. People have a real need to push forward in life and to develop their potentials and capabilities; growth, rather than mere adjustment, is the criterion of health. These self-actualizing tendencies are of particular significance to the humanists.

3. *Meaningfulness must precede objectivity in the selection of research problems.* Psychological research, according to the humanists, has in the past centered on methods rather than on problems. Often research topics have been selected chiefly because objective and convenient methods are available. But research projects should be undertaken because they are significant and pertinent to human issues, even if the methods available are weak. Research cannot be value free, psychologists must study the important issues of people's lives.

4. *Ultimate value is placed on the dignity of the person.* Above all, humans are accepted as unique and noble. Psychologists must understand people, rather than predict or control their behavior. Individuals are believed by the humanists to have a higher nature with a need for meaningful work, responsibility, and the opportunity for creative expression.

Many prominent psychologists, representing different theoretical viewpoints but sharing a common belief in the importance of the individual's need for meaning and self-actualization, have been attracted to the humanistic movement. They include figures as diverse as Gordon Allport, who, as previously indicated, spent time with Jung; Erich Fromm, whose social psychological deviation from classic psychoanalysis was reviewed in Chapter 5; and Carl Rogers and Abraham Maslow, whose theoretical views lie at the center of the humanistic movement.

The Person-Centered Theory of Carl Rogers

Carl Rogers (Fig. 7.1) ranks among the most influential contemporary psychologists. Born in 1902, he continues to write, to practice, and to function as

Figure 7.1   Carl R. Rogers (b. 1902) (at extreme right, facing the camera) conducting a group-therapy session in 1968. (Michael Rougier, *Life* Magazine, © 1968 Time, Inc.)

a spokesman for the "third force" in psychology. His conception of personality emerged from his work in psychotherapy and reflects the influence of an early religious background. Rogers, in contrast to the psychoanalysts, communicated a fundamental faith and trust in human nature. While Freud viewed human nature as rooted in the Old Testament, with human beings struggling with the "original sin" of destructive and lustful impulses, Rogers brought the voice of the New Testament to personality. By providing love and fundamental acceptance, Rogers believed, we can help our fellow human beings recognize and ultimately realize their basic goodness.

Self-Actualization

For Rogers, as for the other humanists, a core tendency of a person is to actualize his or her own potential. The motive of *self-actualization,* a concept we encountered earlier in the discussions of Jung and Adler, implies that there is an internal, biological driving force to develop one's capacities and talents to the fullest (see Box 7.1). The individual's central motivation is to grow and to enhance the basic self. Activities that are self-actualizing are satisfying, while activities that are incompatible with self-actualizing tendencies are frustrating.

From the perspective of scientific inquiry, the actualization tendency is a vague, general concept that is not amenable to measurement or tests. The reality of an actualization tendency is an axiom of humanistic psychology which is not subject to proof or disproof. Whereas other motivations vary in intensity between individuals and fluctuate within an individual as a function

Box 7.1 THE ACTUALIZING TENDENCY

Rogers once described expression of the actualizing tendency with the following illustration:

During a vacation weekend some months ago I was standing on a headland overlooking one of the rugged coves which dot the coastline of northern California. Several large rock outcroppings were at the mouth of the cove, and these received the full force of the great Pacific combers which, beating upon them, broke into mountains of spray before surging into the cliff-lined shore. As I watched the waves breaking over these large rocks in the distance, I noticed with surprise what appeared to be tiny palm trees on the rocks, no more than two or three feet high, taking the pounding of the breakers. Through my binoculars I saw that these were some type of seaweed, with a slender "trunk" topped off with a head of leaves. As one examined a specimen in the interval between the waves it seemed clear that this fragile, erect, top-heavy plant would be utterly crushed and broken by the next breaker. When the wave crunched down upon it, the trunk bent almost flat, the leaves were whipped into a single line by the torrent of water, yet the moment the wave had passed, here was the plant again, erect, tough, resilient. It seemed incredible that it was able to take this incessant pounding hour after hour, day after night, week after week, perhaps, for all I know, year after year, and all the time nourishing itself, extending its domain, reproducing itself; in short, maintaining and enhancing itself in this position which, in our shorthand, we call growth. Here in this palmlike seaweed was the tenacity of life, the forward thrust of life, the ability to push into an incredibly hostile environment and not only hold its own, but to adapt, develop, become itself.

Source: Reprinted from 1963 *Nebraska Symposium on Motivation*, edited by Marshall R. Jones, by permission of University of Nebraska Press. Copyright © by University of Nebraska Press

of physiological or situational changes, this is not the case for actualization. Moreover, the form that actualization takes is unique to each individual, making it impossible to establish criteria for the presence or absence of actualization. Despite these methodological limitations, Rogers and other humanists (Maslow, 1971) found the actualizing tendency to be conceptually essential for the understanding of human striving and development.

Rather than focusing on the source or strength of the actualizing tendency, Rogers found it more useful to consider what might stand in the way of, or inhibit, this basic human motivation. Rogers (1959) was particularly concerned with blockage of the tendency toward *self*-actualization, which is one component of the more general actualizing tendency. Rogers (1959, p. 200) defined the *self* as the "organized . . . [whole] . . . of the 'I' or 'me.'" It consists of one's self-perceptions (e.g., attractiveness, abilities, achievements, relationships with others) and the range of values attached to these perceptions (e.g., good-bad, worthy-unworthy). Thus, one's self-concept is very dependent on one's learning experiences, especially the kind of feedback and acceptance one receives from others. According to Rogers, human beings have a basic need for others' positive regard in the form of warmth, love, and acceptance. This regard and acceptance, however, is usually offered on a conditional basis. Typically, an individual receives love or recognition as a result of some particular action. Consequently, one's perception of oneself as a valuable human being often depends on these actions and on the resulting evaluations of other people. In contrast, the truly healthy personality perceives his or her whole self in a positive manner; specific actions can be regarded as good or bad, but the self is always unconditionally valuable.

To attain this level of adjustment, the individual needs the experience of *unconditional positive regard,* of being valued for oneself regardless of the degree to which specific behaviors are approved or disapproved. The love of a parent for a child often has such an unconditional quality. A mother may disapprove of her four-year-old's hitting a younger sibling or of the child's sloppy table manners, but she will nevertheless communicate her fundamental love and acceptance of the child. According to Rogers, one should criticize the action, not the person.

The warmth and affection displayed by this elderly couple convey the feeling of unconditional positive regard advocated by Rogers. (Bruce Davidson/Magnum Photos, Inc.)

Conditional positive regard, that is, acceptance that is dependent on the positive or negative evaluation of a person's actions, leads to the development of *conditions of worth.* The person experiences "do" or "do not" and "should" or "should not" as necessary in order to feel appreciated and accepted. A condition of worth, in turn, leads to defensive functioning or to the closing off of experiences. The person loses contact with real experiences, reporting what one "should" feel, not what was actually felt. It is quite normal to behave in a way one doesn't feel, in order to avoid the disapproval of friends, parents, and other important figures; for instance, you may act as if you enjoy a particular movie or a rock group that you actually dislike because you fear that your friends would think less of you if you expressed your real feelings. The clinical problem arises when one begins to deceive oneself and dissociate the true feelings. This generates discrepancies between the objective and the subjective worlds, producing anxiety and threat, which in turn block self-actualization.

Client-Centered Therapy

Corresponding to Rogers's theory of personality is a psychotherapeutic approach he developed, known as *client-centered therapy.* A key element in this therapy is the therapist's manifestation of unconditional positive regard for the client. The Rogerian therapist is trusting, accepting, and empathic, conveying to the client an understanding and acceptance of the client's perception of and feelings about the problem. Through the therapist's acceptance and empathy, the client becomes better able to accept real feelings that may previously have been distorted or denied because they conflicted with self-perceptions based on the conditional regard of others.

One of Rogers's most important contributions was his initiation of efforts to evaluate client-centered therapy. While studies of the effectiveness of various forms of therapy are now quite common, prior to Rogers's pioneering studies (Rogers and Dymond, 1954), assessment of psychotherapy depended primarily on unsystematic patient and therapist reports. Rogers's investigations both helped stimulate research in psychotherapy and contributed to personality theory.

The investigations by Rogers's research group of the efficacy of client-centered therapy focused on the self-concept. Rogers and Dymond (1954) were in part concerned with changes during the course of therapy in the discrepancy between the client's self-concept and *ideal self:* the person the client would like to be, who possesses certain positive attributes and does not have certain negative characteristics. One of the instruments most frequently used to access both self-concept and ideal self is the Q-sort (Stephenson, 1953). In the Q-sort, a large number of statements, such as:

- I am satisfied with myself.
- I have a warm emotional relationship with others.
- I have a few values and standards of my own.
- I don't trust my emotions.

are presented to the person. These descriptive statements are written on separate cards, which the test taker then sorts into categories from "least like me" to "most like me," under either "self" (as one is) or "ideal" (as one would like to be) instructions. Typically, there are from nine to eleven categories, each one assigned a number of points—say, from one to eleven. The respondent is required to place a certain number of cards in each category. This procedure permits specific percepts about both the self and the ideal self to be quantified. It is then possible to compare numerically the sorts for the self and the ideal self. The difference between the two sorts is called the *self-ideal discrepancy.* Large discrepancies, a lack of correlation, or a negative correlation reveal feelings of low self-esteem and lack of personal worth, one index of maladjustment. By administering the Q-sort at various times during the course of psychotherapy, the effectiveness of therapy can be examined.

In one frequently cited investigation guided by these ideas, Butler and Haigh (1954), as part of Rogers and Dymond's project, reported that the self-ideal correlation of individuals seeking psychotherapy averaged −.01; that is, their perceptions of the real self were essentially unrelated to the desired, ideal self. This correlation increased to +.58 following therapy, while that of a control group not receiving psychotherapy did not change. The perceived real self changed so that it was closer to the ideal self. This finding provides evidence for the effectiveness of client-centered therapy, gives the Q-sort some validity, and illustrates one of the better research endeavors guided by a concern with the self and acceptance of the notion of a highly general self-concept.

Therapeutic processes. Rogers, along with his collaborators and students, addressed the process of psychotherapy in great detail and attempted to link therapeutic processes, or what is done during therapy, with therapeutic outcomes. Scales were developed that could be used to assess the openness of the therapists' communications with the client and the degree of acceptance of the client by the therapist (Rogers et al., 1967). The question of the therapist's ability to empathize with the client, to experience the world as the client experiences it, has important implications for the selection of therapists as well as for understanding the process and progress of client-centered therapy. As a result, observational scales have also been developed to assess therapists' degree of empathy (Truax et al., 1966).

Rogers extended his basic ideas concerning self-actualization and unconditional positive regard to a variety of settings. The principle that self-acceptance and self-actualization are facilitated by full acceptance from others and impeded by conditional regard holds true, according to Rogers, in small-group situations, in educational programs, and in families. In short, it applies to any interpersonal interaction: openness to experience and acceptance of others foster effective interpersonal relations, as well as personal growth.

In opposition to Freud's belief that some repression is essential for mental health, Rogers argued that defenses help neither adaptation nor successful functioning in life; on the contrary, they interfere with satisfaction. In addition, Rogers was much less pessimistic than Freud regarding the inevitability of conflict between personal growth and society's needs. Society need not be restrictive, but can instead enhance mental health through the development of institutional attitudes of acceptance and trust.

Maslow's Organismic Humanism

Unlike Rogers, whose theory grew out of his mode of therapy, Abraham Maslow (1908–1970), another major contributor to humanistic psychology (Fig. 7.2), has no particular form of therapy associated with him. When Maslow first embarked on a psychological career, he was drawn to behaviorism and carried out studies on primate sexuality and dominance. He gradually left the confines of the behaviorist method and, after the birth of his first child, remarked that "anyone who [observes] a baby could not be a behaviorist." He was influenced by psychoanalysis, but eventually became critical of the psychoanalytic theory of motivation as well. In developing his own model of motivation and behavior, he incorporated the humanistic notion of self-actualization and eventually embraced humanistic philosophy totally.

The Need Hierarchy

Rather than postulating just one source of motivation, Maslow acknowledged a multiplicity of need systems. More specifically, he delineated a hierarchy of five basic classes or categories of needs, which he defined as physiological, safety, love, esteem, and self-actualization. Arkes and Garske (1977) have pointed out that these needs have common characteristics, such as:

Figure 7.2   Abraham Maslow (1908–1970) in 1968, two years before his untimely death. (Ted Polumbaum, *Life* Magazine, © 1968 Time, Inc.)

1. Failure to gratify a need results in a related form of dysfunction or disturbance. For example, just as lack of vitamins can produce malnutrition, lack of love can produce depression.

2. Restoration of gratification remedies the dysfunction.

3. In a free-choice situation, gratification of lower needs will normally take precedence over gratification of higher needs. Maslow (1943, p. 372) stated:

If all the needs are unsatisfied, and the organism is then dominated by physiological needs, all other needs may become simply non-existent or pushed into the background. It is then fair to characterize the whole organism as saying simply that it is hungry, for consciousness is almost completely preempted by hunger. . . . The urge to write poetry, the desire to acquire an automobile, the interest in American history . . . are . . . forgotten or become of secondary importance.

Table 7.1 shows the hierarchy of needs postulated by Maslow, conditions of deficiency and fulfillment, and a common example of such fulfillment. As already suggested, there is a prepotency of needs, with the lower, physiologically based needs having greater strength and the higher, psychologically based needs relatively weaker. Hence, lower needs must be satisfied before higher ones can be fulfilled. Schultz (1976, pp. 221–222) listed a number of other distinctions between the higher- and lower-order needs:

1. *The higher needs appeared later in the evolutionary development of mankind. All living things need food and water, but only humans have a need to self-actualize and to know and understand. Therefore, the higher the need the more distinctly human it is. . . .*

2. *Higher needs are less necessary for sheer survival, hence their gratification can be postponed longer. Failure to satisfy a higher need does not produce as much of an immediate emergency or a crisis reaction as failure to satisfy a lower need. . . .*

3. *While they are less necessary for survival, the higher needs nevertheless contribute to survival and growth. Higher-level need satisfaction produces better health, longer life, and a generally enhanced biological efficiency. For this reason, the higher needs are also called* growth *needs.*

4. *Higher-need satisfaction is productive or beneficial not only biologically but psychologically as well, because it produces deeper happiness, peace of mind, and fullness in one's inner life.*

5. *Higher-need gratification involves more preconditions and greater complexity than lower-need satisfaction. The search for self-actualization, for example, has the precondition that all the other needs have first been satisfied and involves more complicated and sophisticated behavior and goals than, say, the search for food.*

6. *Higher-need gratification requires better external conditions (social, economic, and political) than lower-need gratification. For example, greater freedom of expression and opportunity are required for self-actualization than for safety.*

D values versus B values.   The list above seems to indicate that lower and higher needs are in some respects qualitatively distinct. Maslow characterized the lower needs as *deficit* (D) *values:* attainment of their desired goal results in tension reduction and returns the organism to a state of equilibrium. Freud was concerned exclusively with D values.

Maslow also postulated that there are *being* (B) *values.* B values are associated with growth motivation, increased tension, and expanded horizons.

Table 7.1 Need hierarchy and levels of personality functioning

Need hierarchy	Condition of deficiency	Fulfilment	Illustration
Self-Actualization ←	Alienation Metapathologies Absence of meaning in life Boredom Routine living Limited activities	Healthy curiosity Peak experiences Realization of potentials Work which is pleasurable and embodies values Creative living	Experiencing a profound insight
Esteem ←	Feeling of incompetence Negativism Feeling of inferiority	Confidence Sense of mastery Positive self-regard	Receiving an award for an outstanding performance on some project
Love ←	Self-consciousness Feeling of being unwanted Feeling of worthlessness Emptiness Loneliness	Free expression of emotions Sense of wholeness Sense of warmth Renewed sense of life and strength Sense of growing together	Experiencing total acceptance in a love relationship
Safety ←	Insecurity Yearning Sense of loss Fear Obsession Compulsion	Security Comfort Balance Poise Calm Tranquility	Being secure in a full-time job
Physiological ←	Hunger, thirst Sexual frustration Tension Illness Lack of proper shelter	Relaxation Release from tension Experiences of pleasure from senses Physical well-being Comfort	Feeling satisfied after a good meal

Source: From Personality Theories: Guide to Living by Nicholas S. DiCaprio Copyright © 1974 by W. B. Saunders Company. Reprinted by permission of Holt, Rinehart and Winston

Among the B values identified by Maslow are wholeness, perfection, justice, beauty, uniqueness, creativity, and truth. One experiences tension from the need to create or to produce beauty, but this tension, Maslow asserted, is associated with positive rather than negative affects.

The Actualized Person

Maslow's wide appeal both within and outside the psychological community has been due largely to his description and elaboration of self-actualization. The B values are associated not only with self-actualization, but also with such qualities as spontaneity and peak experiences, the latter being moments of great ecstasy or awe. Maslow believed that the *peak experience* is elicited by the achievement of real excellence or the movement toward perfect values, not by the "high" attained through the use of drugs.

Maslow attempted to demonstrate the properties of self-actualization by studying individuals who he believed best displayed the qualities of the actualized person. Maslow (1971, p. 7) contended:

> *If we want to answer the question of how tall the human species can grow, then obviously it is well to pick out the ones who already are tallest and study them. If we want to know how fast a human being can run, then it is no use to average out the speed of a "good sample" of the population; it is far better to collect Olympic gold medal winners and see how well they can do. If we want to know the possibilities for spiritual growth, or moral development in human beings, then I maintain that we can learn most by studying our most moral, ethical, or saintly people.* [Maslow identified anthropologist Ruth Benedict and the Gestalt psychologist Max Wertheimer as two of these "saintly people."]

There are a number of characteristics associated with such self-actualizing or fully functioning individuals. They include such positive qualities as self-awareness, creativity, spontaneity, openness to experience, self-acceptance, and the more specific qualities of democratic character structure and social interest. Adjectives such as *happy* and *satisfied* are less appropriate in describing the lives of these individuals, Maslow contended, than are words like *challenging, exciting,* and *meaningful.*

One may well question whether these characteristics are a consequence of a psychological process called self-actualization or merely are reflections of the particular value systems held by Rogers and Maslow. One might also wonder whether anyone displays these idealized attributes in a consistent manner. Nonetheless, the descriptions of actualizing behavior provided by Rogers and Maslow have called attention to significant aspects of experience and behavior that other personality theorists have neglected.

Existential Humanism

Existential personality theory is an outgrowth of the existentialist philosophy developed by Sören Kierkegaard (1813–1855) and subsequently expanded by a number of twentieth-century philosophers and writers, including Paul Tillich, Martin Heidegger, Jean Paul Sartre, Albert Camus, and Martin Buber. We can touch only briefly on the major psychological ideas reflected in these philosophical writings and in the work of personality theorists and clinicians who are identified with the existentialist approach. (For a review of existential psychology, see Kobasa and Maddi, 1977.)

Key words for the existentialists are *freedom, choice, anxiety, meaning, authenticity,* and *struggle*. By virtue of our capacity for self-reflection and to perceive our uniqueness and our mortality, we are able to make choices and affect our fate and, thus, must also assume responsibility for the decisions we make. The German term *Dasein* is used to denote this higher, human level of consciousness that captures the whole psychological person. To face the future and contemplate change creates *existential anxiety;* to review the past and one's errors creates *guilt*. While either excessive anxiety or excessive guilt can be crippling, the experiences of anxiety and guilt are conditions of human existence. To change, to grow, and to choose entails *anxiety,* but the willingness or courage to confront anxiety and choose to change is the basis for personal development and the attainment of true maturity, or *authenticity*.

The existential psychologists do not permit us to escape responsibility for our actions, as might the psychoanalysts and the Skinnerians, by attributing the cause for our actions to some past experience or early conditioning. Rather, the cause lies in our present experience. Two Swiss psychiatrists, Ludwig Binswanger (1881–1966) and Medard Boss (b. 1903) pioneered in the development of a form of psychotherapy referred to as existential analysis (Binswanger, 1963), or *Daseinanalysis* (Boss, 1963), which is based on existential ideas. The existential therapists view their primary task as the analysis and clarification of the client's subjective world, of the meanings that the client attributes to events and relationships, and of the alternatives that they believe are available. Existentialists make use of the psychoanalytic method, but they reject psychoanalytic theory, maintaining that theoretical concepts such as the superego, Oedipus complex, and the like bias the therapist's perceptions and diminish openness to the reality of the client. In addition, the existentialists contend that Freud's views *justify* pathology, rather than giving the person responsibility and choice.

It is the person's existence, his or her "being-in-the-world" (Binswanger, 1963) or consciousness that defines what it is to be human. From an existentialist point of view, there is a unity or wholeness between the human being and the environment. The person's experiences of the external world of people and objects and of his or her psychological self and body are the essence of being human. This notion of oneness with the physical world reflects the influence of Eastern religious thought on existential psychology (see also Chapter 15). There are many conditions that diminish this wholeness, such as being treated as a thing or object by social institutions, self-preoccupation interfering with full awareness of people and of nature, and unwillingness to face the anxiety of making difficult choices. These conditions lead to feelings of alienation, loneliness, and despair.

To be authentic, the human being must be willing to recognize his or her unique potentials, desires, and freedom of choice. Authenticity also entails consciousness of the limitations imposed by the environment and one's personal capacities. All things are not possible for all people, but there are individual meanings and choices that can be made even in very limiting circumstances such as in prison or when facing impending death. Victor Frankl (1963) is a well-known existential theorist and therapist whose views were formulated following his experiences in a concentration camp during World War II. His observations led him to conclude that prisoners who were reflective, fully conscious of their experience, and capable of finding personal meaning in even these extreme circumstances were best able physically and psychologically to survive the concentration camp ordeal.

The existentialists' emphasis on personal struggle, courage, and the unavoidability of anxiety and guilt distinguishes their views from those of self-actualization theorists. Rogers's portrayal of personal growth makes the assumption of a biologically programmed self-actualizing tendency that will result in self-fulfillment if the individual receives unconditional positive regard. The existentialists, however, see the individual as a much more active agent for whom struggle and anxiety are necessary precursors of authenticity. These theoretical differences between the existentialist and self-actualization theorists are a matter more of assumptions and worldviews than of issues that can be put to empirical test. In general, the existentialists see the empirical approach of psychology as irrelevant, although one can find occasional examples of research efforts guided by existentialist theory (Kobasa and Maddi, 1977).

Kelly's Personal Construct Theory

Humanistic psychologists are particularly concerned with how individuals feel about and perceive themselves in terms of personal value or worth, and with the consequences of disparate self-concepts. *Personal construct theory* addresses how the perceiver organizes his or her world and interprets, or *construes,* events. Thus, personal construct theory is as much a part of the phenomenological approach in psychology as is humanism. However, in contrast to humanistic psychology, thought rather than feeling is stressed, and affect is considered simply one of the consequences of particular thought processes.

The Human as Scientist

George Kelly (1905–1966), the originator of personal construct theory, contended that the underlying goal of the individual is to predict and control experienced events. Thus, he conceived of individuals as scientists seeking to understand and forecast the events around them.

Kelly noted that it is puzzling that, while psychologists try to explain the behavior of their clients or of people in general, the theories they have formulated cannot account for their own scientific activity. For example, if people are impelled by sexual and aggressive instincts and if all behavior is directed toward the reduction of these primary urges, as the Freudians argue, then what motivated Freud to formulate his theory of personality? Freud did contend that higher intellectual activities, such as scientific pursuits, are derivatives of instinctual drives and are in service of these basic drives. But this analysis is far from convincing. In a similar manner, if humans are mere robots, as behaviorists like Skinner would have us believe, then how did the new ideas formulated by Skinner originate? In sum, the psychoanalytic and strict behaviorist theory that dominated psychology for so many years cannot readily account for the scientific behavior of Freud and Skinner.

As intimated above, Kelly's theory of personal constructs can explain scientific endeavors, for Kelly considered the average person to be an intuitive scientist with the goal of predicting and understanding behavior. To accomplish this aim, naive individuals formulate hypotheses about the world and themselves, collect data that confirm or disconfirm these hypotheses, and then alter their theories to account for the new data. Hence, the average person operates in much the same manner as a professional scientist, although professional scientists may be more accurate and self-conscious in their attempts to achieve cognitive clarity and understanding. Just as scientists sometimes hold bad theories, individuals may entertain bad theories, that is, beliefs that hinder effective behavior and lead to bias in data collection and interpretation. For example, assume that a woman (Nancy) believes that a man (John) has strong negative feelings toward her. When Nancy meets John at a party, she expects that he will ignore her, make an insulting remark, or embarrass her in front of her friends. However, assume that, to Nancy's surprise, John acts friendly and seems happy to see her. Assume, too, that this disconfirmation is repeatedly experienced so that John's displayed friendliness cannot be due to some temporary mood state or to the immediate social pressures of acting "nice." On the basis of these new data, Nancy should reformulate her hypothesis and perceive that John really likes her. The new construction more accurately predicts behavior and allows Nancy to correctly anticipate her interactions with John.

In discussing his conception of the person as a seeker of truth, Kelly (1955, p. 5) asserted:

It is customary to say that the scientist's ultimate aim is to predict and to control. *This is a summary statement that psychologists frequently like to quote in characterizing their own aspirations. Yet, curiously enough, psychologists rarely credit the human subjects in their experiments with having similar aspirations. It is as though the psychologist were saying to himself, "I, being a* psychologist, *and therefore a* scientist, *am performing this experiment in order to improve the prediction and control of certain human phenomena; but my subject, being merely a human organism, is obviously propelled by inexorable drives welling up within him, or else he is in gluttonous pursuit of sustenance and shelter.*

Many other psychologists besides Kelly implicitly accept the conception of the individual as an intuitive scientist. Of great concern to experimental psychologists is the possibility that the subject will infer what the experimenter is trying to prove and then will consciously or unconsciously comply with this hypothesis (Orne, 1962). The *demand characteristics* of an experiment therefore must be carefully controlled or concealed in many psychological investigations. But the very existence of such controls intimates that subjects search for meaning in their environment, formulate hypotheses, and act on the basis of these belief systems. Of course, if a subject were to perceive the experimenter as a nasty or intrusive person, then he or she might try to "ruin" the experiment by disproving the experimenter's hypothesis. This behavior is also in service of the subject's goal and is based on a particular belief system, as well as on inferences about the purpose of the investigation.

Bannister and Fransella (1971, p. 16), commenting on the human-as-scientist formulation, noted:

One of the effects of this is to make the model man of personal construct theory look recognizably like you: that is, unless you are the very modest kind of man who can see himself as the stimulus-jerked puppet of learning theory [or] the primitive infant of psychoanalytic theory. . . . If you do not recognize yourself at any point in personal construct theory, you have discovered a major defect in it and are entitled to be suspicious of its claims.

One of the interesting similarities between humanistic theory and personal construct theory is a consequence of the human-as-scientist model. Both the psychologist and the client or an experimental subject are now equal parts of a dyad. That is, the psychologist is no "higher" than the so-called naive person. Hence, psychology is now a metadiscipline, seeking to make sense out of the way that individuals make sense out of the world. The psychologist therefore is engaged in the same interpretive endeavor as nonpsychologists.

Note, then, that Kelly proposes a rational image of humans: to understand thoughts is to understand the person. Bruner (1956) speculated that this theory of personality was in part a product of the particular clinical experiences that Kelly encountered. For many years Kelly was a counselor of college students. Rather than facing patients with hysterical paralysis or bizarre dreams, "the young men and women of Professor Kelly's clinical examples are worried about their dates, their studies, and even their conformity" (Bruner, 1956, p. 357). Hence, Kelly spent relatively little time considering the unconscious, deep-seated urges, or even defenses. As with other conceptions presented in this book, he therefore was able to account well for some aspects of behavior, but could not readily explain other phenomena.

Constructive Alternativism

Kelly labeled his basic philosophical assumption *constructive alternativism.* Meaning, Kelly asserted, is not inherent in an event, but depends on how a person construes or interprets that event. Thus, there is no "reality"; reality truly exists in the eyes of the beholder. As a result, some of Kelly's ideas are, perhaps surprisingly, associated with the psychoanalytic notion that needs and values influence our perception of the world.

Because meaning is subject to change, Kelly reasoned that individuals are personally responsible (able to respond) for their own future. Nature does not dictate one's life or, as Kelly contended, "No one needs to be the victim of his biography." This position again links personal construct theory with humanistic and existentialist thinking by placing change processes within the grasp and the capability of the individual. Credit for a successful life and blame for an unsuccessful life are thus placed directly on the actor.

Formal Theory

Kelly outlined a formal theory with one fundamental postulate and eleven corollaries. Here we examine only the postulate and three of the corollaries, selecting those that shed the most light on Kelly's conception of behavior.

Fundamental postulate.   Kelly stated that an individual's life or conduct is guided by how the world is construed. Furthermore, the predictive power of that construal is demonstrated or proved by how much sense one has made out of the world, or the accuracy with which one is able to predict future events. Confirmation or disconfirmation of predictions was accorded much greater significance in Kelly's thinking than, for example, drives and drive reduction or reward and punishment.

Individual corollary.   Kelly asserted that people differ from one another in their construction of events. For example, one person might judge others according to their sincerity or wit, while another might use intelligence or kindness as bases for perceiving others. Furthermore, there are individual differences in the complexity of one's construal system, which can be illustrated by considering the perceived properties of light. Humans judge light on the basis of three distinct dimensions: brightness, saturation, and hue. Lower organisms, on the other hand, may have only one dimension or construct available (brightness) to distinguish various light stimuli. Thus, humans have greater cognitive differentiation in their perception of light than some lower organisms. Similarly, some individuals perceive more discriminations, or use more dimensions in their construals, than others.

Inasmuch as individuals perceive the identical objective situation in a different manner, it follows that behavior will also differ between individuals. Furthermore, since no two constructions are exactly alike, each person is unique. This position is in keeping with the humanist position.

Range corollary.   A given construction is not appropriate for all events. For example, the construct "tall-short" may be appropriate for anticipating play on a basketball court but is likely to be quite irrelevant in predicting an individual's honesty. Kelly distinguished between the range of convenience and the focus of convenience of a construct. The *range of convenience* indicates the breadth of different phenomena to which a construct may be applied; the *focus of convenience* refers to the area in which the construct is maximally useful.

Scientists frequently employ the range and focus notions when describing and evaluating psychological theories. Freudians, for example, would argue that the range of convenience of their theory includes war, wit, and slips of the tongue; such generalizability is a positive attribute of any theory. But the Freudian model's focus of convenience concerns sexual and aggressive conflicts. A similar description of the range and convenience of all the theories presented in previous chapters could be made and would prove instructive for comparison and evaluation.

Experience corollary.   A person's construct system is subject to change as a result of successful or unsuccessful construal of events. Given Kelly's perspective, psychotherapy is a process in which one's construct system is altered with the aid of a therapist. The therapist must first discover how the client is perceiving the world and then assist the client in reorganizing the old system and finding new, more functional constructs. The therapist might help the client to design and implement "experiments" to test particular hypotheses. For example, if an individual perceives a parent or a spouse as aggressive or dominating, then special behaviors might be suggested to test whether this perception helps rather than hinders the anticipation of events. Role playing and modeling are frequently used to help alter construct systems. The therapist might suggest, for example, that the client act as if the parent or the spouse were not aggressive or dominant, in order to test an alternative hypothesis. (At an earlier time in his life Kelly was a drama coach, which may account in part for his selection of role playing as a technique for altering construct systems.)

In one social experiment involving the change of constructs, the participants were teachers who believed that the children in their classrooms were not learning because they were "lazy" (Kelly, 1958). The experimenters suggested that the teachers give the children nothing to do in the classroom and see what happened. Of course, the pupils would not sit still without any activity. On the basis of this contradictory evidence, the teachers began to consider the school environment and their own inadequacy as causes of poor learning, rather than blaming the problems entirely on the children.

The Role Construct Repertory (REP) Test

Kelly devised an ingenious testing instrument to ascertain an individual's personal construct system. The test reflects Kelly's belief that the tester should not impose his or her constructs on the test taker; rather, the testee should be allowed to display constructs that are naturally used to give meaning to the world.

In the REP test, the test taker first lists the names of individuals who play or have played certain roles in his or her life, such as mother, father, rejecting person, threatening person, and so on (see Fig. 7.3). On the standard REP grid, shown in Fig. 7.3, the three circles in each row designate three roles that each subject is to consider as a group. For each triad, the subject determines the construct, such as cold-warm or dominant-submissive, in which two

Figure 7.3   Simplified grid form of the REP test.

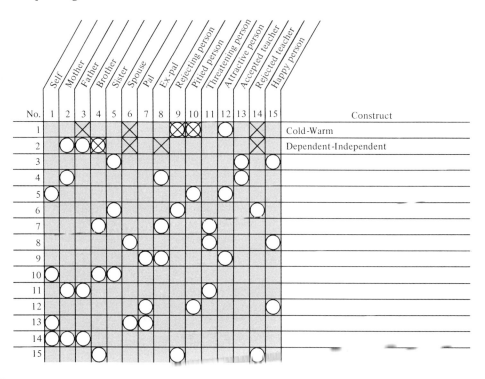

members of that triad are similar yet different from the third. The construct selected by the test taker is assumed to represent a dimension of thought or a construct along which significant people in the respondent's life are ordered or compared. In row 1 of the grid, for example, a respondent might perceive individuals identified as rejecting and pitied to be cold, while attractive people are warm. The respondent then judges the remaining twelve people as having or not having the quality (coldness) of the two linked individuals in the triad, placing an X in the box of that row if that particular characteristic is possessed. Figure 7.3 shows that father, spouse, and rejected teacher are perceived as cold. The remaining fourteen rows are completed in this manner, with a different construct selected for each triad. Using mathematical techniques, the tester reduces the chosen constructs to a few basic ones representing the respondent's typical way of perceiving and classifying others.

Emotions

Critics have often charged Kelly with ignoring affective states, or "the human passions." This is somewhat incorrect. Kelly focused brief attention on certain specific emotions, namely, anxiety, hostility, guilt, threat, fear, and aggression, but he defined them all as consequences of construct systems that are in transitional states.

Anxiety, according to Kelly, occurs when one's construct system provides no means for dealing with an experience. Bannister and Fransella (1971, p. 35) elaborated on anxiety as follows:

We become anxious when we can only partially construe the events which we encounter and too many of their implications are obscure. Sex for the chaste, adulthood for the adolescent, books for the illiterate, power for the humble and death for nearly all of us tend to provoke anxiety. It is the unknown *aspect of things that go bump in the night that give them their potency.*

In a similar manner, interacting with a person whom we cannot understand often gives rise to vague feelings of uneasiness. And even greater anxiety is experienced when starting a new job or confronting a new environment. If anxiety reactions are frequent and severe, then the range of constructs must be broadened so that more phenomena can be incorporated. Disconfirmation of a belief also arouses anxiety because it reveals an inadequacy in the construct system. Anxiety, therefore, is not necessarily bad, for it is one precondition for construct change.

Kelly distinguishes between *threat* and anxiety, even though both result from defective, and therefore transitional, construct systems. Threat is experienced when a fundamental change is about to occur in one's construct system, when major beliefs about the nature of one's personal and social world are invalidated. For example, questioning the purpose of life is threatening for it is likely to lead to basic conceptual change. Similarly, a deeply involving extramarital affair may alter one's conception of what it is to be a parent or a spouse, thus engendering a threat. Psychotherapists must be aware of the possibility that they may also be viewed as threatening inasmuch as they are perceived as agents of construct change.

Finally, in Kelly's system *guilt* results from a discrepancy between one's ideal self and one's actions. Thus, one suffers guilt when doing things that are discrepant with the kind of person you thought you were or would like to be.

Overview of Kelly's Theory

Kelly has contended that humans are intuitive scientists, construing the world in idiosyncratic ways to give it meaning. Meaning is the interpretation of events with particular constructs, enabling one to predict, or anticipate, the future. One's construct system is not immutable; individuals have alternative construction possibilities and are personally responsible for their own well-being. Finally, certain emotions, such as anxiety, threat, and guilt, are products of inadequate and changing construct systems.

Kelly's conception is unique among the theories of personality and provides an alternative language for understanding or construing human action. It has not generated a great deal of research, but it has given rise to new and valuable insights, as well as to a novel method of measurement, and is gaining in popularity.

Implicit Psychology

Psychologists are becoming increasingly interested in a distinction between *science* and *ethnoscience:* the reasons people behave the way they do versus *perceived* reasons they behave the way they do, or what is known positively as "folk wisdom" and negatively as "grandma psychology" (see Wegner and Vallacher, 1977). It is evident that individuals have ideas and often elaborate theories about what people are like and what motivates them. Although these theories are "implicit" (Bruner and Tagiuri, 1954), they nevertheless determine social reality.

Implicit theories concerning the interrelationships of traits or attributes have already received much attention from psychological researchers (see Schneider, 1973). Beliefs like "Fat people are jolly," "People who wear glasses are introverts," and "Intelligent people are witty" are examples of such implicit theories of personality. People are often unaware that they hold such theories and thus do not put them systematically to test. Nevertheless, such notions greatly influence expectations and actions.

Kelly's REP test represents one attempt to measure implicit theories of person perception by ascertaining the constructs people employ as well as the perceived interrelationships among these constructs. Indeed, Kelly's entire theory rests on the presumption that people are naive scientists, formulating their own idiosyncratic psychological theories. Kelly further contended that at times these theories do not work and that the individual must be aided in the construction of better theories.

In addition to implicit theories of person perception, there are implicit theories of child psychology, abnormal psychology, psychodynamics, and virtually any other area within the broad domain of personality psychology. For example, we exhibit our implicit ideas about children in the ways in which we communicate with them. As Wegner and Vallacher (1977, p. 303) state:

The hostess at a dinner party is not likely to say "Hot, hot!" when she places a steaming dish before a guest, but often makes similar remarks to her five-year-old. She does not say "Look both ways, now" when she sends the guests across the street to their cars, but often will repeat this warning to her child. . . . Many of these wholesome and insipid expressions would be totally inappropriate in adult conversation. [see Gleason, 1973]

In a similar manner, implicit theories of abnormal psychology abound. Since the layperson has been introduced to Freudian theory, often through "pop psychology" sources, early childhood experiences are typically perceived as an important cause of abnormal adult behavior. For example, schizophrenia or autism is attributed to "bad" child-rearing practices, sibling rivalry, Oedipal wishes, and so forth. The naive psychology of the layperson and the "true" laws of personality, child psychology, and abnormal psychology may or may not be identical. For example, most laypersons are unaware that certain types of schizophrenia have a strong genetic component and that schizophrenia, particularly among this group, may be little related to such early experiences as parent-child interactions (see Chapter 2).

An investigation by Whiteman (1967) illustrates some of the differences between the science of defense mechanisms and defenses as perceived (or not perceived) by younger children. Whiteman presented children with a number of scenarios, such as that for displacement (Whiteman, 1967, pp. 145–146):

There was once a little girl named Jane. One day her mother promised that Jane's favorite dessert, ice cream, would be served at supper. But Jane's mother forgot to buy the ice cream, and so there wasn't any ice cream for dessert. Jane didn't say anything to her mother about the ice cream. After supper Jane went to play with her dolls and did something she never did before. She spanked her dolls. Why did she spank her dolls?

While the displacement mechanism might be obvious to adults and older children, Whiteman reported that a large percentage of the younger children (ages five to six) did not relate the psychological reaction (spanking the dolls) to the given psychological cause (ice cream deprivation). Rather, in the displacement scenario, the younger children attributed the spanking to, for example, the naughtiness of the doll. In sum, the science of defense mechanisms outlined by Freud and subsequent ego psychologists contrasts with the laws of behavior *perceived* by younger children.

Summary

In this chapter a variety of phenomenological theories have been introduced, including humanism, existential humanism, and personal construct theory. Humanistic theory stresses the subjective experience of the actor. Humanists like Rogers and Maslow presume that individuals strive to maximize their inborn potentials. Existentialist theory shares many of the characteristics of humanism, but concentrates on personal struggles and responsibility.

Personal construct theory, which is considered one of a number of implicit psychologies, is related to humanistic theory because both approaches are concerned with perceptions of self and others, assume that individuals are personally responsible for their fate, and place the subject (client) and the experimenter (therapist) on equal levels.

The humanistic, existentialist, and personal construct theories have generated few testable hypotheses and relatively little experimental research. But they have nonetheless contributed to the study of personality in many ways. First, they have called attention to problems ignored in the more traditional approaches; second, they have suggested novel theoretical concepts and have generated a new scientific vocabulary; and third, they have given the subjects of study greater dignity and prestige.

Specific Points

1. *Humanistic psychology* is governed by the tenets that the experiencing person is of primary interest, that creativity and self-actualization are the preferred topics of investigation, that meaningful research topics should

be selected, and that the dignity of the person is an essential aspect of research inquiry.

2. *Self-actualization* denotes the internal driving force to develop one's capacities and talents to the fullest. It is central in the theory of Carl Rogers.

3. *Unconditional positive regard,* or being valued for oneself, facilitates self-actualization. On the other hand, *conditions of worth* where acceptance is dependent on particular actions decrease the possibility of self-actualization.

4. The *self-ideal discrepancy* refers to the differences between how one perceives oneself and how one would like to be. There is some evidence that this discrepancy decreases following *client-centered therapy.*

5. Maslow postulated a need hierarchy with physiological needs at the bottom and self-actualization needs at the highest level. Lower needs must be gratified prior to the full pursuit of higher-order needs. Higher needs appear later in evolutionary development and, although aiding adjustment and satisfaction, are not necessary for survival.

6. There is a distinction between *deficit* (D) and *being* (B) *values,* the former associated with tension reduction and the latter, with increased tension and expanded horizons.

7. Existentialists contend that we must assume responsibility for our actions and that we cannot escape anxiety and guilt.

8. *Personal construct theory* as formulated by George Kelly addresses the issue of how an actor construes (perceives, organizes) his or her world. It is based on the assumption that individuals act as scientists, formulating hypotheses and gathering data relevant to those hypotheses.

9. Individuals differ in their construction of events and these constructions are not fixed. The REP test was devised to assess construct systems.

10. The emotions of *anxiety* and *threat* have been interpreted by Kelly with the aid of personal construct theory. Anxiety indicates that one's construct system does not allow one to deal with an experience, while threat is experienced when the construct system is about to undergo fundamental change.

11. *Implicit psychology* refers to the theories of behavior held by untrained psychologists or laypersons.

Thought Questions

1. Who among your acquaintances is the most self-actualized? On what evidence do you base this judgment?

2. What do you think of the humanistic belief that people are fundamentally good? How do the humanists account for evil?

3. Many psychologists believe that the humanistic approach to personality can never attain the status of a science. Do you agree with this belief and, if so, is it a "fatal" flaw?

4. Do you believe that our significant behaviors are primarily (1) conscious and rational, (2) mechanistic, or (3) conscious and irrational?

PART III
Personality Development

Part III is concerned with the genesis or antecedents of personality and with changes in personality that occur during the course of life. There is a vast gap in behavior and personality between the newborn and the adult. Children must be socialized through the process of childrearing and other influences so that they function effectively in a particular social and cultural setting. As children grow older, they are confronted with new requirements and new problems that must somehow be mastered. And personality development does not end in childhood or adolescence; the adult years also present unique demands and opportunities for personality growth and change.

The chapters in Part III examine the major changes in personality that take place over the developmental life span and the various processes involved in bringing about these changes. Developmental issues are examined from the perspectives of (1) behavior changes that characterize most individuals in an age group and (2) individual differences in personality development.

Part III begins with a review of basic issues and processes in personality development. Chapter 8 addresses such issues as developmental stages and critical periods and examines some fundamental developmental processes, among them attachment and separation, the mechanisms of identification, and sex typing. In Chapter 9, the socialization of the child is considered through such topics as moral development, the antecedents of other prosocial behaviors such as generosity and caring, and the influence of child-rearing practices on socialization. Chapter 10 begins with a discussion of the self, a construct that provides an important link between early and subsequent periods of personality development. Later periods in the life span are then considered, specifically adolescence, adulthood, and old age. Personality is seen as undergoing constant change and development, with particular experiences associated with particular ages. A principal objective of all three chapters is to convey the relevance of a developmental perspective for the understanding of personality. We will have frequent occasion to refer back to developmental matters in subsequent chapters of the text.

Personality Development: Issues and Processes

8

The study of adult personality inevitably leads back to the study of personality development. One reason for this is the assumption, made by most personality theorists, that the roots of adult personality are laid in childhood. A second, related reason is that a number of issues and processes that are central to the understanding of adult personality are encountered in the study of personality development. One such issue, the nature/nurture question reviewed in Chapter 2, becomes immediately salient as one explores behavior among infants, young children, and adults. Another recurring issue throughout the life span is whether there are critical periods of development and developmental stages, characterized by relatively marked transitions from one level of development to another, as contrasted with a process of gradual, continuous change.

These issues will be considered in this chapter along with several processes basic to personality development and later personality functioning. Particular attention is paid to the process of attachment, a key construct in personality development with implications for phenomena that will be discussed later in the text. Identification and imitation, important processes in the socialization and development of a wide range of personality attributes, are also considered. The chapter concludes with a review of sex role identity and the role of sex differences in personality development.

Issues in Personality Development

Nature or Nurture?

Examining personality from a developmental perspective highlights certain issues in the emergence and development of personality. One familiar and significant issue is the question of nature versus nurture. Forces of nature are involved in the child's progression from a state of helpless infancy to that of an autonomous individual with language, logic, familial attachments, and social involvements. But, as many of the points raised in Chapter 3 suggest, nature does not operate in a vacuum. Children in different cultures learn to speak very different languages and, if deprived of social contact, will develop only the most primitive of communication skills. Children raised outside a social milieu are not likely to develop ambition, conscience, and social concern. The tracing of interactions between biology and environment, between the given and the experiential, and the determination of each influence's role are the primary scientific tasks of developmental psychologists.

The nature/nurture question is illustrated by the often striking individual differences among children. Some babies are highly active, others are calm and placid, and still others are sensitive and easily distressed (Chess, Thomas, and Birch, 1965). What parents with a "different" child have not wondered what mistakes they made in bringing up the child? Other parents, whose children are quite unlike, wonder if they played any role at all in influencing the personality of each child. Developmental studies bear directly on the question of the causes or antecedents of individual differences and on the analogous question of group differences, such as those between males and females. We will be examining these issues in depth later in this chapter.

The observation of marked differences in temperament among children at infancy strongly suggests the influence of biological factors on personality. The calmness of some infants is reminiscent of the phlegmatic temperament described by the Roman physician Galen (see Chapter 1), while the irritability of other infants is suggestive of a choleric temperament. However, there are many features of infants' differences in temperament that do not correspond neatly to the ancient classification of temperaments. There are some babies—about one out of every ten (Thomas, Chess, and Birch, 1968)—who, for want of a better term, have been categorized as "difficult." These infants are characterized by extensive crying, unpredictable fluctuations in emotional state, intense reactions when aroused, and resistance to consolation and soothing. They are more likely than other infants to develop a subsequent behavior disturbance.

Although infants with difficult temperaments have a higher probability of manifesting later behavior problems, it would be misleading to conclude that these children display behavioral problems solely because "they were born that way." The data show only a weak relationship between early infant disturbances and subsequent psychopathology (Sameroff and Chandler, 1975). Whether such infants will later develop behavior problems very much depends on the parents' response to an infant's behavior, on cultural resources and values, and on the particular experiences of the child with peers, in school, and in other contexts. This is not to say merely that a good environment will modify the effects of poor endowment or a birth injury; rather, there is a constant interaction over time between the child and its environment. The characteristics of a child may influence its environment; a difficult infant will evoke a range of responses from its caretakers different from those evoked by an infant with a more placid temperament. The responses from others will in turn modify the child; one mother's patient, warm, and consistent pattern of responding may, after time, foster positive changes in the child's emotional response, which in turn may reinforce the mother's behavior. Another mother's ambivalent response of oscillating beween oversolicitousness and avoidance may exacerbate the infant's difficult behaviors, which in turn may intensify the mother's ambivalence.

There are many other factors that influence the transactions between a child and its environment. A child with a biological handicap may develop a compensatory skill (cf. Adler, Chapter 5). Among a group of infants with difficult temperaments, one difficult child who initially had a very negative interaction with her father subsequently developed a strong interest in the piano. Her excellent skills as a pianist helped change her father's attitude from anger and rejection to pride and acceptance (cited in Sameroff, 1979).

This formulation of the nature/nurture issue in terms of a continuous series of reciprocal interactions between the child and its environment is referred to as the *transactional model* (Sameroff, 1975). The essential elements of the transactional model are shown in Fig. 8.1, which illustrates the continuing interaction between constitution and environment over time.

Figure 8.1   Transactional model. (Adapted from Sameroff, 1975, p. 282.)

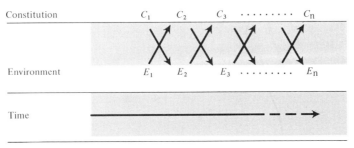

Continuity or Stages?

A related developmental issue of importance to personality is whether the changes in behavior observed during childhood reflect a gradual, continuous process or are marked by discrete stages that introduce new patterns of behavior. For example, most children at the age of seven display a strong sense of conscience, internalized standards of conduct, and guilt feelings. In contrast, three-year-olds display only the barest rudiments of conscience, with few signs of guilt. Psychologists who perceive development as continuous, that is, as developing gradually, account for this change in terms of the specific learning experiences to which a child has been exposed. Conversely, those who consider development as discontinuous, discrete developmental stages favor an interpretation based on changes in the child's psychological structure. The role of learning is not ignored, but the emphasis is on interactions of learning and biological maturation that produce new capacities and relationships that are *qualitatively* different from those that existed before. These emergent stages make possible very different types of behavior than those the child could exhibit before entering the new stage of development.

The personality theories reviewed in Chapters 4 through 7 hold disparate positions on the continuity/discontinuity controversy. Perhaps the two most opposing views are represented by the psychoanalytic and the learning theory schools. Psychoanalytic theory, which views the libido as progressing through a series of transformations in the oral, anal, phallic, and genital stages, reflects the discontinuity position. Learning theories, on the other hand, portray development as a continuous process of change, determined by the particular behaviors that are reinforced or learned by the child. From a learning theory standpoint, personality development is not inherently "progressive"; rather, the direction that development takes is a function of the child's socialization experiences.

Piaget's theory.   In general, the phenomenological or cognitive theories of personality, reviewed in Chapter 7, have not addressed developmental questions beyond proposing a generally forward-moving impetus, such as the drive toward self-actualization. However, cognitive personality theories are certainly compatible with the stage conception of development, as exemplified in the developmental theory (1928, 1929) of Jean Piaget (1896–1980). Piaget, probably the most influential contemporary developmental theorist, was concerned primarily with issues of cognitive development, rather than with personality development. Nevertheless, his ideas have great relevance for personality theory. Piaget described a number of progressive stages in the development of a child's thought processes, extending from simple reflex actions to complex logical thought. Each of these stages involves new abilities and a different way of thinking about events. According to Piaget, from about birth to two years of age the child is at the *sensorimotor* stage of intellectual development. During this stage the child reacts to objects primarily in terms of their physical characteristics and in terms of motor feedback, rather than in terms of objects' symbolic or conceptual properties. Thus, a child will react to a pillow reflexively or as a soft, comforting object rather than as a symbol of a set of objects instrumental to sleep or rest. During the *preoperational* period (from about ages two to seven), the child recognizes the instrumental use of a pillow—as a "sleepy-time" object, along with bed and blanket—and can also use the pillow in a more flexible, symbolic manner, acting toward it as if it were a doll or a friend. However, the child in this stage is still strongly influenced by the perceptual properties of objects. Thus, water poured from an average glass tumbler into a tall, narrow cylinder will be seen as being greater in amount when in the cylinder simply because the cylinder is taller than the tumbler. It is only when the child passes into the next stages of thinking (*concrete operations* at about age seven and *formal operations,* or mature conceptual thought, at about age eleven) that he or she recognizes that the amount of water remains constant, or invariant, regardless of the shape and other perceptual features of the container. The child proceeds through these stages in an orderly, invariant sequence, functioning at an earlier stage before advancing to a more mature level. Although the later stages are built upon the earlier ones, the stages themselves are seen as discontinuous and discrete.

According to Piaget, the child's stage of cognitive development regulates and defines the influence of environmental experiences. Thus, for example, one cannot develop a strong sense of morality and conscience in a three-year-old because the relevant concepts, such as intention, are not comprehended at that age. One can reinforce specific cooperative responses in a preschool child, but one cannot teach the child to behave according to the principles of cooperation and reciprocity. The child, according to Piaget, exercises an enormous influence on how environmental information is perceived and processed. That is, children are active organizers and interpreters of their experience, rather than passive objects controlled by the external reinforcers stressed by learning theory or by the internal drives posited by psychoanalytic theory. How they organize and interpret their experience depends, in large part, on biological and maturational principles.

Critical periods. The concept of *critical periods* suggests another way of looking at the continuity-discontinuity issue or the question of stages. Experiences occurring during critical periods are believed to have greater impact than those occurring at other times during development. Psychoanalysts, for example, believe that the first five years of a child's life are critical for personality development. The basic features of one's personality are believed to be formed during this early period, with later experiences having only a secondary impact. A less extreme view held by most psychologists asserts that, while early childhood experiences are especially influential, significant changes in personality can occur throughout life.

A second implication of conceptualizing critical periods as a significant factor in development is the view that certain skills and competencies can be acquired during these periods. If they are not, then the child may suffer a permanent deficit or one that is extremely difficult to remedy. These deficits may be emotional and social as well as cognitive. For example, according to

Erikson (cf. Chapter 5), a child who does not experience affection and nurturance during the oral-sensory stage will develop a basic mistrust of others and will have difficulty in responding to love and affection in later years. For some behaviors and competencies, the critical period may cover a wide age range. Thus, it has been proposed that language must be acquired by early adolescence. If not, which may be the case if a child is raised in isolation, then language can never be taught to that child (Lennenberg, 1967). Exploration of this issue is one reason that feral children (children raised by packs of animals like wolves) are of such great psychological interest. Unfortunately, these children are typically brain damaged as well, limiting the clear testing of the critical period–language acquisition hypothesis. Although the conception of critical periods seems reasonable and is in keeping with a good deal of animal and human data, many questions remain regarding the specification of critical periods and the kinds of behaviors and skills to which the critical period notion is relevant. For example, the idea that early stimulation of the child is especially critical for later cognitive development has been contested in a study of a Guatemalan village where infants were subjected to severe stimulus deprivation, including substantial periods spent in relative darkness, with little social contact. Despite this early deprivation and early behavioral indications of severe retardation by Western standards, there was little or no evidence of perceptual and cognitive impairment in ten- and eleven-year-olds (Kagan and Klein, 1973). However, since these findings should be substantiated by a follow-up study of the same children when they are older, the results are inconclusive and thus subject to alternative interpretations. Whether there are critical stages for cognitive, social, and emotional development remains a matter of lively debate.

Personality continuity.   The term *continuity* has another meaning besides that of gradual change. It also refers to the constancy, or stability, of behavior over time. Are traits displayed by children during the early years predictive of similar behaviors during later periods of development? Is a fearful and timid child likely to develop into an anxious adult? Similarly, are aggressive children likely to become aggressive adolescents and adults? Are other traits such as intelligence and dependency relatively enduring over the life span?

The answers to these questions, like those for most psychological questions, depend on a number of factors, including the age at which a trait is first assessed or observed, the sex of the child, the age period over which the prediction is being made, and the measures used to assess the trait at different ages. It should be noted that observed continuity or stability of a trait could be a function of any number of factors, such as genetic variables, potent early experiences that leave permanent effects, or a family environment that is constant with respect to behaviors reinforced over the span of a child's development.

The sheer numbers of factors that can influence the stability of a behavior pattern over time make it difficult to interpret the relationship between the childhood manifestation of a trait and later displays of that trait. It is known that certain traits, such as intelligence and aggression, are stable over time; that is, a child who is aggressive at age five also tends to be aggressive at age ten and age sixteen (see also Chapters 13 and 18). This finding of continuity in aggression is particularly true for boys. Similarly, children having high IQs at the age of five tend to score high on IQ tests during the rest of their lives, as well. This continuity can be accounted for by genetic factors. Psychoanalytic theory also argues that the early formation of personality accounts for similar manifestations of personality in later life. According to Freud, basic personality is formed in the first five or six years of life. Subsequent experiences are of secondary importance compared to the overwhelming influence of those early experiences. One might also assume a less extreme position, acknowledging the importance of experiences later in life, while maintaining that early influences are much more powerful than later ones.

A contrasting position, and one held by many social learning theorists, asserts that behavior is continuously shaped by the reinforcements in our environment and by the models to whom we are exposed. From this perspective, personality is largely environmentally determined (see Chapter 6) and therefore subject to major changes throughout life. Hence, whereas psychoanalytically or genetically oriented theorists expect stability in personality over time, social learning theorists anticipate situational influences. But even if personality stability in social behavior is uncovered, social learning theorists still may contend that, in these instances, there has been constancy in environmental reinforcers and external stimuli. There are some family environmental factors that influence aggression, for example, and it may be that the continuity of these family influences is responsible for the continuity observed in this personality disposition. Thus, the stability observed in aggressive behavior over long periods could be due to consistency of the deprivation and frustration experienced by the child or to the family's consistent reinforcement of aggressive responses.

The research strategy most often used to address the question of stability is the *longitudinal study*. Measures of personality are taken in the child's early years and again at subsequent periods of development. A number of longitudinal studies have extended through adolescence and well into adulthood (Block, 1971; Kagan and Moss, 1962; Macfarlane, Allen, and Honzik, 1954). The data yielded by these investigations have not proved conclusive, partly because some personality traits are more stable over time than others, partly because stability decreases as the time period between testings is extended, and partly because of the limitations of the measures used to assess personality. It is difficult to find measures of introversion or achievement that are comparable for young children and adults. Nevertheless, recent investigations using sophisticated analyses have yielded substantial correlations between personality measures obtained at different times (Baumrind, 1972; Block, 1971; Olweus, 1979). For example, in the investigation by Baumrind, children's social behaviors were assessed both at nursery school age and again in the third or fourth grade. The degree of measured competence, social responsibility, and prosocial behaviors manifested by the children at both times were similar.

A major longitudinal project at the Institute of Human Development of the University of California, Berkeley, has been able to provide data for a number of investigators interested in the continuity issue. One of these studies (Block, 1971) compared personality ratings obtained at three different times: when the subjects were in junior high school, in senior high school, and thirty to forty years old. The data provided impressive evidence of consistency. About 60 percent of the personality items on which the subjects were assessed in junior high school were substantially correlated with the senior high school ratings, and about 30 percent of the senior high school ratings were comparable to the ratings obtained during adulthood. For males, substantial consistencies emerged on ratings of such items as, "Is a genuinely dependable and responsible person," "Tends toward undercontrol of needs and impulses, unable to delay gratification," and "Enjoys aesthetic impressions, is aesthetically reactive." Examples of items on which stable ratings were obtained for females include "Basically submissive," "Emphasizes being with others, gregarious," and "Rebellious and nonconforming."

The consistency of personality over time indicates both stability and change. There is a link between childhood and adulthood, but the connection is far from being a solid chain. Our personality structure in childhood predisposes us toward particular choices in our activities, friends, and the way we solve social problems. But these predispositions often can be modified and overridden by new experiences, opportunities, and rewards. As George Kelly contended, we need not be slaves to our biology or our past.

In sum, the question—Is there continuity and stability in personality from childhood to adulthood?—needs to be rephrased. A more productive question is: What are the factors that make for stability or discontinuity? Some attitudes and behaviors are likely to be more stable than others. For example, child behaviors that are closely related to physiology, such as activity level and emotionality or what is commonly called temperament, are one personality characteristic that is likely to remain relatively stable over time (Chess, Thomas, and Birch, 1965). The scientist's task is to be able to predict which kinds of behaviors for which kinds of individuals under which kinds of circumstances will show stability.

Processes of Personality Development

Attachment

We turn now from an examination of the continuity of personality to a key process in the infant's early socialization and personality development: the formation of attachments to others. We will find evidence of continuity here as well; the kinds of attachments established in infancy are reflected at subsequent developmental periods.

Among the special characteristics of infancy are the infant's helplessness and prolonged dependency on its parents and other caretakers for food, protection, satisfaction of needs, and relief of discomforts. Prolonged dependency is one of the hallmarks of human as opposed to infrahuman development. There is evidence that the greater the cognitive ability of a species, the longer the period of dependency. A human infant could not survive for very long without the support and care provided by others. To facilitate survival in the first few months of life, an infant is equipped with a set of reflexive biological responses, such as crying, sucking in response to lip stimulation, head movements, thrashing about, babbling, and smiling. These behaviors directly modify the environment and function as signals to caretakers, informing them of distress and satisfaction. A caretaker must, of course, be able to interpret the signals correctly and to be appropriately motivated. Indeed, what sound is more compelling to parents than their baby's crying?

There are two broad implications of the infant's situation and behavior that warrant special notice. First, the human infant is thrust into a social situation from the moment of birth; social interaction is the normal state of affairs. Second, although dependent, the infant is not a passive creature totally subject to the whims of the environment. Through its cries and smiles the baby can significantly influence the behavior of its caretakers. While the

Infants' reactions of smiling and crying communicate states and needs to those who care for them, and elicit attention and care. (above—Copyright © Ken Robert Buck, 1981; right—Copyright © Harvey Stein, 1981)

mother's control of reinforcement contingencies is much greater than that of the infant, the baby's responses can also be said to shape the mother's behavior (Cairns, 1977; Gewirtz and Boyd, 1977). While the mother has control over such reinforcements as food, attention, and relief of irritation, the infant can reinforce the mother and other caretakers through its responsiveness, the skills it acquires, and a pleasant versus an unhappy disposition. The amount of attention or even affection that parents give their infant will be influenced by the infant's reinforcing and aversive reactions. There is much evidence that the child-rearing practices of parents are to a great extent *determined by* the behavior of the child (Bell, 1968), as well as the more often discussed opposite sequence of child-rearing practices *determining* the behavior of the child.

During the first few months of development, the infant attends to the presence of people, observing them and perhaps smiling or becoming excited in their presence. But the infant does not yet discriminate between its mother or father or other people. There is no innate *attachment* by the infant to the mother, although this early period of social responding may be considered the first phase in the development of attachment to significant people in the infant's world (Bowlby, 1958, 1969). The formation of selective attachments to caregivers, or *bonding,* is usually manifested after three months of age. This bonding is considered to be of paramount importance for the infant's social development and, in the views of many personality theorists, is a prime determinant of the child's basic personality structure.

Characteristics of attachment.   How do we know when a child is attached to someone, and exactly what does it mean to say that a child has an attachment? These questions have been the subject of considerable theoretical debate and investigation, and there are no simple answers. The most comprehensive and influential analysis of attachment has been provided by British psychiatrist John Bowlby. The essence of attachment, according to Bowlby, is the maintenance of proximity to the caregiver, usually the mother. This proximity can be in terms of physical contact (e.g., touching the mother) or psychological contact (e.g., seeing the mother and knowing that she is close by). In addition, to maintain proximity, the baby performs a set of attachment behaviors, including babbling, smiling, looking at the caretaker, and following or clinging to him or her.

One main characteristic of attachment to a person, then, is an effort to approach or maintain proximity to that person. A second characteristic is distress and protest when the infant is separated from the individual to whom it is attached. The same person is able to soothe the child when it is upset. Finally, when the caretaker is present, the infant is able to explore novel surroundings without displaying anxiety. It is as if the special caretaker provides the infant with a base of security that enables it to leave the safe and familiar and to explore new, potentially threatening environments.

The child's early attachments, although formed in infancy, are evident in later periods of development as well. How these attachments are manifested will depend on the age, the particular culture, and the idiosyncratic avenues of expression of the child. Consider, for example, the following expression of a young boy's attachment to his father (Lewis, 1961, p. 65):

Although I haven't been able to show it, I not only love my father, I idolize him. . . . My father was always very dry with us; he didn't talk much. . . . Only twice in my life did my father speak intimately to me. He asked me, "Son, what troubles you? What is the matter? Tell me your trouble." I felt the most important and happy person in the world to hear him call me "son" so affectionately.

The universality of attachment.   Attachment behaviors are characteristic not only of infants in every culture, but also of many infrahuman species, especially mammalians. The comparability between the attachment behaviors of primates and those of human infants has stimulated extensive primate investigations of the variables involved in the formation of attachments and the consequences of separation (Simonds, 1977; Suomi, 1977). The following description (Jensen and Tolman, 1962, pp. 132–33) of separation in rhesus monkeys conveys the flavor of attachment in an infrahuman primate species:

Separation of mother and infant monkeys is an extremely stressful event for both mother and infant as well as for the attendants and for all other monkeys within sight or earshot of the experience. The mother becomes ferocious towards attendants and extremely protective of her infant. The infant's screams can be heard over almost the entire building. The mother struggles and attacks the separators. The baby clings tightly to the mother and to any object which it can grasp to avoid being held or removed by the attendant. With the baby gone, the mother paces the cage almost constantly, charges the cage occasionally, bites at it, and makes continual attempts to escape. She also lets out occasional mooing-like sounds. The infant emits high pitched screams intermittently and almost continuously for the period of separation.

Similar behaviors have been observed in lambs and puppies (Cairns, 1977). The evidence of attachment behavior in infrahumans suggests that there are important biological factors influencing the human infant's attachment response. From an ethological standpoint, the mother might be considered the stimulus that releases the innate smiling response from the infant while the smile, in turn, releases biologically programmed approach and loving responses. Thus, there is a complex chaining of events. In a similar manner, the baby's cry releases approach and comforting responses from the mother. The attachment responses thus increase the likelihood of the newborn's receiving protection and sustenance, thereby increasing its chances of survival.

The foregoing discussion is not meant to imply, however, that learning does not affect attachment. Bowlby (1969) noted that the child has to *learn* to discriminate mother from other adults and stressed the importance of the quality and pattern of the child's interaction with the mother in determining the nature of the attachment bond between them. If the mother, for example, is depressed or for some other reason unresponsive to the infant's smile, then the attachment relationship will take an atypical course. Some theorists believe that the biological explanation and the notion of an affective bond is superfluous and have attempted to account for attachment behavior on the basis of Skinner's principles of mutual reinforcement and operant conditioning (Gewirtz and Boyd, 1977). However, as we examine variations in attachment, it will become clear that although operant conditioning principles are pertinent, they cannot readily account for many attachment phenomena.

Feeding and attachment. The question of why and how the child becomes attached to the mother, and the mother to the child, has not been fully resolved. Early explanations by learning theorists (Miller and Dollard, 1941) emphasized the primary reinforcement provided by nursing and bottle feeding. This reinforcement then generalizes to the caretaker, so that the mere presence or voice of the caretaker could serve to reduce the child's tensions and elicit positive reactions. However, there is much more taking place in the interaction between child and caregiver than feeding. The infant is typically held and soothed and its attention and motor responses are directed toward the caregiver, usually the mother. Thus, the child receives a great deal of stimulation from the mother, in addition to being fed.

The well-known cloth-versus-wire-mother experiments carried out by Harry Harlow of the University of Wisconsin provide compelling evidence that feeding is not central to the development of attachment. Harlow (1958, 1971) separated infant monkeys from their mothers immediately after birth. The infants were then fed through a bottle connected to a dummy that functioned as a substitute, or surrogate, mother. These "mother" dummies were constructed of either wire mesh or wire mesh covered with terrycloth (see Fig. 8.2). If reduction of the infant's hunger drive is the primary basis for attachment, then the infant monkeys should have become attached to the mother

Figure 8.2 The clinging response of Harlow's monkeys to a cloth "mother" and of a human infant to an adult. (left—Harry F. Harlow, University of Wisconsin Primate Laboratory; right—Joan Menschenfreund/Taurus Photos)

 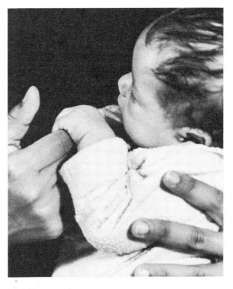

surrogates associated with the giving of milk. But this was not the case. The animals fed by the wire mothers went to them only when they were hungry. But both wire-fed and terrycloth-fed infants preferred the terrycloth mothers and spent most of the day with them. When upset, both groups also were more readily comforted by the terrycloth mothers. Other research has indicated that the critical variable influencing monkey attachment is an opportunity to cling. Monkeys and chimpanzees have a strong tendency to cling, especially when upset, and the terrycloth surrogates were much better than the wire mother substitutes for this response. But, as will be documented later, even the monkeys fed by the cloth mothers manifested severe social problems, demonstrating that a real monkey mother is best.

Imprinting.   In some species, early observation of an object is sufficient to establish an attachment, which occurs through a process called *imprinting.* Imprinting was dramatically demonstrated by noted ethologist and Nobel Prize winner Konrad Lorenz (b. 1903). Lorenz (1935) removed some eggs from the nest of a graylag goose and hatched them in an incubator. The first object that the incubator goslings saw upon hatching was Dr. Lorenz. They then followed him around, ran to him when frightened (even when their mother was near), and maintained this behavior for some time (see Fig. 8.3).

Figure 8.3   Nobel Prize–winning ethologist Konrad Lorenz, with his imprinted goslings, at his research center in Seewiesen, Germany. (Hermann Kacher)

Lorenz and subsequent investigators have found that there is a critical period during which imprinting takes place. For the duckling, the critical period for imprinting on first exposure to an object is between four and fifty-two hours after birth. Before this time, there is insufficient ability to attend to the external world and engage in appropriate responses while, after this time, great fear is elicited by the sight of any novel stimulus. Critical periods do vary with different species and can be somewhat modified by experimental intervention (Moltz and Stettner, 1961).

Not all species manifest critical periods for imprinting like those observed in geese and ducks. While it may seem reasonable to assume that some form of imprinting takes place in the human infant (Bowlby, 1969), there is by no means agreement on this point. Human infants develop attachments to more than one caregiver, exhibiting clear evidence of attachment to the father as well as to the mother (Lamb, 1977). Attachments in humans also seem to develop during many different age periods and are influenced by the feelings and behavior of the other person (Rutter, 1979). At the same time, once attachments are formed, they have considerable strength and persistence. Indeed, whether early attachment can be so completely extinguished that it no longer affects later behaviors is a matter of theoretical debate.

Variations in attachment.   Although individuals in all cultures display attachment behaviors, cultural and individual differences in attachment have been observed. Mary Ainsworth (1967) made detailed observations of mother-child interactions among a group of East African Ganda living in the bush. These children were carried about by their mothers, slept near them, and in general experienced a great deal of physical contact and sensorimotor stimulation. Attachment to the mother appeared earlier and was more intense than for American infants. In addition, the motor development of the Ganda infants was accelerated; the children crawled almost two months earlier than the average American infant. Further, the development of attachment and motor responses in a comparison group of Ganda infants living in the city and raised by Western methods was delayed in comparison to the bush-reared infants and was similar to that for American babies.

Researchers who have placed mothers and children in controlled laboratory situations have found that these investigations yield useful information about the process of attachment and about individual differences in the style and quality of attachment. Ainsworth and her colleagues (Ainsworth, Bell, and Stayton, 1971) employed the following standard series of laboratory episodes in their studies. A mother and an infant enter an unfamiliar room; the infant plays with the mother present; a stranger enters and the stranger and mother are both present for a while; the mother leaves and the infant is left with the stranger; the mother returns and the stranger leaves; the infant is left alone; the stranger returns; and finally, the mother also returns.

Observation of one-year-old infants' behavior during this sequence of events led Ainsworth to classify the babies into three groups: *securely attached, insecurely attached,* and *avoidant* (Ainsworth et al., 1971). Infant crying on separation from the mother is *not* a critical factor in distinguishing the three groups. Rather, the significant factors are the ease with which the infant recovers from the distress of separation upon reunion with the mother; how comforting contact with the mother is; and the degree to which the mother serves as a secure base for the infant's explorations. The infants in these three groups seemed not only quantitatively, but also *qualitatively,* different in their attachment to their mothers (Sroufe and Waters, 1977a). Avoidant infants differ from others in that they are the only babies to avoid proximity with the mother in the reunion situation. But this does not mean that avoidant infants are indifferent to their mothers. Recordings of infants' heart rates in laboratory situations indicate relatively long-lasting heart rate acceleration in avoidant infants when the mother returns, suggesting emotional arousal rather than indifference (Sroufe and Waters, 1977b). In comparison, the heart rates of most attached infants recover to a normal level more rapidly.

Several studies have shown that the classification of infants into securely attached, insecurely attached, and avoidant categories is predictive of their subsequent behavior. In one study of the stability of attachment behavior, fifty infants were classified at both twelve and eighteen months on the basis of their responses in the laboratory (Waters, 1978). Forty-eight of the fifty infants were assigned to the same groups during both of these time periods. A followup on these infants at age two revealed that the securely attached group was more enthusiastic, persistent, cooperative, and effective than the insecurely attached children (Matas, Arend, and Sroufe, 1978).

Researchers have found, too, that the quality of attachment is related to the behavior of the caregiver. Mothers of securely attached children were observed to respond more readily to their infants' crying than mothers of insecure and avoidant children (Ainsworth et al., 1978). Furthermore, securely attached infants do not cry as much as the others. This finding is difficult for learning theorists to explain (Gewirtz and Boyd, 1977), inasmuch as greater responsiveness to crying should reinforce and increase the frequency and duration of crying. Thus, as previously indicated, learning theory cannot account for all aspects of attachment behavior.

The quality of attachment also appears to affect the child's cognitive development. The securely attached child, for instance, tends to be more developmentally advanced (Ainsworth and Bell, 1974) and shows earlier signs of object permanence (Bell, 1970). (*Object permanence* is a Piagetian concept referring to the child's ability to sense that objects have a permanence independent of the child's desires, regardless of whether the child is looking directly at or touching the object. Peekaboo games may delight children because children are surprised at a certain age by the idea of enduring and stable objects that exist even when not in their field of vision.) Clinical evidence also suggests that the security of early attachment has a fundamental influence on subsequent manifestations of security and insecurity. But whether these particular early patterns of attachment are linked to social interaction in later periods of life, reflecting what Erikson called the development of basic trust and mistrust (see Chapter 5), remains to be established in future research.

It is also the task of future research to clarify the theoretical properties of attachment and help resolve theoretical controversies over its usefulness. Some investigators maintain that there is little value in postulating an underlying bond called "attachment" that mediates behavior. Rather, what is significant, they suggest, is the behavioral interaction that takes place between infant and caretaker in a concrete situation and the principles that govern this interaction (Cairns, 1972; Gewirtz, 1972; Weinraub, Brooks, and Lewis, 1977). They point to the weak correlations among different indicators of attachment as evidence that discrete behaviors, rather than a single, underlying dimension, are involved in attachment behavior. Others, amplifying and extending Bowlby's theory, emphasize the affective nature of the attachment bond (Ainsworth et al., 1978; Sroufe and Waters, 1977a). They point to the evidence for stability of attachment-related behaviors and to the indications of goal-directed activity; that is, striving to be near the object of attachment when the organism's security is threatened. It is further proposed that it is useful to think of attachment as a flexible organization of behaviors, mediated by the affective attachment bond (Sroufe and Waters, 1977). How children display and maintain attachments will vary with the individual characteristics of the child, with situational factors, and with developmental level. Consequently, one must distinguish between the underlying attachment bond and the overt attachment behaviors and expect variations in the indicators of attachment. From the perspective of those who see attachment as a key organizing dimension of behavior, attachment bonds not only protect the child and maintain its security, but also form an integral part of subsequent love relationships. "When people are attached to another, they want to be with their loved one. They may be content for a while to be apart in the pursuit of other interests and activities, but the attachment is not worthy of the name if they do not want to spend a substantial amount of time with their attachment figures—that is to say, in proximity and interaction with them" (Ainsworth et al., 1978, p. 14).

Separation

Issues of attachment and issues of *separation* are intimately linked, being essentially two sides of the same coin. For example, the procedure of briefly separating an infant from its mother has been a key experimental method in the study of attachment. Research on separation has been concerned largely with the effects of separation from the mother on the personality development of the child. Separation is ordinarily a disruptive experience, but a distinction must be made between the short-term and long-term effects of separation. The young camper may feel forlorn the first few days away from home, but these feelings can and do change as the child becomes involved in camp activities. On the other hand, if separation is more permanent, as it is, for example, for the child who is sent to an institution for displaced children, then the effects of separation may well be more profound. In addition to the length and permanence of separation, the age of the child at the time of separation and the nature of the child's new environment are important determinants of subsequent reactions.

Isolation.   A number of the influences we have mentioned have been examined in studies of infrahumans. Again, the laboratory investigations of Harlow and his co-workers have provided intriguing data (Harlow, 1971). In addition to the cloth and wire surrogate mother groups, Harlow raised a group of infant monkeys in total isolation, some for as long as two years. The isolation experience seriously damaged the social development of the monkeys, and the longer the isolation, the more severe and resistant to change were the symptoms. These symptoms included a failure to relate to other monkeys or to play and groom, diminished curiosity, and a great deal of time spent in isolated, repetitive activities like those observed in autistic children. Cloth mother–raised infants, in spite of their attachments, also displayed difficulty in later social development. They had problems mating and, after having mated, were unable to care for their own offspring. As previously indicated, cloth-mother surrogates are better than wire-mother substitutes, but they are still poor stand-ins for real mothers!

Harlow did find a substantial improvement in the maternal behavior of cloth mother–raised female monkeys with their second and subsequent offspring (Harlow and Suomi, 1971). In addition, one critical variable determining the effects of isolation from the real mother was degree of social stimulation. If monkeys were provided with the opportunity to play with peers, their later socialization appeared quite normal. Observations also indicated that, to be effective, social stimulation from peers must be provided within the first six months of life. Peer isolation during this critical period appears to lead to irreversible damage.

Early institutionalization.   Many of the behaviors displayed by affection-deprived monkeys also seem to be observed in human infants. However, we do not have the scientific controls at the human level to permit precise statements about critical periods, the effects of separation from the mother, and the consequences of isolation. We must depend on "natural" experiments for data that can provide approximate answers to these complex questions.

A number of natural experiments do occur. The effects of stress can be examined in children raised during wartime. Other children are raised in single-parent versus extended-family households including grandparents and other relatives. And, although they are unusual, there are reports of children raised by infrahumans. Although these settings cannot provide definitive answers because a number of crucial variables have not been controlled, they often provide insights and tentative conclusions.

One of these natural experimental situations involves early institutionalization of children. The pioneering work of Spitz, introduced in Chapter 5, indicated that institutionalization of the infant can have serious negative consequences on development. Other investigations have supported Spitz's observations (Goldfarb, 1945; Provence and Lipton, 1962). In one pertinent investigation, no differences were found between institutionalized and noninstitutionalized infants prior to three or four months of age. But following this period of time, the institutionalized babies began to display marked developmental disturbances. They hardly verbalized, were emotionally and physically unresponsive, and seemed to have lost interest in their environment. Other studies of children reared in institutions indicate more clinging behavior in these children and greater attention seeking and disobedience in school by the age of eight (Tizard, 1977; Tizard and Hodges, 1978; Tizard and Rees, 1975).

Are the negative effects of institutionalization permanent? The experts are not in agreement on this issue. It can be said, however, that young children are quite resilient and show a remarkable capacity to "bounce back" from debilitating environmental experiences. Studies of children adopted later in childhood indicate that environmental improvement in middle or late childhood, well after the presumably "formative" years, can lead to markedly positive changes in social behavior (Kadushin, 1970; Rathbun, McLaughlin, Bennett, and Garland, 1965). It has also been noted that some children appear to be "invulnerable," overcoming great genetic and environmental barriers to lead productive and normal lives (Garmezy, 1978). That is, some children, despite having seriously emotionally disturbed parents and repeated changes in their living situations, still appear reasonably well adjusted and able to function effectively. However, there are also indications that many children may not remain unscathed by their early experiences and that some negative effects, such as school difficulties and emotional problems, may persist (Tizard and Hodges, 1978).

Alternative environments.   The effects of isolation, institutionalization, and early separation from the mother cannot be determined without taking into account the new environment in which the child is placed. Whether one examines immediate behaviors or later development, positive, stimulating, and warm environments can mitigate the deleterious effects of maternal separation. Laboratory studies of separation anxiety and fear of strangers in infants indicate that there are behaviors of strangers that can significantly reduce the level of infant fear (Eckerman and Rheingold, 1974; Ross and Goldman, 1977). Table 8.1 reveals that an active stranger—one who talks to, gestures at, smiles at, and interacts with the child—has a strikingly positive effect on the infant's attachment behaviors. With an active stranger, children spent almost two-thirds less time near their mothers than with a passive stranger, and about four times longer near the stranger. The children also did much less fussing or crying and much more playing when the stranger was active. Thus, the effects of separation can be sharply influenced by situational factors.

Environments also make a difference when there are more prolonged periods of separation. Descriptions of children raised in well-run Russian nurseries (Brackbill, 1962) and in group-care centers in the People's Republic of China (Kessen, 1975) indicate that these children are as well adjusted and socially responsive as children raised at home. The most systematic research concerning the effects of alternative environments, however, involves the Israeli kibbutz. The kibbutz is a collective farm settlement where members

Table 8.1   The influence of strangers' behavior on infants' responses*

Response	Active	Passive
Time near mother	244	639
Latency to leave mother	110	186
Latency to approach stranger	204	592
Time near stranger	580	148
Time in close proximity to stranger	257	65
Number who touch stranger	25	2
Latency to touch toys	213	667
Time touching toys	578	167
Latency to fuss or cry	830	613
Time fussing or crying	9	98

Source: Ross and Goldman, 1977, p. 67. Reprinted by permission.
* Response time is in seconds.

share the resources and the labor and where the children are raised communally. The infant is placed in a nursery where it is tended by a member of the kibbutz whose major responsibility is child care. Initially, the parents visit the nursery daily to play with the child and, in the mother's case, to nurse the child. These visits are characterized by affectionate and positive attachment behaviors in both parent and child (Rabkin and Rabkin, 1974). As children grow older, they move to other cottages where they experience new caretakers and have less frequent contact with their parents. Researchers have found that these kibbutz children are as well adjusted as home-reared children and display similar patterns of social attachment (Maccoby and Feldman, 1972). There are also indications of special positive features of the kibbutz environment: it tends to promote greater autonomy (Rabkin and Rabkin, 1974) and more cooperative behavior (Shapira and Madsen, 1974) than the traditional family environment.

The increased number of Western women who have entered the workforce has entailed varying degrees of separation between mother and infant and between mother and preschool child, requiring the development of alternative daycare arrangements. In the United States, the percentage of mothers employed outside the home with children under six years of age has increased from 18 percent in 1955 to 41 percent in 1977 (Belsky, Steinberg, and Walker, 1981) and is still increasing. Given the several million children involved in alternative daycare arrangements, there is naturally considerable social and scientific interest in the effects of this form of child care and early maternal separation on the child's intellectual and social development. While there has been a body of research addressed to the effects of daycare, the methodological problems and the number of variables involved prevent any definite conclusion concerning the impact of daycare on the infant's and preschooler's development. First and foremost, one must consider the quality of the daycare arrangements. And then there are socioeconomic factors, individual differences, variable marital and familial situations, and significant cultural factors that bear on daycare arrangements and their effects. Recognizing the complexity of daycare effects, it is nonetheless possible to offer a tentative evaluation. In a careful review of the admittedly limited data, the effects were summarized as follows: "Experience in high-quality, center-based day care (1) has neither salutory nor deleterious effects upon the intellectual development of the child, (2) is not disruptive of the child's emotional bond with his mother, and (3) increases the degree to which the child interacts, both positively and negatively, with peers" (Belsky and Steinberg, 1978, p. 929).

In an update of this review some three years later, in which these authors had available the results of an extensive evaluation of daycare in Sweden, as well as a number of additional studies carried out in the United States, the conclusions remained essentially the same (Belsky, Steinberg, and Walker, 1981). The authors noted that, while day or out-of-home care need not be deleterious to child development and can even be beneficial, these effects cannot be taken for granted and depend on high-quality, stable daycare arrangements.

In sum, the opportunity to form stable attachments to nurturant caregivers is important to the child's development. However, there are many possible caretaking arrangements, and different cultures make different arrangements. Some involve close and continuous interaction between mother and child, while others involve relatively little contact between mother and child. These child-rearing alternatives have special social relevance, given the increasing numbers of women entering the labor force, the increasing growth of single-parent families, and the rise in the number of children attending nurseries and other child-care centers.

Identification

Early caregivers, in most instances parents, exert diverse and powerful influences on the child's personality development and social behavior. We have already noted that they function as objects of attachment. The child enjoys their love, seeks them out when distressed, and experiences pain and anxiety when attempting to separate and act autonomously. In addition to the gratification of emotional needs, parents play a major role in shaping and regulating the child's behavior. This influence can be exerted directly, through the administration of rewards and punishments, and indirectly when the child identifies with and imitates a parent.

Identification, a complex concept that is used in several different ways, plays an important role in the psychoanalytic theory of development. It can refer to the similarity in behaviors between children and parents; it may denote the psychological process by which that similarity in behavior comes about; and it sometimes refers to a motive or desire to emulate an important person in the child's life.

The concept of identification was defined by Freud as a defense mechanism that enables the child to resolve the Oedipal conflict. However, psychoanalytic theory also postulates more primitive forms of early identification in which the infant does not separate or distinguish itself from the object of identification. This primitive process is postulated by psychoanalysts to account for adult reactions in which the individual behaves as if his or her own body and that of another person were psychologically merged. For example, in response to the loss of a loved one, some depressed patients report that they have lost a part of their own body.

In the more common usage of identification, the child imitates and subsequently adopts the perceived attitudes and values of the parent, while still maintaining a distinction between its own and the parent's identities. According to psychoanalytic theory, there are two broad reasons why the child identifies with the parent. One reason involves love and attachment, while the other focuses on fear. The former type, called *anaclitic* identification, is based on the child's dependent love relationship with a caregiver, usually the mother. As the child matures and the mother reduces the amount of her attention and nurturance, the child attempts to recapture the mother, as it were, by reproducing in fantasy and behavior the mother's statements and actions. This is illustrated in the following anecdote (Mussen, 1977, p. 277):

I was visiting a nursery school attended by the three-year-old daughter of an old friend. Although I had not seen the girl since she was an infant and she did not look like her mother, it was very easy to pick her out from among the twenty pupils. Her ways of moving were clear duplicates of her mother's: the same erect posture; the same quick, deliberate steps in walking; swinging her arms in the same somewhat loose manner. She also used her mother's expressive gestures and inflections when she spoke, pausing frequently between words just as her mother did. My friend had not trained her daughter to walk, move, and speak as she did. Nor is it likely that she rewarded the child directly for emulating her behavior and mannerisms. Nevertheless, the child adopted these responses through identification with her mother.

One might conjecture that the child, in reproducing the behavior of a loved parent, experiences good feelings like those that the parent directly elicits in interaction with the child. These positive feelings then serve to reinforce the child's modeling of the parent. In addition, the child is developing competence and mastery; the demonstration of skills and powers that are similar to those of important figures in the child's environment is an additional source of reinforcement for identification.

In contrast to anaclitic identification, Freud emphasized a *defensive* form of identification that takes place because of fear of the parent. The prototype of defensive identification is boys' resolution of the Oedipal conflict. According to Freud, the boy has erotic feelings toward his mother and, as a result, fears his father's aggressive retaliation. The boy's anxieties result in repression of his libidinous feelings. However, through the process of identification with the feared father, the boy is able to indirectly satisfy his feelings for his

Like father, like son. (Peter Vander-mark)

mother. As a consequence of this process of identification, the boy internal-izes his idealized perception of his father's attitudes and values, thereby form-ing the basis of the superego, or conscience.

A similar, but weaker, process is also postulated to occur when girls resolve their rivalrous feelings toward their mothers. For girls, however, ana-clitic identification is believed to be more salient. The mother is a less aggres-sive and feared figure than the father. As a consequence, the motive for defensive identification is less strong than in boys, and the resultant superego is alleged to be less harsh and demanding (see also discussions of this issue in Chapters 4 and 9).

The process of defensive identification illustrated in cases of identification with the aggressor can be observed in adults as well as children, as when prisoners in a Nazi concentration camp displayed the sadistic behaviors of the Nazi guards whom they detested and feared (Bettelheim, 1943). Apparently, the only way these prisoners could reduce their anxiety and anger was to become like their tormentors. Defensive identification is the psychological equivalent of "If you can't lick 'em, join 'em."

Evidence supporting the distinction between anaclitic and defensive iden-tification is provided by a study of individual differences in response to two leadership styles (Last, 1975). Last assigned Israeli naval officer trainees to one of two experimental groups. In one group, the training officer assumed a positive, understanding, and relatively nurturant attitude, although still ad-hering to the demanding training requirements and standards established by the military. In the other group, the training officer assumed a strict, authori-tarian role during the several months of training. Measures of similarity between the trainees and their training officer were obtained before, during, and after the training period. In addition, attitudes toward the officer and the

Navy were assessed. Finally, it was possible to estimate by means of questionnaires and other procedures whether the trainee's early identification was based on love or fear. The results of this investigation indicated significantly greater identification with the nurturant than with the authoritarian training officer. Furthermore, morale was better and reenlistments were significantly higher for the trainees in the nurturant group. But among the trainees whose early identification was assessed as largely defensive, identification was stronger with the authoritarian than with the nurturant officer.

Imitation

Some theorists equate identification with imitation (Bandura, 1971; Mischel, 1966). While there is undoubtedly considerable overlap between identification and imitation, a distinction between these two processes is useful. Identification involves the duplication of a wide variety of behaviors, including the parents' major attributes. *Imitation,* on the other hand, typically refers to the reproduction of some discrete action or mannerism. Hence, identification appears to be concerned with more of the child's personality than is imitation. In addition, behavioral similarity is the sole criterion of imitation, while some forms of identification have effects that are not solely behavioral. For example, in addition to behaving like some model whom we value, we may sometimes feel as if what is happening to the model is happening to us. Their joy is our joy and their pain is our pain. When one's hero loses a competition, a child may experience the loss in a very personal way and feel badly not only for the hero, but for himself or herself.

Imitation of a model, or observational learning, is nevertheless a major influence on the child's personality development. As indicated in Chapter 6, the emphasis on observational learning is a key difference between Skinner's operant theory and Bandura's social learning theory. Through the mechanism of observational learning, the child can rapidly acquire and perform complex sequences of behaviors.

As briefly discussed in Chapter 6, there are at least four processes that enter into imitation of a model: attention, retention, reproduction, and motivation (Bandura, 1971). First, the child must attend to the model's actions. Such factors as the novelty of the model's behavior increase attention, while boredom and competing attractions decrease attention. Next, the child must retain or remember what was observed. In addition, imitation cannot take place unless the child has the ability to reproduce the model's behavior. And finally, the child may have learned and retained the observed act, but will not perform it unless motivated to do so.

There are many figures in the child's environment—in the home, at school, in the mass media—whom the child can imitate. Inasmuch as everyone is not imitated, what factors determine whom the child does imitate? Experimental studies of adult and peer models indicate that children tend to imitate the behavior of models who: (1) are nurturant, rewarding, and affectionate toward the child (Bandura and Huston, 1961); (2) have power over resources (Bandura, Ross, and Ross, 1963); and (3) are similar to the observing child, particularly with regard to sex (Wolf, 1973). The characteristics of nurturance, power, and similarity are generally maximized in the same-sex parent. In this respect, then, factors affecting imitation are comparable to those affecting identification.

Observational learning, or imitation, has been shown to influence a wide range of social and emotional behaviors, from aggressive and prosocial acts to the reduction of fear (see Chapter 6). But, although imitation is an important learning mechanism accounting for some aspects of the child's personality development, it also has limitations as an explanatory tool. The tendency to imitate declines as children get older. Furthermore, even in the preschool period children become highly selective in what they imitate, in addition to modifying, reorganizing, and dropping imitative responses. These changes have not been systematically studied and are not readily understood in terms of observational learning. But it is evident that behaviors prevalent during one period of life are not always exhibited in subsequent periods. Finally, observational learning must be considered in the overall context of the child's emotional and cognitive development. Children are not miniature adults; imitative responses are transformed and given meaning by the child's desires, fantasies, and cognitive capabilities.

Sex Typing and Sex Differences

We have already indicated that boys are more likely to identify with and imitate their fathers, while girls are more likely to identify with and imitate their mothers. Some of the most active current research in developmental psychology concerns the development of sex differences and the related issue of sex typing. More boys play with blocks and fire trucks than do girls, who tend to play with dolls and paper cutouts more than do boys; boys prefer football, while girls prefer dramatic play. Later in life, more men than women study to be architects and engineers, while more women become nurses and school teachers than do men. There are many exceptions and, although changes are occurring in traditional sex roles, there are still sex differences in preferred activities and in such diverse domains as child-care responsibilities, work roles, and occupations. These differences are a reflection of the contrasting social roles ascribed to men and women. Comparable kinds of sex differences in social roles are observed in other societies, both modern and preliterate.

We know that these sex differences exist at the social level. The intriguing question is what they are related to at the psychological level. To what extent do boys and girls differ in intellectual abilities, motivation, social skills, and other personality attributes? There are many popular stereotypes concerning sex differences in personality. For example, males are regarded as aggressive, rational, and ambitious, while females are described as passive, emotional, and nurturant. These stereotypes are opinions and are in part responsible for the differential occupational roles, income levels, and statuses of the sexes. But to what extent do these sex stereotypes have a basis in fact?

One task undertaken by psychologists has been to determine possible personality and cognitive attributes that distinguish the two sexes and, in addition, to discern the age levels at which sex differences appear. This empirical task has proved to be far more complex than it initially seemed. First, one must assume that the samples of the sexes are comparable on such variables as socioeconomic status and educational opportunity. It is also important to sample different ethnic and economic groups to establish that the findings are representative of boys and girls in general, rather than restricted to some particular segment of society. To add a further complication, as the culture undergoes economic and social change, there may be corresponding alterations in personality traits. For example, differences in dependency between the sexes seem to have been greater in previous decades, indicating that sex differences reported at one time may not hold for another. Conversely, where there once were similarities, differences may suddenly appear. Finally, some of the psychological attributes distinguishing the sexes are subtle and difficult to measure.

A second and even more challenging task for psychologists is determining how differences between the sexes have come about, or how sex typing occurs. The role of biological versus social factors in determining behavioral differences between the sexes is an especially critical social issue. The phrase "anatomy is destiny" crystallizes the view that women's personality and role in society are fundamentally caused by their biological structure. Right or wrong, this explanation has often been used to justify women's subordination and sex discrimination. It is evident from the extensive amount of research that has been conducted on sex differences that there is a great deal of overlap between the sexes with regard to virtually any behavior. Because of individual variability within a sex and the overlap between sexes, sex discrimination is psychologically, as well as legally, unjustified.

Studies of sex differences.   In a comprehensive review of the literature on human sex differences, Maccoby and Jacklin (1974) concluded that the following differences are well established by research data:

1. Girls excel in verbal ability.
2. Boys excel in visual-spatial ability.
3. Boys are superior in mathematical ability.
4. Males are more aggressive than females.

Although there are conflicting data concerning the age at which girls' verbal superiority first becomes manifest, the prevailing view is that girls' verbal skills, evident even among toddlers, mature earlier than boys'. During the elementary school years, girls show greater proficiency in reading (Feshbach, Adelman, and Fuller, 1977), but it is during the junior high and high school periods that their superiority on tasks involving reading, composition, and complex verbal tasks (e.g., analogies) becomes most evident.

Similarly, differences in mathematical skills, as well as in the ability to perceive and handle objects in three-dimensional space, are not readily apparent in the early and preteen years, but the superiority of males in these areas can be clearly seen by adolescence. Research has not yet provided a satisfactory explanation of the source of these differences in cognitive abilities. It is possible that they are genetically linked, but there is also strong evidence that they are influenced by social experience. For example, in a study of boys separated from their fathers at age four or earlier, a reversal from the usual masculine pattern was found, in that these boys had higher verbal than mathematical abilities (Carlsmith, 1964).

Differences in aggression are observable as soon as children begin to interact and play with peers, around the age of two. Since the male advantage in physical size and strength does not become marked until adolescence, one cannot explain these early differences in aggression in terms of these particular physical variables. Yet the role of other biological factors is controversial and complex. Evidence from primate studies indicates that male monkeys engage in more rough-and-tumble play than females do and that even male infants display more aggressive behavior when attacked than females do (Aldis, 1975; Devore, 1965). But whether these observations of monkey behavior are applicable to humans is uncertain. In humans, the process of treating males and females differently begins at birth, with pink and blue blankets. Girls and boys are not only differently identified through the use of different colors and clothing, but also reacted to with different expectations and behaviors. Thus, even these early sex differences in aggression may be attributed to social rather than biological factors.

In Chapter 18, the question of sex differences in aggression and the role of biological and social factors are examined in more detail. At this point it is useful to keep in mind that the greater aggressiveness noted in males is based on observations of direct physical and verbal aggression. When one examines more indirect, subtle forms of aggressiveness, such as snubbing or ignoring peers, there is some evidence that aggression is greater in females than in males (N. Feshbach, 1969).

Social versus task orientation.   Although experts disagree about sex differences in social behaviors other than aggression, there is a good deal of evidence indicating that females are more people-oriented than males are (Block, 1973, 1976). Girls display greater empathy and responsiveness to the feelings of other children (Hoffman, 1977), are more concerned about the opinions of others, and are more compliant with adults (Block, 1973, 1976). In addition, there are indications that girls are more dependent, fearful, and lacking in confidence than boys are. On the other hand, boys tend to show more curiosity and exploration and are more active and impulsive than girls are.

In the major division of energies and interests between the world of action and achievement and the world of social attachments and family involvement, boys are more active in the former and girls, in the latter. As one author (Block, 1973, p. 515) describes this difference:

Little boys are being taught to control the expression of feelings and affects, while assertion and extension of self are abetted. Little girls are being taught to control aggression, including assertion and extension, while being encouraged to regard the inner, familial world as the proper sphere of their interest.

Theories of sex differences.   Biological versus social explanations for some sex differences have already been considered. There are a number of investigators, particularly those with a sociobiological orientation (see Chapter 2), who emphasize the role of biological factors. But, among the leading personality theorists, only the more traditional psychoanalysts place much weight on biological differences between the sexes as the source of their differences in personality and social role. For Freud, identification was the principal mechanism leading to sex typing. As a result of the process of identification, children acquire the attributes and orientations of their sex. The biological difference between boys and girls leads not only to their making a different choice of which parent to identify with, but also to a less satisfactory identification for females (see Chapter 4). Freud did recognize some influence of learning processes in the development of sex differences, however, and contemporary psychoanalysts acknowledge the importance of social variables to an even greater extent.

The social learning theorists stress the importance of the differential reinforcement boys and girls receive for "appropriately" imitating male and female models and for behaving in accordance with the norms and expectations of society. The behaviors that define the female and male roles are very much influenced by the culture in which a child is socialized. Sex role norms vary from society to society, but in each case children are rewarded for those behaviors that will help them fit the particular roles prescribed by society. This differential reinforcement begins very early. It is manifest in the disparate ways that males and females are handled by their parents, in the unequal rough-and-tumble play of fathers with boys versus girls, and in the reinforcements given for engaging in appropriate sex-typed activities. Studies of child-rearing practices in this and other cultures (Block, 1973; Sears, Maccoby, and Levin, 1957; Whiting, 1963) clearly indicate that parents have different expectations for boys and girls and respond differentially according to the sex of their child. It is inevitable that these socialization practices define and shape male and female behavior.

The powerful influence of learning and cultural variables in sex typing is reflected in studies of *hermaphrodites,* infants born with two sets of genitalia. Some of these infants with external female organs and internal male organs are genetically males according to chromosome tests. Conversely, others are genetically female and have internal female organs and external male organs. Studies of these children consistently indicate that children reared according to their external sexual characteristics develop a sex role and orientation corresponding to the manner in which they are raised, even though this sex role is contrary to their biological constitution (Hampson, 1965; Money, 1965).

But there are at least two major problems with the social learning explanation of sex typing. First, it implies that the many behaviors associated with being male or female have to be differentially reinforced or systematically modeled. It seems unlikely that these vast differences have all been due to reinforcement mechanisms. Second, and perhaps more important, sexual identity is acquired quite early in the child's development and is remarkably stable and difficult to change. The child establishes its *gender identity* and subsequently acquires the set of behaviors that constitutes sex role identity. Guided by this observation, Kohlberg (1966) proposed that the child first learns to identify itself as a boy or a girl and then models itself after males or females. That is, after having learned the category of boy or girl, the child then wants to do whatever it is that boys and girls do. There is much to be said for Kohlberg's cognitive labeling theory, although one difficulty is that it cannot account for the great variation in masculinity-femininity qualities within each sex.

It is quite likely that sex typing is a function of all the mechanisms that have been discussed: identification, selective reinforcement, and cognitive labeling. In addition, one cannot ignore the contribution of biological factors, even if they may be overridden by social reinforcement. In sum, sex typing is the result of the interaction between social and biological processes, leading to personality differences between the sexes and variations within each sex.

Summary

Several basic issues raised by the study of personality development have been discussed, including the role of nature versus nurture; the question of gradual, continuous change versus discrete stages of development; the concept of critical periods; and the continuity of personality over time. In addition, basic developmental processes were examined. The process of attachment is seen as fundamental to the child's emotional and social development, and particular attention is paid to the factors influencing attachment. These include biological factors, variations in characteristics of the caregiver, and social and cultural influences. The conditions under which separations from the caregiver lead to emotional disturbance or to healthy patterns of adjustment have also been considered. Early caregivers who are objects of the infant's attachment also become objects of identification. The role of identification in personality development and several theories and types of identification have been reviewed. Both identification and imitation are significant processes influencing the development of sex differences in personality. The chapter concluded with a review of those sex differences that have been substantiated by research and with a discussion of the factors and processes that determine these sex-related differences in personality.

Specific Points

1. The *transactional model* of development views the interaction between nature and nurture, or the organism and its environment, as a reciprocal and continuous process.
2. Both psychoanalytic theory and Piaget's cognitive theory offer a stage or discontinuity conception of development, while learning theories view development as a continuous process of change.

3. According to Piaget, the stage of a child's cognitive development has a major influence on how the child perceives the environment and organizes its experience.

4. While many developmental psychologists believe that early childhood experiences are critical for the child's subsequent cognitive, emotional, and social development, there is still considerable debate over the usefulness of the concept of *critical periods.*

5. There is no simple answer to the question of the stability or *continuity* of personality traits over time. For some traits, such as aggression, there appears to be considerable stability, an observation supported by longitudinal studies.

6. The evidence of *attachment* behavior in infrahumans suggests that there are important biological factors influencing attachment in human infants. From a biological standpoint, the infant's attachment to a caregiver increases the likelihood of receiving nourishment and protection and therefore increases the infant's chances of survival.

7. Harlow's studies indicate that the reduction of an infant's hunger through the caretaker's provision of food is not a critical factor in the development of attachment in monkeys. Comforting physical contact, particularly the opportunity to cling, appears to be the major contributing element.

8. Research indicates that there are significant differences among infants in the quality of their attachment behavior and that the classification of infants into *securely attached, insecurely attached,* and *avoidant* categories is predictive of subsequent attachment behavior and adjustment.

9. Institutionalization of the young child—one form of *separation*—can have serious negative effects on the child's subsequent emotional and cognitive development. However, there are significant individual differences in children's responses to institutionalization, and the nature of the institutional environment is also a major variable that must be considered.

10. There is some evidence consistent with the Freudian hypothesis regarding the resolution of the Oedipal conflict through *identification* with the parent of the same sex. Identification with a positive, nurturant authority figure was distinguished from identification stemming from fear.

11. Children are more likely to imitate models who are similar to them, are nurturant, and have power over reinforcement. Also, *observational learning* or *imitation* has been shown to influence a wide range of social and emotional behaviors. However, even young children are selective in what they imitate and become more discriminating as they grow older.

12. Aside from sex differences in cognitive skills, the primary behavioral sex difference that has been consistently observed is the manifestation of more physical aggression by boys than by girls. There is also evidence that girls are more social or people oriented, while boys are more achievement or task oriented.

13. While biological factors undoubtedly contribute to observed sex differences in behavior, there is substantial evidence that cultural, experiential

variables exert a profound influence on the behavioral sex typing of males and females.

Thought Questions

1. What are some of the processes that make for stability or continuity of behavior between early childhood and later periods of development? What are some of the processes that make for instability or for lack of relationship between early and later personality attributes?
2. There are some philosophies, mostly Eastern, that argue that we must unlearn attachments and that attachments limit our freedom of choice. How do you feel about this position?
3. What is your view about making daycare centers available to all infants and toddlers, much as elementary schools are available now? What might the advantages and disadvantages of such a program be?
4. In your ideal society, would you socialize children so as to eliminate sex differences in personality? Are there some sex differences in personality that you feel are inevitable? Are there some that you feel society should reinforce and foster?

Social Development and Patterns of Child Rearing

9

In the previous chapter, we reviewed several processes that are basic to the child's personality and social development. We saw how the infant develops significant attachments to adult figures, usually its parents, and the complex effects of separation from these figures. We also noted that these significant others, in addition to becoming the objects of the infant's affections and attachments, also serve as models with whom the child imitates and identifies. The process of identification, in turn, contributes to the development of sex differences in personality, although sex differences are also influenced by differential social reinforcement and by biological factors.

In this second chapter on personality development, we will consider the influence of identification on moral development. After reviewing alternative explanations of moral development, we will go on to examine the broader topic of the development of positive, prosocial behaviors. Moral development and prosocial behavior are two related and important objectives of society's efforts to socialize the child. Finally, in the concluding section of the chapter, we will consider the question of the family's effect on socialization.

Moral Development

How does the infant develop from a creature dominated by biological urges, seeking immediate satisfaction, to an individual with a sense of right and wrong? How does a child become a moral being? The major theoretical approaches to personality—psychoanalytic, cognitive, and social learning theory—offer very different explanations of the process of moral development. In part, these different theoretical explanations arise from their emphases on different aspects of morality. The psychoanalysts have been concerned with the emotional and motivational aspects of morality, particularly the acquisition of guilt and conscience. Cognitive theorists have focused on the development of understanding of moral conduct or rules, or changes in the child's perception of right and wrong. Social learning approaches have been more concerned with the child's moral behaviors and good or bad actions, as well as with mechanisms for the acquisition of these behaviors.

The Superego and Moral Development

The key element in the psychoanalytic theory of moral development is the superego. As noted earlier (see Chapter 4), the superego refers to an internalized set of prohibitions and standards acquired by the child in the resolution of the Oedipal conflict through identification with the same-sex parent. There are a number of interesting implications of Freud's formulation that have led to considerable debate. These implications have to do with the role of identification in superego formation, sex differences, and the age at which superego formation takes place. Specifically, Freud's theory implies that:

1. Identification plays a major role in the development of the internalized moral standards that comprise the superego.
2. Defensive identification (identification out of fear) is more central in superego formation than is anaclitic identification (identification out of affection).
3. Boys develop a stronger, more integrated superego than girls do because the Oedipal conflict is more intense in boys than in girls and because boys fear their fathers more than girls fear their mothers.
4. Superego formation, or the internalization of moral standards, is characterized by rapid development around the age of four or five, during the phallic period.

Only the first of these implications is supported by empirical evidence, and even in that instance the support is slight. The other three derivations from psychoanalytic theory are contradicted by the available evidence.

Concerning defensive versus anaclitic identification, neither has been shown to be linked directly to moral behavior. However, in contrast to the psychoanalytic expectation, defensive identification, which is associated with a more primitive household in which fear of physical punishment prevails, tends to be related to weak moral development in the child, while children raised in affectionate, nurturant households tend to have greater internalization of moral standards (Hoffman, 1970). The latter children are influenced primarily by fear of loss of parental love rather than by fear of parental aggressive coercion. Since the two types of households differ in other respects, such as social class (see Chapter 3), the data must be interpreted with caution. It also has been suggested by psychoanalytic theorists that the combination of affectionate parenting with strong punitive disciplinary practices is likely to result in a rigid and harsh superego that cannot cope with problems for which there are no simple right or wrong answers. But here, too, more supportive data are needed before this hypothesis can be accepted.

With regard to the implication that boys display a more integrated set of moral standards and behaviors than girls do, the evidence suggests the contrary: girls tend to be more consistent in their moral attitudes and behavior than are boys (Maccoby and Jacklin, 1974). Finally, concerning the psychoanalytic belief that superego formation does not occur until the age of four or five, it is evident that children show indications of conscience well before those ages. Younger children use self-monitoring to resist forbidden acts and often "confess" when the resistance was insufficient to inhibit the act (Sears, Rau, and Alpert, 1965).

Given the available evidence, one can conclude only that the classic Freudian explanation of the acquisition of conscience or superego is seriously inadequate and, in important respects, incorrect. Moreover, the concept of the superego as an unconscious, unrelenting internal censor that blocks and punishes the expression of id and egoistic impulses requires modification. Even Freud tempered this fire-and-brimstone image of the nature of conscience by introducing the concept of *ego ideal* to convey the positive aspects of conscience. The ego ideal refers to standards that guide behavior because they are believed to be worthy. Other analysts have suggested that the positive ideals and moral values reflected in the ego ideal arise out of the child's identification with the loving aspects of the parents (Schafer, 1960) and that the ego ideal is a part of the superego that is in harmony with healthy personality development. More generally, however, psychoanalysis offers an inconsistent and ambiguous picture of the neurotic versus healthy implications of guilt, conscience, and responsibility. There is the suggestion in psychoanalytic writings, as well as in the writings of some self-actualization and cognitive theorists, that "ought" and "should" rules of behavior have no place in a truly healthy personality.

Stages of Moral Development: The Cognitive Approach

In addition to feeling guilty, confessing wrongdoings, telling the truth, and not cheating, conscience involves an understanding of moral issues, including what it means to be good or bad.

Piaget's studies.   Piaget was the first to clearly formulate this issue and to undertake the systematic investigation of the development of children's moral concepts. Piaget's studies focused on moral understanding rather than on moral behavior. To examine moral understanding, Piaget used interviewing techniques, asking children of different ages such questions about moral issues as "Why shouldn't you cheat in a game?" and then asking them to give examples of unfair or bad behavior. In addition, Piaget used judgments to examine moral development. For example, in one type of judgment research, he constructed pairs of stories in which an intentional act that resulted in small damage was compared to an unintentional act that resulted in large damage. The child was then asked to judge which of the acts was "naughtier." In one such story a child is called to dinner and, upon opening the dining room door, slams into a hidden tray, causing fifteen cups on the tray to break. In the comparison story, a boy wants to get some forbidden jam from a cupboard while his mother is away. To reach the jam he has to climb a chair and, in the process, reaches over a cup and breaks it. Piaget found that younger children tended to see breaking the larger number of cups as naughtier, basing their judgments on the objective fact of amount of damage done. On the other hand, older children tended to see the intentional act in which only one cup was broken as naughtier, basing their judgments on the subjective motive or intent of the child.

The younger child is also more absolute in his or her moral judgments. Younger children consider lying as always wrong, regardless of the circumstances, and without question accept the standards of parental authority as the criteria for what is moral. Piaget refers to this period of rigid rules and unquestionable reliance on authority, lasting until the age of seven or eight, as the stage of *moral realism.* A second moral stage, from approximately eight to eleven, is characterized by belief in equal treatment and reciprocity, or taking turns, as the basis for determining what is fair. Finally, around the age of eleven or twelve, children enter the third and highest stage, in which judgments become more relativistic (the stage of *moral relativism*); the same action can be judged as good or bad depending on the particular situational circumstances and the events that led to the action.

Piaget's theory of moral development has stimulated a great deal of research. The outcomes of his investigations do not permit a simple verdict that the theory is true or false. It is correct in some respects and deficient in others. Children's sense of justice and their moral evaluations do develop and change with age in general correspondence with the descriptions offered by Piaget (Lee, 1971; Lickona, 1976). There is also a clear relationship between the child's cognitive development or growth of mental functioning and moral judgments. For example, children between the ages of seven and thirteen whose thinking reflects the capacity to assume the point of view of another (*decentration*) are more likely to base their moral judgments on the principle of reciprocity, while children who have difficulty in perceiving the world from another's viewpoint are more likely to apply rigid standards of authority when making moral judgments (Stuart, 1967).

However, the evidence does not support the notion of discrete stages that describe the different kinds of moral judgments that children make. For example, beliefs about the inevitability of punishment for wrongdoing (*immanent justice*) and greater use of outcome than intention information are only weakly correlated, although Piaget assumes that both are manifestations of the same stage of cognitive development. In addition, whether a child or an adult evaluates an act on the basis of the actor's intention or on the basis of outcome depends on a number of situational factors. For example, when the outcome of an unintentional act is extremely damaging (e.g., when a loaded gun accidentally goes off and kills someone), both adults and children advocate punishment for the act (Weiner, Kun, and Benesh-Weiner, 1980). Finally, both adults and children use intent and outcome information in their judgments, although they may "weight" or use the information differently.

Moral judgments are also subject to more modification than a cognitive stage theory would lead one to expect. In an experimental demonstration of the effects of modeling on moral judgment, Bandura and McDonald (1963) first determined children's orientation to intentionality versus outcome as the basis of moral judgment. Children who initially made more use of intent information were then exposed to a model who made judgments based on outcomes, while children making more use of outcome information were exposed to a model who made judgments based on intent. Children in both groups subsequently displayed significant shifts so that their judgments were more like that of the model, even when the model was not present. However, it is also the case that shifts in the direction of intentionality (the "natural" developmental sequence) are more stable than shifts in the direction toward outcomes (Cowan et al., 1969; LeFurgy and Woloshin, 1969).

Kohlberg's contribution.   Piaget's approach has been extended and revised by Lawrence Kohlberg (1969b). Kohlberg expanded the number of stages to six, each characterized by qualitatively distinctive modes of thinking. In addition, the time period over which moral development takes place was extended into adolescence. In the course of development, more advanced stages supercede earlier, more immature stages. The six developmental stages, described in the following paragraphs, are grouped into three moral levels: the preconventional, or premoral; the conventional; and the postconventional, or principled.

At level 1, rules and expectations are perceived as external to the self. The child does make a distinction between right and wrong, but defines right first on the basis of what authorities such as parents and the law demand (stage 1) and subsequently on the basis of *concrete reciprocal hedonism*, characterized by the phrase, "If I do something for you, then it's right that you do something for me" (stage 2). Level 2 begins at approximately age nine and, according to Kohlberg, is the level of most adolescents and adults. Morality here is based on good intentions and obtaining social approval (stage 3) and on a recognition of the importance of laws and rules as means of maintaining the social order (stage 4). The minority of individuals achieving level 3 do so in late adolescence, supposedly around the age of twenty. At this highest level, morality is perceived in terms of contractual obligations and laws based on democratic participation (stage 5). Ultimately, morality is a matter of individual conscience and universal ethics (stage 6). Stage 6 morality is characterized by reasoning from a set of principles that both are universally acceptable and stem from the individual's formulation of moral standards. Kohlberg (1976) has even suggested the existence of a seventh stage, not yet studied, in which moral judgments are based on a philosophical and nonegoistic understanding of the meaning of existence.

Kohlberg derived these stages from an analysis of responses to a series of stories that posed moral dilemmas. Children of different ages and cultures had to arrive at moral judgments based on the content of these stories. For example, in one story a man's wife is desperately in need of a drug recently discovered by a local druggist. The druggist, however, has priced the drug very high in order to make a substantial profit. The husband cannot pay the price and breaks into the man's store to steal the drug for his wife. The question posed is whether the husband should have stolen the drug.

Kohlberg and his associates have found that the stages observed in samples of American children also characterize the developmental pattern of moral understanding in children from other cultures, including those of Mexico, Taiwan, and Turkey. There is also some empirical support for the assumption that the sequence of stages is invariant, maintaining the same sequential order, and that most of a child's moral judgments consistently reflect a particular stage (Kohlberg, 1976; Turiel, 1966).

However, much more evidence is required to substantiate the notion of a moral stage and the implication that stages follow a fixed developmental sequence. It is often difficult to determine the stage of a particular story response. There is also some question as to whether the superiority of the highest stage is a function of social and cognitive development or is largely a matter of an arbitrarily imposed cultural value. In addition, there is evidence that people use different rules for different situations and that the stages are not sequential (Kurtines and Greif, 1974). Finally, the stage approach does not consider the motivational and affective aspects of moral actions.

The moral and the social world.   Piaget's and Kohlberg's models of moral development assume that the child's reactions to rules and to the transgression of rules depend on the child's moral stage, which, in turn, is related to the child's more general level of cognitive development. Turiel and his colleagues, also working within a cognitive framework, have shown that the nature of the transgressed rule is an important determinant of moral judgment, even at the preschool level (Nucci and Turiel, 1978). Turiel distinguishes between transgression of *moral* rules, such as hitting another person without provocation, and transgression of *social* rules, such as appearing nude in public. Moral transgressions are intrinsic to social interaction and are seen as wrong regardless of the existence of a specific rule prohibiting them. Social transgressions, on the other hand, are seen as dependent on more arbitrary rules and can be changed by authority or consensus. Thus we must distinguish between these types of rules when studying stages of moral thinking.

The Social Learning Approach

For social learning theorists, moral behavior is not fundamentally different from any other class of social behavior. It is acquired through punishment for deviation from social rules and through reinforcement for conforming to these standards. Through a process of conditioning, in which rule breaking is first followed by punishment, the child learns to experience discomfort and fear even when thinking about or anticipating breaking a rule. This discomfort inhibits the deviant action even in the absence of likely discovery and punishment. Furthermore, the child comes to feel guilty following a transgression and learns to reduce that guilt through self-punitive remarks and confession (Aronfreed, 1964). Finally, the child also learns to covertly verbalize statements that help control and inhibit socially disapproved actions. These statements, such as "Don't hit the baby" or "Don't take the candy" are often initially voiced aloud. But they eventually become silent and provide the basis for the voice of conscience.

As indicated previously, there are a number of studies indicating that moral behaviors and judgments in children can be influenced through the observation and imitation of models (Bandura and McDonald, 1963). From a social learning standpoint, each society's norms and models form the primary source of moral behavior, but social influence is insufficient to account for all aspects of morality. Social learning theorists point out that the child must develop the cognitive competence required to understand moral rules, as well as the behavioral competence, such as self-control, required to comply with those rules (Mischel and Mischel, 1976). It has been suggested by social learning theorists that variations in mental age and IQ might account for the developmental stage sequence postulated by Kohlberg. However, while IQ is undoubtedly one determinant of moral level, it has also been demonstrated that there are meaningful differences between children at different moral stages even with the influence of IQ eliminated (Kohlberg, 1958).

Social learning theorists also favor a specificity model of moral behavior, maintaining that behaviors such as stealing, cheating, and lying are differentially reinforced and depend on the situation. A classic pioneering study addressed to the question of the generality versus specificity of moral behavior was conducted many years ago by Hartshorne and May (1928). Their study bears on the broader issue of the trait/situation controversy (see Chapter 13), as well as on the more pointed question of the generality of moral behavior. Hartshorne and May obtained a variety of different measures, on a very large sample of children, of lying, cheating, and stealing in several different settings, such as home, school, and so on. The correlations between the different measures were unimpressive, and it was concluded that honesty is essentially situationally determined; that is, it is not meaningful to describe one child as honest and another as dishonest.

Reanalyses of these data (Burton, 1963; Epstein, 1979), using the more reliable of their measures or multiple measures, yielded greater evidence of consistency than was initially reported (see also Chapter 13). Yet some psychologists remain unimpressed by the results of the reanalyses and argue that the data from Hartshorne and May's study are still consistent with a social learning, specificity position. Whether one is more impressed by the fact that disparate moral behaviors are significantly related or by the relative weakness of the relationship is very much dependent on one's theoretical orientation and beliefs, a case of a cup that is half empty also being perceived as half full. Efforts to relate Kohlberg's all-encompassing stages of moral development to specific moral behaviors have yielded similarly small but significant correlations (Schwartz, Feldman, Brown, and Heingartner, 1969).

In any case, many people are able to articulate the higher levels of Kohlberg's stages, but behave in a less moral fashion than do individuals at lower levels. Thus, "ripping off" was a not uncommon practice among sophisticated college students during the late 1960s and early 1970s. The gap between cognitive stages and moral behavior poses a problem for stage theory. On the other hand, it is difficult for learning theorists to account for individuals who maintain moral beliefs and actions that are contrary to the prevailing norm and that may even subject them to ridicule and physical retaliation. What is requred in this important area of personality development is a better understanding of the social and individual factors that make possible the attainment of the highest stages of moral judgment and the courage to behave in accordance with those moral beliefs.

Prosocial Behaviors

The discussion of moral behavior focused on prohibitions, conformity to social rules, and developmental changes in children's concepts of what constitutes good and evil. We now turn to positive social behaviors, such as generosity, caring, and helping, which frequently are socially prescribed and viewed as moral kinds of actions. The four-year-old preschooler sharing her

"Here, have some of mine!" This photograph shows an example of prosocial behavior. (Frank Siteman/Stock, Boston)

lunch with a peer is engaging in prosocial behavior, as are the young opponents of an injured football player who pat him on the back as he is helped from the field. There are, of course, many other behaviors that are included in the prosocial category, such as dedication to improving the lot of the poor, efforts to overcome social injustice, and struggles to eliminate brutality. More generally, "pro-social behaviors refer to actions that are intended to aid or benefit another person or group of people without the actor's anticipation of external rewards" (Mussen and Eisenberg-Berg, 1977). One can never completely eliminate the possibility of "anticipation of external rewards"; even in the biblical parable of charity, the bread cast upon the waters ultimately benefits the giver. Nevertheless, the definition is a useful one. It helps orient research toward investigating the internal reward systems—the pride, the sense of obligation, the intrinsic satisfaction, and perhaps even the reduction of guilt—that may motivate or accompany prosocial behavior.

Evolution of Positive Social Behaviors

Whenever the question of what human beings have inherited from their animal ancestors arises, characteristics such as aggression, sex drive, and territorial competition are typically cited. Rarely does one think of such positive social behaviors as cooperation, generosity, and altruism as part of our animal heritage. Yet there is no doubt that many animal species display cooperative social patterns; even instances of self-sacrifice are not uncommon. However, whether the same biological factors that govern infrahuman prosocial behaviors are relevant to human prosocial behaviors is debatable.

The complex cooperative societies of social insects like the ant and the bee have been described in countless popular articles, and the interaction of genetic programming with environmental influences in these insects has been extensively studied. But cooperation and sharing are by no means restricted to social insects. Chimpanzees, for example, display unusual cooperation and coordination when in pursuit of prey (Teleki, 1973). Also, when the food supply is limited, chimpanzees will beg from one another and share food (Wilson, 1975). Positive social behaviors are common even among African elephants. "Young calves of both sexes are treated equally and each is permitted to suckle from any nursing mother in the group. Adolescent cows serve as 'aunts', restraining the calves from running about and nudging others awake from their naps" (Wilson, 1975, p. 494). When a young bull elephant was felled with an anesthetic dart, "the adult cows rushed to his aid and tried to raise him to his feet" (p. 494). The African wild dog provides a striking contrast between savage behavior displayed when attacking prey and gentle, nurturant behavior extended to others in its pack. When the pack have eaten their prey, they return to the den and regurgitate, making it possible for the young and other adults who remained behind to share in the bounty. The sick and the crippled, unable to participate in the hunt, are thus maintained by the pack. As the incident described in Box 9.1 illustrates, a similar kind of cooperative behavior can be observed in dolphins.

Many of these behaviors can be considered instances of altruism, since, in

---

Box 9.1   PROSOCIAL BEHAVIOR IN DOLPHINS

A school of approximately 50 *Delphinus delphis* was sighted. As soon as the Zodiac (our boat) approached, they increased speed, dived and changed direction under water. The school reassembled behind the Zodiac. The yacht took over the chase and an animal was wounded by the harpoon. We saw quite clearly how other dolphins came immediately to the help of the wounded animal on the starboard side of the yacht. They supported the wounded dolphin with their flippers and bodies and carried it to the surface. It blew 2–3 times and then dived. The whole incident lasted about 30 seconds and was repeated twice when the animal appeared unable to surface alone. All the animals including the wounded dolphin then dived and swam quickly out of sight.

Source: Pilleri and Knuckey, 1969, from Wilson, 1975, p. 475.

---

an effort to save members of their own species, these animals risk their own well-being. But perhaps the most striking examples of altruism are provided by the social insects. Honeybee workers that embed their barbed stings in an intruder threatening the hive will die as a result but, in the process, perhaps save the rest of the hive. Similarly, termite soldiers spray predators with a glandular secretion fatal to both themselves and their enemies. The colony's king and queen are thereby protected and remain able to preserve and expand the colony through breeding. The insects sacrificing themselves are relatives of and share common genes with the surviving insects. The altruistic organism is therefore contributing to the survival of its own gene pool (see also Chapter 2). Sociobiologists argue that such acts of altruism are built into organisms because they are survival-relevant.

Sociobiologists like Wilson have extended this argument to suggest that there is a genetic basis for altruism and other prosocial behaviors among humans. However, while one can draw a crude analogy between self-sacrifice in infrahumans and humans, it is pure speculation to propose that the same mechanisms are operative in both species. Human altruism takes many different forms and is affected by a great range of social influences. A genetic approach to human altruism does not seem very promising. Rather, the importance of animal studies lies in their demonstration that prosocial behaviors are as natural to many animal species as are the more often cited examples of destructive, antisocial behaviors. Human tenderness, caring, attachment, and self-sacrifice are, then, just as "animalistic" as are human competitiveness, selfishness, and brutality.

Cooperation

Describing behavior as "natural" does not necessarily mean that it is inborn; rather, it implies that the organism has the potential for developing this pattern of behavior and will do so under normal environmental circumstances. Infants are not cooperative, but preschool children display sharing, reciprocity, and other forms of cooperation in their play behavior. These positive social behaviors are related to the child's general mental development (Emmerich, Cocking, and Sigel, 1979) and personal adjustment (Block and Block, 1980). An extensive longitudinal study of nursery school children indicated that children rated by their teachers as high in such characteristics as helpfulness and cooperativeness obtained low scores on measures of impulsiveness and high scores on an index of their capacity to recover to a state of normalcy after a stressful experience (Block and Block, 1980). Moreover, four-year-old children described as dependable, calm, and cooperative tended to behave generously at age five on a measure of sharing and distributing rewards, while four-year-old children described as overreactive and not competent in handling stress tended to be low in generosity at age five.

Cooperative methods in the classroom.   There are a number of studies indicating that the implementation of cooperative methods in the classroom may help reduce social prejudice, facilitate other forms of positive social behavior, and even lead to improvement in basic academic skills. In one of these methods, the jigsaw technique (Aronson et al., 1978), the classroom is divided into small groups of about five to six members. The lesson material is then divided into as many parts as there are group members. Each group member is responsible for teaching his or her part to other members of the group. The group members are thus dependent on one another for mastery of the material, and only through cooperation with others can effective learning of all the material take place. This process appears to foster favorable attitudes toward other members of the group and the class, as well as to enhance learning. Similar effects have been found with techniques that combine cooperation within a group with competition between groups or techniques that have group members engage in cooperative planning on a common project involving a variety of activities and skills (Sharon, 1980). The effectiveness of these procedures over more extended periods of time, and the specific factors and mechanisms responsible for the observed changes, must be established by future research.

Cross-cultural cooperative behaviors.   Since the culture of the classroom can influence cooperation, it is not surprising that cooperative behaviors are also strongly influenced by the larger culture. Whiting and Whiting (1975) gathered detailed, naturalistic, observational data of children between the ages of three and eleven in six different cultures: Kenya, Mexico, the Philippines, Okinawa, India, and a New England community. The majority of the children observed in Kenya, Mexico, and the Philippines were above average on such behaviors as "offers help" and "offers support," while the children in the other three cultures scored low on this constellation of prosocial responses. Children from Okinawa, India, and the New England community were more self-seeking and dominance oriented in their social interactions.

Laboratory studies of cooperation and competition by Madsen and his colleagues (Kagan and Madsen, 1971; Madsen and Shapira, 1970) have helped sharpen our understanding of the nature of some of these cultural differences. In several experimental studies of Mexican and American children, in which a child must choose either to cooperate or to compete with a peer, Mexican children were found to be much more cooperative than Americans. These laboratory findings therefore are consistent with the cultural differences reported by the Whitings, using naturalistic observations, and illustrate how both laboratory and field research methodologies can mutually contribute to understanding. However, it is still unclear whether the greater cooperativeness of the Mexican children was due to the fact that they were less competitive or was an indication of a stronger disposition to be cooperative. In one study bearing on this issue, children were given a task in which they could prevent their partner from receiving a toy. This was done twice as often by American as by Mexican children. In another investigation it was revealed that, in an effort to avoid conflict, Mexican children would give their toys up to their partner when only one could receive a toy, while this was not the case with the American children. Hence, the Mexican and the American children apparently differed in competitiveness. But why these Mexican and American children differed in their behavior—whether the critical factors were cultural norms, family structure, or rural-urban background—remains an unresolved question.

Antecedents of cooperation.   As already suggested, cooperation and other prosocial behaviors are related to the child's cognitive and social-emotional competence. In addition, cooperative behavior is affected by situational factors, particularly the presence of competitive goals. A dramatic demonstration of the role of situational context in determining cooperative versus competitive behavior is provided by a classic social psychological field experiment conducted at a camp (Sherif et al., 1961). After the male campers arrived, they were assigned to one of two groups, either the Bull Dogs or the Red Devils. A series of cooperative activities was introduced *within* each group to promote intragroup solidarity. In addition, competitive games and contests were initiated *between* the two groups. Strong hostility between the Bull Dogs and the Red Devils began to accompany competition.

Several methods for reducing hostility and competition and fostering cooperativeness were then introduced. One of the most effective involved taking both groups on an overnight camping trip and having an old food truck break down. Both groups then worked together to pull the truck, using a heavy rope that had previously been used for tug-of-war contests between the groups. When this truck later appeared with the food, the two groups spontaneously engaged in cooperative behavior by preparing meals together.

Members of a culture may also perceive themselves as either Bull Dogs or Red Devils in competition with each other, or they may perceive themselves as part of a larger cultural group cooperating to achieve mutual goals. How different cultures instill a self-centered, competitive orientation versus a socially oriented, cooperative orientation has not been precisely determined. However, some characteristics of society have been described (Mussen and Eisenberg-Berg, 1977) that could enhance cooperation, social responsibility, and other prosocial behaviors:

1. Stress by parents, peers, and other agents of socialization on consideration for others, sharing, and group orientation.
2. A simple social organization like that found in traditional, rural settings.
3. Members of extended family living together.
4. Early assignment of tasks and responsibilities to children.

Generosity and Caring

People who are cooperative also tend to be more generous in their willingness to come to the aid of others in distress. In addition, many of the variables that influence cooperation, such as personal adjustment, cognitive level, imitation, and cultural background, also influence generosity and caring behavior. However, generosity toward others and responsiveness to distress are sufficiently different from cooperation to warrant separate discussion.

A common experimental procedure in the study of generosity is to have children win a prize or earn some reward, such as crayons, pennies, or candy. Then the children are asked to make a donation from their earnings to help needy children. The amount that each child donates serves as a measure of generosity. This procedure has the advantage of providing an objective, quantitative measure that can be readily used in experimental settings, but it also has the disadvantage of a lack of naturalism, for children are not usually called on to make donations to charity. Their generosity is more typically expressed in interactions with playmates and siblings. Nonetheless, this methodology has yielded some interesting findings. For example, relatively brief exposure to an adult model who donates generously has been shown to have a surprisingly strong positive effect on children's generosity. This increased generosity has been reported even months after the observation of the model (Midlarsky and Bryan, 1972; Rushton, 1976). It therefore seems reasonable that children with a generous parent or parents, who identify with that parent, will be high in generosity. In support of this, it has been found that when parents place a high value on prosocial behaviors, their children are more generous and caring (Feshbach, 1975; Hoffman, 1975).

A common method used by teachers, ministers, and others to encourage generosity is exhortation and preaching. How effective is this approach with children? Mild exhortations, simply stating what the child ought to do, are generally ineffective. On the other hand, strong, forceful preaching, especially when reasons for the request and the positive consequences of a donation are made explicit, can have some positive effects on children's generosity. In one pertinent investigation (Eisenberg-Berg and Geisheker, 1979), third- and fourth-grade children observed a model donating some money to a UNICEF collection bank. The collection bank was placed next to a poster showing poor children. The model made either an *empathic* appeal including reasons ("They would be so happy and excited if they could buy food and toys.") or a *normative* appeal ("Sharing is the right thing to do."). The data revealed that children hearing the empathic appeal donated more money. In addition, fourth graders donated more than third graders did, which is consistent with the general finding that generosity increases with age. But the effects of

Sister Teresa, recognized for her devotion to the poor and unfortunate of Calcutta. (Jean-Claude Francolon/Gamma-Liaison)

preaching are weak when compared to the behavior of a model. In one investigation (Bryan and Walbek, 1970), third- and fourth-grade girls were exposed to either a model who preached charity but acted in a stingy manner or a model who preached stinginess but behaved generously. The children followed the model's behavior rather than the preaching!

The Good Samaritan Phenomenon

The following news item appeared in an eastern United States newspaper ("A Social Disaster," 1971, in Lickona, 1976, p. 269):

Carmen Colon, a 10-year-old kidnapped while she was on an errand for her mother, temporarily escaped from her captor along a busy highway near Rochester, New York. Half-clad and obviously distraught, she cried out for help. More than a hundred motorists passed her by. Shortly thereafter, Carmen was murdered.

The unwillingness to come to the aid of someone in distress is not restricted to motorists on highways. The most famous incident of this kind, which has stimulated a great deal of psychological interest and research, involved Kitty Genovese, a young woman in Queens, New York, who was attacked when walking home one night. A subsequent investigation of the incident revealed that thirty-eight people came to their windows, heard the screaming, and saw her being attacked. Yet no one came to her aid. In fact, no one even called the police during the half-hour it took for the assailant to kill her.

Box 9.2   THE GOOD SAMARITAN

The biblical parable of the Good Samaritan contains many ingredients of what may be regarded as the ideal moral response to emergency situations:

A man was going from Jerusalem to Jericho, and he fell among robbers, who stripped him and beat him, and departed, leaving him half dead. Now by chance a priest was going down that road; and when he saw him he passed by on the other side. So likewise a Levite, when he came to the place and saw him, passed by on the other side. But a Samaritan, as he journeyed, came to where he was; and when he saw him, he had compassion, and went to him and bound up his wounds, pouring on oil and wine; then he set him on his own beast and brought him next to an inn, and took care of him. And the next day he took out two denarii and gave them to the innkeeper, saying, "Take care of him; and whatever you spend, I will repay you when I come back." (Luke 10:29–37)

Source: Lickona, 1976, p. 270.

The issue of not assisting someone in distress is by no means a modern phenomenon; it was a matter of concern even in biblical times (see Box 9.2). Social psychologists have carried out many experiments in both field and laboratory to determine the factors influencing bystanders' responses to people who appear to be in distress (e.g., Darley and Batson, 1973; Latané and Darley, 1970). These studies reveal that if there are many bystanders, if someone else is perceived as more expert or as having more responsibility, if the situation is ambiguous, or if the person in distress is considered responsible for his or her own plight, then the observer is less likely to intervene. All these conditions diminish personal responsibility. But bystanders are not merely indifferent; they are beset by conflicting feelings and perceptions.

Developmental psychologists have addressed a similar issue, although employing less dramatic situations, in examining children's responses to the distress of another child. Exposure to models again proves to have a significant influence on the child's response. In one experiment (Sprafkin, Liebert, and Poulos, 1975), a television film was used as the modeling stimulus. First graders watched either a "Lassie" episode in which a boy risks his life to rescue the dog or a "Lassie" episode without a response-to-stress theme. Subsequently, each child was placed in a conflict situation in which he or she could come to the assistance of some distressed puppies, but at the cost of giving up a game involving a valuable prize. The children who viewed the altruistic "Lassie" episode gave more help to the puppies.

The role of the model's nurturance in the imitation of helping behavior has been explored in an ambitious field study conducted by Yarrow, Scott, and Waxler (1973). This investigation was particularly impressive because of its naturalistic features. An adult, who agreed to serve as the experimental model, acted as a caretaker to preschool children, spending a half-hour each day with the children for a two-week period. For half the children, she acted nurturantly, praising them and responding sympathetically and helpfully; for the remaining children, she acted aloof and detached, frequently ignoring their requests. In addition to varying the nurturance of the model, the experimenters also manipulated the degree of realism in the modeling situation. In one condition, the model used miniature reproductions (called dioramas) to illustrate altruistic behaviors in distress situations involving children, family, or animal figures. In another condition, in addition to displaying altruism with such reproductions, she responded with concern and offered assistance to an adult who entered the room and "accidentally" hurt herself. After two such modeling sessions, the children's responses to distress were tested using a variety of procedures, including a visit to a mother and her baby in which the child could help by picking up some toys the baby had dropped out of the crib or reaching for some other fallen objects. The experimenters reported that exposure to the helpful model was much more effective than mere use of dioramas in promoting help giving; this was especially true if the model was also nurturant.

The Yarrow investigation is consistent with the findings on generosity, suggesting that simply verbalizing altruistic behavior is not very effective with young children. Verbalization has to be accompanied by actual helping behavior if it is to have a substantial enduring effect. Furthermore, nurturance by a model does not enhance more abstract indicators of generosity such as a donation to charity (Grusec and Skubinski, 1970), but does heighten children's helping of a child in visible distress (Staub, 1971).

Empathy

One can be generous, supportive, and cooperative because these responses are encouraged and reinforced by the culture. But one can also engage in these same prosocial behaviors because of an understanding of other people's needs and feelings and because one shares in those feelings. The term *empathy* has been used to describe the process of social understanding and common emotional responses. In some theoretical treatments of empathy, the cognitive or social-comprehension aspect of empathy is stressed, while in other treatments the emotional aspect receives greater emphasis. But it appears that empathic responses involve the ability (1) to discriminate and label feelings in others; (2) to assume the perspective and role of another person; and (3) to experience and respond with feeling (N. Feshbach, 1978).

In one experimental approach to empathy, children were presented with a series of slides depicting happiness, sadness, fear, or anger (N. Feshbach, 1978). After each sequence, the child was asked how he or she felt. The number of times the child's reported affect matched the depicted emotion was the measure of empathy. Children scoring high on this measure of empathy were rated by their teachers as high in cooperation, and children scoring low in this measure were rated as high in competitiveness (Barnett, Matthews, and Howard, 1979; Marcus, Telleen, and Poke, 1979). Empathic children tend to be low in aggressiveness (N. Feshbach, 1978; Feshbach and Feshbach, 1969).

Situational factors also influence empathic responses. For example, higher empathy scores appear to be a function of the degree of similarity between the person depicted in the slide sequence and the child; boys respond with more empathy to slide sequences of boys, girls to girls. Even black children respond more to pictures of blacks, and white children to pictures of whites (Feshbach and Roe, 1968; Klein, 1970). Thus, it might be expected that children will be less cooperative and caring when interacting with other children of a different sex or race.

There have been a number of attempts at empathy training which demonstrate that this approach holds considerable promise for the development of prosocial behavior (Feshbach, 1979; Pitkänen-Pulkkinen, 1979; Staub, 1971). For example, Staub (1971) had children participate in training sessions in which they played the role of helper to an individual in need of aid. Girls with role-taking experience subsequently responded more frequently to cries of distress on a recording in an adjacent room than did girls without such experience, while boys with experimental training displayed more subsequent sharing than did boys with no role-playing experience.

Socialization and the Family

It has been indicated that children do not automatically behave in a moral, cooperative, and generous manner. These characteristics have to be acquired and reinforced through a process of socialization. There are a number of socializing agents in society, such as school, church, peers, and the mass media. We turn now to an examination of probably the most powerful socializing agent: the family. Families in which children are reared are very complex social systems, varying in size, stability, economic status, stress, misfortune, the personalities of and relationships between parents, openness of communication, and the practices used to train children. Since we cannot do justice to this complexity here, we will focus on one major source of family influence: child-rearing procedures.

It is useful to distinguish two related categories of child-rearing or socialization practices. The first encompasses broad characteristics or overall patterns of child-rearing activities, such as degree of warmth, control, or punitiveness. The second refers to the specific practices used to train certain behaviors; for example, the methods used to wean or toilet train the child, control aggression, inhibit sexuality, and so on. The broader patterns are obviously reflected in the more specific training practices, but to varying degrees and with varying relevance to the behavior being trained.

Child-Rearing Patterns

Society assigns parents the critical role of child care and child training. It is a parent's responsibility to ensure that the child is adequately fed, clothed, and sheltered. A parent is also responsible for the child's health and safety and may not neglect the child by leaving it unattended, isolated in a locked room, or subjected to comparably severe experiences. If a parent fails to meet these responsibilities, then society may remove a child from the parent's care. In addition, the culture expects much more from a parent than mere adherence to these basic responsibilities. A parent is expected to provide emotional security, guidance, and instruction, as well as to train the child to control bodily functions, act independently, and abide by the standards and values of the culture. While these responsibilities are enormous and although many parents are quite unprepared for them, they are assumed by parents when they decide to have a child.

There are many differences between parents' approaches to the task of child rearing. Some are warm and affectionate, others are cold and aloof; some are strict, others are permissive; some believe that the child should participate in decisions, others favor a more authoritarian style; some are anxious, others are assured; many are gentle, a few are cruel. Parents bring to their child-rearing role completely different personalities, values, and expectations. A basic theoretical and empirical question for the psychologist concerns the influence of all these factors on the personality development of the child.

Chapter 8's review of attachment and separation has indicated that extreme environments, in which the child does not experience the warmth and security of attachment, can have quite negative effects on development and adjustment. But there are significant variations within the less extreme, more normal range of child-rearing practices that also warrant attention. In assessing these child-rearing practices by interviewing parents or directly observing parent-child interactions, it has been found that many aspects of child rearing are interrelated and tend to cluster together. Thus, it is possible to describe the differences in child-rearing practices between families with reference to just a few basic characteristics. One such characteristic is degree of permissiveness versus strictness; another is degree of warmth and nurturance versus coldness and hostility (Becker, 1964). With just these two dimensions, a given child-rearing pattern could be described as permissive and warm, strict and warm, permissive and cold, or strict and cold.

Is it better for the child's development if parents are strict in their demands and discipline, or will the child have better psychological adjustment if parents are more permissive and less authoritarian in their behavior? Research has not provided a consistent or simple answer to such questions. It is known that the effects of both permissiveness and strictness are negative if the family environment tends to be cold and hostile. A hostile and permissive environment is likely to produce an aggressive and delinquent child, while a hostile-suppressive or restrictive family environment fosters children who are anxious and inhibited. In warm and nurturant family environments, the effects of permissiveness versus strictness are less clear. Several early studies (e.g., Baldwin, 1949; Watson, 1957) revealed that children raised in warm and reasonably permissive, democratic families that allowed the child freedom of choice tended to be friendly, assertive, and creative, whereas children raised in warm but strict and controlling homes tended to be conforming, low in curiosity, and well behaved.

However, the results of more recent work by Baumrind (1967, 1971, 1972) suggest that the exercise of strong parental controls may have more positive developmental consequences than a permissive approach. Baumrind divided a sample of nursery school children into three personality groups on the basis of observations of their behavior. Children in one group were described as competent, self-reliant, content, inquiring, and assertive. A second group of children was described as moderately competent and mature, but also some-what fearful, disoriented, and withdrawn. Finally, the least mature children formed a third group. They were highly dependent, fearful of novel situations, and displayed little self-control. Baumrind then assessed the child-rearing practices of the parents through interviews, home visits, and controlled laboratory observations. She found striking differences in the child-rearing procedures used by the parents in the three groups of children. Child-rearing practices among the mature, competent children were characterized by high levels of control and maturity demands (parental pressures to behave at intellectual and social levels congruent with the children's capacities). But control and demands were accompanied by a high degree of communication clarity; explanations and reasons were used to influence the children's behavior and feelings. The communication dimension most differentiated the parents of this mature group of children from the parents of children in the two other groups. The parents of the highly mature children were also the most nurturant, displaying warmth and involvement with their children. Baumrind's description of the parents of well-adjusted children is partially inconsistent with earlier data on the effects of permissiveness. Consistent with prior evidence, the "better" parents used reason and communicated openly with their children, but were higher in control than the permissive parents described in earlier studies. These data suggest that control is not necessarily associated with arbitrary or highly punitive discipline; one can be authoritative without being authoritarian.

In sum, it appears that children will thrive with considerable variation in strictness or permissiveness, provided that parents are nurturant, warm, use reason, take into account their children's feelings, and have expectations for their children that suit their developmental levels and capacities.

Specific Practices: Testing Some Psychoanalytic Hypotheses

As already suggested, broad characteristics of child rearing, such as parental warmth and permissiveness, are reflected in a wide range of training practices, such as how the parent weans the child away from bottle or breast, toilet trains, responds to aggression, and the like. Yet two parents similar in warmth and permissiveness may use very different strategies in weaning, toilet training, and control of aggression.

Psychoanalytic theory has a good deal to say about the effects of weaning, toilet training, and sexual stimulation and inhibition, and there has been a reasonable amount of research examining the validity of these psychoanalytic hypotheses. Much of this research has made use of cross-cultural studies. Anthropological observations and research have shown that cultures vary in age of weaning, severity of toilet training, age of separation from caretaker, and other significant child-rearing factors. Data available in cross-cultural research files frequently permit the assessment of both a culture's personality traits and its child-rearing practices. One can thus determine the relationship between these specific cross-cultural variations in child-rearing practices and some personality dimension of the children and adults under investigation. An analogous method, used in studying differences in child-rearing practices between parents *within* a culture, links these differences to personality differences among the offspring.

The oral period.   Psychoanalytic theory places great importance on the events that occur during the oral period, particularly the extent of gratification or frustration of oral impulses. It is believed that basic attitudes of optimism and pessimism are rooted in an infant's oral frustration or gratification. Some psychoanalysts, in fact, believe that there is an *oral personality:* a passive, dependent individual for whom oral activities like drinking and smoking are still very pleasurable. But evidence for the concept of an oral personality type is mixed (Barnes, 1952; Wolowitz, 1964), and efforts to link oral personality characteristics to such variables as age of weaning and abrupt versus gradual weaning have generally met with negative outcomes (Sears, Maccoby, and Levin, 1957; Sewell and Mussen, 1952).

It may be that psychoanalytic hypotheses regarding oral satisfaction and frustration are entirely invalid or that the effects are very weak. But one might also contend that the interrelations are complex and that more extensive analyses are required. The feeding situation prior to weaning involves at least four different processes or reinforcements. First, there is satisfaction of the child's hunger and thirst. Second, different kinds of satisfaction are derived from sucking. There is evidence of both an innate sucking drive that has no connection with nutritive intake and a learned sucking drive that is acquired through conditioning during the course of feeding (Yarrow, 1954). Third, the child is typically held during feeding, an action facilitating the development of strong attachment to the caretaker. Finally, the child is placed in a highly dependent relationship. Some of these components of the feeding situation might have opposite implications for the development of security and independence, since satisfaction of basic needs can also give rise to strong feelings of dependence on the caregiver. Thus, one can understand the results of a cross-cultural investigation indicating that both early and late weaning are associated with a lesser degree of emotional disturbance (Whiting, 1954). This is probably because early weaning separates the child before it develops a strong dependency on the caretaker, while late weaning takes place when the child is sufficiently mature and secure to cope with separation from the mother and disruption of its dependent attachment.

The anal period. The data on toilet training are consistent with some expectations based on psychoanalytic theory, but not with others. According to psychoanalytic theory, frustration of anal impulses facilitates the development of a constellation of personality traits concerning overcontrol of impulses. Such traits include orderliness, stinginess (the retention of money), punctuality, obstinacy (the retention of ideas), and conscientiousness. A number of personality studies have indeed found many of these traits to be interrelated, lending credence to the concept of an anal character type (Barnes, 1952; Hetherington and Brackbill, 1963; Stagner, Lawson, and Moffitt, 1955). However, the results of studies attempting to link anal traits to aspects of toilet training have been largely negative. What does appear to be the case is that anal character traits in the child are related to similar character traits in the parents (Beloff, 1957; Hetherington and Brackbill, 1963). Parents who are concerned with orderliness may reinforce behaviors related to orderliness, including toilet-related activities. Thus, even if a relationship were found between toilet-training practices and personality traits, the relationship would not necessarily be causal. Rather, the two might be related because both are linked with a parental emphasis on cleanliness and order. Parental reinforcement and modeling of the parents appear to be much better explanations of the development of anal traits than the psychoanalytic hypothesis.

The phallic-genital period. It would appear that the primary value of psychoanalytic hypotheses about psychosexual socialization has been the stimulation of research. However, before we completely dismiss psychoanalytic hypotheses, it is important to keep in mind that scattered empirical findings are consistent with some of the predictions derived from psychoanalytic theory (see Whiting and Child, 1953). For example, one study (Whiting, Kluckhohn, and Anthony, 1958) determined the extent to which fifty-five primitive societies had male initiation rites, such as painful hazing, genital operations, and seclusion from women. In addition, the investigators assessed mother-child sleeping arrangements and the length of sexual taboos restricting the mother following the birth of a child. These taboos are often most strict in nomadic tribes, for the obvious functional reason that mobility would be greatly hampered if any family had a number of smaller children. The investigators reasoned that mother-son sleeping in proximity and long postpartum sexual taboos should intensify incestuous impulses between mother and son. The function of male initiation rites would then be to inhibit these impulses directed toward the mother and ensure identification with the adult males of the society. These investigators reported that almost every society with close mother-child sleeping arrangements and a long postpartum sexual taboo had a male initiation rite, whereas almost all societies without male rites had alternative mother-child sleeping arrangements and practically no postpartum sexual restrictions. These findings are thus consistent with psychoanalytically based predictions.

It would be premature, then, to conclude that psychoanalytic hypotheses concerning the effects of early socialization practices on subsequent personality development are entirely invalid. However, it is also evident that difficult methodological problems arise in attempting to verify either these hypotheses or any theoretical position that claims a causal link between early socialization and later personality patterns. Furthermore, socialization does not end in early childhood; people are continuously involved in educating, training, and disciplining the child and the young adult. Thus, parents and other socializing agents may be maintaining or extinguishing behaviors from early childhood through adolescence, thereby producing continuities or discontinuities between the effects of early socialization and adult personality.

Observations of Parent-Child Interactions

There has been a great deal of research interest in recent years in direct observations of parent-child interactions as a means of understanding the process of socialization. The observations may be of parental responses to an infant's smile (Gewirtz, 1965), the reinforcement patterns displayed by mothers when instructing their children (Feshbach, 1973), or more complex sequences of actions and reactions between parents and children. For example, complex parent-child interactions have been observed regarding aggressive behaviors. A number of studies indicate that children high in aggression tend to be raised in households in which the parents use a good deal of physical punishment and related coercive behaviors in disciplining the child (Eron, Walder, and Lefkowitz, 1971; Feshbach, 1970). There are several possible interpretations of this relationship:

1. Parental coercion is caused by the child's aggression; that is, the child's disobedient, aggressive behavior elicits parental use of strong coercive punishments as a means of control.
2. Parental coercion causes the child to behave aggressively.
3. Parents and child are locked in a relationship that tends to reinforce or escalate both parental coercion and the child's aggression. A child's aggression may elicit from the parents a highly punitive coercive reaction that in turn stimulates further aggression by the child, which leads to more severe punishment, and so on until one of the two sides yields.
4. Both coercive, physical punishment and the child's aggression are caused by a third factor, such as a common genetic inheritance or social norms and frustrations that encourage violence in both adults and children.

Home observations of aggressive children and their parents provide some data on this issue that are consistent with the third interpretation. A parent's coercive response to a child's aggressive act tended to escalate the child's aggressive pattern, which in turn escalated the level of parental punishment (Patterson, 1979).

One of the consequences of observational procedures has been increasing recognition of the role of the child, even the infant, in influencing the behavior of the parent (Bell, 1968). Infants vary in activity level and other temperamental characteristics. They also differ in their responses to parental handling and play. By means of smiles, cries, and attention, the infant can reinforce some parental behaviors and discourage others. This is not to say that the infant has the same power over the parent as the parent has over the infant; parental control over reinforcers and the environment is far greater than comparable control available to the child. Nevertheless, direct observation of the socialization process has revealed that the child is not a helpless, passive creature. Rather, the child selects and influences its environment, including the behavior of the parents.

Summary   Several aspects of the socialization of the child have been addressed in this chapter, with particular attention to moral development and prosocial behaviors. Different theoretical approaches to moral development are provided by psychoanalytic theory, Piaget's cognitive theory, and social learning theory. The distinctive characteristics of each theory are reflected in their different emphases: psychoanalysis focusing on the origins of guilt; cognitive theory, on the thought processes and level of understanding determining moral judgments; and social learning theory, on the factors influencing moral behavior.

In comparison to the work on moral development, research and theory concerned with such positive or prosocial behaviors as cooperation, generosity, and altruism have given more attention to possible biological antecedents. Prosocial behaviors have been shown to be as fundamental to infrahuman behavior as competitive and antisocial behaviors. Humans have a similar capacity for positive social interactions, in which learning plays a significant role. The frequency and strength of these behaviors vary with cultural background, with reinforcement history, and with exposure to models. Parental child-rearing practices play an important role in the development of prosocial behaviors and other personality characteristics. The complexity of family influences makes it difficult to establish simple cause-and-effect relationships between aspects of child rearing and personality development.

Specific Points

1. There is little empirical support for the psychoanalytic view that resolution of the Oedipal conflict through identification with the same-sex parent plays a major role in moral development.
2. Piaget's theory of stages of cognitive development has had a major influence on research in moral development.
3. Before about the age of seven, children tend to judge acts as "bad" on the basis of negative consequences rather than on the basis of intention and tend to be more absolute in their moral judgments, disregarding surrounding circumstances.
4. The weak intercorrelations between different measures of moral judgments and the modifiability of moral judgments are inconsistent with the hypothesis of discrete stages of moral development. But cross-cultural studies based on Kohlberg's moral-dilemmas test reflect a similar developmental pattern, consistent with Kohlberg's postulated six stages, in different cultures.

5. Reward and punishment, exposure to models, and verbalization of moral rules and prohibitions are processes that social learning theorists suggest are relevant to moral behavior.

6. The Hartshorne and May studies of the degree of consistency among different measures of honesty are frequently cited as evidence that honesty is situationally determined rather than a general trait reflected in many kinds of situations. However, reanalyses of these data have provided more evidence of consistency or generality than was initially reported.

7. Sociobiologists (citing evidence of altruistic behavior among infrahuman species) have suggested that there is a genetic basis for human altruism. They argue that acts of altruism have evolved because, despite the individual sacrifices involved, the survival of one genetic pool is facilitated.

8. Cooperative behavior in children varies significantly with cultural background and situational factors.

9. Children's generosity is markedly enhanced by exposure to models displaying generosity. Advocacy of generosity by the model is less effective than an actual display of generous behavior. Similar findings have been obtained in studies of helping behavior in response to people in distress.

10. Empathy is facilitated by situational factors such as similarity between people. Empathy also has some of the characteristics of a personality trait, in that children high in empathy tend to be more cooperative and less competitive and aggressive than children low in empathy.

11. The effects of parental permissiveness versus strictness depend on the degree of parental warmth and the clarity of parental communications to the child.

12. Psychoanalytic hypotheses regarding the personality effects of weaning and toilet training have received little confirmation. However, there are scattered empirical findings consistent with some predictions derived from the psychoanalytic theory of psychosexual development.

13. Parental use of physical aggression to punish a child's aggressive behavior is likely to be counterproductive and to exaggerate rather than reduce the child's aggressive behaviors.

Thought Questions

1. Why aren't moral beliefs and moral understanding more closely related to actual moral behaviors?

2. Is teaching children to be cooperative and generous likely to handicap them if the culture at large is highly competitive and self-oriented?

3. If you were fated to have an accident and to suffer injuries that would require the assistance of other people, in which part of the United States or in which country would you prefer that this accident happen? Why?

4. Is there a "best way" to raise children, a set of socialization practices that all parents should use? What variations from these child-rearing practices would you allow?

The Self and Development Through the Life Span

10 We begin this chapter with a detailed discussion of the concept of the *self*. As we will see, the self provides a link between the socialization experiences and personality structure of the young child and the personality changes and development that continue through adolescence, into adulthood and old age. After a review of the developmental emergence of the self, the theoretical properties of the self are considered. These properties of the self have implications for the personality processes and dimensions to be considered in subsequent chapters, as well as for the personality development that takes place during the course of the life span, a principal concern of this chapter.

Following the discussion of the self, we consider personality development in adolescence (a period marked by substantial changes in the self), adulthood, and old age. Attention is directed to the particular problems and issues that confront most people during maturity and old age and to how resolving these problems and issues can contribute to personality change and growth.

The Self

The idea of the self is fundamental to the history of human thought. The self and the related constructs of self-concept and self-esteem are central to phenomenological theories of personality and to psychodynamic theories like those of Adler, Horney, and Sullivan. Within psychoanalytic theory, the examination of *object relations* (cf. Chapter 5) has led to greater emphasis on the self. Hans Kohut (1971, 1977), a leading contemporary psychoanalyst, has elaborated on and expanded the construct of the self, to propose that disturbances in the development of the self underlie such forms of psychopathology as criminal behavior, alcoholism, and drug addiction. Even social learning theorists acknowledge the significance of processes related to the self, such as the monitoring of one's own behavior, self-evaluation, and perception of self-efficacy (Bandura, 1977a). Yet, despite the theoretical significance of the concept of the self, it remains elusive and ill defined.

Sometimes the term *self* is used as an *object,* in which case an individual is depicted as having knowledge of and evaluating the self-as-object in much the same way one has knowledge of and evaluates another person. One can like and dislike another person; one can like and dislike oneself. We entertain beliefs about and concepts of other people, such as "She's bright," "He's ambitious," "The instructor is fair." Similarly, one has such beliefs about oneself. In this sense, the self becomes the object of one's attitudes, beliefs, and feelings.

Another usage of the self is as an *agent* or *process;* that is, as a mechanism that does something. Thus, the self is said to influence perception and judgment and to screen out threatening or inconsistent information. Related to this usage is the notion of the self as an organized structure or personality component, much like the psychoanalytic concept of the ego. And, as we indicated in the chapter on personality theories, there are even broader usages of self—for example, in the motive for self-actualization and the search for self-identity.

One major objective of personality theory and research is providing a clearer, more precise definition of the self and the self-concept. Better definitions would help improve measuring procedures that are now only barely satisfactory (Wylie, 1974) and also lead to more agreement about the psychological properties of the self. In the meantime, we can review the process of development of the self and examine some of the principal ways in which the self is significant for an understanding of personality, while recognizing that there are ambiguities in how the self is defined and serious difficulties in our methods of assessment. In some overviews of the field of personality, very little attention is given to the self because of these ambiguities and measurement problems. However, in our view, the concept of the self is critical to any comprehensive theory of personality development and function. The self provides a key to much of human motivation, social understanding, and personality disturbances. Basic to the personality development of both the child and the adult are changes in the self.

Beginnings of the Self: Body Image

Our sense of self as a distinct body occupying a specific location in space is so strongly ingrained that we tend to accept it as a given. However, observations of infant behavior indicate that the neonate must learn to know itself. The symptoms of some brain-damaged and emotionally disturbed patients who feel that all or part of their bodies is foreign to them indicate that this knowledge can be seriously disrupted. The infant initially acts as if parts of its body were no different from other objects in the visual field. Through feedback from its movements, from external stimuli impinging on parts of its body, and from its own exploration and touching, the infant learns that it has an independent physical structure, separate from its mother and other figures in its environment. The perception of an integrated, organized physical structure, called one's *body image,* is an important step in the development of the self. This image involves perceptions of the body's shape and size, boundaries, and interconnectedness of parts. The young child also learns that the body is a stable structure that has continuity over time despite developmental changes in physique. In its early months, the infant acts as if objects do not exist when they are hidden from sight. By around eight months of age, the infant has developed the ability to preserve the memory of objects that are no longer present, a capacity Piaget calls *object permanence.* It is likely that this same capacity applies to the self-as-object (Lewis and Brooks, 1975).

Although the child, by the end of its first year, may have acquired a sense of *self-permanence,* the body image is far from complete. For example, the child does not yet have a clear, stable conception of its own gender. More learning about the self must take place before the child has a full understanding of its sex identity and realizes that boys cannot be transformed into girls and vice-versa simply by changing activity or clothing (Gerardo and Bohan, 1971; Kohlberg, 1966). Further, it is not until the infant is about eighteen months old that it gives evidence of recognizing a mirror image or a picture of itself (Amsterdam, 1972; Lewis and Brooks, 1975).

Do Infrahumans Have a Self-Concept?

Most of us have seen a dog staring at, sometimes snarling at, and approaching a reflection of itself. For most animals, seeing their own image in a mirror acts as a social stimulus. But does the dog recognize itself or does the reflection simply signal a potential companion or threat? This question is of interest for a number of reasons. Apart from curiosity about the level of animals' understanding, research on self-recognition in animals provides some insight into the evolutionary significance of this skill, into the level and kinds of cognitive competence that the self-recognition skill requires, and into the kinds of learning experiences that determine the development of self-recognition. In addition, work with animals fosters the use of techniques that are not dependent on verbal responses and that may therefore be suitable for use with preverbal children (e.g., Lewis and Brooks, 1975).

Two-year-old babies recognize their images in a mirror; among infrahumans, only chimpanzees appear to exhibit similar recognition. (left—© Elizabeth Crews; above—Ylla/Rapho-Photo Researchers, Inc.)

The evidence indicates that dogs and almost all other infrahumans do not recognize themselves. However, Gallup (1970, 1975, 1979), in a series of clever experiments, has shown that the chimpanzee does have this capacity. Gallup exposed chimpanzees to a full-length mirror for ten consecutive days in a small cage. It was observed that over this period of time the number of self-directed responses increased (see Fig. 10.1). These behaviors included grooming parts of the body while watching the results, guiding fingers in the mirror, and picking at teeth with the aid of the mirror. Describing one chimp, Gallup (1975, p. 324) said, "Marge used the mirror to play with and inspect the bottom of her feet; she also looked at herself upside down in the mirror while suspended by her feet from the top of the cage; . . . she was also observed to stuff celery leaves up her nose using the mirror for purposes of visually guiding the stems into each nostril."

Then the researchers devised a further test of self-recognition. The chimps were anesthetized and marks were placed over their eyebrows and

Figure 10.1   Total number of time-sampled responses toward the self through the mirror reflection over days. (Gallup, 1975, p. 323. Used by permission.)

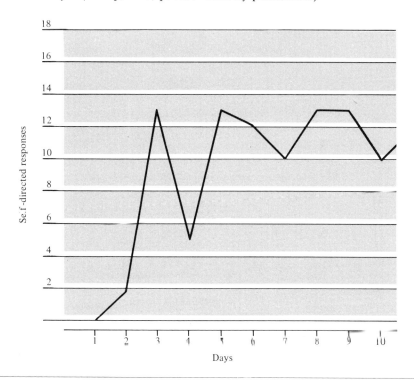

behind their ears, areas the chimps could not directly observe. The mirror was temporarily removed from the room, and baseline data regarding their attempts to touch these areas were recorded. Figure 10.2 shows the number of touch attempts both before and after reintroduction of the mirror. The data clearly suggest that chimps do recognize themselves, or are self-aware, for their attempts to touch the marks increased when they viewed themselves. Citing further evidence for this argument, Gallup noted that chimpanzees with no prior mirror experience did not direct behavior to the marks when first exposed to the mirror (Fig. 10.2). That is, the other chimpanzees appeared to have remembered what they looked like and to have responded to the marks because they noticed changes in their appearance.

An analogous procedure incorporated in a study of human infants clearly reveals the role of developmental influences on this form of self-recognition (Lewis and Brooks-Gunn, 1979). Heavy rouge was applied to the noses of ninety-six infants, ranging in age from nine months to twenty-four months.

Figure 10.2   Number of mark-directed responses made by experimental animals before being exposed to a mirror and by experimental and control animals during the test of self-recognition; controls made no responses. (Gallup, 1975, p. 326. Used by permission.)

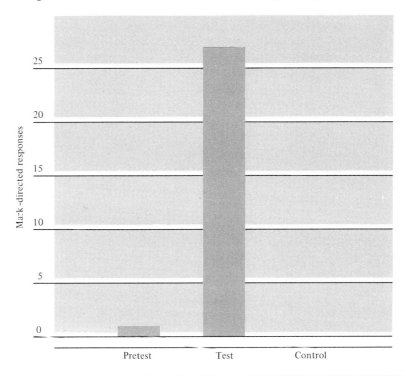

The infants' actions when exposed to a mirror were observed prior to and after the application of rouge. Figure 10.3 indicates the difference between the percentage of infants in each age group who engaged in directed behavior in the rouge condition and the percentage who attempted to touch their noses in the no-rouge condition. While the nine- and twelve-month-old infants were unresponsive to the rouge condition, a dramatic change in responses, indicative of self-recognition, occurred during the latter half of the infants' second year.

Many sociologists have proposed a "looking-glass" concept of self, in which self-concept arises out of social interaction with others. Perhaps the social environment provides information about the self, acting as a mirror for our social selves. While one must be cautious in drawing an analogy between a social and a physical mirror, the chimpanzee and infant findings encourage one to look to social experience as an important contributor to self-concept in humans.

Figure 10.3   Nose-directed behavior: Percentage difference between the no-rouge and rouge conditions by age. (Lewis & Brooks-Gunn, 1979, p. 41. Used by permission.)

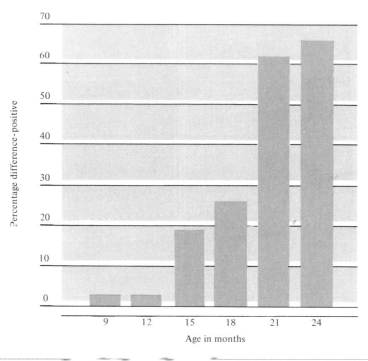

Development of Self-Concept

The physical self is one component of the child's emerging sense of identity. It becomes amplified, enriched by, and integrated with a *psychological self.* By psychological self, we mean those feelings, attitudes, desires, judgments, and behaviors that the individual considers to be characteristic of himself or herself. The psychological aspects of the self are as important a part of one's identity as the physical aspects. Consider what happens when one behaves in a way that is very different from one's typical pattern—for example, a sudden outburst of rage and profanity in a man who sees himself as calm, rational, and well spoken. He might say, "This isn't like me," "Something must have come over me," "I wasn't myself." If these behaviors persist, the person may change his self-concept and integrate these new feelings and behaviors into the conception of his personality. However, this integration is not easily accomplished, and the individual may feel that he is beset by strange, incomprehensible feelings, even that he is going crazy. Alternatively, he may see himself as possessed by demons or controlled by alien forces. This kind of belief system is referred to as *paranoid* thinking. What is important here in terms of the development and dynamics of personality is that psychological attributes are an essential part of the self-concept. We learn to recognize and to count on our psychological selves in much the same way we learn to recognize and count on our physical selves.

The psychological self, like the body image or physical self, has to be acquired. The physical self provides the frame of reference for the psychological attributes that the child sees as characteristic of itself. The body image of a particular face, body, and size becomes a self with such qualities as stupid or smart, careful or careless, strong or weak. Together they constitute the self-concept. The development of language very likely plays a role in this process. Terms like *me* and *I* probably facilitate the organization of traits attributed to the self. And the child's ability to understand and apply self-descriptive labels like "cute," "sweet," and "chip off the old block" is probably also relevant to the formation of the self-concept.

There are individual differences in the accuracy of the self-perceptions that constitute the self-concept. Some children (and adults) exaggerate their failings and underestimate their competencies; others may have an unwarranted positive view of their attributes. The *self-concept* refers to how we see ourselves, not to how we really are. As the poet Robert Burns so aptly stated, "Would that God the giftie gie us to see ourselves as others see us."

Self-concept and self-esteem.   Neither children nor adults feel neutral about these self-characteristics. Positive and negative values are placed on particular attributes that we see in others and in ourselves. It's good to be tall (but not too tall), attractive, strong, intelligent, and socially skillful, and it's bad to be unathletic, shy, or poor. The evaluations we place on these self-attributes contribute to our feelings of self-esteem. It thus becomes evident that self-esteem is closely related to and depends on the self-concept, but self-esteem is not the same as self-concept. We can have beliefs about ourselves that are important elements in our self-concept but that do not affect the value we place on ourselves (self-esteem). For example, one may perceive oneself as introverted or emotionally expressive without feeling particularly good or bad about that self-perception. In a study of sixth-grade children, McGuire and Padawer-Singer (1976) found that only a minimal part of the self-concept involved self-evaluative responses such as "I am smart" or "I am a nice person." The types of self-descriptions given by children in response to the question "Tell us about yourself" are enumerated in Table 10.1. The self-descriptions were consistent with the authors' hypothesis that an especially important determinant of self-concept is distinctiveness. Thus, children born in cities other than the one in which their school was located, and especially in foreign countries, were much more likely to mention their birthplace in describing themselves than were children who were native to the community. McGuire and Padawer-Singer also hypothesized that momentary and situational factors, as well as more stable characteristics and enduring values, will affect the self-concept.

Table 10.1 Categorization of sixth graders' responses to "tell us about yourself"

Category	Percentage of children	Category	Percentage of children
Own activities		*Miscellaneous*	5
Hobbies, amusements	48	*Demographic*	
Sports	43	Age, birthdate	25
Daily schedule	43	Name	19
Places lived	5	Residence	16
Skills	8	Birthplace	11
TV	10	Health	11
Books	6	Sex	10
Jobs	3	Race, ethnic	5
Miscellaneous experiences	6	Religion	3
Significant others		*Self-evaluation*	
Family	38	Moral	20
Friends	43	Physical	15
Pets	22	Intellectual	10
Teachers	16	Emotional	2
Public figures	0	*Physical characteristics*	
Attitudes		Hair color	13
Likes and dislikes	52	Weight	11
Vocational	18	Height	10
Hopes and desires	12	Eye color	11
School (excluding teachers)	71		

Source: McGuire and Padawer-Singer, 1976, p. 748. Adapted by permission.

Self-esteem. While self-concept refers to a complex, multifaceted organization of percepts regarding oneself, *self-esteem* usually connotes a generalized, overall attitude toward oneself. The relationship between overall self-esteem—the degree of high or low regard in which one holds oneself—and the positive and negative values placed on specific components of the self-concept remains an interesting and unresolved issue. Some individuals' view of their academic skills might be the most important contributor to self-esteem while for others, it might be perceived popularity. However, there is a connection between one's appraisal of specific self-attributes and one's overall self-esteem. Studies have shown that the sum of an individual's evaluations of specific attributes—school performance, athletic skills, social interactions, physical attractiveness, and so on—is predictive of the person's overall sense of self-esteem (Coopersmith, 1967).

The experience of being accepted by significant others is also related to overall self-esteem; it may well be the most important factor in self-esteem, as Carl Rogers has proposed. In an extensive study of the antecedents of self-esteem in a group of boys, aged ten to twelve, Coopersmith (1967) found that parents of boys with high self-esteem conveyed total or nearly total acceptance of their children. Other child-rearing factors linked to the boys' self-esteem were "clearly defined and enforced limits, and the respect and latitude for individual acts that exist within the defined limits" (p. 236). Although there are a number of methodological problems with this study (Wylie, 1979, p. 348), the data make intuitive sense.

Self-esteem is, in all likelihood, a function of the regard in which you are held by people you care about. People vary in the degree to which their overall self-esteem is affected by immediate experiences. Some people are highly vulnerable to a minor social slight or to an occasional failure or frustration; others maintain their sense of assurance and positive self-regard in the face of extreme insult and even repeated failure. We need to know more about the antecedents of self-esteem vulnerability, a facet of self-esteem that has important clinical implications for one's emotional adjustment.

Functions of the Self-Concept

The development of self and self-concept is critical for an understanding of human personality; all personality theories eventually have to concern themselves with the psychological processes that stem from the development of the self.

Identity

We have already considered how body image and the psychological self contribute to the child's development of a sense of *identity,* of what is part of him or her and what is alien or part of the environment. In fact, one's sense of identity is generally taken for granted until it becomes disrupted as in cases of amnesia or during adolescence when one must cope with new and intense feelings. The establishment of identity takes place at different levels during the course of development. Infants and toddlers manifest a sense of *physical* identity as they begin to refer to pictures of themselves with their own names during the second year, and as the use of personal pronouns like *me* and *I* becomes commonplace during the third year (Ames, 1952; Lewis and Brooks-Gunn, 1979). And adolescents are manifesting a concern with their *psychological* identity whenever they question who they are and what they will become (Erikson, 1959).

The self-concept and the identity it provides is *time binding;* it helps provide continuity between the past, the present, and the future. Without a sense of identity, the person we were yesterday would be a stranger to us today. The self-concept also links the present and the future in that we can project ourselves into the future, imagining ourselves when older, in different roles and circumstances.

Autonomy and Pride

At some point during the child's second year, it leaves the period of infancy and becomes a toddler. At this point the child shows increased mastery over its body movements, walking, running, jumping, and, if American, eating with utensils and riding a tricycle. The child increasingly attempts to assert itself, to do things for and by itself. As the child smears food over its face and a spoonful of cereal finds its way onto the toddler's neck and clothes, the overburdened parent may find it easier to feed the child, but the toddler will typically insist on feeding itself. According to Erikson (cf. Chapter 5), it is in the stage characterized by striving for *autonomy.* In asserting itself, the child will begin to refuse parental commands and offers of assistance. This expression of negativism has led to the exaggerated but descriptive characterization of this period as "the terrible twos."

The child's efforts at mastery and independence, as well as its negativistic behavior, are likely consequences of its striving to be an independent agent. Parents are not likely to encourage the child to say "no" or to attempt risky tasks that are beyond its competence. Rather, the child's negativism and autonomy appear to be *emergent* behaviors; that is, they arise or emerge as a consequence of some new feature in the child's development. In this case, the new feature is very likely the sense of identity or the self-concept. When the child encounters success, it experiences *pride.* In Chapter 16, we will see that the experience of pride depends on the attribution of success to one's own efforts or abilities rather than to someone else's (Weiner, Russell, and Lerman, 1979). In brief, pride presupposes a self-concept; this affect therefore will not be experienced by infrahumans, except perhaps chimpanzees.

A study of age differences in the response to success and failure reflects different developmental trends in the appearance of self-evaluative reactions to failure or success (Ruble, Parsons, and Ross, 1976). Children in three age groups—six, eight, and ten to eleven years—were given a matching task that contained items of varying difficulty. Regardless of performance, the children were told they had succeeded or failed on the task. (To reduce any possible negative effects of failure, all children were given a success experience following completion of the experiment.) While all groups responded with positive feelings to the success experience, only the two older groups reported feeling badly following the failure. It would appear that, at age six, the process of making self-evaluations of one's stable ability following failure has not yet crystallized.

Emergent Motivation and the Self

Pride and shame are both emotions with important motivational consequences. We engage in behaviors and seek situations that will lead to pride and avoid shame. More generally, we seek to maximize feelings of self-esteem and to minimize threats to our self-esteem. Of course, there are many ways in which self-esteem can be enhanced or threatened, depending on the particular culture and on one's personal values and competencies. One can achieve self-esteem through financial success, through fame, through popularity, through mastery of a difficult task, through social dedication, and so on. How we maintain and enhance self-esteem is very much influenced by learning, but the need for self-esteem is a consequence of the emergent development of the self-concept.

The child's acquisition of a self-concept adds new motivation to behavior. Struggles between parent and child arise not merely because of frustrated gratification, but also because of frustration of the child's autonomy. In a sense, there is a conflict of will between parent and child. It is not, for example, the forbidden ice cream or television program that may be important to the child, but rather the ability to assert himself or herself. Autonomy conflicts are, of course, not restricted to young children; they are common in adult interpersonal relationships as well. A student may resent parental pressure to pursue graduate studies in a particular area, not necessarily because the student's personal preferences differ, but because the decision is not self-determined (see Chapter 17).

Self-Involvement and the Defense of Self

People have varying degrees of self-involvement in their everyday tasks and activities. They can be deeply involved in an activity, say, a political election, without being self-involved. That is, their evaluation of themselves (their self-esteem) is unaffected by the positive or negative outcome of the activity. Tasks differ in the degree to which self-involvement is engaged; academic examinations may elicit more self-involvement than a physical activity. There are also individual differences in extent of self-involvement in a particular task. Some people may feel disappointed when they do poorly on an examination, but do not devalue themselves, while others not only feel badly but also feel less worthy as a result of their performance.

Self-involvement in a task will often call into play such defensive behaviors as repression and rationalization, to ward off the painful feelings of lowered self-esteem. In addition, preoccupation with self interferes with task-relevant, problem-solving behavior and is especially apparent in highly anxious individuals (Sarason et al, 1960). Parents sometimes foster self-involvement in their children without intending to, by making general criticisms of the child like "You're bad" or "You're stupid" whenever the child errs, instead of offering specific criticisms like "That was a wrong thing to do, because. . . ."

Frame of Reference

In addition to introducing major motivational changes in the child's life, the development of the self-concept also leads to profound cognitive changes. First, the toddler and the preschooler are highly *egocentric,* as Piaget has demonstrated; young children assume that other people see the world as they do. The child's egocentricity has been cleverly demonstrated in experiments in which children are presented with three mountains of different heights placed in ascending order so that the tallest one is farthest away. Another person is also present in the room but is situated so that the stimulus is different: the tallest mountain blocks view of the others (Flavell et al., 1968). When asked to describe how the mountains look to the other person, the young child cannot assume the other's perspective. A similar phenomenon holds true for perception of social events. For example, kindergarten children tend to assume that other people have the same information they have; they frequently make this assumption even when a person is a newcomer and hasn't been exposed to conversations and information the child has heard.

While developmental changes occur in the child's ability to assume another person's perspective, important elements of egocentricity or self-centeredness continue even in adulthood. Thus, most of us find it quite difficult to see another person's point of view and understand their feelings when we are in sharp conflict with them. In addition, self-centeredness continues to operate in other, possibly more profound, ways. The self-concept—our body and psychological image—is a relatively constant point in the child's or adult's world, present in many different situations. Hence, it functions as a reference point or scale against which the person evaluates elements in the environment. For example, judgments of how tall, how attractive, how courageous, or how emotionally disturbed other people are can be influenced by how tall, attractive, courageous, and emotionally disturbed we see ourselves.

Although components of the self-concept may serve as relatively stable reference points, other components of the self-concept are modifiable and can be affected by situational circumstances (McGuire and Padawer-Singer, 1976). An experiment illustrating this effect was carried out with male undergraduate students who had applied for a very attractive summer job (Morse and Gergen, 1970). The students were interviewed in the presence of another presumed applicant for the position who was actually a confederate of the experimenter. For half the interviews, the confederate was smartly dressed, well groomed, and impressed one as being an assured, suave individual. For the other half, the confederate was dressed in a sloppy, bedraggled manner— no socks, an old sweat shirt, and torn pants—and seemed confused and ill-mannered. Measures of self-concept were obtained from the subjects as part of the application procedure. Subjects paired with the "Mr. Clean" confederate were much more likely to evaluate themselves as sloppy and inferior than subjects paired with the "Mr. Dirty" applicant. Thus, there is a constant dynamic interplay between one's self-concept and one's perception of others.

The self-concept acts as a frame of reference by which we measure others in the environment; at the same time, as our perception of others changes, so does our self-concept.

Self-Consistency

How we perceive ourselves shapes our judgments and behaviors through still another psychological mechanism: the motivation for self-consistency. Psychologists have found that inconsistencies in one's beliefs or between one's beliefs and behavior are a source of tension and discomfort (Heider, 1958). People are motivated to resolve such inconsistencies and to maintain consistency. For example, a miserly individual who sees himself as very generous can maintain consistency between his behavior and his self-image by perceiving himself as very poor; by exaggerating the significance of any pittance given to charity; by believing that people will be corrupted by gifts; by viewing others as exceptionally greedy and demanding of his resources; and so on. The motivation for cognitive consistency appears to be quite pervasive and is central to a number of personality and social psychological theories (Festinger, 1957; Heider, 1958). Although the development of this motivation has not been systematically studied, the motivations for consistency probably become stronger with developmental changes in the level of cognitive functioning. Inconsistencies have to be understood before one can be concerned about them. In addition, the motivation for consistency is probably influenced by social learning inasmuch as children are encouraged to be logical and consistent.

The motivation for self-consistency is not the same as the motivation to maintain self-esteem, although the two frequently overlap. One important difference is that efforts to maintain consistency may apply to negative self-evaluations. Several decades ago, Lecky (1945) proposed that an important factor governing socially maladaptive behavioral symptoms in children was their tendency to act consistently with a negative self-image. Thus, children who see themselves as poor spellers or stutterers may spell poorly or stutter to maintain consistency with their self-images. Similarly, children who believe themselves to be "bad" may behave delinquently in accordance with their self-concepts, perhaps without being conscious at all of the process. Therapies based on Lecky's approach attempt to help the child become aware of these maladaptive efforts to maintain consistency and, in addition, to help the child modify a negative self-concept.

The Changing Self: Adolescence

Adolescence is a period of transition; the adolescent is in the process of moving from the status of child to the status of adult. It is a period of development marked by profound physical, psychological, and social changes. At the core of this transition is the search for a stable self and a sense of identity (Erikson, 1968). Physical changes in sexuality and body size are often rapid and dramatic; though welcome, they can nevertheless be disquieting until they are fully incorporated in the adolescent's altered body image. At the same time, adolescence brings with it a new social role, with increased independence, choice, and responsibilities. This new role is in fact a reflection of society's recognition of: (1) the psychological development that has taken place when the individual enters adolescence; (2) the adolescent's increased physical and cognitive powers; and (3) the fact that the adolescent has entered a higher level of cognitive and moral development, and can see situations in their full complexity (Elkind, 1970; Kohlberg, 1969b).

These changes in the physical, social, and psychological spheres affect and upset the self-concept and tend to produce a state of uncertainty in the adolescent as to his or her true self. "Who am I?" "What can I do?" "What do I really want?" are questions with which the adolescent is suddenly confronted. Much of adolescent behavior can be understood as efforts to resolve these questions. However, it must be emphasized that the degree of disruption entailed by the changing self-concept, the amount of emotional turmoil experienced by the adolescent, and the extremeness of behaviors are strongly influenced by cultural and familial factors. While adolescence is frequently described as a period of *Sturm and Drang* (the German equivalent of "storm and stress"), this does not have to be the case. Social variables are as important as biological variables in determining the pattern of behavior displayed in adolescence. And, as we will see, even the biological changes that occur in adolescence are influenced by cultural variables.

Biological Changes

Adolescence begins with the onset of puberty, the period of maturation of the sex organs and other sexual characteristics. Actually, two closely related changes in physical development are occurring, both stimulated by an increase in a particular hormonal secretion. The *gonadotropic* hormones, secreted by the pituitary gland, stimulate and enlarge the gonads—the ovary in females and the testes in males—which then release larger amounts of sex hormones. These hormones, in turn, regulate the changes taking place in masculine and feminine bodily characteristics: the enlargement of breasts, the rounded contours and, most dramatically, the menstrual flow in females and the growth of body hair, the deepening of voice, and ejaculation in males. Testosterone (the masculinizing hormone) and estrogen (the feminizing hormone) are necessary for normal sexual development in both males and females. The proportions differ, however, with more testosterone secreted in boys and more estrogen in girls.

At the same time, working in conjunction with the sex hormones, growth hormones secreted by the pituitary initiate a growth spurt. The increase in muscle tissue is greater in boys than in girls so that males, on the average, become biologically stronger than females. Augmenting these biological differences in strength are greater heart and lung size in males than females and corresponding differences in other vital capacities. These changes culminate in the maximum physical size the individual will achieve (excluding weight gains) during the course of his or her development. While it may be an exaggeration to say that one's decline begins as one enters the twenties and adulthood, we certainly cannot look forward to an increase in physical size and capacity at that point. However, in contrast to the pattern for physical development, one can grow psychologically throughout one's lifetime.

Individual Variations

Having experienced the changes of puberty and observed them in our peers, most of us are quite aware of the marked individual variations in the onset and termination of sexual growth. Early-maturing girls may begin to menstruate at age ten while, for some late-maturing girls, menstruation may not begin until age seventeen. Similar variations occur in the initiation and completion of other physical changes. Boys show corresponding variations in their sexual maturation and growth spurts, although as a group they reach puberty about two years later than girls. These differences in rate of physical maturation have consequences for the adolescent's changing self-concept. Late-maturing boys, in comparison to boys who mature earlier, tend to be less popular, are more tense, are perceived as less attractive by others, and generally have negative views of themselves (Jones, 1958; Mussen and Jones, 1957). Similarly, early-maturing girls see themselves more positively than late-maturing girls, although the differences are less pronounced than for boys (Jones and Mussen, 1958). There are, of course, many individual exceptions to these generalizations. The early maturer who is physically awkward or suffers excessively from blackheads and acne will not be viewed as highly attractive. The *very* early-maturing girl, who is already well developed by the sixth grade, may feel at a disadvantage, rather than favored, relative to her classmates (Faust, 1960).

One might think that while there are individual variations in sexual and physical maturation, the average for any particular racial, ethnic, or cultural group would remain more or less constant. This is not the case. Fifteen- and sixteen-year-olds are taller and heavier today—by about 2 inches and 10 pounds for boys and about ½ inch and 1¼ pounds for girls—than their counterparts raised in the United States some forty years ago. Nutrition and other living conditions have affected the physical status of the population, with adolescents in the lower socioeconomic strata showing the greatest change. Especially striking have been the changes taking place in the age of menarche (onset of menstruation). Girls today begin menstruating at a significantly earlier age—around twelve and a half—than their grandmothers, who in turn menstruated earlier than their grandmothers. It is estimated that most females in Western society at the end of the eighteenth and the beginning of the nineteenth centuries did not reach menarche until about age seventeen (Diern, 1974). At earlier times in Western Europe, in the pre-Renaissance period, the age of menarche was much closer to its current level: around thirteen to fourteen. The Industrial Revolution, with its accompanying dietary and health-related changes, apparently resulted in a significant delay in the age of menarche. Psychosexual stimulation and inhibition may also be factors influencing the onset of puberty, but this relationship has not been established (Tanner, 1971).

Autonomy and Conformity

Over a relatively short period of time, the adolescent acquires new physical powers, matching those of the adults who are the controlling forces in society. The adolescent is beset with intense sexual feelings that motivate sexual interests and behaviors that remain largely prohibited by adult society. The drive toward assertion of one's powers and self-definition as an independent decision maker, and toward autonomy from parents and from social rules that are seen as controlling and repressive, is therefore strong. The adolescent may express this drive in a number of different ways: through career choice, political action, sexual experimentation, defiance of speed limits, cigarette smoking, and experimenting with alcohol or drugs. How an adolescent manages his or her independence striving, whether in a socially acceptable or a socially deviant manner, whether with rebelliousness and parental conflict or in the context of maintenance of strong family ties, depends on (1) the stresses and transition structures that exist in the culture, (2) the family atmosphere and response to the adolescent's efforts at independence, and (3) the personality of the individual adolescent.

But the adolescent's search for independence is only half the struggle; the adolescent also needs a support system and a place in society. The adolescent needs feedback on the new self that is in the process of definition (Hamachek, 1976), including answers to questions of self-uncertainty, such as "Am I attractive?" "Am I as powerful as I think I am?" "Can I make intelligent decisions on my own?" "Am I capable of assuming the responsibility of an adult?" In addition, the process of separation from family controls and protection can be painful and isolating. To reduce pain and loneliness, the adolescent is often motivated to seek out some group with which to affiliate. This group can be one's immediate peers, a political organization, a new religious movement, or the military. Paradoxically, in some cases it can even be one's immediate family, which creates an intense but ambivalent attachment.

Thus, the adolescent who is on the one hand striving for independence, on the other hand needs a group that can provide feedback, validation of the self, and emotional support. Under these circumstances, strong attachments to the group can develop, with the group exercising powerful conformity pressures on its individual members. The adolescent asserting his or her independence from adult norms and prohibitions may also adopt every new fad in style of dress, in rock music, in hair length, even in jargon (Remmers and Radler, 1957). In a real sense, the adolescent is dependent on a social group in order to achieve independence. Some psychologists (Riegel, 1975) have used the term *dialectic,* borrowed from philosophers Hegel and Marx, to describe this developmental interplay between two opposing forces. Out of this dialectic between the need for independence and the pressures toward conformity will emerge a more mature individual, able to conform or act independently in a more adaptive, realistic fashion. The struggles and changes of adolescence, then, provide the groundwork necessary for psychological growth in adulthood.

Idealism

One of the striking characteristics of adolescents is a strong measure of idealism (Horrocks, 1969). Of course, not all adolescents are idealists. Some follow conventional values and activities; others are predominantly oriented to self-gratification and may display very little in the way of social conscience. However, the idealism that many adolescents manifest—their dissatisfaction with the state of the world and their desire to improve on society and to adopt life styles that are more genuine and fulfilling—is a special feature of this period of development. How idealism is expressed is as dependent on social conditions and social structure as it is on the degree of individual extremism versus individual willingness to work "within the system."

In the 1940s, the United States was engaged in a war supported by a majority of its population. Adolescents with strong idealistic feelings could express them through participation in the war effort, early enlistment, identification with a noble cause, and often through acts of sacrifice and heroism. Pacifists whose values permitted, joined the medical corps or served in a nonmilitary capacity. In the 1960s, on the other hand, the United States was engaged in an unpopular war in Vietnam. Adolescent idealism could find an outlet more readily through opposition than through support of the war. There were other important social and economic differences between the 1940s and the 1960s that influenced the expression of adolescent idealism. A major step in race relations had taken place in the United States during World War II, with the integration of the armed forces. But progress in this area moved slowly during the postwar years until the civil rights movement emerged, providing adolescents with still another opportunity to work toward a more ideal society. A further difference between these two periods was the long economic depression that preceded World War II, in contrast to the almost two decades of economic prosperity preceding the sixties. The latter situation permitted young people to concern themselves with inner experience and growth, with the development of authentic life styles, rather than with the workaday constraints of striving for economic security and advancement. In brief, the contrast between adolescent behavior during the 1940s and the 1960s illustrates the powerful role that historical and socioeconomic conditions play. As we will see again and again, adolescence is not merely a matter of hormones.

But how do we explain this intensified drive toward a better world, a more just society, a more honest life style that so many adolescents experience? Where does this idealism come from? There are studies linking adolescent involvement in civil rights activities and the student protest movement of the sixties to family background. But, by and large, these studies do not tell us what it is about the adolescent period of development that fosters intense idealistic impulses. There are a number of different factors that one can suggest, but further research is needed to determine which are the critical variables promoting idealism. Probably, it is a combination of several of the following factors:

1. *Greater cognitive skills.* According to Kohlberg, some adolescents during this period attain a higher stage of cognitive and moral development. Adolescents are capable of dealing with statements that have double meanings and enjoy manipulating verbal symbols (Elkind, 1970). One might expect the adolescent to be better able to recognize inconsistencies, which he or she is then motivated to resolve.

2. *Increased independence.* One characteristic of independence is the ability to think for oneself. Adolescents, in establishing their autonomy and independence from parents and authority, can now begin to evaluate critically ideas and values expressed by their parents and by society, which had previously been accepted without question. Seeing imperfections, like recognizing inconsistencies, is the first step toward eliminating these imperfections.

3. *Rivalry with parents and between generations.* Whereas, in the preteen years, the child sees the adult as a source of both support and control, a new ingredient is added in the adolescent years: the adult becomes a rival. Physically, the adolescent is the peer of the parent and is perhaps even stronger and more attractive. Psychoanalytic theory sees adolescence as a period in which the Oedipal impulse and conflicts are reawakened. One difference from the earlier Oedipal situation is that the parents may now feel threatened by the same-sex child: the mother by her sexually mature daughter and the father by his physically adult son. Going beyond the immediate family, rivalry between adult society and adolescents is fostered by the fact that the adolescent is about to enter the labor force and can be an economic threat. In addition, adolescents identify with their peer groups and display tastes and values that may challenge those of the adult society. Thus, part of the fervor of adolescent idealism may be a kind of competitive assertiveness with adult rivals: an "I-can-do-better-than-you-can" response. Contributing to this rivalry with adults and to the adolescent sense of moral superiority is the adolescent's recognition of parental and adult fallibility. This recognition in turn gives rise to *cognitive conceit,* a defensive belief in one's own greater intelligence and insight (Elkind, 1979).

4. *Reaction formation.* Adolescence is a period when impulses—especially sexual ones—whose expression has been prohibited are intensified and

brought to the fore. Aggression, too, may become exacerbated with the stimulation of rivalry and competitiveness, with efforts to establish autonomy, and with an increase in physical strength. Further, the adolescent's attention quite naturally turns inward to cope with these new feelings, powers, and insecurities. The adolescent has to struggle against being self-centered, seeing oneself as the center of the universe. The intensified idealism of some adolescents may then be one way of coping with sexual, aggressive, and egocentric impulses that the adolescent cannot fully accept. To the extent that the defense of reaction formation is operating, the adolescent may display in exaggerated form a concern with the welfare of others rather than oneself, an opposition to any form of aggression, and a search for "pure" relationships in which sexual passion is minimized or absent. Anna Freud (1958) has described the *ascetic adolescent* as in a transitory period in which there is a lack of differentiation between the pleasurable, id aspects of life and the vital biological drives such as the need to eat and to sleep. In defending against id impulses, the adolescent overreacts, rejecting the satisfaction of significant bodily needs. It should be emphasized that we are not saying that asceticism, pacifism, and social concern are necessarily reaction formations, only that these idealistic tendencies can be exaggerated in adolescence through the process of reaction formation.

Continuity Between Adolescents and Parents

We have focused on the adolescent's efforts to separate from the parents and to establish his or her own identity. However, adolescents also have attachments to their parents and, in most societies, the parents have been the most influential adults in the adolescent's life. Consequently, one might expect some similarities between adolescent and parent in attitudes, values, and preferences. In a major study of adolescents, in which fourteen-year-olds were followed through school and, in most cases, through age twenty-two, Offer (1969; Offer and Offer, 1975) found that the values and social orientation expressed by most teenagers were fundamentally similar to their parents'. There were value conflicts, of course, and occasionally severe disagreements and discord, but, on the whole, the teenagers shared their parents' value structures. "The goals they were striving toward were very appropriate in the sense that they fitted very nicely into the cultural milieu in which they were living, and were almost always in accordance with the parents' expectations" (Offer, 1969, pp. 60–61).

We must remember that adolescents share their parents' socioeconomic status, religious affiliation, and residential area—all sociological, demographic factors that exert a powerful influence on social values. In this regard, teenage children of a southern farmer who is a member of a Fundamentalist church are likely to have more in common with their parents than with upper-middle-class, urban adolescents on the East and West coasts. But even when adolescents are matched on demographic factors, one still finds evidence of similarity between parental values and those of their offspring (Troll, Neugarten, and Kraines, 1969). Studies of political activists during the 1960s and early 1970s also revealed a continuity in values between parent and child. The difference between activist students and their parents was most often in the greater willingness of youth to take militant action on beliefs their parents shared (Keniston, 1967). Thus, the difference between generations appears to be more on issues of style than on questions of basic values. But style—how we go about realizing our values, the sacrifices we are prepared to make, the risks we are willing to take—is by no means a trivial matter.

Some Discontinuities in Adolescent Development

Although most adolescents conform in general to the value structure of their parents and to that of the larger society, many deviate and engage in behaviors that are socially disapproved or illegal. Generation differences became especially marked during the 1960s with regard to sex and drugs. We must be especially careful here to distinguish between behaviors that are characteristic of the long period of development we call adolescence and behaviors that are confined to a particular period of history. To understand the "drug revolution" and the "sexual revolution," one would have to go beyond the adolescent, to examine the social, political, and economic forces that were prevalent during the 1960s: economic affluence, an unpopular war, threat of nuclear destruction, and depletion of natural resources, to cite some of the more evident factors. At the same time, it was the youth of the Western nations who sparked the changes in sex practices and use of drugs. For the psychological reasons that have been reviewed—the search for self-identity, increased physical and cognitive competence, the need for autonomy and independence, idealism, and its corollary, disillusionment—young people are likely to be in the forefront of both social and political revolutions.

What is the nature of these changes in adolescent sexual and drug-related behaviors? To what extent have they persisted? What is their relationship to personality development and personality differences? These are some of the questions addressed by an extensive and systematic longitudinal study carried out by Richard and Shirley Jessor (1977). Their project involved over four hundred high school students selected from a predominantly middle-class community. Beginning in junior high school, samples of seventh, eighth, and ninth graders were followed to grades ten, eleven, and twelve, respectively. A parallel study was carried out with two hundred college freshmen, who were investigated through their senior year.

In addition to assessing drug use and sexual behavior, the investigators surveyed other "problem behaviors" such as drinking, protest behavior or activism, and "general deviance," which included such behaviors as aggression, stealing, and lying. All of these activities were viewed as problem behaviors, since, the Jessors argued, even though sexual intercourse and marijuana use might be quite common among college students, these were nonconforming, deviant behaviors for young adolescents. They expected that early participation in these activities would be associated with behaviors that were explicitly recognized as problems, such as drunkenness and general deviance. Their findings for the high school students generally supported their predictions (with the exception of political activism, which was only weakly related to the other categories). Students who used marijuana were much more likely to be nonvirgins, display drunkenness, and generally score high in deviance as compared to nonusers. They further found that early use of marijuana or early drinking behavior predicts the extent to which the adolescent will later display other problem behaviors.

As one might expect, the proportion of individuals who used marijuana, who drank alcohol, and who had had sexual intercourse increased from grade ten to twelve. By the senior year of college, 77 percent of the males and 62 percent of the females in the study had smoked marijuana; 82 percent of the males and 85 percent of the females were nonvirgins; and the percentages for drinking were even higher. The difference between these behaviors in college and in high school was *qualitative* as well as quantitative. These activities are normative in college; they are not problem behaviors in that context. In high school, participation versus nonparticipation is not only indicative of other problem behaviors but is also related to differences in adolescent personality. However, this was not the case for the college sample. High school students who had a high probability of engaging in problem behaviors were found to value independence over academic achievement, to be more critical of society, to be more accepting of social deviance, and to be less involved in religion than students who were unlikely to display these behaviors. In addition, the social environment perceived by the adolescent was an important factor discriminating these two groups. Problem behavior is associated with an orientation toward peers and seeking support from peers, in contrast to the parent orientation characterizing low–problem behavior youth.

In drawing conclusions from the Jessor study, we must realize that there are individual exceptions to these overall trends. There are many adolescents who have tried marijuana, do not drink, and are not high in general deviance. In addition, it must also be realized that the data obtained for any particular problem behavior is dependent on the social context. For example, premarital sexual intercourse before the age of sixteen would not be predictive of the development of problem behaviors in cultures in which early sexual intercourse is the norm for adolescents. It is also possible that the psychological significance of occasional marijuana use may change as exposure to marijuana becomes more common among high school students.

Adolescents and Drugs

What are the facts on changes in marijuana use among high school students in the United States? Do changes in the prevalence of LSD and heroin usage correspond with changes in the proportion of students using marijuana?

Table 10.2   Trends in lifetime prevalence of eleven types of drugs

	Class of 1975 N = (9,400)	Class of 1976 (15,400)	Class of 1977 (17,100)	Class of 1978 (17,800)	1977–1978 Change
	Percentage ever used				
Marijuana	47.3	52.8	56.4	59.2	+2.8
Inhalants	NA	10.3	11.1	12.0	+0.9
Hallucinogens	16.3	15.1	13.9	14.3	+0.4
Cocaine	9.0	9.7	10.8	12.9	+2.1
Heroin	2.2	1.8	1.8	1.6	−0.2
Other opiates[a]	9.0	9.6	10.3	9.9	−0.4
Stimulants	22.3	22.6	23.0	22.9	−0.1
Sedatives[a]	18.2	17.7	17.4	16.0	−1.4
Tranquilizers[a]	17.0	16.8	18.0	17.0	−1.0
Alcohol	90.4	91.9	92.5	93.1	+0.6
Cigarettes	73.6	75.4	75.7	75.3	−0.4

Source: Johnston, Bachman, and O'Malley, 1979, p. 16.

Note: NA indicates data not available.

[a]Only drug use which was not under a doctor's orders is included here.

These are some of the questions addressed by a survey sponsored by the National Institute on Drug Abuse of nearly 18,000 high school seniors in the class of 1978, which revealed a substantial increase in the frequency of marijuana exposure (Johnston, Bachman, and O'Malley, 1979). While about 47 percent of the class of 1975 had used marijuana at least once, this figure had risen to over 59 percent for the class of 1978 (see Table 10.2). However, this increase in marijuana use was not predictive of an increase in general drug usage. The frequency of use of other hallucinogens such as LSD, of amphetamine stimulants and barbiturate sedatives, and of heroin remained relatively unchanged during this period. Cocaine was the only drug to show a sizable increase in usage (from 9.9 percent in 1975 to almost 13 percent in 1978). Although the daily use of marijuana also increased from 6 percent of high school seniors in 1975 to 10.77 percent in 1978 (14 percent for males and 7 percent for females), a substantial majority of high school seniors (68 percent) disapproved of the regular use of marijuana.

It is evident from Table 10.2 that almost every high school senior had a drink at some time in his or her life. Furthermore, almost three-fourths of the seniors reported using alcohol in the past thirty days. Thus, the "deviant" adolescent would appear to be the complete abstainer. At the same time, despite the fact that 30 percent of all seniors reported that most or all of their friends got drunk at least once a week, the regular use of alcohol (one to two drinks a day) was disapproved by two-thirds of the students.

The survey data indicated that the adolescent culture sharply discriminates between the occasional use of marijuana and alcohol and that of other drugs. Occasional experimenting with LSD, heroin, amphetamines, or cocaine was disapproved by at least three-fourths of the high school seniors, and the *regular* use of all drugs, including marijuana and alcohol, was opposed by most seniors. Nevertheless, drinking, and especially drunkenness, showed signs of becoming a significant high school problem. The frequency with which high school seniors reported their friends getting drunk may be a reflection of the increasing tolerance of students for substantial drinking on weekends; 44 percent of the respondents found drinking acceptable. When one considers that alcoholism is a major psychiatric disorder and that drinking is a significant contributor to the automobile accident rate, the increased acceptance of alcohol usage in high schools should be a matter of serious social concern. At the same time, it must be recognized that the adolescent is seeking and asserting the identity of an adult and that it is the adult culture that provides the norms and behaviors that make drinking an acceptable sign of adult status.

Adult Development

Concern with personality development throughout the life span is relatively recent in psychology. Adolescence was recognized as a period of self-uncertainty and self-change that finally culminated in the crystallization of the self upon entrance into young adulthood. There were some studies of personality and attitude change during the college years (Newcomb, 1943), but it was implicitly assumed that by the time one graduated from college, if not before then, personality was more or less "set" until one reached old age. Research on even this latter period remained quite limited until the increase in elderly people in the population gave special social and economic significance to the physical and psychological changes that occur with aging.

Because of the newness of the life-span approach to personality development, there is still uncertainty and debate as to what the important issues and questions are (Baltes and Schaie, 1973). Just what does a developmental approach to personality in the adult years contribute to our understanding, beyond simply studying the changes and continuities in personality over time? Certainly we can expect that the personalities of adults will be affected by repeated experiences of success versus failure, by prolonged unemployment, by tragedies and serious illness, by positions of prestige and responsibility, and so on. What, then, does it mean to talk about personality *development* in the adult years?

There are three kinds, or levels, of answers that have been given to this question, depending on how closely the personality change is linked to a particular age period and how regular or inevitable the change is seen as being:

1. One can examine the effects on adult personality of unusual life events such as a prisoner-of-war experience (Hunter, 1976), an untimely death in the family (Weisman, 1973), or exposure to severe persecution (Ostwald and Bittner, 1968). Developmental considerations become relevant to the extent that one takes into account age-related variations in the social, emotional, and cognitive status of individuals; for example, the fact that these severely stressful events may have occurred to recently married couples, or to men and women with well-established positions and growing families, or to elderly residents of a nursing home.

2. One can focus on the implications for personality change of experiences that occur only or primarily to all those of adult status or to particular age groups within the adult category. Marriage, divorce, becoming a parent, job dissatisfaction, career achievement, and retirement are examples of such experiences. Of course, there is no simple, one-to-one relationship between these experiences and their effects on personality. The personality consequences of marriage, divorce, or a new job depend in part on other personality attributes of the individual. Nevertheless, these events have powerful meanings for adults; they satisfy or frustrate significant needs and may enlarge or narrow one's self-understanding and sensitivity to others.

3. From the most explicitly developmental viewpoint, one can conceive of adult personality as a series of age periods in which specific personality traits are acquired, enhanced, or modified. Some investigators maintain that there is a regular sequence in the patterning and fluctuations of personality over time (Bühler, 1962; Erikson, 1950; Gould, 1972; Levinson, 1978). Just as adolescence and the preceding developmental periods have special significance for the formation of personality, so are the periods of early adulthood, middle adulthood, and old age characterized by their own growth-related issues of marriage, parenthood, career, and retirement. In this section, we will focus largely on research that approaches adult personality from this perspective.

Adult Developmental Stages

In *As You Like It*, Shakespeare described seven ages of man (see Box 10.1). You will recall, too, that Erikson (Chapter 5) proposed a sequence of three psychosocial tasks and corresponding age periods with which the developing adult must deal: intimacy–early adulthood (20–40); generativity–middle adulthood (40–65); and integrity–later adulthood (65–). According to Erikson, the principal problem faced by young adults, in their twenties and thirties, is the

Box 10.1

THE SEVEN AGES OF MAN
William Shakespeare

All the world's a stage,
And all the men and women merely players.
They have their exits and their entrances,
And one man in his time plays many parts,
His acts being seven ages. At first the infant,
Mewling and puking in the nurse's arms.
Then the whining schoolboy, with his satchel
And shining morning face, creeping like snail
Unwillingly to school. And then the lover,
Sighing like furnace, with a woeful ballad
Made to his mistress' eyebrow. Then a soldier,
Full of strange oaths and bearded like the pard,
Jealous in honor, sudden and quick in quarrel,
Seeking the bubble reputation
Even in the cannon's mouth. And then the justice,
In fair round belly with good capon lined,
With eyes severe and beard of formal cut,
Full of wise saws and modern instances,
And so he plays his part. The sixth age shifts
Into the lean and slippered Pantaloon,
With spectacles on nose and pouch on side,
His youthful hose, well saved, a world too wide
For his shrunk shank, and his big manly voice,
Turning again toward childish treble, pipes
And whistles in his sound. Last scene of all,
That ends this strange eventful history,
Is second childishness and mere oblivion,
Sans teeth, sans eyes, sans taste, sans everything.

Source: *As You Like It*, act 2, sc. 7, lines 139–166.

achievement and maintenance of a close personal relationship or, alternatively, the living of one's life as an independent but emotionally isolated individual. On entering the forties, the individual's problems shift. Will one cling to established routines, to old patterns and old habits, or will one look forward to and pursue different satisfactions and future opportunities? Old age presents both the most difficult challenge and possibly the highest level of self-realization: recognizing one's limitations and the ultimate finality of life, while at the same time experiencing life as meaningful and integrating the mosaic of tragedies and joys that life presents.

Erikson, then, saw adulthood as a series of age-related stages, each presenting its own developmental task. The successful resolution of these tasks results in the individual's progressive attainment of higher levels of self-realization. Despite the value that Erikson placed on the greater maturity that

Table 10.3   Bühler's conception of phases and basic tendencies during the life span

| | Basic tendency | | | | |
Age period	Need satisfaction	Adaptation (adjustment)	Creative expansion	Establishment of inner order	Self-fulfillment
0–1.5 yr	Trust and love, evolvement and discovery of self-sameness				
1.5–4 yr		Obedience and superego ideal versus independence			
4–8 yr			Autonomous, value-setting, ego-ideals aspect of task		
8–12 yr				Objective self-evaluation in social roles	
12–18 yr	Sex needs and problem of sexual identity			Review and preview of self-development (auto-biographical)	Fulfillment of and detachment from childhood
18–25 (30) yr		Tentative self-determination to role in society			
25 (30)–45 (50) yr			Self-realization in occupation, marriage, and own family		
45 (50)–65 (70) yr				Critical self-assessment	
65 (70)–80 (85) yr					Self-fulfillment
80 (85)–death	Regression to predominant need satisfaction				

Source: Bühler, 1962, p. 755. Reprinted by permission.

aging offers, however, most adults over thirty in this culture would prefer to be somewhat younger (Kastenbaum, Derbin, Sabatini, and Artt, 1972)! Young adults, the middle aged, and the aged have nevertheless been shown to report the same degree of life satisfaction (Cameron, 1972). Furthermore, in that same study, the middle aged were considered by the other groups to be the happiest.

These studies of satisfaction, age perception, and preferences tell us that people do find meaning in such a division of adult life into different age periods. However, we have to look to other kinds of data to determine whether there are stages of personality development associated with these different age periods. One source of data has been the study of individual biographies. Charlotte Bühler (1962) initiated the collection of life histories from elderly people in Vienna in the early 1930s and continued working on life-span development after emigrating to the United States. Her approach in inferring personality patterns from these life histories was essentially clinical and impressionistic, and her theoretical orientation was in the humanistic tradition. She postulated five basic life tendencies: need satisfaction, adaptive self-limitation or adjustment, creative expansion, establishment of inner order, and self-fulfillment. These life tendencies were assumed to emerge and become dominant at different age periods (see Table 10.3), and the way in which they were reflected in behavior also varied with age period.

Midlife Crisis

The work of Daniel Levinson and his collaborators (Levinson, 1978) is a more contemporary, sophisticated use of biography. In this study, adult males between the ages of thirty-five and forty-five were interviewed. (Due to limited resources, the investigators reluctantly limited their sample to men. Clearly, a comparable study of women in this age range is needed.) The sample of forty individuals was equally divided among four occupational groups: executives, biologists, novelists, and factory workers. Occupation was chosen as a major variable because of the central importance of work to a man's status and income. In the investigators' view, the life cycle as reflected in personality development during this midlife period, as well as in the conflicts and struggles along the way, is affected by the social structure and social context, particularly the work setting and occupational role. As was the case in Bühler's theory, the self played a critical role in Levinson's theoretical formulation, and it is through the self-concept that occupation exerts its influence on adult personality development (Levinson, 1978, p. 45):

Occupation has important sources within the self and important consequences for the self. It is often the primary medium in which a young man's dreams for the future are defined, and the vehicle he uses to pursue those dreams. At best, his occupation permits the fulfillment of basic values and life goals. At worst, a man's work life over the years is oppressive and corrupting, and contributes to a growing alienation from self, work and society. In studying a man's life, we need to understand the meaning of work and the multiple ways in which it may serve to fulfill, to barely sustain or to destroy the self.

To analyze the individual biographies, Levinson found it useful to employ the concept of *life structure,* or the basic pattern at a given developmental period in a person's life: how the person deals with issues concerning work, close relationships, changing perceptions of the self and of the future, and other critical matters that regularly arise as one progresses from youth to old age. The different developmental tasks posed by early, middle, and late adulthood require the individual to build a life structure through certain key choices and decisions, to keep options open or to make commitments, to settle down or to strive to attain greater heights. The most significant conclusion of this study is the finding of an orderly sequence of development, of an evolution of life structure during the adult years, and further that "the essential character of the sequence is the same for all the men in our study and for the other men whose biographies we examined" (Levinson, 1978, p. 49). Whether or not these investigators' findings are as universal as they claimed, they offered many rich observations and stimulating hypotheses regarding the nature of personality development during the adult years. They saw development as marked by stable periods in which the individual copes with particular developmental tasks and by transition periods, or stressful times when one must change from one level of adult development to the next. Although these observations were based on interviews with males, they would seem to have considerable relevance for females as well.

On the basis of the biographies they obtained and others' studies of the later segments of adult life, the Levinson group divided the adult life span into five transition and five developmental periods (see Fig. 10.4). After making the transition from adolescence to early adulthood, one's initial task on entering the adult world is to resolve the struggle between exploring a variety of alternatives—in personal relationships, jobs, life style—and making a commitment to a stable structure—getting married, choosing a career. The next transition period (ages twenty-eight to thirty-three), the so-called age-thirty transition, can be particularly stressful as one begins to move toward "really" settling down. The flaws and mistakes that one may have made—an unsatisfactory marriage, a frustrating occupation, or no commitment at all—take on a more serious quality as one advances from a provisional, "try-out" status to more stable, permanent commitments.

In the next adult stage, which lasts until approximately age forty, a man is most concerned with settling down. This is the period in which he attempts to realize his goals and aspirations, whether in terms of income, status, fame, creative work, or social contributions, and to "build" on his home and family. Then, roughly from age forty to forty-five, he enters the midlife transition period, characterized in a majority of men by a review and questioning of basic life structure. "What have I accomplished?" "Does my work matter?" "What do I really get from and give to my wife and children?" "Am I getting what I want out of life?" "What happened to my dreams?" This is the period of the so-called *midlife crisis,* a theme popularized in films and books in the 1970s (Sheehy, 1976). The turmoil and despair that many men (and women,

Figure 10.4   Developmental periods in early and middle adulthood. (Levinson, 1978, p. 57.)

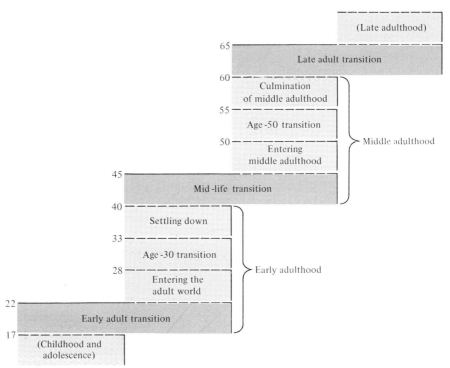

as well) may experience during this period is not to be confused with mental illness. The crisis is normal and, if successfully resolved, healthy. Some men emerge from this crisis defeated and resigned to a life of decline; others emerge with an acceptance of mortality, loss of youth, and realistic limits to aspirations, but with renewed energy and purpose. This period of middle adulthood flows into the age-fifty transition, which can be a period of difficulty for men who have failed to come to grips with the issues of the midlife crisis. However, the decade of the fifties can be a period of rejuvenation and fulfillment as one approaches the later years of one's life span.

The picture of adult development painted by Levinson and his colleagues, although based on intensive biographical studies, must be considered hypothetical until supported by more exact, quantitative data. In one major study of four specific stages of life, from high school seniors to people nearing retirement, it was found that sex was a much more important determinant of issues than age or stage (Lowenthal, Thurnher, and Chiriboga, 1975). In the particular cultural context in which this study was carried out, marriage, parenting, and career achievement were some of the issues that differed in significance for men and women. However, some of the data yielded by this study were consistent with the Levinson observations, particularly the notion of midlife crisis. Experience of a midlife crisis was especially evident in the case of bright, talented women who felt trapped in their parental and housekeeping roles. Roger Gould (1975, 1978), a psychiatrist who has carried out both clinical and questionnaire studies of adults in midlife, reports that men and women in this period no longer feel that "there's still plenty of time to do most of the things I want to do." Gould's clinical observations are consistent with Levinson's research findings. Also, indirect support for one component of the midlife transition period is provided by studies of personality change, which consistently indicate that people become more reflective and self-appraising in the second half of life (Costa and McCrae, 1977; Guttman, 1977).

There is much in literature and history, too, to support the notion of a midlife crisis. Certainly, an ebb in physical powers and other biological changes become clearly noticeable as one enters one's forties. Stamina, reaction time, and strength have all declined. There are also changes in physical contours and in the surface of the skin. If you haven't already won the Davis Cup or a figure skating medal, you will have to adapt to the probability that you never will. There are also biologically linked changes in sexual virility: in males' ability to obtain and maintain an erection, in the force of ejaculation, and so on. It seems reasonable that these biological changes can become linked with the recognition that one's life is at least half over and that this begets a midlife crisis. However, it is also quite likely that crisis is as strongly influenced by cultural features as by individual differences in personality. In cultures with clearly established, age-related social rules and expectations, in which the individual has few alternatives or choices, we might not expect to find a midlife crisis. Individuals living in economically marginal contexts, who are constantly concerned with physical survival, would probably not experience the pattern of adult development that has been described by the adult stage theorists. Concepts such as the midlife crisis are insightful, but our theoretical and research task is to discover the conditions that determine this phenomenon rather than to assume its inevitability as a stage of life.

Old Age

The miracles of modern medicine and public health programs have made possible the extension of the life cycle into old age for increasing numbers of people. More than 25 million residents of the United States were over sixty-five in 1980. Sheer numbers have thus posed enormous medical, economic, and social problems for Western society, which places such a premium on productivity and youth. In addition, the urbanization and mobility of the American family make it difficult for the family to accommodate an elderly parent in the household. To further complicate the role and status of the elderly, the larger society's vision of older people is distorted by myths, half-truths, and stereotypes. The elderly themselves are vulnerable to these commonly held half-truths regarding their own intellectual functioning and emotional life.

Thus, in examining the question of personality change in old age, we do so within a particular social context in which attributes such as the wisdom of the elderly are not highly valued, in which old age is a time of economic hardship for many, and in which large numbers of the elderly live in nursing homes and retirement communities, segregated from younger age groups in society. We have the very difficult task of determining the extent to which behavioral changes in the elderly are due to the process of aging and the extent to which they are attributable to the particular social conditions experienced by the elderly in this society.

Many changes take place simultaneously during old age. There is a noticeable slowdown in reactivity and movement (Hicks and Birren, 1970); the skin is wrinkled and spotted; there is typically a decline in visual acuity and hearing. The aged are very vulnerable to illness and to such chronic diseases as diabetes, arthritis, and heart impairments. Mental illness also increases after the age of sixty-five. Much of this increase is due to biological disorders such as *cerebral arteriosclerosis,* in which the blood vessels thicken and blood flow to the brain is reduced, and *senile brain diseases,* in which there is a decrement in brain cell function. But there are also mental disorders among the aged that are reversible: anxiety, depressive reactions to the loss of loved ones, and disturbances brought on by alcohol or drugs.

Aging versus Illness

The biological and behavioral changes that occur in the aged are closely related (Fillenbaum, 1977; Youmans and Yarrow, 1971), supporting a holistic approach to the problems of aging. The field of *gerontology,* which addresses the phenomena of old age, draws its experts from various biological and behavioral disciplines. A pioneering study carried out by James E. Birren and his colleagues (1963) illustrates the value of a multidisciplinary, gerontological approach to aging. A major objective of the study was to separate the effects of aging from the effects of the illnesses from which old people frequently suffer. Volunteer males, at least sixty-five years old, were screened for evidence of medical disorders, and only the healthier men were retained for inclusion in the study. The mean age of the final group of forty-seven "healthy" individuals was 71.5 and all were living independently in the community, in most instances in households with their wives. Detailed physiological and psychological evaluations of the men were carried out. The results were quite striking. These old men constituted a vigorous, alert, even optimistic group of individuals who were very much involved in their daily lives. The image of rigid, confused oldsters certainly did not apply to this sample. There was evidence of depression and distress in some of the men, but these reactions seemed appropriately linked to personal losses. More intensive analyses and comparisons with a sample of young men reflected

Active senior citizens in marathon competition. Illness, rather than aging per se, accounts for many of the differences observed between younger and older people. (Martine Franck/Magnum Photos, Inc.)

differences on some physiological measures but similarities on many others. For example, elevations in blood pressure did not discriminate between healthy old men and healthy young men and therefore can be taken as a sign of pathology rather than a result of a process of aging. The Birren findings, while based on a small sample and therefore to be taken as preliminary and suggestive, nevertheless point to the importance of separating the effects of illness from the effects of aging. What does seem to be true about the process of aging is that the organism becomes increasingly *vulnerable* to disease, accident, and life's hazards.

Competence and Survival

An interesting followup of survivors in the Birren sample was carried out eleven years after the initial study (Granick and Patterson, 1971). Although the sample of elderly men had been selected on the basis of healthiness, there were still variations in the degree of the men's physical health and in their psychological status. These factors were then examined to determine which factors differentiated survivors and nonsurvivors. As one might expect, physical symptoms such as elevated blood pressure and arteriosclerosis were more common among the nonsurvivors. However, psychological factors also predicted survival. Those among the elderly who had obtained higher scores on an intelligence scale, who were evaluated as more resourceful, and who had more social supports were more likely to be among the survivors. Perhaps this should not be too surprising, since as we have previously noted, physical and psychological functioning are closely interrelated among the aged.

An intriguing experimental study by Judith Rodin and Ellen J. Langer (1977) also bears on psychological factors in the aged that may be associated with survival. A group of elderly nursing home residents were given a talk by the hospital administrator which emphasized the responsibility the residents had for themselves. A contrasting talk was given to a control group of residents in the same institution which stressed the staff's responsibility to the residents as patients of a nursing home. In addition, the experimental group that received the communication emphasizing self-responsibility was offered plants to care for, while the comparison group was given plants that were watered by the staff. There were a number of significant immediate effects of the experimental manipulation of responsibility on the attitudes and behavior of the elderly patients. The elderly residents in the responsibility-induced group became more active, displayed greater alertness, and reported feeling happier than the control group. Patients in the responsibility-induced group also showed an increase in involvement in different kinds of social activities such as movie attendance, social interaction with friends and with staff, and participation in contests (Langer and Rodin, 1976).

Eighteen months later, a followup evaluation indicated that the experimental effects still persisted. The survivors who had been in the responsibility-induced group were judged to be more self-initiating, sociable, involved, and vigorous than those survivors who had been in the control group. The most striking result was the finding that a significantly smaller proportion of patients in the responsibility-induced group (seven out of forty-seven) had died in the eighteen-month period than in the comparison group (thirteen out of forty-four). It would be premature to conclude on the basis of this one study that a single talk, or that responsibility for a plant, will increase longevity. There were all kinds of factors in the nursing home that were not under experimental control that could have influenced the outcome of the study. Nevertheless, the findings indicate that it is possible to improve the psychological status and physical well-being of the elderly; programs designed to encourage the assumption of greater self-responsibility are a promising avenue for accomplishing these goals (see also Chapter 17).

To Disengage or Not to Disengage

For many years, the prevailing view of how to grow old most effectively was a *disengagement* model (Cumming and Henry, 1961). The disengagement theory held that, since slowing down was a natural aspect of aging, the psychologically healthy response for the aging individual was to gradually reduce his or her activities and social involvements. The theory stimulated a good deal of research which nevertheless failed to support the disengagement model. Old people, for example, regret the reduction in their level of activity (Havighurst, Neugarten, and Tobin, 1968) and, in fact, the degree of activity and social engagement is positively related to reports of satisfaction with life.

Subsequent research has revealed that there is no simple prescription— "Keep busy" or "Cut back"—that can be applied generally to the elderly. Although keeping up one's activity tends to go together with positive feelings about life, there are many exceptions to this relationship. Some people need to and should cut back; their heightened activity is often a defense against the idea of growing old. Personality factors, such as the way one relates to one's activity, are more important than activity level (Neugarten, Havighurst, and Tobin, 1968). We have already noted that assuming responsibility for oneself can be a major factor in determining adjustment during old age. The elderly who *choose* to become less active or *choose* particular activities in which to become involved are more contented, better-adjusted personalities than the aged who feel dependent on other people to help and make decisions for them (Neugarten, Havighurst, and Tobin, 1968).

From the perspective of Bühler's and Erikson's conceptions of adult stages of development, old age offers an opportunity to attain a higher level of self-development than is usually possible at younger ages. It entails a level of maturity and wisdom that Erikson refers to as *ego integrity*. Individuals who have achieved this stage have accepted their fate in life, see the inevitability and meaning of their life's course, and realize the inescapability of their triumphs and defeats. They do not engage in fantasies of "If only I had done ——————— rather than ———————." They experience order in their lives. They find satisfaction in life but are also prepared to accept the inevitable finality of life. Young and middle-aged adults may try to approximate some of these attitudes toward life through the adoption of non-Western philosophies such as Zen Buddhism and training in disciplines such as yoga. However, according to Erikson, there is no substitute for the experiences of the life cycle and the review and acceptance of that span of experience if one is to realize this highest stage of self-development.

Summary   This final chapter of three devoted to personality development has been addressed to an examination of the self-concept and developmental changes in adolescence and adulthood. The self-concept is a link between early and later development and is a core personality construct with a number of significant functions and properties. Changes in the self-concept and in other areas of personality can occur throughout the life span. These personality changes are initiated by significant life events, problems, or tasks that tend to be associated with particular age periods. Adolescence, in which the individual must deal with bodily changes and with changes in social status and roles as he or she moves from childhood to adulthood, is one such period. Old age is another period involving bodily changes. In addition, in old age one is typically confronted with the loss of close friends and relatives, with such issues as retirement and, ultimately, with one's own mortality. Between adolescence and old age are several adult developmental periods, marked by divisions regarding career and marriage, by settling down, and by an evaluation of one's achievements and relationships.

Specific Points

1. The *self-concept* consists of a physical self, or *body image,* and a psychological self. There is evidence that adult chimpanzees also have a body image, since they display self-recognition. Human infants begin to manifest self-recognition during their second year.

2. *Self-esteem* is based on one's generalized positive and negative evaluations of the various features of the self-concept. Not all elements of the self-concept contribute to self-esteem, inasmuch as many elements of the self are only descriptive.

3. The development of the self-concept contributes to one's sense of *identity* and continuity over time and acts as a frame of reference in one's perceptions of others. It also provides a basis for the manifestation of autonomy, pride, defensive behavior, and self-consistency.

4. The physical changes of puberty are brought about by an increase in the pituitary gland's secretion of growth hormone and gonadotropic hormone. The latter in turn stimulates the gonads to secrete masculinizing and feminizing hormones in differing proportions for males and females.

5. The adolescent is confronted with a conflict between the need to express sexual feelings and to establish and assert *autonomy* on the one hand and the need for support and *conformity* to social rules on the other. The intensity and mode of resolution of the conflict will vary with cultural, familial, and personality factors.

6. The *idealism* that many adolescents display may be a reflection of their independence, their recognition of adult inconsistencies, and their *cognitive conceit* that they "can do it better." It may also be in part a reaction formation against unacceptable sexual and aggressive impulses.

7. Despite the conflict and discord that may occur in adolescence, there is considerable continuity or similarity between the values of parents and those of their adolescent offspring.

8. Early use of marijuana and alcohol among adolescents is predictive of later deviant behaviors, such as drunkenness and aggression.

9. There is some empirical evidence for the hypothesis proposed by several theorists that adulthood can be divided into a sequence of periods or stages, each posing a particular set of problems and issues. Coping with these issues can stimulate personality change and growth in adults.

10. The *midlife crisis* that many adults are reported to experience during their early forties should not be confused with mental illness, but should rather

be considered as a normal experience for that age group that can result in positive personality development.

11. There are suggestive findings indicating that many of the so-called "effects of aging" are actually a manifestation of the effects of illness to which old people happen to be vulnerable. Relatively healthy elderly individuals do not display the rigidity and mental confusion that often accompanies aging.

12. There is no single prescription for how old people should live their lives. For some, it is best to maintain a certain activity level; for others, it is best to disengage.

Thought Questions

1. Do you think chimpanzees may eventually be shown to have a psychological self? If not, why not?

2. It is better for an adolescent's personality development if the adolescent period is marked by "storm and stress" rather than by relative calm?

3. How might cultural factors influence the stages of adult development observed among samples of adults studied in the United States?

4. Do you think it is wise for society to organize separate residential communities for the elderly? Why or why not?

PART IV

The Structure of Personality

The word *personality* connotes what one is "like": the characteristics, traits, or general manner of thinking and behaving that define who one is. Psychologists sometimes refer to this as the structure of personality. Webster defines *structure* as an arrangement of parts organized in some meaningful way. The next three chapters, then, are concerned with this construction of the parts of the person. This rather analytic aspect of the study of personality contrasts with the explanation of how personality traits develop, which has just been discussed, and with the manner in which personality structures influence behavior, which falls under the dynamics of personality, analyzed in the next part of the text.

The study of the structure of personality is intimately linked with the measurement of personality. To determine the degree to which one is introverted, aggressive, or high in need for achievement, there must be appropriate instruments to assess these concepts. In Chapter 11 the basic principles of measurement are introduced. Reliability, which refers to how well a concept is being measured, and validity, which is concerned with whether a test is measuring what it is supposed to measure, are examined in detail. This is followed, in Chapter 12, by a discussion of the types of instruments used to assess personality. Objective tests are distinguished from projective tests; other ways to measure personality are suggested; and the reliability and validity of these different approaches are considered. Then, in Chapter 13, traits are examined in detail. There is presently a vigorous movement in psychology to deny the existence of traits, based on apparent evidence that behavior is neither general across situations nor enduring. The accuracy of this position is debated and some newer conceptions of traits and their assessment are presented in Chapter 13.

In sum, the chapters in this part of the text progress from the basics of measurement, to an examination of specific measures being employed, to a discussion of traits, or what is being measured. The field of personality structure is exceedingly complex. Because so many issues remain to be resolved, it is one of the most active areas in the field of personality.

Foundations of
Personality Measurement

11 In earlier chapters we frequently referred to specific studies of personality, describing the measures used in these studies and the results obtained. To interpret these results properly, however, it is necessary to be able to evaluate the measures and how well they assess whatever it is they are supposed to assess. One must also have an understanding of the meaning of the numerical relations that are reported. In the next three chapters, we will discuss some of the methods that psychologists use to measure aspects of personality, with measurements typically expressed in terms of scores, ratings, and other quantitative values. Quantitative methods allow us to evaluate theories and hypotheses more systematically. As a result, they also allow us to learn more about characteristics of individuals and how these characteristics are the same as or different from those of other individuals.

In this chapter we present some of the foundations for research in the measurement of personality. First, correlation, which is the basic statistical method used in personality research, is described. Next, we discuss how correlation is used to determine the reliability and validity of psychological assessment procedures. Then we examine behavioral observation methods and the use of rating scales, two of the methods used to collect information about personality.

Before considering these issues, remember that one of the most important purposes of personality assessment is to help investigators make decisions about people. Thus, a college student may be asked to take a test to help a counselor decide what career to recommend; a clinician may administer a test to help decide whether or not a person should be hospitalized or simply placed under psychiatric care. But such decisions involving selection or classification must also take risks and benefits into account. For example, a test score may classify an individual as suicidal. The therapist must then determine whether the person should be placed in a hospital, which is quite costly and has serious implications for both the individual and the community. While making this decision, the therapist takes into account the fact that suicide is quite rare (it has a low "base rate"). Because even good tests are imperfect and the chances of suicide are in general so low, usually the best prediction concerning this individual, regardless of his or her test score, is that suicide will not be attempted. Given only probability or likelihood as the basis for a decision, it would be best not to recommend hospitalization; but in view of the severity of loss in the event of suicide, the therapist may suggest hospitalization in spite of the low probability of that behavior. That is, the clinician would much rather err in the direction of hospitalizing a patient who would not have attempted suicide than in not hospitalizing a client who later does attempt suicide. In sum, testing must be considered within the broader context of decision making and cannot be divorced from the overall values of society.

Correlation

A *correlation* is a mathematical index used to express the degree of association between two variables. For example, suppose one hypothesizes that watching violent television programs is associated with aggressive behavior. To test this hypothesis, aggression in a group of children is measured, and the amount of violence these same children watch on television is also ascertained. Using this information, one can make a precise statement about the association between watching television violence and behaving aggressively.

The *correlation coefficient* is used to evaluate the degree to which these two variables are associated. It takes on values between −1.0 and +1.0, with the value −1.0 representing a perfect *negative correlation* and the value +1.0 representing a perfect *positive correlation*. These values almost never occur in real life, and certainly not in personality study. A correlation of ±1.0 means that the two variables are perfectly associated, so that one variable can be completely predicted from knowledge of the other. Correlations between −1.0 and +1.0 describe associations that are less than perfect. An example of a near-perfect correlation might be found when the most aggressive child also

Figure 11.1   Examples of positive and negative correlations (*r*) of different magnitude.

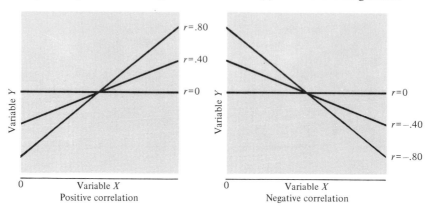

watches the most television violence; when the second most aggressive child is, say, third in the amount of violence watched; and so on, until the least aggressive child, who watches almost the least violence. This would yield a high, but not perfect, positive correlation. A correlation of zero means that the variables are totally unrelated to one another. To say it another way, they are related randomly. Several correlation coefficients are shown in Fig. 11.1.

Another way to evaluate a correlation is to ask how much variation in one variable can be explained by knowing its correlation with another variable; that is, how well one variable can predict the other variable. This is found by squaring the correlation coefficient. If the correlation between aggression and television violence is ±1.0, then all of the variance in aggression (i.e., differences between children in aggression) is explained by how much violence the child watches on television. Now suppose that the correlation between aggression and TV viewing was .30, a figure much closer to the correlations obtained in actual studies of the relationship between amount of exposure to television violence and aggressive behavior. Squaring this, we obtain .09 (.30 × .30 = .09). This tells us that about 9 percent of the variation in aggression is explained by how much violence children watch on television and that about 91 percent is not explained by knowing about TV-viewing patterns. Thus, it is clear that just having information about TV viewing will not tell us anywhere near all there is to know about violence.

Before we leave the topic of correlation, it is important to point out one well-known, but often overlooked, fact. It is not possible to determine *causation* from correlation. If the amount of exposure to television violence and aggression are correlated, then we cannot infer that exposure to television violence *caused* the aggression. Instead, we are left with many possible alternative explanations, among them:

1. TV viewing causes aggression.
2. Being aggressive causes a preference for violent television programs.
3. Some third variable is causing both the watching of aggression on television and aggressive behavior.

Many potential third variables are possible. For example, conflict with parents might cause both aggressive behavior and a preference for violent television shows. These three explanations are diagramed in Fig. 11.2.

There are some situations in which one direction of causation can be ruled out as very improbable. For example, there is a known correlation between rainfall and traffic accidents. The more it rains, the more accidents are reported. In this situation, one direction of causation is more plausible than the other: it is quite likely that rainfall causes accidents and not very likely that accidents cause rainfall. In personality research, however, there are few circumstances in which one causal explanation is so easily ruled out. As a result, many psychologists prefer experimental research in which they intentionally cause variation in one of the variables and maintain strict control over the situation in order to rule out third-variable explanations. These experiments usually allow investigators to make the stronger statement that changes in one variable *cause* changes in the other variable. Unfortunately, such an experimental method is not feasible for many of the questions asked in personality research. If one wanted to study the effects of corporal punishment on aggression in children, it would not be possible to use an experimental method, because it is unethical to manipulate the methods parents use to discipline their children.

While correlational methods may not be ideal for establishing causal relationships, they are of considerable importance in personality research.

Figure 11.2   Three causal interpretations of the correlations between television viewing and aggression.

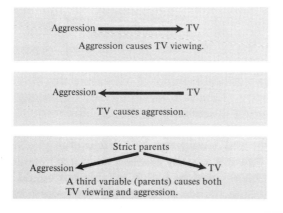

They play a vital role in the initial descriptive and exploratory phases of research. For example, suppose one were interested in uncovering the factors behind professional success. One might begin with an effort to determine the personality characteristics of successful professionals and how they differ from individuals who have not achieved distinction in their professions (Mac-Kinnon, 1962). To just what extent is professional success related to intelligence, to social skills, to self-centeredness, to perseverance, to creativity, to material values, to competitiveness, to anxiety, and to neurosis? The answers to these questions are provided by the degree of correlation between the measure of professional success and the measures of these personality dimensions. These correlations in turn provide a description of the successful professional. They do not tell us what causes professional success but they do tell us where to look and which variables ought to be investigated further.

In addition to their descriptive and exploratory value, correlational methods also help clarify theoretical questions. For example, it has been proposed by Eysenck that the basis for the personality difference between Jung's extraverts and introverts is neurophysiological; specifically, that introversion is a reflection of a tendency toward cortical excitation and that extraversion is a reflection of cortical inhibition (Eysenck, 1955). Since there is reason to believe that cortical excitation facilitates conditioning, Eysenck's theory leads to a prediction of a positive correlation between rate of conditioning and degree of introversion. The absence of a significant positive correlation would provide evidence, albeit inconclusive, against the theory and a positive relationship would tend to support the theory. A substantial number of investigators have in fact obtained correlations consistent with the predicted relationship, although several have not (Eysenck, 1967; Millett, 1960). A great deal of investigation is required to clarify the bases for inconsistencies in findings and to test other theoretical predictions to determine the validity and usefulness of Eysenck's theory of introversion and extraversion. Correlational as well as experimental studies constitute an important part of personality research on this and other personality dimensions.

Reliability and Validity

Beyond providing one of the basic methods used in personality research, correlational procedures are used to assess the quality of psychological measures. There are two critical features of a measure that determine its quality: reliability and validity. *Reliability* refers to the consistency or measurement error of the measuring instrument. A test of introversion that yielded very different scores for a sample of individuals every time they were tested would have low reliability and would not be very useful. *Validity* refers to the degree to which a measure actually assesses what it is intended to assess. The measure of introversion could be highly reliable but would lack validity if it were precisely assessing anxiety or fatigue or nonconformity, attributes other than introversion. A major concern of personality investigators is the reliability and validity of the measures they use.

Reliability

Measurement error occurs in almost all forms of observation. It is assumed that for each quality we attempt to measure there is a *true* score; the researcher's task is to make an observation that is used as the measure of this true quality. The *observed score* is usually not exactly the same as the true score. The deviation of the observed score from the true score is regarded as *measurement error*. In some fields of inquiry the measurement error may be quite small, whereas in other fields it tends to be great. An example of a situation in which measurement error might be minimal would be the measurement of height. In this case there is a standard measurement device such as a ruler or yardstick. The true height of an object or a person might be the number of inches it stands above the floor. Using a yardstick, it is possible to obtain a measure of height which is close to, if not exactly the same as, the true score. Even in this example, however, there might still be some sources of error. For instance, the person using the yardstick might have made some small error in applying the stick to the second three feet after the first three feet had been marked. In addition, he or she might have recorded, say, 69 inches even though the true measurement was 69½ inches, or have made some clerical error in recording the measurement. All things considered, however, there is little error in the recording of height, because height is clearly defined and can be measured quite simply.

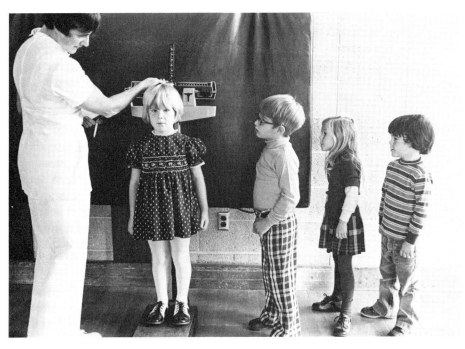

Height can be measured accurately because a valid and reliable measuring instrument exists. Unfortunately, in the study of personality traits, such unambiguous yardsticks are not yet available. (© Peter Vandermark)

Contrast this with some of the qualities that the social sciences attempt to measure. Usually, the concept under consideration is not defined in terms of any single measure. There is no unambiguous yardstick to tell us how depressed or aggressive someone is, but we can attempt to build yardsticks to measure these characteristics. Developing a measure that correctly measures what it is supposed to is a problem of *validity*. Assessing the error in application of the yardstick is a problem in *reliability*.

The scores yielded by a measure are of interest only if they vary between people. If they did not vary, then all persons would be scored exactly the same. However, not all of the variability in a score is really what we want it to be. We are interested only in true variability, or real differences between people. Usually, some observed variability is unwanted, random variability, or *error variance*. The study of reliability can help determine how much of what is being measured is such unwanted error.

Sources of error.   There are many potential sources of error. Concepts like depression and aggressiveness include many kinds of behaviors and ways of thinking; it is unlikely that any small set of items will accurately represent all that is implied by these concepts. The first major component of measurement error occurs when items do not fully represent a concept.

A second source of error results from inconsistent use of the measure by different test takers. For example, a questionnaire may contain ambiguous items that permit varying interpretations by different individuals. On the item "I like to fight," respondents are permitted two alternatives: "Yes" or "No." Some test takers might interpret this item as referring to fist fights; others, to verbal arguments. Some might read standing up for one's rights into the item, and some who like to box in amateur prizefights, but dislike fighting in other contexts, might be uncertain how to answer the question. And, if a third alternative to the item, such as "?" or "Unsure," were permitted, as is sometimes the case, there might be significant individual differences in the tendency to use this alternative. In fact, some people tend to mark items "Yes" when they are confused, while others mark them "No."

A third source of error is introduced when a measure is used in different settings. For instance, a person might score as more depressed if a test were given in a hospital than if it were administered in a private clinic or at home. All of these problems cause a measure to become less accurate than is desirable. In effect, measuring aggressiveness with an unreliable measure would be like trying to measure height with a rubber yardstick: sometimes the yardstick would be stretched too long, sometimes it would be squeezed too short (Nunnally, 1978).

Since the turn of the century, psychologists have attempted to formalize theories of measurement error and to express how error affects other aspects of investigations. Some of these ideas are discussed in the following sections.

Variability.   Reliability is one of the most fundamental concepts in science. If personality measures are unreliable, it becomes impossible to find correlations between the variables that are assessed by these measures. Suppose, for example, we hypothesize that people with high anxiety have a poorer memory of immediate events than people with low anxiety. Suppose further that every time we administer the measure, with repeated administrations only a few minutes apart, the scores vary so widely that the same person sometimes obtains the highest anxiety score, a middle-range anxiety score, or the lowest anxiety score. Since individual scores on the anxiety measure are so unstable, it would be impossible to establish a correlation between memory and anxiety, even if the hypothesis relating memory and anxiety were true.

Another way of describing our anxiety measure is in terms of the meaning of the different individual scores obtained on the measure. Let us suppose that some individuals obtain very high scores on the measure, others score in the middle range, and others fall into the lower range. These score differences can reflect the exact or true differences among individuals, if the measure is completely accurate, or they can reflect measurement error. The variability, which is based on individual differences, can therefore be divided into two components: *true variability* (representing real differences) and *error variability*. The reliability of a measure can be stated in terms of the relationship between these two components of variability; the greater the proportion of true variability relative to error variability, the more reliable the measure. This relationship can be expressed in simple quantitative form as follows:

$$\text{Reliability} = \frac{\text{True variability}}{\text{True variability} + \text{Error variability}} \text{ or}$$

$$= \frac{\text{True variability}}{\text{Observed variability}}$$

As can be seen in this formula, reliability expresses the percentage of the total variation that is true variability. The greater the error, the smaller the reliability ratio will be.

It is, of course, desirable to improve measures so that the proportion of total variability that is true variability increases, while the proportion that is error decreases. Unfortunately, it is no simple matter to find out which aspects of variability are true and which aspects are error.

Evaluating reliability.   There are many methods for evaluating reliability, with the choice of method depending on the potential source of measurement error. One source of error is time sampling. Errors arise from time sampling when a test is given at only one point in time and when a different score might be obtained if the test were given at some other time. Differences in an individual's responses might arise because of differences in mood, in interpersonal relationships, in physical condition, and in myriad other factors that can influence responses on a set of personality items. For example, consider the following items:

1. I like to spend a good deal of time by myself.
2. I feel uncomfortable in large social gatherings.
3. I have many friends.

Let us assume that, at time A, life is running fairly smoothly for a given extravert. At time B, however, he or she has just experienced a very distressful break in a close relationship. At time A, the extravert responds "No" to items 1 and 2 and "Yes" to item 3. But at time B, because of preoccupation with the disrupted relationship, he or she responds "Yes" to items 1 and 2 and, although hesitant, still responds "Yes" to item 3. Another extravert, who might have responded in the direction of extraversion at time A, could have just moved to a new community at time B. He or she might have no friends in the community and might have just attended a social gathering that was cliquish and unresponsive to strangers. While still answering "No" to item 1, this person would answer "Yes" to item 2 and "No" to item 3. There are many other factors that can influence the consistency of responses from time A to time B: inattentiveness on one of the testing occasions; different interpretations of an ambiguous item (Does "friends" mean "close friends"? How many is "many friends"?); the sex of the tester; the degree of rapport with the tester; ad infinitum. One of the reasons for having many items on a test is to reduce the influence of changes on a few items on the overall test score.

For a measure to be reliable, there must be some individual stability in the responses given. If people changed their responses every time a test was administered, the measure would be highly unreliable. A quantitative determination of a test's degree of reliability can be made by giving the measure on two occasions to the same group of individuals. The correlation between scores obtained at two times is an estimate of *test-retest reliability.* However, there are certain inherently unstable personality attributes for which the test-retest method of assessing reliability may be inappropriate. Emotions and moods such as joy, sadness, anger, fear, boredom, and fatigue are expected to fluctuate even though there may be individual differences in the basic tendency to be happy, angry, bored, or tired.

A second method of determining reliability, which is applicable to measures of mood and emotional change, is evaluating the *internal consistency* of a test, using a variety of methods. One method is *split-half* reliability in which test items are divided into two groups (such as odd- and even-numbered items), and the correlation between scores for these halves is obtained. The higher the split-half correlation, the greater the reliability.

Reliability of observations. In addition to the reliability of tests, psychologists are also interested in the reliability of behavioral observations, which are used in many kinds of situations. Behavioral observations have the advantage of being closer to the actual behaviors of individuals than self-report questionnaires. However, if they are to be useful, they must meet the same criteria of reliability. Here the sources of error are associated with different observers' recording the same behavior and with time-sampling issues.

The Skinnerian psychologist who is studying the effects of a particular reinforcement program on attentive behaviors in a primary-grade classroom needs to define attention in terms of behaviors that can be reliably scored by classroom observers. The investigator who wishes to determine whether a questionnaire measure of aggression in hospitalized patients is related to the actual frequency of aggressive behaviors observed on the ward is confronted with a similar problem. If a single observer is used, it is important that the observer score the same behavior in the same way whenever it occurs. Inconsistency in observer scoring can become especially problematic when different observers are used. To ensure the reliability of observations, observers typically are required to take a training program in which they practice the observational scoring system and correct inconsistent scoring of the same behavior before the observational procedure is used in an actual experiment.

In addition to minimizing potential observer error, it is also important to observe representative samples of behavior. If some preschool children are aggressive primarily before mealtime and others when they arrive each morning after being left by the parent who has brought them, it is important that both of these time periods are sampled in addition to other times.

Validity

It is not acceptable for scientific psychology to merely offer opinions about human behavior; psychologists must substantiate their claims, just as lawyers must provide evidence for the particular positions they advocate. There are many personality tests and it is important that psychologists become good consumers of these materials, which requires careful evaluation of the evidence used to support the claims of any given test.

Validity defines the meaning of a test or measure. What does it mean to have a test that measures anxiety, moral values, leadership potential, manic-depressive psychosis, or the likelihood that one will fail a flight training program? The meaning, or validity, of a test of anxiety is determined by the behaviors considered to be indicative of anxiety that the test uncovers. Thus, high scorers on a test of anxiety might be more likely than low scorers to forget painful events, to manifest increased heart rate and trembling of the hands while taking an examination, and to be heavy smokers. If high scorers were no different from low scorers on these and other measures, our anxiety test would have no validity. Alternatively, if the anxiety test was found to be correlated with aggressive behaviors and not with anxiety indicators, we would then have to change its name and its claim.

Evidence for validity is derived from demonstrating clear associations between a test and other measures of behavior. These associations or correlations define the meaning of the test. The same principle applies to our test of flight-training success even though the criterion is more evident than in the case of anxiety. Does our test predict success and failure in any kind of flight training context, or only in one particular military flight school? The more behaviors and measures that are associated with a test, the more confident we can be and the more things we are willing to say about its connotations. There are several types of validity that give different types of evidence about the significance of tests: content, criterion, and construct validity.

Content validity.   A test has *content validity* if it adequately covers the content area it is supposed to measure. For example, if you are being tested on what you learned in a personality course, the test is content valid to the extent that it represents all the material covered in the course. Traditionally, content validity has been of greatest concern in the area of educational testing. However, there are many instances in personality testing in which content validity is important. For example, if it is concluded that someone is compulsive solely on the basis of responses to a set of test questions, then, at the very least, there must be some assurance that the items on the test of compulsiveness adequately represent the behaviors encompassed by the diagnostic label "compulsive."

Content validity is the only type of validity for which the evidence is logical rather than statistical; inferences are often more about test construction than about test scores (Tenopyr, 1977). Establishing whether a test has content validity with regard to the inferences a test constructor wants to make requires good logic and intuitive skills. Establishing content validity for tests of knowledge, such as spelling competency, is more straightforward than for a test of a personality dimension like anxiety, where there is less agreement about the range of content that the test should sample. However, there can also be disagreement over the content validity of a test of knowledge. For instance, students often disagree with an instructor about whether the items on a particular examination adequately represented the material covered in lectures and readings. As will be shown in the following sections, other types of validity depend more on statistical methods, such as correlation, and less on intuition. Content validity is insufficient in itself to establish the validity of a test; other types of validity must also be used as the basis of making inferences about validity.

Criterion validity.   Some psychological tests have a very specific purpose; many are used exclusively to make predictions. A good example of a test used for a predictive purpose is the Scholastic Aptitude Test (SAT). Most of you took SATs to allow colleges and universities to evaluate your potential. To justify using SATs, the Educational Testing Service and the College Board, which are responsible for this instrument, had to provide some evidence that the test really was successful in forecasting future success in college. To do this they chose some index of success, such as grade-point average (GPA) during the first year of college, as the criterion against which the test was to be validated; thus the term *criterion validity.* The variables used to forecast the criterion are called predictor variables. The correlation between the predictor variables and the criterion defines the criterion validity of a test.

Tests should not be labeled as simply valid or invalid. Validity is not absolute; rather, it defines what can be inferred on the basis of a test or measure. Usually, tests have some validity for making certain specific statements. The SAT example will help illustrate this point. At one large California university, it was shown that high school SAT scores correlated .40 with success in the first year of college. This means that the SAT can be expected to forecast about 16 percent of the variability in the first-year college GPA and that 84 percent of the variability cannot be explained by SAT scores.

Is the SAT valid for predicting who will do well in the first year of college? Yes, the test predicts performance better than just guessing. However, most of the variation in college performance is left unexplained. If the validity or the correlation between SAT score and first-year college GPA had been 1.0, then the SAT would be considered the perfect predictor of college success. Thus, a wise college might want to continue using the SAT because it gives them one significant predictor of college success, allowing admissions officers to make better predictions about who will do well in college than they would have been able to make without the test information. However, the Educational Testing Service also advises colleges that the evidence for validity suggests they consider other information about potential students in addition to SAT scores.

When a test is used to predict some criterion that will occur in the future, the problem is one of *predictive validity*. The SAT example is a problem in predictive validity because the test is given to high school students to predict how well they will do in college. Studies of predictive validity are also common in industry, where tests are given to potential employees to predict which people will have the most success on the job.

A related type of criterion validity does not attempt to forecast what will happen in the future. Instead, the criterion measurement and the assessment of the predictor may occur at the same point in time. This is called *concurrent validity*. The Minnesota Multiphasic Personality Inventory (MMPI), a measure discussed more extensively in the next chapter, is an example of a test based *primarily* on concurrent validity. The MMPI is used to diagnose specific forms of psychopathology and covers both the less severe forms of mental disturbance (neuroses) and more severe forms in which there is disruption in thought processes and contact with reality (psychoses). For example, the test might be used to screen a large sample of military recruits. On the basis of scores on particular subscales of the test, some recruits might be diagnosed as schizophrenic (a psychosis characterized by disordered thinking and a split, or dissociation, between one's thoughts and feelings). This diagnosis might be validated through concurrent psychiatric interviews. The MMPI might also be used for predictive purposes, e.g., to predict which students, independent of college grades and measures of ability, will succeed in a clinical psychology graduate training program. We often find both concurrent and predictive procedures used to validate a test.

Construct validity.   About ten years ago, psychologist Zick Rubin (1970) wanted to develop a measure of romantic love. To do this, he had to define exactly what it was that he was attempting to measure. The problem Rubin faced was quite perplexing. After reviewing what many popular authors, playwrights, and famous people had to say about love, Rubin discovered that nearly everyone had their own definition. The index of *Bartlett's Familiar Quotations* lists more citations for *love* (769) than for any other word except *man* (843) (Rubin, 1973). Among all these quotations about love, there were some common themes, but no standard definition.

The problem Rubin faced is quite common among psychologists. Frequently, we want to measure something but are not clear about exactly what it is we want to measure. Measuring the width of a table or the length of a car is straightforward because we can directly observe cars and tables and there is little disagreement about what their length and width are. There are also standardized instruments for such measurement, like the familiar yardstick. The problems of psychological measurement are much more difficult because psychologists try to measure unobservable and ambiguous constructs like assertiveness or intelligence. In *construct validity*, there is a simultaneous attempt to define these constructs and to develop assessment devices to measure them.

There is a constant interplay between the validation of the measure of a psychological construct and the specification of the properties of the construct. Consider a questionnaire such as the Repression-Sensitization (R-S) scale, designed to differentiate individuals who tend to be repressors and those who tend to be sensitizers (Byrne, 1961) in their defenses against anxiety (see Chapter 4). Repressors are hypothesized as using a cluster of defense strategies characterized by avoidance of a threatening stimulus. Thus, they can be expected to deny threats; to forget painful, anxiety-evoking events; and to have difficulty verbalizing feelings of anxiety. Sensitizers, in contrast, are hypothesized as being especially wary of and attuned to possible threatening stimuli. They are likely to be overly preoccupied with threat, to be worriers, and to be obsessed with ideas and possibilities that evoke anxiety. They try to cope with threat, not by avoidance, but by preoccupation with the potential consequences of danger. They err on the side of alertness.

The measurement of this construct of repression-sensitization simultaneously poses two sets of issues. One set of issues has to do with the specification and demonstration of the properties of the construct. Does the concept apply to all threatening events or only to particular kinds of threats, such as threats to self-esteem? What are the specific ways in which avoidance and sensitization are manifested behaviorally? Do individuals consistently avoid or consistently behave in an oversensitized manner? Are some people repressors when faced with certain threatening stimuli and sensitizers when confronted with another type of threat? A second, related set of issues has to do with the validity of the Repression-Sensitization scale in differentiating between individuals who display the characteristics of repressors and those who manifest the characteristics of sensitizers. The two sets of issues are interconnected because, in order to study the construct of repression–sensitization, we must first have some way of determining the degree to which an individual is a repressor or a sensitizer. So we begin with one test that we have reason to believe might be a useful measure of this personality dimension. As we find out more about the correlates of the measure with other behaviors, we learn more about the properties of the construct. On the basis of a number of research studies (e.g., Bell and Byrne, 1978; Haley, 1974), it has been possible to gain a better understanding of the validity of both the R-S scale and the repression-sensitization construct.

It is evident that the construct validation of a test is a complex process with several steps. First, the concept of interest is carefully considered and items are generated that represent various aspects of the concept. At this point, the real work of construct validation begins. In a series of studies, scores on the test or measure are correlated with scores on other tests, measures, and behaviors. Each time a correlation is demonstrated, the meaning of the test is further defined and amplified. For example, if a measure of test anxiety is found to correlate $-.40$ with grade-point average and $+.30$ with number of illnesses experienced per year, then two new implications for the anxiety scale are found. The observed correlations define what the test measures; each time a new correlation is observed, the test takes on some new meaning. In this way, the test itself and the underlying theory or significance of the test develop together (Kaplan and Saccuzzo, 1981).

Construct validation is a never-ending process, in many ways similar to amassing evidence in support of a scientific theory. The researcher continually advances hypotheses, such as "If I am really measuring anxiety, then I would expect those scoring high on the anxiety scale to have more psychosomatic problems than those scoring low on the scale." This hypothesis is then evaluated in a systematic study, with each new study adding some meaning to the test.

In construct validation, two types of correlation are important to observe: convergent and discriminant. *Convergent validity* comes from demonstrating that a test measures the same thing as other tests. However, if the test correlates too well with other measures, then it might be unnecessary. If, for example, our anxiety scale correlated perfectly with one used for psychosomatic illness, then it might not be needed; the psychosomatic measure could be used in its place.

Discriminant validity, on the other hand, establishes that a test is measuring a different construct than that assessed by other measures. For example, if the anxiety scale correlated highly with a well-established test of achievement, it could be measuring achievement motivation instead of test anxiety. But a moderate or low correlation would tell us that the tests are distinctive and thus that the anxiety scale is measuring something other than achievement motivation.

How Low Reliability Affects Validity

As previously indicated, a scientific investigator is working under a handicap when reliability is less than perfect. In most studies, one attempts to find relationships between variables. Finding these relationships is greatly hampered if one or more of the variables is measured unreliably. Over the years, psychologists have systematically defined the ways in which measurement error serves to hamper other aspects of research. To have validity, there must be a reasonably high correlation between two measures of a construct. An earlier example of the relation between a test of anxiety and a measure of immediate memory indicated that, when one of the measures is not reliable, the observed correlation will be lowered. This means that the correlation is less than would be expected if the quantities were measured without error.

Measurement theory allows one to estimate the maximum correlation between variables if one or both variables is assumed to have been measured with some error. For example, if television violence and viewer aggression were correlated perfectly in nature but the reliability of each measure were .60, then the observed correlation would be only .36. Thus, 64 percent of the variance or predictability of one measure from the other would have been lost due to measurement error. A measure with a reliability of .50 cannot correlate more than .50 with any other measure, even if the true association between them were perfect (+1.0). This tells us that, without reliability, it is impossible to obtain convincing evidence for validity. In other words, reliability is required in order to demonstrate that a measure has meaning.

Collecting Information

Validity involves making inferences on the basis of a score or a measure. Of course, measures of personality require that information be gathered for input into the measurement device. There are a variety of procedures used to obtain the needed evidence that comprises a score.

Direct Observation

Psychologists with a behavioral or learning theory orientation prefer not to make any inferences on the basis of test scores. Instead, they favor *direct observation* of specific behaviors and limiting their statements to exactly what they have observed. A good example of this sort of behavioral assessment

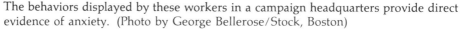

The behaviors displayed by these workers in a campaign headquarters provide direct evidence of anxiety. (Photo by George Bellerose/Stock, Boston)

was provided by Paul (1966) in a study of anxiety in public speakers. Paul needed a way to assess anxiety on the basis of overt behaviors which did not require asking the public speakers any questions about how they felt. To do this, he created a list of twenty specific behaviors that might be regarded as indications of anxiety. Then he asked subjects in his experiment to deliver a speech in front of an audience. Included in the audience were trained observers who recorded the frequency of different behaviors every twenty seconds. Table 11.1 shows the checklist for performance anxiety that was used in the Paul study. It lists the behaviors that were recorded, which then served as objective indicators of anxiety.

Rating Scales

A *rating scale* is a very helpful instrument for quantifying the impressions obtained in an interview or in observing behavior in a natural setting. Assume that an observer is asked to rate the trait of hostility. He or she is given the scale consisting simply of the trait name and a sequence of numbers, with 1 indicating a very low degree and 7, a very high degree, of hostility:

To increase the reliability and validity of the scale, the observers usually discuss the definition and scoring of the trait in advance. Before using the scale, they may be given behavioral examples of the varying degrees of hostility. Thus, indicators of very high hostility might be "angry remarks; gets into fights frequently," while indicators of very little hostility might be "acts friendly; rarely gets into arguments."

One of the problems with rating scales is the *halo effect:* the rater may judge an individual high on one trait simply because that person is high in another trait. Thus, if the rater finds the person very friendly, then that person might also be rated as highly intelligent, even though there is no good, objective reason for the latter rating. There are *negative halos* as well; if a subject is unfriendly, then a rating of unintelligent might be given. In general, great care must be taken in the construction of rating scales and in the training of observers, in order to lessen possible halo effects.

Another widely used technique related to the rating scale is the *adjective checklist.* The rater or the test taker is given a long list of adjectives, such as *active, ambitious, intelligent, strong,* and *zestful,* and checks off those that are considered characteristic of the person being rated. Each item on an adjective checklist is really a rating scale with two points: 0 and 1 (characteristic or uncharacteristic). In one study, the assessment staff of a research institute

---

Table 11.1   Timed behavioral checklist for performance anxiety

| | Time period | | | | | | | | |
Behavior observed	1	2	3	4	5	6	7	8	Σ
1. Paces									
2. Sways									
3. Shuffles feet									
4. Knees tremble									
5. Extraneous arm and hand movement (swings, scratches, toys, etc.)									
6. Arms rigid									
7. Hands restrained (in pockets, behind back, clasped)									
8. Hand tremors									
9. No eye contact									
10. Face muscles tense (drawn, tics, grimaces)									
11. Face "deadpan"									
12. Face pale									
13. Face flushed (blushes)									
14. Moistens lips									
15. Swallows									
16. Clears throat									
17. Breathes heavily									
18. Perspires (face, hands, armpits)									
19. Voice quivers									
20. Speech blocks or stammers									

Source: Reprinted from *Insight vs. Desensitization in Psychotherapy* by Gordon L. Paul with the permission of the publishers, Stanford University Press. © 1966 by the Board of Trustees of the Leland Stanford Junior University.

rated forty graduate students in various fields, half of whom had been designated by their instructors as outstandingly original and half as low in originality (Gough, 1960). Among the adjectives describing the highly original students were *adventurous, alert, curious, quiet, imaginative,* and *fair-minded.*

Among those descriptive of the less original subjects were *confused, conventional, defensive, polished, prejudiced,* and *suggestible.*

In contrast to the adjective checklist, which reduces the rating scale to two points, the *Q-sort* technique is an elaborate rating procedure in which the rater is given a set of adjectives or statements (see Chapter 7). These are sorted into piles according to the degree to which they are descriptive of the subject (Block, 1961; Stephenson, 1953). The California Q-sort developed by Block (1961) consists of one hundred statements on separate cards, such as:

- Has a wide range of interests.
- Is productive; gets things done.
- Seeks reassurance from others.
- Overreacts to minor frustrations; is irritable.

The rater is required to place the items in nine piles. Cards containing statements about the subject that really "hit home" are placed in pile 9; statements not at all descriptive are placed in pile 1. Most of the statements are to be placed in the middle piles, and fewer of the statements are to be placed at the extremes. Figure 11.3 shows a plot of the frequencies that are required, which are similar to what is called a *normal,* or *bell-shaped, curve.* Examination of the

Figure 11.3   The California Q-sort.

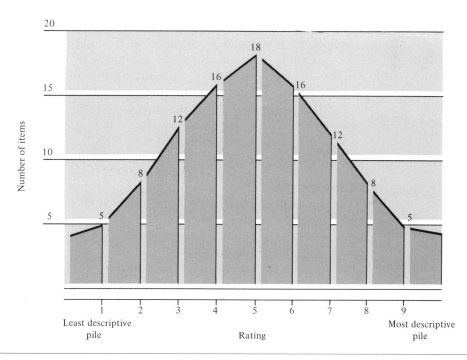

statements in the various piles provides a rich description of the subject's predominant qualities. In addition, rating scales such as the Q-sort can be used by the subject to describe him- or herself. When used in this manner, the scales reflect the person's self-concept and become self-report personality instruments.

Summary   To demonstrate correlations in psychology, as well as in other sciences, the variables under consideration must be measured. In the field of personality, measurement typically refers to the measurement of personality traits, which are usually difficult to assess with accuracy. To interpret results properly, it is necessary to be able to evaluate measures and how well they assess what they are supposed to measure. The variety of methods used to establish reliability and validity are tools to this end.

Specific Points

1. A *correlation* is a mathematical index that indicates the degree of association between two variables. A *correlation coefficient* may range from -1.0 to $+1.0$. The square of this value indicates the amount of variation in one score, or variable, that can be predicted knowing the value of the second variable. Correlation reveals the degree of association between two variables, but does not allow for inferences about *causation*.

2. *Reliability* refers to the degree of measurement error, or the degree to which the observed score deviates from the true score. Sources of error include inconsistent interpretation of items by test takers and the effects of the testing environment on test answers.

3. Types of reliability include *test-retest reliability*, in which the source of unreliability is differences in testing times, and *internal consistency*, which refers to the degree of consistency within a test at any given time period.

4. *Validity* defines the meaning of a test or measure; it indicates whether a test is in fact measuring what it is supposed to measure.

5. *Content validity* refers to whether a test adequately represents the content it is supposed to assess. The evidence for content validity is logical rather than statistical.

6. *Criterion validity* refers to the degree to which a test predicts (correlates with) a subsequent factor (*predictive validity*), as well as the degree to which a test is associated with other indexes that exist at the same point in time (*concurrent validity*).

7. A more complex type of validity is known as *construct validity*. In *construct validation* the meaning of a construct and the test measuring the construct are developed simultaneously. Test validation provides better understanding of the construct, while elaboration of the construct results in changes in the test.

8. Reliability places constraints on validity; for an instrument to have validity, measurement error must be minimized.
9. There are a variety of methods used to gather information about personality and to determine a test score or measure. These include *direct observation* of specified behaviors, self- or other reports on *rating scales, adjective checklists,* and *Q-sort* techniques.

Thought Questions

1. Can you think of examples of correlation being incorrectly interpreted as indicating causation?
2. What advice would you give teachers who want to make their examinations more reliable and valid?
3. Describe a test that would have appropriate content validity as an instrument for selecting a good teacher or a good executive.
4. SAT scores predict subsequent grade-point averages, but leave much of the variation in grades unaccounted for. What factors might be responsible for this less-than-perfect validity? Could a test be constructed to assess these other factors?

Personality Assessment

12 Psychologists frequently use tests to obtain information about clients. There are now thousands of personality tests that attempt to measure every imaginable human characteristic. It would not be feasible to describe each of them, but we will focus on some of the best-known general approaches to testing and the most widely recognized tests.

With few exceptions, traditional approaches to assessment assume that human characteristics can be measured independently of the situation or environment. If, for example, someone scores high on a personality assessment instrument of outgoingness, it is assumed that this individual is outgoing in many different situations and that the tested characteristic is one that the person brings to any situation. Such environment-independent characteristics are typically referred to as *traits*, or enduring tendencies to respond in a particular manner. As we will see in the following chapter, it is most useful to think of traits as dispositions to respond to specific types of situations in specific ways. For example, an individual might be described more accurately as having a disposition to respond aggressively to authority figures, to threats to self-esteem, or to competition, rather than simply as having aggressive tendencies. It is interesting to note, however, that few personality measures take situational factors into account when assessing individual differences in traits.

Personality measures designed to assess traits also view these characteristics of personality as *stable over time*. The developers of many measures assume, as did Freud and other psychoanalytic theorists, that personality is formed early in life. Once characteristics are established, they are not expected to change significantly. If, for example, a personality test reveals that Fred is aggressive, then it is expected that Fred will also be aggressive in the future. Fred will supposedly not display aggression for one month, followed by two months of passivity, followed by one week of aggression, and so on. The aggression should occur with some stability, or it will be concluded that Fred is unpredictable.

Most personality assessment techniques also assume that all humans possess the *same* characteristics. People differ from one another only in the degree to which they possess these common traits, such as anxiety, aggression, or the need for achievement. On the other hand, there are some personality assessment techniques that allow for the possibility that, while certain characteristics exist to some degree in all humans, there are some specific characteristics that may occur in only a few. For example, perhaps only a few people display true altruism, the sacrifice of personal pleasure for the betterment of others. This assumption is consistent with the position that humans are at the same time like all other humans, like some other humans, and like no other humans. In addition to these assumptions, the predominant view is that a person's personality represents the sum total of the variety and degrees of the relatively stable, consistent traits that he or she possesses.

Most personality assessment instruments are referred to more simply as personality tests. Traditionally, two major types of personality tests have evolved: objective and projective. In recent years, however, a number of newer approaches to human personality assessment have appeared. The two major types of personality tests, as well as the newer approaches (which are not really "tests" in the traditional sense) are discussed in this chapter.

Objective Personality Tests

You no doubt already have a good idea of what an *objective* test is; most college instructors give objective exams, with questions of the multiple-choice or true-false variety. This type of question requires that students recognize or remember items, rather than produce anything original, as in a term paper or essay test. In an objective test, one usually chooses from two or more designated alternatives. The response can be made on a standard answer sheet and can be machine- or computer-scored. The scoring is objective rather than subjective, with no judgments or evaluations required.

Like objective college exams, objective personality tests provide a written stimulus. The test taker is then asked to choose among two or more alternative responses, or to compare one written stimulus with one or more alternatives, selecting one or more of these choices according to a set of criteria. In some personality tests, people are asked to indicate which of two statements is more characteristic of them. For example, the following pair of alternatives appears in a test (the internal-external (I-E) locus of control scale) designed to assess individual differences in whether people believe that one can influence and control rewards and punishments or that they are externally controlled:

a. Many people can be described as victims of circumstances.
b. What happens to other people is pretty much of their own making.

The test taker is asked to select the alternative in which he or she more strongly believes. Another test provides three statements and asks the individual to indicate which is most and which is least characteristic. In all objective personality tests, the stimulus is a word, phrase, or statement, and the response requires selection among provided alternatives. Unlike objective college exams, however, there are no right or wrong answers. Subjects simply recall or determine the responses they believe are the best according to the instructions given. The test usually contains a number of items related to each of several personality characteristics. All items related to a single personality characteristic are known collectively as a *scale*. Some objective personality tests contain only one scale; however, most consist of several. If a person marks a greater than average number of items in the appropriate or scored direction on a scale, then that person is assumed to possess a greater than average degree of the trait measured by that scale.

Although they are widely used, there are many problems with objective personality tests. Early objective personality tests were particularly crude and inadequate by today's standards. But even the best of modern objective personality tests are not without recognized flaws. Psychologists continually strive to improve them, either through revision of existing scales or through development of new ones. Efforts to develop accurate objective personality tests have produced four major models or approaches to objective personality testing, each with its own unique assumptions.

Tests Based on Face Validity

Personality testing was used on a large scale in the United States during World War I. These early tests assumed that a person's response to an objective test item could be taken at face value. This assumption of *face validity* viewed the content of a test item as a straightforward indicator of a person's personality. If a person endorsed the item "I am outgoing," then it was assumed that this person was indeed outgoing. Linked to the assumption of face validity are the additional assumptions that people are honest, aware of their own characteristics, objective in evaluating these characteristics, and interpret the word *outgoing* in the same way as others taking the test and evaluating the test responses.

The first objective personality test to assume face validity of test responses (see. Chapter 1) was the Woodworth Personal Data Sheet (Woodworth, 1920). By the 1930s, however, many of the problems with the face validity approach had become apparent. Some of the problems were that people differ in their interpretations of an item's meaning and are limited in their ability to accurately observe and objectively report their own behavior. Other problems concern honesty. Tests based on face validity assume that a person is so open, flexible, and nondefensive that he or she responds as honestly as possible to each item. However, when tests are used to select people for jobs or, more dramatically, in criminal cases, honesty is not always in the test taker's best interests!

Closely related to the honesty of a test response is the notion of *social desirability*. A person might be honest but, without even being totally aware of it, might endorse the response believed to be the one the examiner wants to hear or the response that reflects most favorably on the subject. Edwards (1957, 1962, 1964) has most clearly articulated the importance of this factor in a person's response to an objective personality test. He argued that the meaning of any response on an objective personality test is influenced by the number of acceptable, expected, flattering, and complimentary responses that are selected. When endorsing the socially desirable rather than the true or realistic alternative response, the test score simply reflects the individual's need to present desired and culturally valued qualities. If correct, Edwards's notion of social desirability suggests that objective personality tests measure the need to be accepted and approved, which tends to be confounded with the other behavioral tendencies that the tester wants to assess. Although not without criticism (see Block, 1965; Norman, 1967), the concept of social desirability has been a problem with which practically every major objective personality test has had to cope.

Related to the concept of social desirability is the problem of response tendencies or biases. A *response bias* is the tendency to respond in a particular way, regardless of item content. Some individuals, for example, tend to agree or to say "Yes" regardless of the content of an item (see Jackson and Messick, 1962; Messick and Jackson, 1961). This tendency to agree with or mark "True" on an item regardless of the item's content is called *acquiescence*. There are many other biased response dispositions as well. For example, the corresponding negativistic response bias is the tendency to say "No," while the tendency to endorse the opposite of what a person believes to be true is known as *oppositional bias*. These response tendencies may in themselves reflect an individual's personality characteristics; e.g., acquiescence may reflect a tendency toward conformity and compliance, while a negativistic response bias may indicate hostile, oppositional tendencies. However, the main implication of response bias is that objective personality tests may measure factors other than those the test constructor intended to measure; that is, the possibility always exists that these response patterns have influenced a person's test score to such an extent that the meaning of a test score is subject to some doubt.

Empirical Approaches

The psychologists who developed early personality tests were unaware of problems like social desirability and response bias. However, years of research gradually eroded faith in face validity approaches to personality testing. Twenty years of experience with these early tests gave way to the introduction of various *empirical* approaches, which began around 1940 (see Dahlstrom, 1969). Objective personality tests based on face validity were replaced by tests such as the Minnesota Multiphasic Personality Inventory (MMPI), Cattell's Sixteen Personality-Factor Questionnaire (16 P-F), and other personality measures whose validity was based on research procedures and findings.

Objective personality tests vary in the extent to which they are based on theoretical considerations as well as empirical findings. Some tests are almost completely empirically based, with the theoretical rationale for the content and structure of the test items irrelevant. The critical question is the relationship of test responses to some criterion; e.g., a test of depression should differentiate depressed and nondepressed populations, and a test of the successful salesperson's personality should differentiate known groups of good and poor salespeople.

The empirical approach to objective personality testing attempts to find the behavioral correlates of certain test responses. For example, a test constructor interested in developing a measure of aggressiveness might identify a group of people assumed to be aggressive because they have been in three or more fights during the past year. Then a second group of nonaggressive people might be selected from individuals who have never been in a fight. A set of items is given to both groups and the items or scales marked more often by the aggressive than by the nonaggressive individuals could be used as an indicator or "test" of aggressive tendencies. It need not matter what the actual content of the items is; perhaps aggressive individuals tend to endorse the item "I like carrots" more often than the nonaggressive. This nevertheless becomes a valid test indicator of aggressiveness under the empirical approach. In most instances, however, one can perceive the connection between items on empirically based tests and the criterion behavior.

The MMPI.   The *Minnesota Multiphasic Personality Inventory* (*MMPI*) is perhaps the best-known and most widely used empirically based personality test. This test was introduced at a time when the problems facing objective personality tests seemed all but insurmountable. The MMPI not only came to the rescue, but actually kindled new interest in objective personality testing by providing solutions to the problems intrinsic to the earlier, face validity approach.

The MMPI is a true-false questionnaire consisting of more than five hundred self-reference items. The subject is instructed to respond true or false to each item as it applies to him or her. The items vary widely in content, such as:

- I like to read news magazines.
- I never have trouble falling asleep.
- People are out to get me.

The test contains four validity scales and ten clinical scales. The validity scales of the MMPI were designed to meet the problems inherent in its predecessors. The first validity scale, the "cannot say" scale, records the number of items in which no response is made. This scale is related to the person's level of defensiveness, that is, his or her tendency to avoid revealing personal information. As more items are omitted, the validity of the MMPI results becomes increasingly questionable. If too many items are omitted, then no effort is made to interpret the test, since what has been measured cannot be a true reflection of the person's personality. In more recent uses of the MMPI, respondents are encouraged not to omit any of the items.

A second validity scale, perhaps the most important MMPI scale, is the F scale. The F scale consists of sixty-four items that are rarely endorsed by the general population, such as:

- Everything tastes the same.
- I see things, animals, or people around me that others do not see.

The items cover many content areas, ranging from paranoid thinking to hostility and poor health habits. On the average, the general population endorses about four F-scale items per test (Dahlstrom, Welsh, and Dahlstrom, 1972), while psychiatrically disturbed individuals might endorse eight to sixteen of them, reflecting the nature and severity of their psychological impairment. Furthermore, persons who see themselves as in need of assistance may indicate this by responding to as many as twenty-five of the sixty-four F-scale items in the scored direction (Graham, 1977). However, even the most severely emotionally disturbed individual rarely, if ever, would have enough symptoms to justify marking more than sixteen to eighteen items, and even this many endorsements on the F scale is questionable.

By determining the number of F-scale items endorsed in the scored direction, it becomes possible to evaluate possible response tendencies, as well as a person's approach to the test. If the subject fails to comply with the instructions or cannot read and understand the items, then about half the F-scale items would be endorsed, since these problems result in a random response to the items. In a similar manner, if a person deliberately fakes, in order to appear more disturbed than is warranted, then again there would be far more items endorsed in the scored direction than would realistically be justified.

The F scale is used in combination with the two remaining MMPI validity scales, the K and the "Lie" (L) scales. The K scale is related to social desirability and includes items like:

- At times I feel like swearing.
- At times I feel like smashing things.

Extremely high scores ("No" responses) suggest a defensive approach in which the person is trying to fake a "good" profile. The L scale is similar to the K scale, but much less subtle. An example of an L-scale item is "I always tell the truth." It is assumed that everyone has lied at some time. Thus, responding "Yes," in which case the person claims that he or she never lies, would in fact indicate that the person is lying in order to look good. With the use of these validity scales, errors in measuring a person's personality can be markedly reduced so that the test user can feel more confident that the test scores actually reflect designated behavioral tendencies or personality characteristics.

The ten clinical scales of the MMPI (see Table 12.1) are used to measure specific personality disorders and related personality characteristics. It should be noted, however, that the MMPI was originally designed to measure abnormal or disturbed personality. Eight of the clinical scales of the MMPI were formed by the criterion-keying method, in which, as we mentioned, groups of people known to manifest a certain abnormal behavior, such as depression or schizophrenia, were given the items of the MMPI. Items that were more frequently endorsed in a certain direction by these groups than by a control group were then selected to form a scale that purportedly measured the characteristics (e.g., depression or schizophrenia) of the criterion groups. In other words, each scale consisted of those items discriminating the criterion groups from the normal group.

In spite of its apparent strengths and widespread use in clinical settings (Lubin, Wallis, and Paine, 1971), the MMPI also has a number of important limitations and problems. A detailed analysis of its limitations in terms of the various types of reliability reveals that test-retest reliability over short periods of time is acceptable, but often marginally so. And for longer time intervals, there is substantial unreliability. For most of the scales, individual scores are not stable (Dahlstrom and Welsh, 1960). The reasons for the poor long-term reliability of the MMPI have not been clearly established. One important factor that must be taken into consideration in interpreting the long-term unreliability of the MMPI is its dual use as a measure of psychopathology and as a measure of personality attributes. One would expect fluctuations over time in the degree of psychological disturbance as individuals seek treatment, as they mature and develop better skills in coping with their problems, as crises disappear, and as new stresses arise. These fluctuations in the individual's psychological state may obscure relative stabilities of the psychological traits that are also assessed by the MMPI.

In addition to poor long-term reliability, there are other significant problems with the MMPI. First, many items can be found on more than one scale, in some cases on as many as six. Paralleling this problem, the ten clinical scales are highly intercorrelated, so that some analyses of the interrelationships among the scales indicate that as few as two underlying dispositions are being measured (Dahlstrom, Welsh, and Dahlstrom, 1975): a general psychological adjustment variable and the degree to which the individual exercises control over feelings and actions. Furthermore, the meaning of MMPI scores varies as a function of demographic characteristics such as age and sex (Webb, 1970). For example, standardized interpretations of specific MMPI

Table 12.1   The Meaning of the Clinical Scales of the MMPI

Scale number	Scale name	Important meanings
1	Hypochondriasis	Preoccupation with body and fears of illness
2	Depression	Symptomatic depression; dissatisfaction; low morale
3	Hysteria	Immaturity; denial of problem
4	Psychopathic deviate	Delinquency; antisocial tendencies; family problems
5	Masculinity-femininity	Male and female interests
6	Paranoia	Suspiciousness; hostility; paranoid symptoms such as delusions (false beliefs)
7	Psychasthenia	Anxiety; psychological discomfort
8	Schizophrenia	Alienation; bizarre behavior or thoughts
9	Hypomania	Elevated mood; hyperactivity
10	Social introversion	Tendency to withdraw or become uninvolved in social relationships

Source: Adapted from *The MMPI: A Practical Guide* by John R. Graham. Copyright © 1977 by Oxford University Press, Inc. Used by permission of the author and the publisher.

profiles seem to fit males better than females (Kelley and King, 1979). In addition, as personality measures, most of the subscales can have several different meanings. For example, the overall masculinity-femininity score obscures the important distinction between a person's *identity* as a male or female and his or her *interests,* which may be socially defined as masculine or feminine. A well-adjusted female may be interested in math and sports, and a male with no sexual identity problems may have interests in cooking and art. In fact, one study has shown that well-adjusted college students of both sexes have strong interests in both traditionally feminine and traditionally masculine activities (Bem, 1975).

Nevertheless, despite these limitations, the MMPI has proved to be a useful instrument. More than six thousand studies have been conducted using the MMPI (Dahlstrom et al., 1975), providing ample documentation of its validity. Most of the studies demonstrate that the MMPI does sort people into appropriate diagnostic categories. Newer investigations also attempt to find relationships between MMPI categories and personality types that were not included in the original scales. A recent study of *anhedonia* (a term used to describe the inability to experience pleasure) exemplifies this type of research. Although it is common to think of anhedonia as a form of depression, it has been suggested that groups experiencing this condition share many of the same characteristics as schizophrenics. Thus, it was hypothesized that anhedonia would be associated with an MMPI profile pattern that included a high score on the schizophrenia scale. Data have tended to confirm this pattern (Penk, Carpenter, and Rylee, 1979), thus defining a new meaning for a particular MMPI pattern. In addition, because the MMPI has a large number of items, it has become possible to derive new personality scales using subsets of these items. These new measures include several important research instruments such as the previously cited Repression-Sensitization scale (Byrne, 1961) and the Taylor Manifest Anxiety scale (Taylor, 1953).

Factor Analysis

Some approaches to the study of personality depend on sophisticated methods such as *factor analysis,* a statistical procedure taking large amounts of data from tests, rating scales, or behavioral observations and reducing them down into smaller, more manageable, chunks.

Factor analysis reduces the redundancy or overlap in a set of scores or data. If two variables are correlated, this means that the two overlap in measuring some common characteristic. For example, there is a correlation between how fast a person runs and how far he or she can jump. If we took a group of people and recorded their speeds in the hundred-yard dash and their distances in the broad jump, we would no doubt find a positive correlation. This correlation would mean that those who run faster also jump farther. The association or correlation between performance on these two track events suggests that some common process or ability, such as leg strength, underlies both running and jumping. Each event requires its own unique abilities, or the two would be perfectly correlated; however, a common factor, such as leg strength, is related to both. The correlation tells us the extent to which some common factor or factors underlie performance in both events; the higher the correlation, the more the two have in common.

It may be helpful to think of factor analysis as analogous to finding basic elements in chemistry. A chemist might use technical methods to find what elements or combinations of elements are parts of a given compound. In factor analysis, the "compounds" are large samples of behaviors or responses to tests and scales. Submitting such sets of data to factor analysis is like reducing a large array of information to its basic elements. Objective personality tests based on factor analysis assume that all the descriptive characteristics found in personality test scales can be reduced to just a few common factors that describe the underlying and fundamental aspects of human personality. Factor-analytic procedures are used to ascertain these fundamental aspects of human personality.

Guilford's work.   The pioneer in the factor analytic model of objective personality assessment was J. P. Guilford. Guilford's approach was to intercorrelate the results of a wide variety of existing personality tests to develop a single test that measured the essentials of all the other existing tests. Guilford's initial efforts were published in the early 1940s (Guilford, 1940; Guilford and Martin, 1943) and culminated in the Guilford-Zimmerman Temperament Survey (Guilford and Zimmerman, 1956). Presumably, the Guilford-Zimmerman scale reduced human personality to ten basic characteristics or dimensions: general activity, restraint, ascendance (leadership), sociability, emotional stability, objectivity, friendliness, thoughtfulness, personal relations, and masculinity. But despite the careful work and laborious effort that went into the Guilford-Zimmerman scale, the test failed to find widespread acceptance from either researchers or test users. Part of the problem may have been the measure's limited utility for clinical populations. The test market was far greater for tests like the MMPI, which measured abnormal personality and was appropriate for clinical settings. Another problem with the Guilford-Zimmerman scale was that very limited data were produced in support of the test's stability over time. In other words, if Guilford's ten factors did indeed represent the basics of human personality, there was little evidence that what was being measured remained stable features of the individual whose personality had been assessed.

The 16 P-F.   Following Guilford's early work, R. B. Cattell also used the factor-analytic method to ascertain and measure the fundamental characteristics of human personality. Cattell's starting point consisted of an analysis by Allport and Odbert (1936) of over 4,500 adjectives applicable to human beings listed in an unabridged dictionary. Cattell first added to this list other descriptive adjectives taken from psychiatric and psychological literature and then reduced the list to approximately 170 items which he believed were relatively independent and captured the meaning of all the words on the original list. He then asked college students to describe their friends according to the terms on the reduced list and factor analyzed the results. Cattell reported that the items could be reduced to 36 dimensions that were labeled *surface traits* (see Cattell, 1957). Subsequent attempts to further reduce this list ultimately uncovered 16 dimensions, or factors, labeled *source traits.*

Presumably, Cattell's 16 source traits, including intelligence and ego strength, provided the same information that Guilford's ten dimensions of personality supposedly measured. In 1949, the items most strongly related to each of the 16 factors were identified and selected for inclusion in the 16 Personality-Factor Questionnaire, better known as the 16 P-F (see Cattell, 1949). However, even the factors of the 16 P-F intercorrelated, so that these 16 factors were themselves factor analyzed. The results of these additional factor analyses of the 16 P-F scale have yielded from 4 to 8 so-called second-order factors. Among the factors that were identified are introversion-extraversion, anxiety, affectivity, and free will versus resignation (Cattell, Eber, and Tatsuoka, 1970). Of these, the first two factors are best replicated, that is, most often found in other factor-analytic studies.

In considering the reliability of the 16 P-F, the question of stability over time is again at issue. For the short term, the test-retest scores are relatively higher than for the MMPI. Indeed, the 16 P-F is perhaps the soundest and most carefully constructed personality trait test. Nevertheless, as in the case of the MMPI, long-term stability is lacking. This issue will be explored in greater detail in the next chapter.

The Theoretical Model

The fourth model of objective personality assessment uses theories of human personality in selecting test items. If, for example, a given theory divides human personality into three components—mood, thought, and behavior—then items would be selected to measure each of these components. One of the best-known and most popular of these instruments is the Edwards Personal Preference Schedule (EPPS; Edwards, 1954, 1959).

Murray (1938) theorized that a number of basic needs underlie human personality, including such motivations as the need to achieve, conform, affiliate, gain power, and be nurtured. Selecting from Murray's list of human needs, Edwards chose fifteen and constructed items to assess the extent to which each of these was present in any person. Like the MMPI and the 16 P-F, the resulting EPPS contained a number of validity items designed to detect response biases. Furthermore, to eliminate social desirability, the EPPS was constructed so that each person had to choose between two items in a pair, selecting the more characteristic one. Each item in the pair reflected a different need, and an effort was made to equate the items on social desirability, in order to reduce the influence of this bias on the test results. An example of an item pair is:

a. I feel depressed when I fail at something.
b. I feel nervous when giving a talk before a group.

One difference between the EPPS and other objective tests is that the scores assessing each need are interdependent, reflecting each individual's own preference hierarchy. If some needs receive high scores, then others must receive low scores for a given person because of the forced-choice methodology that is used. For example, in pairing an achievement and an affiliation item, selection of the achievement item augments the achievement scale score while not adding to the affiliation scale score. In contrast, on other tests it is possible to obtain high scores on all the subscales. Although the EPPS is a well-designed instrument from a technical standpoint, it also does not have a good record for long-term stability. Thus, like the MMPI and the 16 P-F, it is subject to some of the same factors that limit the usefulness of these tests as measures of enduring personality traits.

Summing Up

Objective personality tests have been guided by a variety of techniques in search of a method of ascertaining and measuring the fundamental aspects of human personality. There is little doubt that these tests do measure important individual differences in behavior. However, just what is being measured

Box 12.1   FUN WITH PERSONALITY TESTS

Objective personality tests include questions about a wide array of beliefs, feelings, and experiences. At times certain questions may be perceived by the test taker as trivial or inconsequential. The apparent pointlessness of some test items has generated a parlor game of devising personality inventories composed of only facetious queries. One publicized true-false list, in part created by the humorist Art Buchwald, contains the following questions:

1. When I was younger, I used to tease vegetables.
2. Sometimes I am unable to prevent clean thoughts from entering my mind.
3. I am not unwilling to work for a jackass.
4. I would enjoy the work of a chicken flicker.
5. I think beavers work too hard.
6. It is important to wash your hands before washing your hands.
7. It is hard for me to say the right thing when I find myself in a room full of mice.
8. I use shoe polish to excess.
9. The sight of blood no longer excites me.
10. It makes me furious to see an innocent man escape the chair.
11. As a child, I used to wet the ceiling.
12. I am aroused by persons of the opposite sexes.
13. I believe I smell as good as most people.
14. When I was a child, I was an imaginary playmate.

Source: *American Psychologist* 20, 1965, p. 990. Reprinted by permission.

is frequently unclear. If human personality is stable over long periods of time, then objective personality tests fail to reflect it. On the other hand, there may well be changes in personality over time. In addition, if personality attributes can be measured only in the context in which these traits are manifested, then the tests may be "accurate" and test theory must be modified to deal with this difficult issue.

Projective Personality Tests

Long before objective personality tests based on face validity were replaced by better objective instruments, an entirely new and different idea about personality assessment had emerged. This second major traditional approach is known as the *projective* method. In projective methods, the person's task is to produce something spontaneously, through such procedures as associating to test stimuli. Rather than selecting among written alternatives, the test taker has few guidelines for the type of response required; therefore, almost any response can be obtained. Given such a wide range of possible responses, it is difficult to formulate a set of rules for scoring purposes; subjective evaluation is often the most workable solution. As a result, agreement in scoring between testers and between responses is often far from perfect, even though some objective scoring techniques have been developed (see Chapter 16).

Projective tests begin by presenting a person with an ambiguous stimulus like an inkblot or a picture with some indeterminate elements. The examiner might ask a question as simple as "Tell me what this might be," or the subject might be asked to make up a story about an ambiguous picture. In either case, the person must use his or her creative and analytical capacities in providing an answer; alternatives are not provided. In exchange for the loss of objectivity in scoring and evaluating a person's response, projective tests provide much more opportunity for the expression of individuality. They therefore are thought to be potentially capable of detecting more subtle and varied aspects of personality than is possible with objective tests.

All projective tests are based on the projective hypothesis (Frank, 1939), which has its roots in Freud's theory of personality (see Chapter 4). This hypothesis states that the person's response to an ambiguous or vague stimulus is a reflection (i.e., projection) of his or her own needs and feelings. That is, the person, in giving meaning to an ambiguous stimulus, "projects" onto that stimulus his or her needs, feelings, strivings, and thought processes. Moreover, the projection can take place without the individual's being aware that significant aspects of the personality are being revealed. Thus, it is assumed that projective tests provide more access to the kinds of unconscious impulses and attitudes with which psychoanalysis is concerned.

The Rorschach Inkblot Test

The *Rorschach Inkblot Test,* in which subjects are asked to respond to ambiguous inkblots, was the first formal projective method. One of the earliest references to the possibility of using inkblots to assess individual differences dates back to the Civil War (Keiner, 1857). Keiner noted that, when asked to interpret the meaning of an inkblot, each individual tended to produce unique and idiosyncratic responses. Inasmuch as responses to inkblots were different for each individual, it seemed reasonable to conclude that different interpretations reflected differences between individual interpreters. If most subjects had provided the same or even similar responses to the same inkblot stimulus, then the obvious conclusion would have been that the interpretations were simply a reflection of the characteristics of the inkblot. For example, asking subjects to describe a table or a chair would not reveal much about the subjects because all responses would be relatively similar.

Objective personality tests attempt to measure individual differences in specific attributes. The Rorschach Inkblot Test, on the other hand, makes no assumptions concerning the characteristics that should or will be measured. Instead, the Rorschach is so flexible that it leaves open the possibility of assessing the most unique aspects of an individual. There are, however, certain broad dimensions of personality, including impulse control, sensitivity to internal thoughts and feelings, sensitivity to external inputs, and the tendency to distort reality, that the test attempts to assess in all individuals.

Figure 12.1   An inkblot similar to those used in the Rorschach test. (Mussen and Rosenzweig, 1977), p. 152. Used by permission.)

The Rorschach consists of ten cards, each displaying a meaningless, bilaterally symmetrical inkblot. To get an idea of what the cards look like, you can simply repeat the same method Hermann Rorschach used to construct the original test (Rorschach, 1921). Place a few drops of ink on a white card or piece of paper, carefully fold the card in half, open it, and then let it dry. What emerges is an apparently meaningless blob that is symmetrical on both sides of the crease, so that each half looks like the mirror image of the other half. A little inspection soon seems to reveal meaning, and all or parts of the inkblot will begin to resemble familiar shapes and objects (see Fig. 12.1).

The Rorschach test contains five black-and-gray inkblots; two that are black, gray, and red; and three cards consisting of a variety of pastel colors. The Rorschach is administered with minimal instructions, since it is designed to be ambiguous and unstructured. Unlike objective personality tests, the Rorschach is typically administered individually, testing one person at a time. Throughout the sometimes-lengthy testing period, the examiner writes down each response, at the same time offering no clues to the type of response required. In the typical situation, the card is presented and the examiner asks,

"What might this be?" The subject is then free to give one or several responses to each of the ten cards, responding to the entire inkblot, to some portion of it, or to both.

After the subject has responded to each of the ten cards, without information or comments from the examiner, the examiner goes through the cards a second time and asks a set of carefully worded questions, often getting the subject to elaborate on responses. The purpose of this second phase is to provide the examiner with sufficient information to score the test. Scoring is evaluated in terms of location (what area of the blot is used); whether or not color or shading is used in formulating a response; the kind of object described (animal, human, inanimate); the presence of activity or movement; the correspondence of the percept to real objects; and how typical or atypical the response is. Each of these dimensions of scoring is believed to be associated with personality characteristics.

The person's scores, which can be summarized in terms of the frequency of each of the various dimensions, are referred to as the quantitative aspects of the test. Of equal significance, however, is an analysis of the actual content of the person's responses, which is referred to as the qualitative aspect of the test. Rorschach interpretation is based on an evaluation of each scoring category as well as the quality and specific content of each response and how this

This man is responding to a Rorschach inkblot, one of the principal methods of projective measurement. (Ken Robert Buck/The Picture Cube)

varies from card to card. Considering the scoring categories, the human movement response (for example, "A man dancing") is thought by some to reveal introversion, in that the perception of movement is believed to indicate inner-directedness. A response like "That is a bat, but not a good one" might lead to inferences about obsessiveness. According to a proponent of the Rorschach, an experienced examiner can make some rather detailed and specific descriptions of the person's personality and emotional functioning. Although it is suitable for assessing normal personality, the Rorschach, like the MMPI, finds its most extensive use in clinical settings in which there is a need to assess maladaptive thought processes, motivational conflicts, and problems in emotional and behavioral control.

The Rorschach is an extremely complex and subjective method of personality assessment. From the very start, it has been a highly controversial personality instrument. It has been extremely difficult to evaluate its reliability and validity, in part because there are no universally accepted methods of administration, scoring, and interpretation. In addition, because the number of responses can vary widely, it is difficult to be certain of the meaning of the frequency of particular response characteristics. For example, the number of human movement responses in a Rorschach record will vary with the total number of responses given as well as with the tendency to perceive human movement in the blots. Also, test-retest studies reflect considerable instability in Rorschach responses over time. As a result of these and other problems, there is little consensus among psychologists concerning the soundness of the Rorschach and its validity as a measure of human personality. In the case of an instrument as flexible and complex as the Rorschach, one must ask: validity for what? For each dimension of personality? For the assessment of psychopathology? For the prediction of reactions to the stress of pilot training? The evidence bearing on the utility of the Rorschach in various personnel selection programs has been largely negative, while evidence for its utility as a personality measure has been variable. For example, its validity is questionable as an indicator of self-concept and sensitivity to others, but the Rorschach has proved to be somewhat effective in assessing self-control and ego strength (Klopfer, 1954; Zubin, Eron, and Schumer, 1965). In addition, there are also data indicating that specified combinations of Rorschach scores can reliably distinguish schizophrenics from neurotics (Fisher, 1967), even though there are many negative findings concerning the assessment of psychopathology. The Rorschach Prognostic Rating Scale, an index based on the assignment of weights to such features of the response scale as human movement and the match between the response and the ink-blot stimulus, has proved to be a promising predictor of response to therapy (Fisher, 1967; Klopfer and Taulbee, 1976). In general, however, the Rorschach is a better instrument for assessing the person as he or she is currently functioning, not as he or she will function at some future time (Exner, 1974).

It is interesting to note that a projective test like the Rorschach is subject to some of the same difficulties as objective measures; both reflect substantial instability over time. An individual's response to an inkblot (projective test) or to an MMPI item (objective test) can be seen as a function of one's personality disposition, a more temporary personality state, the specific stimulus (inkblot or test item), and the situational context in which the test takes place. When the stimulus remains constant, as in test-retest studies, variability in the subject's response can reflect changes in any of the remaining three determinants of test performance.

The Thematic Apperception Test (TAT)

The *Thematic Apperception Test* (*TAT*) was first published in 1935 by Christiana Morgan and Henry Murray of Harvard University (see Chapter 1). Like the objective EPPS, the TAT is based on Murray's (1938) theory of needs. Murray proposed that human beings have to deal with the expression, satisfaction, and frustration of a number of psychological needs such as aggression, nurturance, affiliation, achievement, dependency, power, and sex. The TAT was specifically developed as a vehicle that would permit individuals to express these needs. The TAT purports to be a measure of human personality functioning that can be used in the assessment of normal as well as abnormal personality. Unlike the Rorschach, the TAT is not widely used in determining the extent of emotional disturbances, although it is used to ascertain the content of an individual's conflict and the defenses employed in coping with psychological conflicts.

The TAT contains twenty-nine cards, each showing a picture or scene. In addition, one blank card is included. Although vague, each picture contains a specific type of content in which the dominant feature is usually one or more humans; e.g., a picture of a seated boy and a violin resting on a table. Some pictures contain only a child and others, only adults. The ages and sexes of the characters are sometimes mixed, such as a middle-aged woman and an older girl, or a young man and an older woman. Although some of the cards can be used for any age group or either sex, others are specifically designed for men, women, boys, or girls. Inasmuch as the pictures of the TAT are more meaningful or structured than the Rorschach inkblots, each picture tends to elicit a certain type of response. Thus, for example, a picture of an older and a younger man together typically elicits stories about father-son relationships. However, there is sufficient variability between individuals' interpretations of the cards to yield information about personalities and problems. A card similar to some of the TAT stimulus cards is shown in Fig. 12.2.

When administering the TAT, the examiner presents the cards one at a time. The subject is requested to make up a story about each picture, stating what led up to the story, what is happening, what the characters are thinking and feeling, and what the outcome will be. Responses are recorded word for word.

The TAT is similar to the Rorschach in several respects. Neither test has a universally accepted, standardized scoring or interpretation. However, both have a number of commonly accepted scoring techniques. Scoring of the TAT can be more difficult and complex than scoring of the Rorschach. Most scoring systems tend to require that the hero, needs, environmental forces or

Figure 12.2   A card similar to TAT stimulus cards. (Mussen and Rosenzweig, 1977, p. 153. Used by permission. Photo by Ted Polumbaum.)

press, themes, and outcomes be identified. The hero is the central character in each picture; it is assumed that the storyteller will identify with the hero. Therefore, the needs and motives of the hero, particularly those that recur from story to story, are assumed to reflect the needs and motives of the storyteller. *Press* refers to the environmental forces or obstacles facing the hero. Again, as the same types of such obstacles recur in several stories, the likelihood increases that the storyteller perceives similar difficulties in his or her own life. Recurrent conflicts and outcomes also are believed to reflect characteristics of the storyteller. In sum, what the examiner looks for in the TAT are themes concerning needs, motivations, obstacles, conflicts, or outcomes that recur in the individual's stories for different pictures. These repeated themes are interpreted as reflecting the basic underlying motivations and conflicts of the storyteller.

As an example of how the TAT is used, consider the following story told by Robert Cooper, the husband described in Chapter 1. The stimulus card to which his story was given depicts a young man with bowed head and an older woman looking into the distance.

The fellow has just told the woman some bad news. He is a friend of her son who was living in another town. I'm not sure why. Perhaps he was in the service or maybe he had taken a job in that town. The son has been in an accident. He was a passenger in the car that his friend was driving. His friend had been drinking, not heavily, but had taken a couple for the road, as it were. Anyway, he was driving pretty fast and didn't see the sign for an approaching S curve. When he tried to slow down, he skidded into a tree. He luckily had only a few scratches, but the woman's son was badly injured and is in a coma. The friend naturally feels guilty and it was very hard for him to tell the mother about the accident. (Q: What happens?) The mother is extremely upset but she manages to maintain her self-control. She rushes to the hospital where she keeps watch at his bedside. After 24 hours, he comes out of the coma and eventually recovers.

There are a number of themes and needs that can be inferred from this story. One might be the untrustworthiness of friends and frustration of the need for affiliation. However, this possible theme is secondary in the story and did not appear in any of Robert's other stories. A more central theme to this and several of Robert's other TAT responses bears on the relationship of a young man to a mother figure. The core sequence of events consists of a son separated from his mother; a very negative, painful experience; reunion with the mother; and then a positive outcome. One might infer from this sequence that separation from his mother is very painful for Robert. He cannot acknowledge the frustration of his dependency needs and can express it only indirectly, through physical injury and through the visit of his friend in the story. The guilt expressed by the friend, a central character in the TAT picture, may be a displaced expression of his own guilt about his anger over frustration of dependency needs. There are other features of the story that might also be revealing: drinking, self-destruction, displacement of responsibility (the accident was the friend's fault). In the case of both subordinate themes and central theme, however, one looks for repeated expressions of a theme in a number of stories before drawing inferences about an individual's basic needs and conflicts.

In reviews of the TAT, Exner (1974) and Murstein (1963) noted that test-retest reliability can be quite high under the specific condition that only a particular variable is studied. But even under such a specific condition, data are still insufficient for drawing firm conclusions about the test's value. There is nevertheless extensive research bearing on the validity of the TAT. For example, several experimental studies have manipulated such needs as hunger, aggression, and sex in order to examine the effects of need arousal on stories elicited in response to a subset of TAT stimuli. In general, the results of these studies indicate that aroused subjects make more responses relating to the aroused need than do nonaroused subjects (McClelland and Atkinson, 1948). These findings contribute to the construct validity of the TAT. At the same time, though, they indicate that the TAT is subject to situational or temporary influences, a fact inconsistent with the traditional assessment goal of measuring enduring personality traits. An enormous amount of data also bears on the relation between TAT measures of need and behaviors reflecting that same need. This literature is too complex and extensive to be reviewed here (see Chapter 16).

In general, as in the case of the Rorschach, validity studies have yielded variable findings. It is clear that there are circumstances under which the

TAT and the Rorschach are predictive of significant aspects of personality. The problem lies in specifying those circumstances in order to tell in advance when the TAT and the Rorschach will provide valid pictures of a subject's personality.

Box 12.2   CLINICAL VERSUS STATISTICAL PREDICTION

In the clinical method of predicting behavior, the assessor uses various sources of information, such as the TAT and interview data as well as structured tests. There are no set rules for combining this information, and so judgments are guided by intuition, hypotheses about personality dynamics, and common sense. In the statistical procedure, relationships are established between particular tests and a behavior. Then a formula is uniformly applied to predict individual behavior.

Adherents to the clinical approach describe it as dynamic, global, meaningful, configural, and sensitive, as opposed to mechanical, artificial, academic, static, and oversimplified. On the other hand, advocates of the statistical procedure describe it as verifiable, objective, scientific, precise, and empirical, as opposed to vague, subjective, unscientific, unreliable, and private.

Which procedure in fact has proved more effective in predicting behavior? Carefully conducted research studies using a variety of predictor variables and sources of information have repeatedly found evidence supporting the superiority of the statistical method. In general, the greater the involvement of humans in the assessment process, the less the validity of the prediction.

Critical research studies typically involve predictions of one of three kinds of behavior: grade point average, recidivism (committing criminal acts after release from prison), and recovery from psychoses. In one representative investigation involving predictions of college grade point average (Sarbin, 1942), adherents to the statistical method applied a formula derived from prior studies relating high school rank, aptitude test score, and grade point average. Supporters of the clinical approach interviewed the students and used other kinds of information, such as projective test scores—as well as the high school rank and aptitude scores used in the statistical method. The results of this investigation favored the statistical procedure; predictions were more accurate when based upon the previously derived formula.

Sometimes, however, clinical judgments allow one to take account of data never before used. The following case, reported by the noted psychoanalyst Theodore Reik, illustrates one prediction that could not have been made with a statistical procedure:

One session at this time took the following course. After a few sentences about the uneventful day, the patient fell into a long silence. She assured me that nothing was in her thoughts. Silence from me. After many minutes she continued about a toothache. She told me that she had been to the dentist yesterday. He had given her an injection and then had pulled a wisdom tooth. The spot was hurting again. New and longer silence. She pointed to my bookcase in the corner and said, "There is a book standing on its head." Without the slightest hesitation and in a reproachful voice I said, "But why did you not tell me you had an abortion?" (Meehl, 1954).

Source: Adapted from Meehl, 1962. Reprinted by permission

Other Approaches to Personality Assessment

The Interview

The *interview* is without doubt the oldest technique for assessing personality. The original objective personality test, the Woodworth Personality Data Sheet (1920), was actually an attempt to develop a standard psychiatric interview. Before the Woodworth, the only substantial tool available for assessing personality was the interview, which was most commonly employed by psychiatrists in determining an individual's emotional stability. The Woodworth attempted to specify a number of questions common to the psychiatric interview and to put these questions in paper-and-pencil form.

Interview techniques are commonly used in conjunction with objective and projective tests in the assessment of personality. Like the tests themselves, interview techniques have improved, and considerable data have accumulated in recent years concerning the nature of the interview (e.g., Marsden, 1971; Wiens, 1976). The evidence suggests that effective interviews are those in which the interviewer is able to display such attitudes as warmth, involvement, interest, and commitment (Orlinsky and Howard, 1967; Saccuzzo, 1975; Tyler, 1969). It is also important for the interviewer to communicate a feeling of empathy or understanding to the person being interviewed (e.g., Truax and Mitchell, 1971). The success of the interview has been shown to be related to the feelings, mood, nonverbal behavior, and even activity level of the interviewer (Bandura, 1971; Heller, Davis, and Myers, 1966). Good interviewers tend to remain calm, relaxed, and confident throughout the interview, while communicating interest, concern, and a sense of mutual sharing.

Although much is known about effective interviewing, there is no standard or universally accepted method for conducting an interview. As a result, interviewers have practically unlimited opportunity to explore any area they believe will aid in the assessment of personality. Interviews vary from the highly structured to the totally unstructured. In the most structured type of interview, the interviewer asks the same set of questions in a particular order. This type of interview is much like a test such as the Woodworth except that the examiner reads the questions and then records the responses. A totally unstructured interview, on the other hand, might begin anywhere, proceed in any direction, change topic at any time, and focus on whatever content the interviewer wishes.

There are little available data concerning the long-term reliability and validity of conclusions based solely on interview data. The variety of interview procedures, the wide differences among interviewers, and the unlimited focus of interviews have limited researchers' ability to produce convincing results concerning the interview's value. There is general consensus, however, that the less structured the interview, the less reliable the information it yields (Wiens, 1976). The less structured the interview, the greater the inconsistency between the information obtained by different interviewers. If different questions are asked with different goals in mind, then the results cannot help but be different. On the other hand, it is difficult to conceive how even the most structured interview can be any more reliable than the best-constructed personality test. At best, an interview might approach the reliability of personality tests, but no real evidence exists that this is the case.

Among the problems of assessing personality via interview is that the interviewer can and does affect the verbal (Greenspoon, 1962) as well as the nonverbal (Matarazzo, Wiens, Matarazzo, and Saslow, 1968) behavior of the person being interviewed (see also Matarazzo and Wiens, 1972). The interviewer can influence the interviewee through subtle expression of interest, approval, or disapproval conveyed by movements of the head and the body, and by voice intonation—without either interviewer or interviewee being aware of the interaction or its effects. Also, a specific explanation or theory held by the interviewer may create a set in which those beliefs are artificially confirmed. As a result, the validity of interview data is often suspect.

The interview is a valuable tool that will no doubt continue to play a role in efforts to assess human personality. However, in providing the most flexible method for assessing individuals, the interview is grossly limited in terms of the true meaning of its results. In its major strength also lies its most serious weakness. Consequently, even though our knowledge of it has grown rapidly in the last two decades, the interview, like traditional personality tests, leaves much to be desired in the area of personality assessment.

Behavioral Techniques

In an effort to solve the difficult problems inherent in the assessment of personality, there has been new and increasing interest in more nontraditional techniques. Perhaps the most important and best developed of these are the *behavioral techniques*, which tend to make few assumptions about the nature of human personality (see Chapter 6). Indeed, contrary to traditional tests, these newer approaches do not necessarily assume that the characteristics being measured are even stable. Nor do they assume that human personality can be assessed independently of the environment. On the contrary, most behavioral procedures are based on the assumption that situations play an integral role in behavior, so that human behavior and thus human personality can be measured only within the context in which they occur. The behaviorist approach to assessment, therefore, is that behavior should be studied directly, rather than determined indirectly through test or talk procedures.

Common to most procedures that employ behavioral observations is the recording of behavioral samples that can be readily quantified. Typically, an observer notes and records the actual behavior of a subject, making no inferences like those usually involved in a rating scale. In assessing a child's aggression, for example, an observer might count the number of fistfights, arguments, destructions of objects, and similar behaviors over a particular time period (Feshbach, 1970; Lovaas et al., 1965). The experimental modification of behavior stemming from the application of learning theories has facilitated the development of systematic and sophisticated behavioral observation techniques. Before an experimental procedure is introduced to modify some designated behavior—e.g., rewarding a withdrawn child whenever an approach response to another child is made—the frequency of the behavior is recorded over a particular time interval, to provide a *baseline*. Stimulus events that precede, coexist with, or follow the designated behavior can also be recorded. Following the experimental intervention, changes in these stimulus events (e.g., friendly actions by other children) and any corresponding changes in the frequency of the designated behavior can be determined through analysis of the behavioral observations. By recording those factors that maintain or reduce particular behaviors, behavioral observation techniques provide a different perspective than traditional tests. This process is specifically illustrated in Box 12.3.

Box 12.3   BEHAVIORAL ASSESSMENT IN ACTION

The following is a report of a behavioral assessment procedure in a natural environment:

Issue. Investigation of the feasibility of treatment in the natural setting (the home) where the child's behavior problem appeared, with the mother serving as the therapeutic agent. The child (C), a four-year-old boy, was brought by his mother (M) to the university clinic because she felt helpless to deal with his frequent tantrums and general disobedience.

Observations. Experimenters (Es) observed M and C in the home and noted that many of C's undesirable behaviors appeared to be maintained by attention from the mother. If C behaved objectionably, M would try to explain to him why he shouldn't do something or would try to distract him by offering him toys or food. Observation in the home indicated that the following responses made up a large portion of C's repertoire of undesirable behavior: (1) biting his shirt or arm, (2) sticking out his tongue, (3) kicking or biting himself, others, or objects, (4) calling someone or something a derogatory name, (5) removing or threatening to remove his clothing, (6) saying no loudly and vigorously, (7) threatening to damage objects or persons, (8) throwing objects, (9) pushing his sister. These nine responses collectively are called objectionable behavior (OB). The frequency of occurrence is measured by recording, for each ten-second interval, whether or not an OB occurred. Observations are made during one-hour sessions conducted two to three times a week. Two Es are employed as observers on eight occasions and three on one occasion to check the reliability of the response scoring. Reliability is found to range from .70 to 1.00 with an average of .88, indicative of high observer reliability.

Treatment. After an initial *baseline period* of sixteen sessions during which C and M interact in their usual way, the *first experimental period* is begun. Every time C emits an OB, M is signalled by E to tell him to stop or to put him in his room by himself and without toys. (This isolation is viewed as a period of "time out" from stimuli associated with positive reinforcement.) When E notices that C is playing in a particularly desirable way, M is signalled to give C attention and approval. During the *second baseline period* M is told to interact with C as she did prior to the experimental period. This is followed by the *second experi-*

mental period, which is the same as in the first except that special attention for desirable play is excluded, save for one accidental instance. Finally, there is a *follow-up period* after twenty-four days without contact between E and M.

Results.   During the baseline period OB varied between 18 and 113 per session (one hour). During the first experimental period the rate of OB ranged from 1 to 8 per session. Special attention was given ten times. During the second baseline period the rate of OB varied between 2 and 24 per session. M reported that she had trouble responding in her previous way because she now felt more sure of herself. She now gives C firm commands and does not give in after denying a request. She also gives more affection, mostly in response to an increase in affectionate overtures from C. During the second experimental period the rate of OB varied between 2 and 8 per session. The rate of OB remained low after the twenty-four-day interval (follow-up period) and M reports C is well-behaved and less demanding.

Figure 12.3   Number of ten-second intervals, per one-hour session, in which objectionable behavior occurred. Asterisks indicate sessions in which reliability was tested.

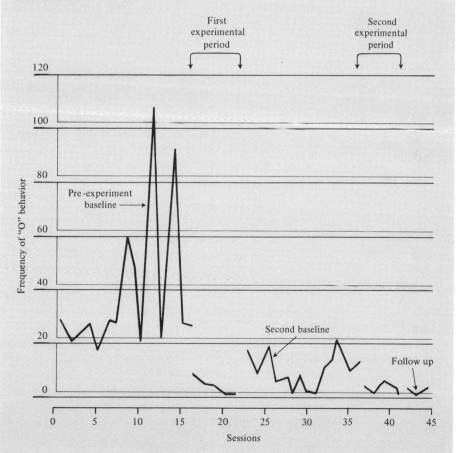

Summary. The results of this study show that it is possible to observe and treat behavioral problems in the home, with the parent as the therapeutic agent. Since it is widely held that many of the child's problems originate in the home environment, direct modification of this environment (including the behavior of other family members) may arrest the difficulty at its source.

Source: Hawkins, Peterson, Schweid, and Bijou, 1966, p. 105. Reprinted by permission.

Behavioral assessment procedures are relatively new and many of their problems have yet to be solved. First, like the interview, there is no standard or universally accepted technique for observing behavior. Guidelines do not exist to indicate which behaviors should be recorded and which are irrelevant. Furthermore, just as an interview can influence the person being interviewed, so too can an observer influence the behavior of the person being observed. As early as 1949, a study by Polansky and his colleagues provided strong evidence that the presence of an observer does alter the behavior of the individual being watched. This has been confirmed in a number of more recent studies (Goldfried, 1976; Wiggins, 1973).

Kanfer and Saslow (1969) have presented a model and guidelines for observing behavior. These authors contend that behavior can be viewed as adaptive (facilitating the accomplishment of goals) or maladaptive. In addition, behavior can be defined in terms of excesses or deficits. Behavioral excesses occur with such frequency, duration, or intensity that they impede the individual in some way. Behavioral deficits, on the other hand, would enhance goal attainment if they occurred more frequently. In attempting to define the components of behavioral observations and to identify the important elements, Kanfer and Saslow have taken positive steps in the development of behavioral observation as a technique in personality assessment. Other steps are following, inasmuch as this remains an area of rapid growth and change.

Physiological Assessment

Another relatively new behaviorally oriented approach to personality assessment involves the evaluation of such physiological changes as heart rate, blood pressure, skin temperature, and perspiration (Lang, 1971). The rationale for *physiological assessment* is that changes in bodily processes reflect changes in psychological, particularly emotional, states (Kallman and Feuerstein, 1977). The major tool for such assessment is the polygraph, an instrument used to monitor various physiological indicators. The lie detector, for example, is a polygraph. It uses a number of physiological recordings and its application is based on the assumption that a lie will produce a marked emotional reaction. Perhaps the most commonly used physiological measure in personality assessment is the galvanic skin response (GSR). The GSR reflects relatively minute changes in the electrical characteristics of the skin related to sweating and therefore is frequently used as an indicator of emotional arousal or anxiety. While self-descriptions of emotional states and even actions can be altered to disguise true feelings, it is extremely difficult to control one's GSR or other physiological responses.

A variety of new techniques for measuring bodily changes have recently been developed (Epstein, 1976). For example, following Masters and Johnson's (1966) finding establishing a link between human sexual arousal and the flow of blood into the genitalia, a number of tools have been developed to measure this flow of blood in order to assess sexual arousal (Kallman and Feuerstein, 1977). These physiological measures made studies of the antecedents and consequences of sexual arousal possible that could not otherwise have been carried out.

Physiological methods, no less than other personality assessment techniques, are subject to the requirements of reliability and validity. However, in terms of development and supporting evidence, many physiological techniques are only in their infancy. Much more research is needed before even the first steps can be taken in evaluating their role and value as personality assessment devices.

Summary   Personality measurement is a procedure to gain information about individuals. This information can be useful in a variety of ways: to aid clinical psychologists in making appropriate diagnoses, to aid in personnel selection, and even to help in the choice of a marriage or dating partner. Over the years, a variety of diverse techniques have been developed to facilitate personality measurement, and a number of different tests have been devised. In spite of many years of work and study, however, many problems remain to be surmounted for the construction of reliable and valid measures of personality.

Specific Points

1. Psychologists measuring personality typically assume that personality *traits* are stable, general (exhibited regardless of situation), and relatively enduring over time.
2. *Objective* personality tests provide a set of responses to a particular item, to which the test taker responds by selecting the most appropriate alternative. The construction of the test may be guided by *face validity*, empirical evidence, or the search for underlying structure (*factor analytic* instruments).

3. Tests having face validity suffer from a number of problems because items may be interpreted differently or not honestly answered by the respondents. There may be a tendency to answer in a way that reflects most favorably on the self (*social desirability*). In addition, *response biases* have been identified, such as *acquiescence* (agreeing with an item regardless of its content) and *oppositional bias* (disagreeing with an item regardless of its content).

4. Tests based on *empirical* approaches first identify groups that differ on a particular behavior or set of behaviors. Items given to both groups that are differentially endorsed are then included in the measuring instrument, regardless of the specific content or meaning of that item.

5. The *MMPI* is the most widely used of the empirically based questionnaires. In addition to ten clinical scales, the MMPI includes four validity scales: (a) the "cannot say" (the inability to endorse either alternative); (b) the F scale (items rarely endorsed by the general population); (c) the K scale (socially desirable items); and (d) the "Lie" (L) scale (less subtle, socially desirable items).

6. *Factor analysis* is a statistical method that enables the investigator to identify the fundamental aspects of personality. Instruments constructed by Guilford and Cattell are among the best-known factor-analytic batteries.

7. In *projective* tests, the test taker spontaneously produces a response, such as a story, for which scoring is often subjective. Projective tests are based on the assumption that a person's response to an ambiguous stimulus reflects his or her own needs and conflicts.

8. The *Rorschach Inkblot Test* was the first formal projective instrument. Responses to symmetrical inkblots are evaluated in terms of location, inclusion of color, the kind of object described, movement, the "accuracy" of the percept, and how typical the response is. The validity of this test is questionable, although it appears to have validity for the assessment of personality characteristics like self-control and ego strength.

9. The *Thematic Apperception Test* (*TAT*) is also one of the most widely used projective instruments, in which subjects tell stories about a set of somewhat ambiguous pictures. As with the Rorschach, the validity of the TAT is unclear.

10. All the traditional tests of personality suffer in that long-term, test-retest reliabilities are low, a fact in conflict with the traditional belief in enduring personality traits.

11. Included among additional approaches to personality assessment are the *interview*, which is generally believed to be a poor assessment technique, *behavior techniques,* and *physiological assessment.*

Thought
Questions

1. Why do you think personality measures have low long-term reliability? Is personality unstable, or does the fault lie in the measures? If the latter, what might these faults be?

2. Can you think of a time when you were less than completely honest on a personality test, or when you answered in a socially desirable manner? Under what conditions are these types of responses most likely?
3. Different factor-analytic batteries tend to find different underlying personality structures. Do you think that there are certain basic aspects of personality that describe all individuals? What do you think they are?
4. Tell a story about the TAT picture shown in this chapter. Do you think that your response is meaningful and reveals your current needs and conflicts?

Traits, Situations, and Their Interaction

Suppose that someone is about to introduce you to one of her best friends. A common inquiry in such circumstances is "What is she like?" In other words, what *traits* characterize her? Is she kind, aggressive, honest? Traits provide us with convenient methods of organizing information about others, of describing how they have behaved in the past, and of making predictions about how they will behave in the future (Jones and Nisbett, 1971; Kelley, 1967). Throughout the history of the study of personality, considerable effort has been devoted to building taxonomies of traits, developing methods for measuring traits, and finding the ways in which groups of traits cluster together. Indeed, the very concept of personality assumes that there are characteristics or traits that remain stable over time.

Even though the search for traits has a long and rich history, their utility has been questioned since at least the turn of the century. Edward Thorndike, one of the pioneers of measurement, wrote in 1906 (p. 248):

Training the mind means the development of thousands of particular, independent capacities, the formation of countless particular habits. . . . The amount of identical elements in different mental functions and the amount of general influence from special training are much less than common opinion supposes.

In this short passage, Thorndike challenged the predominant trait orientation as well as the notion of general intelligence, suggesting instead that behavior is influenced more by situations or training for specific situations than was acknowledged in his time.

By 1934, trait approaches to personality were under serious question. For example, the use of personality tests was attacked at that time because they were unreliable and undependable in classifying individuals (Lehman and Witty, 1934). It was suggested that it was not necessarily the tests that were at fault, but rather the concept of traits. The question arose as to whether people really were consistent over time and between situations. Nevertheless, the trait approach remained dominant in personality theory for several decades. World War I saw the development of huge testing batteries for the classification of servicemen. World War II was also an impetus for expansion of psychological assessment, and the development of trait classification systems flourished in the period immediately after the war.

A variety of other events helped to establish the stature of trait psychology. First, Harvard personologist Gordon Allport (1937) was an extremely influential psychologist who was also a firm believer in traits. In addition, prominent factor-analytic methodologists like Raymond Cattell, whose work was introduced in the preceding chapter, were concerned with trait classification. During the period after the second world war, there was also a growth spurt in clinical psychology. Following the medical model, clinical psychologists began to find traits useful for classifying people, in much the same way physicians classified patients into disease categories.

However, a major critique of trait psychology appeared with the publication of Mischel's (1968) book, *Personality and Assessment*. Mischel's review of the personality literature indicated that personality measures were very poor at predicting behavior in specific situations. Following the publication of Mischel's book and his severe criticisms of the trait notion, the field of personality had to rethink many of its most basic assumptions. As the issues were argued and debated, some clarification began to emerge, but the debate about the existence of traits continues to be one of the most active areas of research in personality psychology. In this chapter we present some of the basic issues in the trait-situation debate and consider ways in which the trait concept can be modified to incorporate situational variability while still accounting for consistencies in behavior. Because of the wealth of research in this area, all of the pertinent literature cannot be summarized; however, excellent collections of articles are available on this topic (Endler and Magnusson, 1976; Magnusson and Endler, 1977). In their attempt to categorize different views of personality, Endler and Magnusson classified personality theorists into four groupings on the basis of their adherence to (1) type models, (2) trait theories, (3) situational theories, and (4) interactionism. We will consider each of these in turn.

Personality Types

The origins of theories of personality go back to Hippocrates, who suggested as early as 400 B.C. that there were four basic personality types, associated with the four bodily humors (see Chapter 1). The relationships between these humors and personality are shown in Table 13.1.

The belief in a relationship between body type and personality has persisted into the present (see also Chapter 2). Toward the end of the last century, a German psychiatrist (Kretschmer, 1925) argued that people who were thin had a tendency to become schizophrenic, while those who were fat were more likely to tend toward manic depression (see also Chapter 2). A more recent and better-known effort regarding body types was that of William Sheldon (1954; Sheldon and Stevens, 1942). Sheldon had people rated according to three physical structure types and then attempted to relate these body types to temperaments. Sheldon reported that people who had *mesomorphic* physiques (strong, athletic, and muscular) tended to have somatotonic temperaments (energetic, assertive, and courageous). *Endomorphic* body builds (soft, round, and with large stomachs) were associated with viscerotonic personalities (relaxed, gregarious, and food loving). And *ectomorphic* physiques (tall, thin, and fragile) were common among cerebrotonic personality types (fearful, introverted, and restrained).

In Sheldon's investigations, individuals were photographed and rated on the extent to which they possessed each of the three body types. Then untrained observers rated the personality characteristics of these same people. Sheldon then found correlations between the physique and personality ratings. However, these findings have come into question because the raters may have been biased by predominant contemporary stereotypes, such as that round body types are jolly and athletic body types are aggressive. In fact, studies in which individuals are rated on specific behaviors rather than on global traits tend not to show strong associations between body types and personality (Mischel, 1968). This statement does not mean, however, that everyone has given up on somatotypes. For example, Sheldon's system has

---

Table 13.1 Relationship between bodily humors and personality types as suggested by Hippocrates

Bodily humor	Personality type	Characteristics
Yellow bile	Choleric	Irritable
Black bile	Melancholic	Depressed
Blood	Sanguine	Optimistic
Phlegm	Phlegmatic	Calm; listless

A medieval woodcut portraying the four temperaments and the elements traditionally associated with them: left—phlegmatic (water) and melancholic (earth); right—sanguine (air) and choleric (fire). (Zentralbibliothek Zurich, Ms. C 101)

been extended (Carter and Heath, 1971) to provide more accurate measurements of body type, and George Sheehan, one of the best-known medical advisors for runners, bases his theories of sport motivation on the Sheldon data.

Not all type theorists base their classification system on physique. Although Jung (see Chapter 5) believed that introversion and extraversion are both present in each individual, he speculated that one of these dispositions would be dominant. Thus, he felt it appropriate to categorize individuals as primarily introverts or extraverts. Nevertheless, typologies like those proposed by Sheldon and Jung are used less frequently in current psychology. The complexity of human behavior makes it difficult to fit individuals neatly into a few simple categories. The description of someone as introverted or extraverted gives us too little information about the person. For most personality characteristics, people fit at some point on a continuous distribution of that characteristic rather than into the either-or categories provided by type concepts. A more scientific extension of the typology approach is represented in the work of trait-oriented psychologists.

Trait Theories

There have been many psychologists who have believed that personality is best understood by studying the organization of traits within an individual. Perhaps the most influential of the trait psychologists was Gordon Allport. Trait psychologists believe that there are characteristics of individuals that remain consistent over time and across situations. If you are an aggressive person, for example, trait theories imply that you will be aggressive in many different settings. In their study of behavior, trait psychologists use a trait as the unit of analysis or the basic focus of examination. Their task is to determine which traits occur together and how patterns of traits are organized within an individual.

Cattell and Factor Analysis

To study the organization of traits, many psychologists have turned to complex statistical methods such as factor analysis, discussed in the previous chapter. The work of Raymond Cattell (1965) is among the best-known work of this type. In his search for the basic elements of personality, Cattell performed extensive factor analyses of three types of data: life records (ratings of behavior in everyday situations), self-ratings on personality scales, and scores on objective tests. As indicated earlier, to determine the nature and the organization of traits, Cattell first examined a list of 4,500 trait names and then reduced this list to less than 200 by grouping synonyms or near-synonyms. Then scores were obtained on the degree to which individuals possessed these traits, and the results were factor analyzed. This procedure yielded 36 *surface traits* (clusters of responses or overt behaviors that fit together) and a smaller number of *source traits* (more basic organizing structures that underlie and determine surface traits).

Various investigations by Cattell using life record and self-report data have produced a similar list of basic traits, shown in Table 13.2. It is clear

Table 13.2   Cattell's major personality factors found

Letter symbol	Technical title	Popular label
A	Affectothymia-Sizothymia	Outgoing-reserved
B	Intelligence	More intelligent–less intelligent
C	Ego strength	Stable-emotional
E	Dominance-Submissiveness	Assertive-humble
F	Surgency-Desurgency	Happy-go-lucky–sober
G	Super-ego strength	Conscientious-expedient
H	Parmia-Threctia	Venturesome-shy
I	Premsia-Harria	Tender-minded–tough-minded
L	Protension-Alaxia	Suspicious-trusting
M	Autia-Praxernia	Imaginative-practical
N	Shrewdness-Artlessness	Shrewd-forthright
O	Guilt proneness-Assurance	Apprehensive-placid

Source: Hall and Lindzey, 1970, p. 390. Reprinted by permission.

from Table 13.2 that Cattell had a fondness for coining words, to the extent that his technical titles needed to be translated into more popular labels. For example, the trait label *premsia* is short for "protected emotional sensitivity."

Most of Cattell's research has been directed toward the identification of source traits, some of which he has called *environment mold traits,* or traits formed by the environment. Others, determined by factors within the individual, are called *constitutional source traits.* Another distinction Cattell has made is between *specific* source traits, which describe how a person operates in a particular situation, and *general* source traits, which affect behavior in many different situations. Thus, in interpreting his factor analytic findings, the idea of trait consistency remains fundamental to Cattell's work and is reflected in the concept of a general source trait.

Eysenck's Hierarchy

Hans J. Eysenck is one of the more controversial figures in contemporary psychology. In his many active years as a psychologist he took strong positions against traditional psychotherapy (Eysenck, 1952), was one of the earliest advocates of behavior therapy, and strongly supported the notion of intelligence as an inherited trait.

Eysenck's view of personality is in many ways similar to Cattell's, with behavior viewed hierarchically. At the bottom of the hierarchy are the *specific responses* that are actually observed. Just above these are *habitual responses.* At the next level in the pyramid are *traits* that are analogous to Cattell's source traits, and at the top level are types. *Types* for Eysenck are basic behavior dimensions which are continuous rather than typological categories. Eysenck identified three types or dimensions that he regarded as the basic units of personality: neuroticism, extraversion-introversion, and psychoticism.

Using a variety of data sources, such as ratings, questionnaires, and physiological measures, Eysenck repeatedly identified the same dimensions in factor analytic studies. Most of his attention was devoted to classifying people along the dimensions of neuroticism and extraversion-introversion. Since neuroticism can be viewed as corresponding to emotional stability, individuals were classified along a continuum from stable to unstable. An unstable personality is seen as moody, touchy, anxious, and restless, while a stable person is characterized as calm, even-tempered, and carefree. With regard to extraversion and introversion, extraverts are seen as sociable, active, outgoing, and optimistic, while introverts are characterized as passive, quiet, careful, and unsociable. In many respects, the basic personality dimensions identified by Eysenck are similar to those described by Cattell. Eysenck acknowledged this but also contended that his approach was more dependable and more theoretically meaningful.

Although trait and type classifications are commonly recognized by psychologist and layperson alike, their value has been a matter of serious debate. The next section of this chapter examines the attack on traditional trait psychology and introduces some new approaches to personality assessment that have arisen out of this debate.

The Attack on Traits

Mischel's Argument

Mischel's (1968) book on the assessment of personality has often been interpreted as an all-out attack on the concept of traits. Mischel, however, repeatedly denied this extreme position. Rather, he maintained that the evidence for the existence of traits is weak and that the methods for their assessment need reevaluation. Furthermore, he acknowledged the value of cognitive traits, such as intelligence, and speed of processing and encoding information.

The essence of Mischel's argument is that trait measures are not valid predictors of behavior in specific situations. Although personality tests do well at predicting how people will score on similar personality tests, they do poorly at predicting how someone will actually behave in a given situation. One finds that questionnaire and projective measures of aggression are not very effective predictors of an individual's aggressive behavior on the athletic field, in confrontations with authority, in response to a friend's arriving late for an appointment, and in myriad other concrete situations in which variations in aggressive behavior can be observed. Moreover, observational measures of aggression are not very effective in predicting aggressive behaviors in situations other than the one in which aggression was initially assessed. Similar low predictability of behaviors in specific situations can be found for measures of impulsivity, achievement motivation, anxiety, and other personality characteristics. It can be maintained that if such tests are really meaningful, they should be able to forecast how people will behave in the specific tasks that psychologists create for laboratory studies.

Mischel reported that many investigations demonstrate that the correlation between test scores and behavior in specific situations is rarely greater than .30, or that around 91 percent of the variance in behavior is unexplained by the test score. Furthermore, behavior in one situation tends not to be a good predictor of behavior in another situation. Again, the correlations reported are rarely greater than .30. Mischel called these low correlations *personality coefficients* and suggested that knowledge of personal characteristics tells us little about how a person will actually behave. Mischel was more impressed with the amount of variation that would be explained by knowing about the situation in which the behavior is observed, rather than knowing about the person in that situation.

The *situational* critique of the concept of traits is an important one but, as we will see later in this chapter, there are still other perspectives from which the research literature on traits can be examined. At this point, it may be noted that there is some question as to whether a trait measure should be expected to be a strong predictor of behavior in a specific situation. People's behavior in most situations is determined by multiple factors, of which the assessed trait is only one. These factors include other personality traits as well as situational variables. For example, whether a student will conform to majority opinion as communicated in a laboratory situation may be a function of the traits of affiliation, dependency, anxiety, competitiveness, and autonomy and such situational elements as the importance of the issue, the prestige of the group members, and the cohesiveness of the group. While each trait measure might show only a small correlation with conformity behavior in that situation, trait measures may still be useful if they can be related to trait-relevant behaviors in a variety of situations.

Attribution Theory

Another perspective suggesting the need to modify traditional trait theories derives from research on a relatively new approach to personality and social psychology, known as *attribution theory*. Originally, attribution theory was concerned primarily with the judgments people make about others, in particular their inferences about others' intentions. However, research in this area now covers all aspects of how people attempt to understand the causes of events in their lives.

The basic ideas of attribution theory were first formulated in the mid-1940s and 1950s (Heider, 1944, 1958) but became popular only in the late 1960s (Jones and Davis, 1965; Kelley, 1967). Kelley offered a model to capture how the layperson determines causation. He suggested that events are perceived as caused by three potential sources: persons, entities (aspects of the environment), or circumstances. To determine which of these, or which combination of sources, has caused an event, the person uses three criteria called distinctiveness, consensus, and consistency. If, for example, we wanted to explain why John enjoys the food at a particular restaurant so much, it would be helpful to ask if he always feels this way in restaurants (distinctiveness), whether others in the same restaurant also enjoy the food (consensus), and whether John enjoyed the food when he ate in this restaurant before (consistency). If all people enjoy the food in this eating establishment, then John's enjoyment would be attributed to the entity (it is a good restaurant); if John always enjoys food at restaurants, then the enjoyment would be attributed to him (he is a glutton); and if John usually dislikes this restaurant, then his present enjoyment would be ascribed to special circumstances, such as unusual hunger, the presence of friends, or some special dish (Kelley, 1967; Orvis, Cunningham, and Kelley, 1975).

Actor-observer differences.   Jones and Nisbett (1971) have suggested that the selection of a trait or a situational explanation for behavior also depends on the role played by the person making the judgment. When people are observers and are making judgments about others, they tend to use dispositional or trait explanations. However, they are likely not to use trait concepts to explain their own behavior. Rather, when people are actors they tend to explain their own behavior in terms of the situation. Thus, one might say, "You hit him because you are aggressive" (a trait explanation), whereas "I hit him because he did something wrong" (a situation explanation).

Why should there be a difference between the attributions of actors and observers? Jones and Nisbett suggest that this is so because people know more about their own behavior than they know about the behavior of others. Searching in memory, a person can recall behaving differently in many different situations in the past. Information regarding the distinctiveness and inconsistency of behavior fosters situation attributions. Note, however, that this analysis assumes that individuals find little consistency in their behaviors across situations! Observers, on the other hand, are less likely to have the information available about others to rule out situational causes of behavior, and therefore make trait attributions for other people.

Another explanation of actor-observer differences in attributions is that the sensory apparatus (eyes and ears) of the actor are focused on the environment rather than on the self. Thus, the actor observes the environment, while the observer views the actor. Videotapes have been used to demonstrate that when actors are shown a situation from the vantage point of the observer, they describe their own behavior in terms of traits (Storms, 1973). In a similar manner, when the observer is shown the situation from the vantage point of the actor, situational attributions are more likely. In sum, attributions are in part dependent on the focus of attention and the information available to the observer.

Attribution theory and trait psychology.   Attribution theorists have not been concerned with the inadequacy of traditional trait tests for predicting behavior. Rather, traits are important because people use them to describe the behavior of others; they are part of the implicit or "naive" psychology that the layperson uses (see Chapter 7). Extensive research has demonstrated that both laypeople and experienced clinical psychologists favor explaining behavior in terms of enduring dispositions instead of in terms of the situation. The tendency to overestimate the importance of traits and underestimate the importance of the situation in causing behavior has been labeled the *fundamental attributional error* (Ross, 1977). Indeed, most general trait characteristics have been inferred from merely specific, fragmented bits of information that have been obtained in a limited sample of situations (Borgida and Nisbett, 1977; Nisbett and Borgida, 1975).

Other research even suggests that the manner in which we make judgments about others is not strongly associated with either past experiences or our observations of these others. For example, one study examined peer ratings given by different groups of men (Norman, 1963). One group had lived together in the same fraternity for three years, while another group was less closely associated. Although the two groups had differing amounts of contact, they used very similar dimensions for making judgments about one another. Indeed, these same dimensions of judgment emerge when subjects rate complete strangers (Passini and Norman, 1966). These studies demonstrate that the same dimensions or traits are used to rate others whether or not the subjects are familiar with the people they are evaluating. These findings do not necessarily mean that the trait dimensions are being misapplied; rather, they suggest that trait ratings might tell us more about the raters than about the people being rated. But whether or not traits are valuable for understanding behavior, observers *believe* that they are and tend to perceive information in a manner that supports trait interpretations.

If traits are not useful concepts, then why is there such a persistent need for people to refer to them? The following possible explanations for this behavior have been suggested (Epstein, 1979, pp. 1099–1100):

1. *It is emotionally satisfying to believe that behavior is predictable, particularly when it is someone else's.*
2. *It is simpler to classify behavior by people than by situations.*
3. *People have implicit personality theories that assume stability in personality, and their theories bias their perceptions.*
4. *A primacy effect operates to make new impressions conform to old ones.*
5. *The observer is always present in the situations that he or she observes in real life, thereby presenting the observer with a biased sample* [of behavior].
6. *There is a tendency for observers to equate behavior that elicits the same emotional reactions in them.*
7. *There is a tendency for judges to generalize from a few attributes that are stable, such as intelligence, to others that are not.*
8. *There are more terms for classifying people than for classifying situations, which leads to a bias toward attributing behavior more often to characteristics of people than to characteristics of situations.*

Newer Assessment Strategies

Despite arguments against the notion of traits, few psychologists have actually shelved their faith in personality dispositions. Mischel (1979) and others contend that trait-oriented and clinical psychologists have tended to predict too much from traits alone and to observe too little. While the concept of traits may still have utility, it does appear that trait categorization is an oversimplification that can lead to incorrect predictions of behavior in a variety of situations. Although there is consistency and constancy in our lives, better measurement techniques are needed to forecast future behavior. This requires methodologies that consider and include the evaluations of situations, the interaction of traits and situations, and new approaches to trait assessment.

Situational Assessment

There is little doubt that behavior is influenced by the situation in which it occurs. Certainly most of social psychology is based on this premise. We know, for example, that there is a higher probability of aggression when people are angry (Konecni, 1975), hot (Baron, 1972), or made to feel anonymous (Zimbardo, 1969). In recognition of the role of environment in regulating behavior, a new field known as environmental psychology has developed (see Chapter 3).

Some of the early work in the field of environmental psychology involved building taxonomies of situations, similar to trait taxonomies. Just as trait psychologists attempted to determine which traits predicted behavior, *situational* psychologists attempted to build classification systems to relate environments and situations to behavior. For example, one taxonomy (see Table 13.3) has been developed in which environments are classified according to six characteristics (Moos, 1973). Each aspect of the environment has been shown to have pronounced impact on individual or group behavior.

Table 13.3   Six characteristics of environments

Characteristics	Examples
1. Ecological dimensions	Architectural design, geographic location, weather conditions.
2. Behavior settings	The office, the home, the store.
3. Organizational structure	Percentage of women in the student body, number of people per household, average age of group.
4. Characteristics of milieu inhabitants	Proportion of students in your university who date, drink, or vote.
5. Psychosocial and organization climate	Work pressure, encouragement of participation, orientation toward helping with personal problems.
6. Functional or reinforcing properties of the environment	Is aggression reinforced on the football field? Is it reinforced at home?

Source: Derived from Moos, 1973.

The situational orientation emphasizes the impact of situations over the impact of personality characteristics in determining behavior. For example, consider the question "Is Fred motivated at work?" Trait-oriented psychologists would want to know something about Fred's characteristics. How high does he score on scales that measure need for achievement, need for power, and other work-related traits? In contrast, situation-oriented psychologists would want to measure characteristics of Fred's work environment. What is the psychosocial climate? Are Fred's work efforts appropriately reinforced?

An emphasis on environments or situations brings with it a whole new set of measurement problems. Just as trait psychologists had to struggle with methods for the evaluation of people, those with a situational orientation need to find quantitative expressions for environmental characteristics. Unfortunately, studies have not revealed that studying the characteristics of the environment lead to much better predictions of behavior than studying the characteristics of the people inhabiting those environments (Endler and Magnusson, 1976). However, the study of situations has made it clear that both situational and personal characteristics influence behavior. The obvious next step is to consider both traits and situations as determinants of action.

The Interactionist Position

To a growing number of psychologists, whether traits or situations are more important in determining behavior is a moot question (Endler, 1973). It is meaningless to ask which is more important when it is evident that behavior is always a joint function of characteristics of the person and of the situation. This *interactionist* position is a rapprochement between trait and situational approaches to personality assessment which acknowledges the importance of personality dispositions as well as the role of situations.

The interactionist position takes several different forms, each with different implications. The most complete and sophisticated form is the *transactional* approach (Endler and Magnusson, 1976; cf. Chapter 8). Whenever interaction is described in these terms, it refers to the reciprocal sequence of actions that takes place between person and situation. Each situation poses its own demands and cues and tends to call for a particular set of behaviors. The relaxed setting of an informal gathering will elicit very different behaviors than a formal dinner party; the athletic field elicits different responses than the classroom; and comparable differences are obtained between home and office. Each individual brings his or her own set of unique personality traits to each of these situations. These traits influence how the situation is perceived; different people will see different aspects of the situation as most important. Thus, at the dinner party, person A, who is characterized by anxiety over status and acceptance by others, will be oriented to the seating arrangement and to the amount of attention given by the host and hostess; person B, a "hail-fellow-well-met" extravert, will find the stiffness and formality particularly frustrating.

The transactional process does not end with individual differences in perceptions of situations. Individuals behave on the basis of these perceptions and their behaviors elicit reactions from others; the feedback from these behaviors and reactions will then influence subsequent behaviors. The behavioral outcome that is finally observed is a result of a sequence of reciprocal transactions between the individual, with his or her uniqueness, and the situation, with its uniqueness. This formulation of the trait-situation interaction is consonant with the views of situation-oriented theorists like Mischel, as well as with those of many trait-oriented theorists (Endler and Magnusson, 1976; Magnusson and Endler, 1977).

There is a common but more limited meaning of the term *interaction* that is also applicable to the trait-situation issue. In the statistical sense interaction refers to a *differential* effect that the same situation may have on different people or the differential effect of the same disposition in response to different situations. For example, a highly insulting, frustrating situation will elicit more aggressive behavior than a nonfrustrating situation. However, the effects of the frustration are likely to be much more pronounced in individuals who have a strong disposition to respond with anger and aggression than in individuals who are low on this trait dimension. The difference in aggressive behavior between the high-aggressive and low-aggressive individuals under nonfrustrating conditions may be negligible; it is under conditions of frustration that the difference in personality traits becomes evident.

In comparison to the transactional model, the more limited interactional model is easier to investigate. Using this model, evidence for the interactionist position is obtained by comparing the proportion of variance in behavior that is explained by person, by situation, and by interaction between person and situation. One might think of this by drawing a pie and dividing it to represent all of the different influences on human behavior. Figure 13.1 shows such a pie. One slice represents the proportion of variance attributable to personality traits; another slice represents the proportion of variance caused by situational influences; and a third slice is for the interaction between situational and dispositional influences. The interaction is due to unique combinations of traits and situations. Careful studies designed for application of the statistical method known as *analysis of variance* have separated the proportion of variance attributable to each of these factors. As shown in Fig. 13.1, interaction accounts for a larger proportion of the variance in behavior than either person or situation (Magnusson and Endler, 1977).

Although it is revealing that unique combinations of persons and situations explain more of the variation than either influence by itself, the interaction position still explains only some of the behavior of some of the people some of the time (Bem and Allen, 1974). As Fig. 13.1 reveals, the largest slice of the pie is reserved for error variance: the proportion of the total that is not explained in terms of the three specified sources of influence. After reviewing many studies of the influence of the person versus the influence of the situation versus the person × situation interaction, Sarason, Smith, and Diener (1975) concluded that none of the three sources accounts for an impressive share in the variation of accounted-for behavior, as compared to the amount of variation that is left unexplained. Although the interaction is a better predictor than either the trait or the situation, it is only slightly better. Thus,

Figure 13.1   Factors influencing behavior.

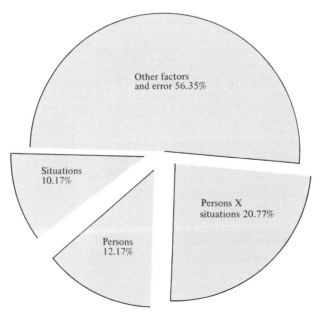

there is still a need for measurement methods that can be used to predict more of the people more of the time. Bem and Funder (1978) have proposed one such method.

The Template-Matching Technique

By 1979, many psychologists were convinced that the interaction between the person and the situation accounts for most of the variance in behavior. However, finding exact person $\times$ situation interactions proved very difficult.

In one study, Bem and Allen (1974) demonstrated that some individuals may be very consistent with regard to some personality characteristics, yet very inconsistent with regard to others. This is an important departure from both situational and traditional trait approaches to personality. Instead, Bem and Allen proposed that some traits characterize some people while other traits characterize other people. And some people may not be characterized by any traits at all. To demonstrate individual differences in consistency, college students rated whether their behavior would be consistent or inconsistent across different situations. These ratings were made for different traits, such as friendliness and conscientiousness. They found that students who identified themselves as consistently friendly did indeed appear to be friendly in a variety of situations. In contrast, those rating themselves as inconsistently friendly were found to be friendly in some situations but unfriendly in others. Thus, the trait of friendliness does not characterize all people; some people are very consistent in displaying friendliness, whereas others are not. Yet the same people inconsistent on friendliness may be consistent on another trait such as conscientiousness. Another exciting aspect of this finding is that subjects are able to predict their own consistencies and inconsistencies very well; fancy testing devices are not needed. Many years earlier Gordon Allport had proposed that if you want to know something about people, you should ask them!

More recently, Bem and Funder (1978) introduced a descriptive system of measurement that could be used to take advantage of the ability to predict our own behavior in particular situations. Their approach, called the *template-matching technique*, attempts to match personality to a specific template of behavior. To employ the technique, one must specify how a person would behave in a particular situation without any information about the particular person. For example, consider the question "Should Cathy see the movie *War Correspondent?*" Perhaps the best way to guide Cathy would be to describe the movie in terms of how several hypothetical people might react to it. People who are squeamish might enjoy the movie but have bad dreams about it for a few nights. Or people with certain political beliefs might not like it because it presents a specific perspective about our involvement in wars. Now Cathy can predict her own reaction to the movie by matching her characteristics with this set of "templates" that have been provided for her.

Bem and Funder (p. 486) proposed that "situations can be characterized as sets of template-behavior pairs, each template being a personality description of an idealized type of person expected to behave in a specified way in that setting." The probability that a particular person will behave in a particular way in a situation will be a function of the match between his or her characteristics and the template. For example, if Cathy's personality characteristics matched the template for those who would hate *War Correspondent*, then she might be best advised to avoid it.

The experiments by Bem and Funder indicated that by asking the appropriate question it is possible to predict the behavior of more of the people more of the time. This research acknowledged that there are personality characteristics that aid in the prediction of behavior in particular situations and is consistent with the findings of Bem and Allen.

The difficulty with a technology of person-situation interactions is that there are so many potential combinations of persons and situations. Bem and Funder were able to demonstrate that they could predict behavior very well in three particular situations, yet the number of potential person-situation combinations staggers the mind (Cronbach, 1975).

Trait Psychology Revisited

It would be worthwhile now to review the various approaches that have already been examined in this chapter. First, we presented the work of traditional trait psychologists who felt that personality measures accurately assess personality traits. Next, Mischel's challenge to personality tests was presented. Although it appeared to many psychologists that personality was neither stable over time nor consistent across situations, it was also suggested that most people do perceive stable and general personality patterns. Bem and Allen and Bem and Funder have now forced us to reconsider whether the notion of traits was ever completely wrong in the first place.

Again there is a paradox. On the one hand, few people seriously deny the importance of personality characteristics. On the other hand, there is still little evidence that personality tests can predict behavior in particular situations. Nevertheless, many psychologists remain unconvinced by Mischel's critique of trait psychology and believe that personality dimensions can be demonstrated to be meaningful predictors of behavior. In a strong defense of traits and the personality tests used to measure them, it has been acknowledged that poor research does not support the existence of traits but that many well-conducted studies are supportive (Hogan, DeSoto, and Solano, 1977). For example, Gough (1965) demonstrated that the sociability scale of his inventory correlated .73 with delinquency in a study of over ten thousand youths. And other investigators have reported that the creativity of architects as assessed by other architects' ratings can be predicted very well on the basis of a few personality variables (Hall and MacKinnon, 1969).

There is also evidence that behavior patterns are stable. Some studies, in which people's self-reports are monitored over the years, have found that people's views of themselves remain constant. However, consistency in self-perception may not mean consistency in behavior. Without resorting to self-report studies, there are well-conducted longitudinal studies that demonstrate the stability of behavioral patterns (see also Chapter 8). Perhaps the most important of these used a set of data maintained at the University of California, Berkeley. As discussed earlier, subjects in this study were first evaluated in junior high school, then again in senior high school, and once again when they were in their midthirties. At each period, the subjects were assessed by observers using the Q-sort technique (Block, 1971; see Chapter 11). In all, persons in the sample were rated on 114 personality variables by different observers at three different points in time. The results clearly demonstrated that many personality characteristics are stable. Indeed, between junior and senior high school nearly 60 percent of the personality characteristics measured remained consistent.

A European study on aggressive behavior in boys produced even more convincing results with regard to personality stability. Over two hundred boys were rated on their tendency to start fights and other characteristics of aggressive behavior. The ratings were obtained when the boys were in the sixth grade and then again three years later. In each case, at least three raters were used. The results showed that aggressive tendencies were quite stable over the three-year period, with a correlation of .66 across the two time periods. When error of measurement was corrected, the correlation became even stronger, reaching a level of .80 (Olweus, 1973, 1974, 1977a, 1977b).

State versus Trait

One factor that has been responsible in part for the low correlations between some trait measures and actual behavior is the failure to distinguish between states and traits. *States* refer to transitory conditions of the organism, to emotions and moods that vary in intensity and fluctuate over time, such as anger, panic, depression, and boredom. *Traits* refer to more enduring individual differences in behavior disposition, in the individual's *tendency* to be angry, afraid, depressed, or bored. A clearer understanding of the manifestations of a trait and of the relationship of the trait to behavior is obtained when a state measure is distinguished from a trait measure. This is best exemplified by the extensive amount of research that has been carried out on the distinction between state anxiety and trait anxiety (Spielberger, 1971a, 1971b; Spielberger, Gorsuch, and Lushene, 1970).

The difference between state and trait anxiety is made evident in the different ways in which they are assessed. Items on the state anxiety scale are answered in terms of the *intensity* of the individual's feelings and how the person feels at the moment. For instance, for the item "I am tense," the individual is given a choice among four alternatives ranging from "Not at all" to "Very much so." In contrast, items on the trait anxiety scale are answered in terms of the frequency of the feeling and how the individual generally feels. For example, for the item "I take disappointments so keenly that I can't put them out of my mind," the individual's four choices range from "Almost never" to "Almost always."

Spielberger and his associates (1970, p. 3) defined trait anxiety in terms of "differences between people in a tendency to respond to situations perceived as threatening with elevations in state anxiety intensity." Whether anxiety will be elicited at any particular time and its manifestation in behavior depends on the strength of trait anxiety and the presence of situational stimuli that will evoke state anxiety. Furthermore, the influence of trait anxiety and of external stimulus stressors are mediated by the process of *cognitive appraisal*. If a stimulus is perceived as nonthreatening (e.g., "He wants to get back at me but he's powerless"), then no anxiety is elicited. If the stimulus is appraised as threatening, then the individual may respond with feelings of anxiety or automatically react with defensive behaviors that minimize the experience of anxiety. Extensive research has been carried out on the process of cognitive appraisal, and it has been shown that it is possible to reduce physiological and other anxiety indicators by manipulating the cognitive appraisal of an ordinarily highly threatening stimulus (see Chapter 14). For example, people exposed to a stressful film depicting the subincision rites of a preliterate culture were asked to perceive the film within an anthropological context. This introduces a method of coping with anxiety similar to that of intellectualization, which lets the viewers detach themselves from a threat that is otherwise reacted to in personal terms (Lazarus and Alfert, 1964; Lazarus and Averill, 1972). In Spielberger's terms, the cognitive appraisal that mediates state anxiety can be modified by situational, experimentally induced, defensive approaches or by variations in trait anxiety and accompanying defensive tendencies.

In accordance with the theoretical attributes of state and trait anxiety, there is a substantial amount of research indicating that trait anxiety is a stable measure while state anxiety varies markedly with changes in situational stresses (Lamb, 1970). There is also evidence that individuals who differ in trait anxiety also differ, as expected, in the intensity of their state anxiety reactions to stressors, particularly to psychological rather than physical threats. These and other relationships indicating the value of the state-trait distinction for the study of anxiety suggest that a similar distinction can be fruitfully applied in helping clarify the trait-situation interaction for other personality attributes. Eliminating state components from the trait measure and taking state changes into account results in more stable trait indicators and stronger relationships between traits and behaviors. Assessing both trait and state also helps reduce measurement error.

Measurement Error

A major influence on the trait-situation controversy was a series of studies conducted many years ago (Hartshorne and May, 1928, 1929; Hartshorne, May, and Shuttleworth, 1930). This large longitudinal study of honesty remains one of the most thorough and widely cited pieces of research in the field (see Chapter 9). Over the course of six years, a national sample of eight thousand children was repeatedly evaluated on a series of measures of honesty which included cheating during a game, cheating at school, cheating on a take-home exam, taking money, lying, and falsifying records. Epstein (1979) noted that this study is widely cited as evidence that personality is not stable, because honesty in any particular situation was not found to be a good predictor of honesty in any other specific situation. What is seldom mentioned, however, is that when several measures of honesty are combined into a single score, honesty at one point in time and across situations becomes a very good predictor of honesty at another time and across situations.

Why would combining several measures of honesty have such an effect? As discussed in Chapter 11, the reliability of measures increases as items are added. Thus, for example, the reliability of a test in personality would be poor if the test consisted of only a few items, but would be relatively higher if the test were composed of many questions. One feels more certain that the same score will be obtained over two occasions as the length of the test increases. When reliability is low, as has been repeatedly warned, it is difficult to show that a measure will correlate well with other measures. But scores on behavior in a laboratory situation usually represent single items of behavior, which might be thought of as a single-item test! Perhaps one reason that Mischel and others may have had so little difficulty demonstrating that personality measures do poorly in predicting behavior in particular situations is that any single situation measure is like a one-item test. That is, situational tests are unreliable reflections of personality. In the studies cited previously, in which individual characteristics were found to be consistent over time, assessments of many items of behavior were averaged together at several points in time. Using aggregate measures of behavior, it is possible to show that personality is indeed stable.

In sum, the problems of inconsistency across situations and of instability over time both may result from measurement error. More reliable indicators can be created by averaging together behaviors in several situations. Thus, personality traits might be more successful in predicting behavior when averaged over several different situations. In addition, the average behavior (across several situations) from one point in time might be a good predictor of the average behavior (over the same situations) at another point in time.

In a series of investigations, Epstein (1979) demonstrated that, as measures of behavior are averaged over an increasingly larger group of items, the stability of personality increases. In these studies, a wide variety of behavioral and self-report measures were used, including objective behavior assessment, self-ratings, ratings by observers, self-report inventories, physiological measures, and standard personality batteries. When an average of behavioral scores taken in a fourteen-day sample was correlated with an average from another fourteen-day sample, the stability of individual behavior was found to be in the range of .80 to .90. Although it is impossible to predict how a person will behave in a particular situation, it is possible to predict average behavior over a variety of situations.

Conceptualizing Traits

We have considered the consistency of traits and the relative influences of traits and situations on behavior. The interaction between traits and situations can provide a basis for conceptualizing the theoretical properties and functions of traits. Figure 13.2, for instance, depicts a chain of processes that can mediate between an observable stimulus and an overt response made to that stimulus. The stimulus first must be perceived and categorized (information processing); the organism's appraisal of the stimulus then has motivational consequences; alternative means for satisfying the motivation elicited may then be considered; and the final link in the chain is the overt response. Individual differences in the overt response may arise from trait differences that can influence any of the processes in the sequence.

Consider the following stimulus situation. A male college student approaches several female students after class and asks each for the class assignment and reading list. Student A sharply tells him to go elsewhere. Student B also refuses, excusing herself to rush to an appointment. Student C agrees to his request. The differences in behaviors among these three students can reflect various trait influences. The students may have reacted differently because they perceived the situation differently. Student C might have a cognitive style characterized by scanning of stimuli rather than focusing on details and might not have perceived subtle cues of intonation and body movement indicative of a social overture. Among other traits that can influence the organism at the information-processing stage, the most extensively studied is the dimension of field dependence–independence (Witkin et al., 1962). The perceptions of the field-dependent person are strongly influenced by the context in which stimuli are presented, while the field-independent person is better able to separate figures from their context.

Returning to our example, the students may have interpreted the information similarly but the information may have elicited different feelings and motivations. Student A might be high in aggressive motivation and might have resented the indirect social approach that was taken. Student B might have anxiety over sexual impulses and reacts with avoidance to most social overtures by members of the opposite sex. The dotted arrow in Fig. 13.2 indicates that motivational traits can also influence information processing. For example, Student B might be a repressive on the repression-sensitization

Figure 13.2   Conceptualizing traits.

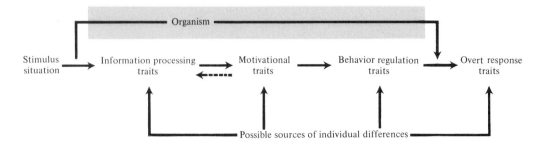

Stimulus situation → Information processing traits → Motivational traits → Behavior regulation traits → Overt response traits

Organism

Possible sources of individual differences

dimension, block out awareness of the heterosexual aspects of the interaction, and fail to recognize her avoidant behavior. Student C might be more comfortable in the sexual area or experience anxiety over asserting her feelings and refusing moderate impositions.

The differences in behavior among the three women could also have arisen from traits operating at the behavior regulation level. Student A might be high on impulsivity and have difficulty in controlling the expression of her feelings, while B might be at the opposite end of this continuum. C might be impulsive or playful or, conversely, overcontrolled. Finally, part of the difference in behavior may be a reflection of behavioral style at the overt response level. Student C might simply have learned to be more polite than A and B. These trait attributes at the overt response level do not influence or cause the behavior; they are intrinsic to it. Traits at this level are *descriptive* of behavior rather than explanatory. However, traits influencing information processing, motivation, or the regulation of behavior can be considered as determinants of or contributing causes to the observed behavioral differences.

Finally, this classification of traits in terms of the nature of their influence is schematic and, in many instances, an oversimplified representation. Trait dimensions such as aggression, anxiety, achievement, introversion, or rigidity are complex constructs with elements and feedback loops that may influence the individual at several points along the sequence between stimulus and response. Thus, individuals with a strong tendency toward anger and aggression might be highly selective in their perception, being quick to perceive slights and humiliations. They also might have difficulty in controlling their behavior and have learned aggressive styles of responding. Nevertheless, the schema in Fig. 13.2 is useful in that it provides a context for the analysis of the functions and modes of influence of different traits.

Summary

Among the most central questions today in the field of personality is whether there are any traits. We have answered this question affirmatively, but we also have indicated that behavior always is a function of both characteristics of the person and the situation in which the behavior is occurring. Furthermore, traits may influence behavior at any place in a behavioral sequence, from what is registered and processed to how a response is expressed.

Specific Points

1. Sheldon contended that three body types—labeled *mesomorphic, endomorphic,* and *ectomorphic*—are related, respectively, to energetic, relaxed, and introverted personality types. Typologies no longer play a central role in psychology because they fail to capture the complexity of personality.
2. Trait psychologists believe that characteristics of individuals are general over situations and endure over time. Cattell distinguished a number of different traits and sources of traits, while Eysenck suggested three higher-order types of traits: neuroticism, introversion-extraversion, and psychoticism.

3. Mischel caused psychologists to rethink the trait issue by documenting that generalized trait measures are poor predictors of behavior in specific situations. The magnitude of the correlation between a trait and behavior tended not to exceed .30.

4. *Attribution theorists* believe that observers tend to see the behavior of others as caused by trait characteristics and their own behavior as due to environmental conditions. This disparity may be due to the greater information held by actors about themselves or to the differential perceptual focuses of actors and observers.

5. Among the newer assessment strategies is *situational* assessment, in which taxonomies of situations, similar to taxonomies of traits, are created. However, situational assessment alone is not sufficient to accurately predict behavior.

6. *Interactionists* contend that behavior is governed by both the properties of the person and the situation in which that person is acting. The *transactional* approach emphasizes the reciprocal influence of the person and the environment on each other. Interactionism, however, typically refers to the fact that variation in behavior is best accounted for by considering both the person and the environment simultaneously.

7. Individuals differ in the consistency of their behavior across situations. In addition, within any individual there may be consistency in some characteristics and inconsistencies in others across different settings.

8. The *template-matching technique* identifies ideal types who would be most likely to behave in a given manner in a given setting. Individuals can then be matched with this ideal type to predict their behavior in that setting.

9. *Traits* are distinguished from *states* in that states are unstable, temporary conditions of the organism. Anxiety is considered to be both a trait and a state. As a state, anxiety is assessed with queries about current intensity of feeling; as a trait, it is measured with questions about frequency and generality across situations.

10. Behavior appears to be more consistent over time and across situations when many instances are sampled. Small samples of behavior, like tests with an insufficient number of items, result in error of measurement, which reduces correlations between the behaviors under study.

Thought Questions

1. Do you believe that body type might "cause" personality characteristics? Why might this be the case?

2. Is your behavior consistent across different settings? Can you think of some behaviors that are consistent and others that are inconsistent?

3. Answer the above question about any friend. Why might the answer be difficult to answer about another person, and what implications might this have for how you perceive that individual?

4. Create a personality template for a good teacher or businessperson. Now predict who among your friends best fits this description.

PART V
Personality Dynamics

So far, we have examined the determinants of behavior that individuals encounter as soon as they enter the world: their genetic predispositions and the physical and social context in which they are placed. Then, after reviewing some of the major theories of personality, we turned to the development and structure of behavior and its measurement. Now we ask: how are these structures expressed in thought and action? What is the dynamic interaction between an individual, attempting to adapt, satisfy needs, and survive, and the environment, which provides the need satisfiers? Here we encounter themes of conflict, impulse control, substitute gratification, frustration, emotion, and stress.

In addition, in this section of the book we deal with questions of consciousness and awareness. Although we must adapt to the environment, often we are not consciously aware of the information that it provides or, for that matter, of the informational signals that our own body sends us. There are multiple levels of awareness. Furthermore, it is often apparent that we are operating within different realms of consciousness, as during dream, hypnotic, or meditational states. In these latter instances, environmental information is almost totally blocked or, on the other hand, there may be a heightened focus of attention.

Dynamics is defined in the dictionary as forces that produce motion. In this Part, we are concerned with the forces acting on the individual that produce psychological "motion": the expression and inhibition of needs and feelings, the entering or leaving of a particular state of consciousness, and the goals and functions of behavior.

The Dynamics of Behavior

14 Why are people motivated to think and behave as they do? One widely accepted and broad answer to this question is that thoughts and actions serve to maximize pleasure and minimize pain, a position most explicitly assumed by Freud (1920, p. 1), who stated: "The impressions that underly the hypothesis of the pleasure principle are so obvious that they cannot be overlooked."

There are two components of the pleasure principle that dictate the directions of our behavior. One indicates that we want to approach and get more of desirable objects and feelings; the second is that we want to avoid or withdraw from undesirable objects and negative emotions. But, to complicate matters, it is often not in our best interests to attain pleasurable goals or to avoid unwanted events *immediately*. That is, it may be functional and adaptive to forgo immediate pleasure in the pursuit of more sustained happiness. Thus, we study to attain a distant career rather than putting down our books and going to a good movie; we do not hit someone when we are angry, because it may lead to retaliation; and so on. In other words, we develop controls over our pleasure-seeking impulses; our defenses inhibit immediate goal attainment but enhance the likelihood of reaching long-term satisfactions. And to further aid in the pursuit of pleasure, if a desired goal is not attained, alternative goals may be established that partially or perhaps entirely satisfy unfulfilled needs. Unfortunately, however, it is also often the case that neither desired goals nor satisfactory substitutes are reached, and frustration is experienced.

Each step in this chain of events—from the arousal of feelings and desires to their frustration and gratification—raises a host of interrelated theoretical and empirical questions. Consider a student who must choose between studying for an exam and going out on a date. Each behavior satisfies a different set of goals related to achievement and academic success versus affiliation and social satisfaction. The student is in conflict between which behavior to choose and which motivation to pursue. What are the properties of such psychological conflict? What kinds of conflict are there? What determines how conflict is resolved? How is the student able to delay the impulse

338

toward being with his girlfriend? The choice the student makes also has important consequences. When a decision is made, some goals are temporarily, or perhaps more permanently, frustrated. Does the desire for the unselected alternative persist? What are the possible responses to frustration? How do these responses influence our student's effectiveness? And how is the unsatisfied desire finally gratified? Through substitute behavior, or even just fantasizing about the postponed desire?

Although a great many questions about the dynamics of behavior have been raised here, the analysis of the situation is still not complete. Given a particular choice, how will the student feel after taking action? Happy? Sad? Angry? Guilty? What determines his emotional response? And, beyond the specific context of choice and the feelings involved, there are further questions about the effects of the tension and stress generated by the experience of conflict. Such stress can accompany the decision and become even more intense following the choice. Of course, in this example the stress might have been minimal, but consider the stress associated with a decision between maintaining a close relationship versus accepting a distant job opportunity.

This chapter is concerned with all of these topics—conflict, impulse control, substitution, frustration, emotion, and stress—all of them subsumed under the general heading of the dynamics of personality, or *psychodynamics.*

Conflict

We live in a world of conflict. Should we marry or remain single? Whom should we marry? What career should we pursue? Should we lie about a wrongdoing or honestly take our punishment? At any given moment in time there are many possible alternatives from which to choose, even in everyday activities. For example, you might be deciding now whether to stay in and study or to go join some friends. If your decision is to study, should you continue with psychology or move on to some other subject? These are conscious conflicts that do not involve any violation of social standards or norms. Other conflicts, however, involve unconscious desires and inhibitions and are of fundamental importance to personality.

Conflicts vary in strength. Some are serious and difficult to resolve, while others are relatively meaningless and easy to settle. The magnitude of a conflict is determined by a number of factors. Assume, for example, that you want to go to a movie, that there is only one movie playing that you have not seen, and that it is precisely the movie you have been waiting for. It is intuitively clear that little conflict exists in this situation. But if two movies are showing that you haven't seen, then more conflict is generated. In general, we can state that *the greater the number of alternatives available, the greater the degree of conflict* (see Berlyne, 1960).

There are other determinants of conflict magnitude in addition to number of alternatives. For example, contrast the situation in which none of the movies except one is considered good with the situation in which many of the movies have been favorably reviewed. Again, there is intuitively more conflict in the latter instance. A second law determining the magnitude of conflict therefore is: *the greater the equality in the attractiveness of the alternatives, the greater the degree of conflict.*

Now suppose you are deciding which college to attend, which job to accept, or which person to marry, as opposed to which movie to attend. Much greater conflict will be aroused in the former instances. Thus, *the greater the importance of a decision, the greater the degree of conflict.*

Temporal, Spatial, and Discriminative Conflict

There are many types of conflicts and different schemes have been proposed that group them into categories. This is an essential scientific step, for it points out the underlying similarities and differences between the various conflict types. One interesting classification scheme distinguishes temporal, spatial, and discriminative conflict (Brown, 1957).

Temporal conflict exists when the attractiveness of alternative choices changes over time. For example, an engaged couple might become more and more uncertain about their decision to marry as the date of the wedding draws near. Job shifts and moving also tend to be perceived with increasing or decreasing favorableness as the time of change approaches.

Spatial conflict is a function of physical distance. A teen-ager might decide to fight the neighborhood bully, for example, but as he approaches him begins to doubt the wisdom of his decision.

Discriminative conflict is best illustrated by an experiment conducted by Ivan Pavlov. Pavlov presented dogs with food following a 600-cycle-frequency tone. A second, 800-cycle-frequency tone was also presented to the animals, but was not followed by any reward. Then, on the conflict trials, a tone of 700 cycles was presented. The dogs had to decide if this was a "food" or a "no-food" tone. Pavlov reported that this conflict gave rise to emotionality and disturbance in his laboratory dogs. He compared these behaviors to the neurotic actions of humans and suggested that certain forms of mental illness might be a result of insoluble discriminative conflicts. Other investigators subsequently contended that schizophrenia can be promoted by a mother who sends both acceptance and rejection signals to a child (a *schizophrenogenic* mother), so that the child does not know if rewards or punishments will be forthcoming (Bateson, Jackson, Haley, and Weakland, 1956).

Lewin's Classification System

A more complete taxonomy of conflict has been proposed by Kurt Lewin, who is considered to be one of the founders of experimental psychodynamics. He was among the first psychologists to test some of Freud's ideas in controlled laboratory settings (see Chapter 1).

Lewin (1935) differentiated three types of conflict: approach-approach, avoidance-avoidance, and approach-avoidance. *Approach-approach conflicts* occur when there are two or more positive alternatives from which to choose: for example, the proverbial donkey choosing between two bundles of hay or someone deciding which of two award-winning movies to see. *Avoidance-avoidance conflicts* are created when a choice is confined to two or more unattractive alternatives, such as a command to either wash the dishes or vacuum the rug.

Lewin contended that approach-approach conflicts are easy to resolve and labeled them *unstable conflicts,* whereas avoidance-avoidance conflicts are dif-

They all look great! An unstable approach-approach conflict; they will soon be eating. (J. Schweiker/Photo Researchers, Inc.)

ficult-to-resolve, *stable conflicts.* Lewin reasoned that, in approach-approach conflicts, as one comes closer to one of the goals, the attractiveness of that goal increases. For example, as one drives to a restaurant, enters the door, reads the menu, and finally sees the food, that food is more and more desired. Thus, in an approach-approach conflict, when an alternative is selected, its attractiveness increases, while the attractiveness of the unselected alternative decreases because one is psychologically further from it. The conflict therefore is readily resolved, as illustrated in Fig. 14.1, which shows that the difference in the relative attractiveness of alternatives increases as one comes closer to either of the goals.

On the other hand, given an avoidance-avoidance conflict (see Fig. 14.1), as one of the aversive alternatives is approached, it becomes increasingly negative. For example, anxiety increases dramatically as one gets closer and closer to the edge of a cliff; less dramatically, washing the dishes will appear increasingly unattractive as the soap and hot water are experienced. In addition, the aversiveness of the unselected alternative decreases, for one is getting psychologically further from it. This change in the perceived aversiveness of the alternatives will cause one to oscillate and repeatedly shift choices. This analysis assumes that escape from both negative alternatives is impossible. Lewin argued that one of the great disadvantages of using negative alternatives and punishments is that energy must be expended to ensure that the individual does not attempt to leave the situation, thereby avoiding both alternatives.

To test the idea that approach-approach conflicts are easier to resolve than avoidance-avoidance conficts, Arkoff (1957) presented subjects with a number of hypothetical choices representing both types of conflict, such as "Would you rather be more attractive *or* more intelligent?" and "Would you rather be less attractive *or* less intelligent?" The time taken to make a choice

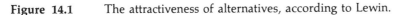

Figure 14.1   The attractiveness of alternatives, according to Lewin.

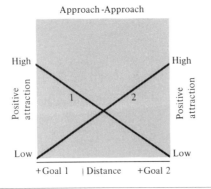
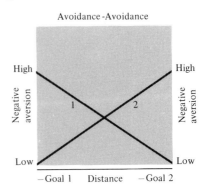

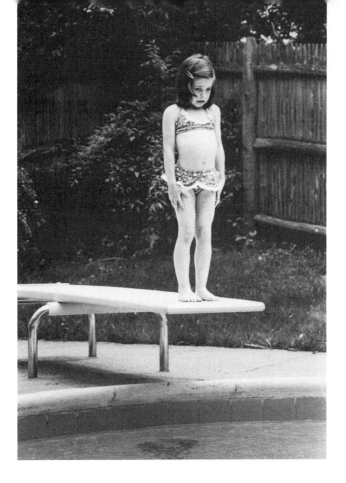

Should I or shouldn't I? A stable approach-avoidance conflict, thus making one wonder how long this young diver will remain on the board. (Peter Vandermark)

or resolve the hypothetical conflicts was much less in approach-approach than in avoidance-avoidance situations.

The third type of conflict identified by Lewin, *approach-avoidance conflict*, was the basis for a well-known theory presented by Neal Miller (1944, 1959). Miller, previously discussed in Chapter 6 on learning theory approaches to personality, used learning theory terminology to explain complex conflicts.

Miller's Conflict Model

The most prevalent type of conflict is *approach-avoidance conflict*, which occurs when both positive and negative consequences are associated with the same action. For example, we like to buy new clothes, but they are expensive; we want to eat a candy bar, but it is fattening; we would like to hit people we are angry at, but this is likely to be punished. Observation of approach-avoidance conflicts often reveals ambivalent behavior; the organism approaches the desired object, only to turn away, reapproach, and so on. The behavior oscillates from approach to withdrawal and hence is labeled *ambivalent*. Miller's model is able to account for this behavior.

In accordance with Fig. 14.1, Miller assumed that the tendency to approach a positive goal, as well as the tendency to avoid a negative goal, is stronger the nearer the organism is to those goals. However, he asserted that the strength of avoidance increases more rapidly with nearness to the goal than does the strength of approach. This process is depicted in Fig. 14.2. The differential steepness of the slopes in Fig. 14.2 is based on the fact that avoidance behavior is determined, in part, by one's level of fear. Fear is a learned drive which varies as a function of one's nearness to the feared situation. For example, fear is great when one is at the edge of a cliff, or perhaps in a dark room, but decreases rapidly when one steps a few feet from the edge of the cliff or turns on a light. On the other hand, approach behavior is typically based on internal drives, such as hunger, which remain relatively constant even though the external environment may change. For these reasons, Miller posited that the avoidance tendency would be steeper than that of approach. Further inspection of the approach-avoidance conflict gradients shown in Fig. 14.2 reveals that the organism should approach the goal until reaching point X, the place where the strengths of both tendencies are equal. Beyond that point, the strength of avoidance exceeds that of approach and the organism should begin to withdraw, thus producing oscillation and the appearance of ambivalence.

Miller, Brown, and others have conducted a number of experiments to test this model. Often rats have been used as the experimental subjects, so that rather severe hours of deprivation as well as the strength of a shock could be varied. In one of the original investigations, Brown (1948) developed a technique for measuring the strength of the approach and avoidance tendencies in rats. The rats were fitted with a harness that allowed the experimenter to test how hard they pulled. Animals had been trained in separate goal boxes either to approach food or to avoid shock and were then placed at various distances from the food or shock. As hypothesized, the strength of pull varied as a function of distance from the goal, and the distance from the

Figure 14.2   Goal strengths in approach-avoidance conflicts.

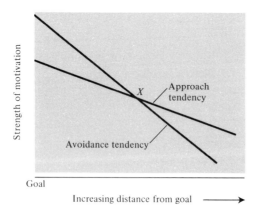

Figure 14.3   Differences in approach gradients.

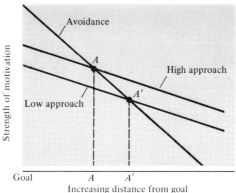

shocked compartment influenced the intensity of pull more than distance from the rewarded compartment.

Other tests and derivations of the model have concerned the effects of the degree of hunger or strength of shock on conflict resolution. Figure 14.3 repeats Fig. 14.2, except that a second approach gradient has been added. The two approach gradients differ in magnitude, showing the difference in intensity of motivation caused by, for example, unequal levels of hunger. The distance between points *A* and *A'* represents the differential distance of approach to the goal. As the figure shows, the intersection of the approach and avoidance gradients occurs at a point closer to the goal when the approach desire is heightened.

The situation depicted in Fig. 14.3 has some interesting behavioral implications. Suppose, for example, that the figure represents strength differences in the aggressive approach tendencies of two individuals. Because the avoidance gradient at the goal is greater than either of the approach gradients, neither individual will engage in overt hostile actions. However, because the individual with the stronger drive comes closer to the goal, he experiences more fear and more conflict. Thus, the amount of fear and conflict displayed by an individual can be an index of his or her attraction to that situation. The Miller conflict model therefore can account for Freud's paradoxical observation that the intensity of avoidance behavior is often a direct reflection of the intensity of temptation.

Conflict and displacement.   The term *displacement* refers to the observation that one's goals may change, even though the desire to reach the original goal has not subsided (see Chapter 4). Freud contended that there are "vicissitudes

Figure 14.4   Displacement.

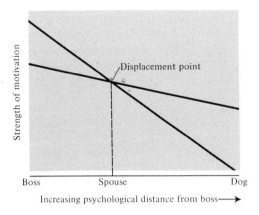

Strength of motivation

Displacement point

Boss   Spouse   Dog

Increasing psychological distance from boss ⟶

of the instincts"; in other words, there are a variety of objects that may satisfy an underlying wish. The most frequently cited example of such displacement activity is in the study of aggression, where it is often pointed out that someone who cannot express anger at his or her boss comes home to take it out on an unsuspecting spouse. Freud (1915, pp. 174–175) used a similar but more humorous example to illustrate displacement;

> *There was a blacksmith in the village who had committed a capital offense. The Court decided that the crime must be punished; but as the blacksmith was the only one in the village and was indispensable, and as on the other hand there were three tailors living there, one of them was hanged instead.*

Displacement activity, or the shifting of goal objects, has been incorporated into Miller's conflict model. Consider the employee angry at the boss but not directly expressing this hostility. Miller would reason that the aggressive tendency directed toward the boss is inhibited by a stronger avoidance tendency. Thus, the person responds aggressively to someone other than the boss, as depicted in Fig. 14.4. In Fig. 14.4, the horizontal or X axis, which represented physical (spatial) distance in previous figures, now depicts "psychological" distance or "similarity" to the figure eliciting hostility. Of course, Fig. 14.4 is a simplified analysis of what can be a very complex process, inasmuch as displacement is affected by a number of psychological factors such as previous experience with the displaced object, the availability of alternative goal satisfiers, and the like.

In situations of conflict, one often must forego a desired goal, as was the case when our hypothetical student decided to study rather than to join his girlfriend. In the next section of this chapter, we examine impulse control and factors that enhance or decrease our ability to delay gratification.

Impulse Control and Delay of Gratification

If all our wishes could be acted on immediately, and if appropriate goal objects existed in the external world, then there would be little conflict of any psychological import. Of course, there are different ways of satisfying desires, and there are competing wishes and goal objects, but approach-approach conflicts typically are easily resolved. Conversely, when avoidance tendencies are elicited and barriers preventing goal attainment are imposed, as is the case when there are social norms prohibiting desired actions, then the potential for severe psychological consequences exists. On the one hand, wishes may be left unfulfilled, while on the other hand, goal satisfaction might entail such great personal cost as retribution, punishment, and loss.

From the perspective of psychoanalytic theory, ego mechanisms recognize the demands of the social world and impose restraints on behavior. Ego constraints postpone goal-directed actions until external conditions are more suitable for the expression of one's drives. Repression, which was discussed in detail in Chapter 4, is the main mechanism responsible for preventing the immediate gratification of wishes. Recall that the defenses often intervene so that a wish does not enter consciousness and thus is not directly acted upon.

Ego controls are necessary if the organism is to function in society and avoid the punishment that might accompany immediate sexual or aggressive gratification. With the individual's increasing cognitive development and maturity, such controls become a virtue as well as a necessity, for the ability to delay enables one to attain highly desirable long-term goals that require the abandonment of immediate gratification. For example, studying to do well on an exam might require forgoing a pleasant social encounter, and enrollment in graduate or medical school necessitates giving up immediate monetary gain for a better position in the future. Thus, ego functions include not only the recognition of appropriate external conditions for drive expression, but also more general self-imposed constraints, or everyday "will power" (Loevinger, 1976).

Hallucinatory Images

Freud (1911) argued that in the absence of satisfying external objects, images of these objects are called forth and pleasure is attained through hallucinations or fantasy activity. Hallucinations, therefore, are one way to cope temporarily with lack of gratification; they bridge the delay between one's desires and their expression—a function frequently referred to as *time binding*.

The effects of mental representations of rewards on the ability to delay gratification have been examined experimentally by Mischel and his colleagues (Mischel, 1974a, 1974b; Mischel and Ebbesen, 1970). In these studies, children were placed in a choice dilemma in which they might have received either a smaller, immediate reward (a candy bar) or a larger reward (two candy bars) at a later time, in exchange for their cooperation at a task. A variety of factors then were manipulated to assess their effects on the choices the children made.

Figure 14.5   Mean minutes of voluntary waiting time for the delayed reward in each attention condition. (From Mischel and Ebbesen, 1970, p. 333. Copyright 1970 by the American Psychological Association. Adapted by permission of publisher and authors.)

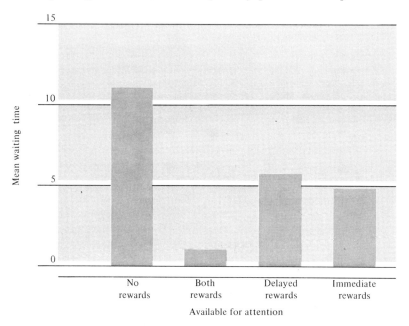

To examine the influence of the visual presence of the reward on delay of gratification, Mischel and Ebbesen (1970) created situations in which the delayed reward, the immediate reward, both rewards, or neither reward was in the subject's visual field during the delay period. In this study, the child could wait for the experimenter to return with the larger reward or signal for him to return and immediately receive the smaller reward. The results of this investigation are shown in Fig. 14.5. The graph clearly reveals that waiting time was maximal when neither of the rewards was visible, and minimal when both rewards could be seen. In a subsequent investigation of the effects of mental representation of a reward, the researchers devised two experimental conditions in which the rewards were not visible and the subjects were instructed to either think about the rewards or think "fun" (Mischel, Ebbesen, and Zeiss, 1972). Figure 14.6 shows that thinking about a reward retards the ability to delay gratification.

On the basis of these and other data, Mischel contended that one consequence of the mental representation of a reward object during the delay interval is frustration. The additional frustration then decreases the ability to delay gratification. Any activity that distracts the person from thinking about the reward should therefore lessen frustration and increase delay behavior.

Figure 14.6　　Mean minutes of voluntary waiting time for treatment conditions and controls. (From Mischel, Ebbesen, and Zeiss, 1972, p. 213. Copyright 1972 by the American Psychological Association. Adapted by permission of publisher and authors.)

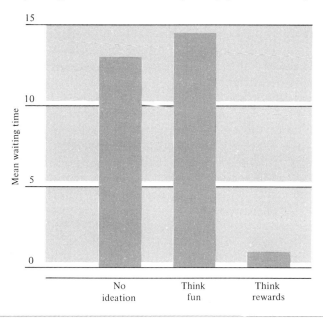

Perhaps we intuitively realize this; when we want something that is unobtainable, we may go to the movies to forget about it. Furthermore, even given the visual appearance of the desired reward, the individual may engage in coping activities that help delay gratification. For example, when children had a potential reward of pretzels and thought about them as logs or other objects, delay ability was enhanced. However, it can be contended that a choice between candy bars does not reflect any strong internalized desires and does not quite capture the problems that Freud addressed. Thus, one must be careful in the generalization of these data to more intense need situations.

Learning Theory Approaches

It is evident from the previous discussion that, according to psychoanalytic theory, delay is an ego function determined by intrapsychic factors. Mischel (1968, p. 153) contrasted this position with that of the social learning theorists:

According to the psychoanalytic theory of delay behavior, aroused impulses press for immediate discharge of tension through overt motoric activity. . . . The psychoanalytic approach . . . leads one to seek determinants of delay behavior in such hypothetical internal events as ego organizations and energy-binding ideations [hallucinations]. In contrast, social behavior theory . . . views manipulable social-stimulus events as the critical determinants of self-controlling behavior.

In the tradition of social learning (see Chapter 6), Bandura and Mischel (1965) examined the role of a model in altering delay behavior. These investigators first identified children who were willing to delay reward and others who sought immediate gratification. The children then observed a model displaying behavior inconsistent with their own delay preferences. For example, the high-delay children observed a model choosing cheaper, plastic chess figures without delay rather than waiting one week for a more attractive chess set. In one condition the model was "live," while in a second condition the model's responses were read rather than actually observed. Both before and immediately after the model's performance, and one month later, delay of gratification was assessed. Figure 14.7, which depicts only the responses of the high-delay children, indicates that their preference for immediate, less valuable rewards increased dramatically in the model conditions. Furthermore, the influence of the live model remained effective at the one-month retest period, or postexposure, and at a related choice task (a "generalization" condition).

Figure 14.7   Effects of modeling on delay of gratification. (From Bandura and Mischel, 1965, p. 702. Copyright 1965 by the American Psychological Association. Adapted by permission of publisher and authors.)

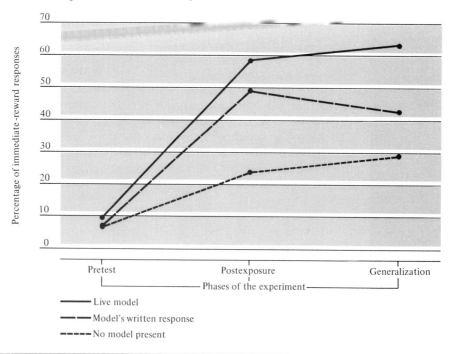

In addition to observational learning, there are other procedures and contingencies that can establish self-control. For example, guided by Skinnerian principles, one woman who had problems controlling her "cussing" fined herself a dollar every time she swore. This money was immediately put aside for charity. Other control techniques that manipulate the environment, like putting a lock on the refrigerator, have been used to prevent impulsive expression. And cognitive behavior modification techniques such as covert self-statements (see Chapter 6) have been used effectively to control motoric discharge ("If I miss this shot, I will not throw my racquet").

Expectancy and Delay of Gratification

Rotter's social learning theory (see Chapter 6) also has been applied to the study of delay behavior. Mahrer (1956) demonstrated that delay behavior is in part determined by the expectation of reinforcement. Children seven to nine years old were offered a choice between a smaller immediate reward and a more attractive delayed reward. Before the choice dilemma, three levels of expectancy for the receipt of a promised reward were induced. On each of five consecutive days the experimenter told the children that for performing an activity they would receive a small balloon on the following day. To develop groups of high, moderate, and low expectancy for delayed reward, this promise was kept variously 100 percent, 50 percent, or none of the time. Three days later, the same subjects were offered a choice between the immediate and the delayed reward. Furthermore, the experimenter offering the choices was either the same one (experimenter A) who conducted the training session or a person differing from A in sex and age (experimenter B). The results of this study are shown in Table 14.1. The table shows that the groups of subjects tested by the different experimenter (E_B) all exhibited the same delay behavior, regardless of prior training. On the other hand, responses to experimenter A (E_A) were consistent with the expectancies based on prior experiences, with higher expectancies leading to greater delay behavior.

Table 14.1 Choices of immediate and delayed reinforcement

Reinforcement choice	Expectancy					
	High		Moderate		Low	
	E_A	E_B	E_A	E_B	E_A	E_B
Immediate	6*	6	15	5	18	7
Delayed	19	14	11	15	6	15

Source: Adapted from Mahrer, 1956, p. 104. Used by permission.
*Number of subjects making that choice.

Individual Differences

Other investigators conducting experimental studies in delay behavior have been particularly concerned with individual differences. For example, Kagan (1966) identified reflective as opposed to impulsive children on the basis of their delay in answering difficult visual discrimination problems. Reflective children were reported as less distractible in school and displayed better attention and concentration on tasks. Subsequent work with this personality dimension suggested that not only response time, but also rate of errors, is important in distinguishing reflective from impulsive children (Kagan and Kogan, 1970). It has been speculated that impulsive children are anxious over their ability and therefore work with excess speed to remove themselves from the task situation. This results in a high rate of errors. However, children working quickly who make many errors must be distinguished from those who work with equal speed but with few errors (see Block, Block, and Harrington, 1974). Indeed, one of the contentions of the Block study was that accuracy, rather than speed, of response has important personality correlates and determinants.

Substitution

If one's wishes are not attained, either because of conflict and impulse control or because the goal object is not available, then psychological processes are elicited to help one cope with the situation. One such process, considered in the previous section, is hallucination. Freud contended that hallucinations about goal objects serve to gratify one's wishes (although the experiments by Mischel and his associates might be considered as evidence contradicting this notion). Other fantasy activity such as dreaming (which is examined in detail in the following chapter) has also been considered to have wish-fulfillment functions. And, as discussed in the chapter on psychoanalytic theory, even such diverse behaviors as slips of the tongue and jokes were thought to reduce aggressive and sexual urges.

But perhaps the most prevalent, most adaptive way of coping with goal frustration is to establish alternative goals. Freudian theory, as has been pointed out, posits that the object of a desire may change. A forbidden, unfulfilled wish can, for example, become directed toward objects that have some similarity to the desired object yet permit expression of the original wish. Freud stated that ultimately a libidinal tendency might even be expressed in cultural activities such as painting or composing. In his analyses of Michelangelo and da Vinci, Freud contended that these great artists had strong unfulfilled sexual urges toward their mothers that were deflected into socially acceptable channels. Freud labeled this defense, included among the defense mechanisms in Chapter 4, *sublimation.*

Displacement activity, examined in the section on conflict, and also one of the defense mechanisms, concerns desires that are deflected from a primary goal because of conflict. Displacement refers to the direction of behavior, or the goals that one selects. The study of alternative goal gratification, or *substitution,* concerns a related, yet different problem; namely, does the attainment of substitute goals satisfy one's desires? That is, is the original wish partially or completely satisfied? More specifically, assume that you want to aggress against an authority figure like your father, but are prevented from doing so by conflict. Aggression is now displaced toward your brother. Is this displacement activity of motivational value; that is, are your aggressive tendencies satisfied through the substitute goal gratification? The latter question is the focus of the study of substitution.

Kurt Lewin and his students conducted a series of experiments that examined the properties and functions of substitute goals. Although these investigations were conducted nearly fifty years ago, they remain classics in the field. Lewin (1935, pp. 180–181) believed that substitution is manifested in many different ways.

There is, for instance, the man who dreams of a palace and brings a few pieces of marble into his kitchen. There is the man who cannot buy a piano, but who collects piano catalogs. Again, we find the delinquent boy who knows that he will not be allowed to leave his reform school but who asks for a traveling bag as a birthday present. . . . These and a hundred other examples make us realize how important and far-reaching the problem of substitution is in regard to psychological needs as well as with reference to bodily needs such as hunger and sex.

To examine the value of substitution in a laboratory experiment, Lewin and his students first allowed their subjects, typically children, to engage in an attractive, gamelike task, such as a building activity, and then interrupted the children before the task was completed. Earlier research had established that there is a strong motivational force to return and complete such interrupted tasks. Then, before allowing the children to finish their task, the experimenters permitted them to engage in some other activity. After this, the children had the opportunity to resume the interrupted activity. If the children resumed the previously unfinished task, then the intervening activity did not serve as a substitute. But if the originally unfinished activity was not undertaken, then the intervening activity had substitute value. Thus, resumption became the behavioral indicator identifying substitute goals and their effects.

One of the first experimental studies of substitution was conducted by Lissner (1933). In her experiment, children were interrupted while making a figure from clay. Then, after they had made a different figure, they were tested for resumption. Lissner identified two factors that influence the substitute value of an activity: its similarity to the first activity and its level of difficulty. The more similar and difficult the intervening task, the greater its substitute value and the less likely the resumption of the unfinished task. Mahler (1933) gave subjects an intervening activity that could be completed in ways that differed in how closely they resembled the original, overt behavior. Subjects could think about doing the task, talk through its completion, or actually do it. In general, substitute value varied directly with the degree of reality of the substitute action, with the least substitution value provided by the imaginative task. This implies that daydreams and other fantasy activity may have little (yet *some*) value for the reduction of persisting desires.

In sum, these studies demonstrate that goals can substitute for one another. Further, some of the relevant dimensions and determinants of substitute value have been identified. There clearly are interrelationships between psychological needs, as Freud and Lewin argued. Unfortunately, while there has been some followup of the work of Lewin and his students, there has been very little recent research on the problem of substitution. One exception has been investigations of the catharsis or discharge of aggression through fantasy, particularly studies that examine the effects of violence on television. This will be discussed in detail in Chapter 18.

One should not conclude from the dearth of research on substitution that it is a minor element in the dynamics of personality. The research techniques developed by Lewin's research team were appropriate to rather minor, experimentally induced motivations and goals, such as cutting out paper dolls, making clay figures, and so on. However, making substitute choices is intrinsic to human experience; questions of the factors determining the value of substitutions are fundamental for human motivation. If we fail to make the football team but play on the baseball team, is our desire to play on the football team thereby less intense? If we aspire to be a novelist but, after a series of rejection slips, shift to a successful career in business, will the desire to write abate? Clearly there are many fundamental unanswered questions concerning the value of substitute choices, and this should be a fertile area of study for future personality psychologists.

Frustration

So far we have examined the dynamics of conflict and how coping with conflict is aided by means of impulse control and the establishment of substitute goals. However, goals must frequently be forsaken. In those cases, there is likely to be frustration, as well as a number of more well-defined emotions, including anger, disappointment, and guilt. First, we will examine the psychological study of frustration and then turn toward the more general topic of emotions.

Frustration has diverse meanings for psychologists. It may refer to an independent variable, or experimental manipulation. Often this involves blocking the attainment of a goal, inducing failure, or delivering a personal insult. Performance of a "frustrated" group is then compared to the performance of a "nonfrustrated" control group. Frustration may also refer to a dependent variable, in which case the researcher measures the amount of frustrated behavior. For example, one might examine whether individuals high in anxiety display more frustrated behavior than persons low in anxiety. Finally, frustration frequently pertains to an intervening variable, or a complex process inferred from certain observable responses. For example, on the basis of observed aggressive behavior, one might conclude that an individual is frustrated.

Many response indicators of frustration have been observed in laboratory situations. These responses include aggression, fixation, regression, and enhanced goal striving, all of which will be briefly examined here. It is not clear which particular response any individual will choose in reaction to frustration. The choice depends on a number of factors, including the degree of frustration, past reinforcement history, situational constraints, and so forth.

Frustration and Aggression

The best-known work on frustration concerns what is called the frustration-aggression hypothesis. In a manner similar to the analysis of approach-avoidance conflict, this work was stimulated by translating Freudian ideas into the terminology of learning and motivational theory. In so doing, experimentally testable ideas could be formulated.

Dollard and his colleagues at Yale (Dollard et al., 1939) postulated a linkage between frustration (defined as a goal response that has been interrupted) and the instigation to aggression (defined as an act that has a goal of injury to another organism). Miller (1941, p. 337) described, in its least extreme form, the hypothesized relation between frustration and aggression:

The frustration-aggression hypothesis is an attempt to state a relationship believed to be important in many different fields of research. It is intended to suggest to the student of human nature that when he sees aggression he should turn a suspicious eye on possibilities that the organism or group is confronted with frustration; and when he views interference with individual or group habits, he should be on the look-out for, among other things, aggression.

This relatively simple formulation has generated a great deal of research. The kinds of phenomena explained by the frustration-aggression hypothesis, its limitations, and the revisions of this hypothesis will be considered in detail in Chapter 18, which is addressed to the topic of aggressive behavior. For the present, we merely want to indicate that one possible reaction to frustration is aggression.

Frustration and Fixation

Psychologists have long noted what is called the *neurotic paradox,* which refers to *fixation,* or the persistence of responses that apparently result in repeated failure and nonreward. For example, if one wanted to do well in school, yet studied very little and failed repeatedly, this would be considered maladaptive behavior. Such responses do not fit within explanations given by traditional learning theories, for negative reinforcement does not appear to decrease the response's occurrence.

Norman Maier (1949) conducted a series of experiments demonstrating that frustration can lead to persistent maladaptive behavior. Maier made use

Figure 14.8

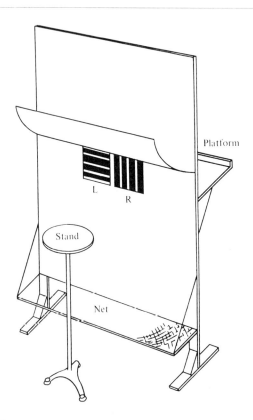

Lashley's jumping stand. (Lashley 1930 p 4F6 Used liy permission.)

of an apparatus known as the Lashley jumping stand (see Fig. 14.8). An animal, typically a rat, is placed on the stand facing two cardboard doors, each marked with a distinctive design. An aversive stimulus, such as a puff of air to the tail or a tail pinch, forces the rat to jump, and it strikes one of the two cards with its body. If it strikes the door that the experimenter has selected as "correct," then the door falls over and the rat lands on a platform with a food reward. If it strikes the other card, it gets a bump and falls into the net below, a rather traumatic punishment. When the reward is randomly assigned to each card and position, many of the animals adopt a stereotyped response and jump to either the left or the right position, regardless of which card design is there. If the problem is then made soluble, the animal does not abandon its earlier response. Even if the reward is made clearly visible by opening one of the doors, many animals continue to exhibit a position habit.

Maier labeled these stereotyped responses *fixated* inasmuch as the organism seems unable to switch to more adaptive behavior. Fixated responses are quite stable and resistant to change. For example, rats taught to *walk* to the correct location by placing a plank between the jumping stand and the other side will continue to *jump* to the fixated side when the plank is removed.

Rat jumping from platform of the Lashley jumping stand to one of the alternative windows. If incorrect, the door does not open and the rat falls into a net. (Frank Lotz Miller/Black Star)

To alter a fixated response, guidance is required. During a trial, animals are pushed toward the open door until gradually they are allowed to make a free choice. In sum, Maier contended that (1) frustration-instigated behavior is characterized by fixation and compulsivity; (2) such behavior is not altered by rewards; and (3) fixated behavior can be abandoned only by using the technique of guidance. Based on these conclusions, Maier argued that frustration-instigated behavior is qualitatively different from motivationally instigated or normal behavior. We will return to these ideas in Chapter 17 on personal responsibility, for the currently popular concept of learned helplessness is closely related to the notion of fixation. *Learned helplessness*, it will be disclosed, is exhibited when an organism does not respond (for example, escape a shock) because of an apparent belief that the response will be ineffective.

Frustration and Regression

Freud specified that during childhood the individual selects certain problem solutions to cope with conflict and stress. During times of later stress, according to Freud, there is a tendency to repeat these earlier modes of behavior, even though they might be inadequate in the present situation. A mild *regression* might involve running home to mother in difficult times, while a more extreme form could result in constant thumb sucking, as may be exhibited by people in a severe psychotic state.

Kurt Lewin also experimentally investigated the Freudian concept of regression by studying the effects of frustration on play activity. The play of older children involves a future time perspective and many distinct subparts. These qualities are much less characteristic of the play of younger children. Thus, conditions that lessen the future time perspective and cause play to be simpler are seen as promoting regression, or "negative development" (Barker, Dembo, and Lewin, 1943).

The experiment conducted by Barker et al. (1943) to produce regression was relatively straightforward. Children were brought into an experimental room and allowed to play with attractive toys (prefrustration period). Then they were separated from the toys by a partition. The children could still see the toys, but were prevented from handling them by a wire fence (frustration period). During the forced separation the children could play with other objects in the room. Throughout the prefrustration and frustration periods, the experimenters measured the constructiveness of their play. The results of the investigation revealed that the play did change between the prefrustration and the frustration periods. During the frustration period, the children's play was more primitive, less elaborate, and so forth. Thus, it was concluded that frustration could lead to regression. (See Lawson, 1965; and Yates, 1962, for further discussion of this research and some methodological criticisms. The main research criticism has been that this study did not include a "no frustration" control group. Thus, the regressive behaviors might have been due to fatigue or boredom rather than to frustration.)

Frustration and Enhanced Goal Striving

The experience of frustration need not lead to maladaptive behaviors such as aggression, fixation, and regression. Rather, frustration might result in increased vigor in pursuit of one's goal. For example, a low grade might lead one to study even harder; failure to get a hit in a baseball game might mean more batting practice, and so forth.

In addition to enhancing the practice and vigor of a particular response, frustration can also act as a goad for creative problem solving to achieve a desired end. The history of scientific discoveries and inventions typically reflects a series of frustrated efforts to resolve a problem, eventually culminating in a creative and successful solution. Thus, frustration may act as an additional incentive and energizer, providing a stimulus for new and adaptive problem-solving behavior (Child and Waterhouse, 1953). In sum, the responses to frustration vary greatly, depending on the availability of alternative responses and the personality characteristics and resources of the frustrated individual. Frustration may elicit maladaptive behaviors, such as fixation and regression, or more positive, goal-oriented actions.

Emotion

If one feels "frustrated," then a certain negative state is being experienced. Thus, frustration, which was defined as a complex internal process, also is an emotion. Anticipated emotional states, broadly conceived as pleasure and pain, guide our conduct; following attainment or nonattainment of a desire, a variety of positive and/or negative feelings are experienced that determine the perceived quality of our lives. Hence, emotions also are a central topic in the study of personality and psychodynamics.

The word *emotion* is derived from the Latin *emovere* ("to move out"). Young (1943), as noted in Cofer and Appley (1964, p. 25), described how the word *emotion* found its way into the field of psychology:

Originally the word meant a moving out of one place into another, in the sense of a migration. Thus: "The divers emotions of that people (the Turks)" (1603). . . . The word [then] came to mean a moving, stirring, agitation, perturbation, and was used in a strictly physical sense. Thus: "Thunder . . . caused so great an Emotion in the air" (1708). . . . This physical meaning was transferred to political and social agitation, the word coming to mean tumult, popular disturbance. Thus: "There were . . . great stirres and emocions in Lombardye" . . . . Finally, the word came to be used to designate any agitated, vehement, or excited mental state of the individual. Thus: "The joy of gratification is properly called an emotion" (1762).

Distinguishing Characteristics

Emotions have a cluster of characteristics that distinguish them from pure thoughts (e.g., contrast "I feel rage" with "This is a table"). Any given property of a "hot" emotion can also describe a "cold" thought, but if all the characteristics are in evidence, then an emotional state can be inferred.

1. Emotions have a positive or negative experiential quality. That is, they are something the person likes and wants to get more of (joy, love, pride) or something the person dislikes and wants to be rid of (sadness, hatred, guilt).

2. The positive and negative characteristics vary in magnitude. Thus, one can feel a little or a great deal of happiness, somewhat sad or very sad, and so on.

3. The feelings might be accompanied by certain facial expressions and body postures. Smiling often accompanies positive emotions; curled lips and tightened facial muscles are linked with anger; and pride may be displayed with an upright posture.

4. The emotions signal certain types of behavior. Thus, for example, one strikes out in order to "eliminate" the object of anger; gratitude gives rise to a reciprocal favor; and so on. Tomkins (1970) has proposed that emotions, not drives or desires, are the chief movers of behavior. He made his point powerfully with the following anecdote (1970, pp. 101–102):

Consider anoxic deprivation. Almost any interference with normal breathing will immediately arouse the most desperate gasping for breath. Is there any motivational claim more urgent than the demand of one who is drowning or choking to death for want of air? Yet it is not simply the imperious demand for oxygen that we observe under such circumstances. We also are observing the rapidly mounting panic ordinarily recruited whenever the air supply is suddenly jeopardized. . . . We have only to change the rate of anoxic deprivation to change the nature of the recruited affect. . . . Thus, in the Second World War, those pilots who refused to wear their oxygen masks at 30,000 feet suffered a more gradual anoxic deprivation. They did not panic for want of oxygen. They became euphoric. It was the affect of enjoyment which the more slowly developing anoxic signal recruited. Some of these men, therefore, met their death with smiles on their lips.

5. Emotions often follow particular thoughts. For example, if you fail an exam because you believe that others hindered you, anger is a likely reaction; success ascribed to help from others elicits gratitude; both success and failure believed to be due to luck bring about surprise; and so on. Thus, one's feelings are determined in part by one's thoughts. The subjective interpretation, not the objective facts, determines emotions. For example, one may fail because of insufficient studying, yet anger (rather than, say, guilt and self-blame) is experienced if the failure is believed to be due to the teacher's bias.

Arousal and Emotions

There have been a number of different approaches to the psychology of emotions. The Darwinian tradition stressed the innate basis of emotional expression. Cross-species facial characteristics that relate to behavioral expression have been identified, such as the similar baring of fangs by wolves and sneering by humans. Innate indicators of anger and other emotional expressions were examined in Chapter 2.

A second influential approach to the study of emotions stems from the Freudian position. As indicated in Chapter 4, the Freudian viewpoint emphasizes unconscious determinants of affect, as well as negative emotions such as anxiety and guilt. More recently, however, the concept of *arousal* and the interrelation of arousal and attribution have been the most dominant concerns in the study of emotions. *Arousal* refers to the intensity, state of activation, or drive characterizing an individual.

An early theory of emotion specified that too high an activation level would result in overexcitement, while too low a level would produce depression. Furthermore, emotions were believed to lead to either behavioral organization or disorganization, depending on the intensity of the emotion or the person's level of arousal. Schlosberg (1954, pp. 82–83) illustrated this position with the following vignette:

[A sleeping man] . . . is near the zero level of action. . . . As a result of this general condition, he doesn't respond to ordinary stimuli; he is unconscious.

Now let the alarm clock ring. . . . The individual is awake and responsive to stimulation. . . . Let us assume that our hero has reached an optimum level of activation by 10:00 A.M. He is alert, and responds efficiently to his environment. But now he finds that a book he needs is missing from his shelf. This frustration produces an increment in level of activation, perhaps not high enough at first to be dignified by the name of anger. But as he continues to search for the book the level of activation builds up until he is "blind with rage."

This conception of emotions, however, proved to be inadequate. First of all, emotions do not necessarily disrupt behavior. As indicated in Tomkins's quote about pilots, even emotions of great intensity may be quite adaptive and survival relevant. Equally important, given the same level of arousal, there are different emotional reactions. For example, high arousal might be accompanied by intense hate, intense love, or excitement. Arousal is therefore not a sufficient explanation of experienced emotions; it does not provide the conceptual tools to distinguish between emotions.

Schachter (1964) and Schachter and Singer (1962) supplemented arousal theory so that it could differentiate between emotions. They proposed that emotions are a function of two factors: level of arousal and cognitions about the arousing situation. In real-life situations the situational cues that arouse an organism also provide the information necessary for understanding the event. For example, the appearance of a birthday cake may heighten arousal and act as a stimulus for positive affect (joy); the sight of a gun is likely to cause heightened arousal and act as a cue for fear. However, in laboratory settings, Schachter and his colleagues were able to manipulate arousal and cognitive factors independently and thereby study their joint effect on emotional expression.

In the best-known of their studies, Schachter and Singer (1962) injected subjects with epinephrine (an activating agent that often produces autonomic arousal and a general "high" feeling), under the guise of studying "how vitamin supplements affect the visual skills" (p. 382). Some subjects were told of the effects of the drug and could thus appropriately label the source of their feelings. But other subjects were either uninformed or misinformed about the drug's effects, and control subjects were injected with a placebo. The subjects then awaited their "visual test" in the presence of a stooge subject. The stooge either acted in a very euphoric manner or feigned anger at some personal inquiries that were part of a questionnaire administered during the waiting period. During this interval, the subjects' behaviors were observed and rated for euphoria or anger. The main reported findings were that uninformed, epinephrine-injected subjects (aroused, but "unlabeled") were relatively angrier in the anger-inducing situation and relatively more euphoric when the stooge acted in a euphoric manner than control subjects. Thus, emotion is a function of arousal level, and individuals in an aroused state may experience disparate emotions as a function of the social (cognitive) situation in which they find themselves.

Schachter's theory suggests that emotional experience results from the following sequence:

1. There is a bodily reaction (arousal).
2. The individual becomes aware of this reaction.
3. There is a need to seek a reason or explanation of the reaction.
4. An external cue is identified and the internal reaction is labeled. This labeling provides the quality or the naming of the emotional feeling and is thus a key determinant of experienced emotions.

A number of other so-called "misattribution" paradigms have evolved to study emotional experience. In an experiment by Nisbett and Schachter (1966), subjects were given a placebo after being told that they were about to receive a series of electric shocks. All of the subjects were informed that the placebo had side-effects. In one condition, the side-effects were described as tremors, shaky hands, pounding heart, and other effects identical with symptoms of fear arousal. In a second condition, the side-effects were described as itching, headache, and other reactions unrelated to fear. Subjects were then given a series of shocks that progressively increased in intensity. The dependent variables included the point at which pain was first experienced and the intensity at which the shock was reported to be unendurable. The data revealed that, within the range of shock at which the subjects reasonably could attribute their arousal symptoms to the two possible causal sources (shock or pill), the individuals in the pill-attribution condition reported that they first experienced pain at a higher level of intensity and had a higher tolerance level than subjects who could attribute their arousal reactions only to the fear of shock. That is, the misattribution of the fear symptoms (which were objectively due only to the shock) to the pill resulted in a reduction of fear itself.

Studies in the aggression area have shown the influence of misattribution on hostile responding and feelings of anger (see Rule and Neasdale, 1976). In these studies, a subject is treated badly by another (typically, a confederate). In addition, there is heightened arousal from an extraneous source, such as loud noise, erotic stimuli, or physical exercise. Under the heightened arousal conditions, angered subjects acted more aggressively than subjects who lacked additional arousal. However, the additional arousal did not have this effect if it was attributed to its true source (see Zillman, 1978).

Some criticisms.   The arousal-plus-cognition theory of emotions proposed by Schachter has been severely challenged (see Marshall and Zimbardo, 1979; Maslach, 1979). These investigators pointed out some of the weaknesses in the data analysis carried out by Schachter and Singer and were unable to replicate their reported results. In addition, Maslach and Marshall and Zimbardo offered the following strong objections to the Schachter position:

1. Unexplained arousal is akin to free-floating anxiety and has a negative quality, rather than being a neutral state to which any emotional label can be applied.
2. When individuals seek to explain a state of arousal, they do not use merely the behavior of others in their environment. Rather, many other sources of information are called on, particularly their own personal histories. That is, they search for prior occasions on which they felt this negative arousal state to explain its occurrence now. The behavior of others may dictate or suggest how one should behave in the situation, but it does not provide information for why one feels as one does. For example, if a confederate were behaving in a completely inappropriate manner, the subject would not use this action to infer something about his or her own emotional state. In this instance, the attribution for the confederate's behavior may not be at all applicable to the subject.

Is arousal necessary? A number of other investigations contradict Schachter's position and suggest that cognitions are sufficient to produce emotional behavior. To demonstrate that the energizing, physiological effects of arousal do not influence emotional expression, Valins (1966) presented fraudulent information to his subjects. At times the subjects overheard bogus heart-rate information indicating that they were in a heightened state of arousal while viewing slides of seminude females. After viewing the stimuli, the subjects rated the attractiveness of the nudes. It was found that the nudes associated with a perceived change in heart rate were rated more attractive than the pictures of nudes not linked with this bogus information. Valins therefore concluded that internal events such as arousal act only as a source of information to the actor; actual arousal is not necessary for emotional experience. Thus, cognitions (information) are sufficient to produce feeling states.

Weiner and his colleagues (Weiner, Russell, and Lerman, 1978, 1979) reached a similar conclusion. They examined emotions experienced following success and failure in achievement-related contexts. Distinctive emotions were found to accompany different causal perceptions. For example, given success, attribution of the positive outcome to ability produced feelings of competence; ascriptions to long-term effort gave rise to relaxation and calmness; ascriptions to others generated thankfulness, and so on. In addition, emotions such as pride require that one take personal credit for a positive outcome. Because certain attributions, such as long-term effort, influenced arousal, it appeared that arousal was determined by thoughts, rather than preceding and eliciting thought and search processes, as Schachter had suggested. Of course, the fact that thoughts might determine subsequent arousal does not preclude the possibility that arousal will also give rise to thought processes.

Investigators in the area of stress have documented that fear, which is one type of emotional arousal state, also is a function of cognitive appraisal and cognitive understanding. We will now shift to this body of research and the general literature on stress, for stress is an important source of emotions that has profound influence on the person and his or her level of functioning.

Stress

In physics, *stress* is a force that acts on a body, producing some kind of strain. In the social world, it also is the case that stressors such as war, fire, and impoverished conditions put a "strain" on the organism. In addition, there is accumulating evidence that any circumstances requiring a change in life pattern, such as marriage, a new job, or the birth of a child, are stressors.

Stress connotes an organism's response to stressful conditions. Stress reactions are determined by many factors, including the characteristics of the stressor, such as its intensity and duration; the availability of social support systems, such as the family and the church; and characteristics of the person, such as prior experience and the ability to use coping defenses.

Life-Event Stress

The role of stressful life events in the etiology of various illnesses has been a prominent field of investigation in the last decade, although the possibility of a connection between stress and illness has long been suspected (see Kobasa, 1979). This research has focused on the relationship between recent life events that require personal change and the onset of an illness. It has been contended that the more such events have occurred in the recent past, the greater the likelihood that one will become seriously ill.

Most of these investigations have used some version of a scale constructed by Holmes and Rahe (1967); see Table 14.2. The items on the scale represent typical incidents of stressful change; the respondent reports which of these events happened within the last six to twenty-four months, depending on the study. Each stressor is given a value, usually determined by judges' ratings, indicating the necessary readjustment that the event requires. Note from Table 14.2 that death of spouse and divorce were judged to require great readjustment, whereas a vacation or a minor law violation were believed to involve little change in one's normal routine.

A great deal of research has demonstrated that scores on the scale shown in Table 14.2 relate significantly to the onset of illness. For example, Rahe (1974) found that sailors who began a cruise with a high score on the scale suffered more illnesses at sea than sailors who started the voyage with low stress scores. This general finding has been replicated many times (see review in Rabkin and Struening, 1976).

Although the reported research findings have been quite consistent, the investigations are not without their critics. The scale includes both positive and negative, and controllable and noncontrollable, events. Many investigators have argued that these should be separated, and that uncontrollable negative events are the important precursors to illness. In addition, respondents often do not answer the questions in the same way at a second testing session (low test-retest reliability), and it has been found that the correlation between a wife's responses about her husband and a husband's responses about himself are lower than desired (low interrater reliability). That is, there is likely to be inaccuracy of reporting. Another problem is that both a life event and an illness could be due to a third cause (see Chapter 11). For example, both being fired from work and subsequent illness might be brought about by fatigue, in which case job change does not *cause* illness, even though the two factors vary together. Finally, some of the question items, such as mortgage payment and pregnancy, may be irrelevant to particular classes or groups. Most people in the lower class are renters rather than owners and, of course, pregnancy is not applicable to males. These are all reasonable criticisms that require careful consideration before the meaning of the reported findings can be fully understood.

If one were to accept the life stress reports fully, then it would be best to forgo any life changes to remain healthy! It is, of course, impossible to avoid the stresses of everyday living, and stress also brings with it the possibility of leading fuller, better lives because of new opportunities. Hence, it is not best

Table 14.2   The Holmes-Rahe schedule of recent life events

Life event	Scale value	Life event	Scale value
Death of spouse	100	Son or daughter leaving home	29
Divorce	73	Trouble with in-laws	29
Marital separation	65	Outstanding personal achievement	28
Jail term	63	Spouse begins or stops work	26
Death of close family member	63	Starting or finishing school	26
Personal injury or illness	53	Change in living conditions	25
Marriage	50	Revision of personal habits	24
Fired from work	47	Trouble with boss	23
Marital reconciliation	45	Change in work hours or conditions	20
Retirement	45	Change in residence	20
Change in family member's health	44		
Pregnancy	40	Change in schools	20
Sex difficulties	39	Change in recreation habits	19
Gain of new family member	39	Change in church activities	19
Business readjustment	39	Change in social activities	18
Change in financial state	00	Mortgage or loan less than $10,000	17
Death of close friend	37	Change in sleeping habits	16
Career change	36	Change in number of family gatherings	15
Change in number of arguments with spouse	35	Change in eating habits	15
Mortgage over $10,000	31	Vacation	13
Foreclosure of mortgage or loan	30	Christmas season	12
Change in responsibilities at work	29	Minor violations of the law	11

Source: Reprinted with permission from *Journal of Psychosomatic Research, II,* T.H. Holmes and R.H. Rahe, "The Social Readjustment Rating Scale," copyright © 1967, Pergamon Press, Ltd.

to avoid all stress; rather, individuals need to develop and use mechanisms that better enable them to cope with threat and subjective danger.

Coping with Stress

Hans Selye (1956) contended that there are various stages in stress reactions. Following the perception of a stressor, there is an initial stress response of alarm and shock, which includes increased heart rate and lowered body temperature. These physiological changes are accompanied by psychological alterations, such as feelings of threat and distress. Following these initial reactions, defense mechanisms are activated, in an attempt to cope with the subjectively harmful, aversive situation. A number of adaptive coping mechanisms have been identified by researchers. If an individual is able to adapt and deal effectively with the stressor, then the alarm reaction and anxiety state subside. But if the mechanisms fail, then a state of exhaustion sets in. The failure of coping can give rise to any number of psychological reactions, including depression, withdrawal, and even suicide.

Stress and experience.   The reader surely has experienced psychological stress reactions in a threatening situation, such as the first ride on a roller coaster, the first job interview, or starting college. But after repeated experience, riding a roller coaster is fun, a job interview can be interesting, and returning to college in the fall is something that most students anticipate happily. Experience clearly aids the individual in adapting to stressors.

Figure 14.9   Parachutists' self-ratings of fear experienced. (Adapted from Epstein and Fenz, 1965, pp. 1, 5.)

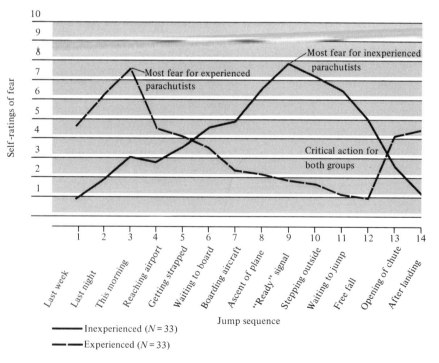

Inexperienced sky divers feel greatest fear just before their jump, which can interfere with their responding appropriately. This is not the case for experienced divers. (Stern/Black Star)

In one experiment (Epstein and Fenz, 1965), sport parachutists were interviewed before and after a jump and were asked to rate their fears. Half the parachutists had previously made more than one hundred jumps; the other half were inexperienced. The fears reported by the parachutists as a function of time from jump are shown in Fig. 14.9. The figure shows that following the decision to jump, experienced parachutists report becoming less and less fearful as the time for the jump draws near, but naive jumpers become more and more fearful. When action must be taken and danger is confronted (the "critical action" period shown on the graph), the experienced parachutist is less likely to experience anxiety that could interfere with performance. It also appears that an active adaptive mechanism is operating, for once the jump is made, the level of fear for the experienced parachutist rises again. Experience provides the actor with knowledge about the action. We learn just when the roller coaster will plunge, what a job interviewer is likely to ask, and what college is like. Thus, the environment becomes predictable and we are aware of how our own behavior will affect and be affected by the circumstances.

Figure 14.10

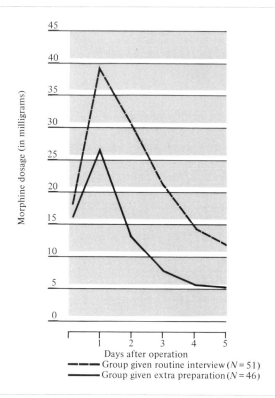

Postoperative narcotic treatment for two groups of surgical patients. (Adapted from Egbert, Battit, Welch, and Bartlett, 1964. Reprinted by permission of *The New England Journal of Medicine*, Vol. 270, p. 826, 1964.

Irving Janis has extensively studied the effects of information on reactions to stress, particularly with regard to surgical operations. Janis (1958) contended that a moderate amount of anticipatory fear facilitates adjustment after the operation and that preparatory information describing the operation and the postoperative pain also aids both psychological and physical recovery. In one experiment supporting this position, conversations were held with patients before an operation (Egbert, Battit, Welch, and Bartlett, 1964). One group of patients was given extra operation-relevant information, while a second group merely participated in a typical preoperation discussion. After the operation it was found that the informed group required less morphine in postoperative treatment and was released from the hospital sooner than the uninformed group (see Fig. 14.10). In sum, information aids adaptive reactions to stress. An informed patient experiencing pain will probably think of the pain as a normal reaction rather than as a sign that the operation was not a success. The latter conclusion could increase fear and emotional disturbance, which might in turn impede improvement. In a similar manner, the experienced parachute jumpers may have learned to deal with their emotions and have become aware that these reactions are normal. Such an attribution would naturally decrease fear and personal feelings of inadequacy.

Defenses against stress.   Research has also clearly demonstrated that defense mechanisms, particularly denial and intellectualization, perform essential functions in protecting individuals from stress. As indicated in Chapter 4, denial occurs when the implications of a thought are rejected so that, for example, the existence of the threat is not accepted, as when one refuses to believe that one can be killed during battle. Intellectualization, or isolation, occurs when an idea and its emotional accompaniment become detached; that is, an emotional event is dealt with in an overly intellectual manner, neutralizing its affective significance. A doctor's ability to perform an autopsy coolly is often cited as a good illustration of the power of intellectualization.

Richard Lazarus (1966) has conducted a systematic program of research in which denial and intellectualization were experimentally manipulated to demonstrate their controlling effects on stress reactions. The general experimental procedure is to have subjects view a film that gives rise to stress reactions. Lazarus used two films that yield similar results: an anthropological movie showing a stone-age subincision ritual (similar to circumcision) and a safety movie depicting workshop accidents. While subjects view either movie, various measures of autonomic arousal, such as heart rate and galvanic skin response, are continuously recorded. A sound track preceding or accompanying each film presentation evokes the psychological defenses of denial or intellectualization. The denial theme indicates that the subincision operation is not harmful or that the participants in the safety film are only actors. The intellectualization sound track offers a detached view of the situations. The subincision film apparently is narrated by an objective anthropologist simply observing strange customs, while during the safety film the viewer is asked to take an objective look at the dynamics of the situation. Lazarus then examined whether emotional reactivity to each film was lowered when the defenses were introduced.

Figure 14.11 shows the results of one study that induced the defensive orientation of denial (Lazarus and Alfert, 1964). The subincision film was used, and the denial theme was introduced either as a denial orientation before the film or as a denial commentary during the film. Skin conductance (change in the electrical resistance of the skin) was used to measure emotional reactivity. The figure shows that (1) the denial defense reduced reactivity to the stressor among subjects in the experimental groups, compared to subjects in the control group, who did not receive the defensive sound track; and (2) the reduction of emotional reactivity was greatest when the defense was introduced in its entirety before the subjects viewed the film. These data indicate that the amount of emotion we experience in fear-inducing situations will be influenced by how we cope in that situation. The activation of defenses results in disparate ways of thinking about the situation, which will often determine the way we end up feeling.

Figure 14.11   Skin conductance curves. "Denial orientation" indicates that the sound track was presented in its entirety before the film began. "Denial commentary" indicates that the denial sound track accompanied, rather than preceded, the film. The control condition is designated as "silent"; that is, there was no accompanying sound track. (Adapted from Lazarus and Alfert, 1964.)

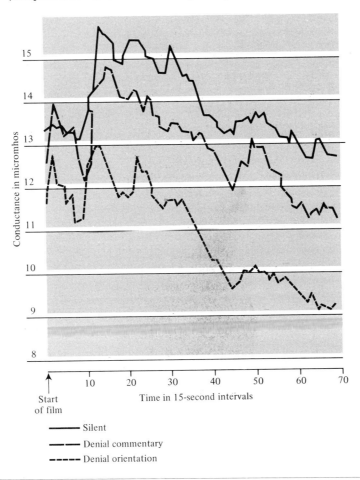

Individual Differences in Stress Reactions

Inasmuch as there are individual differences in the preference and use of defenses, it might be expected that some persons are better able to cope with stress than others. Kobasa (1979) examined the impact of stressful life events on the onset of illness among two groups of executives: those reporting high stress not followed by illness and those who became ill after stressful encounters. She found that the high stress–low illness executives, as compared with the high stress–high illness executives, were characterized by:

1. A clearer sense of values and goals and a belief in their personal importance (commitment rather than alienation).
2. A stronger tendency toward more active involvement with the environment (vigorousness rather than vegetativeness).
3. A general life plan and priorities (meaningfulness rather than meaninglessness).
4. A belief in personal, rather than external, control (see Chapter 17).

These findings also relate to a growing literature linking personality dispositions and behavior to the likelihood of heart attack (see Glass, 1977). A "type A" personality has been identified, characterized by extremely competitive achievement striving, time urgency, aggression, and extreme proneness to coronary heart disease. The type A individual also suppresses fatigue, shows little tolerance for interruption, and exerts great effort to control the environment. These behaviors apparently alter one's biochemistry and increase proneness to coronary heart disease. An opposite, type B individual has also been identified by the absence of type A characteristics and less likelihood of coronary heart disease.

Approaching Stress

The basic assumption guiding this chapter has been that humans strive to increase pleasure and to decrease pain. Thus, given the possibility that the fulfillment of positive goals will be followed by punishment, defenses are likely to be activated that will inhibit the approach behavior. And, given aversive events, defenses are likely to be activated to mitigate their negative consequences. However, it is not the case that all behavior is in service of the pleasure-pain principle. For example, it is evident that there are many altruistic actions that promote the survival of the species, but could result in the death of the helper. These actions cannot be explained with the principle that individuals strive only to maximize personal pleasure. Rather, individuals often act to increase stress, as when riding a roller coaster, jumping into the water to save someone else, and seeking a more challenging job.

Freud also considered a second motive force, akin to what we now think of as mastery behavior or competence seeking. Recall that mastery is a basic motivational principle postulated by ego psychologists and other critics of psychoanalytic theory (see Chapter 5). Freud noted that some behaviors, such as traumatic dreams, games of disappearance (peekaboo), and transference (the patient acting as if the analyst were a parental figure) are engaged in even though they apparently do not increase pleasure, but rather augment stress. Concerning traumatic dreams, for example, he stated (1920, p. 26):

But it is not in the service of the pleasure principle that the dreams of patients suffering from traumatic neurosis lead them back with such regularity to the situation in which the trauma occurred. We may assume, rather, that dreams are here helping to carry out another task which must be accomplished before the dominance of the pleasure principle can even begin. These dreams are endeavoring to master the stimulus retrospectively.

In sum, Freud recognized two fundamental principles of action, or motive forces: (1) hedonism and (2) mastery and understanding of the environment and oneself, which can be temporarily or even permanently painful and stress-inducing. Pleasure-pain has been the principle dominating the field of psychodynamics and it seems reasonable that it will not be supplanted as a source of action. But in recent years it is increasingly being supplemented by notions of mastery and information gain (see Chapters 7 and 17).

Summary

A major area of study within the field of personality concerns the dynamics of behavior, or psychodynamics. A broad array of topics falls under this heading, including conflict, impulse control, substitution, frustration, emotion, and stress. What these topics have in common is the assumption of an organism with needs and goals, acting within an environment that can facilitate or impede the attainment of its desires. These areas are all concerned with the individual's adaptation to the physical and social world; the interrelation of thinking, feeling, and acting; and the resolution of behavior in the face of conflicts between desires and personal or social inhibitions.

Specific Points

1. The strength of a *conflict* is in part determined by the number of available alternatives, the relative attractiveness of those alternatives, and the importance of the decision involved.
2. *Approach-approach conflicts* involve a choice between two or more attractive alternatives; *avoidance-avoidance conflicts* involve a choice between two or more aversive alternatives. The latter are especially difficult to resolve.
3. *Approach-avoidance conflicts* occur in situations where an alternative has both positive and negative characteristics; they tend to produce ambivalent behavior. According to Miller, the observed ambivalence can be accounted for by postulating that the gradient of avoidance, or the change in motivational strength as a function of distance from the goal, is steeper than the gradient of approach.
4. Contrary to Freud's beliefs, evidence suggests that the visual presence of desired goals increases frustration and reduces the ability to delay gratification. Hallucinatory images, the behavior of models, social engineering techniques, and expectancy of future goal attainment all influence delay of gratification.
5. *Substitution* refers to the gratification provided by goals attained in place of the original one. Substitution is greatest when the substitute goal is similar to the original goal and is actually attained, rather than imagined.
6. *Frustration* can refer to an independent (manipulated), an intervening (inferred), or a dependent (measured) variable. It produces behaviors as disparate as aggression, fixation, regression, and enhanced goal striving.

Fixated responses do not appear amenable to change with the use of reward alone.

7. *Emotion* can be defined as having a positive or negative quality of a certain intensity, may be accompanied by facial expressions and body postures, acts as a signal for certain types of action, and often follows from particular thoughts.

8. Schachter and Singer contended that the process of emotion begins with a state of *arousal*. The individual then labels this arousal according to cues in the social situation. This conception is now under question, however.

9. Life-event *stress* produces a susceptibility to illness. Several distinctions between types of life event stress, such as controllable versus uncontrollable events, have been suggested.

10. Experience and information better enable individuals to cope with stress. In addition, experiments have demonstrated that the defenses of denial and intellectualization help reduce stress reactions.

Thought Questions

1. Think of some conflicts you have had recently. Can you classify them according to any of the types of conflict discussed in this chapter? If so, does your classification help you to understand the dynamics of your conflict better?

2. Individuals trapped in an approach-avoidance conflict sometimes resolve the conflict after a few drinks. How does the ingestion of alcohol make conflict resolution possible?

3. In what ways are the concepts of conflict, frustration, displacement, and substitution interrelated?

4. Emotions are often hard to label. How do you "know" what your true feelings are?

Consciousness

At any given moment we are bombarded with a variety of external and internal stimulation. Although humans can process much information, there are limits to our capacities. It therefore follows that some information from the environment, or even from our own bodies, will be overlooked or will not attract our attention. Conversely, other information will be the focus of attention and we will be well aware of it. What is selected depends on our own biological receiving mechanisms, our needs, and our past histories. For example, a number of voices are likely to be heard at any given moment at a party, but only one or two of them will be of concern and will be the focus of attention; other sounds will be ignored. These other inputs are likely to be registered, but they are not further processed or held in memory. Similarly, when we view a landscape, much will be "seen" or registered, but we will be aware of only a limited portion of the scene and only a small part of what meets the eye will be retained or recognized later. And on other occasions, as when auditioning for a part in a play or posing for a picture, we might be acutely aware of ourselves and even fewer external factors will be noticed. Thus, our personal consciousness represents only a small portion of reality.

When psychologists speak of *consciousness*, they are often referring to awareness, or what one knows about his or her experience and how reality is constructed. Consistent with this approach, John Locke defined consciousness as "the perception of what passes in a man's own mind" or, as Ornstein (1972) put it, "subjective life." As just indicated, we are frequently unaware of many aspects of our environment and, as Freud so clearly pointed out, individuals are also unaware of many of the important internal determinants of behavior. These inner causes are considered to be "unconscious." On other occasions, however, our consciousness may be "expanded"; that is, there is heightened sensitivity to external sounds and colors or increased awareness of our own feelings, past experiences, and thoughts. Repeated exposure to a new rock group may make us conscious of variations in the music of which we were not initially aware. Introspection about a problem in an important personal relationship can lead to the recognition of feelings toward the person that we never knew we had. One of the goals of psychoanalytic and Rogerian therapies (cf. Chapters 4 and 7) is to expand consciousness of our inner life. Eastern philosophies of Yoga and Zen Buddism share this same goal and also place great emphasis on enhancing our experience of the physical world.

Instances of heightened inner awareness, as might be experienced when under the influence of a drug or during deep meditation, are referred to as *altered states of consciousness.* Altered states are truly evident in physical objects, as when liquid water changes to solid (ice) or gas (steam). But whether the human mind can be "altered" to a state qualitatively different from the normal waking state is less clear. It is evident, however, that modifications in awareness are often accompanied by a number of profound physiological and psychological changes. It is also clear that individuals can readily pass from one level of consciousness to another, as from waking to daydreaming or reverie and then back to alert consciousness again. We thus move through different levels of consciousness during the normal course of our lives.

In this chapter we first examine diminished awareness, or circumstances in which there is a lack of consciousness concerning certain aspects of experience and behavior. These circumstances can be as simple as when an act is automatically performed or as complex as when there exist multiple personalities that are often completely unaware of one another. We will then consider techniques like biofeedback or even the introduction of a mirror, which increase awareness of internal bodily outputs and focus attention on the self. Following this discussion, some of the better-known examples of heightened awareness or "altered states" are examined. These include sleep and dream states, hypnotic trances, and drug and meditational experiences. The chapter then shifts to a presentation of split-brain research and the possibility of different forms of consciousness residing in different parts of the brain, and concludes with a brief consideration of fantasy activity.

Diminished Awareness

Few would quarrel with the idea that the environment is full of stimuli that we do not attend to, that we cannot label or describe, in brief, of which we are unaware. The intriguing question, however, is whether these stimuli are somehow registered by the brain and influence our thought processes and behavior without our being conscious of them. In an earlier discussion of perceptual defense (Chapter 4), studies were cited indicating that people are able to block the recognition of emotionally threatening stimuli.

However, researchers have demonstrated that even nonthreatening stimuli can be recorded by the brain despite the person's inability to tell what the stimulus is. A technique commonly used in these demonstrations of limited awareness is *subliminal* stimulation (Shevrin and Dickman, 1980). A word or picture is presented on a screen for so short a time that the subject cannot tell what it is. For example, in one experiment a picture of a bee was flashed for one-thousandth of a second. All the subjects "saw" was a flash of light. Yet, measurements of the brain's electrical responses (evoked potentials) indicated that the unrecognizable flash of a bee produced a stronger evoked potential than a similar flash of an abstract geometric shape. Moreover, when subjects were asked to say what came to mind following the flash, associations like "bug," "sting," and "honey" were given significantly more often in response to the flash of a bee than to a geometric shape.

Findings like these raise fears about the deliberate manipulation of our minds, a sort of brainwashing through use of subliminal messages. Although studies of subliminal advertising indicate that such techniques have quite weak effects and often do not work at all, there is little question that the brain can register stimulus events that affect thought processes, even though these events are outside of consciousness.

Automatic Actions

Limitations in awareness extend to our actions as well as to the registration of external stimuli. It is quite evident that we are often unaware of the process of completing many minor acts which are undertaken automatically and without conscious scrutiny. It is often difficult to recall actually engaging in such activities. For example, can you remember the act of turning out the light before going to bed? Flushing the toilet before you left the bathroom?

What is even more surprising is the mindlessness or lack of awareness of even complex social behaviors. For example, consider the following experiment by Langer, Blank, and Chanowitz (1978), in which a person about to use a copying machine was approached by an experimental confederate who asked for permission to use the machine first. The requestor stated that she had either a small or a large number of copies to make and made the request in one of three ways (Langer et al., 1978, p. 635):

1. Request only: *Excuse me, I have 5(20) pages. May I use the Xerox machine?*
2. Placebic information: *Excuse me, I have 5(20) pages. May I use the Xerox machine because I have to make copies?*
3. Real information: *Excuse me, I have 5(20) pages. May I use the Xerox machine because I'm in a rush?*

Condition 2 is called "placebic information" because the reason offered is entirely redundant of the request. After all, "What else would one do with a copying machine except make copies of something?" (Langer et al., 1978, p. 48). The point is that condition 2 offers essentially the same information as condition 1. If subjects were really conscious of the information given, then the rate of compliance with the request should have been the same in the "placebic information" and "request only" conditions. The results of this investigation are shown in Table 15.1. The table shows that if the favor was small (few copies), then the rate of compliance was the same whether the information was placebic or real and in both cases was higher than compliance in the no-information condition. That is, given relatively unimportant events, individuals may be unaware of the information provided by others. But if a favor is large, then they become conscious of the phrasing of the request and comply more in real than in the placebic condition and no-information conditions.

Box 15.1   LEARNING WITHOUT AWARENESS

A controversy in psychology that generated much attention in the late 1950s and 1960s examined whether verbal behavior can be directly manipulated with reinforcement techniques. In a typical experiment, subjects were given a series of cards, each containing a verb and six personal pronouns (Taffel, 1955). The subjects were asked to make up a sentence using the verb and any pronoun. The experimenter then rewarded each sentence starting with *I* or *we* by saying "good" when the sentence was completed. It was found that during the reinforcement phase of this experiment the use of *I* and *we* greatly increased, but, when reinforcement was later withheld, the use of these pronouns decreased. The subjects in the initial investigations reported that they were unaware of the contingency between their response and the reinforcement. It appeared that the learning took place because of the automatic strengthening property of the reinforcer. These research studies were interpreted as supporting both the Skinnerian position and, surprisingly, the Freudian notion of the unconscious.

Subsequent research, however, using more sophisticated, postexperimental interview techniques and indirect assessment procedures, found that only subjects who were aware of the contingency between the response and the reinforcement increased their rate of "correct" responding (see Spielberger, 1962). Subjects who remained unaware of the experimental linkage between *I* or *we* and *good* responded in a random manner. Cognitive psychologists contend that these findings refute the behaviorist belief in mechanical, stimulus-response connections.

Table 15.1   The proportion of subjects who agreed to let the experimenter use the copier

	Reason		
	No info.	Placebic info.	Real info.
Small	.60	.93	.94
Big	.24	.24	.42

Source: Adapted from Langer, Blank, and Chanowitz, 1978, p. 637. Used by permission.

Dissociative Phenomena

Vivid demonstrations of diminished awareness come from the study of pathology. In earlier chapters (see Chapters 4 and 14) the defense mechanisms, including repression, perceptual defense, and denial, were discussed. It was contended that such mechanisms prevent forbidden wishes, fears, and other feelings and thoughts from entering consciousness. But even more dramatic evidence concerning inhibited awareness is illustrated in what are called *dissociative phenomena*. These include:

1. *Somnambulism*—walking or carrying out acts while apparently in a sleeping state.
2. *Amnesia*—a loss of both identity and recall of the past.
3. *Multiple personality*—two or more seemingly well-organized personalities functioning relatively independently of one another in the same person.

It seems inconceivable that multiple and independent personalities within the same person are possible. Yet, it is common that some limited aspects of ourselves, such as our "true" feelings toward others, are blocked out, particularly under conditions of great conflict. In cases of split personality, these mechanisms are carried to an extreme: it is as if the individual were an actor playing several different roles. The difference is that the split personality, unlike acting, is not within the individual's control. In addition, when the individual is in one role, he or she may have complete amnesia for the other roles.

Reported cases of split personality are rare; there are about one hundred known cases in the literature, and these are mostly of young women. Perhaps the most famous split personality is Eve White, Eve Black, and Jane: the "three faces of Eve." Typically, the individual assumes two or three different personalities (although as many as sixteen have been reported), each personality with a distinct and stable pattern of cognitive and emotional behavior and different scores on tests of emotion. The separate personalities may or may not be aware of one another. In addition, a person may maintain one pattern of behavior for years, or change back and forth in a matter of minutes.

In earlier times, such multiple personalities were attributed to demonic possession by a distinct entity that could enter the body. Today the condition is most often interpreted as an attempt to escape from frustration and unhappiness, with conflict leading to the expression of wishes through an alternative personality. While relatively little is known about the dynamics of split personality, it is clearly an example of greatly constricted awareness.

Becoming Aware

One of the main goals of psychotherapy is to make the client more aware of his or her needs and feelings or to bring material from the unconscious into consciousness. Therapists with an analytic orientation speak of "attaining insight," while more humanistic theorists state that one should get more "in touch with feelings." The issue of awareness extends beyond psychotherapy, however. A number of areas in psychology are concerned with the problem of unawareness and the effects of increasing awareness on a variety of psychological states and processes.

Biofeedback

For many years psychologists believed that the mind could not directly influence certain bodily functions. For example, if there was a need to increase heart rate, this could be indirectly accomplished by running up a flight of stairs. But heart rate was not believed to be amenable to direct control, by "willing" it to increase. More generally, autonomic system activities such as blushing or blood pressure level were not considered subject to volitional control, while muscular acts like running were perceived as controllable or modifiable.

But this set of beliefs has changed recently with the introduction of *biofeedback* (short for "biological feedback"). Biofeedback concerns voluntary bodily regulation by means of increased feedback or information from internal organs. Ordinarily we are unaware of the state of many of our bodily outputs, such as blood pressure, heart rate, and level of brain activity. One reason for this is that the necessary feedback concerning these states has been missing. A spinoff from the growth of space technology was development of a cluster of techniques for readily monitoring most autonomic functions.

Increasing feedback could conceivably be accomplished in one of two ways: augmenting the signal from the body or decreasing the "noise," or distractions, that interferes with awareness of the signal. For instance, in the party example given at the beginning of this chapter, one could better hear an attended-to voice by asking the person to speak louder (increasing the signal) or by asking others to speak more softly (decreasing the noise). The study of biofeedback has concentrated on increasing the availability of signals from the body by continuously monitoring bodily output.

This information is then simultaneously fed back to the subject, thus increasing the signal. But, given this augmented personal awareness, is the individual now able to gain control over the body's output? Clearly, learning to control the output would be highly unlikely without such feedback, but it intuitively seems extremely difficult, if not impossible, to control bodily functions such as heart rate or blood pressure even with the possibility of feedback. Yet psychologists first interested in this possibility were impressed with the fact that yogis seemed able to gain control over normally involuntary responses. Yogis have even been known to survive for long periods of time in completely closed spaces by reducing their oxygen consumption to remarkably low levels. (See also the later section of this chapter that discusses meditation.)

Some of the early experiments testing the possibility of control over autonomic activities used infrahuman subjects. For example, it was demonstrated that electrical stimulation of the "pleasure center" in some rats whenever their heart rate went up and in other rats whenever it went down produced, respectively, subsequent increases or decreases in heart rate (Miller and Banuazizi, 1968). That is, the rats learned to control their heart rates to get a reward. Other autonomic controls in a variety of infrahuman species have also been reported (see DiCara, 1970).

Research with humans has demonstrated similar phenomena. Indeed, the control of blood pressure and especially heart rate has not proved difficult in laboratory settings, with control evident after only a half-hour's training. Of particular interest has been the possibility of gaining control over brain activity, or actually regulating one's state of consciousness. In this research, the individual's brain activity is monitored with an electroencephalogram (EEG). Audio or visual information conveys the nature of the brain activity to the subject. Research has concentrated on the possibility of inducing *alpha* waves, one of the main types of brain activity that has been identified. Subjects report that high alpha activity is often accompanied by feelings of detachment and tranquility, and describe themselves as conscious but "nonthinking" (Kamiya, 1969). With biofeedback training, subjects can learn to control alpha activity and hence alter their level of consciousness, although it may be easier to turn alpha off than on.

The biofeedback findings could have far-reaching medical, as well as psychological, implications. For example, in one case study a patient experienced a severe drop in blood pressure every time he stood up, which caused him to faint. With the aid of biofeedback training, the patient learned to control his blood pressure so that standing and walking became possible. In a similar manner, control of migraine headaches, epileptic seizures, and heart constriction has been reported. However, as Ornstein (1972) has indicated, electric Zen is not just around the corner, and the beneficial claims of biofeedback have often been exaggerated. For example, it has been found that the maintenance of self-regulation of blood pressure over a sustained period of time is a much more difficult matter than demonstrating such control for relatively brief periods in a laboratory setting. Nonetheless, this research clearly demonstrates that we can become aware of the unaware, a new direction for psychological research and application.

A biofeedback experiment. The television screen shows blood flow, which is the biological function under study. (Copyright © Ken Robert Buck, 1981. Courtesy University Hospital, Boston)

Self-Awareness

One implication of the previous discussion seems to be that increased awareness is always psychologically beneficial. Clearly, self-insight in a clinical context and biofeedback to increase internal awareness are likely to aid psychological functioning, while evidence of gross unawareness, as exhibited in amnesias and split personalities, is a sign of maladjustment. But it is not the case that complete awareness is always most adaptive. The psychological defenses have the important function of keeping certain material from consciousness, a function in service of psychological well-being. Furthermore, during activities such as tests or athletic events it is important to concentrate completely on the immediate task and block out all competing information and stimulation, like the sun or rain outside the classroom and the cheering or booing of the fans.

Another aspect of awareness that athletes attempt to blot out is awareness of the self. A baseball hitter cannot be conscious of every aspect of his batting technique while swinging the bat and still be successful. There is a movement among athletic coaches to emphasize the Zen aspect of the sport; that is, to have players transcend any awareness of the self and to lose their identity by completely merging with the game. A recent best-selling tennis book stressed that the player should be aware of the seams on the tennis ball and nothing else. Self-statements after missing a shot, such as "I am a lousy player" or "I can't seem to hit a backhand today," are believed to impede performance.

There is an increasing body of research addressing the effects of self-awareness on personal functioning. One clear finding is that focusing awareness on the self produces more acceptance of oneself as the cause of events. For example, Duval and Wicklund (1973, p. 26) had subjects read several scenarios, such as:

1. *Imagine that you have selected and purchased a race horse. You enter the horse in a major race and hire a good jockey to ride him. The horse wins first place. To what degree did your actions cause the victory and to what degree did the actions of the jockey cause the victory?*
2. *Imagine that a friend of yours wants to get you a date. You tell her what characteristics you like in a date and she selects one of her friends. You go out with him and have a very good time. To what degree did your actions cause the successful date and to what degree did the actions of your friend cause the successful date?*

Half of the subjects read these stories under normal conditions; the remainder read the passages in front of a conspicuous mirror. The presence of a mirror was expected to shift the focus of attention to oneself. In accordance with their predictions, Duval and Wicklund found that individuals in the mirror condition made relatively more self-attributions than did subjects in the normal condition.

Duval and Wicklund (1972) also proposed that heightened self awareness is an aversive state, inasmuch as it makes us consciously aware of our shortcomings. In a related theoretical development, Wine (1971) and Sarason (1978) contended that when a stressful event arouses self-preoccupying thoughts, there will be performance decrements because task-relevant thoughts are diminished. Further, they stated that highly anxious individuals focus on the self during test performance, which may account for their relatively poor scores in stressful test situations.

However, the effects of self-awareness on behavior are far from settled. Carver, Scheier, and their colleagues (e.g., Carver, Blaney, and Scheier, 1979a, 1979b) have argued that if self-confidence and performance expectancy are high, then self-focus of attention will increase performance, whereas low confidence combined with self-focus will give rise to performance decrements. To test these ideas in an experimental investigation, people with snake phobias were asked to approach and pick up a snake. Some of these individuals were confident about their ability to overcome the phobia, while others were quite apprehensive and doubting. In one of the experimental conditions a mirror was present to heighten self-awareness. The data were as predicted: the mirror enhanced the likelihood of picking up the snake among the confident subjects but impeded snake handling among the nonconfident subjects, relative to the behavior of persons without feedback from a mirror.

In sum, just as biofeedback can enhance awareness of bodily outputs, common situations such as placement in front of a mirror, camera, or audience can heighten self-awareness. Changes in awareness or self-consciousness can have profound positive or negative behavioral effects.

Altered States of Consciousness

Our normal waking state is but one form of consciousness. In this state, knowledge is communal, or consensual; that is, we share information with others and are mutually aware of the stimuli in the environment. In addition, the passage and constraints of time are recognized. Normal waking states are considered the primary condition of the mind; other types of consciousness are thought of as "unreal" or as "imaginary."

There are a number of states of mind that fall within the rubric of the "unreal." These include sleep and dream states, delirium, hypnotic trances, and drug and meditational experiences. In these conditions, new mental functions and capabilities are experienced that may not have counterparts in normal experience. Time is distorted, illogical events are perceived as real or possible, and there may be a loss of self-awareness. These altered states may be externally induced, as in drug conditions, or part of our natural lives, as in sleep, dreaming, and daydreaming. They may be of long or short duration. They may be passive experiences, with increased awareness of, openness to, and preoccupation with the environment, or active and creative states with preoccupation with inner sensations. They may give rise to positive or negative emotions. And they can be produced by under- or overstimulation. But in all such cases consciousness is perceived as somehow different.

Sleep

All mammals sleep, although there is great variety in the amount of sleeping activity (see Table 15.2). Among humans, there is also a wide range of individual differences in sleep habits, with the amount of sleep for college students averaging 7.4 hours during the week and 8.5 hours on the weekend (White, 1975). Contrary to popular belief, research has not substantiated the hypotheses that sleep is affected by physical exercise, viewing violent television programs, or studying before bedtime. Indeed, there appears to be great stability in the sleeping process.

One of the main characteristics of sleep is that the sleeper is relatively unresponsive to the external world. However, there is not complete unawareness of environmental stimulation. For example, it has been found that important names are more likely to awaken the sleeper than irrelevant ones. A second characteristic of the sleeper is a great reduction in activity. The decreased behavior that accompanies sleep is thought by some to be the key to sleep's function (Webb, 1975). Such nonresponding could be instrumental to survival if it kept one protected from a hostile world and occurred when

Table 15.2   Sleep lengths among mammals

Animal	Length per 24 hours
Bat	19
Hamster	14
Cat	14
Chimpanzee	11
Jaguar	11
Mole	10
Man	7.4
Cow	7
Sheep	6
Bottle-nose dolphin	5
Elephant	4

Source: From *Foundations of Contemporary Psychology,* edited by Merle E. Meyer. Copyright © 1979 by Oxford University Press, Inc. Reprinted by permission.

responding would be unlikely to result in goal attainment. Among humans, hunting was extremely hazardous at night because of our primary dependence on vision. Thus, it may have been survival relevant to "keep the curious quiet and the frightened still" (Webb and Bonnet, 1979, p. 465) until daylight. An alternative to this explanation of the function of sleep is that sleep enables the organism to restore body chemicals, a hypothesis that has not been substantiated. Furthermore, it takes as much energy to sleep as it does merely to lie quietly awake.

A number of sleep disorders have been identified (see Table 15.3). These disorders vary in intensity and frequency of occurrence for any given individual. Night terrors, the first disturbance indicated in Table 15.3, apparently do not originate in bad dreams, as is often thought, but result from abrupt awakening from deep sleep. Similarly, sleepwalking is also not dream related and is typically outgrown by adolescence; it is now considered a developmental disorder rather than a psychological disturbance. Table 15.3 also indicates that a small percentage of the population are victims of *narcolepsy,* or sudden "sleep attacks" that often occur without warning, particularly during times of heightened excitement, and last from a few to fifteen minutes. Narcolepsy is likely to be a genetic disorder; dogs bred from narcoleptic parents show exacerbation of this sleep tendency. Thus, it is not necessarily a sign of psychopathology. Finally, the table indicates that a large percentage of the population suffers from a perceived lack of sufficient sleep. However, this figure is prob-

Table 15.3   Sleep disturbances

	Age range primarily affected	Usually outgrown	Percentage of primary age range
Night terrors	3–5	Yes	2–5%
Enuresis	4–7 (bedwetting considered normal before bladder control learned)	Yes	15–25%
Sleepwalking (Somnambulism)	5–12	Yes	15%
Nightmares	Peak at 8–10	Lessen	95%
Narcolepsy	Onset 15–25	No	.05%
Sleep talking	All ages, primarily less than 25	Lessen	40–60%
Insomnia	All	No	14–20%

Source: From *Foundations of Contemporary Psychology*, edited by Merle E. Meyer. Copyright © 1979 by Oxford University Press, Inc. Reprinted by permission.

ably inflated because the elderly seem to need less sleep and indeed do sleep less, yet are more likely to report sleep problems. Studies have been unable to uncover any personality differences between long- and short-duration sleepers.

Dreams

Sleep is also characterized by dream activity. Dreams exemplify primary process thinking (see Chapter 4): they are illogical, are not bound by the constraints of time, there is fusion of objects into one, and they may include symbolic representations of thoughts and objects. Clearly, dream activity differs from normal waking thought.

Freud contended that sleep is preserved by dreams. According to Freud, the antecedent for all fantasy behavior, including dreaming, is deprivation (unfulfilled wishes); the consequence of fantasy behavior is need reduction. By providing the opportunity for substitute or hallucinatory wish fulfillment, dreams "drain off" internal stimulation and preserve sleep. A simple illustration can clarify this idea. Assume that you go to bed without dinner. After some period of time, hunger cramps are felt that might cause awakening. During sleep, however, you dream about eating food. The content of the dream might be disguised, with the food appearing in symbolic form (e.g., string rather than spaghetti). Such a wish-fulfilling dream produces a diminution in subjective hunger, thereby reducing stomach cramps and preserving sleep.

The study of dreams.   As you might expect, it is extremely difficult to gather scientific evidence that dreams are wish fulfillments and that they preserve sleep by reducing internal stimulation. But recent advances in dream research have generated data that are pertinent to some of Freud's presumptions.

Useful scientific research on dreaming was initiated about twenty-five years ago. One reason for this relatively recent start was that, prior to this time, only the dreamer had direct access to the dream. Therefore, it was not possible to assess the reliability of dream reports (that is, whether or not a dream had occurred, as opposed to the content of the dream). There was a need for a witness to the onset of the dream in addition to the dreamer.

An objective technique for the detection of dreams was discovered in the early 1950s (see Dement and Kleitman, 1957). During sleep, *rapid eye movements (REM)* were discovered, with the eyes exhibiting quick, side-to-side motions under the lids. Individuals awakened during these REM periods reported dreams more frequently than people awakened at other times. Some mental and cognitive activities do occur during non-REM (NREM) periods, but reports of visual and hallucinatory experiences occur only during REM sleep. NREM reports are more like thinking, being less visual and less unusual.

Figure 15.1   Sample EEG patterns for the waking state and the four stages of sleep. (From *New Directions in Psychology Two* by Frank Barron, William C. Dement, Ward Edwards, Harold Lindman, Lawrence D. Phillips, and James and Marianne Olds, foreword by Theodore M. Newcomb. Copyright © 1965 by Holt, Rinehart and Winston.)

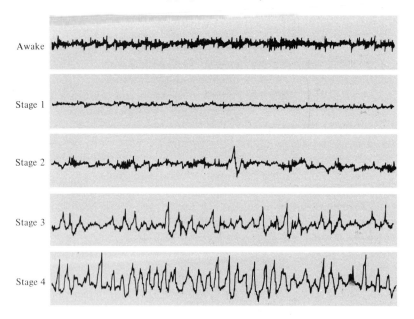

Figure 15.2   Minute-by-minute display of the course of sleep, in terms of sleep stages. The sleep pattern shown is an average of one subject's patterns on three nights.

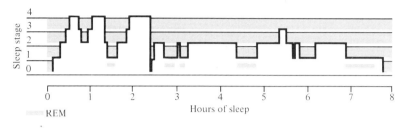

Research has also revealed that there are cyclical patterns of brain activity during the course of sleep (see Dement, 1965). This activity can be monitored with the recording of brain waves (EEG readings). Four different patterns of brain waves have been detected during sleep (see Fig. 15.1). Stage 1 sleep, in which there is a lack of long and narrow waves, as well as *delta*, or large, waves, is highly associated with REM periods and dream reports. It is now quite clear that REM observations and particular patterns of brain waves provide reliable, observable criteria for identifying internal dream processes.

Figure 15.2 depicts a typical night's sleep for a young adult. During the course of an eight-hour sleep period, an individual has five or six dream episodes, or an average of about one dream every eighty to ninety minutes. In general, the longer one sleeps, the greater the total dream activity. The average dream lasts around fifteen minutes, with the length of the dream increasing as the night progresses. The initial episode lasts between five and ten minutes, while final dreams may continue for as long as fifty or sixty minutes. Figure 15.2 also indicates that an individual progresses through a regular nondream-dream sequence during the course of the evening. To enter a REM stage, there first is passage through stage 2 of the sleep cycle.

The percentages of both sleep and dream time are systematically related to maturation (see Fig. 15.3). Figure 15.3 reveals that infants sleep more than half the time and that nearly half of this sleeping time, or around eight hours, is spent in REM activity. However, this percentage drops off rapidly; by early adolescence, the percentage of time spent dreaming begins to stabilize at around 20 percent. However, the total amount of sleep continues to decline very gradually.

The function of dreams.   Freud believed that through dream analysis we could learn about unfulfilled wishes and desires, as well as about the symbolic manifestations of needs. Given an objective dream index, one might expect that the "royal road to the unconscious" (which is how Freud characterized

Figure 15.3   Changes, with age, in total amounts of daily sleep. (From *Foundations of Contemporary Psychology,* edited by Merle E. Meyer. Copyright © 1979 by Oxford University, Press, Inc. Reprinted by permission.)

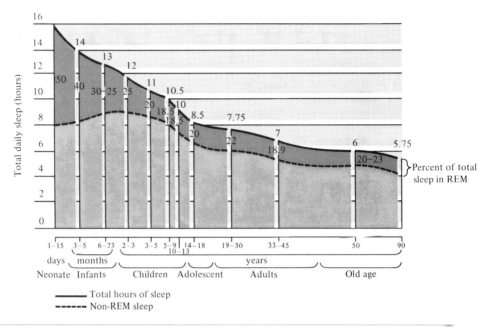

dreams) would become a superhighway and that Freud's speculations would be either confirmed or discarded. Although this has not been the case, inferential data have been gathered that bear on some of the issues raised by Freud.

First, it appears that all individuals dream. The universality of the dream experience was anticipated by Freud. Indeed, many infrahuman species exhibit dream-state sleep (see Table 15.4). But if it is inferred from REM observations that lower organisms also dream, then it is difficult to contend that the function of dreams is to drain internal stimulation. It is generally assumed that infrahumans have few social inhibitions and fewer conflicts regarding sexual and aggressive matters than humans. It therefore seems unlikely that their dreams preserve sleep, but rather that the presence of sleep ensures dreams.

One finding in support of the Freudian conception of dreams is that there appears to be a need to dream (Dement, 1960). If the sleeper is awakened every time a REM period is entered, then the REM periods are more frequent on subsequent evenings, and it subsequently takes more vigor to awaken the sleeper. The organism seems to be making up for a REM deficit.

Table 15.4 Dream state in various mammalian species (young adult animals)

Species	Average length of dream period (min)	Average cycle length (min)	Dream time as percentage of total sleep
Man	14	80–90	20–24
Monkey	4–10	40–60	11–20
Cat	10	20–40	20–60
Sheep	—	—	2–3
Rabbit	—	24	1–3
Rat	4–7	7–13	15–20
Mouse	—	3–4	—
Opossum	5	17	22–40

Source: E. Hartmann, 1965, p. 32. Reprinted by permission of *The New England Journal of Medicine 273, 32, 1965.*

But if there is a need to dream, then dream deprivation should affect psychological functioning. At present it is uncertain whether this is the case. Some investigators do report that individuals become more emotional and less psychologically balanced after losing REM sleep, but other investigators find no such disturbing psychological effects. Furthermore, there are perfectly well-adjusted individuals who sleep less than one hour a night! Whether REM deprivation has adverse psychological effects may be dependent on the personality of the individual. A number of studies suggest that repressors (individuals prone to forget conflictual material) are more disturbed by REM interruption than nonrepressors (Cohen, 1977).

As already indicated, Freud stated that dreams preserve sleep by draining off internal stimulation. It is evident that what Freud labeled "day residues," or memory traces of experiences during the day, influence the content of dreams. In addition, stimulation during sleep, such as a flash of light or tactile input, is sometimes incorporated into dreams. But such stimulation does not instigate dreams. That is, the onset of stimulation that might awaken the sleeper does not initiate a REM episode. Furthermore, emotional upsets during the day, reported frustrations, and unfulfilled desires are unrelated to the amount of time spent in dream activity. Indeed, the vast majority of dreams involve commonplace activities in commonplace settings, and their emotional tone is often negative.

In sum, it appears that dreaming is primarily a biological function. There is a cyclical course of sleep during the night which is relatively uniform across individuals. The question of the dream's psychological function remains moot. One must certainly question the notion of the dream as having substitute value and reducing internal stimulation. It seems more probable that dreams aid in thinking through problems and providing creative solutions that have escaped us during normal waking thought (see Singer, 1974). That is, dreams may have a cognitive rather than a stimulus-reducing function. There is suggestive evidence from both animal and human studies that REM sleep may facilitate new learning and emotionally adaptive waking behavior (McGrath and Cohen, 1978). For example, a number of studies have demonstrated that groups deprived of REM sleep have poorer learning and retention than control groups deprived of an equal amount of sleep, but allowed to engage in REM (dream) sleep. Nevertheless, further evidence appears to be needed before the Freudian conception of dreams as wish fulfillments can be entirely discarded.

Hypnosis

Hypnosis was introduced in the first chapter of this text. Remember that Freud was led to the use of free association as a therapeutic technique after observing the curative effects of hypnosis. However, not all of his patients were able to be hypnotized, and he eventually found free association more suitable for his goals (see Chapter 1). In addition, in Chapter 4 it was revealed that a hypnotic demonstration was responsible for crystallizing Freud's idea that conscious beliefs may be quite inconsistent with unconscious desires.

The word *hypnos* is Greek for "sleep." For a long time hypnotic trances were thought to be akin to sleep, but this similarity is more apparent than real. Brain recordings and a variety of other indicators taken during hypnotic states are the same as those recorded in waking conditions, and both differ from the responses of a sleeping person. Furthermore, during hypnosis an individual can acquire and retain new information and be normally active or even hyperactive. Thus, the two main characteristics of sleep (nonresponsiveness to stimulation and lack of activity) do not describe the hypnotic subject.

Hypnotic trances have rather unique features:

1. The person ceases to make plans. There is a loss of initiative and the individual is generally passive, giving him- or herself over to the care of the hypnotist.
2. There is selective attention. Although this also is true in waking states, hypnotic subjects exhibit an even narrower range of focus.
3. Reality testing is reduced, and distortions and inconsistencies are accepted. This is sometimes called *trance logic.*
4. There is increased suggestibility and a compulsion to please and to follow the biddings of the hypnotist.
5. The subject readily enacts unusual roles, such as rowing a boat while in a room. Antisocial behavior may also be undertaken if it is not construed as antisocial by the person under hypnosis.

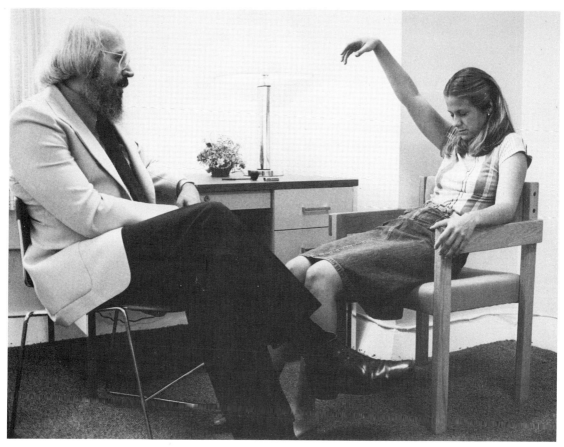

A patient under hypnosis at a psychiatric clinic. (Copyright © Ken Robert Buck, 1981. Courtesy, Mt. Auburn Hospital, Cambridge, Massachusetts)

6. Subjective experience is altered in accordance with the hypnotist's suggestions.
7. There is increased control over bodily functions, such as the capacity to hear, see, and feel pain. This will be elaborated on in the subsequent discussion.
8. There is typically posthypnotic amnesia. The extent of memory loss varies among individuals and according to the depth of the trance. This blockage is unique to hypnotic states.

There are differences in the extent to which these characteristics describe the state of any given individual during hypnosis. Around 10 percent of the population does not respond to hypnotic induction and, at the opposite pole, about 5 to 10 percent can enter deep trances in which even the commands of the hypnotist are no longer processed. A wide array of humans, including children and retardates, can be hypnotized. Furthermore, a single attempt is usually sufficient to determine if a person is susceptible to hypnosis. Performance scales have been developed to indicate the possible depth of trance that one can sustain. Such scales require individuals to attempt experiences ranging, for example, from simple falling forward without stiffening to blockage of smells and voices (Weitzenhoffer and Hilgard, 1962).

One question that immediately comes to mind is whether there are traits that distinguish good hypnotic subjects from poor ones. J. R. Hilgard has suggested that a good subject must have the capacity to become deeply involved in imaginative experiences. For example, one highly susceptible subject described herself as follows (Hilgard, 1970, p. 24):

When I get really involved in reading, I'm not aware of what is going on around me. I concentrate on the people in the book or the movie or in imagination as it is in hypnosis. Reading a book can hypnotize you.

After each book, I'm completely washed out. After hypnosis, it was the same. I was completely washed out and couldn't keep my eyes open. I lacked the ability to communicate.

Although traits that clearly distinguish good from poor hypnotic subjects have not been convincingly demonstrated thus far, a capacity for total absorption and losing oneself does seem to correlate with depth of hypnotic susceptibility (reported by Kimble, Garmezy, and Zigler, 1974).

It is also interesting to speculate about child-rearing practices that might account for differences in hypnotic susceptibility. J. R. Hilgard has conjectured that punitive upbringing might foster susceptibility because this type of child rearing promotes unquestioning obedience and escape through the use of imagination. Again, however, there is insufficient evidence to substantiate or discard this hypothesis.

Control of bodily functions.   The most dramatic reports concerning hypnosis involve control over basic sensory and cognitive functions. For example, in an experiment by Blum (1961), participants were instructed not to see a particular design on a card. This design, which had elicited great anxiety, gave rise to no physiological reactivity whatsoever after the hypnotic instructions.

However, hypnotic subjects do not become literally blind at the moment blindness is suggested; they will blink at a bright light. In a similar manner, apparent deafness can be easily induced in a hypnotic subject, but it can be demonstrated that the individual does process sound. In one such demonstration, individuals were tested in a delayed auditory feedback context, in which personal voice feedback is delayed by about one second, a delay that typically causes speech impairment. The adverse effects of auditory speech delay were not erased under hypnotic "deaf" instructions (Barber and Calverley, 1964).

As previously indicated, there is also apparent hypnotic influence on memory, for hypnosis is perhaps most often identified with amnesia for events during hypnosis. Yet even this aspect of hypnosis is not without ambiguity. For example, although participants are unable to consciously recall events during hypnosis that they have been instructed to forget, traditional measures of recognition and relearning are not affected by suggested amnesia (see Williamsen, Johnson, and Eriksen, 1965). The effects on delayed auditory feedback or on relearning lists of words, which circumvent the possibility of mere compliance with the hypnotized role, indicate that there is less control over basic bodily processes than might at first be apparent (see Cooper, 1972). Indeed, it has even been suggested that posthypnotic amnesia is not real, but is "pretended" by subjects (Coe, 1978). However, even if hypnotic amnesia is real, it is unclear whether the individual cannot retrieve the memories or whether the memories are not "stored" (Evans and Kihlstrom, 1973).

Most of the research on sensory blocking during hypnosis has examined pain reactions. In these experiments, subjects may be shocked or have their arms placed in very cold water. Control groups are hypnotized and either told nothing about pain or allowed to remain in a normal state. If normal, awake subjects are highly paid for this experience, they may tolerate a great deal of pain, like the hypnotic subjects. But, unlike the hypnotic subjects, they are aware of and remember the feeling. The hypnotic subjects appear neither to be consciously aware of nor to recall the pain. In one quite dramatic experiment, J. R. Hilgard (1970) told hypnotic subjects that they had lost their hands; when shock was administered to either hand, pain was not reported. However, in these experiments brain activity in response to pain was not altered.

Another attempt to demonstrate the apparently powerful effects of hypnosis concerns age regression. During hypnotic trance, subjects are told to return to an earlier period in their lives. This suggestion does produce experiential change, in that subjects might act and feel like children. But there are important differences between hypnotic regression and subjects' actual behavior as children. For example, age-regressed subjects' reports of what happened at particular birthday parties differ from reports by adults who attended those parties. Similarly, results of tests administered to age-regressed subjects and of actual tests taken at the earlier age do not correspond (see Orne, 1975).

What is hypnosis?   Given this array of observation, it is now reasonable to ask, "What is hypnosis?" First of all, many aspects of the hypnotic state seem also to be part of the basic equipment of waking consciousness. These aspects include the capacity to become completely absorbed in an activity and to follow the suggestions of another. Second, it is evident that some role playing is involved in hypnosis. For example, in one investigation subjects were falsely told that the arms stiffen under hypnosis (Orne, 1959); more than half the subjects exhibited this reaction when hypnotized. In sum, hypnosis seems to be a complex phenomenon involving interpersonal relationships, the relinquishing of personal control, some role playing, and the ability to imagine and hallucinate.

Hilgard (1973) has further suggested a *neo-dissociative* theory of hypnosis that calls attention to the similarities between hypnotic trances and such dissociative states as multiple personality and amnesia. In one demonstration, Hilgard placed one of the arms of hypnotized subjects in cold water following "no-pain" instructions. The subjects under hypnosis indeed did not report experiencing pain. But with the other hand they were told to report what they felt simultaneously, through automatic writing. These reports indicated feelings of pain (see Fig. 15.4).

Figure 15.4   Reported pain during hypnosis. (From *Introduction to Psychology*, 6th ed., by Ernest R. Hilgard, Richard C. Atkinson, and Rita L. Atkinson. Copyright © 1975 by Harcourt Brace Jovanovich, Inc. Reproduced by permission of the publisher.)

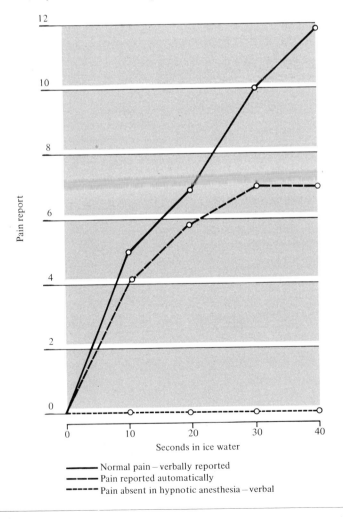

Hilgard thus contended that there is a "hidden observer" during hypnosis, and that information is placed under some sort of barrier before entering consciousness. This implies, as Freud did much earlier, that there are multiple levels of awareness and that the levels may not be in communication with one another, a situation that is apparently not unique to hypnotic trances. In sum, it is still unclear whether hypnosis is or is not a "special" state.

Drugs

Consciousness may be changed by natural occurrences like sleep or by external sources like hypnotic induction. One frequent and controversial method of consciousness alteration through artificial induction is the ingestion of chemical substances. Any substance that affects the structure or function of the body can be considered a drug, including tobacco and caffeine. But here our attention is restricted to drugs that might alter consciousness by causing some combination of:

1. Distortion of thought.
2. Change in the sense of time.
3. Alteration of emotional responses.
4. Perceptual distortion.

Table 15.5 includes a list of drugs differentiated into four classes (narcotics, hallucinogens, stimulants, and depressants) and their typical characteristics. The effects of drugs on any particular person, of course, are dependent on many factors, including the personality of the drug taker, the amount of previous drug experience, the purity of the drug, the social climate during the drug experience, whether the drug is taken singly or in combination with other drugs, and so on.

The use of a number of these drugs for nonmedicinal purposes has increased enormously over the past three decades. Moreover, as indicated in Chapter 10, this trend has extended down the age range into early adolescence. How drugs work, who takes them, the mechanisms behind addiction, and the effects of drugs on behavior have become topics of great interest to the public and the scientist alike. In terms of the major focus of this chapter, the aspect of drugs that is of special interest to us is their influence on consciousness. It is claimed that certain drugs "expand" consciousness; facilitate clearer, sharper perceptions of the physical world; help provide deeper insights into the psyche; expose hidden, repressed materials; and under some circumstances, enable the individual to achieve a more integrated self and sense of spiritual unity. These claims all require careful scientific scrutiny.

Not all of the drugs listed in Table 15.5 are alleged to have positive, consciousness-altering effects. Alcohol may produce a pleasant euphoric state and relax inhibitions, but it predominantly fosters inner confusion, perceptual distortions, and a narrowing rather than an expansion of consciousness. Narcotics like heroin also tend to produce changes in mood and self-confidence, with little else in the way of desirable psychological consequences. The class

Table 15.5 Drugs and their characteristics

Category	Name	Source	How taken	Medical use	Effect lasts (hours)	Typical dose
Narcotics	Morphine	Opium from opium poppy	Injected	Relieves pain	5–7	10–20 mg
	Heroin	Extracted from morphine	Injected; sniffed	None in U.S.	3–6	Variable
	Codeine	Extracted from opium and morphine	Swallowed; injected	Relieves pain	3–5	10–30 mg
	Methadone	Synthetic	Injected; swallowed	Relieves pain	4–6	10 mg
Hallucinogens	LSD (D-lysergic acid)	Ergot alkaloids	Swallowed	Experimental	5–15	100–500 μg
	Mescaline	*Peyote* cactus	Swallowed	None	5–15	200–400 μg
	Psilocybin	*Psilocybe* mushroom	Swallowed	None	4–10	25 mg
	Marijuana	*Cannabis sativa* plant	Smoked; swallowed	Experimental	2–5	1–2 cigarettes
Stimulants	Cocaine	From coca plant	Sniffed; injected; swallowed	Deadens pain	10–60 minutes	Varies
	Amphetamines { Benzedrine Dexedrine Methedrine	Synthetic	Swallowed; injected	Relief of depression	3–5	2–10 mg
Depressants	Barbiturates { Phenobarbital Nembutal Seconal Amytal	Synthetic	Swallowed; injected	Sedation	3–5	20–100 mg
	Alcohol	Fermented or distilled grains, potatoes, etc.	Swallowed	Antiseptic	1–5	Varies

Category	Name	Desired Effects	Long-term Effects	Physical Dependence	Mental Dependence	Physical Damage
Narcotics	Morphine	Sense of well-being; prevention of withdrawal symptoms	Addiction; constipation; loss of appetite	Yes	Yes	No
	Heroin	Same as above	Same as above	Yes	Yes	No
	Codeine	Same as above	Same as above	Yes	Yes	No
	Methadone	Prevention of withdrawal symptoms	Same as above	Yes	Yes	No
Hallucinogens	LSD (D-lysergic acid)	Distortion of senses; insight; euphoria	Can precipitate psychosis	No	Perhaps	Unknown
	Mescaline	Same as above	None known	No	Perhaps	Unknown
	Psilocybin	Same as above	None known	No	Perhaps	Unknown
	Marijuana	Increases perceptions and sense of well-being	None known	No	Perhaps	Unknown
Stimulants	Cocaine	Exhilaration; excitement; sociability	Psychosis; convulsions; depression	No	Yes	Yes (?)
	Amphetamines { Benzedrine Dexedrine Methedrine	Alertness; activeness; confidence	Loss of appetite; depression; psychosis	No (?)	Yes	Yes (?)
Depressants	Barbiturates { Phenobarbital Nembetal Seconal Amytal	Tension reduction; sense of well-being	Addiction; convulsions; psychosis	Yes	Yes	Yes
	Alcohol	Tension reduction; sociability; sense of well-being	Neurological damage; cirrhosis of liver; psychosis	Yes	Yes	Yes

Source: Houston, Bee, Hatfield, and Rimm, 1979, pp. 154-155. Reprinted by permission.

of drugs called the hallucinogens is most likely to give rise to unusual visual experiences and inner feelings. There is no doubt that the hallucinogens can dramatically alter consciousness. The problematic question is whether, in this alteration, any raising or expanding of consciousness takes place. The characters in the following story (Kukla, 1980, p. 520) illustrating some of the differences between the effects of LSD and marijuana hardly display psychological insight or perceptual acuity.

The difference between being stoned and being spaced out is illustrated in a story about two men who arrive at the closed gates of a city at night. One has taken lysergic acid, which is the spacer-out par excellence; *the other has smoked marijuana, which usually gets you stoned. "Let's sprout golden wings and fly over the gates into the city!" suggests the acid-head. The pothead, after a very long pause, replies, "Why don't we just sit down and wait till they open in the morning?"[1]*

The hallucinogens have been known for many centuries, with the exception of lysergic acid diethylamide (LSD), which was first synthesized in 1938. The American Indians used peyote, whose active ingredient is mescaline, to induce states of ecstasy and mystical experience. In his book *The Doors of Perception*, Aldous Huxley (1954, pp. 16–18) helped popularize the consciousness-altering effects of mescaline.

I took my pill at eleven. An hour and a half later, I was sitting in my study, looking intently at a small glass vase. The vase contained only three flowers. . . . I continued to look at the flowers, and in their living light I seemed to detect the qualitative equivalent of breathing— but of a breathing without return to a starting point, with no recurrent ebbs but only a repeated flow from beauty to heightened beauty, from deeper to even deeper meaning; words like "grace" and "transfiguration" came to my mind, and this, of course, was what, among other things, they stood for.

The possibility that hallucinogens could help individuals break through the ordinary barriers of consciousness and achieve a deeper level of self-understanding has been explored by some psychotherapists (Caldwell, 1968). One patient, following a therapeutic session in which she had taken LSD, described her experience (Aaronson and Osmond, 1970, p. 330):

After I had felt that hours must have gone by and then learned that it was only five minutes; after I had seen flowers open and close their petals and held in my hand a peeled grape that became, before my eyes, a tiny brain; and after I had closed my eyes and seen one beautiful vision right after another; well, then I decided that anything must be possible, including the transformations of character and personality I had heard about, and to some extent believed, but which only now I really felt confident could happen.

Although there are very occasional clinical reports of insights achieved through hallucinogenic drugs, there is no systematic evidence demonstrating

---

[1] Andre Kukla, "The Modern Language of Consciousness," in *The State of the Language*, L. Michaels and C. Ricks, © 1980; published by the University of California Press, Berkeley, CA.

their psychotherapeutic utility. As a result, therapists rarely use these drugs in practice. In addition, the hallucinogens can produce very unpleasant experiences. "Bad trips" are not uncommon and experts (Caldwell, 1968) emphasize the necessity for careful supervision of the individual who takes hallucinogens, particularly LSD or mescaline. Huxley also stresses the need for monitoring, portraying mescaline as opening the door to either heaven or hell.

To evaluate the hallucinogens, their immediate effects on consciousness must be separated from their long-term effects. A vivid, dramatic, or ecstatic experience is not the equivalent of personality growth, of a new insight into oneself and the world. Thorough evaluation studies of the effects of LSD have not supported the hypothesis that taking LSD facilitates creativity, produces self-insight, or enhances one's perceptions of the surrounding environment (McGlothlin and Arnold, 1971; McGlothlin, Cohen, and McGlothlin, 1967). A similar conclusion applies to marijuana. The principal scientific uncertainty concerning the effects of repeated use of marijuana and other hallucinogens is over the likelihood of such negative personality effects as decreased energy and goal striving and subtle disturbances in thinking. Moreover, whatever the subjective experiences provided by marijuana, at the objective level marijuana intoxication interferes with motor coordination, visual perception, and reaction time (*Marijuana and Health*, 1977). In brief, aside from the alterations in mood and perception that hallucinogens produce, their consciousness-expanding effects have yet to be demonstrated.

Meditation

There is a close historical association between altered consciousness as induced by drugs and the growth of the meditational movement in America. This connection is explained, with added humorous touches, in the following quote (Kukla, 1980, pp. 516–517):

There also now exists a sizeable American following for every religious sect in the world, not excluding denominations which were thought to be extinct, like Druidism and the worship of Pan. I recall the amazement of a scholar from India who, returning to America in 1970 after several years' absence, found that the Vaishnavaite devotees of Krishna, with their painted foreheads, shaven pates, cymbals and drums, whom he had been studying in remote Indian villages, had arrived before him and were dancing in the streets of Cleveland and Chicago! By now, the average downtown shopper has ceased to find their presence at all remarkable. Even the Balinese fire-walkers elicit no more than a raised eyebrow. As the seventies come to a close, the number of Hindu, Buddhist, and Sufi teachers residing in America is beyond tallying; and it is a commonplace among them that Americans are more ardent, if also more naive, in their pursuit of inner experience than are their own countrymen. Perhaps we will soon see the children of Japanese industrialists and Arab oil magnates, unfulfilled by the materialism of their elders, setting off on holy pilgrimages to the West in search of enlightenment. They will no doubt collect native American trinkets, marvelling at how cheap everything is.

This inward turn of the American psyche is surely related to the general decay of Western civilization, but a specific cause may be found in the large-scale experiment with mind-altering drugs which began to occupy American society in the sixties, and which ultimately led to a reappraisal of the nature of consciousness. Until recently, the popular conception of consciousness did not permit of qualitative variation—either one was conscious, or one was unconscious—but the experience of marijuana, lysergic acid, and amphetamines introduced us to the idea of qualitative differences. In the long run, it scarcely mattered what these differences were, or whether the drugs were considered to be "psychedelic," [or] "hallucinogenic." The main lesson was that ordinary consciousness is alterable; and the immediate corollary is that altered states of consciousness are more satisfactory than the dismal ordinary one. In this way, the door was opened to any teacher or system that promised to effect a radical psychic improvement. Thus the drug culture of the sixties generated the American yogis [and] Buddhists . . . of today. Of course the contemporary situation was anticipated by the English and French Romantics, who were also interested in mind-altering drugs; and an experience with nitrous oxide led William James to conclude, as far back as 1902, that "our normal waking consciousness . . . is but one special type of consciousness, whilst all about it . . . there lie potential forms of consciousness entirely different." But these were avant-garde ideas. What is new in our time is the movement of these ideas from literary salons to the living rooms and laundromats of America, from symbolist poems to network television and the newspapers.[2]

Meditation broadly includes any attempt to alter consciousness by means of systematic concentration and sustained self-regulation of attention. The procedures used and their associated values are derived from Eastern religions; yoga is a system of thought based on Hindu philosophy, while Zen is derived from Chinese and Japanese Buddhism. Many meditational techniques have been advanced, but sitting quietly or chanting a *mantra* (a word kept in constant awareness) are among the most popular methods for altering consciousness with meditation. These methods help block out external sensations, thus aiding the individual in focusing inward. Whether chanting or just sitting without sound, the individual seeks a calm environment and assumes a comfortable position to keep bodily and environmental stimulation from awareness. A water metaphor has been called upon to describe the process of meditation: the ripples on the water are quieted in order to see the depths below.

Many activities, including *kendo* (Japanese fencing), *kado* (flower arranging), and *Kyudo* (archery) offer opportunities for mental self-control, self-actualization, or even *satori* (enlightenment). In each of these disciplines, the ceremony stresses ritualized control of muscular movements, particularly respiration, as a means of self-control. Participants in the tea ceremony, for example, can achieve a kind of altered state of consciousness as a result of altered patterns of sensory stimuli resulting from fixed postures; refined, graceful movements; the regulation of respiration; the smell of burning incense; the monotonous but peaceful sound of boiling water in an iron teapot; the delicate taste of tea; and other tranquilizing aspects of the special tearoom.

---

[2] Andre Kukla, "The Modern Language of Consciousness," in *The State of the Language*, L. Michaels and C. Ricks, © 1980; published by the University of California Press, Berkeley, CA.

Upon this background one is taught the philosophy of the tea ceremony, expressed in the words "one chance, one meeting." Such a philosophy accepts the idea that the ceremony may be the first and last chance of making tea and meeting certain guests in the same room. It is a lesson of nature that everyone is destined to death, even though people are apt to forget it in their daily life. Such a lucid acceptance of nature and the laws of existence makes participants do their best in making each bowl of tea with deep affection for each guest. The tea ceremony is therefore considered to be a way to enlightenment, such as Zen, and not a mere social pastime.

The experience striven for or attained in meditation has been described by William James and others as "ineffable"; that is, defying expression. In addition, the meditational state is transient in that it cannot be sustained for too long, with one's will held in abeyance. Individuals indicate that they experience their "mind going blank," that there is "no-thought," or that their thoughts are "watched" without emotional identification, stress, or cognitive elaboration.

A comparison is often made between the meditation experience and an unusual visual effect that has been produced in the laboratory (see Ornstein, 1972). It has been found that if one visually focuses on a single point or object, then that point or object disappears from sight. This happens because, once a neuron has fired, there is a refractory period during which it cannot be reactivated without intervening rest. Hence, when staring at an object, there is constant shifting of focus and repeated eye movements to keep the image activated. In an experimental setting, it is possible to fix the image of the object on one part of the eye by having the image move in synchrony with eye shifts. Given an unchanging focus of stimulation, awareness of the object "shuts off." Similarly, it is said that when the mind focuses on an idea or word, thoughts disappear, leaving pure thought or "thoughtless consciousness." In this state, feelings are described as restful, floating, and empty. Schwartz (1975, p. 156) characterized the meditational experience as follows:

During meditation one "transcends" normal consciousness, going beyond the act of thinking to arrive at the source of the thought—a state of pure awareness; of nothingness. As a result, practitioners say, one experiences the world directly and profoundly, yet one is relaxed and peaceful.

Consequences of meditation.   Research on meditation is growing rapidly and includes the effects of meditation on physiological responsiveness, reactions to stress, relaxation, personality, mental health, drug use, and basic cognitive processes.

During hypnosis, the physiology is the same as in a normal waking state. On the other hand, meditation produces a slowing of normal physiological processes. The earliest research on this effect was sensational, to say the least: yogis who were able to stay alive when buried in airtight boxes were studied. Since then, more systematic research has been undertaken that has demonstrated, for example, that there is reduced oxygen consumption during medi-

A yoga class. Participants often find that this practice enhances relaxation. (Arthur Grace/Stock, Boston)

tation, less carbon dioxide elimination, and a slowing of heart rate (Wallace and Benson, 1972). As indicated previously, these observations formed the foundation of biofeedback research. In addition, it has been reported that when meditators listen to unpleasant sounds, they decrease physiological responsiveness faster than do nonmeditators (Orme-Johnson, 1973), which suggests that they might be adapting more effectively to aversive sounds. These meditators do not exhibit a drop in activation given repeated sounds of some neutral stimulus. However, these data characterize only a limited number of meditators and much more data need to be gathered before these scattered findings can be considered facts. Furthermore, experienced and deep meditators must be distinguished from inexperienced, more surface meditators, for it appears that physiological reactions to meditation depend on the type of meditation used and the level of proficiency (Woolfolk, 1975).

In addition to these physiological observations, meditators report becoming calm, relaxed, and happier and exhibit more positive personal functioning (e.g., Ferguson and Gowen, 1976; Seeman, Nidich, and Banta, 1972). However, it must be noted that people who have continued meditation training are motivated to find the experience rewarding, so that their reports might be biased. Furthermore, many individuals stop meditating, and it is unclear whether they have experienced any benefits. And whether meditation promotes more relaxation than other techniques, including jogging, has been questioned (Shapiro and Giber, 1978).

In sum, the use of meditation as a means of experiencing new forms of consciousness is increasing. Positive benefits have been reported for a variety of indicators, but much more research is needed before the process and its effects will be fully understood. Furthermore, there is a clear need to separate the process of meditation and what it involves from the subsequent behavior of meditators, who might be a unique group of individuals.

The Divided Self: Split-Brain Experiments and Consciousness

The human brain is divided into two halves. The left side (or *hemisphere*) controls the right side of the body, while the right hemisphere controls the left side of the body. In humans, these halves of the brain are functionally different, with the left side specialized in language functions such as speaking and writing, and the right half more limited in terms of language abilities. It has also been found that the right hemisphere is superior at visual-spatial tasks such as spatial orientation.

Under normal circumstances, information is relayed between the two halves of the brain. However, the connections can be severed experimentally, so that there is disruption of the knowledge flow and each half of the brain may be independently examined. Split-brain operations are typically performed on laboratory animals such as cats or monkeys. But very occasionally this operation is performed on humans, for it has been found that splitting the brain reduces the severity of epileptic seizures. Some individuals suffer such extreme forms of this illness, with as many as twelve seizures daily, that the operation is of great benefit in spite of negative side effects. In addition, through accidents some individuals have greatly damaged one side of their brains, thus permitting the experimental study of half the brain.

Split-brain experiments have revealed that each half of the brain can process information outside the realm of the other half's consciousness. For example, if a word is flashed to a split-brain patient's left (typically major) hemisphere, the patient is able to say the word and write it with his or her right hand. But if the right (typically minor) hemisphere receives this information, then the word cannot be verbalized or written with the left hand (see Sperry, 1968).

On the basis of these data, some individuals have argued that there are two independent spheres or modes of consciousness; that there is a duality in human consciousness, with the "conscious" left side of the brain specializing in verbalization capacities, and the "unconscious" right side not having this function. One might *experience* with the right hemisphere, but that experience would not be part of conscious (verbalizable) awareness. For example, in one experiment a patient was shown a picture of a nude. When the nude was presented to the left hemisphere, there was affect along with verbalization about the picture. But when it was viewed by the right hemisphere, there was affect without any apparent understanding of why. Indeed, the patient appeared to search for a reason to justify and make sense of his feelings.

These data led not only to speculation about the independent modes of consciousness, but also to the belief that there is a duality in human nature, with each aspect of a person having independent representation in the brain. Table 15.6 characterizes the suggested duality in human consciousness and human nature. In a humorous but thought-provoking extension of these ideas, Kimble et al. (1974, p. 614) related the following scenario (based on Gazzaniga, 1970):

Emotions can be different in the two hemispheres. One of these patients once got angry with his wife, grabbed her with the left hand, and shook her violently while the right hand tried to intercede and bring the other half under control. Suppose that the right hand had been unsuccessful and that the left hand had murdered the wife. Who would be guilty in such a case?

It now appears, however, that there has been an overdramatization of the uniqueness of the two sides of the brain (Gazzaniga and LeDoux, 1978). First of all, the hemispheres are typically intact and there is mental unity. If there really were two independent brains, where and how would they be integrated and synthesized? Furthermore, the right hemisphere can perform logical op-

Table 15.6	The two dimensions of consciousness: A dichotomy	
	Right side of the body	*Left side of the body*
	Left hemisphere	Right hemisphere
	Intellectual	Sensuous
	Masculine: yang	Feminine: yin
	Day, light	Night, dark
	Time, history	Eternity, timeless
	Verbal	Spatial
	Western culture	Eastern culture
	Reason, logic	Passion, intuition

Source: Adapted from *The Psychology of Consciousness*, Second Edition (p. 37), copyright © 1977 by Robert Ornstein. Reprinted by permission of Harcourt Brace Jovanovich, Inc.

erations. For example, if the left hemisphere is damaged early in life, the right develops linguistic capabilities. In addition, although the right hemisphere cannot verbally label objects, if the left hand is allowed to feel an object, a correct match to an object flashed on a screen can be made. Thus, although response production through the linguistic mode is not possible by the right hemisphere, it is not without consciousness.

In sum, there are localized differences and specialization of brain functions, primarily due to linguistic development that is typically localized in the left hemisphere. But there is unity and integration in mental functioning, the two hemispheres do not oppose one another, and the differences between the hemispheres are quantitative rather than qualitative. The romance associated with split-brain research may be waning. For example, claims that the right brain is the seat of creativity and that artists are more oriented toward this hemisphere have not been substantiated. But it is evident from this research that there can be experience without verbalization, which is consistent with the theme presented throughout this chapter.

Fantasy and Consciousness

Most of you have had the experience of finding yourself on the same page of a book after a half-hour supposedly spent studying. You wonder where the time went and what happened during the interval. You then realize that your mind has "wandered." Perhaps you were thinking about an upcoming date or a recent party, or imagined yourself reaching a goal or occupying a position of power and status. Our thought processes are engaged in this kind of fantasy activity a surprising amount of the time; our minds are rarely blank or idle. Engaging in such fantasies or daydreams does not entail as radical an alteration of consciousness as that produced by drugs, hypnosis, or dreaming. However, there is a relation between these altered states of consciousness and fantasy activity. In all these experiences attention is directed toward or dominated by the inner, rather than the outer world. In reality-directed activity, we attend to real physical stimuli—sounds, odors, visual displays, and the like—while in fantasy or imaginary activity, we attend to internal representations of physical stimuli—thoughts and ideas. Hence, in fantasy our inner life plays the important role in determining the contents of consciousness.

One important element of daydreams and related fantasy experience is the notion of *imagery,* or "pictures in the mind." Vivid imagery is readily induced by hypnosis, is one of the consequences of hallucinogens, and is a common characteristic of dreams. Thinking in images has been shown to have different properties than thinking in words. For example, images facilitate memory and appear to be understood and stored differently than words (Paivio, 1971). There is also some evidence that thinking in pictures is associated with right-brain activity, while thinking in words is associated with left-brain activity (Robbins and McAdam, 1974). However, the evidence concerning the relationship between imagery and brain hemisphere activity is not conclusive. One problem of interpretation is that the right brain appears to be more responsive to emotions than the left brain, and images frequently elicit strong emotional responses. Hence, it is difficult to disentangle whether the right brain is responding to imagery or to the emotions produced by imagery (Ley, 1979).

There is evidence among both children and adults that individuals who engage in fantasy experience are less impulsive and display more positive adjustment patterns than individuals who engage in very little fantasy activity (Singer, 1966, 1973). But the term *fantasy* is a broad construct embracing many different kinds of activity such as imagery, constructing stories, engaging in play, and even reading fiction and watching theatrical productions. It is not unlikely that the effects of these disparate types of fantasy may be quite different.

In terms of the issues with which we have been concerned in this chapter, it is of interest that the effects of an event portrayed on television differ dramatically, depending on whether children viewing the event perceive it as real or as a fantasy. In one experiment (Feshbach, 1972), children nine to eleven years old were individually shown a six-minute segment of a campus riot, made up by combining shots of a real campus riot with parts of a movie about a campus riot. Before seeing the television program, children assigned to a reality-set condition were told that the program was taken from a television newscast, while children assigned to a fantasy-set condition were told that the program was part of a film made in Hollywood. A control group was not shown a program. Each child was then given the opportunity to aggress against the experimenter by administering an aversive noise that varied in its loudness and severity. The data revealed that children in the fantasy-set condition were less aggressive, while children in the reality-set condition were more aggressive than the no-television control group. The importance of this finding lies in its demonstration that the same event has a different impact when experienced as a fantasy than when experienced as reality.

Summary   In this chapter different varieties of consciousness have been examined. Consciousness is equated with awareness, or subjective life, and can be diminished (e.g., as in amnesia), enhanced (e.g., with biofeedback), or perhaps changed qualitatively in form or type. Normal waking thought is only one form of consciousness. There are a number of so-called "altered" states of consciousness, including dream states, hypnotic trances, and drug and meditational experiences. Under these conditions, time is distorted, unreal events may be perceived as real, and there can be a loss of both personal and social awareness. Finally, split-brain research and fantasy are two areas of study related to consciousness.

Specific Points

1. *Consciousness* refers to awareness, or what is known, about one's experiences. We are not consciously aware of all the internal and external sensations that impinge upon us.
2. *Dissociative phenomena* include somnambulism, amnesia, and multiple personality. In these states there is dramatically diminished awareness of selected aspects of behavior.
3. The process of monitoring and providing personal information about autonomic functioning is called *biofeedback* (biological feedback). Biofeedback allows people to control various normally involuntary responses, such as heart rate, blood pressure, and brain activity, controls that are difficult to sustain for long periods of time outside the laboratory.
4. Self-awareness has been heightened experimentally by placing a mirror in front of subjects. Often self-awareness impedes functioning, but if expectations of positive outcomes are high, then increased self-awareness may enhance performance.
5. Dreams are one of a number of *altered states of consciousness*. The presence of a dream is inferred by *rapid eye movements* (*REM*) and a particular pattern of brain activity. Humans and many infrahuman species pass through a typical dream cycle during the night.
6. Freud's speculations about dreams are not confirmed by dream research. Dream deprivation does not necessarily impede psychological functioning; the onset of external stimulation during sleep does not initiate a dream; and most dreams appear quite commonplace and somewhat unpleasant. Dreams may have a biological or problem-solving, rather than a wish-fulfilling, function.
7. Physiological activity during a hypnotic state corresponds to that in a normal waking condition. However, the individual is highly suggestible, reality testing is reduced, there may be heightened control over bodily functions, and there is posthypnotic amnesia. The hypnotic influence over seeing and hearing is not evident in subtle tasks related to these processes, such as delayed auditory feedback. The *neo-dissociative* theory of hypnosis accepts the notion of multiple layers of consciousness.
8. There are a variety of drugs. Hallucinogens have vivid and immediate effects on consciousness, but there is no evidence that they produce any long-term positive effects.
9. *Meditation* is any attempt to alter consciousness by means of systematic concentration and sustained self-regulation of attention. It may result in a "turning off" of the mind and a slowing of normal physiological processes. The long-term effects of meditation have not been established.
10. The brain has two hemispheres: the left specializing in language function and the right specializing in spatial orientation. Research has shown that presentation of visual material to the right side of the brain results in an experience that cannot be verbalized.
11. In fantasy, as in altered states of consciousness, attention is directed toward or dominated by the inner, rather than the outer, world.

Thought Questions

1. There are times, as during sporting events, when we are under great pain, but are able to "forget" that pain and continue striving. How might this be explained?

2. What stimuli in the environment lead you to focus more on yourself? Under what circumstances do you "lose" yourself?

3. In what ways are dreams, hypnotically induced images, and daydreams similar? How do they differ?

4. Are there any American equivalents to the Japanese tea ceremony which might produce an altered state of consciousness?

PART VI

Complex Personality Processes

Chapters 16–18 focus on complex personality processes and behaviors: achievement strivings and the effects of success or failure (Chapter 16); the influence of one's sense of freedom, or lack of it, on one's own behavior and the attitudinal and behavioral effects when others are perceived as responsible for their actions (Chapter 17); and the theoretical and empirical literature on human aggression (Chapter 18). These topics are fundamental to human personality and represent active research areas. Other significant personality processes and behaviors, such as anxiety, have been considered at various points in the text.

Chapters 16–18 also illustrate different aspects of personality research. The discussion of achievement motivation, for example, includes an illustration of how a simple mathematical model can generate personality-relevant hypotheses and integrate diverse experimental data. In addition, personality methods and concepts in the achievement domain have been used to investigate socioeconomic change and development in the larger culture. Chapter 17, on personal freedom, illustrates how concepts that are central to humanistic views of personality, such as freedom and responsibility, can be systematically investigated with objective, quantitative procedures. It thus demonstrates both the utility of these ideas and the advantages of incorporating them within a scientific framework. Chapter 18, on human aggression, illustrates the multidetermined basis of personality and the interplay of diverse biological and social factors.

Attempts to explain complex personality processes and behaviors in terms of single causes are simplistic and misleading. There are many antecedents to major personality dimensions, and an adequate understanding of achievement, personal responsibility, and aggression requires analysis of the roles of each of them.

Achievement Strivings

16 Freud contended that there are two main motivations in life: *Arbeit und Liebe,* work and love. If the meanings of these terms are somewhat broadened to include what is called achievement and affiliation motivation, then Freud's statement seems to be correct. A count of our day's activities would reveal that, in general, most of the time is spent in maintaining or expanding friendships or intimacy, and in accomplishing tasks and goals. Of course, humans also strive for power, seek entertainment, engage in acts of aggression, attempt to satisfy curiosity, and so on. But affiliation and achievement motivation appear to be dominant concerns within our culture. Thus, it is not surprising that the study of achievement strivings has played a major role in the psychology of personality.

The motivation to achieve takes many different forms. The college student working late into the night to "crack" the next day's examination, the teenager practicing each day in the schoolyard to perfect a basketball shot, the aspiring executive investing funds in a promising venture, and the scientist persisting in the effort to solve a difficult theoretical problem despite repeated frustration and failure are all displaying achievement motivation. What are the roots of achievement motivation? Why do some individuals strive to reach as high as their abilities will permit, while others are satisfied with much lower levels of accomplishment? What is the relationship between the culture or the economic structure of a society and achievement motivation? Why are some people so unrealistic in the goals they set for themselves? Do men and women differ in their levels of achievement motivation and, if so, why?

The starting point for the systematic psychological study of achievement motivation was in the work of Henry Murray, although other psychologists like Freud and Lewin also played significant roles. Murray has already been introduced to you at a number of points in the text. In Chapter 1, it was noted that he was the head of the influential Harvard Clinic and one of the founders of the experimental approach to the study of personality.

Murray (1938) devised a taxonomy that included twenty basic human

410

needs. These needs were thought of as personality traits, or stable dispositions of the person. Individuals were assumed to vary along these personality dimensions, so that some persons had "more of" or stronger dispositions than others. One of these needs, called *achievement,* was conceived as the desire (Murray, 1938, p. 164):

To accomplish something difficult. To master, manipulate or organize physical objects, human beings, or ideas. To do this as rapidly and as independently as possible. To overcome obstacles and attain a high standard. To excel one's self. To rival and surpass others. To increase self-regard by the successful exercise of talent.

These desires, Murray said, are accompanied by the following actions (p. 164):

To make intense, prolonged and repeated efforts to accomplish something difficult. To work with singleness of purpose towards a high and distant goal. To have the determination to win. To try to do everything well. To be stimulated to excel by the presence of others, to enjoy competition.

The Measurement of Achievement Needs

For scientific progress, it is not sufficient merely to indicate that there is a predisposition to strive for achievement. Rather, a measure must be constructed to assess this characteristic accurately, so that individuals can be assigned a score indicating the *magnitude* of their need or motivation. Murray developed an instrument, called the Thematic Apperception Test (TAT), to assess need states (see Chapter 12); it was readily adapted for the assessment of achievement needs. One of the main reasons for its widespread use was that early influential investigators were guided by the Freudian belief that a good place to find indications of motivation is in the fantasy life of individuals. In free responses to ambiguous situations, like those portrayed in Rorschach cards or the TAT, just as in dreams and daydreams, it was believed that individuals revealed their underlying desires and true wishes. In support of this belief, it was found that superficial verbal responses, in which individuals merely introspect and report their levels of achievement desires, did not predict achievement-oriented behavior, whereas the fantasy-based measure seemed to have predictive validity.

The Procedure

The general TAT methodology used to assess achievement needs has remained virtually unchanged since its inception. Four to six pictures are projected on a screen, typically in a group setting, with subjects responding to four directing questions (What is happening? What led up to this situation? What is being thought? What will happen?) The pictures, like the one shown in Fig. 16.1, vary in content, portraying one or two individuals engaging in tasks, having an apparently serious or a casual discussion, and so forth. Four minutes of writing time are allowed for each story, and a total achievement need score is obtained for each person by summing the scores of the individual stories.

The scoring for achievement needs is a two-step process. First it is decided whether a story contains achievement-related imagery. Examples of such story imagery include unique accomplishments, such as inventions or novels; long-term achievement concerns, such as wanting to be a success in

Figure 16.1   Typical scene used to assess achievement needs.

life or a doctor; and competition with some standard of excellence, such as building the best model. The following protocol for the card shown in Fig. 16.1 contains achievement imagery:

Two inventors are working on a new type of machine. They need this machine in order to complete the work on the new invention, the automobile. This takes place some time ago and the necessary tools are not available. . . . They want to do a good job and improve transportation. After years of hard work they are successful; they feel elated.

If the written production contains achievement-related imagery, such as a unique accomplishment or a long-term achievement concern, then the story receives a numerical score of $+1$, and ten other subcategories, each having possible credit of $+1$, are analyzed for particular kinds of achievement-related content. These subcategories include, for example, expressions of affect ("feel elated"), instrumental activity ("years of hard work"), and obstacles to achievement ("necessary tools are not available"). The complete scoring scheme can be mastered with twenty to forty hours of training. However, it has been pointed out that a simple 0 or 1 scoring scheme based only on the presence of achievement imagery correlates quite highly with a system that uses all of the subcategories (see Entwisle, 1972).

Some Criticisms

Some of the disadvantages of projective measures have been presented in Chapter 12. The TAT measure of achievement needs is also beset with a number of measurement problems. For example, the choice of which pictures to use from the many that are available remains uncertain. And the question of match between the respondent's sex, age, or race and those of the people in the TAT pictures remains unresolved. Thus, it is not known if females or children should be presented TAT cards portraying, respectively, only females or children.

More serious questions about the TAT concern its reliability. Its reported internal consistency (recall that this is the correlation between the parts of a test, such as the first and second halves) and its test-retest reliability (described in Chapter 11 as the correlation of the test with itself on different occasions) are quite low (see Entwisle, 1972; Klinger, 1966). Individuals upholding the use of the TAT as a measure of achievement needs have naturally come to its defense, pointing out that the TAT pictures often portray scenes unrelated to achievement (such as men or women sitting around a table drinking coffee) but associated with affiliation or power. Little achievement imagery is elicited by pictures highly associated with motives other than achievement, thus decreasing the measure's internal consistency.

And, concerning test-retest reliability, it has been argued that the TAT is presented as a test of "creative imagination" and that subjects are thus reluctant to give the same general response on successive occasions. Test-retest unreliability therefore may be due to the effect of previous administrations of the test. When one first hears a good joke, one tends to respond with a hearty laugh. When the joke is heard a second time, it seems less funny, and less laughter will be elicited. In this instance, test-retest reliability is a proper index of neither the joke's quality nor the adequacy of laughter as an indicator of how humorous a joke is. As Atkinson and Raynor (1974, p. 9) noted, "Instead of returning on a second occasion like the constant and unchanging block of metal presumed by traditional test theory borrowed from physics, the subjects might be substantially spoiled for a retest." These notions raise fundamental questions regarding personality testing in general and give the flavor of some of the arguments between advocates of projective tests and those espousing objective measurement techniques (see Chapter 12).

Alternative Measures

In addition to suspicions concerning its reliability, there are practical reasons for replacing the TAT as a measure of achievement needs. To obtain a written protocol, the respondent must be literate and fairly articulate. As a result, many individuals, like young children, cannot be tested. Furthermore, writing stories about four to six pictures is extremely wearing and time consuming. But, in spite of the disadvantages of this projective measurement instrument, the TAT has not yet been supplanted by an objective measure. To date, simple verbal report instruments have not proved to be as useful.

More recently, other systematic programs of achievement testing, which are promising as replacements for the TAT, have been undertaken. Helmreich and Spence contend that achievement needs are multidimensional, including mastery desires as well as competitiveness, which are independent of one another. Investigations have revealed that mastery desires, but not competitiveness, are predictive of performance in school settings. The measures used by Helmreich and Spence (1978) contain such objective verbal report statements as:

- It is important for me to do my work as well as I can, even if it isn't popular with my co-workers.
- I prefer work situations that require a high level of skill.

A great deal of work is being conducted to demonstrate the usefulness of this objective method of measurement.

Achievement Needs as a Personality Structure

It has been indicated that Murray conceived of an achievement need as a trait or an enduring personality disposition. Therefore, two issues are of immediate relevance: (1) what is the generality (or extensiveness, or breadth) of the need for achievement? and (2) is this disposition stable, or at least relatively enduring? Unfortunately, neither question has been adequately answered. It is not known, for example, whether a person who strives for success in a particular occupation also exhibits such achievement drives on the tennis court, in night-school accounting class, or in other situations. It certainly seems reasonable to believe that there are circumscribed avenues or outlets for achievement expression in a given individual. For example, we might expect the driven athlete to exhibit competition on the playing field, but not in the classroom; on the football field, but not in a less central sport such as bowling or ping-pong. On the other hand, it is equally plausible that desires to achieve are expressed across a range of achievement-related situations. However, these questions have not been investigated and at present the generality or specificity of achievement as a trait is unknown. It may be, as Bem and Allen (see Chapter 13) have suggested, that there are individual differences in the generality of this disposition.

The stability of achievement needs has been the subject of more research than the issue of generality. This is perhaps surprising, inasmuch as longitudinal studies are difficult to conduct. An overview of this research suggests significant but weak correlations between scores on need achievement scales when the measures are taken as many as six years apart (Feld, 1967; Kagan and Moss, 1959; Moss and Kagan, 1961). Clearly, however, research of this type is hampered because of the uncertain test-retest reliability of the TAT. That is, it is impossible to determine if achievement needs are stable if the test-retest reliability of the measure employed is low. Note, therefore, how closely related the fields of personality structure, measurement, and development are. For example, the demonstration of stable structures and antecedents of development requires valid and reliable measurement instruments.

The question of motive stability is beset with other difficulties as well. For example, it has been found that parents of low-achievement-orientation adolescents react to their children's lack of achievement concern by stressing independence and achievement. These reactions then influence subsequent achievement concerns and alter the stability of the need system, so that retesting will indicate low trait stability. Therefore, stability is in part dependent on the type and the consistency of socialization experiences.

The essential questions of generality and stability are unanswered. The next question is: what is known about people who are labeled as high in need for achievement, or high in the desire to achieve success? The clearest, most understandable correlates of achievement needs have been derived from the various theories of achievement motivation that are examined later in this chapter. However, there are several personality characteristics associated with achievement motivation that can be noted at this point. For example, there is evidence that, given the choice among tasks of high, intermediate, or low difficulty, tasks of intermediate difficulty are more attractive to individuals highly motivated to succeed than to those lower in achievement needs. In a similar vein, individuals high in achievement needs have been characterized as realistic and have occupational goals that are congruent with their abilities (Mahone, 1960; Morris, 1966). The desire for intermediate risk may indicate a preference for personal feedback or knowledge about oneself. This informational explanation is consistent with the high achiever's reported preference for business occupations, where feedback (profit) is immediately evident (McClelland, 1961; Meyer, Walker, and Litwin, 1961). In addition, individuals high in need for achievement apparently are better able to delay gratification (Mischel, 1961) and get higher grades in school than individuals low in achievement needs, if the grades are instrumental to long-term success (Raynor, 1970). Furthermore, they are thought of as hope rather than fear oriented. For example, there is some evidence that they are especially optimistic about their chances of success (Feather, 1965). Finally, individuals high in achievement needs take personal responsibility for success and generally perceive themselves as high in ability (Kukla, 1972). This self-attribution for success increases their feelings of worth and may account, in part, for their high self-concept reported by some investigators (Mukherjee and Sinha, 1970).

The Development of Achievement Needs

What, then, are the antecedents of the trait to strive for achievement? In Chapter 8 a distinction was drawn between nature and nurture, or genetic versus experiential factors that account for personality dispositions. Concerning achievement strivings, questions of inheritability have not been addressed because it seems intuitively so unlikely that genetic factors could contribute to this need state. Thus neither monozygotic versus dyzygotic twin studies of the type reviewed in Chapter 2 nor investigations that trace family histories have been conducted.

Maturational Factors

On the other hand, maturational factors are believed to contribute to the growth of achievement strivings. There appear to be universal processes that are necessary precursors of the tendency to strive for success. For example, it has been contended that the development of achievement needs requires that the child be able to "direct the pleasure or the disappointment after success and failure. . . . at the self, so that with success the child experiences pleasure about his competence and with failure experiences shame about his incompetence" (Heckhausen and Roelofsen, 1962, p. 378). This suggests that developing self-attribution is a necessary antecedent to achievement striving.

There has been speculation that some kind of primitive self-attributional process and resultant pride over accomplishment may be in evidence among children as young as two months. Watson (1966, 1967), for example, placed eight-week-old infants in a crib with an overhead mobile. When they turned their heads to the right, an electrical apparatus in their pillows was activated, causing the mobile to move. For other (control group) children the mobile was merely turned by the experimenter. Watson then measured the frequency of head-turning responses. Representative data (from Watson and Ramey, 1972) clearly revealed that children in the personal causality condition learned the "correct" response, for their head turning increased over time, while the head turning of the children unable to control the movement of the mobile remained relatively constant (see Fig. 16.2). But of greater importance in the present context was the finding that infants in the self-controlling con-

Figure 16.2   Pillow responses across two weeks for the two groups. (Reprinted from "Reactions to Response-Contingent Stimulation in Early Infancy," by J. S. Watson and C. T. Ramey, in *Merrill-Palmer Quarterly of Behavior and Development*, 1972, Vol. 18, p. 222, by permission of the Wayne State University Press.)

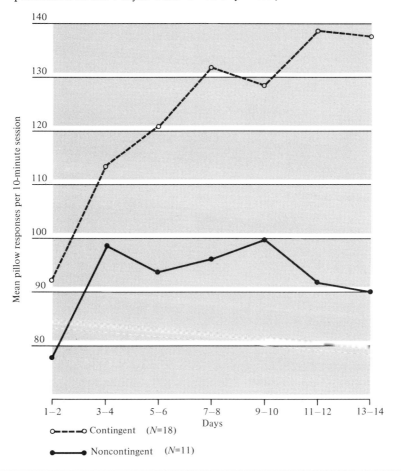

dition displayed more positive affect (smiling and cooing) when the mobile moved than children in the condition in which the mobile was controlled by the experimenter. This suggests that the children were able to perceive themselves as the cause of the accomplishment and that this increased their "pride."

A different cognitive analysis of achievement proposes three stages in the development of achievement strivings: (1) an intrapersonal competition, or autonomous, stage in which the child competes with itself; (2) an interpersonal competition, or social comparison, stage in which competition is with

A parent helping a child accomplish a task. It seems reasonable to believe that the amount of unsolicited help will influence later achievement strivings, but the empiri cal evidence is unclear in this regard. (Copyright © Susan Lapides, 1981)

others rather than with the self; and (3) an integration of the two previous stages (Veroff, 1969). Passage from stage 1 to stage 2 typically takes place when the child enters school and acquires the ability to use social norm information in making comparative judgments. Clearly, the suggestions of Heckhausen and Roelofsen and of Veroff are compatible with the stage position advocated by Piaget and others.

Social Learning

The American research tradition in developmental psychology has been to search for the experiential (social) determinants of personality and to focus on early parental interactions as the prime influence of later behavior. Two early social learning investigations provided the models for the bulk of subsequent research in the achievement area. Winterbottom (1953) obtained TAT achievement scores from a group of boys eight to ten years old and also interviewed their mothers to ascertain prior parental attitudes toward independence training. She reported that the mothers of sons high in achievement needs expected earlier independence (crossing the street without an adult, for instance) than did the mothers of boys scoring low in need for achievement.

A second influential study, conducted by Rosen and D'Andrade (1959), related the present behaviors of parents to the need achievement scores of their sons, rather than relying on retrospective reports. In an experimental setting, children were given tasks to complete, but parents could interact with the children and come to their aid. It was found that the parents of the highly achievement-oriented sons were more involved in the task, gave more reward and punishment, and had higher expectations than the parents of children scoring low in need for achievement. Therefore, the investigators contended that achievement training (doing something well), not independence training (doing something by oneself), is the important antecedent for the development of achievement needs.

Unfortunately, the high expectations spawned by these influential studies have not been met. Subsequent research has produced as many nonconfirmatory as confirmatory results regarding the alleged influence of achievement and/or independence training on the development of achievement needs. Thus, although the investigations of Winterbottom and of Rosen and D'Andrade were creative attempts at demonstrating that social learning is related to achievement needs, the hypothesized relationships remain to be clearly demonstrated. This search is obviously of great practical importance, for if antecedent experiences were identified, then, if one desired, achievement motivation could be promoted.

The lack of satisfactory conclusions should not be discouraging, for there are enormous complexities within the social learning research studies and many years of work will be required before definitive answers will be reached. For example, the encouragement of achievement and independence is likely to be intertwined with other aspects of child rearing, such as general permissiveness and restrictiveness, beliefs about the child's competence, physical affection and reward giving, general affective climate, warmth and trust in the home, and so on. All of these, at one time or another, have been found related to achievement needs by some investigators, while other researchers have reported no relations between these variables and achievement needs. In addition, as previously indicated, parental practices are responsive to the behavior of the child, so that parent-child interactions and rewards change over time. In sum, it is reasonable to believe that what takes place in the home influences the achievement dispositions of the child. But the pertinent research is plagued by a variety of problems; at present the social antecedents of the development of need for achievement have not been clearly demonstrated.

Atkinson's Theory of Achievement Motivation

The most dominant theory of achievement motivation was formulated by John Atkinson (1957, 1964). This theory was influenced by Miller's conflict model (introduced in Chapter 14) as well as by the cognitive theoretical approach. Achievement-oriented behavior was viewed by Atkinson as a conflict between approach and avoidance tendencies. Associated with every achievement-related action is the possibility of success (with the consequent emotion of pride) and the possibilty of failure (with the consequent emotion of shame). The strengths of these anticipated emotions determine whether an individual will approach or avoid achievement-oriented activities. That is, achievement behavior involves an emotional conflict between hopes for success and fears of failure. A significant feature of Atkinson's theory is that it can be stated in quantitative form. Quantitative formulations in the personality area are rare and, for this reason, it is especially instructive to consider this formulation in some detail. In so doing, we can reach a better understanding of the possibilities and limitations of simple mathematical models applied to particular personality issues.

Hope for Success

The tendency to approach an achievement-related goal (T_S) is seen as determined by three factors: the need for achievement, also known as the motive for success (M_S); the probability that one will be successful at the task (P_s); and the incentive value of success (I_s). It is postulated that these three components are multiplicatively related:

$$T_S = M_S \times P_s \times I_s$$

In this equation, M_S represents the relatively stable disposition to strive for success and, as indicated previously, is typically measured with the TAT. The probability of success, P_s, refers to a cognitive goal expectation, or the perceived likelihood of success. It is influenced by factors such as one's past history in the activity and the performance of others at the task. The third determinant of approach behavior, I_s (the incentive value of success), is believed to be inversely related to P_s; that is, $I_s = 1 - P_s$. Thus, the incentive value of success increases as P_s decreases. Atkinson contends that the incentive value of an achievement goal is an affect called *pride in accomplishment*. It is argued that greater pride is experienced following success at a difficult task than after success at an easy task. For example, little pride should be experienced over a grade of A in an easy course, but much pride would be felt if this grade were earned in a difficult course. Similarly, strong positive affect should be experienced when defeating a superior, rather than a poor, athletic team.

Fear of Failure

Achievement-related activities elicit positive affective anticipations because of past successful accomplishments and experienced pride, as well as negative affective anticipations learned from prior failures and experienced shame. Thus, both fear of failure and hope for success are aroused in achievement-related situations.

The determinants of fear of failure, or the tendency to avoid achievement tasks, are seen by Atkinson as analogous to those for hope of success. It was postulated that the tendency to avoid failure (T_{AF}) is a multiplicative function of the motive to avoid failure (M_{AF}), the probability of failure (P_f), and the negative incentive value of failure (I_f):

$$T_{AF} = M_{AF} \times P_f \times I_f$$

Just as M_S is conceived as a personality disposition to hope and strive for success, M_{AF} is considered a disposition to fear and avoid failure. Two environmental factors also influence the avoidance of achievement activities, namely, the probability of failure and the incentive value of failure. It is assumed that the incentive value of failure is a negative affect, shame. Greater shame is believed to be experienced following failure at an easy task than after failure at a difficult task. Therefore, I_f is conceived of as equal to 1 $- P_f$.

Finally, the resultant tendency to approach or avoid an achievement-oriented activity is postulated to be determined by the strength of the tendency to approach the task minus the strength of the tendency to avoid the task:

$$T_A = (M_S \times P_s \times I_s) - (M_{AF} \times P_f \times I_f).$$

Derivations of the Theory

We turn now from the abstract presentation of Atkinson's theory to some hypotheses derived from his conception and some empirical studies testing those hypotheses. Let us take the situation in which a person is confronted with a number of alternative choices varying in difficulty. For example, at an athletic event, a tennis player might choose to play against a competitor of equal skill, one who would be very difficult to beat, or one who should be fairly easy to beat. Or a student might have to decide among three sections of a course that vary in difficulty, such that the chances of getting an A or a B are very low in one section, intermediate in a second section, and almost a sure thing in the third section. Although some cynics might feel that most people would choose the easy section or the easy competitor, there are significant individual differences in the extent to which people select tasks of high, moderate, or low difficulty, that is, there are differences in their *level of aspiration* (Frank, 1935; Lewin, Dembo, Festinger, and Sears, 1944). The Atkinson model enables us to predict the choices that different people make.

Most importantly, according to the Atkinson model, attraction to a sure thing, to a long shot, or to a moderate challenge depends on the relationship between the levels of success motive and fear of failure. In Table 16.1, three levels of success motivation and fear of failure are indicated. For the "High" group ($M_S > M_{AF}$), hope for success is greater than fear of failure. An arbitrary value of 2 is given to M_S and 1 to M_{AF} to illustrate the derivation of hypotheses from the theoretical formulation. When the need for achievement is intermediate ($M_S = M_{AF}$), each motive is assigned a value of 1. For the "Low" group ($M_{AF} > M_S$), M_{AF} is given a value of 2 and M_S a value of 1. To indicate how the strength of resultant achievement motivation is affected by

Table 16.1 Strength of resultant achievement motivation related to task difficulty (probability of success) for hig intermediate, and low achieving groups

Motive Classification

High $(M_S > M_{AF})$							Intermediate $(M_S = M_{AF})$							Low $(M_{AF} > M_S)$						
M_S	P_s	I_s	M_{AF}	P_f	I_f	$T_A{}^*$	M_S	P_s	I_s	M_{AF}	P_f	I_f	T_A	M_S	P_s	I_s	M_{AF}	P_f	I_f	T_A

$2 \times .1 \times .9 - (1 \times .9 \times .1) = .09 \qquad 1 \times .1 \times .9 - (1 \times .9 \times .1) = 0 \qquad 1 \times .1 \times .9 - (2 \times .9 \times .1) = -.09$

$2 \times .3 \times .7 - (1 \times .7 \times .3) = .21 \qquad 1 \times .3 \times .7 - (1 \times .7 \times .3) = 0 \qquad 1 \times .3 \times .7 - (2 \times .7 \times .3) = -.21$

$2 \times .5 \times .5 - (1 \times .5 \times .5) = .25 \qquad 1 \times .5 \times .5 - (1 \times .5 \times .5) = 0 \qquad 1 \times .5 \times .5 - (2 \times .5 \times .5) = -.25$

$2 \times .7 \times .3 - (1 \times .3 \times .7) = .21 \qquad 1 \times .7 \times .3 - (1 \times .3 \times .7) = 0 \qquad 1 \times .7 \times .3 - (2 \times .3 \times .7) = -.21$

$2 \times .9 \times .1 - (1 \times .1 \times .9) = .09 \qquad 1 \times .9 \times .1 - (1 \times .1 \times .9) = 0 \qquad 1 \times .9 \times .1 - (2 \times .1 \times .9) = -.09$

* T_A = resultant achievement motivation.

task difficulty, different probabilities of success and failure are entered into the formula. Note that it is assumed that the probabilities of success and failure total one (e.g., .1 + .9, .7 + .3, .5 + .5).

Close analysis of Table 16.1 reveals that achievement motivation varies systematically as a function of motive level and probability of success or failure at the task. Among those considered high in achievement needs, resultant motivation (approach motivation minus avoidance motivation) is maximum at tasks of intermediate difficulty; that is, when $P_s = .50$. Furthermore, the strength of resultant motivation *decreases* symmetrically as P_s increases or decreases from the level of intermediate difficulty. Hence, these individuals should be most attracted to intermediate-difficulty tasks.

Turning attention to those who are relatively high in fear of failure, it can be seen that, among these individuals, motivation is most inhibited at tasks of intermediate difficulty. All achievement tasks are aversive in that they elicit predominantly fear (hence, the "negative" motivation). But tasks that are very easy, where one will not fail, and tasks that are very difficult, where failure does not elicit great shame, are mildly aversive in comparison to tasks of intermediate difficulty. Thus, these individuals should prefer easy or difficult activities.

An Experimental Test of the Model

We have seen that the Atkinson model predicts that high-achievement individuals will prefer tasks of intermediate difficulty and that low-achievement individuals will prefer tasks of high or low difficulty. How do these predictions measure up when compared with empirical data? An experiment by Atkinson and Litwin (1960) bears directly on this question. In this investigation, subjects attempted to toss rings over a peg. They were allowed to stand at varying distances from the peg and could change position (increase or decrease aspirations) following each toss. It was assumed that a position close to the target corresponded to a high probability of success and that P_s decreased as the distance from the peg increased. Thus, distance from the peg was the observable indicator of choice and of task difficulty. The subjects were classified into motive groups on the basis of individual differences measures, including the TAT. The data on choice behavior are shown in Fig. 16.3, indicating that intermediate task preference was greatest for the high-motive group, least for subjects highly fearful of failure, and intermediate for subjects high or low in both motives.

The data reported by Atkinson and Litwin are typical of most of the research in the study of risk preference. Three research questions that guided these studies, and their answers, are (see Meyer, Folkes, and Weiner, 1976):

1. Do individuals high in achievement needs exhibit a preference for tasks of intermediate difficulty? Definitely yes.
2. Do individuals low in achievement needs exhibit a preference for tasks that are comparatively easy or comparatively difficult? Apparently not.
3. Do individuals high in achievement needs exhibit a greater preference for

Figure 16.3   Percentage of ring-toss attempts as a function of distance from the peg. (Adapted from Atkinson and Litwin, 1960, p. 55. Copyright 1960 by the American Psychological Association. Reprinted by permission.)

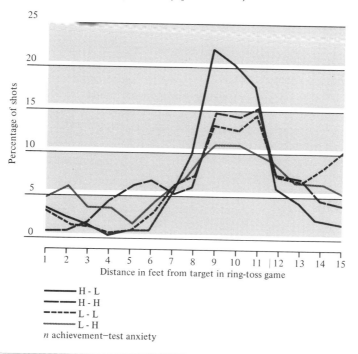

tasks of intermediate difficulty than individuals low in achievement needs? Most likely yes.

In sum, all individuals seem to prefer intermediate difficulty, although this preference is somewhat more evident among individuals highly motivated to succeed. These data pose some problems for Atkinson's theory, but they nevertheless tend to support the broad hypothesis that groups classified according to strength of achievement needs will display differential task preferences.

An Alternative Explanation

Atkinson's prediction of disparate personality-group preferences is based on the belief that choice among achievement tasks follows the principle of maximization of positive affect, for the highly achievement oriented person, and minimization of negative affect, for individuals low in achievement needs. That is, anticipatory emotions and hedonistic concerns determine which tasks one will attempt to perform. As indicated in Chapter 14, most psychologists consider hedonism to be the main source of motivation and behavior.

An alternative interpretation of risk-preference appeals more to informational and self-concept principles than to hedonism, reflecting the trend toward cognitive explanations of action that is now prevalent in psychology. Research has demonstrated that outcomes at tasks of intermediate difficulty provide performers with the most information about their efforts and capabilities. There are logical reasons why this is the case. Selection of easy tasks typically results in success and the outcome is ascribed to the ease of the task. In a similar manner, selection of very difficult tasks generally results in failure, with blame placed on the characteristics of the task. Thus, selection of very easy or very difficult tasks usually confirms our knowledge about the external world. Success on tasks at which almost everyone succeeds and failure on tasks at which almost everyone does poorly tell very little about the skills of the individual engaged in those tasks. However, tasks of intermediate difficulty are just as likely to produce success as failure, and performance at such tasks provides information about the efforts and abilities of the person undertaking them. From this perspective, differential preference for tasks of varying difficulty between groups differing in achievement needs indicates disparate desires for personal feedback and self-evaluation. Of course, it is quite functional and adaptive to have a realistic view of oneself.

To disentangle hedonic (pride-shame) versus informational (knowledge of self) determinants of risk preference and choice, Trope (1975) gave subjects a choice between tasks that varied in difficulty as well as in diagnosticity, or the information gained about one's ability after task performance. *Diagnosticity* is obtained by taking the difference between proportions of individuals designated as high or low in ability who succeed at the task. Thus, for example, a task at which 90% of a high-ability group and 60% of a low-ability group succeed has greater diagnosticity (30%) than a task accomplished by 52% versus 48% of the individuals respectively high or low in ability (4% diagnosticity). One can learn much more about one's level of ability when

Figure 16.4   Mean number of items chosen from test varying in expected diagnostic value. (Trope, 1975, p. 1008. Copyright 1975 by the American Psychological Association. Reprinted by permission.)

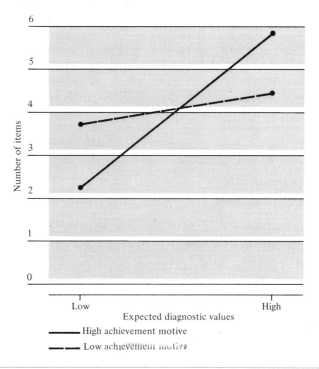

the former task is undertaken. But in this case the task high in diagnosticity, where an average of 75% [(90% + 60%)/2] of individuals succeed, is less intermediate in difficulty than the task low in diagnosticity, where an average of 50% [(52% + 48%)/2] of the persons undertaking the task are successful.

In this investigation it was found that when task choices varied in degree of diagnosticity as well as in difficulty, subjects both high and low in achievement needs preferred the highly diagnostic tasks (see Fig. 16.4). However, this preference was significantly greater among high-achievement subjects. Thus, the two personality groups apparently differ in their information-seeking desires, with the high-achievement group more desirous of diagnostic information so that they can ascertain their relative level of ability.

Attribution Theory and Achievement Strivings

The discussion of choice behavior called attention to the informational or self-evaluative aspects of task selection. It is now apparent that other aspects of achievement motivation are also influenced by cognitive or inferential processes. Foremost among the mental events that affect achievement-related behaviors are causal attributions.

Causal Attributions

Causal attributions in achievement-related contexts refer to beliefs about the reasons for one's success or failure. There are, of course, many possible reasons for a positive or a negative achievement outcome, but research has shown that four factors are perceived as most responsible for success and failure. These factors are ability, effort, task ease or difficulty, and luck. That is, if one succeeds, then the outcome is ascribed to high ability, hard work, the ease of the task, or good luck. In a similar manner, failure is generally ascribed to low ability, lack of effort, a difficut task, or bad luck. Of the four causes, ability and effort are particularly salient. That is, outcomes typically depend on what we *can* do and how hard we *try*. Other, less-used attributions for success and failure include the bias of a supervisor or teacher, mood, illness, fatigue, help or hindrance from others, and home environment.

The perceived causes of success and failure have been incorporated within a few basic causal dimensions which describe the underlying properties of causes (Weiner, 1974, 1979). One dimension, which will be examined in some detail in the following chapter, is labeled *locus of causality*. Causes are perceived as either internal (within the person) or external (in the environment). For example, ability and effort are person causes, whereas task difficulty, help from others, and luck are among the environmental determinants of an outcome. A second dimension of causality has been identified as the *stability* or constancy of a cause. Some causes, such as aptitude, the ease of a task, and conditions in the home, are typically perceived as relatively enduring or stable. On the other hand, causes such as effort expenditure, luck, mood, and illness are generally perceived as subject to momentary or periodic fluctuation. Still a third dimension of causality is the *controllability* of the cause. For example, how much effort we expend is subject to personal influence, whereas luck and illness generally are not. In sum, classifications of causes have been developed that allow each causal factor to be placed within a multidimensional framework.

The Consequences of Causal Attributions

It has been demonstrated that causal attributions are linked to specific psychological consequences. The *locus* of a causal attribution influences affective reactions to success and failure. If, for example, one attributes success to such internal causes as ability or effort, then more pride and self-enhancement are experienced than if that success is attributed to external factors like task ease or good luck. The *stability* of a cause influences the subjective expectancy of success at the task, or how likely the person feels that future success is within reach. For example, if a previous failure is ascribed to lack of effort or bad luck, then future success might be anticipated. But if failure is attributed to a

Figure 16.5  An attributional model of achievement strivings.

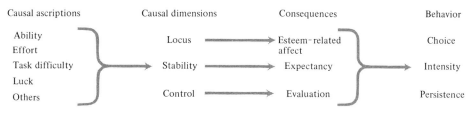

fixed cause such as "no mathematical aptitude," then future failure will be anticipated. The dimension of control is particularly important in interpersonal evaluations. For example, if you are a member of a team and you do poorly for reasons within your control, like lack of effort, then your teammates will be angry with you. On the other hand, poor performance due to an uncontrollable cause, like illness, often elicits sympathy from others.

In sum, causal attributions have many consequences that influence achievement strivings (see Fig. 16.5). Of particular interest is the fact that attributions influence the expectancy of success and failure as well as the affective consequences of attainment or nonattainment of a goal. In the previous section of this chapter it was indicated that Atkinson also specified that expectancy (P_s) and affect (I_s) are the prime determinants of action. Thus, the attributional analysis of causality can be linked with the approach advocated by Atkinson.

Achievement Needs and Causal Attributions

There is evidence suggesting that individuals differing in their level of achievement needs have disparate causal biases or explanations for their success and failure (see review in Weiner, 1979). Persons highly motivated to achieve ascribe success to themselves (their own ability and effort) to a greater extent than do individuals low in achievement needs. Thus, they experience more pride in accomplishment and build up a relatively high self-concept of ability. And, given failure, persons high in achievement motivation tend to ascribe the outcome to a lack of effort, whereas those low in achievement motivation perceive lack of ability as the salient cause. Thus, in achievement-related contexts persons motivated to achieve success believe that effort and outcome go together: high effort produces success and low effort gives rise to failure. This covariation is not exhibited by persons low in achievement need.

It therefore appears that causal attributions may mediate the associations between achievement needs and various indexes of performance. For example, individuals high in achievement needs exhibit more tolerance for frustration and do not quit in the face of failure. This could be due to their tendency to ascribe failure to lack of effort, which is unstable and under personal control. They believe they can succeed if they persist with greater effort. On the other hand, persons low in achievement needs tend to quit in the face of failure. This may be mediated by their tendency to attribute failure to low ability, which is both stable and not subject to volitional control.

In one study demonstrating the influence of causal attributions on performance intensity, Weiner and Sierad (1975) experimentally severed the association between achievement needs and causal ascriptions. Subjects in an experimental condition were induced to blame failure on a drug that was really a placebo. It was found that attributions of failure to this external source augmented the subsequent performance of individuals low in achievement needs. It was reasoned that such attribution to an external source,

Figure 16.6   Mean increments in performance speed (number of digit-symbol substitutions) relative to pretest performance. (Weiner and Sierad, 1975, p. 419.)

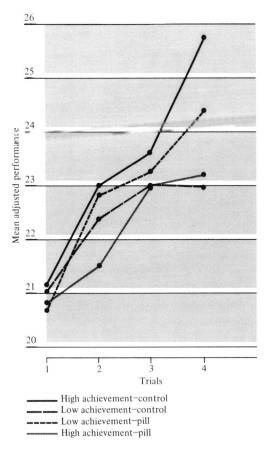

rather than to low ability, lowered their amount of experienced incompetence under failure, thus enhancing performance. On the other hand, in this condition the performance of persons high in achievement needs suffered due to the fact that failure was now ascribed to a relatively stable source (the believed enduring effect of the drug) rather than to a lack of effort. This had one consequence of lowering the expectancy of success, which in turn impeded performance (see Fig. 16.6).

Achievement Needs Among Females

In Chapter 8 we briefly discussed the disparate sex types and roles held by males and females. It was stated that in our culture males are generally perceived as task or achievement oriented, while females are seen as more inclined toward social activities.

Research in achievement has indeed uncovered sex differences, starting with disparities discovered by psychologists who tried to develop adequate measures of achievement needs. For an instrument assessing motive strength to have validity, it must reflect temporary arousal states of the organism. That is, like a thermometer, the instrument should register a higher reading if the "motive temperature" is high. Achievement motive arousal, accomplished through failure induction or special instructions (e.g., "This is a test"), indeed generates higher TAT need-achievement scores as compared with responses under nonarousal conditions. However, this has proved true only for males; females have not exhibited motive score differences in arousal versus neutral conditions. Therefore, it was believed that the TAT motive measure was not valid for females; as a result, female subjects tended to be neglected in early achievement research. Of course, some studies did include females and combined the data from both sexes, but a large number of research investigations either did not test females or reported systematic data for male, but not for female, subjects.

It is uncertain why the few motive arousal studies were unsuccessful for women and why males appear to yield more systematic data than females in studies of achievement motivation. Achievement may be a more complex motivational system for females than for males. This is likely to be true for any number of reasons. For example, because of cultural inhibitions and social norms, females at one time were generally restricted to the home. Furthermore, female success has traditionally been achieved through the spouse's occupation and personal success was achieved, not through movement up the occupational hierarchy, but rather through home management. But little work was conducted to substantiate these intuitively reasonable suppositions and, with the current change in the role of women, these hypotheses may no longer be as relevant as they once were.

Another plausible explanation for these findings was offered by Matina Horner (1968), who postulated a female motive to "avoid success," or *fear of success*. She suggested that success arouses the threat of social rejection or

Sara Simeoni of Italy winning the Olympic medal for high jumping at the 1980 Moscow Olympics. Pride in accomplishment is one of the indicators of high achievement strivings. (Patrice Habans/Sygma)

fears concerning perceived lack of femininity in women. These fears inhibit achievement striving. To test her notion, Horner (1968) had male and female subjects write brief stories to this cue: "At the end of the first-term final, Anne finds herself at the top of her medical school class." Horner found much greater fear-of-success imagery in the female than in the male responses. For example, women tended to write that, "Because of being the top student, the boys in the class would not ask Anne out for a date." These data caused immediate excitement among psychologists and laypeople. They meshed with the rise of the feminist movement and were immediately incorporated into courses on the psychology of women. But the enthusiasm was more a symptom of the void of knowledge about achievement strivings among women and the desire for understanding, rather than a consequence of establishment of a scientific truth. Subsequent research revealed that males exhibit as much fear of success in projective imagery as females (see Tresemer, 1974). Thus, the findings first reported by Horner are now very much in doubt (Zuckerman and Wheeler, 1975). However, these investigations were among the first to call attention to the ambivalence associated with achievement success, as well as the perceived "costs" of success for women.

There are additional interesting sex differences reported in the literature on achievement strivings that do appear reliable. Females generally have lower expectancy of success than males (Crandall, 1969). This is the case in school situations even though females tend to have higher grade-point averages than males. How such biases are formed and what can be done to alter them are central questions to be answered in the study of achievement motivation.

Achievement Motivation and Economic Development

Numerous sociological and anthropological investigations of achievement motivation have gone on outside the laboratory. Foremost among these was an attempt by McClelland (1961) to relate achievement motivation to economic growth.

The initial influences on McClelland's analysis of economic growth were Winterbottom's data relating early independence training to the development of achievement needs and the speculations of Max Weber (1904) concerning the Protestant reformation. Weber noted that the Protestant revolt emphasized the importance of self-reliance and productivity. Furthermore, because of religious beliefs, the results of one's labors could not be spent self-indulgently. Thus, profits were reinvested, resulting in further prosperity.

McClelland perceived a relationship between these notions and the work on achievement motivation. He suggested that Protestant values produced early independence training that, in turn, promoted need for achievement and economic development. This hypothesized sequence is shown in Fig. 16.7, which indicates four relationships: (1) Protestantism and early independence training; (2) early independence training and need for achievement; (3) need for achievement and economic development; and (4) Protestantism and economic development. Of these, the alleged relationship between achievement need and economic development has produced the most extensive, novel, and controversial findings.

Figure 16.7   Hypothetical relationship between self-reliance values and economic development.

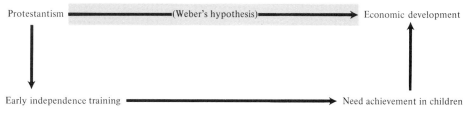

Figure 16.8 Mean frequency of achievement imagery in children's readers and the patent index in the United States, 1800–1950. (Adapted from de Charms and Moeller, 1962, p. 139. Used by permission.)

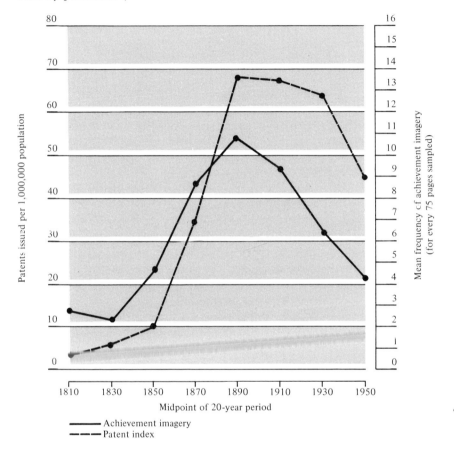

The TAT assessment procedure originated by Murray has a unique advantage in that it is applicable to any prose material. Thus, to examine the relationship between achievement needs and economic growth, McClelland scored prose material, such as children's readers, speeches, folktales, and songs, for achievement needs. These scores were then related to available indexes of economic activity, such as consumption of electrical power, quantity of imports, and number of independent artisans within a society. Data from a wide array of cultures and times, including Tudor England and ancient Greece, provided evidence that increments in need for achievement, inferred from the scoring of the various prose material, precedes economic development, while decreases in need for achievement are predictive of economic decline.

You might be wondering, by this time, about the achievement motivation in U.S. culture. Figure 16.8 indicates that people's achievement needs in America, ascertained from children's readers, increased from 1800 to 1910. Since 1910 the indicators of achievement concerns have steadily decreased. Does this hint that our economy is also going to decline? Figure 16.8 also reveals that the patent index, one indicator of unique accomplishment and achievement needs, and an economic stimulant, is declining as well.

Achievement Change Programs

Inasmuch as high achievement motivation is instrumental to personal success and economic growth, it has generally been considered a positive trait. Thus, high achievement–low achievement as a personality dimension is related to another dimension which might be broadly labeled as winner-loser. Of course, the negative consequences of abnormally high achievement desires, including heart attacks, personal stress, and disregard for others, have been frequently documented. But within the range of normal behavior, concern with success is highly valued in our culture.

Because of this value, attempts have been initiated to increase achievement strivings among individuals who are low in achievement needs or highly fearful of failure. Two quite disparate change programs have been established. To increase achievement concerns, McClelland and Winter (1969) designed a three- to six-week training course in which participants become acquainted with thoughts and actions associated with achievement behavior. They learn to score the TAT for achievement motivation and are taught the beneficial consequences of intermediate risk taking and a future perspective. In addition, the participants undergo a program of self-study in which they describe their life goals, values, self-image, and so forth. The training program assists in the establishment and setting of career goals. These program inputs all take place in a warm and permissive atmosphere in the company of others who then become part of a new reference group. McClelland (1965) described the program as eclectic, using all the psychological principles believed to be effective in behavioral change, including rewards and punishments and suggestions from prestige sources.

Positive results of this program have been reported for underachieving boys (Kolb, 1965) and businessmen (McClelland and Winter, 1969). For example, Kolb (1965) had underachieving boys participate in an achievement change program at summer camp. The participating students had IQs above 120, but were performing below average in school. The effectiveness of the program, assessed by grade-point average, is shown in Fig. 16.9. In addition to being classified in the experimental (training) or control group, the students were subdivided according to their socioeconomic status (SES). Figure 16.9 indicates that both participating and nonparticipating students exhibited unexpected increases in subsequent grade-point average, but that the higher grades were maintained only by students in the experimental group within

Figure 16.9   School grade averages in pretest and followup years as a function of socioeconomic class and participation in the achievement training program. (Kolb, 1965, p. 789. Used by permission.)

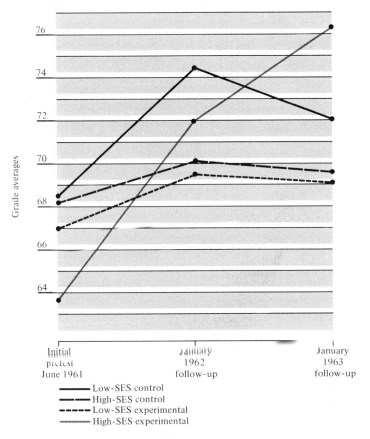

the high-SES group. Presumably, returning to peers who did not share achievement values nullified the gains of the boys in the low-SES group.

In spite of these encouraging findings, the effectiveness of such change programs remains in doubt because many cases of no change, relative to a control group not receiving the program, have been reported. Thus, further evidence is required before this intervention technique can be widely applied. An alternative and much less ambitious achievement change procedure has grown from work on causal attributions. If causal ascriptions for success and failure determine achievement strivings, then it logically follows that a change in these beliefs should produce a change in achievement behavior. The general approach in these studies has been to teach individuals with school problems that achievement outcomes are under their own control. More specifically, it has been the goal of these programs to lead subjects to attribute failure to a lack of effort rather than to the absence of ability. As previously indicated, because ability is a fixed and uncontrollable cause, ascriptions of failure to ability are particularly dysfunctional and debilitating.

One exemplary investigation in this area was conducted by Dweck (1975). Her subjects were eight- to thirteen-year-olds who had been independently identified by their teacher, school psychologist, and principal as having a high expectancy of failure and as displaying performance decrements in failure situations. Dweck's method was to verbalize to subjects that failure during a series of training sessions was due to lack of effort. During these training trials, 20 percent of the responses resulted in failure. The attributional training procedure was compared to the popular program of inducing 100 percent success (without any causal attributions) and, in so doing, supposedly increasing self-confidence. Dweck's data, shown in Fig. 16.10, revealed the efficacy and value of attributional training and its superiority over the success-only treatment. Following training, only the attributional treatment group did not show decrements in responding in the face of failure. However, the interpretation of these findings is somewhat complicated by the fact that the attributional group received partial reinforcement, which might have contributed to their relatively better performance (see Chapter 6).

Figure 16.10   Mean percentage decrease in correct problems. (Dweck, 1975, p. 82. Copyright 1975 by the American Psychological Association. Reprinted by permission.)

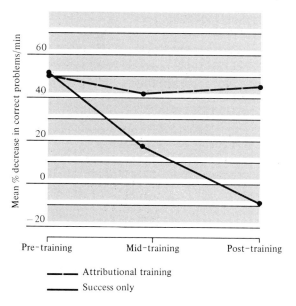

Summary   Achievement striving is one of the central sources of motivation in our culture. This chapter has examined a number of subareas within this topic which relate directly to earlier chapters. There has been concern over the measurement and the personality correlates of the need for achievement; studies have been devoted to its social and cognitive antecedents; experiments have examined the dynamics of achievement striving; and there have been attempts to alter achievement needs. Hence, the components of the study of personality—development, measurement, structure, and dynamics—have all been represented in this chapter. In addition, various theories of achievement motivation have been formulated which make use of mathematical models and cognitive variables such as causal attributions. Finally, achievement motivation has been related to gender and to economic development.

Specific Points

1. Henry Murray played an important role in the study of achievement needs by defining the achievement motive and specifying the actions that it instigates.
2. Need for achievement is typically assessed with a projective technique, the Thematic Apperception Test (TAT). However, this measure has a number of shortcomings, such as low internal consistency.
3. The generality of need for achievement as a trait remains uncertain, and there is only scattered evidence that the trait is relatively enduring.
4. Among the personality correlates of the need for achievement is the tendency for individuals high in achievement needs to (a) prefer intermediate-difficulty tasks, (b) be realistic in their aspirations, and (c) desire performance feedback.
5. Cognitive maturational factors, including self-attribution of success and integration of competitive stages, appear to be necessary precursors for the development of achievement strivings.
6. The effects of early socialization practices, such as early independence training and stress on good performance, have not been convincingly demonstrated as necessary antecedents for the development of high achievement needs.
7. Atkinson proposed a mathematical model of achievement motivation in which achievement tendencies are determined by the difference between hope for success and fear of failure. Hope for success is a product of the need for achievement multiplied by the probability and incentive value of success; fear of failure is a product of anxiety about failure multiplied by the probability and incentive value of failure.
8. Atkinson's mathematical model leads to the prediction that individuals high in achievement needs prefer tasks of intermediate difficulty, while those low in achievement needs are attracted to easy or difficult tasks. Only the former prediction has been confirmed.
9. Studies on *diagnosticity*, or the information gained about one's ability

following task performance, have shown that individuals highly motivated to succeed are especially desirous of feedback about their abilities.

10. *Causal attributions* for success or failure are important determinants of achievement striving. Three basic properties of causes—locus, stability, and controllability—influence, respectively, esteem-related affective reactions, expectancy of success, and evaluation by others. Individuals differing in achievement needs have different causal biases.

11. A fear of success, exhibited by both sexes, indicates that achievement success has costs associated with it. Among the sex differences in achievement contexts is the finding that females have lower expectancies of success in school than males.

12. There is some evidence that increments in need for achievement precede the positive economic growth of a society.

13. A variety of achievement-change programs have been devised, offering some promise that achievement needs may be enhanced. One such program focuses attention on changing attributions for failure from lack of ability to insufficient effort.

Thought Questions

1. Do you think that achievement strivings tend to be expressed across a variety of situations or are specifically channeled into a few activities? Can you think of individuals who meet each of these descriptions?

2. *What Makes Sammy Run?* is the title of a novel describing a highly ambitious young man who needs constant success to maintain his self-esteem. What kinds of behavior might be expected of him in risk situations and in the kinds of tasks used by Atkinson and Trope?

3. When you do well on a test, what attributions do you generally make? How about when you do poorly? Do these influence your feelings and your expectations?

4. How might differences in male and female sex roles produce differences in achievement motivation?

Perceived Freedom and
Personal Responsibility

17 In his provocative book *Beyond Freedom and Dignity,* Skinner (1971) contended that we must give up the illusion of freedom and admit that behavior is controlled by reinforcements (see Chapter 6). According to the principles of operant reinforcement, *external* stimuli paired with rewards are responsible for behavior. For example, if food follows the pressing of a lever, then the appearance of that lever initiates a particular chain of behaviors. If we give up the illusion of freedom, Skinner argued, then our knowledge of behavioral engineering can be used to control human behavior for the betterment of society. But, Skinner went on to state, people refuse to give up this illusion and the false belief that we are autonomous actors, possessing free will and deserving credit for our actions. He concluded that, in order for society to survive, this conviction must be replaced with the acceptance of external control.

Others besides Skinner feel that the belief in freedom has negative implications, perhaps because freedom implies the converse of determinism. Freedom is associated with concepts such as self-determination, spontaneity, or anything that is unpredictable. Conversely, most psychologists advocate that behavior is determined. That is, for any given action there are specified antecedents, and in any given situation it can be argued that the displayed behavior "must" have occurred. Indeed, this belief, which was most clearly pointed out in Chapter 4 on the psychoanalytic approach to personality, is the foundation for scientific advancement and prediction.

The issue of free will versus determinism is an old and persistent philosophical problem which neither philosophers nor psychologists have been able to solve satisfactorily. Consideration of the different ways with which this complex problem has been dealt would take us beyond the scope of this chapter. However, what is directly pertinent are the psychological effects of people's *perceptions* of their freedom of choice. It is evident that the notion of freedom has positive connotations and that individuals do experience free will, or the perceived choice to engage in any one of a number of possible actions. In this chapter we examine this belief system and the wide variety of behaviors affected by perceived free will and self-determination. The chapter will examine predominantly the self-perception of freedom, but also will consider other-perception and how the assignment of responsibility to others influences reward, punishment, and helping.

Perceived Freedom

Locus of Control

Much of the current concern in the field of personality with the notions of freedom and self-responsibility grew from the concept of *locus of control* (Rotter, 1966) and a distinction between *internal* and *external* control (see Chapter 6). Locus of control refers to the perceived influence that one has on the attainment of reinforcement. It has been postulated as a dimension of personality; some persons perceive greater personal (internal) control, while others perceive the situation (external control) as more salient. Rotter (1966, p. 1) defined such internality and externality as follows:

When a reinforcement is perceived . . . as . . . not being entirely contingent upon his action, then, in our culture, it is typically perceived as the result of luck, chance, fate, as under the control of powerful others, or as unpredictable because of the great complexity of forces surrounding him. When the event is interpreted in this way by an individual, we have labeled this a belief in external *control. If the person perceives that the event is contingent upon his own behavior or his own relatively permanent characteristics, we have termed this a belief in* internal *control.*

Similarly, Lefcourt (1976) cited a passage from an interview in Oscar Lewis's (1961, p. 171) classic book on Mexican culture to illustrate the thoughts of a person with an external locus of control:

To me, one's destiny is controlled by a mysterious hand that moves all things. Only for the select, do things turn out as planned; to those of us who are born to be tamale eaters, heaven sends only tamales. We plan and plan and some little thing happens to wash it all away.

Like once, I decided to try and save and I said to Paula, "Old girl, put away this money so that some day we'll have a little pile." When we had ninety pesos laid away, pum! my father got sick and I had to give all to him for doctors and medicine. It was the only time I had helped him and the only time I had tried to save! I said to Paula, "There you are! Why should we save if someone gets sick and we have to spend it all!" Sometimes I even think that savings bring on illness! That's why I firmly believe that some of us are born to be poor.

A number of psychologists have asked whether there are individual differences in beliefs about internal versus external control. Do some individuals have an internal orientation, while others, as illustrated in the above passage, believe that events and rewards are externally controlled?

Assessment procedure.   There are many scales designed to assess the perception of events as internally versus externally controlled, for both children and adults. However, the most frequently used instrument is a 29-item self-report inventory (see Rotter, 1966). This test, called the *Internal-External Control Scale (I-E scale)*, has a forced-choice format with an internal belief pitted directly against an external belief for each item. The items on the scale are classified in six general subcategories on the basis of type of need portrayed and characteristics of described goals. The six categories are academic recognition, social recognition, love and affection, dominance, social-political beliefs, and life philosophy. Some sample items and their keyed responses (italic letters represent externality choices) are:

1. *a.* Many of the unhappy things in people's lives are partly due to bad luck.
   b. People's misfortunes result from the mistakes they make.
2. a. The idea that teachers are unfair to students is nonsense.
   b. Most students don't realize the extent to which grades are influenced by accidental happenings.

It is evident that the questions on the scale are very broad. As Rotter (1975, p. 62) indicated, "[The scale] was developed not as an instrument . . . to allow for a very high prediction of some specific situation, such as achievement or political behavior, but rather to allow for a low degree of prediction of behavior across a wide variety of potential situations." Typically, the situational cues in a setting most influence beliefs and behavior. However, generalized beliefs about control are also presumed, to a lesser extent, to influence a person's specific beliefs and actions.

Personality correlates.   Phares (1976, p. 60) has stated that:

The best single validity of the I-E scale would undoubtedly be evidence showing that internals are more active, alert, or directive in attempting to control and manipulate their environment than are externals. Since locus of control refers to expectancies for control over one's surroundings, a higher level of coping activity would be anticipated from internals.

A reasonable amount of evidence supports this position. In one series of studies, Seeman and Evans (1962) and Seeman (1963) reported, respectively, on information seeking and retention of personally relevant information among institutionalized individuals. It was found that, among hospitalized tuberculosis patients, individuals classified as internals knew more about their illness and asked doctors more questions than patients who were external in locus of control. In addition, prisoners who were internals retained more information pertinent to parole than did externals. In sum, among both patients and prisoners, the behavior displayed by those high in internal control was instrumental to improving their life situations. On the other hand, it appeared that among those low in personal control, the acquisition of information was seen as less likely to serve any useful function.

Other investigators have studied the differential cognitive activity of internals and externals. For example, Wolk and DuCette (1974) presented subjects with protocols to be scanned for errors. It was found that internals were better at incidental learning (remembering the material that had been scanned) and at finding errors. In general, theorists in this area have contended that "the cognitive functioning of internals should enhance their personal effectiveness as compared to externals. And it apparently does" (Phares, 1976, p. 65). It is not at all clear, however, how these disparate dispositions come about, inasmuch as there is little pertinent developmental data. As a result, developmental antecedents of this trait offer a rich opportunity for study.

One of the difficulties faced by researchers in this area is related to the trait-situation controversy examined in Chapter 13. It is quite evident that beliefs about personal control may vary from situation to situation. For example, one might perceive oneself to be personally responsible for positive outcomes in affiliative contexts, yet believe that success in academic affairs is a matter of good luck or help from others. These issues have been relatively neglected by researchers in locus of control and are just beginning to be seriously addressed (see Lefcourt et al., 1979).

Personal Causation

One investigator (de Charms, 1968, pp. 273–274) has proposed a distinction between an *origin* and a *pawn* which is very similar to the differentiation of internal and external control. Nevertheless, de Charms's approach has led to different types of research and appears to be broader in focus than the locus of control work.

We shall use the terms "Origin" and "Pawn" as shorthand terms to connote the distinction between forced and free. An Origin is a person who perceives his behavior as determined by his own choosing; a Pawn is a person who perceives his behavior as determined by external forces beyond his control. . . .

The personal aspect is more important motivationally than objective facts. If the person feels he is an Origin, that is more important in predicting his behavior than any objective indicators of coercion. . . . An Origin has strong feelings of personal causation, a feeling that the locus of causation of effects in his environment lies within himself. . . . A Pawn has a feeling that causal forces beyond his control, or personal forces residing in others, or in the

Humans prefer to be origins rather than pawns, self directed rather than directed by others. In addition, the loss of freedom creates a force to restore that freedom. (Burk Uzzle/Magnum Photos, Inc.)

physical environment, determine his behavior. This constitutes a strong feeling of powerlessness and ineffectiveness.

The concept of origin is associated with behaviors undertaken for their own sake (rather than for the sake of others or an external reward), with freedom, and with the perception of situations as challenging. Conversely, the concept of pawn is linked with extrinsically motivated behavior, restriction of movement, and the perception of situations as threatening. de Charms advocates that it is "better" to be (feel) like an origin than like a pawn.

Experiments have been conducted to manipulate situational factors that influence feelings of being an origin or a pawn. The general approach in these experiments is to induce freedom in one experimental condition and constraint in a comparison condition. For example, in one investigation children were given the task of building models. In the pawn condition, the subjects were told exactly what to do; in the origin condition, they proceeded in any manner they wanted. Subsequent questionnaire data revealed that the origins enjoyed the task more and were more interested in continuing the activity than were the pawns.

Training programs have also been developed by de Charms to augment feelings of being an origin. It is believed that an increase in origin experiences will also enhance achievement strivings. Such training programs are similar to those established by McClelland and Winter (see Chapter 16), although they place greater emphasis on accepting personal responsibility.

One large-scale program of origin training was conducted with black teachers in inner-city schools (de Charms, 1976), in which the effects of the teachers' origin training on the behavior of the *pupils* was examined. It was hypothesized that feelings of being an origin would be transmitted to pupils, in part by allowing students greater freedom of choice. It was anticipated that as a result, the students would enjoy school more and demonstrate increased learning. The data did substantiate the premise that origin-trained teachers were more accepting in the classroom and that their pupils were also more likely to perceive themselves as origins than students in the classrooms of teachers who had not received origin training.

Intrinsic Versus Extrinsic Motivation

Teachers often feel that students do their best, not because of *intrinsic* interest in the material, but rather because of the course grade, or the *extrinsic* motivator that is contingent on their efforts. The concepts of intrinsic and extrinsic motivation are nicely illustrated in an experiment conducted by Harry Harlow (1953). Recall that Harlow's investigations of surrogate mothers were presented earlier in the text (see Chapter 8).

Harlow wanted to demonstrate that monkeys engage in activities that do not reduce basic drives. Such a demonstration would have contradicted the then-dominant drive and need reduction theories advocated by Freud and others. Indeed, Harlow was able to prove that monkeys can learn a complex set of responses to receive a mechanical puzzle, a reward with no apparent biological value. Of greater importance in the present context, the monkeys engaged in endless puzzle-receiving and solving trials. Then new conditions were introduced. Following each puzzle solution, Harlow gave the monkeys a food reward. After this was done for a number of trials, the food was withheld. When this occurred, the monkeys ceased to engage in responses that produced a new puzzle to be solved. That is, the intrinsic attractiveness of the puzzles was no longer sufficient to instigate behavior once food had been introduced. After that point, the monkeys only played with and solved the puzzles in order to receive the extrinsic reward.

A fable reported by Ausubel (1948) provides an amusing illustration of the distinction between intrinsic and extrinsic motivation.

In a little Southern town where the Klan was riding again, a Jewish tailor had the temerity to open his little shop on the main street. To drive him out of the town the Kleagle of the Klan sent a gang of little ragamuffins to annoy him. Day after day they stood at the entrance of his shop. "Jew! Jew!" they hooted at him. The situation looked serious for the tailor. He took the matter so much to heart that he began to brood and spent sleepless nights over it. Finally out of desperation he evolved a plan.

The following day, when the little hoodlums came to jeer at him, he came to the door and said to them, "From today on anybody who calls me "Jew" will get a dime from me." Then he put his hand in his pocket and gave each boy a dime.

Delighted with their booty, the boys came back the following day and began to shrill, "Jew! Jew!" The tailor came out smiling. He put his hand in his pocket and gave each of the boys a nickel, saying, "A dime is too much—I can only afford a nickel today." The boys went away satisfied because, after all, a nickel was money, too.

However, when they returned the next day to hoot at him, the tailor gave them only a penny each.

"Why do we get only a penny today?" they yelled.

"That's all I can afford."

"But two days ago you gave us a dime, and yesterday we got a nickel. It's not fair, mister."

"Take it or leave it. That's all you're going to get!"

"Do you think we're going to call you "Jew" for one lousy penny?"

"So don't!"

And they didn't.[1]

The observations of Harlow and anecdotes like the story of the tailor have been incorporated in a conception called *cognitive evaluation theory* (Deci, 1975). Deci contended that when someone receives extrinsic rewards for engaging in intrinsically motivating activities, there may be a change in beliefs about why one is engaging in the activity. Using the language of locus of control theory, perceived causation may change from internal (intrinsic interest) to external (the extrinsic reward initiates the activity).

An experiment by Lepper, Greene, and Nisbett (1973) demonstrated this phenomenon in the laboratory. In this study, nursery school children interested in a drawing task were selected as the subjects. The children were asked to perform the drawing task under one of three experimental conditions. In an *expected-reward* condition, the subjects were told beforehand that they would receive a Good Player Certificate if they played with the experimental materials. In an *unexpected-reward* condition, the subjects received the same reward, but had no knowledge that they were going to receive the certificate until the drawing activity was completed. Finally, in a control condition, the reward was neither expected nor received.

One or two weeks later the children were given the opportunity to perform the drawing task again during one of their regular classroom hours. The subjects were free to engage in the drawing activity or in other games that were available. No rewards were mentioned, and the teachers did not encourage play with any particular material. To assess the dependent variable (time spent with the drawing task), researchers secretly observed the children in their free-time activities through a one-way mirror. The data revealed that the children in the expected-reward condition exhibited less interest in the task during the free-time period than did the children in the other two conditions (see Condry, 1977).

It seems intuitively unreasonable to contend that reward always decreases interest. One useful distinction in this regard differentiates between the controlling and the informational aspects of a reward. Deci believed that every reward has both controlling and informational aspects. If the controlling aspect is made salient, then there will be a change in perceived locus of causality. But if the informational aspect is salient, then changes in feelings of

---

[1]Reprinted from *A Treasury of Jewish Folklore* by Nathan Ausubel. Copyright ©1948, 1976 by Crown Publisher, Inc. By permission of Crown Publishers, Inc.

competence and self-determination are initiated. Hence, rewards indicating that an individual is competent at a task often enhance, rather than undermine, intrinsic motivation. For example, a medal for the best performance, an indication of superiority, would not be expected to undermine interest. More generally speaking, when reward is not contingent on good performance, but is merely contingent on doing the task, then undermining is likely. In these latter instances the individual merely goes through the task as fast as possible in order to receive the reward.

The so-called "undermining" effect of extrinsic reward appears to be a robust and powerful phenomenon, given a tangible reward. The implication of such a finding for the practices of teachers in the classroom, or even for business managers, is enormous. But, in order for teachers, managers, and parents to effectively apply the principles of extrinsic versus intrinsic motivation, conditions must be specified in which undermining will occur as well as those in which reward will enhance intrinsic interest.

Reactance

Fights for political freedom have occurred throughout history, often involving acts of extreme heroism that dramatically illustrate the motivational effects of loss of freedom. Similarly, we may engage in daily battles to preserve our psychological freedom. Being confined to one's room as a child, being forced to accept a decision, hearing a message that one prefers not to listen to, being pressured by others, and having censorship imposed are some examples of loss of personal, psychological freedom.

According to Brehm (1966, 1972), when a person's freedom to engage in a behavior is threatened or taken away, the motivation to perform that behavior, and therefore to reinstate freedom, increases. As Brehm (1972, p. 1) stated, "A person is motivationally aroused any time he thinks one of his freedoms has been threatened or eliminated. This motivational arousal, or 'psychological reactance,' moves a person to try to restore his freedoms."

Many experimental investigations have demonstrated the motivational effects of *psychological reactance*. In the majority of these research studies, individuals find themselves unable to engage in behaviors that they thought were available. For example, an alternative is eliminated or an expected message is censored. The experimenter then typically measures the perceived attractiveness of the available and unavailable options. It is believed that a change in the desirability of the alternatives, so that the unavailable alternative gains in attractiveness, is one indication of an attempt to restore freedom.

In one of the first such experiments, children were asked to rank-order the desirability of nine different candy bars (Hammock and Brehm, 1966). As a reward for this task, some children were told that they would have a *choice* between two candy bars, while others in a control condition were told that they would be *given* one of two different kinds of candy bars. The children were then shown their third- and fourth-ranked candies, and all were given the more attractive of the two. Thus, reactance was created in the decision

Table 17.1   Mean changes in ranking of the forced and eliminated candy bars

		Choice Alternative		
Conditions	N	Forced (rank 3)	Eliminated (rank 4)	Total reactance
Experimental	13	−1.23*	.23	1.46
Control	14	.00	−.43	−.43

Source: T. Hammock and J.W. Brehm, "The Attractiveness of Choice Alternatives When Freedom to Choose Is Eliminated by a Social Agent," *Journal of Personality 34*, 1966, p. 550. Copyright 1966, Duke University Press (Durham, N.C.).
*A minus indicates a decrease in attractiveness.

condition by telling the children who thought they would have a free choice that they were denied this opportunity. Following the giving of the candy (but before it was eaten), the experimenter had the children re-rate their candy preferences.

If the hypotheses about reactance and perceived attractiveness (attitude) are correct, then the preference for the denied (eliminated) alternative should increase in the choice condition. The data from this investigation are shown in Table 17.1. The findings indicated that the ranking of the eliminated alternative did increase in the experimental or reactance condition. But even more dramatic was the decrease in the attractiveness of the candy bar that the children were forced to take.

Reactance notions have also been tested in field, rather than laboratory, settings. In Miami, Florida, an antipollution law was imposed that prohibited the use of cleaning materials containing phosphates. Reactance theory suggests that shoppers should have had an increased desire for these banned products. To test this idea, purchaser attitudes in Miami were compared with those in Tampa, where the antipollution law was not in effect (Mazis, 1975). The investigator had the experimental participants (housewives) rate the effectiveness of the various detergents they had used during the six months prior to the survey. Table 17.2 shows that the ratings of the phosphate detergents were significantly higher in Miami, where the products were unavailable, than in Tampa. In addition, in Miami there was a strong negative attitude toward the quality of the alternative detergents.

Learned Helplessness

The previous section concerning reactance has revealed that a loss of freedom has psychological consequences. These consequences may often be quite harmful. Two experimental investigations with rats as subjects dramatically illustrate some of these adverse effects. In fact, the procedures used and the

Table 17.2   Means for effectiveness ratings of phosphate detergents

Characteristic	Miami (N = 76) M	Tampa (N = 45) M
Whiteness	8.68*	8.27
Freshness	8.77	7.87
Cleans in cold water	8.52	7.47
Brightness	8.31	7.84
Stain removal	8.00	6.96
Pours easily	9.45	9.07
Gentleness	8.81	8.71

Source: Adapted from Michael Mazis, "Antipollution Measures and Psychological Reactance Theory: A Field Experiment," *Journal of Personality and Social Psychology, 31,* 1975, p. 656. Copyright 1975 by the American Psychological Association. Adapted by permission of publisher and author.

*Based on an eleven-point scale with eleven labeled "absolutely perfect" and one labeled "poor."

consequences observed were so injurious in these particular investigations that lower organisms had to be the experimental subjects.

In one of the investigations, Mowrer and Viek (1948) gave hungry rats the opportunity to eat ten seconds before the onset of a shock. For half the animals, the shock could be terminated by jumping into the air. The second group of rats could not terminate the shock through their own actions. Rather, each was paired with a "controlling" rat and received the same amount of shock that the partner had received before the partner jumped to terminate its own shock.

Since it was known from prior experimental research that fear inhibits eating, the experimenters measured the eating behavior of both groups to examine the effects of the helplessness experience. The data revealed that the noncontrolling, or helpless, rats were inhibited in their eating, whereas the behavior of the controlling rats was not greatly affected. This difference existed even though the two groups received identical amounts of shock.

In the course of subsequent research, Richter (1958) observed cases of sudden death among rats during experimentation. For example, in a study of swimming endurance, many unexplained drownings occurred after the rats swam for only a short period of time. Richter speculated that (pp. 308–309) "the situation of these rats is not one that can be resolved by either fight or flight—it is rather one of hopelessness: Being restrained . . . in the swimming jar with no chance of escape is a situation against which the rat has no defense

. . . . They seem literally to give up." In sum, a loss of control has dramatic and aversive effects on the well-being of an organism (see Lefcourt, 1973).

Further research investigations of helplessness were conducted with researchers administering inescapable shock to dogs for a period of time. The dogs were placed in a harness and shock was administered to one of their hind legs. Then these animals, as well as other dogs not given prior inescapable training, were placed in a two-compartment box. When a tone signaling that shock would follow was sounded, the dogs could move from the shock side to the no-shock side of the box. Seligman and Maier (1967) reported that many of the dogs given prior inescapable shocks did not attempt to escape in this situation. Rather, they passively accepted their supposed fate; they appeared to have "learned helplessness." The untrained dogs, on the other hand, engaged in a variety of responses until the escape response was learned. Similar differences in behavior have been reported in experiments using fish, rats, cats, and other infrahuman species. It must be noted, however, that not all animals exposed to inescapable shock exhibit helplessness, and deficits are displayed on some subsequent tasks but not on others. Furthermore, in some cases helplessness is exhibited if testing immediately follows training, while a waiting period erases helplessness effects (see critique by Levis, 1976). In sum, there are many questions yet unanswered about the existence of this psychological state.

The most systematic and influential analysis of loss of control is that reported by Seligman (1975), who contended that organisms are helpless when their actions are perceived as not influencing outcomes. This is depicted in Fig. 17.1. In the figure, the horizontal axis shows the probability of a reinforcement when a response is made, $p(RF/R)$. The vertical axis shows the probability of the reward given no response, $p(RF/\bar{R})$. According to Seligman, if $p(RF/R) = p(RF)\bar{R}$ (the diagonal line in Fig. 17.1)—if the response does not increase the likelihood of receiving a reinforcement—then conditions for helplessness have been established. For example, assume that a baby goes to sleep after crying for one hour. The harried parents try to shorten this aversive period by rocking, feeding, or even playing music to the baby. Despite all these actions, however, the baby still doesn't fall asleep until an hour of crying has gone by. Thus, the reinforcer (the end of crying and the onset of sleep) is independent of the parents' behavior. The parents, therefore, are helpless in this situation.

To explain observations of learned helplessness, Seligman proposed a three-stage theory:

1. Information is gained about the contingency between outcomes and responding. In the case of helplessness training, this information reveals that there is no contingency or association between actions and reward.
2. This information results in the development of the expectation that responses and outcomes will remain independent in the future.
3. The low expectation causes deficits in future learning as well as motivational and emotional disturbance.

Figure 17.1   Portrayal of the antecedents of learned helplessness. (Adapted from *Helplessness: On Depression, Development, and Death*, p. 17, by Martin E. P. Seligman. W. H. Freeman and Company. Copyright © 1975.)

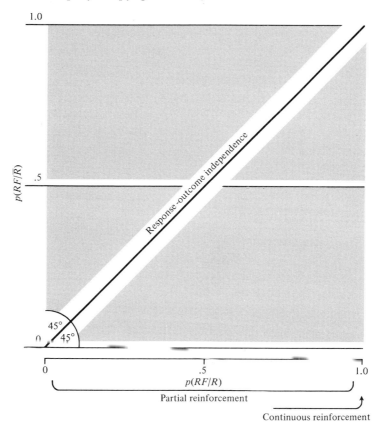

Learned-helplessness research has more recently been expanded to include human subjects. In one exemplary research investigation, Hiroto and Seligman (1975) exposed participants to either an escapable or an inescapable aversive tone. Subjects were then given a different task in which they could escape the noise by making a particular hand movement. It was found that individuals previously exposed to the inescapable tone performed poorly as compared to groups without prior inescapable-tone training.

Learned helplessness and depression.   The research of Seligman and others has called attention to a parallel between helplessness learning in the laboratory and human depression. Table 17.3 lists some of the similarities between the two phenomena. It certainly appears fruitful to think of some kinds of de-

Table 17.3   Summary of features common to learned helplessness and depression

	Learned helplessness	*Depression*
Symptoms	Passivity	Passivity
	Difficulty learning that responses produce relief	Negative cognitive set
	Dissipates in time	Time course
	Lack of aggression	Introjected hostility (hostility turned inward)
	Weight loss, appetite loss, social and sexual deficits	Weight loss, appetite loss, social and sexual deficits
	Ulcers and stress	Ulcers (?) and stress
		Feelings of helplessness
Cause	Learning that responding and reinforcement are independent	Belief that responding is useless
Cure	Directive therapy: forced exposure to responses that produce reinforcement	Recovery of belief that responding produces reinforcement
	Electroconvulsive shock	Electroconvulsive shock
	Time	Time
Prevention	Immunization by mastery over reinforcement	(?)

Source: From *Helplessness: On Depression, Development, and Death*, p. 106, by Martin E.P. Seligman. W.H. Freeman and Company. Copyright © 1975.

pression as akin to learned helplessness, but it must also be remembered that clinical depression is not a unitary illness; many kinds of depression have been identified, and there are many determinants of depression.

More recently, attributional analyses of learned helplessness and depression have been formulated (Abramson, Seligman, and Teasdale, 1978; Miller and Norman, 1979). Recall it was indicated in the chapter on achievement motivation that causal attributions, or why one believes success or failure has been attained, are an important determinant of subsequent expectancies, feelings, and actions. In a similar manner, it has been contended that how one perceives the causes of prior outcomes determines the type and course of depression.

Abramson and her co-workers (1978), guided by attributional tenets, distinguished between personal helplessness and universal helplessness. Universal helplessness is experienced when responses and outcomes are not contingent for any person in that situation. For example, if a child contracts leukemia, despite all efforts of the parents and doctors, the child's life may not be saved. The parents and doctors would probably not perceive themselves as personally responsible, although they would experience helplessness. Conversely, personal helplessness connotes a situation in which a person feels helpless but in which others might be able to attain the desired goal. For example, a person unable to receive passing grades in school in spite of effort will experience personal helplessness, for others obviously can receive passing grades. Although in both cases low expectancies and helplessness are experienced, low self-esteem is likely to be a consequence only of personal helplessness. Depressed patients may fail to make this distinction and may perceive situations of universal helplessness as indicative of personal helplessness and their own shortcomings.

Helplessness and reactance.   It appears that learned-helplessness theory and reactance theory generate opposite predictions about responses to uncontrollable events. Reactance theory states that if one loses control, attempts are made to restore that control. On the other hand, helplessness research suggests that motivation is impaired when control is lost. Organisms are expected to become passive, rather than active, following experiences with uncontrollable events.

Wortman and Brehm (1975) have attempted to reconcile these two positions, contending that the theories are not contradictory, but rather represent part of a temporal sequence of psychological reactivity. When faced with an uncontrollable event (loss of freedom), the initial reaction is an increased motivation to exert control. But when an individual becomes convinced that the outcome cannot be controlled, helplessness arises. Hence, there is a postulated temporal sequence in which reactance precedes helplessness.

Perceived Freedom: An Integration

Five overlapping areas of research have been examined briefly in this section of the chapter. These research topics have been labeled locus of control, personal causation, intrinsic versus extrinsic motivation, reactance, and learned helplessness. It is evident that these topics have much in common. First, all are concerned with the allocation of responsibility along an internal (self) versus external (environmental) dimension. Thus, the concepts of internality, origin, intrinsic motivation, freedom, and controllability are linked, as are the concepts of externality, pawn, extrinsic motivation, lack of freedom, and uncontrollability.

Investigations of these concepts have focused on both the antecedents of these particular feelings and their consequences or effects. Among the many antecedent conditions are the structure of the situation (constrained or free), the amount of external reward that is offered, barriers or interference from external sources, and the contingency between one's responses and the outcomes. These conditions affect many factors, such as the amount of information search, feeling states toward and liking of activities, amount of continued effort, and motivation to learn. The breadth of these findings is one indication of why perceived personal freedom is currently one of the most popular topics in the field of personalilty.

Personal Responsibility and Reactions Toward Others

Individuals perceive not only whether they have freedom and choice, but also whether others in their environment also have these options. Beliefs about others influence how we feel about and evaluate them. In addition, positive social behaviors such as helping are greatly affected by perceptions of responsibility, or the perceived degree of personal control or freedom the needy individual has.

Evaluation

The influence of intention (personal responsibility) on the moral evaluation of children was examined in Chapter 9. In addition, achievement evaluation is affected by the responsibility that is assigned for success and failure. In one experimental demonstration (Weiner and Kukla, 1970), subjects were asked to pretend that they were teachers and were to provide evaluative feedback to their students. The pupils were described as having just completed an exam with one of five possible outcomes: excellent, fair, borderline, failure, and clear failure. In addition, the pupils were described jointly in terms of ability (high or low) and effort (high or low). For example, one pupil was characterized as high in ability, low in effort, and having a borderline test performance. Evaluation was indicated by giving each pupil a score from +5 (highest reward) to   3 (highest punishment).

The results are depicted in Fig. 17.2, which reveals that test outcome, a factor commonly known to affect evaluation, indeed influences feedback in the expected manner: the greater the success, the more favorable the feedback. But pupil characteristics and perceived personal responsibility also affect evaluation. First, high effort results in a more positive evaluation than does low effort, at all outcome levels. And, perhaps surprisingly, low ability produces a higher evaluation than does high ability. This is because low ability coupled with high effort and success is especially rewarded. For example, the handicapped person who completes a marathon or the retarded child who persists in completing a task elicits great social approval because each is considered personally responsible for success. On the other hand, high ability coupled with low effort and failure is maximally punished. For example, the bright dropout or the gifted athlete who refuses to practice and performs poorly generates great social disapproval. Again this is because each is perceived as personally responsible for failure. These individuals did not *have* to fail; they had freedom of choice and could have chosen a different outcome. Because low ability coupled with high effort and success is so strongly rewarded, while high ability linked with low effort and failure is correspondingly punished, lack of ability emerges as a beneficial attribute in this particular kind of experiment.

Figure 17.2   Evaluation (reward and punishment) as a function of pupil ability, motivation, and examination outcome. (Weiner and Kukla, 1970, p. 3.)

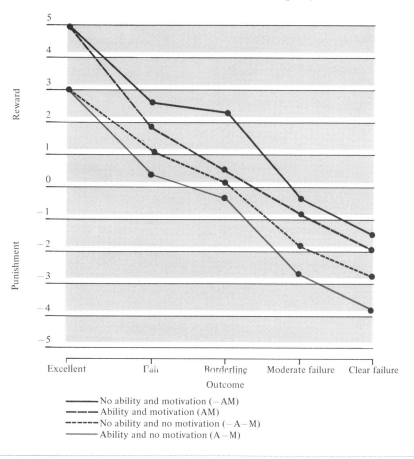

————— No ability and motivation (−AM)
– – – – Ability and motivation (AM)
- - - - - No ability and no motivation (−A−M)
————— Ability and no motivation (A−M)

A handicapped skier participating in the French International Handicapped Ski Championships. We exhibit great admiration toward those who overcome handicaps to accomplish difficult goals. What is your immediate reaction? (SIPA/Editorial Photocolor Archives)

Helping Behavior

It is also evident that whether we help others and the kind of aid we are willing to give are in part dependent on whether we perceive the person in need of aid as responsible for his or her plight. For example, it has been clearly demonstrated that people are more likely to help a disabled person than a drunk (Piliavin, Rodin, and Piliavin, 1969). In a similar manner, it is much easier for a charity to raise money for battered children or the blind than for the obese and alcoholics. This appears to be true because we perceive individuals as personally responsible for obesity and alcoholism; one should be able to control one's own eating and drinking behavior. On the other hand, this is not the case, for example, for blindness and other physical ailments.

There is evidence that differential help giving is mediated by the feelings that are elicited by various persons in need of aid. We typically feel sympathy and pity toward the blind because they are not responsible, but anger and annoyance toward a drunk because he can be "blamed." These opposing emotional reactions guide approach and helping behavior versus avoidance and neglect (see Weiner, 1980). In a similar manner, you might be likely to help a classmate if he or she needed class notes because of illness or hospitalization. But if the same classmate cut class to go to the beach, or said that he or she merely "didn't feel like going to school," then the request for aid might elicit anger and neglect. In sum, our decision to help others and our feelings toward them are in good part determined by why the aid was needed and whether the needy are perceived as personally responsible for their plight.

Summary   This chapter has focused on the topics of perceived freedom and personal responsibility. The issue of free will versus determinism is one of the oldest in philosophy and psychology. This question, rephrased in terms of the effects of perceived freedom versus perceived absence of control or choice, is now one of the most discussed topics in the field of personality. The specific approaches to perceived freedom—locus of control, personal causation, intrinsic versus extrinsic motivation, reactance, and learned helplessness—differ in their particular focus of concern. But all examine the fundamental issue of how the right to be "master of one's fate" pervades our psychological life. Similarly, beliefs about and behavior toward others are influenced by perceptions of others' personal responsibility.

Specific points

1. Skinner has contended that freedom is an illusion and that acceptance of this fact will lead to a better society.
2. *Locus of control* refers to beliefs regarding the perceived influence that one has on the attainment of a reinforcement. Questionnaires have been de-

vised to classify individuals as *internal* versus *external* in locus of control. There is some evidence that persons labeled as internal function more effectively.

3. A distinction has been drawn between acting as an *origin* and acting as a *pawn.* Programs that train individuals to behave as origins have resulted in apparent success.

4. *Intrinsic* motivation indicates that behavior is undertaken for its own sake; *extrinsic* motivation connotes that the action is undertaken because of an extrinsic reward. Use of an extrinsic reward to motivate behavior may undermine or decrease intrinsic interest in the activity. Undermining occurs when the controlling, rather than the informational, aspects of the reward are salient.

5. Individuals attempt to restore freedom if it is taken away, a reaction termed *psychological reactance.* One manifestation of this attempt is demonstrated in attitudes: increased liking of a "forbidden" choice and decreased liking of available alternatives.

6. *Learned helplessness* develops when the likelihood of receiving a reward is unaffected by an organism's response. Learned helplessness impedes subsequent performance. There are some similarities between laboratory-induced helplessness and the state of depression.

7. Reactance and learned helplessness may form a temporal sequence. Initial reactions to a loss of freedom or lack of control may be attempts to restore freedom (reactance), while continued evidence of this loss may then beget helplessness.

8. Evaluations of others are affected and the likelihood of help giving is minimized when others are perceived as personally responsible for their plight.

Thought Questions

1. What do you think of Skinner's position that we have only an illusion of control?

2. What situations in your present environment give rise to origin and pawn feelings?

3. Can you recall a situation in which your freedom was restricted? What were your feelings and subsequent actions at the time? Did you make an attempt to restore freedom?

4. Do grades in school undermine your intrinsic interest in the subject matter? If grading were eliminated, would you have more or less interest in studying the material?

Aggression

18 The study of human aggression touches on all of the major issues involved in the study of personality. The role of biological versus environmental factors, differing theoretical interpretations, developmental antecedents, and trait characteristics of aggression are some of the issues that will be addressed in this chapter. The understanding of aggression, moreover, is a matter of intense social as well as scientific interest. There is a great deal of anxiety in contemporary society concerning the prevalence of aggression and violence. Aggression is hardly new to human affairs, but it poses a more serious problem as societies become more interdependent and easily disrupted and as weapons become more powerful and destructive.

Are humans fundamentally aggressive animals? Are humans by nature warlike? Are hatred and violence learned? Does poverty produce aggression? Is it possible for society to control aggression effectively? Do sports and the entertainment media serve as outlets for aggression? Unfortunately, there are no simple answers to these questions and, in some instances, it is not yet possible to give *any* answers. However, the analysis and investigation of problems of aggression have at the very least provided a framework that enables us to discuss these issues sensibly and systematically. Yet, it must be kept in mind that our approach to human aggression is from the perspective of students of personality; a truly full account of human aggression would involve most of the biological and social sciences.

What Is Aggression?

The term *aggression*, as used by both layperson and scientist, covers many different behaviors. It includes murder, physical attack, verbal insults, and outbursts of rage. To these we might add destruction of property, menacing gestures, social humiliation, prejudice, playful jostling, and violent dreams and fantasies. And the listing is still far from exhaustive (see Box 18.1). While the behaviors embraced by the term *aggression* may have important

456

elements in common, their diversity makes it difficult to establish general laws or principles that apply to all forms of aggression. It also leads to confusion in communication, so that different investigators might mean different things when they refer to aggressive behavior. Biologists, in fact, prefer to use the term *agonistic behavior* as an alternative to aggression. Agonistic behavior refers to offensive and defensive fighting and competitive behaviors, and also includes sounds and gestures that function as threats and may serve to avert

Box 18.1   SOME EXAMPLES OF AGGRESSIVE BEHAVIOR

1. A boy swats at a hornet and gets stung.
2. A cat kills a mouse, parades around with it, and then discards it.
3. A wolf kills and devours a stray sheep.
4. A farmer beheads a chicken and prepares it for Sunday dinner.
5. A hunter kills an animal and mounts it as a trophy.
6. A dog snarls at the mailman, but never bites him.
7. A tennis player smashes his racket after missing a volley.
8. A boxer gives his opponent a bloody nose.
9. A small boy daydreams of beating up the neighborhood bully.
10. A woman nags and criticizes her husband, and he ignores her in return.
11. A firing squad executes a prisoner.
12. A bombardier presses a button and hundreds below are killed.
13. A bank robber is shot in the back while attempting to escape.
14. A politician evades legislation that might help clear up a crime-ridden slum.
15. A man commits suicide.
16. An assassin misses his target.
17. A man dislikes all blacks, Jews, and long-haired college students.
18. Two friends get into a heated quarrel after drinking too much.

Source: From *Aggression: In Man and Animals* by Roger N. Johnson, pp. 4–5. Copyright © 1972 by W. B. Saunders Company. Reprinted by permission of Holt, Rinehart and Winston.

more serious conflicts. While these definitions are useful, the ultimate answer to the question of what aggression is will have to depend on research that tells us which kinds of aggressive behaviors go together and which ones have different properties.

There are certain theoretical distinctions that are helpful in understanding some of the controversies and experimental findings concerning the causes and functions of aggression. First, it is important to distinguish between the response or behavior and the motive or reason for that response. For example, an attack by a mugger is a clear instance of an aggressive response. However, there may be important psychological differences in the reasons for such an attack. The mugger's primary motive might be to steal the victim's wallet. If the wallet falls or can be successfully picked out of the victim's pocket, the mugger will be equally satisfied. In this instance, the aggressive attack is one of a number of possible *instrumental* responses, which may or may not involve aggression, for achieving a basically nonaggressive goal. Suppose, however, that the mugger is angry at his victim and that his primary goal is to humiliate and physically hurt the victim, with theft being incidental. Here, the aggressive response is no longer instrumental to a nonaggressive goal (i.e., money) but is motivated by *aggressive drive,* or *drive-instigated* hostility. What is critical to the mugger is that the victim be injured or publicly disgraced. He would be equally satisfied if he witnessed someone else carrying out the attack or if a member of the victim's family were injured. Other factors also influence the nature of the aggressive response and sometimes instrumental aggression and aggressive drive–motivated behavior may overlap (e.g., the mugger may both hate his victim and want his money). But, as we will try to show, the distinction between instrumental and drive-instigated aggression helps clarify some of the theoretical confusion and debate concerning the causes of human aggression. For example, social learning theorists have been largely concerned with the acquisition and performance of *instrumental* aggression (cf. discussion of Bandura, Chapter 6), while psychoanalytic theorists have focused on the dynamics of aggressive *drive.*

Biological Aspects of Aggression

Do humans have an innate propensity to use instrumental aggressive responses? Do they have an innate aggressive drive that, like hunger and thirst, must somehow be satisfied? There are three areas of biological study that relate to these questions:

1. Ethology, which entails systematic observations of animals in their natural settings.
2. Physiological research on hormones, brain structures, and brain chemistry involved in aggression.
3. Genetic research, with both animals and humans, on the inheritance of aggression.

Two young boys engaging in aggressive behavior, which may not be motivated by aggressive drives if they are only "playing" (note the boxing gloves). (© Frank Siteman MCMLXXX)

Ethological Research

The investigation of the bases for aggression in animals has been and continues to be of major interest to ethologists. A substantial part of the research for which two pioneering ethologists, Konrad Lorenz (1966) and Nikita Tinbergen (1953, 1968), received Nobel prizes involved contributions to our knowledge of aggression. Among these contributions was the discovery that there are stimuli that act as innate *releasers* of aggressive responses. For example, male robins, on perceiving the red patch on the breast of a rival, will respond by attacking him. Removal of the red patch eliminates the aggressive response (Lack, 1943). Another well-known instance is the aggressive response of a male stickleback fish to the red belly of another stickleback who enters his territory (Tinbergen, 1951), although subsequent research has shown this releasing effect to be strongly influenced by other variables (Peeke, Wyers, and Herz, 1969). In some cases, like that of the famous tropical fighting fish (*Betta splendens*), there appears to be no specific releasing stimulus. All it takes for a male fighting fish to put on an aggressive display and begin an attack is the perception of another male *Betta,* or even of his own image in a mirror.

However, ethologists have also discovered that, in most species, fighting between members of the same species rarely escalates to killing or even to severe destruction. Much of the fighting is ritualistic and, in many cases, involves only threat displays, with little or no physical contact. For example, a study of aggression among elephant seals indicated that for every actual fight, there were sixty-seven aggressive encounters that consisted solely of aggressive threat displays (LeBoeuf and Peterson, 1969). These displays vary according to the species under study. In a cat, the back arches, the hackles rise, the teeth bare, and the claws extend, all of which serve to make the cat appear larger. Birds commonly fluff their feathers and spread their wings for the same effect. And wild chimpanzees engage in a variety of rituals, including staring an opponent into submission, stomping the ground, and hooting and screaming (Van Lawick-Goodall, 1968*b*).

These aggressive displays commonly serve to inhibit the behavior of the target animal that provoked the aggressive display. Such provoking behaviors include intrusion on territory, approach to another's female partner or cache of food, and efforts at dominance. If threat gestures do not suffice and an actual fight takes place, in many species ritualized behaviors come into play that act as *inhibitory* rather than releasing stimuli, so that a victorious animal will cease its aggressive attack before the vanquished animal is seri-

Two German shepherds and a husky in combat. Within-species infrahuman aggression rarely results in death. (Julie O'Neil/The Picture Cube)

ously injured. For example, a dog who is the loser of a fight may present its unprotected neck to the mouth of the victor or roll over on its back exposing its vulnerable underside (Lorenz, 1966). Thus, for most animal species a sequence of interactions has evolved to act as a brake on intraspecies fighting and killing. Severe fighting does occur and intraspecies killing does take place; lions of one group have been observed to attack and kill lions of another group (Eibl-Eibesfeldt, 1977, p. 130). However, ethological studies of aggression in infrahuman species do not support the notion that it is biologically "natural" for people to kill each other or, as some maintain (Ardrey, 1967), that we humans have an inborn killer instinct.

What these studies do suggest is that it is possible that some instrumental aggressive responses are innately "wired into" our neuromuscular system. Observations of children born deaf and blind indicate that a number of patterns of aggressive behavior, such as stamping the feet, clenching the teeth, and making fists are present in these children despite lack of opportunity to observe these behaviors (cf. Eibl-Eibesfeldt, 1977, p. 135). It is also possible that these aggressive reactions are wired to releasing stimuli. However, there are no good examples in humans of simple stimuli that automatically release an aggressive response. The possible counterparts of releasing stimuli—restraint of infant movement, intense discomfort, exposure to deliberate frustration, or malicious attack on a loved family member—are complex affective-cognitive situations rather than relatively simple physical stimuli. And, if there are innate aggression inhibitors in humans—for example, tears, pleading, and submissive gestures—they are unfortunately quite weak and all too frequently do not work. The human capacity to experience empathy, the sharing of another's perspective and feelings (cf Chapter 9), may be one mechanism that helps restrain an aggressor from sustaining an attack, but empathy is not automatic and requires experience and training (N. Feshbach, 1979).

Anger and aggressive drive. Several of the innate aggressive reactions that have been described resemble the emotions of anger or rage. Anger, like other emotions, has an important adaptive value: the organism becomes fiercer and more capable of defending itself when angry. Anger adds to one's strength and to the intensity of one's behaviors, as the following comment from a nineteenth-century California preacher conveys: "Although I weigh a hundred and twenty pounds, when I'm mad I weigh a ton!" (cf. Stratton, 1923). Anger, like the other emotions, is also a form of social communication; the facial expressions, sounds, and postures displayed by an angry organism tell another animal or individual to stay away or desist from whatever it is doing. This threat property, noted by Charles Darwin (1872), has probably evolved to ensure adequate territorial spacing of the species, with distributed access to food, and, in primates, to foster the maintenance of a socially stable group with an effective dominance hierarchy (Bernstein and Gordon, 1974).

Darwin, in his above-cited book on emotions, also commented on the possible functions of emotional expression as a means of discharging excess tension. When an emotion is very strong or blocked, the organism is motivated to express that feeling. In the case of rage, the motivation to discharge angry feelings would seem to be related to the notion of aggressive drive. However, it is not aggressive drive in the sense that Freud and others use this concept; namely, as a drive to inflict injury. Rather, the drive is to discharge the feeling through expressing it or getting rid of the tension in some other way. It is the angry, aggressive movements—the snarling, the shouting, the clawing, and the biting—that are critical, rather than seriously hurting the rival. These expressions of anger can lead to serious injury and sometimes killing, but that is the *consequence,* not the purpose, of the action.

Intrinsic aggression.   There is evidence that some animals will seek opportunities for aggression. We will call this motivation toward aggressive response *intrinsic aggression* (Reykowski, 1979) to distinguish it from aggressive *drive,* which traditionally implies the motive to inflict injury. Intrinsic aggression refers to the motivation to perform an aggressive act: to fight, rather than to hurt or inflict damage. When intrinsic aggression is observed, it is usually the result of blocking an aggressive response after exposure to an aggression-releasing stimulus or after interruption of a fight sequence. It is as if the organism has to complete the aggressive sequence (Berkowitz, 1965a), just as there appears to be a need to express emotions once they are aroused. For example, in one experiment demonstrating intrinsic aggression, male mice engaging in a fight were separated and placed in adjacent compartments where one of the mice could initiate resumption of the fight (Lagerspetz, 1979). From Table 18.1, it can be seen that most mice resumed fighting within two minutes. In addition, following fights in which the experimental animal was victorious, or equally matched with an opponent, it was much more likely to resume contact with the opponent than following fights in which it had been defeated or when no fight had occurred. Additional experiments demonstrated that some mice were even willing to cross an electric grid to reach a goal box where they could resume fighting.

Table 18.1   Amount of time elapsing between interruption of fighting and resumption of fighting

Condition	Mean latency (seconds)
Experimental animal victorious	31.5
Experimental animal and opponent equal	31.5
Opponent victorious	95.0
No prior fight occurred	94.8

Source: Adapted from Lagerspetz, 1979. From *Aggression and Behavior Change: Biological and Social Processes* edited by Seymour Feshbach and Adam Fraczek. Copyright © 1979 by Praeger Publishers. Reprinted and adapted with the permission of Praeger Publishers.

Figure 18.1   The effect of victories and defeats on aggression scores. Black dots: 21 animals allowed first to fight with more-aggressive partners (*A*) and, subsequently, with less-aggressive partners (*N*). Open circles: 21 animals allowed first to fight with less-aggressive partners (*N*) and then with more-aggressive partners (*A*). (Lagerspetz, 1961, p. 170. Used by permission.)

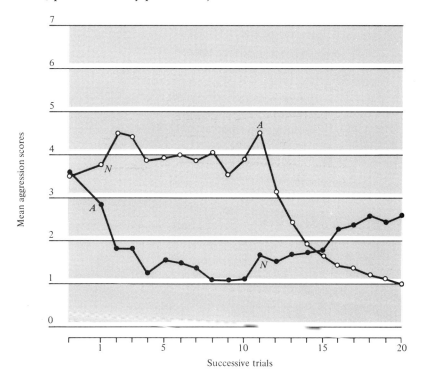

Although the great majority of aggressive behaviors observed in infrahumans are instrumental in character, it also appears that some animals, under some circumstances, seek aggression for its own sake. For the male fighting cock, the simple lapse of time without an opportunity for fighting increases the likelihood of aggressive acts (Kruijt, 1964). Fighting cocks raised in complete isolation displayed periods of agitated, aggressivelike behaviors in which they attempted to attack their own tails and even their own shadows with their spurs and beaks.

A word of caution is necessary at this point. In reviewing the animal literature, the focus has been on innate mechanisms that influence the occurrence and inhibition of aggression. However, it must be emphasized that these patterns of aggressive behavior are strongly affected by learning and social experience. The role of learning becomes more powerful as one ascends the evolutionary ladder. While it can be shown that genetic, physiological, and other biological factors influence aggression in mammals, even within infrahumans, patterns of aggression are sharply affected by learning experiences. For example, victory and defeat are naturally occurring experiences that have a major effect on aggressive response tendencies. In rodents or in primates, these outcomes determine dominance hierarchies and patterns of aggression in social groups. Laboratory studies in which victory and defeat are experimentally manipulated have demonstrated, for example, that mice can be encouraged to fight by matching an experimental mouse with a restrained mouse that is prevented from fighting back. Figure 18.1 (p. 463) shows the striking effects on aggressive behavior of pairing test animals with more or less aggressive partners (Lagerspetz, 1961). The experimental mouse, rewarded by his apparent success, substantially increases the frequency of attack on other mice, including mice with which he would not ordinarily fight (Scott, 1958). On the other hand, punishment decreases the frequency of attack. If learning experiences have been shown to be important in influencing the aggressive behavior of mice, how much more significant their influence is likely to be on human aggression!

Physiological Influences

In a famous novel by Robert Louis Stevenson, the hero, a friendly, gracious, civil English doctor becomes transformed into a hostile, cruel, sadistic monster by simply swallowing a potion. We are all familiar with the Jekyll-and-Hyde story. While there are no chemicals that have this dramatic an effect, a number of chemicals have been identified that significantly influence aggressive behavior. The relationship between alcohol and aggression is one obvious example. Drinking is a major contributor to violent incidents.

Conversely, other drugs decrease rather than enhance aggression. Violent, assaultive behaviors in mental patients have been shown to be markedly reduced by the advent of the use of phenylthiazines, a group of powerful tranquilizing drugs that have made the once-familiar straitjacket obsolete. A novel index of tranquilizers' reduction of aggression is provided by the following statistical comparison. In 1955, before the staff of New York's Rockland State Hospital began to use tranquilizers for their seriously emotionally disturbed patients, 8,000 windowpanes were broken in that one year. Three full-time glaziers were kept busy keeping the windows in repair. By 1960, when phenylthiazines were in widespread use, the level of breakage was down to 1,900 windowpanes (Kline, 1962)! Although the impact of these drugs is quite dramatic, it must be emphasized that their effects are also quite complex. They influence other behaviors and processes besides aggression; for example, they reduce response to pain (Valzelli, 1976). Some tranquilizers affect the motor system and act as muscle relaxants. And, as one might expect, situational factors and individual differences among patients influence the response to tranquilizers.

Sex hormones and aggression.   Still other well-known chemical influences on aggression, familiar even in ancient times, are the male sex hormones, the androgens. The symbol of violence, the bull, is rendered a docile ox through castration. In general, removal of androgens tends to lower aggression while the administration of androgens tends to increase it. Also female hormones, the estrogens, tend to reduce aggressivity (Moyer, 1971). However, the relationships among hormones, sexuality, and aggression are quite complex for both lower animals and humans (Herbert, 1970).

The species and the age at which administration or removal of the hormone takes place are particularly critical variables. Hormonal manipulation during the very early stages of development is generally more effective than at later periods. Thus, adult female mice rarely fight, even when administered the androgen testosterone. However, administration of either male or female hormones, androgens or estrogens, shortly after birth makes mice sensitive as adults to the aggression-inducing effects of testosterone (Edwards and Herndon, 1970). Age, however, is a less critical factor for hens. Even when first injected with male hormones as adults, hens develop the secondary sex characteristics of roosters and, more pertinently, become more aggressive (Allee, Collias, and Lutherman, 1939).

Moving up the phylogenetic ladder, a study of testosterone levels in a group of adult rhesus monkeys indicated that monkeys with higher testosterone levels were the more aggressive and the more dominant (Rose, Holaday, and Bernstein, 1971). But the relationship between sex hormones and level of aggression in humans has not been well established and remains a matter of debate. One study of young male prisoners indicated higher levels of testosterone in prisoners who had engaged in more aggressive crimes such as armed robbery, assault, and murder during adolescence. The testosterone levels in prisoners whose offenses had been restricted to more routine offenses of burglary and larceny were, on the other hand, relatively low (Kreuz and Rose, 1972). However, the meaning of this finding is unclear since there was no relationship between testosterone levels and the amount of fighting and other aggressive behaviors displayed in prison.

Although the connection, if any, between the sexual biological system and the aggressive biological system has not yet been resolved in humans, there has been some medical interest in hormonal treatment of male sex offenders who commit aggressive acts. In most modern societies, castration of sex offenders is not permissible either as a punishment or as a treatment. However, scientific ingenuity has made possible a form of "chemical castration" through administering a female sex hormone to the offender. There have been several reports of a substantial decline in aggressive sex offenses following such treatment (Chatz, 1972; Field and Williams, 1970). Apart from lack of well-controlled studies, the mechanisms by which a female sex hormone such as estrogen affect the aggressive behavior of an offender is not understood. Estrogen has been shown to reduce the sexual drives and virility of the young males in these studies. Consequently, the occasion for using physical force (e.g., in child molestation) is reduced since the aggressive behavior was in service of a sexual goal that is no longer desired. Whether such hormonal treatment would affect the behaviors of rapists whose primary goal is the humiliation and injury of their victim is, at best, uncertain. Quite apart from our ignorance of how these hormones work and their possible side-effects, these treatments raise serious ethical issues. Questions of irreversibility of the effects and of the informed and free consent of the prisoner are involved. These same ethical questions arise when other biological treatments for aggression are considered.

When should drugs be used?   Should tranquilizers or other drugs affecting aggression be used in prisons as they are in mental hospitals? Should they be used for all difficult prisoners? Only for prisoners with a diagnosed psychiatric problem? Who is to determine when the aggressive behavior in a prison is the prisoner's problem and when the behavior is a legitimate response to an abusive prison regimen? As the following extract from an investigator (Moyer, 1976, p. 263) working with one of the mild tranquilizers indicates, the ethical issues extend beyond prisons and mental hospitals.

In my laboratory at Carnegie-Mellon we have squirrel monkeys which are vicious and untameable. A hand put in the cage to touch or pet them will be savagely and repeatedly bitten. . . . it is possible to put a few thousands of a gram of diazepam in the milk that we give them; they evidently cannot taste it, nor could I. When the drug begins to take effect, they lose their hostility and can be handled with bare hands. As others have reported, the drug does not sedate them, it simply makes them more friendly. Most of the milk available today is pasteurized and homogenized and has vitamin D added. Will the milk available tomorrow have an anti-hostility drug added, or will such a drug be added to the water supply? Will this make for a peaceful population, and if so, will it be worth it?

Brain mechanisms and aggression.   Between the pathway of drugs that are absorbed into the bloodstream and the performance or inhibition of an aggressive response lies the brain. One of the most exciting research areas in contemporary science is the study of the relationships between the brain and behavior. And within this extraordinarily rich and rapidly expanding research area, a good deal of attention has been given to brain structures and processes involved in aggressive behavior. It has now been well established that the limbic system plays a significant role in the excitation and inhibition of rage and aggression and, more generally, in emotional behavior. The limbic system is located beneath the cerebral cortex and is part of the old brain, having evolved earlier than the cortex. It is composed of a number of substructures including the hypothalamus and the amygdala. Investigations have attempted to determine how each of these structures influences aggressive behavior.

The principal research techniques used have been surgical removal (ablation), electrical stimulation, and chemical stimulation of specific brain areas. For example, stimulation by electrodes implanted in the lateral hypothalamus of selected cats that normally ignored rats resulted in the cats' pouncing on a rat and biting the back of its neck (Wasman and Flynn, 1962). Such attacks are organized, directed, and relatively unemotional. In contrast, stimulation of another area in the hypothalamus (the medial section) produced an enraged, clawing, hissing animal (Egger and Flynn, 1963). Thus, the task of mapping out areas of the brain related to aggression is quite complicated, since different segments of the same limbic system substructure can have markedly different functions. Furthermore, the same sections can have different functions for different species. For example, vicious wildcats have been rendered docile through removal of the amygdala (Schreiner and Kling, 1956) while surgical lesions in the amygdala produce a rage reaction in cats (Bard and Mountcastle, 1948).

These animal studies, covering a wide range of mammals, indicate that it is possible to exert a strong influence on aggression through stimulation or surgical removal of specific brain areas. In addition, modern techniques in brain chemistry make it possible to stimulate or inhibit aggression by applying chemicals to brain sites, thereby influencing the action of neurotransmitters (chemicals that transmit nerve impulses) at that site. In one study, normally peaceful rats became mouse killers when one drug was injected, while a drug with opposite chemical effects suppressed killing in killer rats (Smith, King, and Hoebel, 1970).

Although the effects of brain stimulation and surgery on violent behavior in infrahumans can be quite dramatic, caution must be exercised in extrapolating these data to humans or to all forms of aggression. It may be possible to eliminate one attack behavior while leaving other forms of aggression intact. Second, limbic structures and neurotransmitters are not specific to aggression; they also affect other behaviors. Third, the effects of these biological procedures are not as automatic as they may appear. José Delgado (1979), one of the pioneers in the area of brain stimulation, demonstrated that the effects of such stimulation can be strongly influenced by features of the environment. In one study, electrodes were implanted in the brain of a female monkey who was placed at various times in three different colonies of four animals. In the first group (A), she had the lowest dominance rank (fourth), in group B she ranked third, and in group C she ranked second. The monkey was radio-stimulated, through a remote control device, at the same brain site and with the same electrical stimulus when interacting with each of the three groups. The frequency of the monkey's aggressive acts and the frequency with which she was attacked by the other group members is shown in Table 18.2. These data reflect a striking variability in aggressive behavior as a function of the monkey's dominance status in the group. With high dominance status in group C, electrical stimulation produced a marked increase in aggressive activity. But when dominance status was low, this same stimulation resulted in less aggression than that directed toward the animal by other group members.

Although one cannot be certain how a particular brain lesion or brain stimulation will affect aggression, there has been some medical interest in the use of these procedures for the treatment of individuals who are prone to uncontrollable violent outbursts (Mark and Erwin, 1970). When a patient has a clearly diagnosable brain disorder that is probably responsible for the aggressive outburst, then the case for medical intervention is reasonable. However, ethical problems arise when using these procedures with assaultive individuals with no apparent brain malfunction.

Table 18.2   Aggressive behavior in different colonies of monkeys where the same stimulated animal had different hierarchical status

Group	Rank of stimulated monkey	Aggressive acts of stimulated monkey	Aggressive acts of other colony animals against stimulated monkey
A	4	8	20
B	3	41	17
C	2	84	0

Source: Delgado, 1967. From *Aggression and Behavior Change: Biological and Social Processes* edited by Seymour Feshbach and Adam Fraczek. Copyright © 1979 by Praeger Publishers. Reprinted and adapted by permission of Praeger Publishers.

Genetics and Aggression

Infants display striking differences in temperament (see Chapter 2). Longitudinal studies suggest that these temperamental differences interact in time with environmental experiences to form the child's personality (Thomas and Chess, 1976). Some of these temperamental traits appear closely related to aggression. For example, the pattern of unpleasant moods, unfriendly social responses, and intense motor reactions may be a precursor to aggressiveness. There are a number of possible prenatal factors that may be the principal causes of these aggression related temperamental differences: mother's diet, activity level, smoking, and ingestion of alcohol or other drugs. But perhaps the most likely places to look for the cause of temperamental differences are genetic disparities.

At the infrahuman level, the genetic influence on aggression is evident to any dog breeder. To demonstrate the aggressivity of terriers, litters of fox terriers and beagles were raised together. The terriers, although smaller, dominated access to food and male terriers had primary access to females (James, 1951). In addition to studying aggressive differences between existent breeds, it is also possible to create strains of aggressive and nonaggressive animals through selective breeding for aggression (see Chapter 2). The most aggressive animals are mated with each other; similarly, for the least aggressive. This process is repeated with each generation of offspring until there is little or no overlap between the strains in aggression. Again, it must be emphasized that genetically based temperamental differences in aggression can be strongly influenced by environmental factors. For example, when mice are reared together, genetic influences on aggression are less evident than when they are reared in isolation. Punishment and defeat also decrease aggressivity (Lagerspetz, 1969).

It has been more difficult to conclusively demonstrate genetic influences on aggression at the human level. In the late 1960s, there was a flurry of excitement over a presumed connection between male criminality and a certain genetic abnormality: an extra Y chromosome added to the normal male XY sex chromosome. Since the X chromosome comes from the female and the Y chromosome from the male, the added Y factor suggested to some scientists the notion of more maleness and therefore more aggressiveness. But systematic studies failed to substantiate earlier claims concerning the XYY connection to aggression. A large-scale survey carried out in Denmark did reveal a marginal tendency for XYY males to be overrepresented in the criminal population as compared to XY males. However, there was no evidence of any tendency on the part of XYY males to commit aggressive, violent offenses (Witkin et al., 1976).

There have been many efforts to determine whether there is a genetic basis for criminality. The most systematic and extensive of these have been series of studies carried out in Denmark, where the excellence of national records of social deviance, psychopathology, identical and fraternal twins, adoption, and divorce permit systematic, detailed analyses of the role of genetics and environment in various behavioral disorders and social problems (Mednick and Christiansen, 1977). These data provide us with some evidence for a genetic factor in criminality: the concordance rate for identical twins is about twice that for dyzygotic or fraternal twins (cf. Chapter 2). In addition, a study of adoptees indicated that sons whose biological fathers were criminals were twice as likely to have criminal records as sons whose biological fathers were not criminals. But, as Table 18.3 indicates, environmental factors also exert an influence; the adopted son is most likely to have a criminal record when both the adopted father and the biological father are criminals known to the police (Hutchings and Mednick, 1977).

In view of the animal literature demonstrating the genetic contribution to aggression, it seems plausible that genetic factors also influence aggression in humans. The differences in aggression manifested by males and females, which appear to be related to genetically linked differences between the sexes in such factors as physique and hormones, also support the genetic position concerning the innate determinants of aggression. But, given that the evidence on criminality suggests only a modest genetic influence, and given the

---

Table 18.3   "Cross-fostering" analysis: Percentage of adoptive sons who are registered criminals

		Is biological father criminal?	
		Yes	No
Is adoptive father criminal?	Yes	36.2 (of 58)	11.5 (of 52)
	No	22.0 (of 219)	10.5 (of 333)

Source: Hutchings and Mednick, 1977, p. 137. Reprinted by permission.

fact that this genetic influence may reflect factors other than aggression, such as low IQ and various mental disorders, the literature on criminality fails to provide definitive support for the proposition that aggressive tendencies are genetically transmitted.

Cultural Influences

Some cultural groups are peaceful; others are warlike. In some cultures, violent solutions of conflicts are common; in others, they are rare. For some groups, killing is a sin; for others, it is a virtue. The enormous variations in the level of violence between societies underline the importance of social influences on human aggression. Biological factors, as we have seen, exert a significant influence on aggressive behavior. But the influence of biological factors is very much dependent on the social context and the organism's past experiences.

The importance of cultural influences on aggressive behavior is readily illustrated by a simple inspection of national differences in homicide rates. In Table 18.4, homicide rates for selected countries are presented for 1974 to 1976. Suicide rates are also included for comparison purposes. It is noteworthy that the United States is consistently among those countries with the highest homicide rates. When the United States is compared with other English-speaking nations, it can be seen to have about ten times the homicide rate of Ireland or England, and four to six times that of Australia, Canada, or Scotland. Of this English-language group, only Northern Ireland, beset by civil war, has a higher rate of killings than the United States. It has been argued by some theorists that the amount of violence in any culture is a constant, so that if violence is not expressed outwardly, as in homicides, then it will be expressed inwardly in the form of suicides. From this perspective, the amount of violence is largely biologically determined, while the role of culture is to shape the form or direction in which the violence is expressed. However, homicide and suicide are not inversely related; in Table 18.4 one can find every combination of high, middle, and low homicide and suicide rates among these nations. The amount as well as the form of violence varies with the culture.

Since homicide and suicide are but two of the many ways in which aggression can be expressed, it is possible that if other manifestations of aggression were taken into account, much smaller cultural differences in total aggression would be observed. But the fact remains that there is little evidence for such a position. Studies of preliterate cultures reflect similar variations in aggression; some seem to be permeated with violence and aggressive ideation; some have mixed patterns; and there are a few where very little aggression is evident. An example of the latter are the Senoi, an isolated tribe found on the Malay Penninsula. Because neighboring tribes fear the presumed magical powers of the Senoi, they are never attacked by these tribes. At the same time, they have no interest in initiating attacks on others. This pattern of

Table 18.4 Homicide and suicide rates, selected countries: 1974 to 1976 (homicide rates per 100,000 population of all ages, suicide rates per 100,000 population 15 years old and over)

Country	Homicides 1974	1975	1976	Suicides 1974	1975	1976
United States	10.2	10.0	9.1	12.1	16.9	16.4
Australia	1.8	1.6	1.3	11.7	15.2	14.8
Austria	1.5	1.6	1.3	23.7	31.3	29.2
Belgium	1.0	.9	.9	15.6	20.8	21.2
Canada	2.5	2.7	(NA)	12.9	16.8	(NA)
Denmark	.7	.6	.7	26.0	31.1	30.7
Finland	2.6	3.6	(NA)	25.1	31.9	(NA)
France	.9	1.0	.9	15.6	20.5	20.4
Germany, Fed. Rep.	1.2	1.2	1.3	21.0	26.4	27.2
Greece	.6	.8	.7	3.4	3.6	3.6
Ireland	.7	1.0	(NA)	3.8	6.9	(NA)
Israel[1]	1.0	1.3	1.4	5.5	11.9	11.8
Japan	1.3	1.3	1.3	17.5	23.6	23.1
Netherlands	.8	.7	.8	9.2	11.9	12.5
Norway	.6	.7	.7	10.4	12.8	14.1
Philippines	1.3	1.4	(NA)	1.2	1.5	(NA)
Poland	.9	1.0	1.2	11.3	14.7	15.7
Portugal	1.3	1.9	(NA)	8.5	11.6	(NA)
Puerto Rico	17.7	16.1	(NA)	7.7	11.8	(NA)
Spain	.4	.6	(NA)	4.0	5.3	(NA)
Sweden	1.2	1.1	1.3	20.1	24.4	23.8
Switzerland	1.0	.9	.9	20.6	28.8	28.1
United Kingdom:						
England[2]	1.0	1.0	1.1	7.9	9.7	10.0
Northern Ireland	13.6	11.4	13.7	4.0	5.1	6.2
Scotland	1.2	1.5	1.9	8.4	10.8	10.8

NA = not available. [1]Jewish population. [2]Includes Wales.
Source: U.S. Bureau of the Census, *Statistical Abstract of the United States* (Washington, D.C.: U.S. Government Printing Office, 1979), p. 182.

peace has apparently endured for over a century. More significant is the absence of violence between members of the Senoi tribe. They are described as psychologically integrated, emotionally mature, and socially constructive. "In the realms of family, economics, and politics, their society operates smoothly on the principle of contract, agreement and democratic consensus, with no need of police force [or] jail . . . to reinforce the agreements or to confine those who are not willing or able to reach consensus" (Stewart, 1969, p. 160).

While this image of the Senoi may be idealized, profound differences remain between this peaceful and relatively conflict-free society and the violence and social conflict that characterize so many other cultures. The challenge for the psychologist is to determine those features of the culture that are primarily responsible for the observed cultural differences in aggression. Is it the child-rearing practices? the type of social organization? economic resources? the type of living arrangements? In the ensuing sections, we will examine various factors contributing to aggression which could account for cultural and individual differences in aggressive behavior.

The Physical Environment

As we saw in Chapter 3, the physical environment in which people live may exert a significant impact on their personality and social behavior. Aggressiveness is commonly cited as an example of a significant personality component that is strongly affected by features of the physical environment; for example, by heat, crowded living conditions, urban noise, and so on. It should be noted that statements about the behavioral effects of particular physical conditions also imply assumptions concerning the biological properties of the organism. It is assumed that the organism is so constructed that particular features of the environment either directly or indirectly heighten or diminish aggression. For example, suppose we found a relationship between smog level and aggression, such that when the smog level goes up, aggression also increases. This connection is presumably unlearned, although it may possibly be modified by learning. In this context, we will focus on properties of the physical environment that may be the source of variations between individuals and between cultures in aggressive behavior.

Territoriality

The relationship between the amount of physical space and the number of its occupants is a fundamental ecological matter. Space limits food supply and other resources and these, in turn, limit the size of the population that can be supported. Aggression, as previously noted, helps distribute the members of a species over space and is one of a number of mechanisms that are believed to prevent overpopulation. While this evolutionary function may be valid, one cannot assume that aggression will be evoked whenever space is crowded or intruded upon.

There are many reasons why high population density may foster aggression. There are the obvious factors of increased competition for food and resources. Furthermore, the increased opportunity for contact may increase the frequency of conflicts. In addition, there is the possibility that crowding automatically evokes aggression, even when food supplies and related resources are adequate. Presumably, the automatic aggressive response to crowding would be linked to the territorial behavior that many animal species display. Intense aggression in response to an intruder's violation of an area occupied by an individual or a colony is commonplace in nature.

The fierceness with which many mammal and nonmammal species defend their territory has given rise to loose analogies between animal territoriality and human defense of space (Ardrey, 1966). Humans certainly fight over space. Nations defend their boundaries; adolescent groups in large urban settings designate particular streets or neighborhoods as their personal territory (Yablonsky, 1966). However, it is misleading to conclude that humans are thereby displaying a territorial instinct. There is enormous variability in human attachment to space and in their sharing of space. Human territorial behavior, in comparison to that of infrahumans, is strongly influenced and probably largely determined by learning and experience. Moreover, territoriality is not a universal characteristic of infrahumans. With the exception of gibbons, most primates do not defend territories (Johnson, 1972).

It is helpful to distinguish between territoriality and personal space. *Territoriality* refers to recognized areas and objects that are perceived by a person or group as belonging to them. *Personal space* is invisible and refers to a smaller area than a territory. It has been defined as "the space surrounding an individual within which an entering other causes the individual to feel encroached upon, leading him to show displeasure and sometimes to withdraw" (Goffman, 1971, p. 30).

Personal space is not a fixed entity. How close another person may approach before one feels discomfort and annoyance depends on personality and social factors and, most especially, on one's relation to the person approaching. Several studies have shown that friends consistently approach each other more closely than do acquaintances or strangers (Altman, 1975). Experimenters have also manipulated the positive versus negative features of an "intruder" and have shown that when the other person appears pleasant and acts in a reinforcing manner, the subject interacts at a closer distance with that individual (Altman, 1975).

Territoriality is similarly affected by social experience and situational factors. In one illustrative study, many volunteers who were strangers to each other were assigned to two-person groups and lived in confined, socially isolated quarters for eight to ten days (Altman, Taylor, and Wheeler, 1971). Territorial behavior was assessed by determining the exclusive use of chairs, beds, and areas. The degree of compatibility in the personalities of the two pair members influenced both territorial behavior and the amount of fighting between them. Incompatible pairs, which were defined as both members having a dominant personality, took much longer to establish territories, while displaying much more conflict than did pairs consisting of one member high in dominance and another member low in dominance. These data indicate that territoriality can be a social mechanism that helps *reduce* aggression and conflict between groups by establishing rules about what belongs to whom. It is also noteworthy that, after having established clear ground rules in their space and object usage, the compatible pairs, at a later point in their association, began to relax the territorial boundaries and permitted more intrusions.

Crowding

We have seen that nature permits considerable flexibility in personal space and territorial behavior among humans. Does this flexibility hold when space gets crowded? Is there a built-in aggressive mechanism that is evoked when space is dense with people? Some early studies with infrahumans suggested that aggression and other mechanisms come into play that have the biological function of reducing overpopulation when crowding occurs. In a series of studies by Calhoun (1948, 1950), the population of rats living in a one-block area in Baltimore almost doubled when over 100 new rats were released in the area. Although the food supply could have supported several thousand rats, the increased population pressure caused social disorganization and fighting. Most of the newly introduced rats and some of the older ones were killed so that, after a two-year period, the rat population was estimated to be only 150, a figure close to the initial levels. This field study was followed up by experiments in which rats were confined to a crowded room for a sixteen-month period (Calhoun, 1962). The rats adapted poorly to the crowded conditions, displaying marked social pathology. Infant and female mortality were high and there was a good deal of fighting, with infliction of gashes and cuts.

These findings indicate that crowding *can* lead to violence. But, as we have found for other factors influencing aggression, the effects of crowding depend on a number of other variables. For example, crowding is more likely to foster aggression when rodents are unfamiliar with each other (Wolfe and Summerlin, 1968). At the human level, the relationship between aggression and crowding is even more complicated. On first inspection, such indexes of aggression as juvenile delinquency were found to be greater in those neighborhoods in New York City with higher population density, determined by the number of people living in the area and the number of people per room. However, when neighborhoods were equated for demographic variables, such as educational level, income, and ethnic background, the relationship disappeared. In general, there is little evidence of a causal relationship between urban density and crime, including crimes of violence (Baron, 1977).

In addition to these correlational studies between naturally occurring crowding and aggression, there have also been several experimental efforts to manipulate crowding and determine changes in aggressive behavior. The results have been mixed. Both increases and decreases in aggression have been observed as a consequence of crowding. In one study, groups of six to ten same-sex or mixed-sex individuals listened to tapes of presumedly active

Table 18.5   Sentence scores (in months) as a function of
room size and sex

Room size	Males	Females
Large	37.78	37.10
Small	38.87	32.95

Source: Adapted from Freedman et al., 1972. Used
by permission.

trial proceedings and were given the task of deciding the guilt or innocence of
the defendants and, if guilty, to assign a sentence (Freedman, Levy, Buchanan,
and Price, 1972). The critical manipulation of the experiment was the size of
the room in which the discussion took place. In one condition, the room was
quite small, with about twelve square feet available for each participant. In a
second condition, the corresponding space available was twenty-five square
feet. The critical dependent variable was the severity of the sentence recom-
mended for the defendants. As Table 18.5 makes evident, crowding had a
different effect on females than on males. Whereas males in the smaller room
advocated somewhat more severe punishments than males in the larger room,
an opposite effect was found for the all-female groups. The different response tendencies of the two sexes appear to have canceled themselves out in
the mixed-sex groups, for whom no experimental difference was found.

Can one conclude that crowding increases aggressiveness in males and
decreases aggression in females? The answer is, "It depends." The results
are variable, with one study even finding significantly less aggression in
groups of four- to five-year-old boys when they played in a small area than
when they played in a much larger one (Loo, 1972). A theoretical interpretation accounting for these discrepant findings proposes that crowding serves to
intensify whatever behavior is prepotent at the time (Freedman, 1975). If a
nonaggressive response is stronger, as appears to be most often the case for
females and possibly for the preschool boys who knew each other quite well,
then crowding will enhance nonaggressive responding. On the other hand,
when aggressive responses are stronger, crowding should then increase the
level of aggression.

Noise

The intensification interpretation just suggested has its roots in Hullian, Dollard-Miller learning theory (cf. Chapter 6), which asserts that generalized
tension or arousal has an enhancing effect on whatever responses are prepotent at the time. One advantage of the arousal interpretation is that it helps
predict when noise and other arousers will facilitate aggression. Consider the

Figure 18.2   Effects of low-intensity (65 db) and high-intensity (95 db) noise on aggression. (Based on data from Donnerstein and Wilson, 1976.)

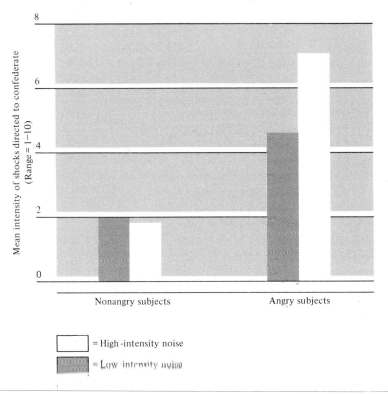

following experiment by Donnerstein and Wilson (1976). Male college students were either angered or treated positively by an experimental confederate. They were subsequently given the opportunity to administer electric shocks of varying intensities to the confederate while wearing earphones through which low-intensity or high-intensity noise was transmitted. From Fig. 18.2, it can be seen that noise enhanced aggression only for the subjects who had been angered, that is, for whom aggressive responses were more dominant. The same effect occurs when physical exercise rather than noise is the source of physiological arousal. Two and one-half minutes of strenuous physical exercise significantly heightened the level of aggression toward a confederate among those subjects who had previously been angered by the confederate, while having no effect on the nonangered subjects (Zillman, Katcher, and Milarsky, 1972).

Of course, the experimental effects of noise manipulation may differ from those of real noise. Real-life noises can be either more or less grating, annoying, louder, and painful than those used in experimental investigations. In addition, the effects of persistent, long-lasting noise may be different than those of the sporadic, short-duration noise used in most research. All of these effects must be evaluated in order to determine whether noise pollution in our urban environments is a significant contributor to urban violence.

Temperature

Another environmental feature with possible effects on aggression is temperature change. There is a widespread belief that prolonged heat increases the level of violence in a community. Common linguistic expressions also suggest an equivalence between heat and anger: "hot-tempered," "hot under the collar," "heated argument." Research exploring the factual basis for this presumed equivalence is relatively recent. In Chapter 3, reference was made to the correlation between ambient temperature and the frequency of major riots occurring in the United States during the period of the late 1960s and early 1970s. When an adjustment is made for the unequal number of days in different temperature ranges, one finds a positive linear relationship between probability of a riot and the temperature at the outbreak of the riot. There have been several experimental investigations of the effects of variations in the temperature of a laboratory on levels of aggression, as assessed by the administration of electric shock. These studies suggest that high temperatures in combination with other sources of unpleasantness, such as verbal insults, tend to have the paradoxical effect of lowering aggression. The subject is apparently more motivated to escape the very unpleasant situation than to aggress (Baron and Bell, 1975; Bell and Baron, 1976).

The complex laboratory findings underline the fact that we have not yet determined the basis for the positive relationship observed between ambient temperature and the probability of a riot. It could be due to the unpleasantness and frustration of heat, to greater numbers of people out on the streets, to teen-agers out of school during the summer months, to physiological changes, and so on. To achieve theoretical coherence and to be able to predict the effects of temperature under a variety of conditions, we need to identify the processes mediating between temperature and aggression; that is, we have to identify the factors that are affected by heat and that in turn influence aggression.

Personality Theories and the Antecedents of Aggression

We have seen that human aggression is influenced by biological and social variables, neurological mechanisms, cultural differences, individual learning experiences, and the physical and social environment. How do the facts on aggression relate to theories of personality? We will find that the personality theories that have given special attention to the problem of aggression differ in the relative emphasis placed on biological versus social variables, and in the particular social influences believed to be of primary importance. A discussion of theoretical views and research on the principal mechanisms causing aggression provides a basis for integrating the diverse data on aggression with other personality issues and for understanding the controversies concerning the development of aggression and its control.

Psychoanalytic Theory

Freud's views on aggression, like his views on other issues, underwent substantial modification during the course of his long career. In his early writings, Freud believed aggression to be primarily an innate reaction to frustration and pain: "the ego hates, abhors and pursues with intent to destroy all objects which are for it a source of painful feelings" (Freud, 1925, p. 81). This view persisted but was made subordinate to a subsequent formulation of aggression as arising from a biological drive. He proposed a new dichotomy in which the libidinal instinct, Eros, was enlarged to embrace all of the positive, constructive, life-enhancing tendencies and was contrasted with the death instinct, Thanatos, which encompassed the organism's tendencies toward aggression, self-destruction, and ultimately death (Freud, 1920). By the late 1920s, partly in response to the destruction of World War I, Freud had elevated aggression urges to a status equivalent to that of libidinal urges.

The death instinct is one of Freud's more speculative concepts and is not an integral part of psychoanalytic theory (see Chapter 4). However, while the concept of a death instinct has gained little acceptance, many psychologists support the assumption of an innate, biologically rooted aggressive drive. This view of aggression has important social consequences. It leads one to emphasize social controls and power as a means of checking human aggression rather than to modify social conditions and relationships that might foster aggression. Concerning the necessity of strong social controls, Freud stated: "Civilized society is perpetually mirrored with disintegration through this primary hostility of men toward one another. . . . Culture has to call up every possible reinforcement in order to erect barriers against the aggressive instincts of men" (Freud, 1930, p. 86).

Broad assumptions about human behavior, such as the view that humans have innate aggressive urges, are difficult to test or disprove. The work of ethologists like Lorenz and Tinbergen is sometimes cited as support for the innate aggressive drive hypothesis. However, as has been noted earlier, there are fundamental differences between the observations of ethologists and the psychoanalysts' conception of innate aggression. These differences may be summarized as follows:

1. Infrahuman aggression is primarily reactive rather than internally generated. Aggression is elicited by specific stimuli, referred to as *releasers*.
2. Innate aggressive responses by animals are primarily instrumental. If the object of aggression ceases the aggression-eliciting behaviors (e.g., intruding on territory, competing for food), then the aggressive attack usually ceases.

3. Withdrawal by or a submissive signal (an inhibitor) from the opponent is usually sufficient to terminate a conflict. Injury to an opponent is not required for an animal to terminate aggression.
4. Consistent with the psychoanalytic hypothesis, aggressive displacement has been observed in some animals. There is also evidence that some animals are motivated to continue or initiate a fight and will cross an electrified grid to do so. However, an animal's drive to complete an aggressive response, to express anger, or even to initiate a fight must be distinguished from the psychoanalytic conception of an innate drive to inflict injury.
5. The desire to hurt, to inflict injury, and to seek revenge is observed primarily in humans, not in animals. It seems quite likely that an aggressive drive in this sense is an acquired or learned motivation (Feshbach, 1974).

We have noted that, in psychoanalytic theory, the theme of reactive aggression coexists but is theoretically subordinate to the theme of innate aggressive drive. Nevertheless, in their writings, and especially in their practice, psychoanalysts also make extensive use of the idea that aggression is a reaction to particular experiences. Thus, in exploring the basis for a particular patient's anger and hostility, the analyst will look for situations in early childhood that might be responsible for the patient's aggression; for example, rivalry with a sibling may be exacerbated by parental favoritism toward that sibling. Psychoanalysts have also believed that frustration of biologically based oral or anal impulses (cf. Chapter 4) is a significant cause of aggression. However, studies investigating the relationship of aggression to the severity of weaning or toilet training have yielded negative or inconsistent findings (Feshbach, 1970). Modern psychoanalytic theory, with its emphasis on object relations and ego development, is more likely to look for the causes of aggression in the child's relationship with its parents and in the factors that promote the ineffective development of self-control, rather than to focus on the biology of the organism.

Learning Theory Models of Aggression

Learning theory models of aggression have in common the effort to establish systematic relationships between antecedent events and aggressive behavior. They differ in the particular antecedents or mechanisms thought to be most important. Adherents of Hullian and the Dollard-Miller theory have focused on frustration as an antecedent to aggressive drive. The elaboration of the relationship between frustration and aggression eventually led to a reformulation of the frustration-aggression hypothesis through the incorporation of significant elements from cognitive theory. In contrast, adherents of Bandura's learning theory have addressed their attention to the acquisition of instrumental aggressive responses and to the role of imitation in the development of aggression. Investigators favoring a Skinnerian model of learning have stressed the role of direct and subtle reinforcements in the acquisition of instrumental aggressive behaviors. In addition, several other theoretical positions will be considered that have incorporated aspects of learning theories but also have some unique features and emphases (Berkowitz, 1978; Feshbach, 1974).

The frustration-aggression hypothesis.   The formulation of the frustration-aggression hypothesis and the publication in 1939 of the Dollard et al. volume *Frustration and Aggression* marked the first systematic treatment by psychologists of aggressive behaviors. In addition, it provided a significant link between psychoanalytic theory and experimental psychology. And finally, the frustration-aggression hypothesis helped integrate a very diverse set of observations, ranging from violent dreams reported during psychotherapy to the frequency of lynchings, by linking these events to frustrations experienced by the individual and by members of a group. Although psychologists have significantly revised the hypothesis, it is still extensively used by social scientists and considered to be a landmark theoretical proposition.

The frustration-aggression hypothesis asserts very simply that the frustration (interference, blocking) of an ongoing activity produces an instigation (drive, motivation) whose goal response is injury to some person or object. No assumption is made regarding how the connection between frustration and aggression comes about, whether it is innate or learned, although it is acknowledged that reactions to frustration can be altered through learning. The initial statement of the hypothesis, namely that "aggression is *always* a consequence of frustration" has two implications: (1) aggression is always due to frustration and (2) frustration always leads to aggression. These statements are not equivalent; one can be false and the other true. For example, it might be that frustration always produces an impetus to aggression but that there are other factors besides frustration that also instigate aggression. It was immediately recognized by critics and also by the authors that, in using such exclusive terms as *always,* these propositions were too strongly phrased. The authors then acknowledged that there are other causes of aggression besides frustration and maintained that frustration produces a tendency to aggress as well as other response tendencies (Miller 1941). Consequently, overt aggression, while likely, is not an inevitable response to frustration, and the relationship between frustration and aggression can be modified through learning. But the hypothesis, even if less strongly stated, still had a number of important properties. The amount of aggression was hypothesized to be quantitatively related to the amount of frustration experienced by the organism. In addition, the authors also proposed that when the instigation to aggression was blocked through, for example, fear of punishment, there would still remain an instigation to aggress toward available targets. Thus, the formulation provided a model for the analysis of the displacement of aggression.

The frustration-aggression hypothesis has stimulated a good deal of research. A very early study, which reflects its potential utility as an explanatory tool, used as the measure of aggression the number of lynchings that took place yearly in the United States, largely in fourteen southern states, during the period from 1882 to 1930. Since cotton was the basic commodity in these states the value of the cotton yield each year during this period was also determined. It was hypothesized that the lower the cotton yield, the greater the economic frustration experienced by the community, and the greater the likelihood of displaced aggression toward an available target (in this case, primarily blacks). An analysis of the data revealed a sizable and significant negative correlation consistent with the hypothesis: the lower the yearly cotton yield, the higher the frequency of lynchings that year. While alternative explanations can be offered to account for this finding, the results are consistent with the frustration-aggression hypothesis and, without the guidance of that hypothesis, it is unlikely that anyone would have thought of correlating these two disparate events.

A more recent test of the effects of the magnitude of frustration employed a simple but clever experimental procedure in a natural setting (Harris, 1974). The experimenter had a confederate cut into a line of individuals who were waiting their turn at places like ticket windows, restaurants, and grocery stores. The critical dependent variable was the amount of aggression displayed by the individual whose place in line the confederate had displaced. Hypothesizing that the amount of frustration would be greater the closer that individual was to the beginning of the line, the confederate cut in front of either the second or the twelfth person in line. The person who had been closer indeed displayed much more aggression (fortunately, mostly verbal) toward the confederate than the person who had been farther along in line.

While these findings point to the usefulness of the frustration-aggression hypothesis, it is also the case that many investigators have failed to find an increase in aggression following frustration (Feshbach, 1970). The difficulty in evaluating these negative findings is that the level of frustration experimentally induced in the laboratory may often be too weak to evoke aggression. However, apart from the question of the adequacy of experimental tests, it is clear that the frustration-aggression hypothesis has serious limitations. First, the concept of frustration is vague. Insults and physical pain have been shown to be powerful elicitors of aggression. But are they frustrations? Failure would seem to be an obvious frustration, yet the frustrating effects of failure are dependent on expectancy. Your reaction to failing an examination would greatly depend on whether you had expected to pass. Second, in addition to the need to establish explicit criteria for what constitutes a frustration, the particular motivations that are frustrated must also be taken into account. Experiences that threaten an individual's self-esteem and sense of security appear to be much more likely to elicit hostility than experiences that interfere with satisfactions of a physiological drive like hunger (Maslow, 1941). It is not surprising, then, that parental rejection of a child or separation of the child from the parents results in more aggressive children than a severe weaning experience (Feshbach, 1970).

Although the frustration-aggression hypothesis has some validity, then, it is too broadly stated. What is required is a determination of the particular properties of interfering events that tend to foster aggressive reactions. Cognitive theories have proved to be very helpful in this regard. Cognitive attributes both determine the meaning of the frustration and strongly influence the likelihood of an aggressive response to the frustration. At least four cognitive attributes of frustration can be specified. While these are related to one another, it is helpful to separate them.

1. *Expectancy.* As has been noted, the degree to which a negative experience is frustrating depends on the degree of expectation of that experience. We expect some amount of discomfort in a crowded subway car and consequently react with less anger to jostling than if the car were half-empty. Expectancy also has significant implications for predicting the response to economic deprivation. Individuals from middle-class backgrounds who are unable to attain the standard of living they experienced when living in their parents' home are likely to feel more frustrated than individuals at the same income level but from poorer backgrounds. The aggression that sometimes accompanies small improvements in economic level in economically disadvantaged groups is also understandable in terms of expectancy, in that the small economic advance may have led to increased expectancies for substantial economic improvement that are subsequently frustrated.

2. *Arbitrariness or inequity.* A frustration is more likely to evoke aggression if it is perceived as arbitrary rather than justified. You are much more likely to get angry at a poor grade if you feel the instructor assigned the grade at random or was otherwise unfair than if you feel the grade was deserved. The roles of both arbitrariness and expectancy are nicely illustrated in an experiment in which subjects were promised a prize and given their first, second, or third choice under one of three anticipatory conditions: (a) they might or might not receive their first choice (no-expectancy); (b) they would receive their first choice (expectancy); or (c) they would be able to select any prize they wished (choice). The subjects were not given a reason when they did not receive their expected choice. This lack of explanation increased the likelihood that they would perceive the frustration as arbitrary. It is evident from Fig. 18.3 that not receiving a desired prize is not, in itself, sufficiently frustrating to provoke verbal aggression (no-expectancy group). It is only when expectancies are violated and the frustration is arbitrary that aggression is evoked.

3. *Intentionality.* We are much less likely to be angered by the same frustrating or painful event (e.g., being tripped while walking down an aisle) if we perceive it as accidental rather than intentional. This effect is clearly demonstrated in an experiment in which subjects received either strong or weak electric shocks administered at the presumed option of a confederate (Nickel, 1974). Half the subjects in each of these two groups were then informed that a switch had been placed in the wrong position and that the shock level actually intended was directly opposite to the one received. The amount of aggression subsequently expressed by the subjects toward the confederate was much more closely linked to the confederate's intended shock than to the actual level of shock inflicted.

Figure 18.3   Reactions to expected and unexpected frustration. (From "The Effect of Three Types of Arbitrary Thwarting on Instigation to Aggression," by Stephen Worchel. *Journal of Personality* 1974, *42*, 300–331. Copyright 1974, Duke University Press, Durham, N. C.)

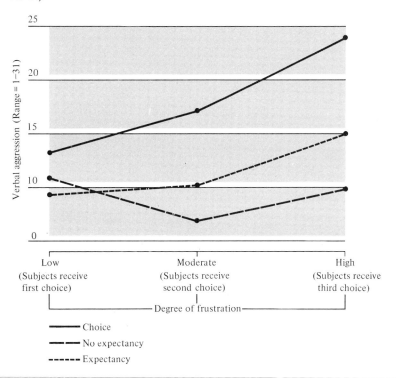

4. *Responsibility*. Related to intentionality is the attribution of responsibility. The greater the perceived responsibility of the frustrating agent, the greater the likelihood of an aggressive response. Given the same frustration, one does not react with equal aggression or punishment when the agent is a two-year-old as when the agent is a twelve-year-old. The role of responsibility is explicitly recognized in our legal code. If the perpetrator of a criminal aggressive act was forced to do so, then he or she is not held "responsible" and the penalty is much less severe.

A full understanding of the relationship between frustration and aggression must consider the cognitive attributes or meaning of the frustration. There are individual differences in the meanings given to frustration. Suspicious, paranoid individuals tend to attribute intentionality to an individual who frustrates them, even when the frustration was due to accident or ignorance. Learning also influences the response to frustration. Children can, for instance, be trained to respond less aggressively to frustrating events (Davitz, 1952). As we will see, learning is a powerful determinant of aggressive behavior.

Figure 18.4   Mean imitative aggressive responses performed by children. (Plotted from data by Bandura, Ross, and Ross, 1963a, pp. 3–11. Used by permission.)

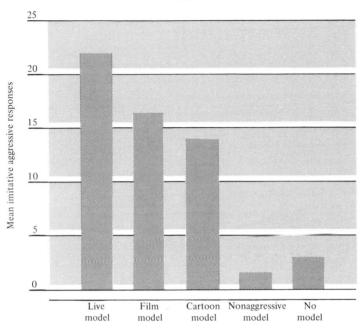

The influence of modeling on aggression.   Several of the basic experiments by Bandura and his coworkers, which provided the foundation for his theory of observational learning, involved the modeling of aggression (Bandura, 1962; Bandura, Ross, and Ross, 1963a; cf. Chapter 6). Preschool children who had observed an adult model carry out a series of discrete aggressive responses toward a Bobo doll (an inflated plastic clown) subsequently displayed a striking degree of imitation of the adult aggressive behavior in interacting with the Bobo doll. As Fig. 18.4 indicates, the children imitated the adult whether the model was live, on film, or dressed as a cartoon cat. The finding that children imitated filmed adult aggression and cartoon aggression suggested that similar effects might occur as a result of children observing televised aggression and has stimulated research and theorizing on the possible modeling influence of television on the aggressive behavior of child and adult viewers.

Although imitation is undoubtedly one process by which children acquire aggressive and other social behaviors, children obviously do not imitate every aggressive act they observe. We need to know the conditions under which they are likely to imitate an aggressive model. There have been a number of studies addressed to this issue. For example, verbalization of aggressive actions increases the amount and persistence of imitation (Bandura, Grusec, and

Menlove, 1966). In addition, children are more likely to imitate an aggressive model if they have had a prior frustrating experience as, for example, when losing in competitive play (Nelson, Gelfand, and Hartmann, 1969). And witnessing a model being rewarded for aggression tends to increase imitation, while punishment of the model's behavior tends to reduce imitation. However, there is some evidence that children learn the punished response and will perform it when inhibitory factors in the situation are lessened (Hicks, 1968).

Figure 18.5   Incidence of hijacking over a span of twenty-five years. (Plotted from data furnished by the Federal Aviation Administration. Adapted from Albert Bandura, *Aggression: A Social Learning Analysis,* © 1973, p. 106. Reprinted by permission of Prentice-Hall, Inc., Englewood Cliffs, N. J.)

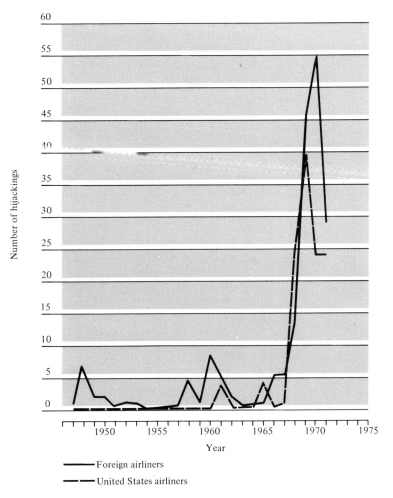

The concept of modeling has been applied to the spread of violent actions. An event can be modeled through verbal description, without visual representation, as in a newspaper report. Learning of a violent event can, under appropriate conditions, facilitate repetition of that event. The rapid spread of airline hijackings (see Fig. 18.5, p. 485) provides an excellent example of this influence (the rapid decline can be attributed to countermeasures). The process of modeling can, in fact, be used to account for a wide variety of aggressive behaviors. However, in view of the enormous variability in imitation of observed behaviors, we need to know much more about the situational and individual factors that determine when a model is imitated.

Reinforcement.   Why have some people learned to be aggressive? One reason may be that they have been exposed to models of aggressive parents, peers, and perhaps favorite television characters. Another, probably more potent, reason is that they have found that aggression "pays off," that it gets them the rewards of money, sex, status, and power over others that they seek. There is a good deal of evidence that aggressive behavior is governed by the same principles that govern instrumental responses. Aggression increases when reinforced and declines when not rewarded or when punished (Brown and Elliott, 1965; Walters and Brown, 1963). We have seen, in our discussion of infrahuman aggression, that victory and defeat play a powerful role in determining the level of aggressive behavior. A naturalistic study in which preschool children were observed over a nine-month period indicated that similar effects are at work at the human level (Patterson, Littman, and Bricker, 1967). The effects of reinforcement and punishment were especially noticeable in passive children who entered nursery school with weak aggressive tendencies. The passive children who were attacked by other children and whose counterattacks were unsuccessful remained submissive in their behaviors. However, the initially passive children whose counterattacks were successful showed a significant increase in aggressive tendencies.

There has been a great deal of interest in the use of reinforcement procedures for the modification of aggression in highly aggressive youngsters. These reinforcement programs have been carried out in institutional settings, in classrooms, and in the home. The programs are characterized by the careful monitoring of the child's behavior, the administration of positive rewards (e.g., prizes and privileges) for prosocial behaviors, and either ignoring of or mild punishment (e.g., brief isolation periods, loss of privileges) for aggression and related negative behaviors. Patterson and his colleagues have pioneered in the development of methods for training parents to cope more effectively with aggressive problem children through the appropriate utilization of reinforcement procedures (Patterson, 1979). Their findings indicate that after twenty-five to thirty treatment hours with parents and children, over a period of several months, significant reductions occur in the level of the children's aggression and other aversive behaviors (e.g., whining).

One of the contributions of the behavioral method developed by Patterson and others on the basis of Skinnerian principles is that it requires close attention to the behavior that is to be discouraged or rewarded. The parent, teacher, and other authority figures thus become more conscious of the subtle ways in which they may be reinforcing an undesired behavior: for example, they may reinforce aggression by paying attention to a child whenever he is difficult or by finally yielding to demands after an escalating sequence of aggression and punishment. In addition, aggression may be rewarded quite directly. Bandura and Walters (1959) found that fathers of aggressive adolescent boys tended to urge their sons to fight their peers even though they discouraged aggression in the home; the attitude of these fathers is not very far from the ambivalent attitude toward male aggression that prevails in American culture. Aggression is, to be sure, discouraged, but it is also admired. The "he-man," virile cowboy image remains a significant component of the American conception of what it is to be a man (*New York Times,* 1980).

Aggressive cues.   When individuals are frustrated, have strong aggressive tendencies due to reinforcement, or are otherwise aggressively disposed, they are not aggressive all the time. An *aggressive cue* is usually required in order for the aggressive tendency to be expressed in behavior. Leonard Berkowitz (1978) proposed that these aggressive cues have acquired the property of eliciting aggression through the learning mechanism of classical conditioning. It is assumed that aggressive words and aggressive instruments have accompanied frustration and other stimulus events that evoke aggressive responses and, through this pairing, become conditioned stimuli or cues for aggression. Berkowitz and his students have carried out an extensive series of ingenious experiments demonstrating the importance of such cues in the regulation of aggressive behavior (Berkowitz, 1965b; Berkowitz and Geen, 1966). For example, subjects who had seen a film depicting a brutal prize fight and who had previously been angered by a confederate administered a greater number of shocks to the confederate when he was described as a college boxer than when he was described as a speech major. Several control conditions that were included indicated that this difference in cue labeling was not effective unless the subject had seen the fight film and was also angry. A similar effect was obtained when the confederate was introduced to the subject merely with the same first name as the major character in the boxing film (Berkowitz and Geen, 1966).

In another provocative demonstration of the role of aggressive cues, angered or nonangered subjects were given the opportunity to shock a confederate either while observing a .38-caliber revolver and a 12-gauge shotgun placed in the vicinity of the shock button or with these objects absent (Berkowitz and LePage, 1967). The amount of shock delivered by the subjects who had been angered was significantly greater when the weapon cues were present than with the weapons absent. These findings, if confirmed, would suggest another reason why the reduction of available firearms in the community should result in a reduction in the amount of violence, particularly on the part of angry individuals. But subsequent efforts to repeat these findings have yielded mixed results. Some investigators have obtained the "weapons effect," while others have not. Nevertheless, there is little doubt concerning the role of aggressive cues in the facilitation of aggressive behavior.

Social influence. Social norms and social influences can be considered aggressive cues that may directly encourage aggressive behavior. Even nonaggressive individuals may participate in aggressive actions because of conformity to social expectations and social pressure. A dramatic demonstration of the power of an authority figure to elicit conformity and obedience to rather extreme demands and expectations is provided in a famous experiment by Stanley Milgram (1963). Adult volunteers were requested and then commanded to use increasing levels of shock whenever a confederate made an error on a learning task. The switches controlling shock levels were clearly labeled, with the indicator ranging from 15 to 450 volts. Protesting subjects augmented the shock levels under pressure from the experimenter, even when the presumed "victim" pounded on the wall that separated himself from the subject, as if in great pain. Whenever the subject wanted to stop the proceedings, the experimenter would exert additional pressure. Under these circumstances, 65 percent of the subjects proceeded to the final 450-volt shock. Perhaps because of the experimental situation and the belief that a university professor would not encourage a violent act that was truly painful or destructive, the 65 percent compliance figure is inflated. Nevertheless, the Milgram study suggests that conformity pressures can induce individuals to carry out extreme aggressive acts. Many individuals who participated in implementing the atrocities ordered by the Nazis were probably doing so out of such obedience and fear.

It is evident from this review of the diverse explanations that have been offered for human aggression that there are many different processes mediating aggressive behavior. There is no single mechanism that one can point to as *the* cause of aggression. The various personality theories have tended to focus on different processes rather than offering rival interpretations of aggression. Thus, frustration, particularly when perceived as intentional or arbitrary; rewards and punishments; modeling; the presence of aggressive cues; and conformity to social norms are all determinants of aggression. The least satisfactory hypothesis is the psychoanalytic assumption of an instinctive aggressive drive, or innate hostility. However, there are undoubtedly biological factors involved in some forms of aggression. In other respects, as in its focus on the family's role in the development of aggression, the psychoanalytic contribution to our understanding of aggression has been substantial.

Developmental Influences

Child-Rearing Practices

On the basis of the antecedents of aggression that have been discussed, we might expect that a history of frustration and parental rejection, or of parental permissiveness and reinforcement of aggression, would be associated with the development of aggression in offspring. This is indeed the case (Feshbach, 1970). Parents who are permissive about aggression or, like the fathers cited earlier, encourage some forms of aggression; parents who make few demands of their children with regard to positive social behaviors and who are lax in their supervision; and parents who essentially reject the child through their coldness or actual hostility are likely to have highly aggressive children. What about the effects of parental punitiveness, particularly the use of physical punishment? There is some disagreement among investigators on this issue. From a theoretical standpoint, physical punishment can affect aggression in several different ways. First, because of its aversive features, it has an inhibitory function for the disapproved behavior. However, physical punishment is painful, frustrating, and frequently humiliating—all of which are likely to stimulate aggression. In addition, the parent, while physically punishing the child, is serving as a model to the child. Imitation of the parent's behavior would enhance aggression. And, in this connection, the parent may be teaching the child a social norm that essentially states that if you are injured or frustrated by someone, you respond by physically punishing them.

With few exceptions, studies of child-rearing practices have indicated that the frequency of parental use of physical punishment is one of the best predictors of aggression in children. Differences arise in the interpretation of this relationship since these studies as a rule do not clearly distinguish between physical punishment that is limited and restrained and punishment that is brutal. In addition, it may be that more aggressive children elicit more severe and more frequent punishment from their parents.

The report of a major ten-year longitudinal study of the development of aggression (Eron, Walder, and Lefkowitz, 1971; Lefkowitz, Eron, Walder, and Huesmann, 1977), indicated that "moderate punishment by parents in the long run produced less aggressive children than either no punishment or harsh punishment" (p. 192). Thus, permissiveness of aggression and severe punishment had the same consequence: highly aggressive children.

Child Abuse

Other evidence of the relationship between physical punishment and aggression pertains to the commonly cited observation that parents who physically abuse their children were themselves physically abused as children (cf. Gerbner, Ross, and Zigler, 1980). Child abuse is a form of aggression that is particularly distressing in that young children are the objects of physical abuse and adults, most often parents, are the abusers. It is a problem that unfortunately is not rare; estimates of the number of children in the United States who are physically abused each year range in the hundreds of thousands (Gil, 1970). Moreover, the parents cannot be considered psychotic or suffering from serious psychopathology. Personality studies of child abusers have reported some differences between this group and nonabusing parents, but the differences are not great and are outnumbered by the similarities (Parke and Collmer, 1975; Spinetta and Rigler, 1972).

There is some evidence that the same factors associated with aggression in general are also involved in child abuse. Thus, frustrations like job dissatisfaction are more common among abusive parents (McKinley, 1964). In addition, abusive parents tend to expect more of their children than is age appropriate. They are more likely to see the child as a fully responsible agent and perceive the child's failure to conform to parental requests as intentionally motivated. In addition, one of the personality characteristics of abusive parents that does distinguish them from other parents is low self-esteem; threats to self-esteem are generally considered to be among the most powerful instigators of anger and hostility.

Aggression as a Personality Trait

The literature that has been reviewed provides substantial evidence of situational factors influencing aggression. But data have also been cited reflecting individual differences in aggressivity. The evidence of the stability of aggressive behavior over long periods of time (cf. Chapter 8 and Lefkowitz et al., 1977) provides strong support for viewing aggression as a personality dimension in which individuals differ. In a detailed review of sixteen studies on the stability of aggressive behavior patterns, an impressive degree of consistency in aggressive characteristics was observed over periods ranging from six months to as much as twenty-one years (Olweus, 1979). Although the correlation between the level of aggression displayed at one age and that assessed at a later period decreased as the length of the time interval increased, there was nevertheless a significant relationship between the degree of aggression that an individual manifested as a preschooler and the level of aggression characterizing that same individual as a young adult. There is substantial evidence for stable individual differences in aggression, whether aggression is assessed through direct observations of behavior or by means of ratings by peers, teachers or clinicians.

These findings do not necessarily mean that a person's level of aggression is fixed in early childhood or is biologically determined. We have already noted that aggressive behavior can be markedly influenced by a great many situational and social factors including frustration, heat, noise, humiliation, victory, defeat, aggressive cues, and social norms. What the data on individual differences do indicate is that relatively stable individual differences in the tendency to respond aggressively in particular kinds of situations can be observed at a fairly early age. Aggression is thus a personality trait as well as a response to the situational factors enumerated above.

Data from these and other studies indicate that aggression is not only relatively stable over time but that there are also consistencies among different indicators of aggression. Self-report questionnaires have been shown to be related to peer ratings of aggression and to the judgments of authority figures, while these measures in turn are related to aggressive choices and to aggressive behaviors (Feshbach and Singer, 1971; Lefkowitz et al., 1977; Olweus, 1978). Although there is evidence for the consistency of aggressive behavior, the role of situational factors should not be minimized. A very aggressive person at home and among peers may be unaggressive in a work situation because the job is particularly satisfying or because of fear of losing the job.

Fear of punishment and guilt or anxiety over aggression complicate the findings on the consistency of aggressive behavior. As one might expect, individuals who experience guilt (Knott, Lasater, and Shuman, 1974) and anxiety (Feshbach and Singer, 1971) over aggression are less aggressive than individuals with little guilt and anxiety. However, there is evidence that individuals who express a good deal of anxiety over aggression are struggling with strong aggressive tendencies. Their aggression is expressed in indirect ways or only when it is completely safe to do so (Eron et al., 1971; Feshbach, Stiles, and Bitter, 1967). Aggression-anxious persons would appear, at a superficial level, to be inconsistent in their aggressive behavior, displaying very little aggression in some situations and exaggerated aggression in other contexts. But by taking into account both their conflict over aggressive impulses and the presence of situational cues that elicit anxiety, one can find order and consistency in their behavior (cf. Miller's conflict model, Chapter 14).

Other data bearing on the question of aggression as a trait address the question of the personality of aggressive individuals. Are they fearful? bored? suspicious? impulsive? With regard to the personality correlates of aggression, conflicting findings are reported by different investigators and it is likely that there is more than one "aggressive personality." For example, there is clinical theory and some empirical findings suggesting that people who are overtly aggressive suffer from underlying anxiety (Feshbach and Singer, 1971). However, Olweus (1978), in an intensive study of sixth-grade Swedish boys who were classified as "bullies" or "whipping boys," found that the bullies were low in anxiety and evaluated themselves quite positively. They were quite comparable on these measures to a group of well-adapted boys. Olweus also found that the bullies had less positive attitudes toward their fathers than did the other boys, had less close contact with their mothers, and were more likely to feel rejected by their parents.

As one might expect, the personality correlates of aggressiveness vary with the type of aggression involved. Thus, willingness to retaliate when aggressed against is associated with a hard-driving, competitive personality— a so-called type A personality (Baron, 1977)—and with a belief in one's ability to influence one's own fate (Dengerink, O'Leary, and Kasner, 1975). However, the most striking example of the relationship of personality correlates to the type of aggressive behavior is provided by Megargee's studies of extremely assaultive individuals (1966). Megargee found that the moderately aggressive criminal has weak inhibitions against aggression, a low threshold for aggression, and a history of aggressive behavior: an *undercontrolled aggressive* type. In contrast, an extremely assaultive person whose criminal aggressive act was of homicidal intensity is more likely to fall into the *chronically overcontrolled* category (Megargee and Mendelsohn, 1962).

The extremely assaultive person is often a fairly mild-mannered long-suffering individual who buries his resentment under rigid but brittle controls. Under certain circumstances he may lash out and release all his aggression in one, often disastrous, act. Afterwards he reverts to his usual overcontrolled defenses. Thus he may be more of a menace than the verbally aggressive "chip-on-the-shoulder" type who releases his aggression in small doses.

The Megargee findings and those reported by other investigators provide a picture of extreme violence that is in greater accord with a psychodynamic model and with concepts of frustration-produced aggressive drive and repression than with the learning models of Bandura and Skinner which focus on the imitation or reinforcement of instrumental aggression.

Megargee's image of the overcontrolled assaultive type also is an interesting contrast to Toch's (1969) personality description of prisoners and parolees with a history of violent encounters. Toch arranged for other prisoners and parolees to conduct extensive interviews with this sample of undercontrolled aggressive persons. A large subgroup consisted of individuals whose violence stemmed from basic insecurity and low self-esteem. Some expressed this insecurity in their excessive sensitivity to any sign of a slight, while others tried to convey an exaggerated image of fearlessness. Other subgroups were characterized by infantile expectations of indulgence, by a sense of being in danger and becoming a victim, and by a need to defend their status as tough and powerful. Still another subgroup fell into the category of bullies or sadists who seemed to enjoy inflicting pain on helpless victims.

In summary, the response to the question of the personality characteristics of aggressive individuals depends on the degree and type of aggression. Instrumental aggression, reactive aggression, aggressive drive, and repressed hostility are interwoven in various combinations and shades; each pattern of aggression seems to have a different constellation of personality factors.

The Influence of the Mass Media

Up to this point, aggression has been seen as rooted in a complex personality structure of low self-esteem, profound frustration, and suppressed rage that are, in turn, related to such child-rearing factors as the reinforcement of aggressive behaviors, the use of extreme punishment, lax demands, hostility, and rejection. However, the family is only one of the many socializing influences on a child's development. Another socialization influence that has received a great deal of attention as a potential antecedent of aggression and crime is the mass media, particularly the depiction of violence on television.

Television Violence

Observation of television violence can foster aggression in the viewer through a number of possible mechanisms including:

1. Imitation of aggressive television character models.
2. Disinhibition of aggression; sending a "message" that violence is "okay."
3. Providing aggressive cues.
4. Adaptation to and acceptance of violence after constant exposure.

There is experimental evidence, some of which has been cited earlier, for each of these potential aggression-facilitating mechanisms.

On the other hand, exposure to violence in the mass media could conceivably have the opposite effect of reducing aggression through:

1. Serving as a substitute for direct aggression by providing an opportunity for the vicarious expression of angry feelings, or *catharsis.*
2. Reinforcing fantasy behavior by providing entertainment and associating pleasurable feelings with television viewing.
3. Providing recognition of and insights into aggressive feelings.
4. Associating punishment with antisocial aggressive behaviors.

There is some experimental evidence consistent with the first and second of these potential aggression-reducing influences. But if one compares the amount of empirical support for mechanisms that result in the augmentation of aggression with those that might reduce aggressive behavior, there is clearly much more support for aggression-enhancing effects of television viewing. Bandura's findings on the imitation of an aggressive film model and Berkowitz's investigations of exposure to the fight film in conjunction with aggressive cues are examples of studies indicating that violence on television and in films can facilitate and augment aggressive behavior. However, one must still distinguish between these potential effects of television violence as determined in the laboratory and the actual effects of observing television violence in the complex natural context in which most viewing takes place.

Although many, if not most, behavioral scientists believe that the depiction of violence on television is a significant contributor to violence in the society, the evidence from more naturalistic field studies is quite mixed and not nearly as persuasive as the data based on laboratory experiments. The primary field method used has been correlational. These studies have found that the frequency with which aggressive television programs are viewed is positively correlated with the degree of aggressive behavior. One of the limitations of these studies is the difficulty of determining the direction of cause and effect (see Chapter 11). Do aggressive children prefer and select aggressive programs to view or does the observation of aggressive programs cause the viewer to be aggressive? Some investigations have made use of longitudinal methods that permitted the analysis of changes in behavior over time and concluded that viewing violence on television was a significant cause of aggressive behavior. However, other correlational studies, equally well controlled, have found a negligible relationship between television viewing and aggression or find that the relationship disappears when relevant variables are controlled (Hartnagel, Teevan, and McIntyre, 1975; Jessor and Jessor, 1977).

In an experimental effort to control television viewing in a natural setting, Feshbach and Singer (1971) arranged for preadolescents and adolescents living in private schools or boys' homes to be exposed to a predominantly aggressive or nonaggressive television diet for a six-week period. The private school students were unaffected by the television manipulation but the boys' home sample actually displayed a significant decline in aggression relative to controls. Still another well-known and ambitious series of field experiments

A child watching violence depicted on television. This could increase violence if it leads to modeling and imitation. But the effects of watching television violence on actual behavior are complex and uncertain. (Alice Kandell/Photo Researchers, Inc)

by Milgram and Shotland (1973) failed to provide any evidence for modeling a television theft of money from a charity box or the use of obscene language in a telephone call. Each of these field experiments has methodological limitations, as do the few field studies that report an increase in aggression following television viewing (Leyens, Camino, Parke, and Berkowitz, 1975; Stein and Friedrich, 1971).

Rather than trying to decide whether television violence causes aggression, we might address the more properly phrased question of the conditions under which television violence facilitates aggression, decreases aggression, or is likely to have no effect on aggressive behavior. The experiment described earlier, contrasting the effects of a reality set versus a fantasy set in responding to an aggressive television sequence (cf., Chapter 15), suggests that a reality orientation enhances the aggression-stimulating effect while a fantasy orientation is more conducive to a reduction in aggression, or catharsis. There are undoubtedly many other relevant variables, such as the age and personality of the viewer and the structure and emotional tone of the television program, that warrant investigation.

A related question that has barely been addressed but which has at last begun to be examined is why children and adults are attracted to violence in the mass media. The response to this question will undoubtedly be related to the deeper issue of why people watch drama at all.

Erotica

Violence in the mass media is not the only type of content that may influence the viewer's level of aggression. There has also been some interest in the effects of erotic themes on viewers' aggressive behavior. This interest stems in part from the social relevance of determining the effects of erotic stimuli and in part from its relevance to the broader personality question of the relationship between the sexual and the aggressive behavior systems. There are a number of experiments indicating that watching an erotic film or reading a highly erotic story, in comparison to exposure to neutral stimuli, results in elevated levels of aggression (Jaffe et al., 1974; Zillman, 1971). However, other studies have also reported a decrement in aggression following exposure to sexual materials (Baron, 1974; Frodi, 1977; Malamuth, Haber, and Feshbach, 1980).

One hypothesis that has been offered to account for the diverse effects of sexual arousal on aggression asserts that when sexual arousal is accompanied by anxiety, aggression is inhibited. Conversely, when sexual arousal is not accompanied by inhibitory feelings, aggression is facilitated. Jaffe (1975) provided evidence to support this hypothesis by demonstrating that when an erotic film that had resulted in lowered aggression was presented in a less anxiety evoking context, aggression was facilitated. He also found that the introduction of a fifteen-minute delay between the observation of the erotic stimulus and the measurement of aggression had no effect on reducing the subject's level of aggression. Since physiological arousal—elevated heart rate, blood pressure, respiration, and galvanic skin response—returned to normal during the fifteen-minute period following sexual arousal to the film, these data indicate that the increase in aggression was not attributable to physiological arousal. Rather, it was suggested that the implicit disinhibitory message of the erotic film, that taboo behaviors are permissible, facilitated the expression of aggression (Malamuth, Feshbach, and Jaffe, 1977). It was further proposed that the reciprocal influence of sex and aggression occurs only for cultures and individuals whose training and experience have led to a link between the two systems of behavior.

An interesting offshoot of these experiments has been the investigation of factors influencing the response to the depiction of rape. One series of studies suggests that males are motivated to reinterpret the pain cues expressed by the rape victim. In one experiment, a relatively mild sadomasochistic story taken from a popular sex magazine was adapted so that two forms were available: the sadomasochism version and a similar sexual, but nonviolent, version. After reading one of these two versions and completing a questionnaire assessing level of sexual arousal, all subjects were given the same rape story to read. Male subjects who had read the sadomasochistic story were more sexually aroused in response to the rape story than males who had read the nonviolent version. It was as if the significance of cues of female pain that ordinarily would be expected to function as inhibitors had been altered so that they now became indicators of female sexual arousal.

Catharsis and the Regulation of Aggression

At various points in this chapter reference has been made to factors relevant to the control and reduction of aggression. There are a number of methods for modifying anger and the response to aggressive provocation. It would be misleading if the presentation of these alternatives suggested that it is a relatively simple matter to modify aggression. The methods are intended only as guides. They offer a basis for designing procedures to cope with and hopefully mitigate destructive social behaviors.

Catharsis

Originally, the term *catharsis* referred to the discharge of feelings resulting from witnessing a dramatic play. Currently, it is used to refer to the reduction of aggression through any aggressive activity, whether shouting epithets, witnessing the depiction of violence on the stage or in film, inflicting injury on an innocent target, or directly aggressing against the instigating source. There are a number of studies indicating that, in order for a reduction in aggression to occur, the individual must be angry at the time of the aggressive act (Doob and Wood, 1972; Feshbach, 1964; Konecni, 1975). Hitting a punching bag will not reduce aggression toward an irritating supervisor unless one is angry at the supervisor while punching the bag. The evidence for catharsis is also stronger when fantasy aggression is expressed directly toward the instigating target rather than toward a displaced target. While there are several studies indicating that the expression of aggression in fantasy or imagination can be cathartic (Feshbach, 1956; Manning and Taylor, 1975), there are others that question this effect and suggest that only direct, overt expressions of aggression are cathartic (Hokanson and Burgess, 1962).

It is significant that an aggressive act in which too much or too little pain is inflicted will not provide drive reduction (Fromkin, Goldstein, and Brock, 1977). This finding is in keeping with the proposition that aggressive drive is based on social norms or rules that regulate retaliation; these rules state essentially that if you have been injured by someone, you are supposed to reciprocate by inflicting an equivalent injury on that person (Feshbach, 1974).

Incompatible Responses

The second mode of reducing aggression is through training a response that is incompatible with anger. Various studies have successfully demonstrated the training of incompatible overt responses using reinforcement procedures and imitation (Donnerstein and Donnerstein, 1977). A very promising program for the training of mediating cognitive responses that are incompatible with anger has been developed by Novaco (1975). In that program, Novaco trained angry individuals to relax when provoked and to rehearse nonaggressive statements.

Cognitive Control Mediators and Prosocial Expression of Anger

Experienced anger can be controlled through the subject's empathy with the frustrating agent and through the capacity to delay expression of anger and contemplate alternatives. If one can take the perspective of those with whom one is in conflict and understand their feelings, their behavior is less likely to seem frustrating and arbitrary and therefore is less likely to evoke aggression. The ability to think before acting, to consider a range of possible responses to a provocative situation, is also likely to increase the probability of nonaggressive, prosocial alternatives. There have been several recent reports of promising programs designed to enhance prosocial behavior and reduce aggression through empathy training (N. Feshbach, 1979), social understanding (Pitkänen-Pulkkinnen, 1979), and problem-solving skills (Spivack and Shure, 1974).

Altering Stimulus Meaning

Aggression and anger can also be modified by changing the meaning of a stimulus. For example, an individual may be perceived as not being responsible for or not having intended some injurious act. An example of this procedure is provided by a study in which an experimenter acted in a rude and obnoxious manner. The subjects were informed that the experimenter was very "uptight" about a forthcoming midterm examination. This information resulted in a sharp reduction in subjects' verbal aggression and blood pressure. The latter finding suggests that the subjects were not simply inhibiting their anger (Zillman and Cantor, 1976).

Punishment

The last of the methods for modifying aggression is punishment, which may inhibit the aggressive response but leave the underlying anger unaffected. Mild punishment or punishment that is meaningfully related to the aggressive infraction, e.g., having someone do something positive for the injured person, coupled with one of the other procedures, could prove to be a very effective method for reducing aggression.

Summary   Human aggression consists of a complex set of social behaviors that have many antecedents. These include genetic, neurological, and biochemical factors, as well as varied influences in the physical and cultural environments. For humans, there is no simple one-to-one relationship between aggression and such factors as territorial space, crowding, noise, heat, and frustration. The extent and even direction of the effects of these factors are very much dependent on other variables. Aggression, in addition to being influenced by these situational and environmental variations, can also be acquired through systematic reinforcement of aggressive behavior and through exposure to aggressive models. The effects of these different learning mechanisms and of repeated exposure to punitive, frustrating experiences on individual differences in aggression are reflected in investigations of the development of aggression and of the personality of aggressive individuals. A full understanding of the development of aggression must take into account the effects of such diverse socializing forces as individual family child-rearing practices, mass media content, and exposure to prevalent cultural norms.

Specific Points

1. The term *aggression* includes a great many behaviors that may have different functions and causes. Distinctions should be made between the emotion of anger and the motivation to inflict injury, or *aggressive drive,* and the *instrumental* use of aggression to obtain nonaggressive goals.

2. For many infrahuman species, intraspecies aggression is regulated by stimuli called releasers that elicit innate aggressive responses and inhibitory stimuli that serve to terminate an aggressive interaction.

3. Although there is evidence that male sex hormones will, under certain conditions, increase aggressive behavior for several infrahuman species, no clear relationship between male sex hormones and aggression has been established for humans.

4. Brain surgery and brain stimulation studies have shown that specific areas of the brain are involved in some types of aggressive behavior. However, the effects of brain stimulation can also be markedly influenced by features of the environment.

5. There is some evidence that genetic factors influence criminality and possibly aggression as well. However, in either case environmental factors have been shown to exert much more powerful effects.

6. Crowding and noise have been shown to both increase and decrease aggressive behavior. These factors apparently intensify whatever behavior, aggressive or nonaggressive, is prepotent at the time.

7. The extent to which frustration elicits aggression depends on the nature of the motivation that is frustrated and on such cognitive factors as expectancy of frustration and whether the frustration is perceived as arbitrary, intentional, and caused by a responsible agent.

8. Imitation of a model's aggressive behavior may account for such diverse phenomena as the positive correlation between parental use of physical punishment and children's aggression, and the recent dramatic increase in airplane hijacking.

9. Violent, extremely assaultive behaviors are associated with a history of strong punishment for and extreme inhibition of aggression.

10. The majority of laboratory studies indicate that observation of aggression in films and on television tends to stimulate and facilitate aggressive behavior. The results of field studies reflect a more complex relationship between aggression and exposure to violence in the mass media.

11. Exposure to erotic stimuli has been shown to both enhance and decrease aggressive behavior. A critical variable appears to be the degree of anxiety and related inhibitory reactions elicited by the erotic situation.

Thought Questions

1. To what extent is modern warfare a result of biologically based aggressive tendencies?
2. If a drug were discovered that practically eliminated violent behavior through chemical action on brain sites, would you favor its administration to violent criminals?
3. Among the factors discussed in the text that contribute to or elicit aggression, which ones, in your opinion, are the principal contributors to the high level of violence that exists in a number of U.S. urban areas?
4. Some people maintain that rock music, especially when played to large audiences, is a significant source of violence in adolescents and young adults. What studies bear on this contention? What is your own opinion on this issue?

Summing Up

19   In the preceding eighteen chapters, we have discussed a great many ideas, research approaches, and experiments. It is impossible to review and integrate this extensive material within a few final pages. The summaries at the end of each chapter can be of some help, but what is most useful and feasible at this point is to consider some of the major themes in human personality that are represented in this text. Four major themes recur: interactionism, the multidimensionality of the person, the self, and personality as a science. After identifying these recurrent themes and reaching some general conclusions about them, we look to the future. Using a combination of a crystal ball and our own sense of current trends, we will suggest the directions in which the field of personality is moving and which problems we think should be addressed in the years to come.

Interactionism

Human behavior and personality are a function of the interaction between the person and the environment. The important theme of interaction is present throughout this text. It appears in the early chapters on the biological versus the physical, social, and cultural determinants of personality. These chapters make it evident that both nature and nurture exert significant influences on personality. For example, how can one possibly argue that all the determinants of behavior reside in the environment, given the similarities between the traits of monozygotic twins, or given the differential concordance rates for schizophrenia among monozygotic versus dizygotic twins? On the other hand, how can one logically believe that genetic determinants of behavior account for cultural and social class differences? Individuals strictly committed to either an environmental or a genetic approach cannot give satisfactory answers to these questions.

But the concept of interaction implies even more; it indicates that the influences of nature and nurture do not work in isolation, but rather are interdependent. For example, both infrahuman and human data indicate that a predisposition to alcoholism can be inherited. But the genetic predisposition alone cannot produce alcoholism. An environment in which alcohol is available is also necessary. In certain cultures, such as Moslem communities where alcohol consumption is forbidden, an inherited vulnerability to alcoholism is not likely to emerge. Aside from the availability of alcohol, the development of alcoholism may also depend on the interaction of a genetic predisposition with other environmental factors such as repeated situational stress.

Another example of the interaction between biological and environmental factors is the relationship between physique and personality. A child's physique is influenced by environmental as well as genetic factors. He or she must have the appropriate diet and exercise if a genetic predisposition toward athletic (mesomorphic) body build is to be manifested. Because of muscularity, there may in turn be increased likelihood of the child's experiencing success in aggressive encounters or sports. The culture may also share certain stereotypes about mesomorphic individuals, like the belief that they are dominant, courageous, and aggressive. The child may then acquire these behaviors in the process of living up to stereotyped expectations. Thus, it would be just as wrong to say that a child's assertiveness is due to his or her inherited physique as to view the attribute as solely determined by environmental experiences. Both biological and environmental factors contribute to personality traits. In this example, the interaction between the child's body structure and subsequent experiences is critical.

The theme of interaction extends beyond the nature-nurture controversy. It is also intrinsic to the dynamics of behavior. For example, different periods of life pose special problems for adaptation and development. By knowing that someone is an adolescent or in midlife, we glean some information about the kinds of problem situations that person will confront. Clearly, the situations encountered by a teenager are very different from those of an adult in midlife crisis. But there are also significant individual differences between and among adolescents and adults in approaching problem situations, in the intensity of developmental crises, and in how the situations are resolved.

Numerous other instances of the person-situation interaction can be found in the text. Many reactions to frustration have been identified. For example, frustration may increase the probability of aggression or of immature, regressive behavior. But this effect is more marked in children who are "undercontrolled" than in children who are labeled as "overcontrolled" (Block and Martin, 1955). In addition, while some individuals react to frustration with hostility, childishness, and disruptiveness, others may withdraw and become apathetic, while still others respond with increased problem-solving activity that can lead to new, creative solutions for overcoming the source of frustration. You are encouraged to look for other experimental examples of person-situation interactions that are cited or implicit in the text.

At one level, it may appear that the interaction notion is so obvious that it hardly requires special emphasis. However, it is all too easy to view behavior as determined by either situational or person factors. Indeed, the procedures used in investigating personality frequently lend themselves to a one-sided perspective. To simplify their studies, researchers may concentrate on the effects of the situation and ignore differences in personal attributes or, conversely, they may focus on individual differences while ignoring the properties of the situation that are relevant to those individual differences. For example, consider the following experiments which have demonstrated a situational focus: exposure to a television episode depicting altruism or to a nurturant caretaker increases prosocial behavior in young children; the visual presence of a prospective reward reduces delay of gratification; frustration decreases the constructiveness of play; and precise instructions for completing a task lead to decreased satisfaction. In these and many more studies, the investigators manipulated some situational property and determined its effects on behavior, but the attributes of the person that were essential to these situational effects were ignored. Because subjects are not equally affected by experimental manipulations, psychologists conduct experiments with many subjects, rather than simply generalizing from the responses of one particular individual. A few subjects, in fact, may respond in a manner opposite to the general trend. For some, very precise instructions and a high degree of structure may result in heightened, rather than decreased, satisfaction. This does not mean that the experiments are flawed or uninformative, or that the experimenters were unaware of the importance and possible interactions of subject attributes. Rather, it is easy to forget that one is really dealing with interactions even when an investigation has focused on situational variables.

A comparable problem arises when experimenters center on person variables. In these instances, the situational component of the interaction is neglected. You may recall that there is a tendency to overestimate the importance of personal traits and to underestimate the importance of the situation as a determinant of others' behavior. We tend to characterize people in trait terms that are independent of situations, such as introversion-extraversion or high achievement need–low achievement need. The situations in which introversion or high achievement strivings are evoked are typically unspecified. This is also the case in experimental studies. For example, reports that high achievement-oriented persons are more realistic than those low in achievement needs ignore the fact that this finding was obtained under particular circumstances, in a specific situation.

Although traits are often considered properties of the person, they may be better conceptualized as predispositions to respond to particular classes of situations in certain ways. Thus, when an individual is labeled high in anxiety, this should not be taken to mean that that person is always anxious; rather, he or she is predisposed to become anxious in certain situations. The range of situations can be quite broad, such as becoming anxious whenever competing, or more narrow, such as becoming anxious whenever taking a test in a classroom. But whether the range of situations in which a trait is manifested is broad or narrow, trait effects, like situational effects, always imply an interaction.

In phenomenological theory, the interaction between person and situation is exhibited in the subjective perceptions and meanings that individuals impose. Theorists in the phenomenological tradition tend not to be concerned with traits or with external physical events, but assume instead that the individual's subjective experience is of fundamental interest. This experience reflects an interaction between the objective stimulus situation, or what is "out there," and the attributes of the person that filter the external environment and provide meaning to the world. Thus, phenomenological theorists are concerned with interactions at the level of subjective perception and personal understanding.

The Multidimensionality of the Person

Human beings are thinking, feeling, motivated, behaving organisms. Some theoretical approaches, notably the learning theories, have placed primary emphasis on overt behavioral responses, largely because these are observable and subject to direct verification. Psychoanalytic theorists, on the other hand, stress largely the feelings and motivations of the organism, while the phenomenological, cognitive theorists are particularly interested in the individual's thoughts and perceptions. In the approach to personality that has been followed in this text, all these dimensions of human functioning are considered significant.

The term *eclectic* is sometimes used for an approach in which elements of different theories are incorporated, without strong identification with one particular theoretical model. Unfortunately, *eclectic* also has the connotation of unwillingness to make the hard choice of selecting among theories. In reviewing the empirical findings that have been presented in this text, however, it becomes evident that thoughts, feelings, desires, and response tendencies are all essential to an understanding of human personality. Hence, the various theoretical approaches contribute positively to an understanding of the person, while being incomplete in and of themselves.

Some theorists might argue that, while all of these components are necessary, one is primary and the others are secondary. For example, it could be argued that cognitions determine feelings, motivations, and behavior. Thus, if you believe that someone deliberately humiliated you (cognition), then you are likely to become angry (emotion) and wish to retaliate (desire). If you believe that you have a good chance of retaliating without punishment (cognition), then you might act aggressively toward the person who injured you (behavior). In this example, cognitions are primary, producing certain feelings, motivations, and behaviors. But motivations are sometimes primary. For example, an extremely ambitious person might perceive other people as obstacles and threats, in which case motivations determine cognitions. And overt responses or behaviors can also be primary: a boy may act aggressively because he has been repeatedly reinforced for aggressive acts. When acting aggressively, he may rationalize his behavior, perceiving other children as initiators of the hostile exchange.

Under certain circumstances, then, each component might be of central importance and determine the other processes. At a more fundamental level, the cognitive, affective, motivational, and behavioral aspects of human personality are interrelated. For example, a highly aggressive person not only has a low threshold for responding with aggressive behaviors, but also tends to perceive others as threatening. Thus, the disparate aspects of personality form an organized whole; each aspect has a significant role and none can be considered sufficient to account for the complexity of human action.

There is an apparent contradiction in human behavior that also highlights the necessity of accepting an eclectic approach and the shifting primacy of the components of human behavior. On the one hand, humans are quite rational. They can consciously employ coping strategies to handle threat and anxiety; goal expectancies are calculated and logical decisions are made; information is sought out and processed; causal inferences are made; and self-insight can be attained. On the other hand, it is also evident that we are frequently irrational. Motivations are unconscious and we defend ourselves in ways unknown to us; in times of stress and frustration, distinctions may be blurred and fixated behavior is displayed; overgeneralizations are made when there have been prior unfavorable outcomes and perceived lack of control; information is not properly processed; illogical decisions are reached; and there is personal delusion.

A list of the contradictions in human behavior could go on and on. Because logical and rational or illogical and irrational behavior might be exhibited in any given situation, the creation of a general theory of personality is indeed a difficult undertaking. And, given this diversity, one must accept that many equally important components or processes play an active role in human personality and behavior.

The Self

The self and related ideas of self-concept and self-esteem were discussed in some depth in Chapter 10. However, research and theories about the self are by no means restricted to the contents of that chapter; in virtually all the other chapters of this text, issues involving some aspect of the self have been addressed.

Theoretical Views

Consider first the place of the self in the various theories of personality. Clearly, the self is a central construct for phenomenological theorists, with their concentration on self-worth, self-perception, the ego ideal, and self-actualization. But the other theoretical approaches also place considerable importance on the self. Psychoanalytic defenses such as regression, reaction formation, and projection are mechanisms for maintaining self-esteem and preventing the individual from awareness of painful attributes of the self (Hilgard, 1949). And social learning theory gives considerable attention to self-monitoring processes. Another attribute of the self that has assumed central importance in social learning theory is the sense of self-competence or self-efficacy.

In a very general way, phenomenological theorists have focused on the cognitive, experiential aspects of the self (who am I?); psychoanalytic theorists have been oriented toward the motivational properties of the self (how can I protect myself?); and the social learning theorists have stressed the response properties of the self (what are the response consequences of high or low self-efficacy?). Remember, though, that these differences are a matter of emphasis, inasmuch as all the theoretical approaches recognize the cognitive, motivational, and behavioral components of the self.

The various aspects of the self have assumed a significant role in personality research. For example, we have reviewed studies in this text that concern self-control, self-esteem, self-focus, discrepancies between perceived and ideal self, and the relations between self-attributions and affect. Furthermore, how we believe we appear to others and the avoidance of guilt and shame are among the most powerful of human motivations and determinants of human striving. But the importance of the concept of the self has perhaps been best revealed in the discussion of perceived freedom and personal responsibility. An impressive amount of data indicates that self-determination and the perception that one has choice and control over life events have profound behavioral consequences.

The Self and Consciousness

The relevance of the self to personality and behavior is particularly evident when there are disturbances in consciousness. For example, in cases of multiple personality, unacceptable impulses become attributed to another self that has its own personality. Organized patterns of behavior that constitute a separate self are rare, but dissociated fragments of behavior are quite common. Following some unusual behavior it is common to feel "that wasn't me" and to experience the event as outside one's personality and self-control.

An intriguing approach to the loss of self is provided by the meditative practices and philosophies of a number of Eastern religions. Through a program of meditation, relaxation, and self-mastery, one can apparently lose one's sense of a separate self or ego during the meditation experience. The individual is said to become one with the larger universe. The phenomena of dissociation and merging of the self refer to the discrimination between what is "me" and what is "not me", or to the perception of the self as a distinct psychological entity.

The opposite of dissociation is self-insight, or increased awareness of one's feelings, drives, and attitudes. An important goal of some forms of psychotherapy is the attainment of insight, where information is brought into consciousness and new forms of understanding are reached. The important effects of self-understanding are also evident in other human endeavors. For example, self perception of skill and competence are particularly important determinants of realistic achievement striving.

But self-awareness is not always functional. Repression is a necessary defense enabling one to adapt and function within society. In addition, a distinction must be drawn between awareness of the self as an object or agent and awareness of the stimuli or information that come from the environment and one's own body. An athlete's awareness of the self—of body movements, of the desire to win and the fear of losing,—can interfere with concentration and impede effective task performance. This seems to be particularly true if expectations of success are initially low.

The role of the self in the analysis of personality often goes unrecognized. But close inspection reveals that it is one of the unifying themes in the study of personality. It stands alongside interactionism and the multidimensionality of the person as a strong motif in this text.

Personality as a Science

At the outset, we indicated that the study of personality must be guided by experimental procedures and empirical evidence. Certainly, many of the complex issues in personality are difficult to investigate. Manipulation of antecedent conditions thought to influence personality development, such as parental warmth, are neither feasible nor ethical, and precise measurement of constructs such as parental warmth are exceedingly difficult. Nonetheless, the study of personality is not exempt from the scientific method.

Throughout this book we have asked if assumptions or conclusions are supported by appropriate evidence. For example:

1. Psychoanalytic theory postulates a death instinct and conceptualizes humans as closed energy systems. It was pointed out that these presumptions are not supported by empirical evidence, but rather are theoretical assumptions not subject to proof or disproof. On the other hand, there is some empirical support for the existence and function of psychoanalytic defenses, such as repression, denial, and intellectualization.

2. Social learning theorists hypothesize that exposure to a model influences learning and behavior. This has been well established. In addition, other social learning theorists accept the belief that rewards and punishments alter behavior. This is certainly true, but there are exceptions or contradictions to this fundamental principle. For example, rewards and punishments do not appear to influence frustration-induced fixation, and an extrinsic reward might actually undermine an intrinsic interest.

3. The humanistic principle of self-actualization is not subject to scientific proof or disproof. On the other hand, in support of humanistic hypotheses, there is evidence that the discrepancy between the ideal self and the perceived self does change during the course of psychotherapy.

The number of known and established facts about personality is truly enormous. At the same time, our ignorance is all too apparent. We have tried to indicate what the facts are and when we are ignorant, what is speculation and what is established. One must constantly try to remain aware of this distinction. A major theme of this book is that appropriate data should always be brought to bear on statements concerning personality.

The Future

The field of personality is constantly changing. New theoretical approaches are being developed, new content areas are being explored, new methodologies are evolving, and new empirical findings are being reported every year. It is extremely difficult to predict future developments in the field, given this constant ferment and change. What we can do, however, is suggest some future directions that the study of personality may take, as well as indicate the topics that we would like to see pursued.

It is evident from the text that many issues remain to be resolved. Some broad and fundamental empirical questions still at issue include the role of nature and nurture and their interaction in determining human personality; the degree of trait consistency and generality; the extent to which personality is crystallized in childhood; and the modifiability of basic personality attributes in later life. There is also disagreement on many quite specific issues. Psychologists are not in agreement on the extent of sex differences in personality, the validity of self-report personality scales, the major antecedents of aggression, and the effects of factors such as anxiety, stress, meditation, and self-esteem on performance quality and intensity. Clearly, many more disagreements can be added to this short list of examples.

The fact that so many issues remain unresolved does not mean that there has not been significant progress in the investigation and understanding of personality. In the study of personality, it is true that similar questions have been examined again and again. But when the questions do reappear, they are in improved forms that make more meaningful answers possible. As one looks at the history of inquiry into personality issues, it can be seen that there have been profound changes in the sophistication of the questions asked and the methods of research employed.

These positive trends are illustrated in the study of aggressive instincts. Questions regarding the instinctiveness of aggressive behavior have been addressed for many years by philosophers and early psychologists. In previous eras it was believed that aggression was a product of an aggressive instinct and that one either had or did not have such an instinctive tendency. Research first revealed that aggressive behavior is not an either-or matter, but involves degrees or amounts of aggression; that is, there is variability in the extent of aggressive actions. It was later determined that environmental variables, such as aggressive models, frustration, and the presence of weapons in the environment, may contribute to aggressive actions. The investigation of the contribution of learning and situational factors to aggressive behavior caused still further revision of thought on the matter. It became clear that, for a genetic predisposition to be manifested, particular environmental conditions were required. Thus, regardless of the relative contributions of personal and situational determinants of hostility, aggression is always determined by both innate qualities and the environment. In addition, more precise analyses of aggressive phenomena revealed that the phrase *aggressive instinct* is far too vague and undifferentiated. The internal determinants of aggressive responses that appear to be instinctive, like those studied by ethologists, must be distinguished from aggressive drives, and these drives must, in turn, be distinguished from simple expressions of anger.

There is no fully satisfactory answer to the question of the instinctive nature of human aggression. But the systematic study of personality has enabled us to provide a more sophisticated answer than was possible in the prescientific era. A similar statement can be made about virtually any of the topics reviewed in this text. In accordance with this analysis, we do not expect that developments in the immediate future of personality will provide final answers to the difficult and unresolved issues. However, we do believe that they will help provide better, more sophisticated answers.

Personality Structure

A *structure* refers to something made up of interdependent elements or parts, with a fixed pattern of organization. Thus, when we discuss the structure of personality, we mean the relatively fixed and interdependent components of the person. There have been many references in this text to various aspects of personality structure. *Introversion, need for achievement,* and *aggressive inclination* are structural terms; id, ego, and superego are also structural concepts, as is the self, including the "split" within the self. In some cases, the meaning of these terms is clear and procedures are available for measuring and studying them. However, in other instances the concepts are unclear and difficult to assess, as is the case for the concepts of ego and split personality.

But an even greater shortcoming is the absence of a coherent system that specifies the interrelationships among the many structural terms. Part of the difficulty here is that psychological structure is analogous to physical structure; it is easy to equate and confuse the two. But a psychological split is not the same as a physical split, and psychological distance cannot be measured in physical dimensions of inches or feet. Indeed, psychological direction may be opposite to physical direction, as when one runs toward a fire in order to escape from it. Furthermore, passing an examination or getting married involves psychological movement, even though there may be no change in physical location.

In spite of these difficulties, there is some utility in thinking of personality in terms of structural concepts derived from the physical sciences. The chapters on the development of the self, traits, and consciousness all have to do with the structure and organization of personality. The issue, then, is not one of establishing that there is a structure to personality. Rather, the task is to formulate a logical set of constructs relating to personality and to develop a clear set of procedures for measuring and making inferences about these constructs.

Individual Differences and Their Development

Psychologists have devoted a great deal of attention to the study of individual differences in personality. Measures have been developed for traits like introversion, aggression, achievement, and the belief in internal versus external control, to cite a few. After establishing a trait category or dimension of individual difference, a logical next step is to identify the antecedents of a trait. There have been some investigations of the effects of differences in socialization practices on personality development. And, especially in recent years, there has been considerable interest in the role of biological variables in personality development. But, in general, insufficient attention has been paid to the causes of individual differences, and much more research has been directed toward establishing trait categories and trait measures than toward sources of individual differences.

We can anticipate that there will be more extensive and coordinated efforts in this area. In particular, what is needed in addition to more research on social and biological variables is an integration of these two research traditions. Much of the biologically oriented research has been devoted to the demonstration that there are genetic and physiological factors influencing personality. In a similar manner, socialization research has focused on demonstrating the role of child rearing and cultural variables. But more attention must be given to the interplay of both sets of variables. We anticipate that there will be an increasing number of investigations tracing the interaction over time between a child's biologically based inclinations and the behaviors encouraged by parents, peers, and other socializing agents.

An additional source of personality influence that contributes to this interaction is the character of the physical environment, both natural and artificial, in which the child is reared. Because of the complexity of the interactions among these three sets of influences, one can expect that new research methods will be formulated to facilitate investigations of personality development.

Personality Dynamics

A close inspection of the studies in Chapter 14 concerned with psychodynamics will reveal that they were conducted earlier than the experiments discussed in other chapters of this text. The investigations of substitution undertaken by Kurt Lewin and his students took place, for the most part, in the 1920s and 1930s; studies of conflict were conducted primarily in the 1940s and 1950s; and the same is true of experiments examining the effects of frustration, including aggression, regression, fixation, and renewed goal strivings. We find it unfortunate that the experimental study of these topics is only weakly represented in contemporary psychology, inasmuch as behavioral dynamics encompasses extremely important and interesting issues for the field of personality.

There are many understandable reasons why investigators do not continue to pursue a particular phenomenon. First, there are diminishing payoffs for the study of any given problem or theory. Second, there are many other interesting ideas and issues competing for attention. Third, scientists quite naturally want to establish their own reputations in uncharted areas. Finally, the problems of psychodynamics are especially difficult to solve, discouraging investigators who then seek more fruitful fields elsewhere. These are valid reasons and the goals of the investigators are laudable. But as a result of premature diminution of research in an area, problems are left behind before sufficient scientific progress has been made.

We believe that there should and will be a return to the study of basic psychodynamic phenomena, such as substitution and displacement, in the future. Lewin and Freud both pointed out the importance of the interrelationships of need systems and the fact that attainment of one goal can serve to satisfy other unfulfilled needs. This and related problems in psychodynamics are key issues for the field of personality and are in need of systematic investigation.

An Integrated Theory of Personality

The current state of personality theory is unsatisfactory. Chapters 4 through 7 presented a number of alternative conceptions of human behavior. In some reviews of personality, as many as twenty-five different theories are presented, one chapter after the other, with little or no theoretical integration or connection. Inasmuch as one of the tasks of science is to provide a general theory with as few constructs as possible, one hopes that in the next decade there will be a significant reduction in the number of theories of personality that are offered. Of course, for this to be true there must first be an increase in the availability of pertinent data that permit one to reject certain theories and accept others.

It is unrealistic, however, to expect that the field of personality will be able to settle on one theory that is acceptable to all. As has already been indicated, some of the differences between theories are primarily philosophical. Whether one views the person in mechanical terms or in self-determining, cognitive terms is more a matter of philosophical bias than an issue that can be resolved by firm data.

Although one can therefore anticipate that competing theories will be with us for a long time, it is both possible and valuable to begin to formulate a comprehensive theory of personality based on an integration of compatible elements drawn from extant theories. Each theory—Freudian, Jungian, Rogerian, social learning, and so on—has important statements to make that are consistent with the available data about personality. These propositions about personality can begin to be incorporated within a common framework and a common terminology.

The matter of language is not a simple obstacle to overcome, since the theories employ such different concepts. However, for a number of reasons we feel that a common theoretical language can now be formulated. Contemporary psychological thinking is more flexible and broader than was the case a decade or two ago; cognitive psychology has achieved respectability; there is a general interest in affects and their relation to motivation and behavior; the concept of self is widely used; and both the mind and the emotions have been readmitted to formal, scientific psychology. With increasing agreement about the appropriateness of structural, cognitive, emotional, motivational, and behavioral terms, it may well be possible to start the task of a more integrated and comprehensive theory of personality.

Summary

Four themes that are represented throughout this text have been pointed out: interactionism, multidimensionality, the self, and personality as a science. In addition, future directions in the areas of structure, development, dynamics, and theory have been suggested. The field of personality is vital and growing; this growth is evident in the increasing sophistication of the questions asked and in the increasing refinement of the answers provided.

Thought Questions

1. Which personality areas do you feel are most in need of study?
2. In which personality areas do you feel that the most progress has been made and the most knowledge has been generated?
3. Which personality areas discussed in the text most interested you and motivated you to find out more about them? Why?
4. Do you think that any one of the personality theories discussed in the text will be dominant in the future? Defend your answer.

Glossary

adolescence The transitional period of human development between childhood and adulthood, from the onset of puberty to the early twenties.

aggression Hostile, injurious, or destructive behavior.

agonistic behavior Offensive and defensive fighting and competitive activity; a term used by biologists to define aggression.

altered states of consciousness Instances of heightened inner awareness, as might be experienced when under the influence of a drug or during deep meditation.

altruism Concern for the welfare of another without regard for oneself.

ambivalent behavior Behavior that oscillates from approach to withdrawal.

amnesia A loss of both identity and recall of the past.

analytic psychology Jung's personality theory that deviates from psychoanalysis in its emphasis on the collective unconscious and on the human striving toward self-fulfillment.

anxiety A state of unrealistic fear.

approach-approach conflict Lewin's classification for conflict in which there are two or more positive alternatives to choose from.

approach-avoidance conflict Lewin's classification for conflict that occurs when both positive and negative consequences are associated with the same action.

archetypes In Jungian theory, the primeval contents of the collective unconscious.

arousal The intensity, state of activation, or drive characterizing an individual.

associationist learning theory A learning theory that views humans in terms of stimulus-response variables and as essentially creatures of habit.

attribution theory A theoretical approach based on the view that people attempt to explain and understand behavioral events through attributing the causes of those events to characteristics of the person or to factors in the environment; these causal ascriptions significantly influence goal expectancies and behavioral responses.

autism A severe mental illness of early childhood, characterized by absorption in fantasy, isolation, and extremely defective thinking and language abilities.

autonomy The ability to act for and by oneself.

avoidance-avoidance conflict Lewin's classification for conflict in which a choice is confined to two or more unattractive alternatives.

behavior Any activity, covert or overt, of an organism.

behavior modification Therapeutic techniques that use Skinnerian methods of changing behavior to modify disturbed behaviors.

behavior therapy Psychotherapeutic techniques based on learning principles.

biofeedback The process of monitoring and providing information to the person about involuntary body functioning, usually as a therapeutic method for learning how to control maladaptive physiological responses.

body image The organized perception of one's physical structure.

bonding (attachment behavior) The formation of stable attachments to particular caregivers.

catharsis The reduction of emotional tension through expressive release activity; sometimes restricted to release through vicarious activity, such as watching a play or film.

cathexis The psychic energy that has been invested in a desired object.

causal attributions A term used in achievement-related contexts to connote beliefs about the reasons for one's success or failure—for example, ability, effort, task ease or difficulty, or luck.

client-centered therapy The psychotherapeutic approach used by Rogers, which employs trust, acceptance, and empathy to help clients realize their goals.

cognitive behavior modification A modified Skinnerian approach to human behavior, derived from modified Skinnerian principles, that stresses the role of cognitive factors in mediating behavior and attempts to bring about change through alteration of these cognitions.

cognitive conceit A defensive belief in one's own greater intelligence and insight.

cognitive style A person's consistent ways of perceiving in relation to himself or herself and the surrounding world.

cognitive theory The theory of personality that focuses on human thought processes and levels of understanding as a major determinant of behavior.

collective unconscious In Jungian theory, the site of inherited primitive, universal attitudes and ideas (archetypes) of which we are not conscious.

complex In Jung's theory, a group of feelings, ideas, memories, and behaviors organized around a significant object.

concrete reciprocal hedonism The view that if one person does something for another, it is right for the other to do something in return.

conditions of worth The conditional positive regard—the "do's" and "don'ts," "shoulds" and "shouldn'ts"—that people live by in order to feel appreciated and accepted by others.

conflict A psychological state in which two or more varying forces or alternatives are present simultaneously.

consciousness Awareness, or self-knowledge, of one's experiences.

construct validity The degree to which a test represents the meaning of the construct it is designed to measure.

constructive alternativism Kelly's basic tenet that "meaning" and "reality" are dependent on the person's interpretation and therefore are subject to change.

content validity The degree to which a test adequately represents the content it is designed to assess.

convergent validity The degree to which a test measures the same construct as that assessed by other tests.

correlation A mathematical index used to express the degree of association between two variables.

criterion validity The degree to which a test predicts, or correlates with, a subsequent factor (*predictive validity*), as well as the degree to which it is associated with other indexes that exist at the same point in time (*concurrent validity*).

cue Any stimulus, often a subtle one, that directs behavior.

decentration The cognitive capacity to assume the point of view of another.

defense mechanisms In psychoanalytic theory, unconscious strategies that enable a person to avoid awareness of unpleasant or anxiety-arousing experiences.

depression A disturbing condition involving feelings of sadness, lowered initiative, and an attitude of self-blame.

diagnosticity The information gained about one's ability following task performance.

discriminant validity The degree to which a test measures a different construct than that assessed by other tests.

discriminative conflict As noted in Pavlov's studies, a conflict in which similar stimuli are associated with different consequences so that it is difficult to distinguish whether the outcome of a choice will be favorable or unfavorable.

displacement A defense mechanism in which a person shifts a reaction from an original target person or situation to some other person or situation.

dissociation An altered state of consciousness in which a person lacks awareness of significant segments of his or her behavior or identity.

drive Any motive or need that impels action.

drive reduction A decrease in the intensity of a motive or need force, which, according to associationist learning theory, also strengthens the stimulus-response connection.

ectomorph A person with a tall, thin physique, whom Sheldon observed as also tending to have an introverted temperament.

ego In Freudian theory, the part of the personality that mediates between the demands of id impulses, superego, and external reality.

ego ideal In Freudian theory, standards that guide behavior because they are believed to constitute worthy goals to strive toward.

egocentricity A self-centered frame of reference in which one assumes that others perceive the world from the same perspective as oneself.

emotion A subjective feeling state, with cognitive, physiological, and/or behavioral components.

empathy The ability to discriminate and label feelings in others, to assume the perspective and role of another person, and to experience and respond with feeling.

endomorph A person with a rounded physique, whom Sheldon observed as also tending to have a relaxed and gregarious temperament.

environmental psychology The study of the role of environment in regulating behavior.

existential humanism A personality theory that views the individual as responsible for his or her own actions and as having to cope with guilt and anxiety.

expectancy-value theory A motivational theory emphasizing that behavior depends on the probability that an act will lead to a goal and upon the value of that goal.

extraversion From Jung, the tendency to be strongly oriented toward other people and social situations.

extrinsic motivation The undertaking of an activity for an expected external reward.

face validity The degree to which a person's response to an objective test item can be taken as a valid personality indicator.

factor analysis A statistical method of reducing a large amount of data from tests, rating scales, or behavioral observations to a smaller and presumably more basic number of dimensions or personality factors.

fixation The persistence of responses that apparently result in repeated failure and nonreward.

frustration A state of arousal that occurs when a person is unable to reach his or her goal and produces behaviors as disparate as aggression, fixation, regression, and enhanced goal striving.

genotype A person's set of inherited characteristics, as determined by genetic makeup.

gerontology The study of the phenomena of aging in humans.

hallucination Perception of visual images or audible sounds that are not actually present in the environment.

hallucinogen Any drug that produces hallucinations.

homeostasis Equilibrium or balance among internal processes.

humanistic psychology The system of psychology that focuses not only on what a person is, but also on what a person has the potential to become.

hypnosis A trancelike state in which the cooperative subject is highly responsive to suggestions made by the hypnotist.

hysteria A psychological reaction state (for example, dissociation) characterized by high excitability and anxiety, incapacitating bodily symptoms, and altered states of consciousness.

id In Freudian theory, the most primitive and inaccessible part of the personality, made up of sexual and aggressive instincts, which strive continually for gratification.

idealism A dissatisfaction with the state of the world, a desire to improve it and to make life more fulfilling.

identification The process by which the child imitates and subsequently internalizes the perceived attitudes and values of the parent while still maintaining a distinction between its own and the parents' identities.

identity The sense of being a physical and psychological self separate from the environment.

imagery Pictures one visualizes or imagines, which can facilitate memory and alter feelings and behaviors.

implicit psychology The perceived laws of behavior held by naive observers, or the personality theories of individuals who are untrained psychologists.

imprinting The process of establishing an attachment on first exposure to an object (noted in Lorenz's studies of newborn infrahumans).

instinct   An innate, biologically based mode of response to certain stimuli.

interactionism   The personality theory that views behavior as governed by both the properties of the person and the situation in which the person is acting.

internal consistency   A measure of test reliability; the degree of consistency within a test during any given time period.

intrinsic aggression   Aggressive behavior motivated by the satisfaction of engaging in aggressive activity, as contrasted with behavior motivated by the desire to inflict injury.

intrinsic motivation   The undertaking of an activity for its own sake without expectation of external reward.

introversion   In Jung's theory, the tendency to be attentive and interested in one's own thoughts and feelings.

isolation paradigm   The experimental procedure used to study innate behaviors in which infant infrahumans are isolated so that they cannot observe others' responses and hence exhibit only innate responses.

learned helplessness   The acquired expectation that one's actions will exert little control over outcomes.

learning theory   As applied to the area of personality, a set of assumptions that the development and functioning of the personality is based on experimentally derived principles of learning.

libido   Freud's term of psychic energy, derived primarily from the sexual, pleasure-seeking instincts of the id.

life structure   Levinson's term for the basic pattern governing a person's adult life stages.

measurement error   The degree to which the observed score on a measuring instrument deviates from the true score.

mediated generalization   An unobservable association process by which dissimilar situations elicit the same mediating response.

mediating response   Any unobservable internal response that intervenes between the observable stimulus and the overt response.

meditation   Any attempt to alter consciousness by means of systematic concentration and sustained self-regulation of attention.

mesomorph   A person with an athletic physique, whom Sheldon observed as also tending to have an energetic and assertive temperament.

midlife crisis   In Levinson's theory, a transitional period in adult development (the forties) during which one assesses his or her basic life structure.

modeling (imitation) (observational learning)   The process of acquiring new behaviors through observation of another person performing them.

narcolepsy   Sudden "sleep attacks" that often occur without warning, particularly during times of heightened excitement, lasting from a few to fifteen minutes.

natural behavior   Patterns of behavior that one has the potential for developing and that will develop under normal environmental circumstances.

neurosis   An emotional, nonpsychotic disorder characterized by anxiety and other symptoms and resulting in partial impairment of functioning.

object permanence   A Piagetian concept referring to the child's ability to sense that objects have a permanence independent of his or her desires, regardless of whether the child is looking directly at or touching the object.

object relations theory   In psychoanalytic ego psychology, the theory that ego development and subsequent interpersonal relationships are based on the infant's attachment to the mother and other figures.

object representation   A person's internalized image of a significant object.

oedipal conflict (Oedipus complex for boys; Electra complex for girls)   In Freud's psychosexual theory of development, sexual attraction to the opposite-sex parent, and jealousy and hostility toward and fear of punishment from the rival, same-sex parent.

operant conditioning (operant reinforcement)   A manipulation of behavior in which the response is controlled by the reinforcement following it.

operants   Behaviors that "operate" on and change the environment—for example, releasing a latch that opens a door.

organismic humanism   Maslow's theory of personality and human motivation describing a hierarchical human needs system, from strong physiological needs to self-actualization needs.

partial reinforcement   An intermittent reward schedule that strengthens a response.

peak experience   A moment of great ecstasy or awe that is experienced without the use of drugs or other stimulants.

personal construct theory   Kelly's personality theory that focuses on how a person, as perceiver, organizes his or her world and interprets, or construes, events.

personal space   A small, invisible area surrounding a person, within which an intrusion by another person causes discomfort and annoyance.

personality   Relatively enduring behavior patterns and traits that distinguish people, groups, and cultures; the overall organization and structure of these enduring patterns and traits; and the interactions among these patterns and the interactions of these patterns with fluctuations in the internal state and with changing external stimuli.

personality continuity   The stability of personality traits and behavior over time.

personality measurement   A system of assessing the extent of specific personality traits and other characteristics.

personality structure   The organization of the basic components of the personality.

personification   The image of oneself or another based on one's personal feelings and attitudes.

phenomenology   The study of subjective experience, or the "meaning" that a person gives to events.

phenotype   The totality of observed characteristics or behaviors of an organism that result from the interaction between genotype and environmental influences.

polygraph   An instrument used to monitor various physiological indicators.

pride   A sense of self-satisfaction typically arising from the attribution of success to one's own efforts and abilities.

primary drive   An innate, biologically based motivational force, such as hunger or thirst.

projection   In Freud's theory, a defense mechanism involving the unconscious attribution of one's own unacceptable feelings or motives to others.

projective test   A test consisting of ambiguous stimuli, to which an individual produces spontaneous responses whose is often subjective.

prosocial behavior   Positive social behavior, often socially prescribed and viewed as moral action, that is enacted to help others.

psychoanalysis   A system of psychology and psychotherapy, founded on Freud's theory of conflict in relation to unconscious libidinal impulses.

psychodynamics (personality dynamics)   The psychological "motion" of the personality produced by forces acting on the individual: the expression and inhibition of needs, the entering or leaving of a particular state of consciousness, and the functions or goals of behavior.

psychological reactance   A motivational arousal state in which a person increases behavior to secure that which is threatened or has been experienced but made unavailable.

psychopathology   The science of the study of mental disorders.

psychosis   Severe mental disorder involving personality disorganization and impairment of contact with reality.

psychosocial stages   In Erikson's theory of personality, the periods from birth to maturity posing particular developmental tasks and providing the basis for specific personality characteristics.

puberty   The period of maturation of the sex organs and other sexual characteristics.

Q-sort   A rating technique in which a set of adjectives or statements is categorized into piles according to the degree to which they are descriptive of an individual.

radical behaviorism   The approach to psychology that views human behavior as controlled by external stimulus situations.

reaction formation   In Freud's theory, a defense mechanism in which a person behaves in a way directly opposite from some underlying anxiety-provoking impulse.

regression   In Freudian theory, a return to some earlier stage of psychosexual development in the face of some current frustration.

reinforcement   Stimulation following a response, which increases the probability that the same response will occur again in the same situation.

reliability   The consistency, or degree of accuracy, of a measuring instrument.

repression   A defense mechanism in which an anxiety-arousing memory or impulse is prevented from becoming conscious.

repression-sensitization continuum   An approach-avoidance stylistic dimension of individual differences in defense reactions.

response bias   The tendency to respond to a test item in a particular way regardless of item content.

schizophrenia   A severe psychosis characterized by major disturbances in thought, emotion and behavior, often reflected in withdrawal and a fantasy life of delusions and hallucinations.

self   A person's fundamental sense of identity.

self-actualization   A principle of human behavior stating that individuals strive to develop their capacities and talents to the fullest—that is, growing and enhancing the basic self.

self-concept   The organized set of perceptions and ideas that the individual has of himself or herself.

self-consistency   The relationship between one's concept of oneself and one's behavior.

self-efficacy   A person's expectation that he or she can effectively cope with and master situations and bring about desired outcomes through personal efforts.

self-esteem   The value, respect, and honor one has for oneself.

self-ideal discrepancy   The differences between how one perceives oneself and how one would like to be.

self-insight   Increased awareness of one's feelings, drives, and attitudes.

sex role   The pattern of behavior expected of a male or female by society.

shame   A sense of devaluation, dishonor, or loss of respect based on the attribution of misbehavior to the self.

shaping   The process of establishing a behavior by rewarding successively closer approximations of that behavior.

situational theory   The personality theory that emphasizes the impact of situations over the impact of personality characteristics in determining behavior.

social desirability   A factor, to be considered on personality tests, that connotes a person's tendency to respond in a socially approved or favorable manner.

social deviance   Nonconforming, socially unapproved behavior(s).

social learning theory   Several related personality approaches that emphasize an individual's expectancy that certain behaviors will be rewarded by parents and society.

social stratification   The ranking of individuals into groups within a culture.

socialization   The process of developing the motivations and behaviors that are appropriate in one's culture.

somnambulism   Walking or carrying out acts while apparently in a sleeping state.

source traits   In Cattell's factor analyses of personality traits, basic organizing structures that underlie and determine surface traits.

state anxiety   Temporary anxiety that varies in intensity, fluctuates over time, and is strongly influenced by situational factors.

stress   Any force acting on a person that produces psychological or physiological strain.

sublimation   In Freudian theory, a defense mechanism in which libidinal (sexual) energy is redirected from an unacceptable to a socially approved mode of expression.

substitution   The gratification provided by goals attained in place of one's original goal.

superego   In Freudian theory, the part of the personality representing the morals, values, and ideals of one's society.

surface traits   In Cattell's factor analyses of personality traits, clusters of responses or overt behaviors that are related or fit together.

symbiosis   A state of a rewarding attachment and interdependence between two organisms.

temperament   Behavioral characteristics that are present at an early age and that are believed to have some basis in biological processes partly determined by heredity.

template-matching technique   Bem and Funder's measurement of personality that matches individuals with ideal types (those that are most likely to behave in a given manner in a given situation) to predict specific behaviors.

test-retest reliability   The correlation between scores obtained by administering a test on two occasions to the same group of individuals.

time-binding   A process that helps delay the immediate gratification of a need.

trait   A distinguishing personal characteristic that is relatively stable and enduring.

trait anxiety   An enduring tendency to be anxious.

trait psychology   The system of psychology based on the study of personality characteristics that are believed to be general over situations and enduring over time.

transactional model   An approach to human development that views the interaction between the child and its environment as a reciprocal and continuous process.

unconditional positive regard   Rogers' term for the accepting and valuing of a person per se, regardless of the degree to which he or she exhibits specific behaviors that are approved or disapproved.

validity   The degree to which a test actually measures what it is intended to measure.

variability   In personality testing, individual differences reflecting both true differences and error.

variable   In personality testing, an individual characteristic that can be measured.

References

Aaronson, B., and Osmond, H. *Psychedelics: The use and implications of hallucinogenic drugs.* Garden City, N.Y.: Anchor Books/Doubleday, 1970.

Abramson, L. Y., Seligman, M. E. P., and Teasdale, J. D. Learned helplessness in humans: Critique and reformulation. *Journal of Abnormal Psychology,* 1978, *87,* 49–74.

Adler, A. *Practice and theory of individual psychology.* New York: Harcourt, Brace & World, 1927.

Adorno, I. W., Frenkel-Brunswick, E., Levinson, D. J., and Sanford, R. N. *The authoritarian personality.* New York: Harper & Row, 1950.

Ainsworth, M. D. S. *Infancy in Uganda.* Baltimore: Johns Hopkins, 1967.

———, **and Bell, S. M.** Mother-infant interaction and the development of competence. In K. Connolly and J. Bruner (Eds.), *The growth of competeness.* New York: Academic Press, 1974.

———, **and Stayton, D.** Individual differences in strange situation behavior of one-year-olds. In H. R. Schaffer (Ed.), *The origins of human social relations.* London: Academic Press, 1971.

———, **Blehar, M. C., Waters, E., and Wall, S.** *Patterns of attachment.* Hillsdale, N.J.: Lawrence Erlbaum, 1978.

Aldis, O. *Play fighting.* New York: Academic Press, 1975.

Allee, W. C., Collias, N., and Lutherman, C. Z. Modification of the social order among flocks of hens by injection of testosterone propionate. *Physiological Zoology,* 1939, *12,* 412–420.

Allen, K. E., and Harris, F. R. Elimination of a child's excessive scratching by training the mother in reinforcement procedures. *Behavior Research and Therapy,* 1966, *4,* 79–84.

Allen, M. J., and Yen, W. M. *Introduction to measurement theory.* Belmont, Calif.: Brooks/Cole, 1979.

Allport, G. W. *Personality: A psychological interpretation.* New York: Henry Holt, 1937.

———. *Pattern and growth in personality.* New York: Holt, 1961.

———, **and Odbert, H. S.** Trait-names: A psycho-lexical study. *Psychological Monographs,* 1936, *47*(1, Whole No. 211.)

———, **and Vernon, P. E.** *Studies in expressive movement.* New York: Macmillan, 1933.

Altman, I. *The environment and social behavior.* Belmont, Calif.: Brooks/Cole, 1975.

———. Environmental psychology and social psychology. *Personality and Social Psychology Bulletin,* 1976, *2,* 96–113.

———, **Taylor, D. A., and Wheeler, L.** Ecological aspects of group behavior in social isolation. *Journal of Applied Social Psychology,* 1971, *1,* 76–100.

American Psychologist, 1965, *20,* 990.

Ames, L. B. The sense of self of nursery school children as manifested by their verbal behavior. *Journal of Genetic Psychology,* 1952, *81,* 193–232.

Amsterdam, B. Mirror self-image reactions before age two. *Developmental Psychobiology,* 1972, *5,* 297–305.

Anastasi, A. *Psychological testing* (4th ed.). New York: Macmillan, 1976.

Ansbacher, H. L., and Ansbacher R. R. (Eds.). *The individual psychology of Alfred Adler.* New York: Basic Books, 1956.

——— **(Eds.).** *Superiority and social interest by Alfred Adler.* Evanston, Ill.: Northwestern University Press, 1964.

Archer, J. Effects of population density on behavior in rodents. In J. H. Croobe (Ed.), *Social behaviors in birds and mammals.* New York: Academic Press, 1970.

Ardrey, R. *The territorial imperative.* New York: Atheneum, 1966.

————. *African genesis.* New York: Dell, 1967.

Arkes, H. R., and Garske, J. P. *Psychological theories of motivation.* Belmont, Calif.: Brooks/Cole, 1977.

Arkoff, A. Resolution of approach-approach and avoidance-avoidance conflicts. *Journal of Abnormal and Social Psychology,* 1957, *55,* 402–404.

Aronfreed, J. The origins of self-criticism. *Psychological Review,* 1964, *71,* 193–218.

Aronson, E., Blaney, N., Stephan, C., Silva, J., and Snopp, M. *The jigsaw classroom.* Beverly Hills, Calif.: Sage Publications, 1978.

Atkinson, J. W. Motivational determinants of risk-taking behavior. *Psychological Review,* 1957, *64,* 359–372.

————. *An introduction to motivation.* Princeton, N.J.: Van Nostrand, 1964.

————, and Litwin, G. H. Achievement motive and test anxiety conceived as motive to approach success and motive to avoid failure. *Journal of Abnormal and Social Psychology,* 1960, *60,* 52–63.

————, and Raynor, J. O. (Eds.). *Motivation and achievement.* Washington, D.C.: V. H. Winston, 1974.

Ausubel, N. (Ed.). Applied psychology. In *A treasury of Jewish folklore.* New York: Crown, 1948.

Ayllon, T., and Azrin, N. H. The measurement and reinforcement of behavior of psychotics. *Journal of Experimental Analysis of Behavior,* 1965, *8,* 357–383.

Baldwin, A. L. The effect of home environment on nursery school behavior. *Child Development,* 1949, *20,* 49–62.

Baltes, P. B., and Schaie, K. W. *Life-span developmental psychology: Personality and socialization.* New York: Academic Press, 1973.

Bandura, A. Social learning through imitation. In M. R. Jones (Ed.), *Nebraska Symposium on Motivation.* Lincoln: University of Nebraska Press, 1962.

————. Behavior modifications through modeling procedures. In L. Krasner and L. P. Ullmann (Eds.), *Research in behavior modification.* New York: Holt, 1965.

————. *Principles of behavior modification.* New York: Holt, 1969.

————. Psychotherapy based upon modeling principles. In A. E. Bergin and S. L. Garfield (Eds.), *Handbook of psychotherapy and behavior change.* New York: Wiley, 1971.

————. *Aggression: A social learning analysis.* Englewood Cliffs, N.J.: Prentice-Hall, 1973.

————. *Social learning theory.* Morristown, N.J.: General Learning Press, 1976.

————. Self-efficacy: Toward a unifying theory of behavioral change. *Psychological Review,* 1977, *84,* 191–215.

————. *Social learning theory.* Englewood Cliffs, N.J.: Prentice-Hall, 1977. (b)

————, Adams, N. E., and Beyer, J. Cognitive processes mediating behavioral changes. *Journal of Personality and Social Psychology,* 1977, *35,* 125–139.

————, Grusec, J. E., and Menlove, F. L. Observational learning as a function of symbolization and incentive set. *Child Development,* 1966, *37,* 499–506.

————. Vicarious extinction of avoidance behavior. *Journal of Personality and Social Psychology,* 1967, *5,* 16–23.

————, and Huston, A. Identification as a process of incidental learning. *Journal of Abnormal and Social Psychology,* 1961, *63,* 311–318.

————, and Jeffrey, R. W. Role of symbolic coding and rehearsal processes in observational learning. *Journal of Personality and Social Psychology,* 1973, *26,* 122–130.

————, and McDonald, F. J. Influence of social reinforcement and the behavior of models in shaping children's moral judgments. *Journal of Abnormal and Social Psychology,* 1963, *67,* 274–281.

————, and Mischel, W. Modification of self-imposed delay of reward through exposure to live and symbolic models. *Journal of Personality and Social Psychology,* 1965, *2,* 698–705.

————, Ross, D., and Ross, S. A. Transmission of aggression through imitation of aggressive models. *Journal of Abnormal Social Psychology,* 1961, *63,* 575–582.

————. Imitation of film-mediated aggressive models. *Journal of Abnormal and Social Psychology,* 1963, *66,* 3–11; *67,* 527–534. (a)

————. Vicarious reinforcement and imitative learning. *Journal of Abnormal and Social Psychology,* 1963, *67,* 601–607. (b)

————, and Walters, R. H. *Adolescent aggression.* New York: Ronald, 1959.

————. *Social learning and personality development.* New York: Holt, 1963.

Bannister, D., and Fransella, F. *Inquiring man.* Baltimore: Penguin, 1971.

Barber, T. X., and Calverley, D. S. Experimental studies in "hypnotic" behavior: Suggested deafness evaluated by delayed auditory feedback. *British Journal of Psychology,* 1964, *55,* 439–446.

Bard, P., and Mountcastle, V. B. Some forebrain mechanisms involved in expression of rage with special reference to suppression of angry behavior. *Research Publications, Association for Research in Nervous Mental Disease,* 1948, *27,* 362–404.

Barker, R. G. Ecology and motivation. In M. R. Jones (Ed.), *Nebraska Symposium on Motivation* (Vol. 8). Lincoln: University of Nebraska Press, 1960.

————. Explorations in ecological psychology. *American Psychologist,* 1965. *20,* 1–13.

————. *Ecological psychology.* Stanford, Calif.: Stanford University Press, 1968.

————, Dembo, T., and Lewin, K. Frustration and regression. In R. G. Barker, J. S. Kounin, and H. F. Wright (Eds.), *Child behavior and development.* New York: McGraw-Hill, 1943.

Barnes, C. A. A statistical study of the Freudian theory of levels of psychosexual development. *Genetic Psychology Monographs,* 1952, *45,* 105–174.

Barnett, M. A., Matthews, K. A., and Howard, J. A. Relationships between competitiveness and empathy in 6- and 7-year olds. *Developmental Psychology,* 1979, *15,* 221–222.

Baron, R. A. Aggression as a function of ambient temperature and prior anger arousal. *Journal of Personality and Social Psychology,* 1972, *21,* 183–189.

————. The aggression-inhibiting influence of heightened sexual arousal. *Journal of Personality and Social Psychology,* 1974, *30,* 318–322.

————. *Human aggression.* New York: Plenum, 1977.

————, and Bell, P. A. Aggression and heat: Mediating effects of prior provocation and exposure to an aggressive model. *Journal of Personality and Social Psychology,* 1975, *31,* 825–832.

————. Aggression and heat: The influence of ambient temperature, negative affect, and a cooling drink on physical aggression. *Journal of Personality and Social Psychology,* 1976, *33,* 245–255.

————, and Ransberger, V. M. Ambient temperature and the occurrence of collective violence: The "long hot summer" revisited. *Journal of Personality and Social Psychology,* 1978, *36,* 351–360.

Barry, H., Child, I., and Bacon, M. Relation of child training to subsistence economy. *American Anthropologist,* 1959, *61,* 51–63.

Barzun, J. *God's country and mine.* Boston: Atlantic Monthly, 1954.

Bateson, C., Jackson, D. D., Haley, J., and Weakland, J. H. Toward a theory of schizophrenia. *Behavioral Science,* 1956, *1,* 251–264.

Baumrind, D. Child care practices anteceding three patterns of preschool behavior. *Genetic Psychology Monographs,* 1967, *75,* 43–88.

————. Current patterns of parental authority. *Developmental Psychology Monographs,* 1971, *1,* 1–103.

————. Socialization and instrumental competence in young children. In W. W. Hartup (Ed.), *The young child: Reviews of research* (Vol. 2). Washington, D.C.: National Association for the Education of Young Children, 1972.

Beach, F. The descent of instinct. *Psychological Review,* 1955, *62,* 401–410.

Beck, A. T. *Depression: Clinical, experimental, and theoretical aspects.* New York: Hoeber, 1967.

Becker, W. C. Consequences of different kinds of parental discipline. In M. L. Hoffman and L. W. Hoffman (Eds.), *Review of child development research* (Vol. 1). New York: Russell Sage, 1964.

Bell, P. A., and Baron, R. A. Aggression and heat: The mediating role of negative affect. *Journal of Applied Social Psychology,* 1976, *6,* 18–30.

————, and Byrne, D. Repression-sensitization. In H. London and J. E. Exner, Jr. (Eds.), *Dimensions of personality.* New York: Wiley, 1978.

Bell, R. Q. Developmental psychology. *Annual Review of Psychology*, 1965, *16*, 1–38.

———. A reinterpretation of the direction of effects in studies of socialization. *Psychological Review*, 1968, *75*, 81–95.

Bell, S. The development of the concept of object as related to infant-mother attachment. *Child Development*, 1970, *41*, 291–311.

Beloff, H. The structure and origin of the anal character. *Genetic Psychology Monographs*, 1957, *55*, 141–172.

Belsky, J., and Steinberg, L. D. The effects of day care: A critical review. *Child Development*, 1978, *49*, 929–949.

———, **and Walker, A.** In M. Lamb (Ed.), *Childrearing in nontraditional families*. Hillsdale, N.J.: Lawrence Erlbaum, 1981.

Belson, W. A. *Television violence and the adolescent boy*. Teakfied Limited, England: Saxon House, 1978.

Bem, D. J., and Allen, A. On predicting some of the people some of the time: The search for cross-situational consistencies in behavior. *Psychological Review*, 1974, *81*, 505–520.

Bem, D. J., and Funder, D. C. Predicting more of the people more of the time: Assessing the personality of situations. *Psychological Review*, 1978, *85*, 485–501.

Bem, S. L. Sex-role adaptability: One consequence of psychological androgyny. *Journal of Personality and Social Psychology*, 1975, *31*, 634–653.

Bentham, J. (1779) An introduction to the principles of morals and legislation. Oxford: Blackwell, 1948.

Berkowitz, L. The concept of aggressive drive: Some additional considerations. In L. Berkowitz (Ed.), *Advances in experimental social psychology* (Vol. 2). New York: Academic Press, 1965. (a)

———. Some aspects of observed aggression. *Journal of Personality and Social Psychology*, 1965, *2*, 359–369. (b)

———. External determinants of impulsive aggression. In W. W. Hartup and J. de Wit (Eds.), *Origins of aggression*. The Hague: Mouton, 1978.

———, **and Geen, R. G.** Film violence and the cue properties of available targets. *Journal of Personality and Social Psychology*, 1966, *3*, 525–530.

———, **and Le Page, A.** Weapons as aggression-eliciting stimuli. *Journal of Personality and Social Psychology*, 1967, *7*, 202–207.

Berlyne, D. *Conflict, arousal, and curiosity*. New York: McGraw-Hill, 1960.

Bernstein B. Linguistic codes, hesitation phenomena and intelligence. *Language and Speech*, 1962, *5*, 221–240. (a)

———. Social class, linguistic codes and grammatical elements. *Language and Speech*, 1962, *5*, 221–240. (b)

———. Elaborated and restricted codes: Their social origins and some consequences. In J. Gumpery, and D. Hymes (Eds.), *The ethnography of communication* (American Anthropologist Special Publication), 1964, *66*, 55–69.

Bernstein, I. S. and Gordon, T. P. The function of aggression in primate societies. *American Scientist*, 1974, *62*, 304–311.

Berry, J. W. Independence and conformity in subsistence-level societies. *Journal of Personality and Social Psychology*, 1967, *7*, 415–418.

———. *Human ecology and cognitive style*. New York: Russell Sage, 1976.

Bertelsen, A., Harvald, B., and Hauge, M. A Danish twin study of manic-depressive disorders. *British Journal of Psychiatry*, 1977, *130*, 330–351.

Bettelheim, B. Individual and mass behavior in extreme situations, *Journal of Abnormal and Social Psychology*, 1943, *38* (4), 417–452.

Bickman, L. The effect of another bystander's ability to help on bystander intervention in an emergency. *Journal of Experimental Social Psychology*, 1971, *7*, 367–379.

Binet, A., and Henri, V. La psychologie individuelle. *Année psychologique*, 1895, *2*, 411–463.

Binswanger, L. *Being-in-the-world: Selected papers of Ludwig Binswanger*. J. Needleman, trans. New York: Basic Books, 1963.

Birren, J. E., Butler, R. N., Greenhouse, S. W., Sobolofe, C., and Yarrow, M. R. *Human aging: A biological and behavioral study*. Bethesda, Md.: U.S. Public Health Service, 1963

Block, J. *The Q-sort method in personality assessment and psychiatric research*. Springfield, Ill.: Charles C Thomas, 1961.

———. *The challenge of response sets: Unconfounding meaning, acquiescence, and social desirability in the MMPI*. New York: Appleton-Century-Crofts, 1965.

———. *Lives through time*. Berkeley, Calif.: Bancroft, 1971.

———. Advancing the psychology of personality: Paradigmatic shift or improving the quality of research. In D. Magnussen and N. S. Endler (Eds.), *Personality at the crossroads: Current issues in interactional psychology*. Hillsdale, N.J.: Lawrence Erlbaum, 1977.

———, **Block, J. H., and Harrington, D. M.** Some misgivings about the matching familiar figures test as a measure of reflection-impulsivity. *Developmental Psychology*, 1974, *10*, 611–632.

Block, J. H. Conceptions of sex role: Some cross-cultural and longitudinal perspectives. *American Psychologist*, 1973, *28*, 512–529.

———. Issues, problems and pitfalls in assessing sex differences. *Merrill-Palmer Quarterly*, 1976, *22*,

283–308.

———, and Block, J. The role of ego-control and ego-resiliency in the organization of behavior. In W. A. Collins (Ed.), *Minnesota Symposium on Child Development* (Vol. 13). Hillsdale, N.J.: Lawrence Erlbaum, 1980.

———, and Martin, B. Predicting the behavior of children under frustration. *Journal of Abnormal Social Psychology*, 1955, *51*, 281–285.

Blum, G. S. *A model of the mind*. New York: Wiley, 1961.

Borgida, E., and Nisbett, R. The differential impact of abstract vs. concrete information on decisions. *Journal of Applied Social Psychology*, 1977, *7*, 258–271.

Boss, M. *Psychoanalysis and daseinanalysis*. L. B. Lefebre, trans. New York: Basic Books, 1963.

Bowers, K. S. Situationalism in psychology: An analysis and critique. *Psychological Review*, 1973, *80*, 307–336.

Bowlby, J. The nature of the child's tie to his mother. *International Journal of Psycho-Analysis*, 1958, *39*, 350–373.

———. *Attachment and love: Attachment* (Vol. 1). New York: Basic Books, 1969.

Brackbill, Y. *Research and clinical work with children*. Washington, D.C.: American Psychological Association, 1962.

Bradburn, N. M. Achievement and father dominance in Turkey. *Journal of Abnormal and Social Psychology*, 1963, *67*, 464–468.

Breger, L. *From instinct to identity*. Englewood Cliffs, N.J.: Prentice-Hall, 1974.

Brehm, J. W. (Ed.). *A theory of psychological reactance*. New York: Academic Press, 1966.

———. *Responses to loss of freedom: A theory of psychological reactance*. Morristown, N.J.: General Learning Press, 1972.

Breland, K., and Breland, M. The misbehavior of organisms. *American Psychologist*, 1961, *16*, 681–684.

Broadhurst, P. L. Analysis of maternal effects in the inheritance of behaviour. *Animal Behaviour*, 1961, *9*, 129–141.

Brown, J. S. Gradients of approach and avoidance responses and their relation to level of motivation. *Journal of Comparative and Physiological Psychology*, 1948, *41*, 450–465.

———. Principles of intrapersonal conflict. *Journal of Conflict Resolution*, 1957, *1*, 135–154.

Brown, P., and Elliott, R. Control of aggression in a nursery school class. *Journal of Experimental Child Psychology*, 1965, *2*, 103–107.

Bruner, J. S. A cognitive theory of personality. *Contemporary Psychology*, 1956, *1*, 355–357.

———, and Tagiuri, R. The perception of people. In G. Lindzey (Ed.), *Handbook of social psychology*. Reading, Mass.: Addison-Wesley, 1954.

Bryan, J. H., and Test, M. A. Models and helping: Naturalistic studies in aiding behavior. *Journal of Personality and Social Psychology*, 1967, *6*, 400–407.

Bryan, J. H., and Walbek, N. Preaching and practicing generosity: Children's actions and reactions. *Child Development*, 1970, *41*, 329–353.

Bühler, C. Genetic aspects of the self. *Annals of the New York Academy of Science*, 1962, *96*, 730–764.

Burton, R. V. Generality of honesty reconsidered. *Psychological Review*, 1963, *70*, 481–499.

Buss, A. H., Plomin, R., and Willerman, L. The inheritance of temperaments. *Journal of Personality*, 1973, *41*, 513–524.

Butcher, J. N., and Tellegen, A. Common methodological problems in MMPI research. *Journal of Consulting and Clinical Psychology*, 1978, *46*, 620–628.

Butler, J. M., and Haigh, G. V. Changes in the relation between self-concepts and ideal concepts consequent upon client-centered counseling. In C. R. Rogers and R. F. Dymond (Eds.), *Psychotherapy and personality change*. Chicago: University of Chicago Press, 1954.

Byrne, D. The repression-sensitization scale: Rationale, reliability, and validity. *Journal of Personality*, 1961, *29*, 334–349.

Cairns, R. B. *Antecedents of social reinforcer effectiveness*. Unpublished manuscript, Indiana University, 1962.

———. Attachment and dependency: A psychobiological and social learning synthesis. In J. Gewirtz (Ed.), *Attachment and dependency*. New York: Winston, 1972.

———. Beyond social attachment: The dynamics of interactional development. In T. Alloway, P. Pliner, and L. Krames (Eds.), *Attachment behavior: Advances in the study of communication and affect*. New York: Plenum, 1977.

Caldwell, W. V. *LSD psychotherapy: An exploration of psychedelic and psycholytic therapy*. New York: Grove, 1968.

Calhoun, J. B. Mortality and movement of brown rats (*Rattus norvegicus*) in artificially supersaturated populations. *Journal of Wildlife Management*, 1948, *12*, 167–172.

———. The study of wild animals under controlled conditions. *Annals of the New York Academy of Science*, 1950, *51*, 1113–1122.

———. Population density and social pathology. *Scientific American*, 1962, *206*, 139–146.

Cameron, P. Stereotypes about generational fun and

happiness versus self-appraised fun and happiness. *The Gerontologist,* 1972, *12,* 120–123.

Campbell, J. (Ed.). *The portable Jung* (R. F. C. Hull, trans.). New York: Viking, 1971. (Other editions Baltimore: Penguin, 1976, 1978.)

Campbell, J. P. *Handbook for the Strong-Campbell Interest Inventory.* Stanford, Calif.: Stanford University Press, 1974.

———. Psychometric theory. In M. D. Dunnette (Ed.), *Handbook of industrial and organizational psychology.* Chicago: Rand McNally, 1976.

Carey, G., Goldsmith, H. H., Tellegen, A., and Gottesman, I. I. Genetics and personality inventories: The limits of replication with twin data. *Behavior Genetics,* 1978, *8,* 299–313.

Carkhuff, R. R. *Helping and human relations. Vol. 1: Selection and training. Vol. 11: Practice and research.* New York: Holt, 1969.

———, **and Berenson, B. G.** *Beyond counseling and therapy.* New York: Holt, 1967.

Carlsmith, J. M., and Anderson, C. A. Ambient temperature and the occurrence of collective violence: A new analysis. *Journal of Personality and Social Psychology,* 1979, *37,* 337–344.

Carlsmith, L. Effect of early father-absence on scholastic aptitude. *Harvard Educational Review,* 1964, *34,* 3–21.

Carter, J. E., and Heath, B. Somatotype methodology and kinesiology research. *Kinesiology Review,* 1971, *2,* 10.

Carver, C. S., Blaney, P. H., and Scheier, M. F. Focus of attention, chronic expectancy and response to a feared stimulus. *Journal of Personality and Social Psychology,* 1979, *37,* 1186–1195 (a).

———. Reassertion and giving up: The interactive role of self-directed attention and outcome expectancy. *Journal of Personality and Social Psychology,* 1979, *37,* 1859–1870 (b).

Cattell, R. B. *Manual for forms A and B: Sixteen Personality Factor Questionnaire.* Champaign, Ill.: Institute for Personality and Ability Testing, 1949.

———. *Personality and motivation, structure and measurement.* Yonkers, N. Y.: World Book, 1957.

———. *The scientific analysis of personality.* Baltimore: Penguin, 1965.

———, **Eber, H. W., and Tatsuoka, M. M.** *Handbook for the Sixteen Personality Factor Questionnaire (16 PF).* Champaign, Ill.: Institute for Personality and Ability Testing, 1970.

Caudill, W., and Plath, D. W. Who sleeps by whom? Parent-child involvement in urban Japanese families. *Psychiatry,* 1966, *29,* 344–366.

Cautela, I. R. Lowest conditioning: Assumptions and procedures. *Journal of Mental Imagery,* 1977, *1,* 53–64.

Chatz, T. L. Recognizing and treating dangerous sex offenders. *Journal of Offender Therapy,* 1972, *16,* 109–115.

Chess, S., Thomas, A., and Birch, H. G. *Your child is a person.* New York: Viking, 1965.

Child, I. L. Personality in culture. In E. F. Borgatta and W. W. Lambert (Eds.), *Handbook of personality theory and research.* Chicago: Rand McNally, 1968.

———, **and Waterhouse, I. K.** Frustration and the quality of performance: III. An experimental study. *Journal of Personality,* 1953, *21,* 298–311.

Clemes, S. R. Repression and hypnotic amnesia. *Journal of Abnormal and Social Psychology,* 1964, *69,* 62–69.

Coe, W. C. The credibility of posthypnotic amnesia: A contextualist's view. *International Journal of Classical and Experimental Hypnosis,* 1978, *26,* 673–681.

Cofer, C. N., and Appley, M. H. *Motivation: Theory and research.* New York: Wiley, 1964.

Cohen, D. B. Neuroticism and dreaming sleep: A case for interactionism in personality of research. *British Journal of Social and Clinical Psychology,* 1977, *16,* 153–163.

Condry, J. Enemies of exploration: Self-initiated versus other-initiated learning. *Journal of Personality and Social Psychology,* 1977, *35,* 459–477.

Cooper, L. M. Hypnotic amnesia. In E. Fromm and R. E. Shor (Eds.), *Hypnosis: Research developments and perspectives.* Chicago: Aldine-Atherton, 1972.

Cooper, R. M., and Zubek, J. P. Effects of enriched and restricted early environments on the learning ability of bright and dull rats. *Canadian Journal of Psychology,* 1958, *12,* 159–164.

Coopersmith, H. S. *The antecedents of self-esteem.* San Francisco: Freeman, 1967.

Costa, P. T., and McCrae, R. R. Age differences in personality structures revisited: Studies in validity, stability and change. *International Journal of Aging and Human Development,* 1977, *8,* 261–276.

Covington, M. V., and Beery, R. G. *Self-worth and school learning.* New York: Holt, 1976.

Cowan, P., Langer, J., Heavenrich, J., and Nathanson, M. Social learning and Piaget's cognitive theory of moral development. *Journal of Personality and Social Psychology,* 1969, *11,* 261–274.

Crandall, V. C. Sex differences in expectancy of intellectual and academic performance. In C. P. Smith (Ed.), *Achievement-related motives in children.* New York: Russell Sage, 1969.

Cronbach, L. J. Beyond the two disciplines of scientific psychology. *American Psychologist,* 1975, *30,* 116–127.

Cumming, E., and Henry, W. H. *Growing old.* New York: Basic Books, 1961.

Dahlstrom, W. G. Recurrent issues in the development of the MMPI. In J. N. Butcher (Ed.), *MMPI: Research developments and clinical applications.* New York: McGraw-Hill, 1969.

———, **and Welsh, G. S.** *An MMPI handbook: A guide to use in clinical practice and research.* Minneapolis: University of Minnesota Press, 1960.

———, **and Dahlstrom, L. E.** *An MMPI handbook: Clinical interpretation* (Vol. I) (Rev. ed.). Minneapolis: University of Minnesota Press, 1972.

———. *An MMPI handbook: Research applications* (Vol. II) (Rev. ed.). Minneapolis: University of Minnesota Press, 1975.

Dallett, J. O. *The effects of sensory and social variables on the recalled dream: Complementarity, continuity and compensation.* Unpublished doctoral dissertation, University of California, Los Angeles, 1973.

Darley, J., and Batson, C. "From Jerusalem to Jericho": A study of situational and dispositional variables in helping behavior. *Journal of Personality and Social Psychology,* 1973, *27,* 100–108.

Darwin, C. *On the origin of species by means of natural selection or the preservation of favoured races in the struggle for life.* New York: Appleton, 1869.

———. (1872) *The expression of the emotions in man and animals.* Chicago: University of Chicago Press, 1965.

———. *The descent of man, and selection in relation to sex.* New York: Appleton, 1873.

Davison, G. C. Elimination of a sadistic fantasy by a client-controlled counter-conditioning technique: A case study. *Journal of Abnormal Psychology,* 1968, *73,* 84–89.

Davitz, J. The effects of previous training on postfrustration behavior. *Journal of Abnormal Social Psychology,* 1952, *47,* 309–315.

de Charms, R. *Personal causation.* New York: Academic Press, 1968.

———. Personal causation training in the schools. *Journal of Applied Social Psychology,* 1972, *2,* 95–113.

———. *Enhancing motivation: Change in the classroom.* New York: Irvington, 1976.

———, **and Moeller, G. H.** Values expressed in American children's readers: 1800–1950. *Journal of Abnormal and Social Psychology,* 1962, *64,* 136–142.

Deci, E. L. *Intrinsic motivation.* New York: Plenum, 1975.

Delgado, J. Neurophysiological mechanisms of aggressive behavior. In S. Feshbach and A. Fraczek (Eds.), *Aggression and behavior change: Biological and social processes.* New York: Praeger, 1979.

Dement, W. C. The effect of dream deprivation. *Science,* 1960, *131,* 1705–1707.

———. An essay on dreams: The role of physiology in understanding their nature. In F. Barron (Ed.), *New directions in psychology* (Vol. 2). New York: Holt, 1965.

———, **and Kleitman, N.** The relation of eye movements during sleep to dream activity: An objective method for the study of dreaming. *Journal of Experimental Psychology,* 1957, *53,* 339–346.

Dengerink, H. A., O'Leary, M. R., and Kasner, K. H. Individual differences in aggression responses to attack: Internal-external locus of control and field dependence-independence. *Journal of Research in Personality,* 1975, *9,* 191–199.

De Vore, I. (Ed.). *Primate behavior: Field studies of monkeys and apes.* New York: Holt, 1965.

DiCaprio, N. S. *Personality theories: Guides to living.* Philadelphia: Saunders, 1974.

DiCara, L. V. Learning in the autonomic nervous system. *Scientific American,* January 1970, 30–39.

Dicks-Mireaux, M. J. Extraversion-introversion in experimental psychology: Examples of experimental evidence and their theoretical implications. *Journal of Analytical Psychology,* 1964, *9,* 117–128.

Diern, C. J. Historical trends in the age at menarche and menopause. *Psychological Reports,* 1974, *34,* 931–937.

Dixon, N. F. *Subliminal perception: The nature of a controversy.* London: McGraw-Hill, 1971.

Dollard, J., Doob, L. W., Miller, N. E., Mowrer, O. H., and Sears, R. R. *Frustration and aggression.* New Haven: Yale University Press, 1939.

Dollard, J., and Miller, N. E. *Personality and psychotherapy.* New York: McGraw-Hill, 1950.

Donnerstein, E., and Wilson, D. W. The effects of noise and perceived control upon ongoing and subsequent aggressive behavior. *Journal of Personality and Social Psychology,* 1976, *34,* 774–781.

Donnerstein, M., and Donnerstein, E. Modeling in the control of interracial aggression: The problem of generality. *Journal of Personality,* 1977, *45,* 100–116.

Doob, A. N., and Wood, L. Catharsis and aggression: The effects of annoyance and retaliation on aggressive behavior. *Journal of Personality and Social Psychology,* 1972, *22,* 156–162.

Dulany, D. E., Jr. Avoidance learning of perceptual defense and vigilance. *Journal of Abnormal and Social Psychology,* 1957, *55,* 333–338.

Dunnette, M. D. Aptitudes, abilities, and skills. In M. D. Dunnette (Ed.), *Handbook of industrial and* *organizational psychology.* Chicago: Rand McNally, 1976.

———, **and Borman, W. C.** Personnel selection and classification systems. *Annual Review of Psychology,* 1979, *30,* 477–525.

Duval, S., and Wicklund, R. A. *A theory of objective self-awareness.* New York: Academic Press, 1972.

———. Effects of objective self-awareness on attribution of causality. *Journal of Personality and Social Psychology,* 1973, *9,* 17–31.

Dweck, C. S. The role of expectation and attribution in the alleviation of learned helplessness. *Journal of Personality and Social Psychology,* 1975, *31,* 674–685

Ebel, R. L. Comments on some problems of employment testing. *Personnel Psychology,* 1977, *30,* 55–63.

Eckerman, C. O., and Rheingold, K. L. Infants' exploratory responses to toys and people. *Developmental Psychology,* 1974, *10,* 255–259.

Edney, J. J. Territoriality and control: A field experiment. *Journal of Personality and Social Psychology,* 1975, *31,* 1108–1115.

Edwards, A. L. *Manual for the Edwards Personal Preference Schedule.* New York: Psychological Corporation, 1954.

———. *The social desirability variable in personality research.* New York: Dryden, 1957.

———. *Edwards Personal Preference Schedule.* New York: Psychological Corporation, 1959.

———. The social desirability hypothesis: Theoretical implications for personality measurement. In S. Messick and J. Ross (Eds.), *Measurement in personality and cognition.* New York: Wiley, 1962.

———. Social desirability and performance on the MMPI. *Psychometrika,* 1964, *29,* 295–308.

Edwards, D. A., and Herndon, J. Neonatal estrogen stimulation and aggressive behavior in female mice. *Physiological Behavior,* 1970, *5,* 993–995.

Egbert, L., Battit, G., Welch, C., and Bartlett, M. Reduction of post-operative pain by encouragement and instruction of patients. *New England Journal of Medicine,* 1964, *270,* 825–827.

Egger, M. D., and Flynn, J. P. Effect of electrical stimulation of the amygdala on hypothalamically elicited attack behaviors in cats. *Journal of Neurophysiology,* 1963, *26,* 705–720.

Eibl-Eibesfeldt, I. *Ethology: The biology of behavior.* New York: Holt, 1970.

———. Evolution of destructive aggression. *Aggressive Behavior,* 1977, *3,* 127–144.

Eisenberg-Berg, N., and Geisheker, E. Content of preachings and power of the model preacher: The effect on children's generosity. *Developmental Psychology,* 1979, *15,* 168–175.

Ekman, P., and Friesen, W. V. *Unmasking the face.* Englewood Cliffs, N.J.: Prentice-Hall, 1975.

Elkind, D. *Children and adolescents: Interpretive essay on Jean Piaget.* New York: Oxford University Press, 1970.

———. *The child and society.* New York: Oxford University Press, 1979.

Ellis, A. The validity of personality questionnaires. *Psychological Bulletin,* 1946, *43,* 385–440.

Emmerich, W., Cocking, R. R., and Sigel, I. E. Relationships between cognitive and social functioning in preschool children. *Developmental Psychology,* 1979, *15,* 495–504.

Endler, N. S. The person versus the situation—a pseudo issue? A response to Alker. *Journal of Personality,* 1973, *41,* 287–303.

———, **and Hunt, J. McV.** S-R inventories of hostility and comparisons of the proportions of variance from persons, responses, and situations for hostility and anxiousness. *Journal of Personality and Social Psychology,* 1968, *9,* 309–315.

Endler, N. S., and Magnussen, D. *Interactional psychology and personality.* Washington, D.C.: Hemisphere, 1976.

Entwisle, D. R. To dispel fantasies about fantasy-based measures of achievement motivation. *Psychological Bulletin,* 1972, *77,* 377–391.

Epstein, L. Psychophysiological measurement in assessment. In M. Hersen and A. S. Bellack (Eds.), *Behavioral Assessment.* New York: Pergamon, 1976.

Epstein, S. Traits are alive and well. In D. Magnusson and N. S. Endler (Eds.), *Personality at the crossroads.* New York: Wiley, 1977.

———. The self-concept: A review and the proposal of an integrated theory of personality. In E. Staub (Ed.), *Personality: Basic issues and current research.* Englewood Cliffs, N.J.: Prentice-Hall, 1980.

———, **and Fenz, W. D.** Steepness of approach and avoidance gradients in humans as a function of experience: Theory and experiment. *Journal of Experimental Psychology,* 1965, *70,* 1–12.

Erdelyi, M. H. A new look at the new look: Perceptual defense and vigilance. *Psychological Review,* 1974, *81,* 1–25.

Ericksen, C. W. Unconscious processes. In M. R. Jones (Ed.), *Nebraska Symposium on Motivation.* Lincoln: University of Nebraska Press, 1958.

———. Discrimination and learning without awareness: A methodological survey and evaluation. *Psychological Review,* 1960, *67,* 279–300.

Erikson, E. H. *Childhood and society.* New York: Norton, 1950.

———. *Young man Luther.* New York: W. W. Norton, 1958.

———. *Identity and the life cycle.* (Psychological Issues Monograph 1, Vol. 1, No. 1). New York: International Universities Press, 1959.

———. *Insight and responsibility.* New York: Norton, 1964.

———. *Identity: Youth and crisis.* New York: Norton, 1968.

———. *Ghandi's truth on the origins of militant nonviolence.* New York: W. W. Norton, 1969.

———. *Toys and reasons.* New York: Norton, 1976.

Eron, L. O., Walder, L. O., and Lefkowitz, M. M. *Learning of aggression in children.* Boston: Little, Brown, 1971.

Escalona, S. K. *The roots of individuals: Normal patterns of development in infancy.* Chicago: Aldine, 1968.

Evans, F. J., and Kihlstrom, J. F. Posthypnotic amnesia as disrupted retrieval. *Journal of Abnormal Psychology,* 1973, *82,* 317–332.

Exner, J. E. *The Rorschach: A comprehensive system.* New York: Wiley, 1974.

———. Projective techniques. In I. B. Weiner (Ed.), *Clinical methods in psychology.* New York: Wiley, 1976.

Eysenck, H. J. *Dimensions of personality.* London: Routledge, 1947.

———. *The structure of human personality.* London: Methuen, 1952.

———. Cortical inhibition, figured after effect and theory of personality. *Journal of Abnormal and Social Psychology,* 1955, *51,* 94–106.

——— *The biological basis of personality.* Springfield, Ill. Charles C Thomas, 1967.

———, **and Eysenck, S. B. G.** *The manual of the Eysenck personality inventory.* San Diego: Educational and Industrial Testing Service, 1964.

———, **and Rachman, S.** *The causes and cures of neurosis: An introduction to modern behavior therapy based on learning theory and the principles of conditioning.* San Diego: Knapp, 1965.

Fairbairn, W. R. D. *Psycho-analytic studies of the personality.* New York: Basic Books, 1952.

Faust, M. S. Developmental maturity as a determinant in prestige of adolescent girls. *Child Development,* 1960, *31,* 173–184.

Feather, N. T. The relationship of expectation of success to *n* Achievement and test anxiety. *Journal of Personality and Social Psychology,* 1965, *1,* 118–126.

Feld, S. Longitudinal study of the origins of achievement strivings. *Journal of Personality and Social Psychology,* 1967, *7,* 408–414.

Ferguson, P., and Gowan, R. TM: Some preliminary findings. *Journal of Humanistic Psychology,* 1976, *16,* 51–60.

Feshbach, N. Sex differences in children's modes of aggressive responses toward outsiders. *Merrill-Palmer Quarterly,* 1969, *15,* 249–258.

———. Cross-cultural studies of teaching styles in four-year-olds and their mothers. In A. E. Pick (Ed.), *Minnesota Symposium on Child Psychology* (Vol. 7). Minneapolis: University of Minnesota Press, 1973.

———. The relationship of child rearing factors to children's aggression, empathy, and related positive and negative social behaviors. In J. de Wit and W. W. Hartup (Eds.), *Determinants and origins of aggressive behavior.* The Hague: Mouton, 1975.

———. Studies on empathic behavior in children. In B. A. Maher (Ed.), *Progress in experimental personality research.* New York: Academic Press, 1978.

———. Empathy training: A field study in affective education. In S. Feshbach and A. Fraczek (Eds.), *Aggression and behavior change: Biological and social processes.* New York: Praeger, 1979.

———, **and Feshbach, S.** The relationship between empathy and aggression in two age groups. *Developmental Psychology,* 1969, *1*(2), 102–107.

Feshbach, N., and Roe, L. Empathy in six- and seven-year-olds. *Child Development,* 1968, *39,* 133–145.

Feshbach, S. The catharsis hypothesis and some consequences of interaction with aggressive and neutral play objects. *Journal of Personality,* 1956, *24,* 449–462.

———. The function of aggression and the regulation of aggressive drive. *Psychological Review,* 1964, *71,* 257–272.

———. Aggression. In P. H. Mussen (Ed.), *Carmichael's manual of child psychology.* New York: Wiley, 1970.

———. Effects of reality versus fantasy in filmed violence. In J. P. Murray, E. A. Rubinstein, and G. A. Comstock (Eds.), *Television and social behavior: Television and social learning* (Vol. II). Washington, D.C.: U.S. Government Printing Office, 1972.

———. The development and regulation of aggression: Some research gaps and a proposed cognitive approach. In W. W. Hartup and J. de Wit (Eds.), *Determinants and origins of aggressive behavior.* The Hague: Mouton, 1974.

———. The environment of personality. *American Psychologist,* 1978, *33,* 447–455.

———. Child abuse and the dynamics of human aggression on violence. In G. Gerbner, E. Zigler, and C. Ross (Eds.), *Child abuse.* New York: Oxford University Press, 1980.

———, **Adelman, H., and Fuller, W.** The prediction

of reading and related academic problems. *Journal of Educational Psychology*, 1977, *69*, 299–308.

Feshbach, S., and Feshbach, N. The influence of the stimulus object upon the complementary and supplementary projection of fear. *Journal of Abnormal and Social Psychology*, 1963, *66*, 498–502.

Feshbach, S., and Singer, R. *Television and aggression.* San Francisco: Jossey-Bass, 1971.

Feshbach, S., Stiles, W., and Bitter, E. The reinforcing effect of witnessing aggression. *Journal of Experimental Research in Personality*, 1967, *2*, 133–139.

Festinger, L. *A theory of cognitive dissonance.* Evanston, Ill.: Row, Peterson, 1957.

Field, L. H., and Williams, M. The hormonal treatment of sexual offenders. *Medicine, Science, and the Law*, 1970, 27–34.

Fillenbaum, G. B. An examination of the vulnerability hypothesis. *International Journal of Aging and Human Development*, 1977, *8*, 155–160.

Fisher, S. Projective methodologies. *Annual Review of Psychology*, 1967, 165–190.

Flavell, J. H., Bothin, P. T., Fry, C. L., Wright, J. W., and Jarvis, P. E. *The development of role-taking and communication skills in children.* New York: Wiley, 1968.

Frank, J. D. Individual differences in certain aspects of the level of aspiration. *American Journal of Psychology*, 1935, *47*, 119–128.

Frank, L. K. Projective methods for the study of personality. *Journal of Psychology*, 1939, *8*, 343–389.

Frankl, V. E. *Man's search of meaning: An introduction to logotherapy.* I. Lasch, trans. New York: Washington Square Press, 1963.

Fransella, F., and Adams, B. An illustration of the use of repertory grid technique in a clinical setting. *British Journal of Social and Clinical Psychology*, 1966, *5*, 51–62.

Freedman, D. G. Smiling in blind infants and the issue of innate vs. acquired. *Journal of Child Psychology and Psychiatry*, 1964, *5*, 171–184.

Freedman, J. L. *Crowding and behavior.* San Francisco: Freeman, 1975.

———, Levy, A. S., Buchanan, R. W., and Price, J. Crowding and human aggression. *Journal of Experimental Social Psychology*, 1972, *8*, 528–548.

Freedman, J. L., Sears, D. O., and Carlsmith, J. M. *Social psychology* (2nd ed.). Englewood Cliffs, N.J.: Prentice-Hall, 1978.

Freud, A. *The ego and the mechanisms of defense.* New York: International Universities Press, 1946.

———. Adolescence. *The Psychoanalytic Study of the Child*, 1958, *13*, 255–278.

Freud, S. (1911) Formulations regarding the two principles of mental functioning. In *Collected Papers* (Vol. IV). New York: Basic Books, 1959.

———. (1915) *A general introduction to psychoanalysis.* New York: Washington Square Press, 1934.

———. (1920) *Beyond the pleasure principle. The standard edition* (Vol. 18). London: Hogarth, 1955.

———. *Collected papers.* London: Hogarth, 1925.

———. (1926) *The problem of anxiety.* New York: W. W. Norton, 1935.

———. (1930) *Civilization and its discontents.* London: Hogarth, 1961.

———. (1933) *New introductory lectures on psychoanalysis.* New York: Norton, 1961.

Freundl, P. C. *When is assertion aggressive?* Unpublished doctoral dissertation, University of California, Los Angeles, 1977.

Frodi, A. Sexual arousal, situational restrictiveness, and aggressive behavior. *Journal of Research in Personality*, 1977, *11*, 48–58.

Fromkin, H. L., Goldstein, I. H., and Brock, T. C. The role of "irrelevant" derogation in hostility catharsis: A field experiment. *Journal of Experimental Social Psychology*, 1977, *13*, 239–252.

Fromm, E. *Escape from freedom.* New York: Rinehart, 1941.

———. *The sane society.* New York: Rinehart, 1955.

———. *The heart of man.* New York: Harper & Row, 1964.

———. *Man for himself.* New York: Rinehart, 1974.

Gallup, G. G., Jr. Chimpanzees: Self-recognition. *Science*, 1970, *167*, 86–87.

——— Towards an operational definition of self-awareness. In R. H. Tuttle (Ed.), *Sociobiology and psychology of primates.* The Hague: Mouton, 1975.

———. Self-awareness in primates. *American Scientist*, 1979, *67*, 417–421.

———, McClure, M. K., Hill, S. D., and Bundy, R. A. Capacity for self-recognition in differentially reared chimpanzees. *Psychological Record*, 1971, *21*, 69–74.

Garcia, J., and Koelling, R. A. Relation of cue to consequences in avoidance learning. *Psychonomic Science*, 1966, *4*, 123–124.

Gardner, R. W., Holtzman, P. S., Klein, G. S., Linton, H. B., and Spence, D. P. *Cognitive control: A study of individual consistencies in cognitive behavior* (Psychological Issues Monograph 4). New York: International Universities Press, 1959.

Garmezy, N. Current status of a sample of other high-risk research programs. In L. C. Wyne, R. C. Cromwell, and S. Mattlynke (Eds.), *The nature of schizophrenia: New approaches to research and treatment.* New York: Wiley, 1978.

Gazzaniga, M. S. *The bisected brain.* New York: Appleton-Century-Crofts, 1970.

————, **and LeDoux, J. R.** *The integrated mind.* New York: Plenum, 1978.

Gerardo, C. J., and Bohan, J. B. Development of a sense of self-identity in children. *Child Development,* 1971, *42,* 1909–1921.

Gerbner, G., Ross, C. J., and Zigler, E. *Child abuse: An agenda for action.* New York: Oxford University Press, 1980.

Gerwirtz, J. L. A learning analysis of the effects of normal stimulation, privation, and deprivation on the acquisition of social motivation and attachment. In B. M. Foss (Ed.), *Determinants of infant behavior* (Vol. 1). New York: Wiley, 1961.

————. The cause of infant smiling in four child-rearing environments in Israel. In B. M. Foss (Ed.), *Determinants of infant behavior (Vol. 3).* London: Methuen, 1965.

————. Attachment, dependence and a distinction in terms of stimulus control. In J. L. Gewirtz (Ed.), *Attachment and dependency.* Washington, D.C.: V. H. Winston, 1972.

————, **and Boyd, E. F.** Experiments on mother-infant interaction underlying mutual attachment acquisition: The infant conditions the mother. In T. Alloway, P. Pliner, and L. Krames (Eds.), *Attachment behavior: Advances in the study of communication and affect.* New York: Plenum, 1977.

Gil, D. G. *Violence against children: Physical child abuse in the United States.* Cambridge, Mass.: Harvard University Press, 1970.

Glass, D. C. *Behavior patterns, stress, and coronary disease.* Hillsdale, N.J.: Lawrence Erlbaum, 1977.

Gleason, J. B. Code switching in children's language. In T. E. Moore (Ed.), *Cognitive development and the acquisition of language.* New York: Academic Press, 1973.

Goffman, E. *Asylums.* Garden City, N.Y.: Doubleday, 1961.

————. *Relations in public.* New York: Basic Books, 1971.

Goldfarb, W. Psychological privation in infancy and subsequent adjustment. *American Journal of Orthopsychiatry,* 1945, *15,* 247–255.

Goldfried, M. R. Behavioral assessment. In I. B. Weiner (Ed.), *Clinical methods in psychology.* New York: Interscience-Wiley, 1976.

Goodwin, D. W., Schulsinger. F., Hermansen, L., Guze, S. B., and Winokur, G. Alcohol problems in adoptees raised apart from alcoholic biological parents. *Archives of General Psychiatry,* 1973, *28,* 238–243.

Gottesman, I. I., and Shields, J. Contributions of twin studies to perspectives on schizophrenia. In B. Maher (Ed.), *Progress in experimental personality research* (Vol. 3). New York: Academic Press, 1966.

————. *Schizophrenia and genetics: A twin study vantage point.* New York: Academic Press, 1972.

Gough, H. G. The Adjective Checklist as a personality assessment research technique. *Psychological Reports,* 1960, *6,* 107–122.

————. Conceptual analysis of psychological test scores and other diagnostic variables. *Journal of Abnormal Psychology,* 1965, *70,* 294–302.

Gould, K. L. The phases of adult life: A study in developmental psychology. *American Journal of Psychiatry,* 1972, *129,* 521–531.

————. *Transformation.* New York: Simon and Schuster, 1978.

Gould, R. Adult life stages: Growth toward self-tolerance. *Psychology Today,* 1975, *8,* 74–78.

Graham, J. R. *The MMPI: A practical guide.* New York: Oxford University Press, 1977.

Granick, S., and Patterson, R. D. *Human aging. II: An eleven-year follow-up biomedical and behavioral study.* Bethesda, Md.: U.S. Public Health Service, 1972.

Gray, H., and Wheelwright, J. Jung's psychological types, their frequency and occurrence. *Journal of General Psychology,* 1964, *34,* 3–17.

Greenspoon, J. Verbal conditioning and clinical psychology. In A. J. Bachrach (Ed.), *Experimental foundations of clinical psychology.* New York: Basic Books, 1962.

Griffitt, W. Environmental effects on interpersonal affective behavior. Ambient effective temperature and attraction. *Journal of Personality and Social Psychology,* 1970, *15,* 240–244.

Grusec, J. E., and Skubinski, S. L. Model nurturance, demand characteristics of the modeling experiment and altruism. *Journal of Personality and Social Psychology,* 1970, *14,* 352–359.

Guilford, J. P. *An inventory of factors STDCR.* Beverly Hills, Calif.: Sheridan Supply, 1940.

————, **and Martin, H. G.** *The Guilford-Martin inventory of factors GAMIN: Manual of directions and norms.* Beverly Hills, Calif.: Sheridan Supply, 1943.

Guilford, J. P., and Zimmerman, W. S. Fourteen dimensions of temperament. *Psychological Monographs,* 1956, *70* (No. 10).

Guttman, D. The cross-cultural perspective: Notes toward a comparative psychology of aging. In J. E. Birren and K. W. Schaie (Eds.), *Handbook of the psychology of aging.* Princeton, N.J.: Van Nostrand, 1977.

Haley, G. A. Eye movement responses of repressors and sensitizers to a stressful film. *Journal of Research in Personality,* 1974, *8,* 88–94.

Hall, C. S., and Lindzey, G. *Theories of Personality* (2nd ed.). New York: Wiley, 1970.

Hall, W. B., and MacKinnon, D. W. Personality inventories as predictors of creativity among architects. *Journal of Applied Psychology,* 1969, *53,* 322–326.

Hamachek, D. E. Development of dynamics of the self. In James F. Adams (Ed.), *Understanding adolescence: Current developments in adolescent psychology.* Boston: Allyn and Bacon, 1976.

Hammock, T., and Brehm, J. W. The attractiveness of choice alternatives when freedom to choose is eliminated by a social agent. *Journal of Personality,* 1966, *34,* 546–554.

Hampson, J. L. Determinants of psychosexual orientation. In F. A. Beach (Ed.), *Sex and behavior.* New York: Wiley, 1965.

Harari, H., and Kaplan, R. M. *Psychology: Personal and social adjustment.* New York: Harper & Row, 1977.

Harlow, H. F. Motivation as a factor in the acquisition of new responses. In M. R. Jones (Ed.), *Nebraska Symposium on Motivation.* Lincoln: University of Nebraska Press, 1953.

————. The nature of love. *American Psychologist,* 1958, *13,* 673–685.

————. *Learning to love.* San Francisco: Albion, 1971.

————, **and Suomi, S. J.** Social recovery by isolation-reared monkeys. *Proceedings of the National Academy of Sciences,* 1971, *68,* 1534–1558.

Harman, H. H. *Modern factor analysis* (2nd ed.). Chicago: University of Chicago Press, 1967.

Harris, M. B. Mediators between frustration and aggression in a field experiment. *Journal of Experimental Social Psychology,* 1974, *10,* 561–571.

Hartmann, D. P. Considerations in the choice of interobserver reliability estimates. *Journal of Applied Behavioral Analysis,* 1977, *10,* 103–116.

Hartmann, E. The D-State: A review and discussion of studies on the physiological state concomitant with dreaming. *New England Journal of Medicine,* 1965, *273,* 30–35.

Hartmann, H. *Ego psychology and the problem of adaptation.* New York: International Universities Press, 1958.

————. *Essays on ego psychology: Selected problems in psychoanalytic theory.* New York: International Universities Press, 1964.

————, **Kris, E., and Loewenstein, R. M.** Comments on the formation of psychic structure. *Psychoanalytic study of the child,* 1946, 11–18.

Hartnagel, T. F., Teevan, J. J., and McIntyre, J. J. Television violence and violent behavior. *Social Forces,* 1979, *54,* 341–351.

Hartshorne, H., and May, M. A. *Studies in the nature*

of character. Vol. 1. *Studies in deceit.* New York: Macmillan, 1928.

————, **and Maller, J. B.** *Studies in service and self control.* New York: Macmillan, 1929.

Hartshorne, H., May, M. A., and Shuttleworth, F. H. *Studies in the nature of character. Vol. 3. Studies in the organization of character.* New York: Macmillan, 1930.

Havighurst, R. J., Neugarten, B. L., and Tobin, S. S. Disengagement and patterns of aging. In B. L. Neugarten (Ed.), *Middle age and aging.* Chicago: University of Chicago Press, 1968.

Hawkins, R. P., Peterson, R. F., Schweid, E., and Bijou, S. W. Behavior therapy in the home: Amelioration of parent-child relations with the parent in a therapeutic role. *Journal of Experimental Child Psychology,* 1966, *4,* 99–107.

Heckhausen, H., and Roelofsen, I. Anfange und Entwicklung der Leistungsmotivation: (I) Im Wetteifer des Kleinkindes. *Psychologisches Forschungen,* 1962, *26,* 313–397.

Heider, F. Social perception and phenomenal causation. *Psychological Review,* 1944, *51,* 358–374.

————. *The psychology of interpersonal relations.* New York: Wiley, 1958.

Heller, K., Davis., J. D., and Myers, R. A. The effects of interviewer style in a standardized interview. *Journal of Consulting Psychology,* 1966, *30,* 501–508.

Helmreich, R. L., and Spence, J. T. The work and family orientation questionnaire: An objective instrument to assess components of achievement motivation and attitudes toward family and career. *JSAS catalog of selected documents in psychology,* 1978, *8,* 35.

Herbert, J. Hormones and reproductive behaviors in Rhesus and Talapain monkeys. *Journal of Reproduction and Fertility* (supplement), 1970, *11,* 119–140.

Hess, E. H. Attitude and pupil size. *Scientific American,* 1965, *212,* 46–54.

Hess, R. D., and Shipman, V. C. Early experience and the socialization of cognitive modes in children. *Child Development,* 1965, *34,* 869–886.

Hetherington, E. M., and Brackbill, Y. Etiology and covariation of obstinacy, orderliness, and parsimony in young children. *Child Development,* 1963, *34,* 919–943.

Hicks, D. J. Effects of co-observer's sanctions and adult presence on imitative aggression. *Child Development* 1968, *39,* 303–309.

Hicks, L. H., and Birren, J. E. Aging, brain damage, and psychomotor slowing. *Psychological Bulletin,* 1970, *74,* 377–396.

Hilgard, E. R. Human motives and the concept of the self. *American Psychologist,* 1949, *4,* 374–382.

————. A neodissociation interpretation of pain reduction in hypnosis. *Psychological Review*, 1973, *80*, 396–411.

————, Atkinson, R. C., and Atkinson, R. L. *Introduction to psychology* (6th ed.). New York: Harcourt, Brace, Jovanovich, 1975.

Hilgard, J. R. *Personality and hypnosis*. Chicago: University of Chicago Press, 1970.

Hinde, R. A. Energy models of motivation. *Symposium of the Society of Experimental Biology*, 1960, *14*, 199–213.

Hirai, T. *Psychophysiology of Zen*. Tokyo: Igaku Shoin, 1974.

Hiroto, D. S., and Seligman, M. E. P. Generality of learned helplessness in man. *Journal of Personality and Social Psychology*, 1975, *31*, 311–327.

Hoffman, M. L. Conscience, personality, and socialization techniques. *Human Development*, 1970, *13*, 90–126.

————. Altruistic behavior and the parent-child relationship. *Journal of Personality and Social Psychology*, 1975, *31*, 937–943.

————. Sex differences in empathy. *Psychological Bulletin*, 1977, *84*, 712–722.

Hogan, R. *Personality theory*. Englewood Cliffs, N.J.: Prentice-Hall, 1976.

————, DeSoto, C. B., and Solano, C. Traits, tests, and personality research. *American Psychologist*, 1977, *32*, 255–264.

Hokanson, J. E., and Burgess, M. The effects of three types of aggression on vascular processes. *Journal of Abnormal and Social Psychology*, 1962, *64*, 446–449.

Hollingworth, H. L. *Psychology of the functional neurotic*. New York: Appleton-Century, 1920.

Holmes, T. H., and Rahe, R. H. The social readjustment rating sale. *Journal of Psychosomatic Research*, 1967, *11*, 213–218.

Holt, E. B. *Animal drive and the learning process, an essay toward radical empiricism* (Vol. 1). New York: Holt, 1931.

Horner, M. S. *Sex differences in achievement motivation and performance in competitive and non-competitive situations*. Unpublished doctoral dissertation, University of Michigan, 1968.

Horney, K. *Neurotic personality of our times*. New York: Norton, 1937.

————. *Our inner conflicts*. New York: Norton, 1945.

Horrocks, J. E. *The psychology of adolescence*. Boston: Houghton Mifflin, 1969.

————. Development and dynamics of the self. In J. F. Adams (Ed.), *Understanding adolescence*. Boston: Allyn and Bacon, 1976.

Houston, J. P., Bee, H., Hatfield, E., and Rimm, D. C. *Invitation to psychology*. New York: Academic Press, 1979.

Howes, D. H., and Solomon, R. L. Visual duration threshold as a function of word-probability. *Journal of Experimental Psychology*, 1951, *41*, 401–410.

Hull, C. L. *Principles of behavior*. New York: Appleton-Century-Crofts, 1943.

————. *Essentials of behavior*. New Haven: Yale University Press, 1951.

————. *A behavior system: An introduction to behavior theory concerning the individual organism*. New Haven: Yale University Press, 1952.

Hunter, E. J. The prisoner of war: Coping with the stress of isolation. In R. H. Moos (Ed.), *Human adaptation: Coping with life crises*. Lexington, Mass.: Heath, 1976.

Hutchings, B., and Mednick, S. A. Criminality in adoptees and their adoptive and biological parents: A pilot study. In S. Mednick and K. O. Christiansen (Eds.), *Biosocial bases of criminal behavior*. New York: Gardner, 1977.

Huxley, A. *The doors of perception*. New York: Harper & Row, 1954.

Inkeles, A. Society, social structure, and child socialization. In J. A. Clausen (Ed.), *Socialization and society*. Boston: Little, Brown, 1968.

————, and Rossi, P. H. National comparisons of occupational prestige. *American Journal of Sociology*, 1966, *61*, 329–339.

Ittelson, W. H., Proshansky, H. M., Rivlin, L. G., and Winkel, G. H. *An introduction to environmental psychology*. New York: Holt, 1974.

Jackson, D. H., and Messick, S. Response styles and the assessment of psychopathology. In S. Messick and J. Ross (Eds.), *Measurement of personality and cognition*. New York: Wiley, 1962.

Jaffe, Y. *Sex and aggression: An intimate relationship*. Unpublished doctoral dissertation, University of California, Los Angeles, 1975.

————, Malamuth, N., Feingold, J., and Feshbach, S. Sexual arousal and behavioral aggression. *Journal of Personality and Social Psychology*, 1974, *30*, 759–764.

James, W. T. Social organization among dogs of different temperaments: Terriers and beagles reared together. *Journal of Comparative Physiological Psychology*, 1951, *44*, 71–77.

Janis, I. L. *Psychological stress*. New York: Wiley, 1958.

Jensen, G. D., and Tolman, C. W. Activity level of the mother monkey, *Macaca nemestrina*, as affected by various conditions of sensory access to the infant following separation. *Animal Behaviour*, 1962, *10*, 228–230.

————. Mother-infant relationship in the monkey, *Macaca nemestrina*: The effect of brief separation and mother-infant specificity. *Journal of*

Comparative and Physiological Psychology, 1962, *55*, 131–136.

Jessor, R., Graves, T. D., Hanson, R. C., and Jessor, S. L. *Society, personality, and deviant behavior.* New York: Holt, 1968.

Jessor, R., and Jessor, S. L. *Problem behavior and psychosocial development: A longitudinal study of youth.* New York: Academic Press, 1977.

Johnson, R. N. *Aggression in man and animals.* Philadelphia: Saunders, 1972.

Johnston, L. D., Bachman, J. G., and O'Malley, P. M. *Highlights from drugs and the class of 1978: Behaviors, attitudes, and recent national trends.* Rockville, Md.: National Institute on Drug Abuse, 1979.

Jones, E. *The life and work of Sigmund Freud* (Vols. I–III). New York: Basic Books, 1953–1957.

Jones, E. E. The rocky road from acts to dispositions. *American Psychologist*, 1979, *34*, 107–117.

———, **and Davis, K. E.** From acts to dispositions: The attribution process in person perception. In L. Berkowitz (Ed.), *Advances in experimental social psychology* (Vol. 2). New York: Academic Press, 1965.

Jones, E. E., and Nisbett, R. E. *The actor and observer: Divergent perceptions of the causes of behavior.* Morristown, N.J.: General Learning Press, 1971.

Jones, M. C. A study of socialization patterns at the high school level. *Journal of Genetic Psychology*, 1958, *92*, 87–111.

———, **and Mussen, P. H.** Self-conception, motivation and interpersonal attitudes of early and late maturing girls. *Child Development*, 1958, *29*, 491–501.

Jung, C. (1904) Studies in word association. In *Experimental researches, collected works* (Vol. 2). Princeton, N.J.: Princeton University Press, 1973.

———. *Analytical psychology.* New York: Moffat, Yard, 1916.

———. (1936) *The concept of the collective unconscious.* In *Collected work* (Vol. 9, Part I). N.J.: Princeton University Press, 1959.

———. *The basic writings of C. G. Jung* (V. de Laszlo, Ed.). New York: Random House, 1959.

Kadushin, A. *Adopting older children.* New York: Columbia University Press, 1970.

Kagan, J. Developmental studies in reflection and analysis. In A. H. Kidd and J. L. Rivoire (Eds.), *Perceptual development in children.* New York: International Universities Press, 1966.

———, **and Kogan, N.** Individual variation in cognitive processes. In P. H. Mussen (Ed.), *Carmichael's manual of child psychology* (Vol. 1). New York: Wiley, 1970.

Kagan, J., and Klein, R. E. Cross-cultural perspectives on early development. *American Psychologist*, 1973, *28*, 947–961.

Kagan, J., and Moss, H. A. Stability and validity of achievement fantasy. *Journal of Abnormal and Social Psychology*, 1959, *58*, 357–364.

———. *Birth to maturity.* New York: Wiley, 1962.

Kagan, S., and Madsen, M. C. Cooperation and competition of Mexican, Mexican-American, and Anglo children of two ages. *Developmental Psychology*, 1971, *5*, 32–39.

Kallmann, F. J. Genetic principles in manic-depressive psychosis. In P. H. Hoch and J. Zubin (Eds.), *Depression.* New York: Grune & Stratton, 1958.

Kallman, W. M., and Feuerstein, M. Psychophysiological procedures. In A. R. Ciminero, K. S. Calhoun, and H. E. Adams (Eds.), *Handbook of Behavioral assessment.* New York: Interscience-Wiley, 1977.

Kamiya, J. Operant control of the EEG and some of its reported effects on consciousness. In C. T. Tart (Ed.), *Altered states of consciousness.* New York: Wiley, 1969.

Kanfer, F. H. The maintenance of behavior of self-generated stimuli and reinforcement. In A. Jacobs and B. Sachs (Eds.), *The psychology of private events.* New York: Academic Press, 1971.

———, **and Marston, A. R.** Determinants of self-reinforcement in human learning. *Journal of Experimental Psychology*, 1963, *66*, 245–254.

Kanfer, F. H., and Saslow, G. Behavioral diagnosis. In C. M. Franks (Ed.), *Behavior therapy: Appraisal and status.* New York: McGraw-Hill, 1969.

Kaplan, R. M., and Saccuzzo, D. S. *Psychological testing: Principles and applications.* Belmont, Calif.: Brooks/Cole, 1981.

Kardiner, A. *The psychological frontier of society.* New York: Columbia University Press, 1945.

Kastenbaum, R., Derbin, V., Sabatini, P., and Artt, S. "The age of me": Towards personal and interpersonal definitions of functional aging. *International Journal of Aging and Human Development*, 1972, *3*, 197–211.

Kaufman, H., and Feshbach, S. Displaced aggression and its modification through exposure to antiaggressive communications. *Journal of Abnormal and Social Psychology*, 1963, *67*, 79–83.

Kazdin, A. E. Artifact, bias, and complexity of assessment: The ABCs of reliability. *Journal of Applied Behavior Analysis*, 1977, *10*, 141–150.

Keiner, J. Klexographien, Part VI. In R. Pissin (Ed.), *Keiners Werke.* Berlin: Bong & Co., 1857.

Keller, S., and Zavalloni, M. Ambition and social class: A respecification. *Social Forces*, 1964, *43*, 58–70.

Kelley, C. K., and King, G. D. Behavioral correlates of the 2-7-8 MMPI profile type in students at a university mental health center. *Journal of*

Consulting and Clinical Psychology, 1979, *47,* 679–685.

Kelley, H. H. Attribution theory in social psychology. In D. Levine (Ed.), *Nebraska Symposium on Motivation.* Lincoln: University of Nebraska Press, 1967.

Kelly, G. A. *The psychology of personal constructs.* New York: Norton, 1955.

———. Man's construction of his alternatives. In G. Lindzey (Ed.), *Assessment of human motives.* New York: Grove, 1958.

———. (1966) A summary statement of cognitive-oriented comprehensive theory of behavior. In J. C. Mancuso (Ed.), *Readings for a cognitive theory of personality.* New York: Holt, 1970.

Keniston, K. The sources of student dissent. *Journal of Social Issues,* 1967, *22,* 108–137.

Kessen, W. (Ed.). *Childhood in China.* New Haven: Yale University Press, 1975.

Kimble, G. A., Garmezy, N., and Zigler, E. *Principles of general psychology* (4th ed.). New York: Ronald, 1974.

King, L. F., Armitage, S. G., and Tilton, J. A therapeutic approach to schizophrenia of extreme pathology. *Journal of Abnormal and Social Psychology,* 1960, *61,* 276–286.

Kinsey, A. C., Pomeroy, W. B., and Martin, C. E. *Sexual behavior in the human male.* Philadelphia: Saunders, 1948.

———, **and Gebhard, P. H.** *Sexual behavior in the human female.* Philadelphia: Saunders, 1953.

Klein, G. S. Peremptory ideation; Structure and force in motivated ideas. In R. Jessor and S. Feshback (Eds.), *Cognition, personality and clinical psychology.* San Francisco: Jossey-Bass, 1967.

———. Freud's two theories of sexuality. In L. Breger (Ed.), *Clinical-cognitive psychology.* Englewood Cliffs, N.J.: Prentice-Hall, 1969.

———. *Perception, motives and personality.* New York: Knopf, 1970.

Klein, M. *The psycho-analysis of children* (2nd ed.). London: Hogarth, 1937.

———. *Contributions to psychoanalysis, 1921–45.* London: Hogarth, 1948.

Klein, R. *Some factors influencing empathy in six and seven year old children varying in ethnic background.* Unpublished doctoral dissertation, University of California, Los Angeles, 1970.

Kline, N. Drugs are the greatest practical advance in the history of psychiatry. *New Medical Material,* 1962, *4,* 49.

Kline, P. *Fact and fancy in Freudian theory.* London: Methuen, 1972.

Klineberg, O. *Race differences.* New York: Harper & Brothers, 1935.

Klinger, E. Fantasy need achievement as a motivational construct. *Psychological Bulletin,* 1966, *66,* 291–303.

Klopfer, B. (Ed.), *Developments in the Rorschach technique.* Yonkers, N.Y.: World Book, 1954–1970.

Klopfer, W. G., and Taulbee, E. S. Projective tests. *Annual Review of Psychology,* 1976, 543–568.

Knott, P. D., Lasater, L., and Shuman, R. Aggression: Guilt and conditionability for aggressiveness. *Journal of Personality,* 1974, *42,* 332–344.

Kobasa, S. C. Stressful life events, personality, and health: An inquiry into hardiness. *Journal of Personality and Social Psychology,* 1979, *37,* 1–11.

———, **and Maddi, S. R.** Existential personality theory. In Raymond J. Corsini (Ed.), *Current Personality Theories.* Itasca, Ill.: F. E. Peacock, 1977.

Kohlberg, L. *The development of modes of moral thinking and choice in the years ten to sixteen.* Unpublished doctoral dissertation, University of Chicago, 1958.

———. A cognitive-developmental analysis of children's sex-role concepts and attitudes. In E. Maccoby (Ed.), *The development of sex differences.* Stanford, Calif.: Stanford University Press, 1966.

———. Stage and sequence: The cognitive-developmental approach to socialization. In D. Goslin (Ed.), *Handbook of socialization theory and research.* Chicago: Rand McNally, 1969. (a)

———. *Stages in the development of moral thought and action.* New York: Holt, 1969. (b)

———. Moral stages and moralization. The cognitive-developmental approach. In T. Lickona (Ed.), *Moral development and behavior: Theory, research and social issues.* New York: Holt, 1976.

Kohn, M. L. Social class and schizophrenia: A critical review. *Psychiatric Research,* 1968, *6* (Supp. 1), 155–173.

Kohut, H. *The analysis of the self: A systematic approach to the psychoanalytic treatment of narcissistic personality disorders* (Monograph Series of the Psychoanalytic Study of the Child, No. 41). New York: International Universities Press, 1971.

———. *The restoration of the self.* New York: International Universities Press, 1977.

Kolb, D. Achievement motivation training of underachieving high-school boys. *Journal of Personality and Social Psychology,* 1965, *2,* 783–792.

Konecni, V. J. Annoyance, type and duration of postannoyance activity, and aggression: The "cathartic effect." *Journal of Experimental Psychology: General,* 1975, *104,* 76–102.

Krasner, L., and Ullman, L. P., *Behavior influence and personality.* New York: Holt, 1973.

Kretschmer, E. *Physique and character.* New York: Harcourt, Brace, 1925.

Kreuz, L. E. and Rose, R. M. Assessment of aggressive behaviors and plasma testosterone in a young criminal population. *Psychosomatic Medicine,* 1972, *34,* 321–332.

Kruijt, J. *Ontogeny of social behavior in Burmese red jungle fowl* (Gallus gallus spodiceus) (Behavior Supp. 12). Leiden: Brill, 1964.

Kuder, G. F., and Richardson, M. W. The theory of the estimation of reliability, *Psychometrika,* 1937, *2,* 151–160.

Kukla, A. Attributional determinants of achievement-related behavior. *Journal of Personality and Social Psychology,* 1972, *21,* 166–174.

———. The modern language of consciousness. In L. Michaels and C. Ricks (Eds.), *The state of the language.* Berkeley: University of California Press, 1980.

Kurtines, W., and Greif, E. B. The development of moral thought: Review and evaluation of Kohlberg's approach. *Psychological Bulletin,* 1974, *81,* 453–470.

Lack, D. L. *The life of the robin.* Cambridge: Cambridge University Press, 1943.

Lagerspetz, K. Genetic and social causes of aggressive behavior in mice. *Scandinavian Journal of Psychology,* 1961, *2,* 117–173.

———. In S. Garattini and E. B. Sigg (Eds.), *Aggressive behavior.* Amsterdam: Excerpta Medica, 1969.

———. Modification of aggressiveness in mice. In S. Feshbach and A. Fraczek (Eds.), *Aggression and behavior change: Biological and social processes.* New York: Praeger, 1979.

Laing, R. D. *The divided self: An existential study in sanity and madness.* Baltimore: Penguin, 1965.

Lamb, D. Anxiety. In H. London and J. E. Exner (Eds.), *Dimensions of personality.* New York: John Wiley, 1978.

Lamb, M. E. Father-infant and mother-infant interaction in the first year of life. *Child Development,* 1977, *48,* 167–181.

Lang, P. J. The application of psychophysiological methods to the study of psychotherapy and behavior modification. In A. E. Bergin and S. L. Garfield (Eds.), *Handbook of psychotherapy and behavior change.* New York: Wiley, 1971.

Langer, E. J., Blank, A., and Chanowitz, B. The mindlessness of ostensibly thoughtful action: The role of "placebic" information in interpersonal interaction. *Journal of Personality and Social Psychology,* 1978, *36,* 635–642.

Langer, E. J., and Rodin, J. The effects of choice and enhanced personal responsibility for the aged: A field experiment in an institutional setting. *Journal of Personality and Social Psychology,* 1976, *34,* 191–198.

Lashley, K. S. The mechanism of vision: I. A method for rapid analysis of pattern-vision in the rat. *Pedagogical Seminary and Journal of Genetic Psychology,* 1930, *37,* 453–460.

Last, U. *Motives, styles, contents and products of identification in the authority figure.* Unpublished doctoral dissertation, Hebrew University, 1975.

Latané, B., and Darley, J. Social determinants of bystander intervention in emergencies. In J. Macaulay and L. Berkowitz (Eds.), *Altruism and helping behavior.* New York: Academic Press, 1970.

Lawson, R. *Frustration: The development of a scientific concept.* New York: Macmillan, 1965.

Lazarus, A. A. *Behavior therapy and beyond.* New York: McGraw-Hill, 1971.

Lazarus, R. S. *Psychological stress and the coping process.* New York: McGraw-Hill, 1966.

———, and Alfert, E. The short circuiting of threat by experimentally altering cognitive appraisal. *Journal of Abnormal and Social Psychology,* 1964, *69,* 195–205.

Lazarus, R. S., and Averill, J. R. Emotion and cognition: With special reference to anxiety. In C. D. Spielberger (Ed.), *Anxiety: Current trends in theory and research.* New York: Academic Press, 1972.

LeBoeuf, B. J. and Peterson, R. S. Social status and mating activity in elephant seals. *Science,* 1969, *163,* 91–93.

Lecky, P. *Self-consistency: A theory of personality.* New York: Island Press Co-operative, 1945.

Lee, L. C. The concomitant development of cognitive and moral modes of thought: A test of selected deductions from Piaget's theory. *Genetic Psychology Monographs,* 1971, *83,* 93–143.

Lefcourt, H. M. The function of illusions of control and freedom. *American Psychologist,* 1973, *28,* 417–425.

———. *Locus of control.* Hillsdale, N.J.: Lawrence Erlbaum, 1976.

———, Von Baeyer, C. L., Ware, E. E., and Cox, C. J. The multidimensional-multiattributional causality scale: The development of a goal specific locus of control scale. *Canadian Journal of Behavioral Science,* 1979, *11,* 286–304.

Lefkowitz, M. M., Eron, L. D., Walder, L. O., and Huesmann, L. R. *Growing up to be violent.* New York: Pergamon, 1977.

LeFurgy, W. G., and Woloshin, G. W. Immediate and long-term effects of experimentally induced social influence in the modification of adolescents' moral judgments. *Journal of Abnormal and Social Psychology,* 1969, *12,* 104–110.

Lehman, C. H., and Witty, P. A. Faculty psychology and personality traits. *American Journal of Psychology,* 1934, *44,* 486–500.

Lehrman, D. S. A critique of Konrad Lorenz's theory of instinctive behavior. *Quarterly Review of Biology,* 1953, *28,* 337–363.

——. Semantic and conceptual issues in the nature-nurture problem. In L. R. Aronson, E. Tobach, D. S. Lehrman, and J. S. Rosenblatt (Eds.), *Development and evolution of behavior.* San Francisco: Freeman, 1970.

Lennenberg, E. H. *Biological foundations of language.* New York: Wiley, 1967.

Lepper, M. R., Greene, D., and Nisbett, R. E. Undermining children's intrinsic interest with extrinsic reward: A test of the overjustification hypothesis. *Journal of Personality and Social Psychology,* 1973, *28,* 129–137.

Levinson, D. J. *The seasons of a man's life.* New York: Ballantine, 1978.

Levis, D. J. Learned helplessness: A reply and an alternative S-R interpretation. *Journal of Experimental Psychology: General,* 1976, *105,* 47–65.

Lewin, K. *A dynamic theory of personality.* New York: McGraw-Hill, 1935.

——, Dembo, T., Festinger, L., and Sears, P. S. Level of aspiration. In J. McV. Hunt (Ed.), *Personality and the behavioral disorders* (Vol. 1). New York: Ronald, 1944.

Lewis, M., and Brooks, J. Infants' social perception: A constructionist view. In L. Cohen and S. Salapatele (Eds.), *Infant perception: From sensation to cognition. Perception of space, speech and sound* (Vol. 2). New York: Academic Press, 1975.

Lewis, M., and Brooks-Gunn, J. *Social cognition and the acquisition of self.* New York: Plenum, 1979.

Lewis, O. *Children of Sanchez.* New York: Random House, 1961.

Ley, R. G. Cerebral asymmetries, emotional experience, and imagery: Implications for psychotherapy. In A. A. Sheilah and J. T. Shaffer (Eds.), *The potential of fantasy and imagination.* New York: Brandon House, 1979.

Leyens, J. P., Camino, L., Parke, R. D., and Berkowitz, L. Effects of movie violence on aggression in a field setting as a function of group dominance and cohesion. *Journal of Personality and Social Psychology,* 1975, *32,* 346–360.

Lickona, T. (Ed.). *Moral development and behavior: Theory, research, and social issues.* New York: Holt, 1976.

Liebert, R. M., and Allen, K. M. *The effects of rule structure and reward magnitude on the acquisition and adoption of self-reward criteria.* Unpublished manuscript, Vanderbilt University, 1967.

Lindzey, G. The Thematic Apperception Test: Interpretive assumptions and related empirical evidence. *Psychological Bulletin,* 1952, *49,* 1–25.

——. Some remarks concerning incest, the incest taboo, and psychoanalytic theory. *American Psychologist,* 1967, *22,* 1051–1059. (a)

——. Behavior and morphological variation. In J. N. Spuhler (Ed.), *Genetic diversity and human behavior.* Chicago: Aldine, 1967. (b)

Lissner, K. Die Entspannung von Bedürfnissen durch Ersatzhandlungen. *Psychologische Forschung,* 1933, *18,* 218–250.

Loeb, A., Beck, A. T., Diggory, J. C., and Tuthill, R. Expectancy, level of aspiration, performance, and self-evaluation in depression. *Proceedings of the 75th Annual Convention of the American Psychological Association,* 1967, *2,* 193–194.

Loehlin, J. C., and Nichols, R. C. *Heredity, environment, and personality.* Austin: University of Texas Press, 1976.

Loevinger, J. *Ego development.* San Francisco: Jossey-Bass, 1976.

Lomangino, L. *The depiction of subliminally and supraliminally presented aggressive stimuli and its effect on the cognitive functioning of schizophrenics.* Unpublished doctoral dissertation, Fordham University, 1969.

Loo, C. M. The effects of spatial density on the social behavior of children. *Journal of Applied Social Psychology,* 1972, *2,* 372–381.

Lorenz, K. Der Kumpan in der umwelt des vogels. *Journal für Ornithologie,* 1935, *83,* 137–213, 289–413.

——. The comparative method in studying innate behaviour patterns. *Symposium of the Society of Experimental Biology,* 1950, *4,* 221–268.

——. *On aggression.* New York: Bantam, 1966.

Lovaas, O. I. Some studies on the treatment of childhood schizophrenia. In J. M. Shlien (Ed.), *Research in psychotherapy.* Washington, D.C.: American Psychological Association, 1968.

——, Freitag, G., Gold, V. J., and Kassorla, I. C. Experimental studies in childhood schizophrenia: 1. Analysis of self-destructive behavior. *Journal of Experimental Child Psychology,* 1965, *2,* 67–84.

Lowenthal, M. F., Thurnher, M., and Chiriboga, D. *Four stages of life-span.* San Francisco: Jossey-Bass, 1975.

Lubin, B., Wallis, R. R., and Paine, C. Patterns of psychological test usage in the United States, 1935–1969. *Professional Psychology,* 1971, *2,* 70–74.

Luborsky, L. Momentary forgetting during psychotherapy and psychoanalysis: A theory and research method. In R. R. Holt (Ed.), *Motives and thought: Psychoanalytic essays in honor of David Rappaport* (Psychological Issues Monograph 18/19). New York: International Universities Press, 1967.

Maccoby, E. E., and Feldman, S. S. Mother attachment and stranger reactions in the third year of life. *Monographs of the Society for Research in Child Development*, 1972, *37*(1).

Maccoby, E. E., and Jacklin, C. H. *The psychology of sex differences*. Stanford, Calif.: Stanford University Press, 1974.

Macfarlane, J. W., Allen, L., and Honzik, M. P. A development study of the behavior problems of normal children between 20 months and 14 years. *University of California Publications in Child Development*, 1954, *2*.

MacKinnon, D. W. The nature and nurture of creative talent. *American Psychologist*, 1962, *17*, 484–495.

Maddi, S. R. *Personality theories: A comparative analysis* (3rd ed.). Homewood, Ill.: Dorsey, 1976.

Maddox, G. L. Fact and artifact: Evidence bearing on disengagement theory. In E. Palmore (Ed.), *Normal aging*. Durham, N.C.: Duke University Press, 1970.

Madsen, M. C., and Shapira, A. Cooperative and competitive behavior of urban Afro-American, Anglo-American, Mexican-American, and Mexican village children. *Developmental Psychology*, 1970, *3*, 16–20.

Maduro, R. J., and Wheelwright, J. B. Analytical psychology. In R. J. Corsini (Ed.), *Current personality theories*. Itasca, Illinois: F. E. Peacock, 1977.

Magnussen, D., and Endler, N. S. Interactional psychology: Present status and future prospects. In D. Magnussen and N. S. Endler (Eds.), *Personality at the crossroads: Current issues in interactional psychology*. Hillsdale, N.J.: Lawrence Erlbaum, 1977, 99–111.

Mahler, M. S. *On human symbiosis and the vicissitudes of individuation*. New York: International Universities Press, 1968.

Mahler, V. Ersatzhandlungen verschiedenen Realitätsgrade. *Psychologische Forschung*, 1933, *18*, 26–89.

Mahone, C. H. Fear of failure and unrealistic vocational aspiration. *Journal of Abnormal and Social Psychology*, 1960, *60*, 253–261.

Mahoney, M. J. *Cognition and behavior modification*. Cambridge, Mass.: Ballinger, 1974.

Mahrer, A. R. The role of expectancy in delayed reinforcement. *Journal of Experimental Psychology*, 1956, *52*, 101–105.

Maier, N. R. F. *Frustration: The study of behavior without a goal*. New York: McGraw-Hill, 1949.

Malamuth, N., Feshbach, S., and Jaffe, Y. Sexual arousal and aggression: Recent experiments and theoretical issues. In A. Peplau and C. Hammen (Eds.), *Journal of Social Issues*, 1977, *33*, 110–133.

Malamuth, N., Haber, S. F., and Feshbach, S. Testing hypotheses regarding rape: Exposure to sexual violence, sex differences, and the "normality" of rapists. *Journal of Research in Personality*, 1980, *14*, 121–137.

Maltzman, I. Awareness: Cognitive psychology vs. behaviorism. *Journal of Experimental Research in Personality*, 1966, *1*, 161–165.

Manning, S. A., and Taylor, D. A. Effects of viewed violence and aggression: Stimulation and catharsis. *Journal of Personality and Social Psychology*, 1975, *31*, 180–188.

Marcus, R. F., Telleen, S., and Poke, E. J. Relation between cooperation and empathy in young children. *Developmental Psychology*, 1979, *15*, 346–347.

Marijuana and Health: Seventh Annual Report to the United States Congress from the Secretary of Health, Education, and Welfare. Washington, D.C.: U.S. Government Printing Office, 1977.

Mark, V. H., and Erwin, F. R. *Violence and the brain*. New York: Harper & Row, 1970.

Marsden, G. Content analysis studies of psychotherapy: 1954 through 1968. In A. E. Bergin and S. L. Garfield (Eds.), *Handbook of psychotherapy and behavior change*. New York: Wiley, 1971.

Marshall, G. D., and Zimbardo, P. G. Affective consequences of inadequately explained physiological arousal. *Journal of Personality and Social Psychology*, 1979, *37*, 970–988.

Martindale, D. A. Territorial dominance behavior in dyadic verbal interactions. *Proceedings of the 79th Annual Convention of the American Psychological Association*, 1971, *6*, 305–306.

Maslach, C. Negative emotional biasing of unexplained arousal. *Journal of Personality and Social Psychology*, 1979, *37*, 953–969.

Maslow, A. H. Deprivation, threat and frustration. *Psychological Review*, 1941, *48*, 364–366.

———. A theory of human motivation. *Psychological Review*, 1943, *50*, 370–396.

———. *The farther reaches of human nature*. New York: Viking, 1971.

Masters, W., and Johnson, V. *Human sexual response*. Boston: Little, Brown, 1966.

Matarazzo, J. D., and Wiens, A. N. *The interview: Research on its anatomy and structure*. Chicago: Aldino-Atherton, 1972.

———, **Matarazzo, R. G., and Saslow, G.** Speech and silence behavior in clinical psychotherapy and its laboratory correlates. In J. Shlien, H. Hunt, J. D. Matarazzo, and C. Savage (Eds.), *Research in psychotherapy* (Vol. 3). Washington, D.C.: American Psychological Association, 1968.

Matas, L., Arend, R. A., and Sroufe, L. A. Continuity of adaptation in the second year: The relationship between quality of attachment and later competence. *Child Development*, 1978, *49*, 483–494.

Mazis, M. B. Antipollution measures and psychological reactance theory: A field experiment. *Journal of Personality and Social Psychology,* 1975, *31,* 546–660.

McClearn, G. E. The inheritance of behavior. In L. Postman (Ed.), *Psychology in the making.* New York: Knopf, 1962.

McClelland, D. C. Methods of measuring human motivation. In J. W. Atkinson (Ed.), *Motives in fantasy, action, and society.* Princeton, N.J.: Van Nostrand, 1958.

———. *The achieving society.* Princeton, N.J.: Van Nostrand, 1961.

———. Toward a theory of motive acquisition. *American Psychologist,* 1965, *20,* 321–333.

———, **and Atkinson, J. W.** The projective expression of needs: I. The effect of different intensities of the hunger drive on perception. *Journal of Psychology,* 1948, *25,* 205–222.

McClelland, D. C., Davis, W. N., Kalin, R., and Wanner, E. *The drinking man.* New York: Free Press, 1972.

McClelland, D. C., and Winter, D. G. *Motivating economic achievement.* New York: Free Press, 1969.

McGinnies, E. Emotionality and perceptual defense. *Psychological Review,* 1949, *56,* 244–251.

McGlothlin, W. H., and Arnold, D. D. LSD revisited. *Archives of General Psychiatry,* 1971, *24,* 35–49.

McGlothlin, W. H., Cohen, S., and McGlothlin, M. S. Long lasting effects of LSD on normals. *Archives of General Psychiatry,* 1967, *17,* 521–532.

McGrath, M. J., and Cohen, D. B. REM sleep facilitation of adaptive waking behaviors: A review of the literature. *Psychological Bulletin,* 1978, *85,* 24–57.

McGuire, W. J., and Padawer-Singer, A. Trait salience in the spontaneous self-concept. *Journal of Personality and Social Psychology,* 1976, *33,* 743–754.

McKinley, D. G. *Social class and family life.* New York: Free Press, 1964.

Mednick, S., and Christiansen, K. O. *Biosocial bases of criminal behavior.* New York: Gardner, 1977.

Meehl, P. E. *Clinical versus statistical prediction.* Minneapolis: University of Minnesota Press, 1954.

———. Schizotaxia, schizotypy, schizophrenia. *American Psychologist,* 1962, *17,* 827–838.

Megargee, E. I. Undercontrolled and overcontrolled personality types in extreme antisocial aggression. *Psychological Monographs,* 1966, *80* (Whole No. 611).

———, **and Mendelsohn, G. A.** A cross validation of twelve MMPI indices of hostility and control. *Journal of Abnormal and Social Psychology,* 1962, *65,* 431–438.

Meichenbaum, D. Cognitive factors in behavior modification: Modifying what clients say to themselves. In C. M. Franks and G. T. Wilson (Eds.), *Annual review of behavior therapy theory and practice* (Vol. 1). New York: Brunner/Mazel, 1973.

———, **and Cameron, R.** Training schizophrenics to talk to themselves: A means of developing attentional controls. *Behavior Therapy,* 1973, *4,* 515–534.

Menzies, E. S. *Preference in television content among violent prisoners* (FCI Research Reports). Tallahassee: Federal Correctional Institution, 1974.

Merton, R. K. *Social theory and social structure.* Glencoe, Ill.: Free Press, 1957.

Messick, S. The standard problem: Meaning and values in measurement and evaluation. *American Psychologist,* 1975, *30,* 955–966.

———, **and Jackson, D. N.** Acquiescence and the factorial interpretation of the MMPI. *Psychological Bulletin,* 1961, *58,* 299–304.

Meyer, H. H., Walker, W. B., and Litwin, G. H. Motive patterns and risk preferences associated with entrepreneurship. *Journal of Abnormal and Social Psychology,* 1961, *63,* 570–574.

Meyer, W. U., Folkes, V. S., and Weiner, B. The perceived informational value and affective consequences of choice behavior and intermediate difficulty task selection. *Journal of Research in Personality,* 1976, *10,* 410–423.

Midlarsky, E., and Bryan, J. H. Affect expressions and children's imitative altruism. *Journal of Experimental Research in Personality,* 1972, *6,* 195–203.

Milgram, S. Behavioral study of obedience. *Journal of Abnormal and Social Psychology,* 1963, *67,* 371–378.

Milgram, S. *Obedience to authority.* New York: Harper & Row, 1974.

———, **and Shotland, R. L.** *Television and antisocial behavior: Field experiments.* New York: Academic Press, 1973.

Miller, D. R., and Swanson, G. E. *Inner conflict and defense.* New York: Holt, 1960.

Miller, I. W., III, and Norman, W. H. Learned helplessness: A review and attribution-theory model. *Psychological Bulletin,* 1979, *86,* 93–118.

Miller M. M. Treatment of chronic alcoholism by hypnotic aversion. *Journal of the American Medical Association,* 1959, *171,* 1492–1495.

Miller, N. E. The frustration-aggression hypothesis. *Psychological Review,* 1941, *48,* 337–342.

———. Experimental studies in conflict. In J. McV. Hunt (Ed.), *Personality and the behavioral disorders* (Vol. 1). New York: Ronald, 1944.

———. Liberalization of basic S-R concepts: Extensions to conflict, motivation, and social learning. In S. Koch (Ed.), *Psychology: A study of a science* (Vol. 2). New York: McGraw-Hill, 1959.

————, **and Banuazizi, A.** Instrumental learning by curarized rats of a specific visceral response, intestinal or cardiac. *Journal of Comparative and Physiological Psychology,* 1968, *65,* 1–17.

Miller, N. E., and Bugelski, R. Minor studies in aggression. II. The influence of frustration imposed by the in-group attitudes expressed toward out-groups. *Journal of Psychology,* 1948, *25,* 437–442.

Miller, N. E., and Dollard, J. *Social learning and imitation.* New Haven: Yale University Press, 1941.

Millett, R. A. Measures of learning and conditioning. In H. J. Eysenck (Ed.), *Experiments in personality* (Vol. II). London: Routledge, 1960.

Mischel, W. Delay of gratification, need for achievement, and acquiescence in another culture. *Journal of Abnormal and Social Psychology,* 1961, *62,* 543–552.

————. A social learning theory view of sex differences in behavior. In E. E. Maccoby (Ed.), *The development of sex differences.* Stanford, Calif.: Stanford University Press, 1966.

————. *Personality and assessment.* New York: Wiley, 1968.

————. *Introduction to personality.* New York: Holt, 1971.

————. Toward a cognitive social learning reconceptualization of personality. *Psychological Review,* 1973, *80,* 252–283.

————. Cognitive appraisals and transformations in self-control. In B. Weiner (Ed.), *Cognitive views of human motivation.* New York: Academic Press, 1974. (a)

————. Processes in delay of gratification. In L. Berkowitz (Ed.), *Advances in experimental social psychology* (Vol. 7). New York: Academic Press, 1974.

————. On the future of personality measurement. *American Psychologist,* 1977, *32,* 246–254.

————. On the interface of cognition and personality: Beyond the person-situation debate. *American Psychologist,* 1979, *34,* 740–754.

————, **and Ebbesen, E. B.** Attention in delay of gratification. *Journal of Personality and Social Psychology,* 1970, *16,* 329–337.

————, **and Zeiss, A.** Cognitive and attentional mechanisms in delay of gratification. *Journal of Personality and Social Psychology,* 1972, *21,* 204–218.

Mischel, W., and Mischel, H. N. A cognitive social learning approach to morality and self-regulation. In T. Lickona (Ed.), *Moral development and behavior: Theory, research and social issues.* New York: Holt, 1976.

Moltz, H., and Stettner, L. J. The influence of patterned-light deprivation on the critical period for imprinting. *Journal of Comparative and Physiological Psychology,* 1961, *54,* 279–283.

Money, J. (Ed.). *Sex research, new developments.* New York: Holt, 1965.

Monte, C. F. *Beneath the mask.* New York: Praeger, 1977.

Moos, R. H. Conceptualizations of human environment. *American Psychologist,* 1973, *28,* 652–665.

Morris, J. L. Propensity for risk taking as a determinant of vocational choice: An extension of the theory of achievement motivation. *Journal of Personality and Social Psychology,* 1966, *3,* 328–335.

Morse, S. J., and Gergen, K. J. Social comparison, self-consistency, and the concept of self. *Journal of Personality and Social Psychology,* 1970, *16,* 148–156.

Moss, H. A., and Kagan, J. Stability of achievement and recognition seeking behaviors from early childhood through adulthood. *Journal of Abnormal and Social Psychology,* 1961, *62,* 504–513.

Mowrer, O. H., and Viek, P. An experimental analogue of fear from a sense of helplessness. *Journal of Abnormal and Social Psychology,* 1948, *43,* 193–200.

Moyer, K. E. The physiology of aggression and the implications for aggression control. In J. L. Singer (Ed.), *The control of aggression and violence.* New York: Academic Press, 1971.

————. The physiology of aggression and the implication for aggression controls. In K. E. Moyer (Ed.), *Physiology of aggression.* New York: Raven, 1976.

Mukherjee, B. N., and Sinha, R. Achievement values and self-ideal discrepancies in college students. *Personality: An International Journal,* 1970, *1,* 275–301.

Murray, H. A. The effect of fear upon estimates of the maliciousness of other personalities. *Journal of Social Psychology,* 1933, *4,* 310–329.

————. *Explorations in personality: A clinical and experimental study of fifty men of college age.* New York: Oxford University Press, 1938.

Murstein, B. I. *Theory and research in projective techniques.* New York: Wiley, 1963.

Mussen, P. H. The development of personality and social behavior. In P. Mussen & M. R. Rosenzweig (Eds.), *Psychology: An introduction.* Lexington: D. C. Heath, 1977.

————, **and Eisenberg-Berg, N.** *Roots of caring, sharing, and helping: The development of prosocial behavior in children.* San Francisco: Freeman, 1977.

Mussen, P. H., and Jones, M. C. Self-conceptions, motivations and interpersonal attitudes of late and early maturing boys. *Child Development,* 1957, *28,* 243–256.

Myers, I. *The Meyers-Briggs Type Indicator.* Princeton, N.J.: Educational Testing Service, 1962.

Nation, J. R., Cooney, J. B., and Gartrell, K. E. Durability and generalizability of persistence training. *Journal of Abnormal Psychology,* 1979, 88(2), 121–136.

Nelson, J. D., Gelfand, D. M., and Hartmann, D. P. Children's aggression following competition and exposure to an aggressive model. *Child Development,* 1969, 40, 1085–1097.

Neugarten, B. L. Personality and aging. In J. E. Birren and K. W. Schaie (Eds.) *Handbook of the psychology of aging.* New York: Van Nostrand Reinhold, 1977.

———, **Havighurst, R. J., and Tobin, S. S.** Personality and patterns of aging. In B. L. Neugarten (Ed.), *Middle age and aging.* Chicago: University of Chicago Press, 1968.

Newcomb, T. *Personality and social change.* New York: Dryden, 1943.

Newson, J., and Newson, E. *Four years old in an urban community.* Chicago: Aldine, 1968.

———. Cultural aspects of child rearing in the English-speaking world. In A. Skolnick (Ed.), *Rethinking childhood.* Boston: Little, Brown, 1976.

The New York Times, Sunday, June 8, 1980, Section 2, p. 15.

Nickel, T. W. The attribution of intention as a critical factor in the relation between frustration and aggression. *Journal of Personality,* 1974, 42, 482–492.

Nisbett, R. E., and Borgida, E. Attribution and the psychology of prediction. *Journal of Personality and Social Psychology,* 1975, 32, 932–943.

Nisbett, R. E., and Schachter, S. Cognitive manipulation of pain. *Journal of Experimental Social Psychology,* 1966, 2, 227–236.

Norman, W. T. Toward an adequate taxonomy of personality attributes: Replicated factor structure in peer nomination personality ratings. *Journal of Abnormal and Social Psychology,* 1963, 66, 574–583.

———. On estimating psychological relationships: Social desirability and self-report. *Psychological Bulletin,* 1967, 67, 273–293.

Novaco, R. W. *Anger control: The development and evaluation of an experimental treatment.* Lexington, Mass.: Lexington Books, 1975.

Nucci, L., and Turiel, E. Social interactions and the development of social concepts in preschool children. *Child Development,* 1978, 49, 400–407.

Nunnally, J. C. *Psychometric theory* (2nd ed.). New York: McGraw-Hill, 1978.

Offer, D. *The psychological world of the teenager.* New York: Basic Books, 1969.

———, **and Offer, J. B.** *From teenage to young manhood.* New York: Basic Books, 1975.

Olim, E. A., Hess, R. D., and Shipman, V. C. Role of mother's language styles in mediating their preschool children's cognitive development. *School Review,* 1967, 75, 414–424.

Olweus, D. Personality and aggression. In J. K. Cole and D. D. Jensen (Eds.), *Nebraska Symposium on Motivation* (Vol. 21). Lincoln: University of Nebraska Press, 1973.

———. Personality factors and aggression: With special reference to violence within the peer group. In J. de Wit and W. W. Hartup (Eds.), *Determinants and origins of aggressive behavior.* The Hague: Mouton, 1974.

———. *Aggression in the schools: Bullies and whipping boys.* Washington, D.C.: Hemisphere, 1976.

———. A critical analysis of the "modern" interactionist position. In D. Magnussen and N. S. Endler (Eds.), *Personality at the crossroads: Current issues in interactional psychology.* Hillsdale, N.J.: Lawrence Erlbaum, 1977. (a)

———. Aggression and peer acceptance in preadolescent boys. Two short-term longitudinal studies of ratings. *Child Development,* 1977, 48, 1301–1313. (b)

———. Stability of aggressive reaction patterns in males: A review. *Psychological Bulletin,* 1979, 86, 852–875.

Opler, M. K. (Ed.). *Culture and mental health.* New York: Macmillan, 1959.

———. *Culture and social psychiatry.* New York: Atherton, 1967.

Orlinsky, D., and Howard, B. The good hour. *Archives of General Psychiatry,* 1967, 16, 621–632.

Orme-Johnson, D. W. Autonomic stability and transcendental meditation. *Psychosomatic Medicine,* 1973, 35, 341–349.

Orne, M. T. The nature of hypnosis: Artifact and essence. *Journal of Abnormal and Social Psychology,* 1959, 58, 277–299.

———. On the social psychology of the psychological experiment. *American Psychologist,* 1962, 17, 776–783.

———. Hypnosis. In G. Lindzey, C. Hall, and R. F. Thompson, *Psychology.* New York: Worth, 1975.

Ornstein, R. E. *The psychology of consciousness.* San Francisco: Freeman, 1972.

Orvis, B. R., Cunningham, J. D., and Kelley, H. H. A closer examination of causal inference: The role of consensus, distinctiveness, and consistency information. *Journal of Personality and Social Psychology,* 1975, 32, 605–616.

Ostwald, P., and Bittner, E. Life adjustment after severe persecution. *American Journal of Psychiatry,* 1968, 124, 87–94.

Paivio, A. *Imagery and verbal processes.* New York: Holt, 1971.

Parke, R. D. The role of punishment in the socialization process. In R. A. Hoppe, G. A. Milton, and E. C. Simmel (Eds.), *Early experiences and the processes of socialization.* New York: Academic Press, 1970.

————, **and Colmer, C. W.** Child abuse: An interdisciplinary analysis. In E. M. Hetherington (Ed.), *Child Development Research,* 1975, *5.*

Parke, R. D., and Walters, R. H. Some factors influencing the efficacy of punishment training for inducing response inhibitions. *Monographs of the Society for Research in Child Development,* 1967, *32* (1, Serial No. 109).

Passini, F. T., and Norman, W. T. A universal conception of personality structure? *Journal of Personality and Social Psychology,* 1966, *4,* 44–49.

Patterson, G. R. Treatment for children with conduct problems: A review of outcome studies. In S. Feshbach and A. Fraczek (Eds.), *Aggression and behavior change: Biological and social processes.* New York: Praeger, 1979.

————, **Cobb, J. A., and Ray, R. S.** A social engineering technology for retraining the families of aggressive boys. In H. E. Adams and I. P. Unibel (Eds.), *Issues and trends in behavior therapy.* Springfield, Ill.: Charles C Thomas, 1973.

Patterson, G. R., Littman, R. A., and Bricker, W. Assertive behavior in children: A step toward a theory of aggression. *Monographs of the Society for Research in Child Development,* 1967, *32*(5, Serial No. 113).

Paul, G. L. *Insight vs. desensitization in psychotherapy.* Stanford, Calif.: Stanford University Press, 1966.

Peeke, H. R. S., Wyers, E. J., and Herz, M. J. Waning of the aggressive response to male models in the three spined stickleback *(Gasterosteus aculeatus L.). Animal Behavior,* 1969, *17,* 224–228.

Pelto, P. The difference between tight and loose societies. *Transaction,* April 1968, 37–40.

Penk, W. E., Carpenter, J. C., and Rylee, K. E. MMPI correlates of social and physical anhedonia. *Journal of Consulting and Clinical Psychology,* 1979, *47,* 1046–1052.

Phares, E. J. *Locus of control in personality.* Morristown, N.J.: General Learning Press, 1976.

Piaget, J. *Judgment and reasoning in the child.* New York: Harcourt Brace, 1928.

————. *The child's conception of the world.* New York: Harcourt Brace, 1929.

Piliavin, I. M., Rodin, J., and Piliavin, J. A. Good Samaritanism: An underground phenomenon? *Journal of Personality and Social Psychology,* 1969, *13,* 289–299.

Pilleri, G., and Knuckey, J. Behaviour patterns of some delphinidae observed in the western Mediterranean. *Zeitschrift fur Tierpsychologie,* 1969, *26*(1), 48–72.

Pitkänen-Pulkkinen, L. Self-control as a prerequisite for constructive behavior. In S. Feshbach and A. Fraczek (Eds.), *Aggression and behavior change: Biological and social processes.* New York: Praeger, 1979.

Polansky, N., Freeman, W., Horowitz, M., Irwin, L., Papanis, N., Rappaport, D., and Whaley, F. Problems of interpersonal relations in research on groups. *Human Relations,* 1949, *2,* 281–291.

Provence, S., and Lipton, R. C. *Infants in institutions.* New York: International Universities Press, 1962.

Rabkin, J. G., and Streuning, E. L. Life events, stress, and illness. *Science,* 1976, *194,* 1013–1020.

Rabkin, L. Y., and Rabkin, K. Children of the kibbutz. *Readings in Psychology Today* (3rd ed.). Del Mar, Calif.: CRM, 1974.

Rahe, R. H. The pathway between subjects' recent life change and their near-future illness reports: Representative results and methodological issues. In B. S. Dohrenwend and B. P. Dohrenwend (Eds.), *Stressful life events: Their nature and effects.* New York: Wiley, 1974.

Rapaport, D. *Emotions and memory.* Baltimore: Williams & Wilkins, 1942.

————. The structure of psychoanalytic theory. In S. Koch (Ed.), *Psychology: A study of a science* (Vol. 3). New York: McGraw-Hill, 1959.

————. *The structure of psychoanalytic theory: A systematizing attempt* (Psychological Issues Monograph 6). New York: International Universities Press, 1960.

Rathbun, C., McLaughlin, H., Bennett, O., and Garland, J. A. Later adjustment of children following radical separation from family and culture. *American Journal of Orthopsychiatry,* 1965, *35,* 604–609.

Raynor, J. O. Relationships between achievement-related motives, future orientation, and academic performance. *Journal of Personality and Social Psychology,* 1970, *15,* 28–33.

Remmers, H. H., and Radler, D. H. *The American teenager.* Indianapolis: Bobbs-Merrill, 1957.

Reyker, J. Hypnosis in research on psychopathology. In J. E. Gordon (Ed.), *Handbook of clinical and experimental hypnosis.* New York: Macmillan, 1967.

Reykowski, J. Intrinsic motivation and intrinsic inhibition of aggressive behavior. In S. Feshbach and A. Fraczek (Eds.), *Aggression and behavior change: Biological and social processes.* New York: Praeger, 1979.

Rheingold, H. L. The modification of social responsiveness in institutional babies. *Monographs of the Society for Research in Child Development,* 1956, *21* (2, Whole No. 63).

Ribble, M. *The rights of infants.* New York: Columbia University Press, 1943.

Richter, C. P. The phenomenon of unexplained sudden death in animals and man. In W. H. Gant (Ed.), *Physiological basis of psychiatry.* Springfield, Ill.: Charles C Thomas, 1958.

Riegel, K. Adult life crises: A diabetic interpretation of development. In M. Dutan and L. H. Ginsberg (Eds.), *Life span developmental psychology: Normative life crises.* New York: Academic Press, 1975.

Rimm, D. C. Thought stopping and covert assertion in the treatment of phobias. *Journal of Consulting and Clinical Psychology,* 1973, *41,* 466–467.

Robbins, K., and McAdam, D. Interhemispheric alpha symmetry and imagery mode. *Brain and Language,* 1974, *1,* 189–193.

Rodgers, D. A. Factors underlying differences in alcohol preference among inbred strains of mice. *Psychosomatic Medicine,* 1966, *28,* 498–513.

———, **and McClearn, G. E.** Alcohol preference of mice. In E. L. Bliss (Ed.), *Roots of behavior.* New York: Harper & Row, 1962.

Rodin, J., and Langer, E. J. Long-term effects of a control-relevant intervention with the institutionalized aged. *Journal of Personality and Social Psychology,* 1977, *35,* 897–902.

Rogers, C. R. A theory of therapy, personality, and interpersonal relationships, as developed in the client-centered framework. In S. Koch (Ed.), *Psychology: A study of a science* (Vol. 3). New York: McGraw-Hill, 1959.

———. *On becoming a person.* Boston: Houghton Mifflin, 1961.

———. Actualizing tendency in relation to "motives" and to consciousness. In M. R. Jones (Ed.), *Nebraska symposium on motivation.* Lincoln: University of Nebraska Press, 1963.

———, **and Dymond, R. F. (Eds.).** *Psychotherapy and personality change.* Chicago: University of Chicago Press, 1954.

Rogers, C. R., Gendlin, E. T., Kiesler, D. J., and Truax, C. B. *The therapeutic relationship and its impact.* Madison: University of Wisconsin Press, 1967.

Rohe, W., and Patterson, A. H. *The effects of varied levels of resources and density on behavior in a day care center.* Paper presented at Experimental Design Research Association, Milwaukee, 1974.

Rorer, L. G., and Goldberg, L. R. Acquiescence in the MMPI? *Educational and Psychological Measurement,* 1965, *25,* 801–817.

Rorschach, H. *Psychodiagnostik.* Bern: Bircher, 1921. (Trans. Hans Huber Verlag, 1942).

Rose, R. M., Holaday, J. W., and Bernstein, I. S. Plasma testosterone, dominance rank and aggressive behavior in male Rhesus monkeys. *Nature,* 1971, *231,* 366–368.

Rosen, B., and D'Andrade, R. C. The psychosocial origins of achievement motivation. *Sociometry,* 1959, *22,* 185–218.

Rosenberg, M. *Society and the adolescent self-image.* Princeton, N.J.: Princeton University Press, 1965.

Rosenthal, D. *Genetic theory and abnormal behavior.* New York: McGraw-Hill, 1970.

Rosenthal, R., and Jacobson, L. *Pygmalion in the classroom: Teacher expectation and pupils' intellectual development.* New York: Holt, 1968.

Ross, H. S., and Goldman, B. D. Establishing new social relations in infancy. In T. Alloway, P. Pliner, and L. Krames (Eds.), *Attachment behavior: Advances in the study of communication and affect* (Vol. 3). New York: Plenum, 1977.

Ross, L. The intuitive psychologist and his shortcomings. Distortions in the attribution process. In L. Berkowitz (Ed.), *Advances in experimental social psychology* (Vol. 10). New York: Academic Press, 1977.

Rotter, J. B. *Social learning and clinical psychology.* Englewood Cliffs, N.J.: Prentice-Hall, 1954.

———. Generalized expectancies for internal versus external control of reinforcements. *Psychological Monographs,* 1966, *80*(1, Whole No. 609).

———. *Applications of a social learning theory of personality.* New York: Holt, 1972.

———. Some problems and misconceptions related to the construct of internal versus external control of reinforcement. *Journal of Consulting and Clinical Psychology,* 1975, *43,* 55–67.

———, **Chance, J. E., and Phares, E. J.** An introduction to social learning theory. In J. B. Rotter, J. E. Chance, and E. J. Phares (Eds.), *Applications of a social learning theory of personality.* New York: Holt, 1972.

Rubin, Z. Measurement of romantic love. *Journal of Personality and Social Psychology,* 1970, *16,* 265–273.

———. *Liking and loving: an invitation to social psychology.* New York: Holt, 1973.

Ruble, D. N., Parsons, J. E., and Ross, J. Self-evaluative responses of children in an achievement setting. *Child Development,* 1976, *47,* 990–997.

Rule, B. G., and Neasdale, A. R. Emotional arousal and aggressive behavior. *Psychological Bulletin,* 1976, *83,* 851–863.

Rushton, J. P. Socialization and the altruistic behavior of children. *Psychological Bulletin,* 1976, *83,* 898–913.

Rutter, M. Maternal deprivation, 1972–1978: New findings, new concepts, new approaches. *Child Development,* 1979, *50,* 283–305.

Saccuzzo, D. P. Canonical correlation as a method of assessing the correlates of good and bad therapy hours. *Psychotherapy: Theory, Research, and Practice,* Menasha, Wisconsin: American Psychological Association, 1975.

Sameroff, A. J. Early influences in development: Fact or fancy? *Merrill-Palmer Quarterly,* 1975, *21,* No. 4, 267–294.

———. *Theoretical and empirical issues in the operationalization of transactional research.* Paper presented at the biennial meeting of the Society for Research in Child Development, San Francisco, March, 1979.

———, and Chandler, M. J. Reproductive right and the continuum of caretaking casualty. In F. D. Horowitz (Ed.), *Review of child development research: Vol. 4.* Chicago: University of Chicago Press, 1975.

Sarason, I. G. The test anxiety scale: Concept and research. In C. D. Spielberger and I. G. Sarason (Eds.), *Stress and anxiety* (Vol. 5). Washington, D.C.: Hemisphere, 1978.

———, Smith, R. E., and Diener, E. Personality research: Components of variance attributable to the person and the situation. *Journal of Personality and Social Psychology,* 1975, *3,* 199–204.

Sarbin, T. R. A contribution to the study of actuarial and individual method of predictions. *American Journal of Sociology,* 1942, *48,* 593–602.

Sarason, S. B., Davidson, K. S., Lightchal, F., Waite, R. R., and Ruebush, B. K., *Anxiety in elementary school children.* New York: Wiley, 1960.

Schachter, S. *The psychology of affiliation.* Stanford, Calif.: Stanford University Press, 1959.

———. The interaction of cognitive and physiological determinants of emotional state. In L. Berkowitz (Ed.), *Advances in experimental social psychology* (Vol. 1). New York: Academic Press, 1964.

———, and Singer, J. E. Cognitive, social, and physiological determinants of emotional state. *Psychological Review,* 1962, *69,* 379–399.

Schafer, R. The loving and beloved super ego in Freud's structural theory. In O. Fenichel et al. (Eds.), *Psychoanalytic study of the child* (Vol. 15). New York: International Universities Press, 1960.

———. *A new language for psychoanalysis.* New Haven: Yale University Press, 1976.

Schlosberg, H. Three dimensions of emotion. *Psychological Review,* 1954, *61,* 81–88.

Schneider, D. J. Implicit theory: A review. *Psychological Bulletin,* 1973, *79,* 294–309.

Schreiner, L., and Kling, A. Rhinencephalon and behavior. *American Journal of Physiology,* 1956, *184,* 486–490.

Schultz, D. *Theories of personality.* Belmont, Calif.: Brooks/Cole, 1976.

Schwartz, G. E. Meditation. In G. Lindzey, C. S. Hall, and R. F. Thompson (Eds.), *Psychology.* New York: Worth, 1975.

Schwartz, S., Feldman, K., Brown, M., and Heingartner, A. Some personality correlates of conduct in two situations of moral conflict. *Journal of Personality,* 1969, *37,* 41–58.

Scott, J. P. *Aggression.* Chicago: University of Chicago Press, 1958.

Sears, R. R., Maccoby, E. E., and Levin, H. *Patterns of child rearing.* New York: Harper & Row, 1957.

Sears, R. R., Rau, L., and Alpert, R. *Identification and child rearing.* Stanford, Calif.: Stanford University Press, 1965.

Seeman, M. Alienation and social learning in a reformatory. *American Journal of Sociology,* 1963, *69,* 270–284.

———, and Evans, J. W. Alienation and learning in a hospital setting. *American Sociological Review,* 1962, *27,* 772–783.

Seeman, W., Nidich, S., and Banta, T. H. Influence of transcendental meditation on a measure of self-actualization. *Journal of Counseling Psychology,* 1972, *19,* 184–187.

Segal, H. *Introduction to the work of Melanie Klein.* New York: Basic Books, 1973.

Seligman, M. E. P. *Helplessness: On depression, development, and death.* San Francisco: Freeman, 1975.

———, and Maier, S. F. Failure to escape traumatic shock. *Journal of Experimental Psychology,* 1967, *74,* 1–9.

Selye, H. *The stress of life.* New York: McGraw-Hill, 1956.

Service, E. R. *The hunters.* Englewood Cliffs, N.J.: Prentice-Hall, 1966.

Sewell, W. H., and Mussen, P. H. The effects of feeding, weaning, and scheduling procedures on childhood adjustment and the formation of oral symptoms. *Child Development,* 1952, *23,* 185–191.

Shakow, D., and Rapaport, D. The influence of Freud on American psychology. *Psychological Issues,* 1964, No. 13.

Shapira, A., and Madsen, M. C. Between and within group cooperation and competitive behavior among kibbutz and non-kibbutz children. *Developmental Psychology,* 1974, *10,* 140–145.

Shapiro, D., and Giber, D. Meditation and psychotherapeutic effects. *Archives of General Psychiatry,* 1978, *35,* 294–302.

Shapiro, D., and Surwit, R. S. Learned control of physiological functions and disease. In H. Leitenberg (Ed.), *Handbook of behavior modification* *and behavior therapy.* Englewood Cliffs, N.J.: Prentice-Hall, 1976.

Shapiro, D. J., and Alexander, I. W. Extroversion-introversion: Affiliation and anxiety. *Journal of Personality,* 1969, *37,* 387–406.

Sharon, S. Cooperative learning in small groups: Recent methods and effects on achievement, attitudes and ethnic relations. *Review of Educational Research,* 1980, *50,* 241–271.

Sheehan, G. *Running and being.* New York: Warner, 1978.

Sheehy, G. *Passages.* New York: Dutton, 1976.

Sheldon, W. H. *Atlas of men.* New York: Harper & Brothers, 1954.

———, **and Stevens, S. S.** *The varieties of temperament: A psychology of constitutional differences.* New York: Harper, 1942.

———, **and Tucker, W. B.** *The varieties of human physique: An introduction to constitutional psychology.* New York: Harper, 1940.

Sherif, M., Harvey, O. J., White, B. J., Hood, W. R., and Sherif, C. *Intergroup conflict and cooperation: The robber's cave experiment.* Norman: University of Oklahoma Book Exchange, 1961.

Shevrin, H. Brain wave correlates of subliminal stimulation, unconscious attention, primary and secondary process thinking and repressiveness. In *Psychoanalytic research: Three approaches to the experimental study of subliminal processes* (Psychological Issues Monograph 30). New York: International Universities Press, 1974.

———, **and Dickman, S.** The psychological unconscious. A necessary assumption for all psychological theory. *American Psychologist,* 1980, *35,* 421–434.

Shields, J. Heredity and environment. In H. J. Eysenck and G. D. Wilson (Eds.), *A textbook of human psychology.* Baltimore: University Park Press, 1976.

Shure, M., and Spivack, G. Means-ends thinking, adjustment and social class among elementary school–aged children. *Journal of Consulting and Clinical Psychology,* 1972, *38,* 348–353.

Silverman, L. H. Psychoanalytic theory: "The reports of my death are greatly exaggerated." *American Psychologist,* 1976, *31,* 621–637.

———, **Bronstein, A., and Mendlelsohn, E.** The further use of the subliminal psychodynamic activation method for the experimental study of the clinical theory of psychoanalysis: On the specificity of relationships between manifest psychopathology and unconscious conflict. *Psychotherapy: Theory, Research and Practice,* 1976, *13,* 2–16.

Simonds, P. F. Peers, parents and primates: The developing network of attachments. In T.

Alloway, P. Pliner, and L. Krames (Eds.), *Attachment behavior: Advances in the study of communication and affect.* New York: Plenum, 1977.

Singer, J. L. *Daydreaming.* New York: Random House, 1966.

———. *The child's world of make believe.* New York: Academic Press, 1973.

———. *Imagery and daydream methods in psychotherapy and behavior modification.* New York: Academic Press, 1974.

Skinner, B. F. *The behavior of organisms.* New York: Appleton-Century-Crofts, 1938.

———. *Walden two.* New York: Macmillan, 1948.

———. *Science and human behavior.* New York: Macmillan, 1953.

———. Operant behavior. *American Psychologist,* 1963, *18,* 503–515.

———. *Beyond freedom and dignity.* New York: Knopf, 1971.

Smith, D. E., King, M. B., and Hoebel, B. C. Lateral hypothalamic control of killing: Evidence for a cholinoceptive mechanism. *Science,* 1970, *167,* 900–901.

Smith, R., Smythe, L., and Lien, D. Inhibition of helping behavior by a similar or dissimilar nonreactive fellow bystander. *Journal of Personality and Social Psychology,* 1972, *23,* 414–419.

Smith, R. T. A comparison of socioenvironmental factors in monozygotic and dizygotic twins. Testing an assumption. In S. G. Vandenberg (Ed.), *Methods and goals in human behavior genetics.* New York: Academic Press, 1963.

Sommer, R., and Ross, H. Social interaction on a geriatric ward. *International Journal of Social Psychiatry,* 1958, *4,* 128–133.

Sommershield, H., and Reyker, J. Posthypnotic conflict, repression and psychopathology. *Journal of Abnormal Psychology,* 1973, *82,* 278–290.

Sorenson, R. C. *Adolescent sexuality in contemporary America: Personal values and sexual behavior ages 13–19.* New York: Abrams, 1973.

Spence, J. T., and Helmrich, R. L. *Masculinity and femininity: Their psychological dimensions, correlates, and antecedents.* Austin: University of Texas Press, 1978.

Sperry, R. W. The great cerebral commissure. *Scientific American,* 1964, *210,* 42–52.

———. Hemisphere deconnection and unity in conscious awareness. *American Psychologist,* 1968, *23,* 723–733.

Spielberger, C. D. The role of awareness in verbal conditioning. In C. W. Eriksen (Ed.), *Behavior and awareness.* Durham, N.C.: Duke University Press, 1962.

————. Anxiety as an emotional state. In C. D. Spielberger (Ed.), *Anxiety: Current trends in theory and research*, Vol. 1. New York: Academic Press, 1971(a).

———— (Ed.). *Anxiety: Current trends in theory and research, Vol. II.* New York: Academic Press, 1971 (b).

————, and DeNike, L. D. Descriptive behaviorism versus cognitive theory in verbal operant conditioning. *Psychological Review*, 1966, *73*, 306–326.

————, Gorsuch, R. L., and Lushene, R. E. *Manual for the state-trait anxiety inventory.* Palo Alto, Calif.: Consulting Psychologists Press, 1970.

Spinetta, J. J., and Rigler, D. The child-abusing parent: A psychological review. *Psychological Bulletin*, 1972, *77*, 296–304.

Spitz, R. A. Hospitalism. An inquiry into the genesis of psychiatric conditions in early childhood. In O. Fenichel et al. (Eds.), *The psychoanalytic study of the child* (Vol. 1). New York: International Universities Press, 1945.

Spivack, G., and Levine, M. *Self-regulation in acting-out and normal adolescents* (Report M-4351). Washington, D.C.: National Institute of Health, 1963.

Spivack, G., and Shure, M. B. *Social adjustment of young children: A cognitive approach to solving real-life problems.* San Francisco: Jossey-Bass, 1974.

Sprafkin, J. N., Liebert, R. M., and Poulos, R. W. Effects of a prosocial televised example on children's helping. *Journal of Experimental Child Psychology*, 1975, *20*, 119–126.

Sroufe, L. A., and Waters, E. Attachment as an organizational construct. *Child Development*, 1977, *48*, 1184–1199.

————. Heart rate as a convergent measure in clinical and developmental research. *American Behavioral Scientist*, 1977, *20*, (3), 295–318.

Stagner, R., Lawson, E. D., and Moffitt, J. W. The Krout Personal Preference Scale: A factor-analytic study. *Journal of Clinical Psychology*, 1955, *11*, 103–113.

Staub, E. A child in distress: The influence of nurturance and modeling on children's attempts to help. *Developmental Psychology*, 1971, *5*, 124–132.

————. Instigation to goodness: The role of social norms and interpersonal influence. *Journal of Social Issues*, 1972, *28*, 131–150.

————. Helping a distressed person: Social, personality, and stimulus determinants. In L. Berkowitz (Ed.), *Advances in Experimental Social Psychology* (Vol. 7). New York: Academic Press, 1974.

Stein, A., and Friedrich, L. K. Television content and young children's behavior. In J. P. Murray, E. A. Rubinstein, and G. A. Comstock (Eds.), *Television and social behavior: Television and social learning* (Vol. 2). Washington, D.C.: U.S. Government Printing Office, 1971.

Stephenson, W. *The study of behavior.* Chicago: University of Chicago Press, 1953.

Stewart, K. Dream theory in Malaya. In C. T. Tart (Ed.), *Altered states of consciousness.* New York: Wiley, 1969.

Stokols, D. On the distinction between density and crowding: Some implications for future research. *Psychological Review*, 1972, *79*, 275–278.

————. Environmental psychology. In L. W. Porter and M. R. Rosenzweig (Eds.), *Annual review of psychology* (Vol. 29). Palo Alto, Calif.: Annual Reviews, 1978.

Stormes, M. D. Videotape and the attribution process: Reversion actors' and observers' points of view. *Journal of Personality and Social Psychology*, 1973, *27*, 165–175.

Stotland, E., and Dunn, R. E. Identification, authoritarian defensiveness, self-esteem, and birth order. *Psychological Monographs*, 1962, *76* (No. 528).

Stratton, G. M. *Anger: Its religious and moral significance.* New York: Macmillan, 1923.

Straus, M. A. Communication, creativity and problem solving ability of middle and working class families in three societies. *American Journal of Sociology*, 1968, *73*, 417–431.

Strong, E. K. *Vocational interests of men and women.* Stanford, Calif.: Stanford University Press, 1943.

Stuart, R. B. Decentration in the development of children's concepts of moral and causal judgment. *Journal of Genetic Psychology*, 1967, *111*, 59–68.

Sullivan, H. S. *The interpersonal theory of psychiatry.* New York: Norton, 1953.

Suomi, S. J. Development of attachment and other social behaviors in Rhesus monkeys. In T. Alloway, P. Pliner, and L. Krames (Eds.), *Attachment behavior: Advances in the study of communication and affect.* New York: Plenum, 1977.

————, Harlow, H. F., and Kimball, S. D. Behavioral effects of prolonged partial social isolation in the rhesus monkey. *Psychological Reports*, 1971, *29*, 1171–1177.

Taffel, C. Anxiety and conditioning in verbal learning. *Journal of Abnormal and Social Psychology*, 1955, *51*, 496–501.

Tagiuri, R. Person perception. In G. Lindzey and E. Aronson (Eds.), *Handbook of social psychology.* Vol. 3. Reading, Mass.: Addison-Wesley, 1969.

Tanner, J. M. Sequence, tempo, and individual variation in the growth and development of boys and girls aged 12 to 16. *Daedalus*, 1971, *100*, 907–930.

Taylor, J. A. A personality scale of manifest anxiety. *Journal of Abnormal and Social Psychology*, 1953, *48*, 285–290.

Teleki, G. *The predatory behavior of wild chimpanzees.* Lewisburg, Pa.: Bucknell University Press, 1973.

Tempone, V. J. Extension of the repression-sensitization hypothesis to success and failure experience. *Psychological Reports*, 1964, *15*, 39–45.

Tenopyr, M. L. Content-construct confusion. *Personnel Psychology*, 1977, *30*, 47–54.

Thomas, A., and Chess, S. Behavioral individuality in childhood. In L. Aronson, E. Tabach, D. Lehrmon, and J. Rosenblatt (Eds.), *Development and evolution of behavior*. San Francisco: Freeman, 1976.

———, Birch, H. G., Hertzig, M. L., and Korn, S. J. *Behavioral individuality in early childhood.* New York: New York University Press, 1963.

———. *Temperament and behavior disorders in children.* New York: New York University, 1968.

Thompson, W. R. The inheritance and development of intelligence. *Association for Research in Nervous and Mental Diseases: Research Pub.*, 1954, *33*, 209–231.

Thorndike, E. L. *Principles of teaching.* New York: Seiler, 1906.

Tinbergen, N. *The study of instinct.* London: Oxford University Press, 1951.

———. Fighting and threat in animals. *New Biology*, 1953, *14*, 9–24.

———. On war and peace in animals and man. *Science*, 1968, *160*, 1411–1418.

Tizard, B. *Adoption. A second change.* London: Open Books, 1977.

———, and Hodges, J. The effect of early institutional rearing on the development of eight-year-old children. *Journal of Child Psychology and Psychiatry*, 1978, *19*, 99–118.

Tizard, B., and Rees, J. The effect of early institutional rearing on the behavior problems and affectional relationships of four-year-old children. *Journal of Child Psychology and Psychiatry*, 1975, *16*, 61–74.

Toch, H. *Violent men.* Chicago: Aldine, 1969.

Tomkins, S. S. *The Thematic Apperception Test: The theory and technique of interpretation.* New York: Grune & Stratton, 1947.

———. Affect as the primary motivational system. In M. B. Arnold (Ed.), *Feelings and emotions*. New York: Academic Press, 1970.

Tongas, P. N. The Kaiser-Permanente smoking control program: Its purpose and implications for an HMO. *Professional Psychology*, 1979, *10*, 409–418.

Tresemer, D. Fear of success: Popular, but unproven. *Psychology Today*, 1974, *7*, 82–85.

Troll, L. E., Neugarten, B. L., and Kraines, R. J. Similarities in values and other personality characteristics in college students and their parents. *Merrill-Palmer Quarterly*, 1969, *15*, 323–326.

Trope, Y. Seeking information about one's own ability as a determinant of choice among tasks. *Journal of Personality and Social Psychology*, 1975, *32*, 1004–1013.

Truax, C. B., and Carkhuff, R. R. *Toward effective counseling and psychotherapy: Training and practice.* Chicago: Aldine, 1967.

Truax, C. B., and Mitchell, K. M. Research on certain therapist interpersonal skills in relation to process and outcome. In A. E. Bergin and S. L. Garfield (Eds.), *Handbook of psychotherapy and behavior change.* New York: Wiley, 1971.

Truax, C. B., Wargo, D. G., Frank, J. D., Imber, S. D., Battle, C. C., Hoehn-Saric, R., Nash, E. H., and Stone, A. R. Therapist empathy, genuineness and warmth and patient therapeutic outcome. *Journal of Consulting Psychology*, 1966, *30*, 395–401.

Turiel, E. An experimental test of the sequentiality of developmental states in the child's moral judgments. *Journal of Personality and Social Psychology*, 1966, *3*, 611–618.

Tversky, A., and Kahneman, D. Belief in the law of small numbers. *Psychological Bulletin*, 1971, *76*, 105–110.

———. Causal schemas in judgments under uncertainty. In M. Fishbein (Ed.), *Progress in social psychology.* Hillsdale, N.J.: Lawrence Erlbaum, 1980.

Tyler, L. E. *The work of the counselor* (3rd ed.). New York: Appleton-Century-Crofts, 1969.

———. *Tests and measurements* (2nd ed.). Englewood Cliffs, N.J.: Prentice-Hall, 1971.

Valins, S. Cognitive effects of false heart-rate feedback. *Journal of Personality and Social Psychology*, 1966, *4*, 400–408.

———, and Baum, A. Residential group size, social interaction and crowding. *Environment and Behavior*, 1973, *5*, 421–440.

Valzelli, L. Drugs and aggressiveness. In K. Moyer (Ed.), *Physiology of aggression and implications for control.* New York: Raven, 1976.

Van Lawick-Goodall, J. Tool-using bird: The Egyptian vulture. *National Geographic*, 1968, *133*, 631–641. (a)

———. The behavior of free-living chimpanzees in the Gombe Stream Reserve. *Animal Behavior Monographs*, 1968(I, Part III). (b)

Veroff, J. Social comparison and the development of achievement motivation. In C. P. Smith (Ed.), *Achievement-related motives in children.* New York: Russell Sage, 1969.

————, Atkinson, J. W., Feld, S. C., and Gurin, G. The use of thematic apperception to assess motivation in a nationwide interview study. *Psychological Monographs*, 1960, 74 (No. 12).

Volosinov, V. N. *Freudianism: A Marxist critique.* New York: Academic Press, 1976.

Wallace, R. K., and Benson, H. The physiology of meditation. *Scientific American*, 1972, 226, 84–90.

Walters, R. H., and Brown, M. Studies of reinforcement of aggression: III. Transfer of responses to an interpersonal situation. *Child Development*, 1963, 34, 536–571.

Washburn, S. L. Human behavior and the behavior of other animals. *American Psychologist*, 1978, 33, 405–418.

Wasman, M. D., and Flynn, J. P. Direct attack elicited from the hypothalamus. *Archives of Neurology*, 1962, 6, 60–67.

Waters, E. The reliability and stability of individual differences in infant-mother attachment. *Child Development*, 1978, 49, 483–494.

————, and Crandall, V. J. Social class and obscured maternal behaviors from 1940 to 1960. *Child Development*, 1964, 35, 1021–1032.

Watkins, R. P., Peterson, R. F., Schweid, E., and Bijou, S. W. Behavior therapy in the home: Amelioration of problem parent-child relations with the parent in a therapeutic role. *Journal of Experimental Child Psychology*, 1966, 4, 99–107.

Watson, G. A. Some personality differences in children related to strict or permissive parental discipline. *Journal of Psychology*, 1957, 44, 227–249.

Watson, J. B. *Behaviorism* (Rev. ed.). New York: Norton, 1930.

Watson, J. S. The development and generalization of "contingency awareness" in early infancy: Some hypotheses. *Merrill-Palmer Quarterly*, 1966, 12, 123–135.

————. Memory and "contingency analysis" in infant learning. *Merrill-Palmer Quarterly*, 1967, 13, 55–76.

————, and Ramey, C. G. Reactions to response-contingent stimulation in early infancy. *Merrill-Palmer Quarterly*, 1972, 18, 219–228.

Webb, J. T. *The relation of MMPI two-point codes to age, sex, and education level in a representative nationwide sample of psychiatric outpatients.* Paper presented at Southeastern Psychological Association meetings, Louisville, Ky., April 1970.

Webb, W. B. *Sleep, the gentle tyrant.* Englewood Cliffs, N.J.: Prentice-Hall, 1975.

————, and Bonnet, M. H. Sleep and dreams. In M. E. Meyer (Ed), *Foundations of contemporary psychology.* New York: Oxford University Press, 1979.

Weber, M. (1904) *The protestant ethic and the spirit of capitalism.* New York: Scribner's, 1958.

Wegner, D. M., and Vallacher, R. R. *Implicit psychology.* New York: Oxford University Press, 1977.

Weiner, B. Effects of motivation on the availability and retrieval of memory traces. *Psychological Bulletin*, 1966, 65, 24–37.

———— (Ed.). *Achievement motivation and attribution theory.* Morristown, N.J.: General Learning Press, 1974.

————. Achievement strivings. In H. London and J. Exner (Eds.), *Dimensions of personality.* New York: Wiley, 1978.

————. A theory of motivation for some classroom experiences. *Journal of Educational Psychology*, 1979, 71, 3–25.

————. A cognitive (attribution)–emotion-action model of motivated behavior: An analysis of judgments of help-giving. *Journal of Personality and Social Psychology*, 1980, 39, 186–200.

————, and Kukla, A. An attributional analysis of achievement motivation. *Journal of Personality and Social Psychology*, 1970, 15, 1–20.

Weiner, B., Kun, A., and Benesh-Weiner, M. The development of mastery, emotions and morality from an attributional perspective. In W. A. Collins (Ed.), *Minnesota Symposium on Child Development* (Vol. 13). Hillsdale, N.J.: Lawrence Erlbaum, 1980.

Weiner, B., Russell, D., and Lerman, D. Affective consequences of causal ascriptions. In J. H. Harvey, W. J. Ickes, and R. F. Kidd (Eds.), *New directions in attribution research* (Vol. 2). Hillsdale, N.J.: Lawrence Erlbaum, 1978.

————. The cognition-emotion process in achievement-related contexts. *Journal of Personality and Social Psychology*, 1979, 37, 1211–1220.

Weiner, B., and Sierad, J. Misattribution for failure and the enhancement of achievement strivings. *Journal of Personality and Social Psychology*, 1975, 31, 415–421.

Weinraub, M., Brooks, J., and Lewis, M. The social network: A reconsideration of the concept of attachment. *Human Development*, 1977, 20, 31–47.

Weisman, A. D. Coping with untimely death. *Psychiatry*, 1973, 36, 366–378.

Weitzenhoffer, A. M., and Hilgard, E. R. *Stanford hypnotic susceptibility scale.* Stanford, Calif.: Standford University Press, 1962.

Wells, B. W. P. The psycho-social influence of building environment: Sociometric findings in large and small office spaces. In R. Gutman (Ed.), *People and buildings.* New York: Basic Books, 1972.

Wells, W. D. Television and aggression: Replication of an experimental field study. Unpublished manuscript, University of Chicago, 1971.

White, R. M. *Sleep length and variability: Measurement and interrelationships.* Unpublished doctoral dissertation, University of Florida, 1975.

Whiteman, M. Children's conceptions of psychological causality. *Child Development*, 1967, *38*, 143–155.

Whiting, B. B. *Six cultures: Studies of child rearing.* New York: Wiley, 1963.

———— (Ed.). *Six cultures series* (Vol. I–VII). New York: Wiley, 1966.

————, and Whiting, J. W. M. *Children of six cultures.* Cambridge, Mass.: Harvard University Press, 1975.

Whiting, J. W. M. The crosscultural method. In G. Lindzey (Ed.), *Handbook of social psychology.* Reading, Mass.: Addison-Wesley, 1954.

————. Methods and problems in cross-cultural research. In G. Lindzey and E. Aronson (Eds.), *Handbook of social psychology* (Vol. 2). Reading, Mass.: Addison-Wesley, 1968.

————, and Child, I. L. *Child training and personality.* New Haven: Yale University Press, 1953.

Whiting, J. W. M., Kluckhohn, R., and Anthony, A. The function of male initiation ceremonies at puberty. In E. E. Maccoby, T. M. Newcomb, and E. L. Hartley (Eds.), *Readings in social psychology* (3rd ed.). New York: Holt, 1958.

Wicker, A. W. Undermanning, performances, and students' subjective experiences in behavioral settings of large and small high schools. *Journal of Personality and Social Psychology*, 1968, *10*, 255–261.

————, and Kirmeyer, S. From church to laboratory to national park: A program of research on excess and insufficient populations in behavior settings. In D. Stokols (Ed.), *Perspectives on environment and behavior.* New York: Plenum, 1977.

Wiens, A. H. The assessment interview. In I. B. Weiner (Ed.), *Clinical methods in psychology.* New York: Wiley, 1976.

Wiggins, J. S. Interrelationships among MMPI measures of dissimulation under standard and social desirability instructions. *Journal of Consulting Psychology*, 1959, *23*, 419–427.

————. Strategic, method, and stylistic variance in the MMPI. *Psychological Bulletin*, 1962, *59*, 224–242.

————. *Personality and prediction: Principles of personality assessment.* Reading, Mass.: Addison-Wesley, 1973.

————, Renner, K. E., Clore, G. L., and Rose, R. J. *The psychology of personality.* Reading, Mass.: Addison-Wesley, 1971.

Williamsen, J. A., Johnson, H. J., and Eriksen, C. W. Some characteristics of posthypnotic amnesia. *Journal of Abnormal Psychology*, 1965, *70*, 123–131.

Wilson, E. O. *Sociobiology: The new synthesis.* Cambridge, Mass.: Harvard University Press, 1975.

————. Biology and the social sciences. *Daedalus*, 1977, *11*, 127–140.

Wilson, G. Introversion/extraversion. In H. London and J. E. Exner, Jr. (Eds.), *Dimensions of personality.* New York: Wiley, 1978.

Wine, J. D. Test anxiety and direction of attention. *Psychological Bulletin*, 1971, *76*, 92–104.

Winston, H. D., and Lindzey, G. Albinism and water escape performance in the mouse. *Science*, 1964, *144*, 189–191.

Winterbottom, M. R. *The relation of childhood training in independence to achievement motivation.* Unpublished doctoral dissertation, University of Michigan, 1953.

Witkin, H. A., Dyk, R. B., Faterson, H. F., Goodenough, D. R., and Karp, S. A. *Psychological differentiation.* New York: Wiley, 1962.

Witkin, H. A., Mednick, S. A., Schulsinger, F., Bakkestrom, E., Christianses, K. O., Goodenough, D. R., Hirschhorn, K., Lundsteen, C., Owen, D. R., Philip, J., Rubin, D. B., and Stocking, M. Criminality in XYY and XXY men. *Science*, 1976, *196*, 547–555.

Wolf, T. M. Effects of live modeled sex-inappropriate play behavior in a naturalistic setting. *Developmental Psychology*, 1973, *9*, 120–124.

Wolfe, J. L., and Summerlin, C. T. Agonistic behavior in organized and disorganized cotton rat populations. *Science*, 1968, *160*, 98–99.

Wolk, S., and DuCette, J. Intentional performance and incidental learning as a function of personality and task dimensions. *Journal of Personality and Social Psychology*, 1974, *29*, 90–101.

Wolowitz, H. M. Food preferences as an index of orality. *Journal of Abnormal Social Psychology*, 1964, *69*, 650–654.

Wolpe, J. *Psychotherapy by reciprocal inhibition.* Stanford, Calif.: Stanford University Press, 1958.

————. *The practice of behavior therapy.* New York: Pergamon, 1969.

Woodworth, R. S. *Personal Data Sheet.* Chicago: Stoelting, 1920.

Woolfolk, R. Psychophysiological correlates of meditation. *Archives of General Psychiatry*, 1975, *32*, 1326–1333.

Worchel, S. The effect of three types of arbitrary thwarting on the instigation to aggression. *Journal of Personality*, 1974, *42*, 300–318.

Wortman, C. B., and Brehm, J. W. Responses to uncontrollable outcomes: An integration of reactance theory and the learned helplessness model. In L. Berkowitz (Ed.), *Advances in experimental social psychology* (Vol. 8). New York: Academic Press, 1975.

Wrightsman, L. *Social psychology* (2nd ed.) Belmont, Calif.: Brooks/Cole, 1977.

Wylie, R. G. *The self-concept: A review of methodological considerations and measuring instruments* (Rev. ed.) (Vol. 1.). Lincoln: University of Nebraska Press, 1974.

———. *The self-concept: Theory and research on selected topics* (Vol. 2). Lincoln: University of Nebraska Press, 1979.

Yablonsky, L. *The violent gang.* Baltimore: Penguin, 1966.

Yarrow, L. J. The relationship between nutritive sucking experience in infancy and non-nutritive sucking in childhood. *Journal of Genetic Psychology,* 1954, *84,* 149–162.

Yarrow, M. R., Scott, P., and Waxler, C. Z. Learning concern for others. *Developmental Psychology,* 1973, *8,* 240–260.

Yates, A. B. *Frustration and conflict.* London: Methuen, 1962.

Youmans, E. G., and Yarrow, M. R. Aging and social adaptation: A longitudinal study of healthy old men. In S. Cranick and R. Ratherson (Eds.), *Human Aging II: An eleven year follow-up study.* Bethesda, Md.: U.S. Public Health Service, 1971.

Young, P. T. *Emotion in man and animal.* New York. Wiley, 1943.

Zigler, E., and Yospe, L. Perceptual defense and the problem of response suppression. *Journal of Personality,* 1960, *28,* 220–239.

Zillman, D. Excitation transfer in communication-mediated aggressive behavior. *Journal of Experimental Social Psychology,* 1971, *7,* 419–434.

———. Attribution and misattribution of excitatory reactions. In J. H. Harvey, W. J. Ickes, and R. F. Kidd (Eds.), *New directions in attribution research* (Vol. 2). Hillsdale, N.J.: Lawrence Erlbaum, 1978.

———, and Cantor, J. R. Effect of timing of information about mitigating circumstances on emotional responses to provocation and retaliatory behavior. *Journal of Experimental Social Psychology,* 1976, *12,* 38–55.

Zillman, D., Katcher, A. H., and Milarsky, B. Exitation transfer from physical exercise to subsequent aggressive behavior. *Journal of Experimental Social Psychology,* 1972, *8,* 247–259.

Zimbardo, P. G. The human choice: Individuation, reason, and order versus deindividuation, impulse, and chaos. In W. D. Arnold and D. Levine (Eds.), *Nebraska Symposium on Motivation.* Lincoln: University of Nebraska Press, 1969.

Zinberg, N. E. (Ed.). *Alternate states of consciousness.* New York: Free Press, 1977.

Zlutnick, S., and Altman, I. Crowding and human behavior. In J. F. Wohlwill and D. H. Carson (Eds.), *Environment and the social sciences: Perspectives and applications.* Washington, D.C.: American Psychological Association, 1972.

Zubin, J., Eron, L. D., and Schumer, F. *An experimental approach to projective techniques.* New York: Wiley, 1965.

Zuckerman, M., and Wheeler, L. To dispel fantasies about the fantasy-based measure of fear of success. *Psychological Bulletin,* 1975, *82,* 932–946.

Index of Names

Index of Concepts